A2
2ND EDITION

Business
Studies

John Wolinski & Gwen Coates

Philip Allan Updates, an imprint of Hodder Education, an Hachette UK company, Market Place, Deddington, Oxfordshire OX15 0SE

Orders

Bookpoint Ltd, 130 Milton Park, Abingdon, Oxfordshire OX14 4SB
tel: 01235 827827
fax: 01235 400401
e-mail: education@bookpoint.co.uk

Lines are open 9.00 a.m.–5.00 p.m., Monday to Saturday, with a 24-hour message answering service. You can also order through the Philip Allan Updates website: www.philipallan.co.uk

ISBN 978-0-340-95934-3

First published 2005
Second edition 2009

Impression number   5
Year   2014   2013   2012   2011

This textbook has been written specifically to support students studying AQA A2 business studies. The content has been neither approved nor endorsed by AQA and remains the sole responsibility of the authors.

All efforts have been made to trace copyright on items used.

All web addresses are correct at the time of going to press but may subsequently change.

Printed in Italy

Hachette UK's policy is to use papers that are natural, renewableand recyclable products and made from wood grown in sustainable forests. The logging and manufacturing processes are expected to conform to the environmental regulations of the country of origin.

Contents

Unit 4: The business environment and managing change

Corporate aims and objectives

Assessing changes in the business environment

Managing change

Introduction

This textbook has been written specifically to meet the needs of students taking the AQA A2 Business Studies course and provides comprehensive coverage of the subject content of the AQA A2 specification, module by module, section by section, as it is laid out in the specification document. It follows on from the authors' AS textbook, *AQA AS Business Studies 2nd Edition* (Philip Allan Updates), subsequently referred to as 'the AS textbook'.

Up-to-date examples and illustrations from real-life organisations and situations are used throughout this book in order to help you to recognise the dynamic and changing nature of business studies and its relevance to society.

The AQA specification does not require real-life cases for its examinations, but we have tried to use real-life case studies as much as possible. For this reason, students are encouraged to read the case study articles as a development of the specification content, even if they do not attempt to answer the questions that accompany them.

Online resources

To access the online resources go to **www.hodderplus.co.uk/philipallan**. Here you will find guidance on exam technique and sample essay-style questions, together with graded answers and detailed commentaries.

Course coverage and how to use this book

Structure

This book follows the order of the AQA A2 Business Studies specification. The specification is divided into two units.

- **Unit 3 (BUSS3): Strategies for success**. This covers the strategic planning of the four main functional areas of a business. Chapter 1 introduces this unit which covers:
  - 'Financial strategies and accounts', covered in Chapters 2–6
  - 'Marketing strategies', covered in Chapters 7–10
  - 'Operational strategies', covered in Chapters 11–15
  - 'Human resource strategies', covered in Chapters 16–19
- **Unit 4 (BUSS4): The business environment and managing change.** Chapter 20 introduces this unit which covers:
  - 'Assessing changes in the business environment', covered in Chapters 21–25
  - 'Managing change', covered in Chapters 26–31

For each unit, the order of the chapters in this book provides a logical progression of learning, with the later chapters building on the theory and understanding acquired in the earlier chapters. Some questions at the end of chapters also assume an understanding of work in previous chapters.

Special features

This book contains several special features designed to aid your understanding of the requirements of the AQA A2 Business Studies course.

Key terms
These are clear, concise definitions of the main terms needed for the course. An accurate understanding of the definitions of key terms will reduce the chances of you producing an irrelevant answer.

Examiner's voice
Both authors have over 20 years' experience of examining and have used this to provide snippets of advice that will help you to present your ideas effectively and to avoid potential pitfalls. Some of this advice is specific to a particular topic; the remainder is general advice on how you should approach the examinations.

Fact files
Topical examples from the world of business are included at regular intervals in order to increase interest and to help you to develop your application skills by showing how the business ideas that you have studied can be applied to real-life situations. These fact files will also help you to increase your awareness of current developments and practices.

Did you know?
These boxes are placed throughout the book. They provide useful insights into the ideas and concepts covered in the A2 course and their use in businesses. The comments will help you to improve your understanding of business activities.

What do you think?
On occasions, facts or comments on business activity are presented in the form of a challenge — what do you think? There is often a range of possible solutions to business problems or many differing consequences to an action. These boxes will get you thinking about possible alternative solutions or consequences.

Group exercises
These are included when a part of the specification lends itself to discussion or a cooperative approach to study.

Practice exercises
Over 80 practice exercises are provided to help you check your understanding of the topics you have covered within each chapter. Many of these exercises are geared towards testing knowledge, but several are based on relevant articles. You can use the latter type to test your higher-level skills, such as evaluation. Although individual questions within a practice exercise may

match the style of AQA A2 questions, overall the practice exercises do not adopt the AQA examination style — the case studies perform this role.

Case studies

A common problem facing both teachers and students is finding suitable material for examination practice. The examinations are based on the whole of the specification and so, on completion of a particular topic, it is not possible to find a past examination paper that sets a realistic challenge. To fill this gap over 60 examination-style questions have been included in this book. The heading 'case study' is used wherever the style of the questions is similar to the AQA A2 examinations.

Assessment

Unit 3

This unit will be assessed by an unseen case study that consists of a story line followed by appendices of data. The unit will be tested through four questions:
- Question 1 will be an analysis question of approximately 10 marks, focused on one of the four functional areas (Finance, Marketing, Operations and Human Resources).
- Questions 2 and 3 will be evaluation questions of approximately 18 marks, each rooted in one of the other three functional areas.
- Question 4 is a final evaluative question based on a major decision. Although this will be based on the fourth functional area it is likely to draw on the other three areas of the unit. The decision will utilise the appendices to a greater extent than the earlier questions, although it will require use of the text also.

Unit 4

In the January/February prior to this Unit AQA will announce a research theme. This theme will be a part of the Unit 4 specification, such as globalisation, the economic environment or leadership. Students will be expected to undertake research on this theme based on organisations of their own choosing, in preparation for the examination.

This unit will be assessed by two 40-marks questions with an element of optional choice:
- The first question will involve a choice of ONE from TWO questions. These questions will be based on an unseen article within the examination paper which will allow students to draw on the research that they have undertaken on the research theme.
- The second question will be an essay (with ONE title to be answered from a choice of THREE essays). These essays will test the whole of the Unit 4 specification and draw on earlier units too, but they are not linked to the research theme.

The hierarchy of skills

Every mark that is awarded on an A2 paper is given for the demonstration of a skill. The following four skills are tested:

- **Knowledge and understanding** — demonstrating knowledge and understanding of the specified content of the course, such as clear definitions or explanation of theories.
- **Application** — relating or applying your knowledge and understanding to a specific organisation or situation. An example might be advising a business to recruit and train a specific category of employee based on recognising the shortage of suitable staff for that business.
- **Analysis** — using theory or business logic to develop a line of thought in relation to the solution of a business problem. An example might be showing how a particular strategy may cause personnel difficulties and low morale in the short term, but more efficient production and higher profit margins in the long run.
- **Evaluation** — making a judgement based on weighing up different evidence and, possibly, recognising the strength, quality and reliability of the evidence before making a decision.

Please note that at A2 the vast majority of questions will test all four skills.

Table 1 Typical mark allocations for a Unit 3 examination

Question	Skills				
	Knowledge	Application	Analysis	Evaluation	Total
1	2	6	2		10
2	4	4	5	5	18
3	4	4	5	5	18
4	6	10	8	10	34
Total	16	24	20	20	80

Table 2 Typical mark allocations for Unit 4

	Skills				
	Knowledge	Application	Analysis	Evaluation	Total
Question 1 or 2	8	8	10	14	40
Essay	8	8	10	14	40
Total	16	16	20	28	80

Demonstrating the skills required

Avoid the temptation to show off your knowledge by listing lots of different points. The AQA examinations reward quality, not quantity. As a general rule of thumb, in Units 3 and 4 it is best to focus on approximately four points per question, but to develop them in great depth.

You should identify the appropriate number of relevant ideas, explain their relevance using arguments that are specific to the situation or organisation featured in the question, and then draw a conclusion or make a decision based on your arguments. If, and only if, time permits, you can add and develop further ideas. In short, move up the skills levels from knowledge to application and analysis and on to evaluation as quickly as possible.

The A2 examinations

Scheme of assessment

Each examination unit is tested in a separate 105-minute examination.

During your revision you are also advised to practise answering actual past papers. AQA A2 Business Studies past papers are available (in pdf format) from the AQA website: **www.aqa.org.uk**. Mark schemes for these examinations can also be downloaded.

Examination advice

Advice is provided throughout the book in the 'examiner's voice' boxes. Some of the key points are noted here:

- **Practice makes perfect.** Examination practice will help you to establish the best approach for you to take in the exam itself.
- **Plan the length of your answers.** After allowing for reading time, you will have more than 1 minute for every mark awarded. Use this as a guideline to the timing of your answers (10 marks = 10 minutes plus; 40 marks = approximately 45–50 minutes).
- **Use the mark allocations and wording of the question.** In Unit 3, question 1 requires analysis, questions 2, 3 and 4 require evaluation. For Unit 4 the mark allocation is a good guide (below 11 marks means that evaluation is not required; 11 marks and above means that evaluation is needed). For Unit 4, *all* questions require evaluation.
- **Move up the hierarchy of skills as quickly as possible.** Do not spend an excessive amount of time on stating points when application, analysis and evaluation are required.
- **Read the wording of the question carefully.** Half a minute spent on deciding exactly what is needed by the examiner can save you 10 to 20 minutes of wasted effort.
- **Do not be tempted to show off unnecessary knowledge.** Be prepared to accept that your favourite topic is not relevant to this examination if there are no questions on it.
- **State the obvious.** Some explanations might seem to be too easy, but they need to be included in your answer. The examiner can only reward what you have written.

- **Leave a space at the end of each answer.** If time permits, you can then add more detail at the end of your answer.

We wish you well in your studies and examinations, and hope that this book helps to provide you with the understanding needed to succeed. Good luck!

Acknowledgements

The authors would like to express their thanks to numerous individuals who have contributed to the completion of this book.

John owes a debt of gratitude to Yvonne for her stoicism and tolerance during the writing, and to Lara, Nina, Dave, Marje, Tricia and Martin for their support over many years.

Gwen is grateful to John and Jessica, both of whom are always calm, relaxed and supportive, allowing her the time and space to complete this work.

Unit 3
Strategies for success

Chapter 1

Using objectives and strategies

This chapter considers the functional objectives of a business and their relationship with its corporate objectives. It also considers the relationship between functional objectives and strategies.

Business objectives

Corporate objectives

Corporate objectives are designed to enable a business to achieve its aims or mission. They are set in order to coordinate business activity and give a sense of direction to, and guide the actions of, the organisation as a whole. They govern the setting of functional objectives (i.e. the targets or objectives of each division or department of the business), and thus provide a mechanism for ensuring that authority can be delegated without loss of coordination.

KEY TERMS

objectives: goals or targets that must be achieved in order to realise the stated aims of an organisation, department or individual team. Objectives tend to be medium to long term.

corporate objectives: the goals or targets of the whole organisation, usually based on its mission or aims.

functional objectives: the goals or targets of each of the functional areas of a business, usually based on its corporate objectives.

FOTOLIA

DID YOU KNOW?

A **mission statement** is a qualitative statement of an organisation's aims and describes the general purpose of the organisation. Corporate aims are the long-term intentions of a business.

Functional objectives

Functional objectives are set for each division or department of a business (including marketing, finance, operations and human resources) and are designed to ensure that the business achieves its corporate objectives and thus its overall aims or mission. Functional objectives are set in order to coordinate the activities of, give a sense of direction to, and guide the actions of the division or department.

FACT FILE

Corporate objectives at Hewlett Packard (HP)

'It is necessary that people work together in unison toward common objectives and avoid working at cross purposes at all levels if the ultimate in efficiency and achievement is to be obtained.' (Dave Packard, co-founder of HP)

HP is a technology company that operates in more than 170 countries around the world. It offers a wide range of technology products for business and for individual consumers.

Its corporate objectives are:

- **Customer loyalty:** to provide products, services and solutions of the highest quality, and to deliver more value to our customers that earns their respect and loyalty.
- **Profit:** to achieve sufficient profit to finance our company growth, create value for our shareholders and provide the resources we need to achieve our other corporate objectives.
- **Market leadership:** to grow by continually providing useful and significant products, services and solutions to markets we already serve — and to expand into new areas that build on our technologies, competencies and customer interests.
- **Growth:** to view change in the market as an opportunity to grow; to use our profits and our ability to develop and produce innovative products, services and solutions that satisfy emerging customer needs.
- **Employee commitment:** to help HP employees share in the company's success that they make possible; to provide people with employment opportunities based on performance; to create with them a safe, exciting and inclusive work environment that values their diversity and recognises individual contributions; and to help them gain a sense of satisfaction and accomplishment from their work.
- **Leadership capability:** to develop leaders at every level who are accountable for achieving business results and exemplifying our values.
- **Global citizenship:** good citizenship is good business. We live up to our responsibility to society by being an economic, intellectual and social asset to each country and community in which we do business.

Source: adapted from information on HP's website, www.hp.com.

Relationship between corporate objectives and functional objectives

Corporate objectives vary from firm to firm, depending on the size of the business and the legal structure. For example, the major objective of a corner shop may simply be to survive, whereas a multinational organisation may be more interested in its corporate image and the possibility of diversifying. Corporate objectives and their contributing functional objectives might include the following:

- **Survival.** Functional objectives that will assist a business's survival might include minimum levels of sales and sales revenue, appropriate levels of stock and the required number of experienced or well-trained staff.

- **Profit maximisation.** Functional objectives that will assist a business in maximising its profits might include effective marketing in order to increase sales, improving profit margins by minimising costs, the effective utilisation of capacity, and reducing staff turnover and staff absenteeism.
- **Growth maximisation.** Functional objectives that will assist a business that wishes to grow might include increasing market share, retaining profit in order to finance growth, increasing capacity by expanding the number of sites, recruiting more staff and improving training provision.
- **Diversification.** Functional objectives that will assist a business that wishes to diversify might include the development of niche markets, raising additional finance via appropriate and cost-effective sources, achieving economies of scale and ensuring effective communication between different production sites.

SMART objectives

To be effective, objectives should be **SMART** — that is, they should be:
- **Specific** — clearly and easily defined.
- **Measurable** — quantifiable (e.g. to increase market share from 15 to 20% within the next 2 years).
- **Agreed** — managers and subordinates are involved in setting the targets.
- **Realistic** — achievable and not in conflict with other objectives.
- **Time bound** — based on an explicit timescale (e.g. to open 20 new stores within the next year).

DID YOU KNOW?

Some texts suggest an alternative explanation of SMART. They state that the 'A' stands for 'achievable' and the 'R' for 'relevant'.

Objectives should be specific, measurable and timed so that it is possible to assess the extent to which they have been achieved and to ensure that people are clear about what it is they are trying to achieve. In addition, objectives must be realistic, otherwise they can be demotivating and counterproductive. Objectives that are agreed by the whole workforce are much more likely to be achieved than those that are imposed.

Business strategies

Objectives form the basis for decisions on strategy. Strategies are the medium- to long-term plans that will allow a business to achieve its objectives. Such plans include details about what is to be done and the financial, production and personnel resources required to implement the plans. Strategies should not be considered until the company's corporate and functional objectives have been agreed.

 KEY TERM

strategy: the medium- to long-term plans through which an organisation aims to attain its objectives.

Relationship between functional objectives and strategies

Functional objectives are set to ensure that corporate objectives are met. Once functional objectives have been set, appropriate strategies or plans can be devised to provide opportunities for such objectives to be met. Functional objectives and appropriate strategies are discussed in detail in later chapters, but some examples are outlined here:

- A functional objective in the marketing division might be to gain market share in order to contribute to the corporate objective of increasing the rate of growth of the business. A marketing strategy to achieve this functional objective might involve lowering price.
- A functional objective in the finance division might be to minimise costs in order to contribute to the corporate objective of maximising profits. A financial strategy to achieve this functional objective might involve introducing zero budgeting.
- A functional objective in the operations division might be to improve economies of scale. An operational strategy to achieve this functional objective might include centralised buying in bulk from the same supplier.
- A functional objective in the human resource division might be to improve labour turnover. A human resource strategy to achieve this functional objective might be to improve motivational techniques.

PRACTICE EXERCISE	Total: 40 marks (35 minutes)

1 What is meant by the term 'objectives' in a business context? *(2 marks)*

2 Distinguish between corporate and functional objectives. *(4 marks)*

3 a Give three examples of corporate objectives. *(3 marks)*
   b State three functional objectives that might contribute to achieving the corporate objectives you have identified in part **a**. *(3 marks)*

4 Identify a functional objective for each functional area of a business (i.e. for marketing, finance, operations and human resources). *(4 marks)*

5 What does the mnemonic SMART stand for in relation to objectives? *(5 marks)*

6 Explain whether the following objective satisfies the SMART criteria: 'to increase sales by 3% over the next 18 months'. *(3 marks)*

7 Explain whether the following objective satisfies the SMART criteria: 'to improve market share in the near future'. *(3 marks)*

8 What does the term 'strategy' mean in a business context? *(3 marks)*

9 Explain the relationship between functional objectives and strategies. *(4 marks)*

10 a Identify any three functional objectives. *(3 marks)*
   b Identify three related strategies designed to achieve the functional objectives noted in part **a**. *(3 marks)*

CASE STUDY Sainsbury plc

J. SAINSBURY PLC MEDIA LIBRARY

In May 2007, new 3-year targets were set in order to build on the strong progress already made and to drive further growth in the business. Five areas of focus were identified:

- Great food at fair prices: to build on and stretch the lead in food. By sharing customers' passion for healthy, safe, fresh and tasty food Sainsbury's will continue to innovate and provide leadership in delivering quality products at fair prices, sourced with integrity.
- Accelerating the growth of complementary non-food ranges: to continue to develop and accelerate the development of non-food ranges following the same principles of quality, value and innovation, and to provide a broader shopping experience for customers.
- Reaching more customers through additional channels: to extend the reach of Sainsbury's brand by opening new convenience stores, developing the online home delivery operation and growing Sainsbury's bank.
- Growing supermarket space: to expand the company's store estate, actively seeking and developing a pipeline of new stores and extending the largely under-developed store portfolio to provide an even better food offer while also growing space for non-food ranges.
- Active property management: the ownership of property assets provides operational flexibility, and the exploitation of potential development opportunities will maximise value.

Achievements 2005–07

- Sales growth of £2.7 billion: exceeding plan to reach £2.5 billion sales growth by March 2008.
- Achieved cost savings target of £440 million.
- Delivered a neutral underlying cash-flow position.
- 13 consecutive quarters of like-for-like sales growth.
- Profit more than doubled (£488 million compared to £238 million), demonstrating strong operational gearing.
- 2.5 million additional customers — now over 16.5 million a week compared to 14 million a week in 2005.

Plan for 2007–10

- Space growth — 10% new space by March 2010.
- Development of grocery and non-food ranges.
- Costs — cost savings of £155 million in 2007/08, thereafter ongoing cost savings to offset half our operating cost inflation.
- Channel growth through online and convenience expansion.
- Profit — profit growth flowing through at a percentage rate in high single digits.
- Sales growth — total additional sales of £3.5 billion by March 2010.
- Capital expenditure of £2.5 billion by March 2010.
- Cash flow neutral over 3 years.

Source: adapted from information on Sainsbury's website, **www.j-sainsbury.co.uk**.

Preliminary questions   Total: 30 marks (35 minutes)

1 Identify two of Sainsbury's corporate objectives.   *(2 marks)*

2 Explain the relationship between Sainsbury's corporate objectives
   and its functional objectives.   *(5 marks)*

3 In relation to any one of Sainsbury's corporate objectives, draft
   and explain three functional objectives that might have been set.   *(9 marks)*

4 Suggest how Sainsbury's corporate objectives could be rewritten
   to comply with the SMART criteria.   *(6 marks)*

5 Define the term 'strategy' and outline any two strategies that might
   assist Sainsbury's in meeting any one of its corporate targets.   *(8 marks)*

Case study questions   Total: 40 marks (50 minutes)

1 Examine the problems that might emerge if Sainsbury's does not set
   SMART objectives.   *(10 marks)*

2 Using examples, discuss the extent to which appropriately set functional
   objectives and well-planned strategies might help Sainsbury's achieve its
   corporate objectives.   *(15 marks)*

3 Assess the extent to which Sainsbury's plan for 2007–10 is likely to
   enable it to meet its corporate objectives.   *(15 marks)*

Chapter 2

Understanding financial objectives

This chapter examines the link between the financial objectives of a business and its broader corporate aims and objectives. The main types of financial objective are identified and explained, and the internal and external factors that influence these objectives are studied. The chapter also provides the background for subsequent chapters that examine the use of financial data in the strategic management and development of a business.

> **KEY TERMS**
>
> **financial aims:** the broad, general goals of the finance and accounting function or department within an organisation.
>
> **financial objectives:** the specific, focused targets of the finance and accounting function or department within an organisation.
>
> **financial strategies:** long-term or medium-term plans, devised at senior management level, and designed to achieve the firm's financial objectives.
>
> **financial tactics:** short-term financial measures adopted to meet the needs of a short-term threat or opportunity.

A financial hierarchy

A firm's financial aims and objectives are the goals or targets of the financial and accounting function or department of the business.

In order to achieve its *corporate* aims and objectives, a business must ensure that its *functional* aims and objectives, such as those of its finance department, are consistent with these corporate objectives.

Financial strategies are used to achieve these objectives, and these strategies may be changed if the targets set out in the objectives are not being met. However, a business should constantly review all its objectives, in case the reason for the failure of the financial strategy is an inappropriate objective, rather than an ineffective strategy.

Types of financial objective

The examples set out below illustrate the types of financial objective that a business might pursue, but they are not an exhaustive list.

Cash-flow targets

Many businesses get into financial difficulties because of a lack of cash flow rather than a lack of overall profitability. Consequently, it is vital that businesses set themselves cash-flow targets to ensure that they are able to keep operating.

Examples of cash-flow targets include:

- **Maintaining a minimum closing monthly cash balance.** For example, a minimum cash balance of £10,000 would be a sensible target for a small newsagent.
- **Reducing the bank overdraft by a certain sum by the end of the year.** For a new start-up it is likely that an overdraft will be needed to support everyday expenses, which can be quite high in the opening few months of the business. However, it is not advisable to maintain a permanent bank overdraft, so reducing the overdraft would be an appropriate target for such a business. The business might set a target of paying off the bank overdraft by a certain date.
- **Creating a more even spread of sales revenue.** To avoid cash-flow problems a business may set an objective to create a more even spread of sales revenue throughout the year. For example, one reason why Mars Ltd introduced the Mars Ice Cream was because sales of chocolate fall in the summer months. This strategy means that it is less likely that Mars Ltd will become short of cash in the summer months.
- **Spreading its costs more evenly.** A business may pay its utility bills, such as gas and electricity, on a monthly basis rather than quarterly or once every 6 months.
- **Achieving a certain level of liquid, non-cash items.** Many businesses set a target for holding certain assets, such as short-term investments or stock. If the business does run low on cash, it can turn these assets into cash quickly.
- **Raising certain levels of cash at a particular point in time.** If the business knows through its cash-flow forecasts that it needs to acquire a higher level of cash at a certain time (for example, a retailer building up stock levels for Christmas), it may set a target of raising a particular level of cash.
- **Setting contingency fund levels.** Most businesses set a target for a contingency fund, which is an emergency source of finance that can be used if unexpected difficulties occur.

Cost minimisation

A business that reduces its costs can benefit in two ways:

- It can keep its price the same and benefit from a higher profit margin.
- It can use its cost reduction to reduce the selling price of its finished product and thus attract more customers.

 EXAMINER'S VOICE

Financial objectives come in many forms, so it is not advisable to memorise a specific list. In the examination, try to work out the financial aims and objectives of the actual business in the case study. This will allow you to apply your answer in a way that is relevant to the particular situation or business concerned.

 **EXAMINER'S VOICE**

Detailed analysis of methods of improving cash flow was given in Chapter 17 of the AS textbook. If you wish to remind yourself of the nature of cash flow, take another look at this chapter.

EXAMINER'S VOICE

When providing suggestions for cost minimisation, it is important to consider the business's financial situation. While each of the examples given will achieve lower unit costs of production, some methods — such as introducing new technology and relocating the business — will incur very high short-term costs. In these cases, cost minimisation will take place only in the long term. Thus the objective of cost minimisation may not be appropriate for a business with short-term cash-flow difficulties.

Examples of cost minimisation objectives include:

- **Achieving a certain cost reduction in the purchase of raw materials.** The business might try to lower raw material purchase costs by 10%, for example, by locating cheaper suppliers overseas, such as in China.
- **Reducing wage costs per unit.** This may be done by improving the productivity of labour or reducing the level of overtime payments.
- **Lowering levels of wastage.** This saves costs by reducing the usage of raw materials or the number of items of finished products that are discarded.
- **Relocating the business to the 'least-cost site'.** This might help to cut costs.
- **Reducing the cost per thousand customers (CPT) of the business's promotion and advertising.** Many businesses are using the internet, rather than more traditional forms of media such as newspapers and television, in order to improve the cost effectiveness of their marketing.
- **Improving the efficiency of production by reducing variable costs per unit.** This might be achieved through introducing new technology.

Targets based on cost minimisation must be used with caution. Cheaper raw materials may be of inferior quality, and this in turn can reduce the quality of the finished products. Lower quality may be acceptable for customers seeking the lowest possible price, but for many customers lower quality would be unacceptable. If cost minimisation has adverse side-effects, it may not be an appropriate objective.

FACT FILE

Porter's generic strategies

According to Michael Porter, firms must try to achieve a 'sustainable competitive advantage'. This is an advantage that can be maintained in the face of sustained competition. Porter's theory suggests that there are two main approaches that can achieve this advantage:

- cost leadership
- differentiation or value leadership

The first of these two approaches can be achieved by a business keeping its costs below those of its rivals, producing standard mass-produced products of an acceptable standard at a much lower cost than its competitors. In the UK, Poundstretcher and ASDA are examples of businesses using this strategy.

To adopt this strategy it is vital that costs are minimised. ASDA has been helped in this strategy by its parent company, Wal-Mart, which is the world's largest supermarket. Wal-Mart has tremendous buying power and is able to keep its costs to a minimum, which helps ASDA's competitiveness.

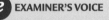 **EXAMINER'S VOICE**

The use of cost minimisation as a marketing strategy is considered in Chapter 9.

ROCE targets

The success of a business is invariably demonstrated by its profit levels. Clearly, large firms will achieve higher profit levels than smaller businesses, so the profit needs to be compared to the size of the business.

The **capital employed** is a measure of the value of the resources used by a business and is an excellent guide to its size. Consequently, profit targets are often expressed as a **return on capital employed** (ROCE), which uses the formula below:

$$\text{return on capital employed } (\%) = \frac{\text{operating profit}}{\text{capital employed}} \times 100$$

Typically, a business will set itself one or more of three types of objective for its ROCE:

- To achieve an ROCE that exceeds the level recorded in the previous year by a certain percentage.
- To achieve an ROCE that compares favourably to the average ROCE achieved in the UK.
- To achieve an ROCE that exceeds the level of a particular competitor or group of competitors.

Note that, on occasions, a business may set a less ambitious objective for its profit. For example, during a recession it is likely that a business will expect a lower level of profit than it would during a time when the economy is growing.

Return on capital employed (%) as a financial objective is discussed in detail in Chapter 4.

Shareholders' returns

A business must satisfy the needs of its owners/shareholders. Many shareholders assess a business in terms of the dividends received because a high dividend is likely to be linked to high levels of profit and a sound financial performance by the business. However, shareholders may have other objectives that need to be considered. Some of these non-financial objectives, such as ethical behaviour on the part of the business, will be considered in Unit 4 (see Chapter 23). This section focuses only on financial objectives.

Some examples of financial objectives that meet shareholders' needs are:

- **A high dividend per share.** The **dividend** is the payment made to each shareholder as their part of the profit made by the business. Usually this target will take the form of a particular level of dividend or a percentage increase on the dividend payment made in the previous year.
- **A high dividend yield.** This shows the dividend paid as a percentage of the market value of the share. For example, suppose that one share in Company X could be purchased for £1 and that Company X is paying a dividend of 7p per share. In this case the percentage return or dividend yield is 7%. Shareholders will usually compare this 7% dividend yield to the interest they could receive from an alternative investment, such as the interest they would receive from a bank account.
- **Increasing the share price.** In simple terms the share price tends to reflect the value of the business. Therefore, if the business retains its profits and grows successfully, the share price should increase, satisfying this objective.

- **High earnings per share.** Earnings per share are measured as the total profit divided by the number of shares. In effect, they show the profit made by each individual share in the businesss and so they provide a good indicator of efficiency.

Other financial objectives

- **Sales maximisation.** Some businesses try to make more profit by maximising their sales revenue or sales volume.
- **Liquidity and gearing targets.** Most businesses set specific objectives that help them to keep sufficient liquidity and thus avoid cash-flow problems. A detailed treatment of these objectives is provided in Chapter 4.
- **Financial objectives for individual projects.** Businesses often set financial objectives for individual projects. Chapter 5 looks at further examples of these objectives, such as the **payback period**, which measures how quickly an investment pays for itself.
- **Financial efficiency targets.** Financial objectives are often set for the performance of a particular aspect of the business's financial management, such as the accuracy of the budgeting process (targeting low variances).

Reasons for setting financial objectives

The reasons for setting financial objectives vary according to the specific objective and the firm's situation. Some major reasons are to:
- act as a focus for decision making and effort
- provide a yardstick against which success or failure can be measured
- improve coordination, by giving teams and departments a common purpose
- improve efficiency, by examining the reasons for success and failure in different areas
- allow shareholders to assess whether the business is going to provide a worthwhile investment
- enable outside organisations, such as suppliers and customers, to confirm the financial viability of a business

Assessing internal influences on financial objectives

Internal factors that affect financial objectives are those within the business, such as its workforce, resources and financial position.

Corporate objectives

The overall aims of an organisation are a key influence on the objectives of a functional area, such as the finance department. The finance department must ensure that its objectives are consistent with the corporate objectives of the business. For example, pizza restaurants are now experiencing greater levels of competition, so profit targets have been reduced for some restaurants.

In contrast, one of Sainsbury's key corporate objectives was to try to persuade customers to spend more on each visit to the store. This required the finance department, in coordination with the other functional areas, to set objectives focused on higher profit margins on a wide range of products.

FACT FILE

Increasing customer spending at Sainsbury's

In 2007 Sainsbury's chief executive, Justin King, set his colleagues a corporate objective that appeared to be too challenging. The target was for Sainsbury's to increase its sales revenue by £25 billion per annum. In order to translate this into what appeared to be a more reasonable target, the number of customer visits per annum was calculated. This was divided into £25 billion and led to a modified target: Sainsbury's aimed to persuade each customer to spend an additional £1.14 every time they visited the store. A promotional campaign was introduced to encourage customers to shift their purchasing habits towards higher-priced items such as nutmeg and exotic fruits. Although this objective was not reached initially, at the end of the year Sainsbury's customers were spending an additional 85p per visit.

J. SAINSBURY PLC MEDIA LIBRARY

Finance

There is a saying that 'money makes money'. A business in a healthy financial situation is in a much better position to achieve high levels of profits and cash flow. It can fund investment into items such as research and development, new technology and marketing campaigns that may help it to improve its overall financial performance.

Consequently, such a business can set more challenging objectives. For example, the high levels of profit achieved by Microsoft have enabled it to spend considerable sums of money on researching and developing new software so that it can stay ahead of competition. These high profits have also enabled Microsoft to diversify into areas of great potential, such as computer consoles.

Human resources (HR)

Achieving financial objectives depends on the efforts and skills of the workforce. Effective planning of the workforce and a good recruitment and training policy can enable a business to increase its profitability, by increasing the efficiency of the workforce.

However, there can be conflict between the needs of the workforce and the business's financial objectives. Cost minimisation is a particular case in point. Workers may resist measures that might endanger their own jobs, such as the introduction of a new IT system, or objectives that require unit costs to be cut by making the workers extend their hours without additional pay.

Operational factors

The finance department relies on each of the other functional areas in order to reach its objectives. If the operations management function of the business is operating efficiently, the firm will be able to produce goods of high quality and low cost. This combination will lead to good sales revenue and high profit margins, and enable the business to achieve quite challenging financial targets.

Resources available

A business which, over time, has built up a strong resource base will be able to target and achieve a strong financial performance. These resources might be in the form of premises, well-known brand names, or the quality of the workforce.

The nature of the product

The success of a business is heavily influenced by its products and services. In many cases, successful businesses have happened to be in the right place at the right time. Some of the most successful companies in the UK in recent years have been the mobile phone networks. However, as the market has reached maturity, companies such as Orange and Vodafone have needed to devise innovation or extension strategies to reach their financial objectives. With continued rapid changes in mobile communications technology, it is by no means certain that the mobile phone, in its current form, will retain its popularity.

Assessing external influences on financial objectives

External factors are those outside the business, such as the state of the economy and the actions of competitors. The mnemonic PESTLE is often used to classify the external factors that can influence a business. The PESTLE (or LE PEST) factors are as follows:

- **Political**
- **Economic**
- **Social**
- **Technological**
- **Legal**
- **Environmental**

> **e EXAMINER'S VOICE**
>
> PESTLE factors are covered in detail in Chapters 21–25. For BUSS3 only an overview of external factors is required. For each of the PESTLE factors *one* example of its influence on financial objectives is provided below.

Examples of external factors influencing financial objectives

Political factors

Financial objectives are often guided towards the wishes of the shareholders. However, greater openness has also led to expectations on businesses to serve the needs of other groups, such as the workforce, customers, the local community and the environment.

Economic factors

The state of the economy is a major influence on the financial performance of businesses. For example if an economy is in recession, customers will purchase fewer products and so lower sales and profit targets will be set. For businesses dealing in luxury products, it is likely that these targets will be significantly lower. For some businesses, such as those selling staple foods, there will be only a limited effect.

Social factors

Society is constantly changing and businesses must adjust to suit society. People now expect access to businesses 24–7 if possible. This change in expectations can make it difficult for businesses to set targets that involve lower costs, but at the same time it opens up opportunities for targeting greater revenue and creating new ways of generating income.

Technological change

Technological change can lead to improvements in communication. A particular benefit is that financial targets can be monitored more regularly and more closely, and objectives or strategies modified in the light of changing circumstances.

Legal factors

In some industries, legal requirements have a big impact on the objectives of a business and changes in these requirements will lead to modified financial objectives. For example, in the motor industry, frequent updates in environmental legislation, covering both the manufacturing process and the end product, have increased the costs of manufacturing a car.

Environmental factors

Growing environmental awareness among consumers and actions by pressure groups have had financial implications for businesses. Acquiring supplies and raw materials from environmentally friendly sources is now an aim for many businesses as they try to minimise their carbon footprint.

Other external factors that can influence financial objectives, but which are not part of the PESTLE model, are described below.

Market factors

The demand for certain types of product goes through cycles of expansion and decline, closely related to the life cycle of that type of product. When a product reaches maturity, high levels of profit will become the main financial objective for that specific product.

Competitors' actions and performance

The level of competition is also an influence on a firm's financial objectives. In recent years, the prices of utilities, such as gas and electricity, have increased substantially, as suppliers have been able to take advantage of the relatively limited levels of competition in those markets. Consequently, utility suppliers have been able to target and achieve very high levels of profit.

Suppliers

Suppliers can have a major impact on a business's financial objectives. The Cooperative Society (Co-op) is one of the UK's major farmers and supplies its shops with food products, particularly from its dairy farms. However, although this has provided the Co-op with a regular supply of food, this food is not among the cheapest in the UK and is more expensive than farm produce from some other countries. As a consequence, this has had an adverse affect on the Co-op's ability to set and achieve high profit targets.

PRACTICE EXERCISE   Total: 40 marks (35 minutes)

1 As financial management is essential to the strategic development of the business, financial objectives and corporate objectives often overlap. State three financial objectives that could also be set as corporate objectives.   *(3 marks)*

2 State two different cash-flow objectives.   *(2 marks)*

3 Why is cost minimisation often an important financial objective? *(5 marks)*

4 Outline two possible disadvantages of prioritising cost minimisation as a major financial objective.   *(6 marks)*

5 What is meant by ROCE (%)?   *(3 marks)*

6 Why are profit targets so important to a business?   *(5 marks)*

7 Identify two different financial objectives based on shareholders' needs.   *(2 marks)*

8 Explain two reasons for setting financial objectives.   *(6 marks)*

9 State four internal factors that might influence a firm's financial objectives.   *(4 marks)*

10 State four external factors that might influence a firm's financial objectives.   *(4 marks)*

CASE STUDY 1 Halfords heads east

Table 2.1 *Halfords' financial objectives, 2007/08*

Financial objective	Commentary on actual performance
Increase the dividend to shareholders	Increase in dividend of 9% — from 13.85p per share to 15.1p per share.
Cutting costs	Achieved by reducing the use of agents and buying more products directly from manufacturers. This reduces unit costs and improves the quality of the service.
	Buying more supplies from the Far East. The percentage of supplies from the Far East increased from 7% in 2003/04 to 21% in 2007/08. The future target is to continue to increase this percentage.
Increase the profit (earnings) per share for shareholders	This has been achieved by: • a continued share buyback programme • increases in the net profit margin
Increase the net profit margin	This objective has been: • helped by improvements in labour productivity in stores • helped by a slowdown in rent increases on property • hindered by setting up costs in eastern Europe
Increase overall net profits	Profit before tax rose from £80.9 million to £90.2 million, an increase of 11.5%, surpassing the target set.
Increase rate of stock turnover	This figure improved by 7.1% in 2007/08.
Maintain a healthy cash flow	High levels of liquidity were maintained in 2007/08, with excellent cash-flow balances.

In 2007/08 Halfords enjoyed a successful year. Its key financial results were:
- an increase in revenue of 7.2%
- profit rising by 11.5%
- store growth up by 5.6%

Table 2.1 summarises the main financial objectives of Halfords, with a comment on the company's actual performance.

Sources: Halfords' annual reports and other sources.

Preliminary questions
Total: 25 marks (30 minutes)

1 a Identify two other financial objectives that Halfords might have set. *(2 marks)*
   b Briefly explain why the two financial objectives that you have selected in your answer to part **a** would have been good objectives for Halfords to set. *(4 marks)*

2 Explain one internal factor that might have influenced Halfords' financial objectives. *(4 marks)*

3 Explain one external factor that might have influenced Halfords' financial objectives. *(4 marks)*

4 Explain one factor that might make it difficult for Halfords to achieve a healthy cash flow. *(4 marks)*

5 Halfords has established new shops in eastern Europe. Examine why this strategy might have led to a decline in profits in the short term but an increase in profits in the long-term. *(7 marks)*

Case study questions
Total: 30 marks (35 minutes)

1 To what extent are Halfords' financial objectives 'SMART'? *(12 marks)*

2 Evaluate the extent to which Halfords has enjoyed a successful year, with respect to its financial objectives. *(18 marks)*

CASE STUDY 2 'Making Sainsbury great again'

J Sainsbury shrugged off some of the gloom surrounding consumer spending as it announced that annual sales rose last year by £1 billion. The company predicted a period of growth after completing its 3-year turnaround programme. The third largest supermarket in the UK boosted its sales by 5.8% to £19.2 billion in the year ending March 2008.

Sainsbury's now plans to expand throughout the UK and has put £15 million into launching an online business to sell non-food items, such as clothing and homeware, in early 2009.

Justin King, the group's chief executive, said the company had equalled all and beaten many of the targets set under the 'Making Sainsbury great again' recovery plan, launched 3 years ago. Sainsbury's staff will share a £47 million bonus after meeting those targets, which included increasing sales by £2.5 billion; cost savings of £440 million; and investments of more than £400 million. Since the strategy was started in 2005, Sainsbury's has more than doubled its profits from £238 million to £488 million.

The 'Making Sainsbury great again' plan was dismissed by many people as fanciful when Justin King unveiled it in 2005. Three years on, he believes that he has done more than enough to prove the doubters wrong. Sales growth has generated an extra £2.7 billion, surpassing his target of £2.5 billion.

Mr King used the opportunity to launch Sainsbury's next 3-year plan. The main financial objective for the next 3 years is an extra £3.5 billion of sales. Sainsbury's will be targeting Tesco and ASDA at their own game, by expanding far more into non-food sales. Last week, Sainsbury's launched a new range of cut-price homeware, with more than 1,700 new products such as bathroom fittings and kitchen implements. Around 70% of the range will cost less than £10. King cites the success of 'Tu', Sainsbury's £300 million clothing range, as proof that Sainsbury's is on the right path by diversifying into non-food products. At the height of the Christmas and New Year 2008 promotion, the supermarket sold a Sony Ravia flatscreen television every 5 seconds.

City analysts take different views on Sainsbury's prospects. Freddie George of Seymour Pierce believes the company has 'a great opportunity to expand in non-food and develop its multichannel activities, with great potential for cost savings, particularly in its transport'.

However, Philip Dorgan of Panmure Gordon believes that 'Profits are still lower than those achieved in 1991 and operating cash-flow growth has been weak. We also believe that the industry environment is about to get a lot tougher.'

King refuted suggestions that customer demand would fall but did acknowledge that economic factors would be an important influence on the success or failure of this latest plan.

Sources: articles by Nick Clark in the *Independent*, 15 May 2008 and by Steve Hawkes in *The Times*, 28 April 2008, and other sources.

Questions

Total: 35 marks (45 minutes)

1 In 2005 Sainsbury's set itself three challenging financial targets: increasing sales by £2.5 billion; achieving cost savings of £440 million; and introducing investments of more than £400 million. Evaluate the possible benefits and problems to Sainsbury's as a result of setting these specific, challenging financial objectives.

(15 marks)

2 Discuss the main internal and external factors that are likely to influence the ability of Sainsbury's to meet its latest 3-year target — to increase sales by £3.5 billion.

(20 marks)

Chapter 3

Using financial data to measure and assess performance

This chapter introduces company accounts by considering the people who use accounting information and scrutinising their reasons for using it. It then studies the two main sources of financial data: the balance sheet and the income statement. This study commences with the balance sheet, focusing on its layout and its main components. The importance of working capital and the significance of depreciation are also examined. The purposes of the balance sheet are considered and the reasons why it balances are outlined. The chapter then looks at the income statement and its purposes. The structure of the income statement is described and the reasons for the structure are explained. The concept of profit quality and the significance of profit utilisation are examined. The chapter then considers the use of financial data for comparisons, trend analysis and decision making. It concludes by assessing the strengths and weaknesses of financial data in judging performance.

 EXAMINER'S VOICE

The AQA A2 business studies specification does *not* require you to construct a balance sheet or an income statement. However, in the opinion of the authors an understanding of the layout of both the balance sheet and the income statement is essential in order to understand their purpose and meaning.

Company accounts

Two key financial documents kept by firms are:

- the balance sheet
- the income statement

These documents are required by law in order to show people the financial strengths and weaknesses of an organisation's recent performance and current situation. They can also be used to assess the potential of a business, particularly when trend analysis is used to estimate future performances based on recent history.

Both documents are based on historical data and show what has happened in the recent past.

KEY TERMS

balance sheet:
a document describing the financial position of a company at a particular point in time, by comparing the items owned by the organisation (its assets) with the amounts that it owes (its liabilities).

income statement:
an account showing the income and expenditure (and thus the profit or loss) of a firm over a period of time (usually a year).

Purposes and users of company accounts

Accounting information serves many purposes and these depend on who is using the accounts. The main users and purposes are summarised in Table 3.1.

At AS, the main focus in the 'Financial planning' part of the course was on management accounting, through examining breakeven analysis, sources of finance, cash-flow forecasting and budgeting.

The A2 course continues the study of management accounting by examining the selecting of financial strategies and the making of investment decisions (see Chapters 5 and 6). However, at A2 there is greater emphasis on financial accounting through the study of company accounts and their significance (this chapter and Chapter 4).

KEY TERMS

management accounting: the creation of financial information for use by *internal users* in the business, in order to predict, plan, review and control the financial performance of the business.

financial accounting: the provision of financial information to show *external users* the financial position of the business; it concentrates on historical data.

Table 3.1 *Purposes of accounting information*

Users	Purpose
Internal users	
Managers	Managers use information to record financial activities, plan appropriate courses of action, control the use of resources, and analyse and evaluate the effectiveness of actions and decisions taken in financial terms.
Employees	Employees can assess the security of their employment and the ability of the firm to provide them with reasonable wages by examining the financial position of the business.
Owners and investors*	Investors want to compare the financial benefits of their investment with alternatives, such as shares in different companies or placing their savings in a bank. Invariably, the financial benefits to owners and investors are closely related to the financial success of the business.
External users	
Government	The government wants to know that the business has met its legal requirements and that it has paid certain levels of tax. In addition, UK firms collect some taxes, such as VAT and the income tax payments of their employees, and pass them on to the tax authorities. Government also uses this information to assess the impact of its economic policies on the sales revenue and profits of businesses, and to plan future policies.
Competitors	Competitors are able to compare their performance against rival companies and benchmark their performances. Government encourages the publicising of results so that firms can learn from each other's strengths and errors.
Suppliers	Suppliers want information about a firm's financial situation before agreeing to supply materials. This may help them to decide if the firm is likely to continue operating. Closer scrutiny may help the supplier to identify the sort of payment terms that are being offered to other suppliers.
Customers	Customers want to know if the company is financially sound and that guarantees and after-sales servicing agreements are secure. Business customers want to establish whether it is advisable for them to draw up long-term supply contracts with this company.
The local community	The local community relies on businesses for employment and wealth creation. The local council may need to modify its housing or road-building plans if a local firm is getting into financial difficulties and is likely to close down or reduce staff. (It may also need to consider the possible consequences if a local firm is becoming very successful and wishes to expand.)

*Investors would be considered external users if they are considering whether to invest in a business, but have not yet invested.

Analysing balance sheets

What is a balance sheet?

A balance sheet looks at the accumulated wealth of a business and can be used to assess its overall worth. It lists the resources that a business owns (its **assets**) and the amounts it owes to others (its **liabilities**).

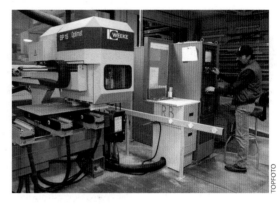

In addition, it shows the **equity** (capital) provided by the owners (the shareholders in a limited company). Equity is provided through either the purchase of shares or the agreement to allow the company to retain or 'plough back' profit into the business, known as **reserves**, rather than using it to pay further dividends to the shareholders.

Elements of the balance sheet

In order to understand the layout of the balance sheet, it is important to understand the different elements listed in it.

EXAMINER'S VOICE

The AQA A2 business studies specification requires students to recognise and understand the layout of the balance sheet (and the income statement) so that a business's performance and potential can be recognised. However, in the examination any necessary accounting information will be provided for you to analyse. You will not be expected to construct either of these accounts.

Assets

Assets can be divided into two main categories according to time:

- **Non-current assets** tend to be owned by an organisation for a period of more than 1 year.
- **Current assets** tend to be owned for less than 1 year.

In general, non-current assets are purchased to allow the business to operate continuously. Land and buildings are acquired so that the firm has the premises from which to operate. Machinery and equipment enable organisations to manufacture and/or sell their goods and services, and to administer their business. Vehicles are required for delivery and staff transport, as appropriate.

DID YOU KNOW?

The balance sheet only shows those non-current assets that are owned by the business. In 2007, HSBC sold its headquarters in Canary Wharf, London for £1.1 billion, a record UK price for a building, and it now rents the property from the new owners for £43.5 million a year. As a consequence, HSBC's fixed assets fell by £1.1 billion (but its cash reserves initially rose by £1.1 billion).

KEY TERMS

assets: items that are owned by an organisation.

non-current assets: resources that can be used repeatedly in the production process, although they do wear out (depreciate) or lose value. Examples are land, buildings, machinery and vehicles.

tangible assets: non-current (fixed) assets that exist physically.

intangible assets: non-current assets that do not have a physical presence, but are nevertheless of value to a firm (e.g. a brand name or patent).

The main intangible asset is **goodwill**, which includes the value of a firm's brand names, patents and copyrights. The value of intangible assets is difficult to assess objectively, so it is customary to exclude them from the balance sheet.

DID YOU KNOW?

Although accounting regulations indicate that businesses should not include intangible assets, such as the value of a brand name, in their balance sheets, there is a major exception to this rule. A business that buys another firm invariably pays for the goodwill/intangible assets belonging to that firm. As money has been paid for these intangible assets, they are included as a fixed asset in the balance sheet.

The value of each tangible fixed asset is reduced annually; this process is known as **depreciation** and is explained in more detail later in this chapter. Similarly, businesses must reduce the value of their goodwill over time; this process is known as **amortisation**.

In 2007–08, Game Group plc bought Gamestation's 217 stores. In addition to physical locations, it also aimed to get hold of Gamestation's goodwill and expertise. As a consequence, its intangible assets are valued at a higher level than its tangible assets, and amortisation of goodwill in 2008 almost doubled to over £20 million.

Examples of current assets are inventories {stocks}; receivables {debtors} — people who owe the business money, usually customers who have been given credit terms; cash and other cash equivalents (mainly the bank balance and cash).

KEY TERM

current assets: short-term items that circulate in a business on a daily basis and can be expected to be turned into cash within 1 year.

EXAMINER'S VOICE

Since 2005 a European regulation requires public limited companies (plcs) to prepare financial statements in compliance with the International Financial Reporting Standards (IFRS). This has led to a number of changes in the terminology used on the IFRS balance sheet:

- Fixed assets are called 'non-current assets' but continue to include tangible and non-tangible assets.
- There are two changes within the current assets section of the balance sheet: stocks are renamed as 'inventories' and debtors are now termed 'trade and other receivables'.
- Under current liabilities, creditors are referred to as 'trade and other payables'.
- Long-term liabilities are renamed 'non-current liabilities'.
- Reserves in the final section of the balance sheet are supplemented by 'retained earnings'. Retained earnings are profits that a company has generated which have not been paid out to shareholders.
- Shareholders' funds are termed 'total equity' or 'total shareholders' equity'.

Note that the overall structure of the balance sheet is the same, even though the terminology varies.

To ease this transition and to allow students to utilise previous papers from the old AQA business studies specification, this book uses the new IFS terminology but frequently shows the previous terminology in {brackets}. For the sake of simplicity and ease of use, the IFRS standard terms are used for the accounts of all businesses in this book, rather than being restricted to plcs only.

Inventories {stocks} consist of finished products, work-in-progress (partially completed goods) and raw materials. In order to meet the accounting concept of prudence, inventories {stocks} are valued at the cost paid, rather than the price they are expected to fetch. Firms regularly update the value of their inventories. If inventories have been damaged, have exceeded their sell-by date or have gone out of fashion, their value is reduced. Similarly, the value of **receivables** {debtors} is reduced if any receivable is behind schedule and unlikely to be paid. (Most firms value their receivables at slightly below their face value to allow for **bad debts**: that is, receivables that are not paid.)

Liabilities

Liabilities are classified according to time, in a similar way to assets:

- **Non-current liabilities** (long-term liabilities) are debts due for repayment after more than 1 year.
- **Current liabilities** are debts scheduled for repayment within 1 year.

Examples of **non-current liabilities** are debentures and long-term or medium-term loans. **Debentures** are fixed-interest loans with a repayment date set a long time into the future. **Loans** are usually provided by banks. These long-term liabilities must be repaid, but they mean that a company does not need to issue more shares to raise funds to purchase fixed assets.

Examples of **current liabilities** are payables {creditors}, bank overdrafts, corporation tax owing and shareholders' dividends due for payment. **Payables** {creditors} are people or organisations that are owed money by the firm. Often these are suppliers awaiting payment, but they may be traders who have supplied services, such as gas, electricity and telephone systems. In the balance sheet, traders and suppliers are combined under the description 'trade and other payables'.

Capital

Capital takes two main forms:

- **Share capital** — the funds provided by shareholders through the purchase of shares.
- **Reserves and retained earnings** — those items that arise from increases in the value of the company, which are not distributed to shareholders as dividends, but are retained by the business for future use.

Most reserves arise because shareholders have voted at the annual general meeting to allow the firm to keep some of the profit, rather than distribute it to shareholders as dividends.

INGRAM

KEY TERMS

liabilities: debts owed by an organisation to suppliers, shareholders, investors or customers who have paid in advance.

total equity or total shareholders' equity {capital}: funds provided by shareholders to set up the business, fund expansion and purchase fixed assets.

_e_ EXAMINER'S VOICE

Remember, reserves are not cash. Usually they are an entry in the accounts that shows how much profit the firm has retained, but invariably the purpose of this action is to purchase non-current (fixed) assets. Any cash held by the business is shown under current assets. Technically, reserves are included to recognise the fact that they are a liability owed to shareholders, not an asset. Reserves represent the sum that shareholders could have taken as dividends, but which was retained in the business for its own use.

Purposes of the balance sheet

The details provided in the balance sheet help stakeholders to assess the financial strength of a business. As with the income statement, the balance sheet should be studied over time and a comparison made with the balance sheets of competitors in order to draw valid conclusions.

Scrutiny of the balance sheet serves the following purposes:

- **Recognising the scale of a business.** Adding non-current assets to working capital (see Table 3.2) gives an overall view of the capital employed by a business and thus its overall worth.
- **Calculating the net assets of a business.** The balance sheet shows the overall worth of a business: its total assets minus its total liabilities. This figure (net assets) shows the value of the business to its shareholders.
- **Gaining an understanding of the nature of the firm.** The structure of a firm's assets may give information about the nature of the business. For example, primary industries, such as agriculture and mineral extraction, often own large areas of land in comparison to other firms, although high-street organisations may own expensive land.

  Shops tend to possess high levels of inventories {stocks}, as they need to display their goods to attract customers. Low levels of receivables {debtors} are shown on the accounts of firms providing personal and financial services, as there is a tradition of immediate payment rather than credit facilities being provided.
- **Identifying the company's liquidity position.** Comparing liquid or current assets (those that can be turned into cash quickly) with current liabilities (those that must be paid back soon) shows whether a firm is going to be able to avoid cash-flow problems.
- **Showing sources of capital.** The balance sheet shows whether a company is raising its finance from retained profits or long-term loans.
- **Recognising the significance of changes over time.** Continual scrutiny of the balance sheet can identify any undesirable changes that take place.

e EXAMINER'S VOICE

There are minor variations in the ways in which a balance sheet can be presented. In order to assist students, AQA has agreed that any balance sheets presented in examination papers will adopt a certain standard approach. The balance sheet for 'Rounded Figures plc' (Table 3.2) shows the *maximum possible* extent of data that could be included on a single paper. This format will be used for all balance sheets in this textbook. It is likely that questions will be asked on balance sheets where only some of the elements included in Table 3.2 are provided.

Actual balance sheets of public limited companies may include other details. These additional details are not required for AQA A2 business studies.

The layout of the balance sheet

The balance sheet allows the **net value** of a company (its **net assets**) to be calculated by working out the **total assets** (non-current assets and current assets) and subtracting **total liabilities** (current liabilities and non-current liabilities). Alternatively, net value could be obtained by adding **non-current assets** to **working capital** and subtracting **non-current liabilities**.

The format also allows the **capital employed** (net assets plus non-current liabilities) to be calculated, by adding **non-current assets** to **working capital** or **net current assets** (current assets minus current liabilities), or by adding **total equity** to **non-current liabilities** (see Table 3.2).

Useful balance sheet formulae

current assets = inventories + receivables + cash and other cash equivalents

working capital = current assets − current liabilities

net assets = non-current assets + current assets − current liabilities − non-current liabilities

net assets = non-current assets + working capital (or net current assets) − non-current liabilities

assets employed = net current assets + non-current assets

capital employed = total equity + non-current liabilities

assets employed = capital employed

The balance sheets below (Table 3.2) refer to a fictitious company called Rounded Figures plc. The company supplies food products and is famous for its cream cakes and doughnuts.

	As at: 30.6.09 (£000s)		30.6.08 (£000s)	
Non-current assets {fixed assets}		890	750	
Inventories {stocks}	60		50	
Receivables {debtors}	150		140	
Cash and other cash equivalents	300		310	
Total current assets		510	500	
Payables {creditors}	(300)		(250)	
Current liabilities		(300)	(250)	
Net current assets (working capital)		210	250	
Non-current liabilities (long-term liabilities)		(200)	(280)	
Net assets (net worth)		900	720	
Share capital			300	280
Reserves			600	440
Total equity			900	720
NB capital employed =				
non-current assets + net current assets =		1,100	1,000	

Table 3.2
Balance sheets of Rounded Figures plc, 30 June 2009 and 30 June 2008

Why the balance sheet always balances

The balance sheet balances because:

assets = liabilities + equity

In 2009 Rounded Figures plc has assets of £1,400,000 (£890,000 + £510,000). It has liabilities and equity of £1,400,000 (£300,000 + £200,000 + £900,000).

PRACTICE EXERCISE 1   Total: 30 marks (30 minutes)

1 What is meant by a 'balance sheet'? *(2 marks)*

2 What are the differences between assets, liabilities and equity? *(6 marks)*

3 Identify three non-current assets. *(3 marks)*

4 Identify three current assets. *(3 marks)*

5 Why is it important to distinguish between non-current assets and current assets? *(4 marks)*

6 Identify three possible current liabilities. *(3 marks)*

7 Explain three uses of balance sheets. *(9 marks)*

PRACTICE EXERCISE 2   Total: 20 marks (20 minutes)

Using the data in Table 3.3, calculate the following values:

1 Non-current assets (fixed assets) *(3 marks)*

2 Current assets *(3 marks)*

3 Current liabilities *(3 marks)*

4 Net current assets (working capital) *(3 marks)*

5 Non-current liabilities *(2 marks)*

6 Net assets (total net assets) *(3 marks)*

7 Total equity (capital) *(3 marks)*

Table 3.3 *Balance sheet data*

	£m
Intangible assets	68
Cash and other equivalents	4
Payables {creditors}	23
Share capital	74
Receivables {debtors}	34
Bank overdraft	3
Bank loans (over 1 year)	16
Land and buildings	88
Inventories {stock}	19
Vehicles	11
Reserves	132
Plant and machinery	24

Capital expenditure, revenue expenditure and depreciation

Classifying business expenditure

Business expenditure can be classified as either revenue expenditure or capital expenditure.

Capital expenditure exists when the spending is on an item that will be used time and time again. For accounting purposes, if the expenditure on an asset continues to help the business in future years, it is capital expenditure.

DID YOU KNOW?

As with many business classifications, the distinction between revenue spending and capital spending is open to interpretation. The key distinction is the length of time that the business benefits from the spending. For marketing spending, it is often argued that this year's marketing can help to build a brand for the future. However, for the sake of simplicity, marketing is taken to be revenue expenditure. Similarly, a business that rents its property is undertaking revenue expenditure, but an organisation that buys its property is making a capital expenditure.

The main categories of revenue expenditure and capital expenditure are listed in Table 3.4.

Revenue expenditure	Capital expenditure
• Wages and salaries to employees	• Freehold property or extensions to premises
• Office consumables such as stationery and ink cartridges	• Machinery for production purposes
• Operating expenses such as power and petrol for vehicles	• Office equipment and furniture
• Marketing expenditure	• Vehicles
• Raw materials and inventories	
• Rental payments	

Table 3.4 Categories of revenue expenditure and capital expenditure

The significance of the distinction between capital and revenue expenditure

When constructing accounts, accountants follow certain agreed principles. One of the basic rules of accounting is the **matching** or **accruals concept**. This states that, when calculating a firm's profit, any income should be matched to the expenditure involved in creating that income. What are the implications of this convention?

For revenue expenditure the implications are reasonably clear. Any wages paid to production-line workers and payments for raw materials are deducted from the income earned from selling the final product. It is assumed that the sales revenue and expenditure take place in the same financial year. Thus, wages and power are always treated as a cost in the year in which the payment is made. In general, payments for raw materials are treated in the same way. However, if there are some raw materials left over at the end of the year, the value of those raw materials is transferred to the next year's accounts, as that is when they will be used. This meets the requirements of the 'matching' principle, because raw material costs are matched to the time period in which the finished product is sold.

For capital expenditure the situation is very different. Fixed assets are used over a long period, so any capital expenditure needs to be spread over the lifetime of the fixed asset in order to 'match' the spending to the income that it creates. For example, a machine that costs £50,000 and lasts for 5 years could be deemed to cost £10,000 a year for the next 5 years. It should not be

KEY TERMS

revenue expenditure: spending on day-to-day items such as raw materials, inventories {stocks}, wages and power to run the production process.

capital expenditure: spending on non-current (fixed) assets — those assets used repeatedly in the production process, such as buildings, vehicles and machinery.

charged as £50,000 in the year in which it is purchased because it will continue to create income in all 5 years.

Another accounting convention (that of **prudence**) states that accounts should ensure that the worth of the business is not exaggerated. This means that a firm must be careful and therefore slightly pessimistic in estimating the value of its assets.

These two conventions (matching and prudence) lead to a system that reduces the value of any fixed asset by a sum equal to the figure that has been agreed as the cost of the item for that year. In the above example, the value of the £50,000 asset will fall by £10,000 per year for 5 years, so that at the end of the 5 years it is worth nothing. This process is known as depreciation.

Depreciation

Causes of depreciation

Assets depreciate for a number of reasons. The main ones are as follows:

- **Time.** Assets such as machinery wear out over time, although some last much longer than others. For reasons of prudence, a business will want to be pessimistic when depreciating an asset, so a shorter period of time is used if there is doubt. Remember, it is the *useful* lifetime of an asset that is important.
- **Use.** The more an asset is used, the quicker it will wear out. Although careful use and regular maintenance can extend the useful life of an asset, there is still a correlation between the amount that an asset is used and the level of depreciation.
- **Obsolescence.** Changes in technology may mean that an asset needs to be replaced as it becomes inefficient in comparison with newer alternatives; this occurs frequently in the field of information technology.

These three factors help a firm to calculate the time over which an asset should be depreciated. Table 3.5 shows the time periods over which specific assets are depreciated by three different organisations.

KEY TERMS

depreciation: the fall in value of an asset over time, reflecting the wear and tear of the asset as it becomes older, the reduction in its economic use or its obsolescence.

obsolescence: when an asset is still functioning but is no longer considered useful because it is out of date.

Table 3.5
Depreciation in three real-life organisations

Organisation	Asset	Period of depreciation	Comment
London Transport	Tunnels	100 years	All these assets will last a very long time, although some maintenance will be required. The lack of any real threat of competition means that each of these assets will have a long economic lifetime too. Recently, London Transport replaced some 50-year-old buses because of poor disabled access rather than because of wear and tear.
	Buses and trains	30 years	
	Signals	15 years	
Wincanton Transport	Lorries	5–10 years	Wincanton Transport purchases specialist lorries for different contracts (e.g. liquids, chemicals, livestock), so although the lorries will last longer, they are depreciated over the length of the contract. For image reasons, company cars are replaced more regularly.
	Office equipment	3–5 years	
	Company cars	3 years	
Next plc	Warehouses	10 years	The introduction of just-in-time deliveries from factories means that Next depreciates its warehouses over 10 years because it may not need them in the future (25–40 years is common practice). Office equipment needs updating every 3-5 years and stock over 3 months old is probably unfashionable or out of season.
	Office equipment	3–5 years	
	Clothing stock	3–6 months	

One of the most widely used calculations is the **straight-line** method. This can be calculated as follows:

$$\text{annual provision for depreciation} = \frac{\text{initial cost} - \text{residual value}}{\text{expected lifetime (in years)}}$$

For example, if a piece of equipment costs £100,000 and the company expects to receive £40,000 when selling it after 4 years (its expected lifetime), then:

$$\text{annual depreciation} = \frac{£100,000 - £40,000}{4 \text{ years}} = £15,000 \text{ per annum}$$

The purposes of depreciation

Depreciation is used to ensure that the accounts meet the principles of accounting. Its purposes can be seen from the impact of depreciation on the main accounts.

In the **income statement**, depreciation spreads the cost of an asset over the lifetime during which it is helping to create income. This overcomes the problem of exaggerating a firm's costs in the year in which an asset is bought, and thus reducing the firm's profits considerably in that year.

In the **balance sheet**, depreciation shows the reduction in an asset's value over its lifetime. This helps the company to show a true and fair valuation of each asset in its balance sheets over the years. The balance sheet shows a steady lowering of the asset's book value over time.

Table 3.6 shows how the asset used in the example would be treated in the main accounts.

Financial year	Annual charge to income statement (£000s)	'Book value' of asset in balance sheet	
		Start of year (£000s)	End of year (£000s)
1 (year of purchase)	15	100	85
2	15	85	70
3	15	70	55
4	15	55	40

Table 3.6 Example: impact of depreciation on financial accounts

Depreciation is one of the reasons why the income statement does not show the cash position of a business. In our example above, the cash-flow statements show an outflow of £100,000 at the beginning and an inflow 4 years later of £40,000: a net outflow of £60,000. The income statements shows 4 successive years in which depreciation has cost £15,000. This represents a total cost of £60,000 over the 4 years, but the figures in each individual year's accounts are very different.

Can you think of any other reasons why cash flow can be very different from levels of profit or loss?

Any information that relies on depreciation calculations should be treated with caution. The calculation itself is based on both facts (**objectivity**) and personal opinions (**subjectivity**).

PRACTICE EXERCISE 3   Total: 15 marks (15 minutes)

1 What is the difference between capital expenditure and revenue expenditure? *(4 marks)*

2 Which three items from this list of six payments would be classified as capital expenditure?
   - buildings
   - raw materials
   - vehicles
   - machinery
   - rent
   - wages
   (3 marks)

3 Explain why revenue expenditure is treated differently from capital expenditure in the income statement and in the balance sheet, but not treated differently in the cash-flow statement. *(8 marks)*

PRACTICE EXERCISE 4   Total: 30 marks (35 minutes)

1 Explain what is meant by the term 'depreciation'. *(3 marks)*

2 Explain three factors that cause assets to depreciate. *(9 marks)*

3 An asset is bought for £6,000 and is expected to last for 6 years, at which point it will be sold for £900. Calculate the rate of depreciation using the straight-line method. *(3 marks)*

4 What is the residual value after 5 years of an asset whose initial cost is £800 and which depreciates by £130 per annum? *(3 marks)*

5 The table below shows the value of fixed assets and the annual depreciation levels of four different organisations in 2008.

Name of organisation	Description of business	Book value of fixed assets (£m)	Level of depreciation (£m)	Depreciation as a % of fixed assets
AstraZeneca	Large-scale pharmaceutical company	8,316	1,304	15.7
London Transport	Provider of bus and underground rail transport	15,349	602	3.9
DSG International	Electrical retailer trading as Dixons, Currys and PC World	531	122	23.0
Wincanton Transport plc	Haulier, supplying lorry transport for businesses	231	39	16.9

Discuss the possible reasons for the differences in the level of depreciation of fixed assets in these four organisations. *(12 marks)*

Working capital (net current assets)

What is working capital?

The formula for calculating working capital (net current assets) is:

  working capital (net current assets) = current assets − current liabilities

As a general rule, firms wish to have working capital equal to current liabilities (that is, twice as many current assets as current liabilities), although in many industries a lower ratio is acceptable.

The working capital of a business provides an indication of the firm's scope to pay its short-term debts, as it includes the most liquid assets (the current assets). Non-current assets, such as property, may take a long time to sell, or may be sold at a loss if the business tries to sell them immediately.

The working capital cycle

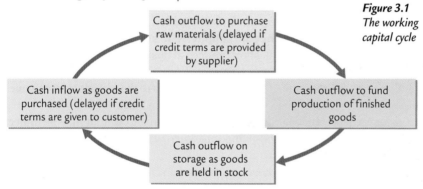

Figure 3.1
The working capital cycle

The length of the working capital cycle can be calculated by studying the three main elements of working capital:

- inventories
- receivables
- payables

The formula is:

  length of working capital cycle = length of time that goods are held +
  time taken for receivables to be paid − period of credit received from suppliers

Here is an example of calculating the working capital cycle:

- Goods are held in stock for an average of 14 days.
- Receivables are given 30 days to pay, on average.
- Suppliers (payables) give the firm 28 days to pay for the supplies that they purchase.
- The working capital cycle is: 14 + 30 − 28 = 16 days.

In effect, the company has to wait 16 days after it has paid for its supplies before it receives payment from the sale of its goods.

KEY TERMS

working capital (or net current assets): the day-to-day finance used in a business, consisting of current assets (e.g. cash, inventories and receivables) minus current liabilities (e.g. payables, bank overdraft, dividends owed and tax owed).

liquidity: the ability to convert an asset into cash without loss or delay.

liquid assets: items owned by an organisation that can be converted into cash quickly and without a loss of value. The most liquid asset that a business can possess is cash.

working capital cycle (or cash operating cycle): the inflow and outflow of liquid assets and liabilities within a business (see Figure 3.1).

FACT FILE

How much working capital?

At certain times of the year, a business must possess a higher than usual level of working capital, as it must hold sufficient liquid assets to pay outstanding short-term liabilities, such as dividends to shareholders and corporation tax payments to the government.

Factors influencing the level of working capital

The time taken to sell inventories (stocks)

A range of factors affect the number of days that inventories are held:

- **The nature of the product.** Items such as clothing that must be displayed in order to entice customers require higher inventory levels than those that do not need display.
- **The durability of the product.** Companies try to have lower levels of inventories of perishable items or finished products that may become unfashionable.
- **The efficiency of suppliers.** If suppliers can supply large quantities at short notice, a business will be able to hold lower inventory levels.
- **Lead time.** If it takes a long time to make a product, companies will be more likely to hold them in stock.
- **Customer expectations.** If the customer is prepared to wait, it may be unnecessary to hold inventories; if the customer wants the item immediately, inventories should be held.
- **Competition.** A business needs to match its rivals, so inventory levels are influenced by the policies of competitors.

The time taken by customers to pay for goods

Factors that lead to delay in receiving payment will lead to the need for greater working capital:

- **The nature of the market.** Commercial products (sold to other businesses) are usually sold on credit, with 28 or 30 days being common credit periods.
- **The type of product.** Expensive, durable items such as vehicles, white goods and electrical products are often offered on credit. Smaller, everyday items are normally paid for immediately.
- **Bargaining power.** The offer of credit may depend on the relative bargaining power of the supplier and the buyer. A large supermarket may demand (and get) a credit period from a small supplier that is desperate for the contract. A small supermarket may be forced to pay immediately for supplies from a major supplier such as Coca-Cola. Recently Tesco successfully demanded 2 months credit from its suppliers instead of 1 month.

The credit period offered by suppliers

The longer the period of credit offered to the business, the better it is for the business, as this means delaying the payment made. The factors influencing the credit period are the same as those listed above. However, the impact on the business is exactly the opposite because in this case the firm is the receivable {debtor}.

Causes of working capital difficulties

Failure to control inventory levels
This worsens a firm's working capital position, as high levels of inventories 'tie up' resources unnecessarily and cost the business money in storage costs. However, a business must balance this factor against the dangers of running out of inventories and upsetting customers.

Poor control of receivables {debtors}
A firm that allows receivables to delay payments needs to hold higher levels of other current assets, such as cash, as a precaution. This reduces the funds available for other activities.

Poor control of payables {creditors}
A firm that pays its payables too quickly will damage its working capital. Ideally, businesses will try to delay payments to payables for as long as possible.

Cash-flow problems
A failure to manage cash flow will cause working capital difficulties, as cash is a major component of net current assets (working capital). (See Chapter 13 of the AS textbook for causes of cash-flow problems.)

Poor internal planning and coordination
If individual departments of a firm are unable to meet targets, working capital problems will occur, for example, if the finance department fails to chase up receivables who do not pay on time.

External factors
Unforeseen changes can affect consumers' tastes. If the business is not able to adapt quickly, this may lead to unsold stock or low levels of cash.

Solving working capital problems

Solutions to cash-flow problems were outlined in Chapter 17 of the AS textbook. Other solutions relate to inventory control and receivables control.

Inventory control
Ideally inventory levels should be maintained at a low level, as this means that less money is tied up in inventories.

Low inventory levels reduce the need for storage space, and the chances of damage, deterioration and obsolescence. **High inventory levels** allow companies to benefit from bulk-buying discounts and minimise the risk of lost sales and lost goodwill through a failure to meet customer needs. Firms that operate **just-in-time** systems of supply can exist with low levels of inventories, but these companies need efficient suppliers that can meet tight deadlines.

Receivables control

Receivables should be kept to a minimum, as they mean a delay in receiving cash. However, the offer of credit may help to increase sales, particularly in markets in which buyers expect credit facilities.

If credit is offered to customers, the company must ensure prompt payment. This can be achieved by:

■ managing credit control so that customers are invoiced and reminded promptly
■ chasing up late payers and being prepared to take receivables to court if payment is not received
■ obtaining a credit rating, which indicates the capability of the potential receivable to finance the debt
■ controlling the quality of the service or product, because a satisfied customer is less likely to delay or dispute payment

Finally, a company can turn its receivables into cash by **factoring**. This means selling the right to collect the debts owed by receivables to another business, usually at a discount. Less money is received, but cash is received much more quickly and the risk of bad debts is reduced.

FACT FILE

High liquidity at Vodafone

Firms will not want excessive, 'unproductive' working capital. In 2008, Vodafone plc had accumulated cash levels of £1.7 billion. Along with many other companies, Vodafone found its share price falling in July 2008. As a result, it used this high level of liquidity to buy back £1 billion of its shares. This action will reduce the value of dividends that it needs to pay to shareholders in future years. However, the continued fall in the share price after July 2008 meant that Vodafone acquired shares that were to lose even more value.

PRACTICE EXERCISE 5   Total: 35 marks (30 minutes)

1 How is working capital (net current assets) calculated? *(2 marks)*

2 What is meant by the term 'liquidity'? *(3 marks)*

3 Calculate the working capital cycle based on the following information:
   ● Goods are held in stock for 23 days.
   ● Debtors are given 15 days to pay.
   ● Creditors give the firm 28 days to pay. *(3 marks)*

4 Explain one factor that might increase the level of working capital in a firm. *(3 marks)*

5 Explain three possible causes of working capital problems. *(9 marks)*

6 Explain how inventory control might overcome a firm's working capital problems. *(6 marks)*

7 Explain how control of receivables might overcome a firm's working capital problems. *(6 marks)*

8 Why is it sensible for a firm to make sure that its level of working capital (net current assets) is not too high? *(3 marks)*

CASE STUDY 1   HBOS plc: countdown to implosion

On 17 September 2008, Lloyds TSB announced that it would be taking over HBOS plc, Britain's biggest mortgage lender. This takeover was supported by the UK government amid fears for the future of HBOS, whose share price had fallen from £9.80 to £0.88 in 1 year. HBOS was the UK's oldest commercial bank, tracing its origins back to the formation of the Bank of Scotland in 1695. HBOS itself was formed by the merger between the Bank of Scotland and the Halifax Bank in 2001.

How was it possible for a business that made a pre-tax profit of £5.5 billion in 2007, and was still showing a half-year profit of £1.45 billion in the year to June 2008, to fail so spectacularly in September 2008?

Analysts put the blame squarely on poor working capital control.

Traditionally, organisations such as HBOS plc raised money from customers' savings accounts and used this money to lend, on a long-term basis, to people requiring mortgages to buy property. Fundamentally, this process created potential for working capital and cash-flow problems because customers could withdraw their money on demand, but the bank was unable to reclaim the money for up to 25 years. In effect, the system depended on trust.

In the early years of the twenty-first century, UK banks tried to extend the amount of lending that they undertook but were held back by the lack of deposits from savers and limited numbers of house buyers. As a result, banks such as Northern Rock and HBOS moved into the sub-prime market, where lending is provided to people who might normally be considered as risky borrowers. This market was booming in the USA, where more people were being encouraged to purchase their own homes. This led to a house price boom which meant that, even if people did get into financial difficulties, they could repay the loan by selling their home.

This changed when the housing market in the USA started to decline. Borrowers in the USA found themselves in a position of negative equity (where the value of their house falls below the amount owed on their loan). This caused the liquidation of a number of

banks in the USA and had a knock-on effect on UK banks, as customers defaulted on loans arranged through American banks such as Lehmann Brothers. The sub-prime market was not limited to the USA. In 2006 HBOS announced that it was prepared to offer 125% mortgages to UK borrowers, who were thus able to borrow 25% more than the value of the property. This increased the risk of bad debts for HBOS.

The first UK bank affected by this was Northern Rock, which was saved from liquidation by the government's decision to nationalise it (take it into public ownership).

The decline in the level of trust in the banking system led to speculators selling HBOS shares. In its 2007 balance sheet, HBOS indicated that it was writing off £227 million of bad debts and stated that it had lost £550 million from US sub-prime lending.

Worried about potential cash-flow problems, HBOS announced a rights issue of shares intended to raise £4 billion. However, with the announcement that HBOS had 'written down' the value of its assets by a further £3.65 billion in the first 3 months of 2008, over 90% of the shareholders declined the share offer, recognising that HBOS would effectively be using the equity capital to boost liquidity rather than profitability.

Over the summer of 2008 there was continued speculation, which forced the HBOS share price down from £2.50 to £0.88. Attracted by the low price of HBOS shares, Lloyds TSB proposed a takeover of HBOS in September 2008. According to BBC business editor, Robert Peston, the government helped to push through the Lloyds TSB–HBOS tie-up because HBOS had voiced concerns that depositors and lenders had begun to withdraw their deposits and credit from the bank. The government was keen to avoid another run on a bank, as had happened at Northern Rock, where savers had queued to withdraw their savings.

Lloyds TSB believes that the potential profitability of HBOS will help it to grow in the future, especially as the takeover will enable Lloyds TSB to achieve cost savings of £1 billion through branch closures and rationalisation at head offices.

Questions

Total: 30 marks (40 minutes)

1 In the context of HBOS plc, analyse the extent to which there is conflict between maintaining good working capital and achieving high levels of profitability. *(12 marks)*

2 Evaluate the main factors that led to the takeover of HBOS plc by Lloyds TSB. *(18 marks)*

Analysing income statements

What is an income statement?

An income statement describes the income and expenditure of a business over a given period of time, usually a year. The income statement shows the profit (or loss) made by the business. The profit (or loss) is the difference between a firm's income and its costs. For many organisations, making a profit is their main objective. Even if other aims are pursued, such as growth, image, workforce welfare and social responsibility, financial success is needed to fund these objectives.

Purposes of the income statement

- Regular calculations of profit throughout the year help managers to review progress before the final end-of-year accounts are completed, while the final accounts allow the firm to assess the success of its policies.
- It allows shareholders to assess whether their investment is beneficial.
- It enables people to see if profit is of high quality.
- It enables people to see if profit is being utilised in a sensible way.
- To satisfy legal requirements, the Companies Act requires firms to publish their income statement.
- Publication allows stakeholders to see if the firm is meeting their needs.
- Comparisons can be made between different firms (inter-firm comparisons) in order to measure relative performance.
- Comparisons can be made over time (temporal comparisons) to see if the firm is improving its performance.
- Comparisons can be made within the business (intra-firm comparisons) to assess the effectiveness of different divisions or branches.
- The income statement can be used to show potential investors that the firm is successful and able to repay loans or provide a good return on investments.

FACT FILE

Accounts and company legal structures
The details provided in the company accounts depend on the legal structure of the business. The government requires more detail from a public limited company than from a private limited company. Accounts of sole traders only need to meet the needs of the tax authorities.

Structure of the income statement

The income statement is divided into sections, each of which provides useful information for users of the accounts.

Revenue and cost of sales

This part of the statement records the revenue (turnover or sales income) of the company and the 'cost of sales' (costs that can be linked directly to the provision of the product or service). 'Cost of sales' includes items such as raw materials and wages of production-line workers for a manufacturer, or the cost of purchasing stock and warehousing and transporting the stock to shops for a retailer. This section calculates the gross profit.

Expenses (overheads)

This part takes the gross profit and deducts those costs that are not directly related to producing the product or service, such as marketing expenditure, general administration costs, rent and depreciation. These costs are termed 'expenses' (overheads). This section calculates the operating profit.

FOTOLIA

Finance income and expenses

This element of the income statement includes information on any interest payments made by the business and any interest received on money lent or saved. This information is useful for shareholders in gaining an understanding of the company's liquidity and the extent to which it borrows or lends money.

After these two items have been calculated, the profit before tax is shown.

Tax paid on the profits made

The final profit is found by the following calculation:

profit for the period = profit before tax − tax on profit (or income)

For a public limited company, corporation tax is charged on profits, but for an unincorporated business, such as a sole trader, income tax is charged.

The income statement concludes by showing how much of this profit is attributable to shareholders (in many cases it will be all of the profit). This figure is converted to 'earnings per share' using the following calculation:

$$\text{earnings per share} = \frac{\text{profit for the period}}{\text{number of shares}}$$

KEY TERMS

gross profit: revenue minus cost of sales. The gross profit shows how efficiently a business is converting its raw materials or stock into finished products.

operating profit: the revenue earned from everyday trading activities minus the costs involved in carrying out those activities.

earnings per share: how much a shareholder would earn if *all* of the profit were given to shareholders as dividends. In practice, this is unlikely to happen as some profit will be retained in the business. Earnings per share is an excellent way of measuring how effectively a business is using its shareholders' money to make profit.

e **EXAMINER'S VOICE**

Always remember to compare like with like when analysing a given profit or loss. The profit recorded may be the overall profit or the operating profit, and it might be shown before or after finance income and finance costs, and before or after tax. Comparing operating profit before finance income and finance costs with operating profit after finance income and finance costs and after tax would lead to an inappropriate conclusion.

Reasons for the structure of the income statement

- The first section enables a business to see how efficiently it is turning materials into sales revenue. A high gross profit level suggests that costs of sales are being kept low or that the business is achieving a high **value added** by creating a product that fetches a high price.
- The next section of the income statement shows the efficiency of a firm in controlling its expenses. If expenses are low, the firm should be able to secure a high operating profit.
- The finance income and finance costs give an indication of how much the business borrows and lends money, and the efficiency with which it handles these financial operations.

What happens to the profit?

'Earnings per share' shows shareholders the effectiveness of the business in using its equity capital to make profits. A breakdown of the use of these earnings is of particular interest to shareholders. A business that is using most of its profits to pay high dividends will please shareholders looking for a quick return. However, shareholders with a long-term interest in the business may prefer to see higher retained profits, as these will be reinvested into the business to boost profits in the future.

The layout of the income statement

It is customary to publish the latest income statement alongside the income statement from the previous year (or the equivalent period from the previous financial year if the account covers less than 1 year). Typically, income statements are published for a period of a year, but it is not unusual for firms to publish 6-month or 3-month income statements.

Useful income statement formulae

gross profit = revenue − cost of sales

operating profit = gross profit − expenses +/− exceptional items

Where there are no exceptional items:

operating profit = gross profit − expenses

profit before tax = operating profit + finance income − finance costs

profit for the year = profit before tax − taxation

$$\text{earnings per share} = \frac{\text{profit for the year}}{\text{number of shares issues}}$$

Example of an income statement: Rounded Figures plc

Rounded Figures plc specialises in cream cakes and doughnuts.

Table 3.7 shows the income statements for Rounded Figures plc for the financial years ending in 2008 and 2009. Note that it is traditional to place the latest year on the left and the previous year on the right.

Years ending:	30.6.09(£000s)	30.6.08 (£000s)
Revenue	2,500	2,000
Cost of sales	(1,150)	(1,050)
Gross profit	**1,350**	**950**
Expenses	(970)	(700)
plus (minus) Exceptional items	0	200
Operating profit	**380**	**450**
Finance income	50	70
Finance costs	(100)	(70)
Profit before tax	**330**	**450**
Taxation	(66)	(90)
Profit for year	**264**	**360**
Earnings per share	£0.88*	£1.29*
*Additional information:		
Number of shares issued (thousands)	300	280

Table 3.7 Income statements for Rounded Figures plc

Profit quality

Although all businesses aim to make a profit, it is possible to distinguish between high-quality profit and low-quality profit.

When analysing accounts, profit is used to assess performance, so it is vital to know if there are any unusual, exceptional or one-off circumstances that are affecting the accounts in the year being studied. For example, if a firm sells many of its non-current assets, this will increase its net profit for this year because of this one-off source of income. However, the sale of these non-current assets may reduce future performance, as non-current assets produce the goods and services that help the business to make a profit. In this case, we can conclude that the profit shown in that year is of low quality.

In contrast, a firm may be undergoing a major restructuring programme, which in the short term could lower profit, as the firm adjusts to the new systems. However, this could lead to greater profit in the long term.

KEY TERMS

profit quality: a measure of whether profit is sustainable in the long run. High-quality profit is profit that will continue; low-quality profit arises from exceptional or extraordinary circumstances that are unlikely to continue.

In October 2008, Shell announced profits of $8.4 billion for the third quarter of the year. It had also made a profit of $1.4 billion from the sale of a subsidiary. Shell argued that these profits were necessary to finance exploration and research to secure future energy supplies. Clearly the £1.4 billion profit that Shell had made through the sale of a subsidiary is of lower quality than its £8.4 billion profit. However, there are differences of opinion about the £8.4 billion.

Some people see it as a short-term, low-quality profit arising from the shortages in oil supply that occurred in the summer of 2008, with petrol prices rocketing to over £1.30 in some garages; others believe that these shortages will remain a permanent feature of the oil market and that companies such as Shell will be able to rely on them into the future. What do you think?

FACT FILE

Profit quality at Morrisons

Sometimes 'profit quality' can only be assessed in the long term. In July 2004, Morrisons, the supermarket chain, issued the first profits warning in its 37-year history, and then gave a repeat warning early in 2005. These were blamed on teething problems resulting from its takeover of Safeways. In the long run, Morrisons expected to benefit from economies of scale resulting from the takeover, and believed that eventual profits would be much higher as a result. This view was reinforced by the announcement in 2008 of Morrisons achieving a record profit of £612 million — double the levels of profit achieved before the takeover.

KEY TERM

profit utilisation: the way in which a business uses its profit or surplus.

Profit utilisation

It is common for a business to use its profit in one of two ways.

Dividends paid to shareholders

Every 6 months, public limited companies usually pay a dividend to their shareholders. This dividend payment represents the share of the profits allocated to shareholders.

Some shareholders depend on the dividend payment as a source of income, particularly retired people who rely on their shares to provide a steady flow of money. These shareholders may have a greater interest in making sure that a high dividend is paid.

Retained profits

In order to fund expansion plans and capital investment, the company directors will wish to keep some of the profits in the business. This avoids the need to pay interest on borrowed money or to sell more shares in order to finance expansion. Retained (or 'ploughed-back') profits increase the assets of a business and should therefore increase the value of the company. Furthermore, retained profits should help the business to increase its future profits (and thus increase future dividends). Consequently, shareholders often support requests to increase the level of retained profit. In practice, most firms will strike a balance between paying dividends and retaining profits.

On occasions, profit may be utilised in different ways. Shell recently used £2 billion of its profit to buy back shares from shareholders. In future years this means it will have to pay dividends to fewer shareholders.

FACT FILE

Profit retention at Rolls-Royce

Decisions to retain profit or pay dividends often depend on recent history and corporate aims. In recent years, Rolls-Royce's policy has varied considerably. In 2002 it made a loss of £53 million but paid dividends totalling £133 million. This was possible because of retained profits from earlier years. Having drained some of the company's funds in 2002, shareholders agreed to a lower dividend in 2003 and received no dividend in 2004 when the company recorded a good profit level. In 2004 the company's finance costs considerably exceeded its finance income as it borrowed money to fund research and development. This investment paid off with record profits in 2007.

UK companies are often accused of taking short-term decisions to satisfy the immediate needs of shareholders, but Rolls-Royce has shown that it can plan long term. Having increased its vulnerability in 2002, it is now reaping the benefits of long-term planning for growth.

PRACTICE EXERCISE 6   Total: 40 marks (35 minutes)

1 Identify three purposes of an income statement.   *(3 marks)*

2 How is gross profit calculated?   *(2 marks)*

3 What is the difference between net or overall profit and operating profit?   *(4 marks)*

4 What is an 'exceptional' item?   *(3 marks)*

5 Explain the meanings of:
   a finance income   **b** finance costs   *(4 marks)*

6 In a public limited company, which tax is deducted from 'profit before tax' in order to calculate the 'profit for year' (or final profit)?   *(1 mark)*

7 Identify the two ways in which profit is utilised.   *(2 marks)*

8 Using the figures below, calculate:
   a the gross profit   *(3 marks)*
   b the operating profit   *(3 marks)*

   Show all of your working.

Cost of raw materials	£400,000
Marketing expenditure	£125,000
General administration	£200,000
Sales revenue	£980,000
Wages of production-line workers	£110,000

9 A company must pay corporation tax of 30% on its profit of £200,000. If it plans to use 60% of its profits (after tax) to build an extension to its factory, how much of its profit will be paid to shareholders?   *(4 marks)*

10 Explain the meaning of profit quality. *(4 marks)*

11 Why might shareholders allow a business to keep all of the profit for its own use? *(4 marks)*

12 Calculate the earnings per share based on the following data:

Profit for year: £300,000
Shares issued: 500,000 at 50p each *(3 marks)*

PRACTICE EXERCISE 7 — Total: 10 marks (10 minutes)

Refer to the income statement for Rounded Figures plc for the year ending 30.6.09 (see Table 3.7).

1 Rewrite the income statement to take into consideration the following changes:

Revenue: increases by 20%
Cost of sales: increase by £100,000
Expenses: increase by £150,000
Finance income and finance costs: no changes
Corporation tax: equal to 20% of profit before tax *(8 marks)*

2 Based on these changes, calculate the amended earnings per share on the assumption that the number of shares remains the same as for 30.6.09. *(2 marks)*

Using financial data for comparisons, trend analysis and decision making

It is difficult to draw meaningful conclusions from a single piece of data. When using financial data to analyse a company's situation, it is best to consider data that:

- allow comparisons with other organisations
- have been compiled over a period of time

Decision making that considers these two factors is likely to be more accurate than a single piece of data, which may be unrepresentative.

Comparisons

To interpret financial data, the data should be compared with other results, so that the company can be judged in relative terms. The main methods of comparison are as follows.

Intra-firm comparisons: comparisons within the company
The efficiencies of different divisions or areas of a company can be compared. Again, comparisons should be made between similar areas of the company. A retailer should compare stores in similar towns where the size of population and levels of competition are matched.

From the balance sheet it is worth comparing the net current assets (working capital) of different divisions or branches within the company. Income statement comparisons may enable the organisation to ascertain which of its branches is generating the most profit.

Inter-firm comparisons: comparisons between companies

A company should compare itself with rival companies in order to assess its relative performance. Ideally, the company should select those competitors with which it has most in common, as any external factors that are helping (or hindering) the company should be having a similar effect on those competitors.

The balance sheet can be used to show the overall worth and therefore the scale of operations of different businesses. The income statement allows a business to compare its revenue and profit against those of its competitors. It also helps the business to discover whether it is controlling certain costs as efficiently as its competitors.

Comparisons to a standard

Certain levels of performance are recognised as efficient within the business community. A company can compare itself with these standards in order to assess its performance objectively. It is often easy to obtain comparable data from other companies too, if such standards are widely used.

The balance sheet can be used to show how a business's liquidity compares to the standard for that industry, while the income statement can allow a business to see whether the growth of the business's sales and profits is matching the overall growth rates for the economy as a whole.

Comparisons over time: trend analysis

A company's data should be compared over time in order to register trends in efficiency and to allow for exceptional circumstances in a particular year. A firm may take a long time to reap the benefits of a restructuring or to devise suitable strategies to fight off a new competitor. For these reasons, it is important to use data to identify trends in performance as well as the performance in one particular year.

KEY TERM

trend: the underlying pattern of change shown within a set of numerical data.

AUTHOR'S NOTE

More detailed coverage of each form of comparison is provided elsewhere in this book.
- Intra-firm comparisons are covered in Chapter 5 (Selecting financial strategies), in the section 'Introducing and implementing profit centres'.
- The use of financial data for inter-firm comparisons and comparisons to a standard are dealt with in Chapter 4 (Interpreting published accounts).
- Trend analysis is explained in detail in Chapter 8 (Analysing markets and marketing).

e EXAMINER'S VOICE

Remember that published accounts, such as the income statement and balance sheet, are historical: they show what has already happened. Consequently, they can be used to analyse the company's actual performance. However, in order to judge the potential of the business, these data need to be extrapolated into the future. External factors also need to be considered.

Taking Rolls-Royce as an example, the case study at the end of this chapter shows that its profit has decreased, suggesting a further decline in the future. However, the additional information available in the case study shows a very large order book, which suggests that the future potential of Rolls-Royce is perhaps better than its current performance shows. On the other hand, knowledge of the external environment reveals a current economic downturn (autumn 2008), and this is likely to damage Rolls-Royce's profits, particularly the profits of its ommercial aircraft engine division.

Assessing strengths and weaknesses of financial data in judging performances

There are strengths and weaknesses involved in using financial data to judge a firm's performance. These strengths and weaknesses are based on the accuracy of the data as a measure of:

- current performance
- potential performance

Strengths of financial data in judging performance

- The balance sheet has been designed to provide data that allow people to judge a company's performance. It can help people to:
  - assess the size of a business
  - calculate the net assets of a business, to assess its overall worth
  - discover the company's liquidity position
  - understand the sources of capital and see how reliant it is on borrowing
- The income statement has also been designed to allow people to judge a company's performance. It can help people to:
  - calculate the profit levels of the firm
  - assess whether it is worth buying shares in the business
  - note if profit is of high quality
  - see if profit is being utilised in a sensible way
- Since 2005, published accounts have had to conform to International Financial Reporting Standards (IFRS). This means that financial data related to public limited companies (plcs) must be based on the same principles.
- IFRS rules also indicate a certain format for the publication of accounts of plcs, so that it is much easier to compare the accounts of different companies.

- Published accounts must be checked by independent auditors. This helps to guarantee high levels of accuracy because it ensures that:
  - companies keep accurate records of their financial transactions
  - companies internally audit their own accounts, to avoid the embarrassment of having external auditors refusing to guarantee their accuracy
  - the external (independent) auditors provide additional scrutiny to ensure accuracy
- Stakeholders expect regular and accurate data. A business that does not provide accurate data may find itself losing customers and suppliers, or alienating the local community.

Weaknesses of financial data in judging performances

- IFRS rules do not cover private limited companies (Ltds), which constitute the majority of companies in the UK, although most Ltds operate on a relatively small scale.
- The growing number of large limited companies that have been bought up by private equity organisations and thus set up as Ltds means that more large companies are not covered by IFRS rules.
- Some valuations are partially subjective. For example, what is the value of a specialist piece of machinery which has no alternative use, and what might be its value if the business is considering closing the factory?
- Different accounting methods may be employed. Straight-line depreciation generally provides higher book values for the balance sheet than alternative methods.
- Accounts show what has happened, rather than why, and so they can only serve to point out potential problems.
- Published accounts focus on the profitability and liquidity of a business. By focusing only on financial measures, they ignore other objectives that may be more important to a business, such as:
  - building a reputation
  - satisfying the needs of its employees
  - improving its relationship with suppliers
  - improving product quality
  - securing long-term growth
- Financial performance is influenced greatly by external factors such as fashion and the economic environment. A business that is successful in a growing economy may fail in a recession. For many firms, trends in profit and revenue can suddenly be reversed by changes in external factors.
- A firm's financial situation changes daily, and it may manipulate its accounts to provide a favourable view on the date on which they are prepared. This practice is known as **window dressing**. Some examples are:
  - revaluing land and buildings to improve the value of non-current assets
  - changing depreciation calculations to boost values (e.g. by predicting a longer lifetime for an asset)

EXAMINER'S VOICE

Private limited companies (Ltds) are free to use IFRS rules and formats. If an AQA A2 business studies examination paper refers to a Ltd, the accounts will use the same format as that of plcs.

- selling non-current assets to boost cash levels
- sale and leaseback
- bringing forward sales or delaying expenditure

PRACTICE EXERCISE 8   Total: 40 marks (35 minutes)

1 What is meant by a 'trend'? *(2 marks)*

2 Explain four types of comparison that can be made using financial data. *(12 marks)*

3 Identify three useful pieces of information that can be obtained from a balance sheet. *(3 marks)*

4 Identify three useful pieces of information that can be obtained from an income statement. *(3 marks)*

5 Explain two other strengths of financial data in judging current performance. *(6 marks)*

6 Analyse three weaknesses in using financial data to judge current performance. *(9 marks)*

7 Explain why it might be difficult to use current performance to judge potential, future performance of a business. *(5 marks)*

CASE STUDY 2 Rolls-Royce wins second $1 billion deal

Rolls-Royce recently celebrated its one hundredth anniversary at the Farnborough air show with a display of aircraft powered by Rolls-Royce engines — from Spitfires to the Airbus A340.

After the disposal of its car division, Rolls-Royce basically had one role: manufacturer of aircraft engines. However, its main product — the Trent engine — has been adapted for ships and power generators. After GE of America, Rolls-Royce is the second biggest engine-maker in the world. Few UK companies can claim such status.

The future looks bright for Rolls-Royce. It has recently been awarded two separate $1 billion contracts with the US military for development of aircraft engines and a jump-jet facility for fighter planes. With its two main commercial customers, aircraft manufacturers Boeing and Airbus, Rolls-Royce is expecting further growth. Rolls-Royce engines are on both of the next generation of commercial aircraft — Airbus's A380 superjumbo and Boeing's 787 dreamliner. Furthermore, it has received advance orders for many other commercial and military projects. In total, the company's order book stretches to £53.5 billion — a very secure level for a company with annual sales of less than £8 billion.

Replacement parts and upgrades on its existing products account for 53% of its total sales, so the order book suggests a significant growth in sales in the near future.

Rolls-Royce has spread its risks well — no single contract accounts for more than 3% of its sales. Furthermore, the company has gained so much cash that its finance income exceeds its finance costs. However, the surplus from this source declined in 2008, partly as a consequence of Rolls-Royce's spending of £380 million on research and development; a vital expense if Rolls-Royce is to stay ahead of its competitors. Despite the current economic climate, the directors are forecasting sales growth of over 12% in 2009, although profit levels are expected to stabilise.

Source: based on recent interim and annual reports of Rolls-Royce plc, articles by Philip Aldrick in the *Daily Telegraph* and BBC website news.

Table 3.8 *Income statements for Rolls-Royce plc*

Years ending:	30.6.08 (£m)	30.6.07 (£m)
Revenue	7,893	7,357
Cost of sales	6,231	5,904
Gross profit	**1,662**	**1,453**
Expenses	968	921
Exceptional items*	(60)	0
Operating profit	**634**	**532**
Finance income	661	859
Finance costs	550	493
Profit before tax	**745**	**898**
Taxation	156	218
Profit for year	**589**	**680**
Earnings per share	32.77p	38.58p

*Restructuring costs of £60 million were incurred in 2008.

Table 3.9 *Balance sheets for Rolls-Royce plc*

As at:	30.6.08 (£m)	30.6.07 (£m)
Non-current assets (fixed assets)	**4,344** (a)	**3,702**
Inventories (stocks	2,453	2,081
Receivables (debtors)	3,069 (b)	2,535
Cash and other cash equivalents	2,374 (c)	2,452
Current assets	7,896	7,068
Current liabilities	(5,180) (d)	(4,198)
Net current assets (working capital)	2,716	2,870
Non-current liabilities (long-term liabilities)	(3,295)	(3,284)
Net assets (net worth)	**3,765** (e)	**3,288**
Share capital	826	709
Reserves	2,939	2,579
Total equity	**3,765**	**3,288**
NB capital employed = non-current assets + net current assets	7,060	6,572

Preliminary question

Total: 10 marks (10 minutes)

1 Study the changes in Rolls-Royce's balance sheet between 30 June 2007 and 30 June 2008 (Table 3.9). Provide brief (1-line) descriptions of the possible reasons for each of the five changes labelled (a) to (e).

(10 marks)

Case study questions

Total: 45 marks (50 minutes)

1 Referring solely to Table 3.8, to what extent can it be concluded that the year ending 30.6.08 was a more successful year for Rolls-Royce plc than the year ending 30.6.07?

(15 marks)

2 Based on the article and the accounts, discuss whether Rolls-Royce's financial position is likely to improve or worsen between 2008 and 2011.

(15 marks)

3 To what extent would the information in the case study provide a reliable basis for future strategic decision making by Rolls-Royce directors?

(15 marks)

Chapter 4

Interpreting published accounts

This chapter introduces the concept of ratio analysis. The importance of comparing ratios is explained and the main types of comparison are identified. The users of ratio analysis are identified and their needs outlined. The chapter describes the main categories of ratios and explains the calculations and significance of the key ratios used to assess businesses. To assist comparisons, data are provided on the key ratios for UK firms in recent years. The chapter concludes with an assessment of the limitations of ratio analysis as a technique.

The concept of ratio analysis

Ratio analysis is based mainly on data extracted from the firm's financial accounting records — usually the balance sheet and income statement. However, for some ratios, information needs to be extracted from the management accounting information or other sources.

> **FACT FILE**
>
> **What is a ratio?**
> A ratio is a comparison of a figure with another figure, where the relative values of the two numbers can be used to make a judgement. Ratios are expressed as, for example, 2.5:1. In this example, the first digit is two and a half times the second digit. In ratios, the second digit is always 1. Despite the name of this technique, most of the 'ratios' featured in ratio analysis are actually stated as percentages or raw numbers, and hence not presented in the format of the example above.

As indicated in Chapter 3, different groups of people use the information provided in a company's accounts in order to judge a firm's situation. Some actual figures in the accounts, such as net profit, can be used to draw conclusions about a company's performance. However, much more meaningful conclusions can be drawn by comparing this figure with another. If a business has doubled its profit in the last decade, is this an indicator of success? Most people would conclude that this does show good performance, but what if the scale of the business has trebled in that time? Should its profits have trebled too? Ratio analysis allows us to compare two sets of data (in this case, profit and scale) in order to try to draw more meaningful conclusions.

EXAMINER'S VOICE

AQA will provide the formulae for the ratios in this chapter as an attachment to the BUSS3 examination paper. Accordingly, the formulae for the ten ratios covered in this chapter are presented as an appendix at the end of this chapter.

KEY TERM

ratio analysis: a method of assessing a firm's financial situation by comparing two sets of linked data.

EXAMINER'S VOICE

When calculating a ratio, always ensure that you present it in the appropriate format (as a percentage, ratio etc.).

Ratio analysis also allows a business to compare itself with other firms, taking into consideration differences in size or circumstances. Similarly, it can be used to compare the relative efficiency of different parts of a business, such as departments, stores or factories. However, no two businesses or departments operate in identical circumstances and so, at best, ratio analysis can only act as a guide to performance.

> **e EXAMINER'S VOICE**
>
> In the A2 course you will be expected to interpret ratios. Many students calculate the ratios but fail to explain their significance. Make sure that you explain the significance for the business of any ratios that you calculate, and comment on any limitations to the conclusions that you have drawn.

Stages in using ratio analysis

If ratios are to prove useful, careful selection and organisation are needed. The following process will help businesses to take full advantage of ratio analysis:

1 Identify the reason for the investigation. Is the information needed to decide whether to become an investor, customer or a supplier, or is it being used by the organisation itself to improve its own efficiency?
2 Decide on the relevant ratio(s) that will help to achieve the purpose of the user(s).
3 Gather the information required and then calculate the ratio(s).
4 Interpret the ratio(s). What is the meaning of the results that have been obtained?
5 Make appropriate comparisons (see the next section) in order to understand the significance of the ratio(s).
6 Take action in accordance with the results of the investigation.
7 Apply the above processes again, to measure the success of the actions taken in stage 6.

Comparisons

Ratios in isolation are rather meaningless. To interpret a ratio, it should be compared with other results, so that the company can be judged in relative terms. The main bases for comparison are as follows:

- **Inter-firm comparisons** — comparisons *between* companies. A company should compare itself with rival companies, in order to assess its relative performance. Ideally, the company should select those competitors with which it has most in common, as any external factors that are helping (or hindering) the company should be having a similar effect on those competitors.
- **Intra-firm comparisons** — comparisons *within* the company. The efficiency of different divisions or areas of a company can be compared. Again, comparisons should be made between similar areas of the company.
- **Comparisons to a standard.** Certain levels of performance are recognised as efficient within the business community. A company can compare itself with these standards in order to assess its performance objectively.
- **Comparisons over time.** Whatever basis is used, a company's ratios should be compared over time in order to register trends in efficiency and to allow for exceptional circumstances in a particular year.

Types of ratio

Ratios can be categorised under five headings, as shown in Table 4.1.

Table 4.1 The main types of ratio and their meanings

Type of ratio	Meaning of ratio type
Profitability ratios	These compare profits with the size of the firm. As profit is often the primary aim of a company, these ratios are often described as **performance ratios**.
Liquidity ratios	These show whether a firm is likely to be able to meet its short-term liabilities. Although profit shows long-term success, it is vital that firms hold sufficient liquidity to avoid difficulties in paying debts.
Gearing	Gearing focuses on long-term liquidity and shows whether a firm's capital structure is likely to be able to continue to meet interest payments on, and to repay, long-term borrowing.
Financial efficiency ratios	These generally concentrate on the firm's management of its working capital. They are used to assess the efficiency of the firm in its management of its assets and short-term liabilities.
Shareholders' ratios	These focus on drawing conclusions about whether shareholders are likely to benefit financially from their shareholding in a company.

ⓔ EXAMINER'S VOICE

Ratios must be used in context. A firm's ratio may compare unfavourably to the 'standard' or to its performance in previous years, but look at the background to the firm. Is there a reason for this unfavourable result? Ensure that you refer to any such reasons in your answer.

ⓔ EXAMINER'S VOICE

A wide variety of ratios can be used to judge a firm's performance (see Figure 4.1). The philosophy behind the AQA A-level specification is that students should understand the significance of ratio analysis and be able to interpret and apply sufficient ratios to draw valid conclusions on a firm's operations.

For these reasons, ten specific ratios have been incorporated into the specification. There are other ratios that can be used to assess a company. However, only those ratios that are identified in the AQA specification are considered in this chapter.

Remember, AQA will provide the formula for each ratio as an attachment to the BUSS3 examination paper. The formulae are presented as an Appendix at the end of this chapter.

Figure 4.1 provides a summary of the types and classification of the ratios used.

Figure 4.1 Classification of financial ratios

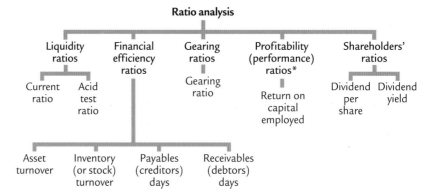

* A second profitability ratio (the net profit to sales % or net profit margin) was covered in the AS course (see Chapter 18 of the AS book).

Users of ratios

Ratios serve a number of purposes, which will be outlined in detail later in this chapter as each ratio is examined. Different ratios meet the needs of a variety of users of accounts. Table 4.2 shows the main groups of users and their reasons for using ratio analysis.

Table 4.2 Users and their reasons for using ratio analysis

Users	Reasons for using ratio analysis
Managers	To identify the efficiency of the firm and its different areas, to plan ahead, to control operations and to assess the effectiveness of policies
Employees	To find out whether the firm can afford wage rises and to see if profits are being allocated fairly
Government	To review the success of its economic policies and to find ways of improving business efficiency overall
Competitors	To compare their performance against rival firms and discover their relative strengths and weaknesses
Suppliers	To know the sort of payment terms that are being offered to other suppliers, and whether a firm can afford to pay
Customers	To know if the future of the firm and therefore any guarantees and after-sales servicing agreements are secure
Shareholders	To compare the financial benefits of their investment with other alternatives, such as owning shares in a different firm or putting savings in a bank

Using ratios

The majority of ratios are based on information from the income statement and the balance sheet. Each of the ten ratios explained in this book is calculated using the figures from the accounts of Rounded Figures plc, a supplier of doughnuts and cream cakes. Thus Tables 4.3 and 4.4 are identical to Tables 3.2 and 3.7 from the previous chapter. To allow *intra-firm* comparisons, the accounts shown are from two successive years — the financial years ending on 30 June 2009 and 30 June 2008. Later in this chapter, *inter-firm* comparisons will be made with Rounded Figures plc's main rival, Doh! Nuts! plc.

	As at:	30.6.09 (£000s)		30.6.08 (£000s)	
Non-current assets {fixed assets}		890		750	
Inventories {stocks}	60		50		
Receivables {debtors}	150		140		
Cash and other cash equivalents	300		310		
Total current assets		510		500	
Payables {creditors}	(300)		(250)		
Current liabilities		(300)		(250)	
Net current assets (working capital)		210		250	
Non-current liabilities (long-term liabilities)		(200)		(280)	
Net assets (net worth)		900		720	
Share capital			300		280
Reserves			600		440
Total equity		900		720	
NB capital employed =					
non-current assets + net current assets =		1,100		1,000	

Table 4.3 Balance sheets of Rounded Figures plc, 30 June 2009 and 30 June 2008

Table 4.4 *Income statements for Rounded Figures plc*

Years ending:	30.6.09 (£000s)	30.6.08 (£000s)
Revenue	2,500	2,000
Cost of sales	(1,150)	(1,050)
Gross profit	**1,350**	**950**
Expenses	(970)	(700)
plus (minus) Exceptional items	0	200
Operating profit	**380**	**450**
Finance income	50	70
Finance costs	(100)	(70)
Profit before tax	**330**	**450**
Taxation	(66)	(90)
Profit for year	**264**	**360**
Earnings per share	£0.88 *	£1.29 *
*Additional information:		
Number of shares issued (thousands)	300	280
Dividends paid (£000s)	100	200
Share price	£2.25	£2

FACT FILE

Financial years
The accounts used in this book so far all show years ending 30 June. This is purely coincidental. Financial years represent 12 successive months and invariably span over two calendar years, in which case they are shown as 2003/04, 2004/05 etc. As the tax year ends in early April, many businesses have a financial year ending 31 March. Other popular days for the end of a company's financial year are 31 July and 31 December.

PRACTICE EXERCISE 1   Total: 25 marks (20 minutes)

1 What is meant by the term 'ratio analysis'? *(3 marks)*

2 Identify five different users of ratio analysis. *(5 marks)*

3 Select two of the five users identified in question 2 and explain the reasons why they might use ratio analysis. *(6 marks)*

4 Distinguish between inter-firm comparisons and intra-firm comparisons. *(4 marks)*

5 Identify two other types of comparison. *(2 marks)*

6 Identify the five main types of ratio. *(5 marks)*

e EXAMINER'S VOICE

In the previous AQA specification for A-level business studies, you were expected to remember the formulae for any ratios that needed to be calculated. In the new specification, the formulae will be provided in the examination paper so you do not need to remember them.

While this might seem to be an easier proposition, it does lead to a different challenge. Whereas in previous papers you were invariably told which ratio to calculate, examination papers from 2010 onwards will expect you to recognise which ratio or ratios need to be used. For example, if the question is about a company's cash flow or a liquidity problem, the current ratio and/or the acid test ratio will discover how serious the problem is. In contrast, if profitability is the main issue, the return on capital employed should be used to make a judgement.

It is vital that you understand the purpose of each ratio so that you can select an appropriate ratio or ratios to calculate, using the formulae given in the examination paper.

Profitability and performance ratios

Most firms aim to make a profit. In order to assess the efficiency of a business in achieving this major objective, two profitability (or performance) ratios may be used: the return on capital employed and the net profit margin. The net profit margin was covered in Chapter 18 of the AS course, so this section will focus on return on capital employed as the key measure of profitability.

> **e EXAMINER'S VOICE**
>
> Net profit margin was covered in the AS course as a ratio for measuring the profitability of a business. It is not one of the ratios required for A2 business studies. Consequently, no formula to calculate it will be included in a BUSS3 examination paper.
>
> Any A2 question requiring a judgement on profitability will be answerable by using the return on capital employed as the only profitability ratio. However, if you do use the net profit ratio in a relevant way, you will be credited by the examiner.

Return on capital (employed)

The return on capital employed (ROC or ROCE) ratio shows the operating profit as a percentage of capital employed; capital employed equates to the value of the capital that a business has at its disposal.

Operating profit is considered to be the best measure of performance, as it focuses only on the company's main trading activities, whereas other measures of profit can include items that are not a reflection of efficiency.

Profit *before tax* is used because tax rates vary between countries, so profit after tax is a less reliable measure of the company's performance.

Capital employed is generally considered to be the best measure of a firm's size. It is calculated by adding the total equity provided by shareholders (in the form of purchases of shares and retained profits that shareholders have allowed the business to retain) to any non-current liabilities (such as long-term loans and debentures). This is not a totally reliable guide as firms are tending to lease many assets rather than purchase them, but in general, capital employed is a good basis for comparing the scale of companies' operations.

Return on capital employed is measured as a percentage, using the following formula:

$$\text{return on capital employed } (\%) = \frac{\text{operating profit or profit before tax}}{\text{total equity} + \text{non-current liabilities}} \times 100$$

Based on Tables 4.3 and 4.4, the ROCE for Rounded Figures plc is:

$$2008\text{: } \frac{450^*}{1{,}000} \times 100 = 45\%$$

*As 200 (£200,000) of the 450 (£450,000) profit was an exceptional item, this would not be deemed high-quality profit. Therefore, a more accurate assessment of operating profit is 250 (450 − 200). Using this figure gives the following ROCE for 2008:

$$\text{2008 (high-quality profit): } \frac{250}{1,000} \times 100 = 25\%$$

$$\text{2009: } \frac{330}{1,000} \times 100 = 30\%$$

Conclusion: in 2008 Rounded Figures plc achieved an ROCE of 45%, indicating a high level of profitability. In 2009 the headline level of profitability decreased to 30%. This is still a very good level of ROCE for most industries, but at first sight it suggests that Rounded Figures plc did not perform as well in 2009 as it did in 2008. However, a closer study of the profit quality indicates that, if we exclude the exceptional items from 2008, Rounded Figures plc improved its basic profitability between 2008 and 2009 from 25% to 30%.

FACT FILE

Benchmarking

Table 4.5 shows the average ROCE for all UK companies in recent years. Companies can use these figures as a benchmark to see if they are making a good profit. These figures apply to *all* firms. However, the performance of manufacturing companies is generally lower than that of the service sector. Therefore, Rounded Figures plc might wish to compare itself to the average ROCE for services, which averaged 18% in this period.

FOTOLIA

It should also be noted that there are considerable variations in performance between regions and industries. For example, the average return on capital is higher in Yorkshire and Humberside and the southwest, but lower in the northwest and Wales. Similarly, the average return on capital was 25% in pharmaceuticals but only 1% in engineering and media.

Ratio	Year		
	2001	2004	2007
Return on capital employed (%)	12.2	13.0	14.2

Table 4.5 *Profitability ratios for UK firms, selected years between 2001 and 2007*

Source: ONS.

PRACTICE EXERCISE 2   Total: 25 marks (25 minutes)

1 Explain why return on capital employed is considered to be a good measure of a firm's performance. *(4 marks)*

2 Explain two reasons why return on capital employed might *not* be a good indicator of a firm's success. *(6 marks)*

Questions 3 to 5 are based on the following information, which is extracted from the accounts of DSG International plc. This group consists of three main retail outlets: Dixons, Currys and PC World.

Years ending:	1.5.2008 (£m)	1.5.2004 (£m)
Operating profit	205	366
Profit including exceptional items	(193)	366
Capital employed	1,737	2,272

3 In 2008 DSG International plc's accounts included an exceptional item of approximately (£400 million), representing the writing-off of an investment. The group had also bought back some shares in previous years. Explain how these two changes are shown in the data above. *(5 marks)*

4 Based on the information above, calculate the return on capital employed for the year ending 1 May 2008 and the year ending 1 May 2004. *(6 marks)*

5 In which year did DSG plc enjoy the best performance? Use the ratios calculated in question 4 to support your views. *(4 marks)*

Liquidity ratios

Two liquidity ratios — the current ratio and the acid test ratio — are used in order to assess the ability of an organisation to meet its short-term liabilities.

Although profit is the main measure of company success, firms can be vulnerable to cash-flow problems, so the ability of a firm to meet its immediate payments is a key test. Liquidity ratios concentrate on balance sheet information. Examination of a firm's short-term (current) assets and its current liabilities allows an observer to analyse a firm's ability to stay solvent in the short term.

KEY TERM

solvency: a measure of a firm's ability to pay its debts on time. A firm that can meet its financial commitments is described as 'solvent'; a firm that cannot meet its financial commitments is described as 'insolvent'.

It is estimated that as many as 30% of all business failures can be attributed to insolvency. Consequently, liquidity ratios are vital in analysing a firm's financial position.

Current ratio

In order to meet its liabilities, a firm can draw on its short-term (current) assets. Cash and bank balances are the most liquid current assets. However, receivables {debtors} will be paying their debts to the company, thus providing a steady source of cash. Similarly, inventories {stock} will be sold continually, providing the business with an additional means to pay its current liabilities.

The ratio is calculated as follows:

current ratio = current assets:current liabilities

If a company has between £1.50 and £2 of current assets for every £1 of current liabilities, it is unlikely to run out of cash. Therefore, the 'ideal' current ratio is between 1.5:1 and 2:1.

It should be noted that a maximum as well as a minimum ratio is recommended. The opportunity cost of holding too many current assets is the lost opportunity to purchase non-current assets such as machinery. The non-current assets are needed to produce the goods that provide the company's profit. Consequently, a high current ratio may be an advantage in the short run but will inhibit the long-term profitability of the company.

Based on Table 4.3, calculation of these ratios for Rounded Figures plc gives the following results:

June 2009:   510:300   1.7:1
June 2008:   500:250   2.0:1

Conclusion: in 2008 the current ratio was at the upper level of the 'acceptable' range. In 2009 it was significantly lower but comfortably in the middle of the 'acceptable' range. Rounded Figures plc would appear to be removing the excess liquidity that it had in 2008, so these changes could be seen as an improvement in its liquidity. It should be cautious that liquidity does not fall too dramatically in 2010.

Acid test (quick) ratio

The current ratio assumes that inventories and receivables are liquid assets. This is likely to be true of receivables, as any receivables who are deemed to be unlikely to pay will be classified as 'bad debts' and not included in the balance sheet. However, for inventories the situation is less clear. Firms cannot be certain that their inventories will sell quickly, so the acid test ratio is used as an alternative to the current ratio. The calculation of the acid test (quick) ratio ignores inventories in its calculation, considering only cash, bank balances and receivables as liquid assets.

The ratio is calculated as follows:

acid test ratio = (current assets − inventories):current liabilities

Again, there is an ideal maximum and an ideal minimum ratio, as explained for the current ratio. If a company has between £0.75 and £1 of current assets (excluding inventories) for every £1 of current liabilities, it is unlikely to run out of cash. Therefore, the 'ideal' acid test ratio is between 0.75:1 and 1:1.

Based on Table 4.3, the acid test ratios for Rounded Figures plc are as follows:

June 2009:   450:300   1.5:1
June 2008:   450:250   1.8:1

Conclusion: in 2008 the acid test ratio was much too high, being significantly above the upper level of the 'acceptable' range. In 2009 it fell significantly, but it was still much higher than the 'acceptable' range. Rounded Figures plc should aim to reduce its acid test ratio in 2010 and put more of its resources into non-current assets, such as new stores. The nature of its business (fresh cakes) suggests that inventory levels should be quite low, so a satisfactory current ratio may mean a high acid test ratio.

WHAT DO YOU THINK?

The 'ideal' levels of the liquidity ratios are based on historical research. Some years ago, an examination was undertaken of the balance sheets of leading companies over a period of years. It found that a number of businesses whose liquidity ratios were below the advisable (ideal) levels went into liquidation. Similarly, those with excessive liquidity tended to make less profit over time because they were not putting enough money into non-current assets.

'Ideal' ratios were set as a result of these observations, but do they still apply today? With businesses using just-in-time inventory control, and having much easier access to funds, many accountants feel that these 'ideal' levels are too high. Retailers that benefit from a constant flow of cash receipts can survive with very low levels of liquid assets. HMV has a current ratio of 0.64:1 and an acid test ratio of only 0.20:1. Tesco's ratios are also low at 0.58:1 and 0.35:1 respectively. These ratios are well below the minimum 'ideal' levels of 1.5:1 and 0.75:1 respectively, but neither business appears to be at risk of insolvency.

A quick glance at Table 4.6 supports this view — the average current ratio of UK companies in 2007 was 1.2:1, well below the recommended minimum level of 1.5:1.

Ratio	Year			Table 4.6
	2001	2004	2007	*Current ratio of UK firms, 2001–07*
Current ratio	1.14:1	1.19:1	1.20:1	

Sources: Experian, Reuters and company reports.

In the light of these data we might wish to reassess the liquidity of Rounded Figures plc, as it appears to have even more excess liquidity than the earlier comments suggest.

PRACTICE EXERCISE 3 — Total: 30 marks (30 minutes)

1 Ideally, the acid test ratio should be between *x*:1 and *y*:1, where *x* and *y* are numbers.
 a What is the ideal value for *x*? *(1 mark)*
 b What is the ideal value for *y*? *(1 mark)*

2 Why should a firm try to avoid a low acid test ratio? *(4 marks)*

3 What is the disadvantage of a high acid test ratio? *(4 marks)*

4 The following information is extracted from the accounts of DSG International plc. This group consists of three main retail outlets: Dixons, Currys and PC World.

Extracts from balance sheets of DSG International plc

Values as at:	1.5.2008 (£m)	1.5.2004 (£m)
Current assets	2,042	2,304
Inventories	1,093	793
Current liabilities	2,120	1,566

Based on this information, calculate the following ratios for the year ending 1 May 2008 and the year ending 1 May 2004.
 a current ratio *(6 marks)*
 b acid test ratio *(4 marks)*

5 In the light of the table and your calculations in question 4, discuss how well DSG International plc has managed its liquidity. *(10 marks)*

Gearing

Gearing examines the capital structure of a firm and its likely impact on the firm's ability to stay solvent. There is one relevant measure of gearing, known as the **gearing ratio** (or capital gearing).

The gearing ratio is measured by the following formula:

$$\text{gearing} (\%) = \frac{\text{non-current liabilities}}{\text{total equity} + \text{non-current liabilities}} \times 100$$

Non-current liabilities normally take the form of loans, such as debentures or long-term loans from the bank.

High and low gearing

If the gearing ratio is greater than 50%, the company is said to have *high* capital gearing. If the gearing ratio is below 25%, the company is said to have *low* capital gearing. Usually, capital gearing between 25% and 50% would be considered to be within the normal range, but the interpretation of 'high' and 'low' gearing can vary over time.

A high capital gearing ratio shows that a business has borrowed a lot of money in relation to its total capital. A low capital gearing ratio indicates that a firm has raised most of its capital from shareholders, in the form of share capital and retained profits.

Based on Table 4.3, the gearing ratios for Rounded Figures plc for 2008 and 2009 are:

$$2009: \frac{200}{1,100} \times 100 = 18.2\%$$

$$2008: \frac{280}{1,000} \times 100 = 28.0\%$$

Conclusion: the gearing ratio for Rounded Figures plc has fallen from a 'normal' level to a 'low' level. The ratios in both 2008 and 2009 suggest that Rounded Figures plc is unlikely to come under any pressure from having to repay loans or pay interest on borrowed money. Furthermore, the lower figure in 2009 shows that there is a reduction in any pressures of this nature.

FACT FILE

UK gearing ratios

Table 4.7 shows the average gearing ratio in the UK in recent years. If interest rates are low and the economy is growing steadily businesses will be eager to take advantage of the opportunity to borrow money at low rates of interest and lenders will be eager to lend, confident that businesses will repay any money that is lent. This led to an unprecedented rise in gearing ratios between 2002 and 2003, when gearing ratios averaged 73.3%. This rise ended in 2004 when interest rates started to rise again.

Ratio	Year			Table 4.7
	2001	2004	2007	*Gearing, selected years, 2001–07*
Gearing (%)	49.8	60.4	57.5	

Sources: Experian and company reports.

WHAT DO YOU THINK?

As the UK entered a recession in late 2008, the Bank of England lowered interest rates. This should encourage borrowing by businesses (and increase gearing ratios), but will lenders restrict loans and will businesses believe that it is too risky to borrow? What do you think?

Benefits of high capital gearing

High capital gearing offers several benefits:

- There are relatively few shareholders, so it is easier for existing shareholders to keep control of the company.
- The company can benefit from a very cheap source of finance when interest rates are low.
- In times of high profit, interest payments are usually much lower than shareholders' dividend requirements, allowing the company to retain much more profit for future expansion.

Benefits of low capital gearing

Low capital gearing also has advantages:

- Most capital is permanent share capital, so with low gearing the company is at less risk of payables {creditors} forcing it into liquidation.
- A low-geared company avoids the problem of having to pay high levels of interest on its borrowed capital when interest rates are high.
- The company avoids the pressure facing highly geared companies that must repay their borrowing at some stage.

We can conclude that there is no ideal gearing ratio. The best gearing percentage will depend on circumstances.

- A highly profitable company will prefer high gearing, as its dividend payments usually exceed its interest payments on loans. High gearing is also advantageous if interest rates are low and if the owners of a business want to limit the number of new shareholders.
- Low gearing tends to exist if companies are less profitable, if interest rates are high and if the business is prepared to expand its number of shareholders. Companies that have retained high levels of profit in the past tend to have low levels of gearing.

PRACTICE EXERCISE 4   Total: 35 marks (35 minutes)

1 Capital gearing is considered to be 'high' if it exceeds what percentage? *(1 mark)*

2 Capital gearing is considered to be 'low' if it is below what percentage? *(1 mark)*

3 Briefly explain two possible disadvantages of high capital gearing. *(6 marks)*

4 Briefly explain two possible advantages of high capital gearing. *(6 marks)*

5 Explain why high levels of capital gearing are likely to coincide with the lowest levels of interest rates in the UK. *(4 marks)*

6 Explain one reason why a firm's gearing levels might be low despite low interest rates. *(5 marks)*

7 The following information is extracted from the accounts of DSG International Group plc.

As at:	1.5.2008 (£m)	1.5.2004 (£m)
Balance sheet:		
Capital employed (total equity plus non-current liabilities)	1,737	2,272
Non-current liabilities/loans	883	804

Based on this information, calculate the gearing ratio for the year ending 1 May 2008 and the year ending 1 May 2004. *(6 marks)*

8 In which year did DSG International Ltd have the best gearing ratio? Justify your view. *(6 marks)*

Financial efficiency ratios

Financial efficiency ratios measure the efficiency with which a business manages specific assets and liabilities. They allow the business to scrutinise the effectiveness of certain areas of its operation. This section analyses the four financial efficiency ratios included in the AQA A2 business studies specification: asset turnover, inventory or stock turnover, receivables (debtors) days and payables (creditors) days.

Asset turnover

This ratio measures how well a company uses its assets in order to achieve sales revenue. A key purpose of a company is to maximise its sales. Companies organise their finances in order to create an efficient balance of non-current assets and working capital. Non-current assets, such as machinery and retail premises, enable a firm to generate sales revenue from providing and selling goods and services. A healthy level of current assets within the firm's working capital also helps it to increase sales revenue. Current assets, in the form of inventory (stock), must be held to meet customers' needs and, for retailers, to entice buyers. The existence of receivables (debtors) also helps to increase sales, as many customers are attracted by the offer of credit when they buy goods.

Asset turnover is calculated by the formula below. It should be noted that it is measured as a number and not as a ratio or percentage.

$$\text{asset turnover} = \frac{\text{revenue (annual sales turnover)}}{\text{net assets}}$$

A *high* figure shows that the business is using its assets efficiently to achieve sales. A *low* figure shows that the business is not using its assets efficiently to achieve sales. However, care needs to be taken when using the asset turnover ratio, as it can be misleading. Capital-intensive firms will have lower asset turnover figures than labour-intensive firms. This is because any capital owned by a business will be included in its net assets, thus lowering the value

J. SAINSBURY PLC MEDIA LIBRARY

Table 4.8 Asset turnover of UK firms, selected years, 2001–07

of the ratio. In contrast, labour-intensive firms do not own their labour forces, so their net asset figures will be lower, leading to a higher asset turnover figure.

If comparisons are made between firms with similar asset structures, however, a valid conclusion can be drawn. For this reason, asset turnover is used by firms to make intra-firm comparisons between branches. Supermarkets, for example, use this ratio to see which branches are the most efficient at generating sales. In this way, underperforming branches can copy the techniques used by the more efficient ones.

Table 4.8 shows the average asset turnover figures for UK businesses in recent years.

	Year		
Ratio	2001	2004	2007
Asset turnover	2.4	3.0	3.3

Sources: Experian and company reports.

From Tables 4.3 and 4.4, Rounded Figures plc's asset turnover figures are:

2009: $\dfrac{2,500}{900} = 2.8$

2008: $\dfrac{2,000}{720} = 2.8$

These figures show that Rounded Figures plc maintained a consistent level of asset turnover between 2008 and 2009. However, these figures are lower than the UK average, suggesting that the company is not using its assets to generate sales as efficiently as most UK companies.

Inventory turnover or stock turnover

This measure of financial efficiency indicates how quickly inventory (stock) is converted into sales. A high figure means that stock is sold quickly, thus bringing money into the company more rapidly.

$$\text{inventory (stock) turnover} = \frac{\text{cost of goods sold}}{\text{average inventories held}}$$

Sales are valued at cost to provide a fair comparison, as inventory values in the accounts are based on the cost paid for them rather than the price at which they will be sold.

The inventory turnover figure represents the number of times in a year that the firm sells the value of its stock. A value of 3 means that it sells its stock three times a year (that is, once every 4 months). Thus it will take 4 months, on average, to convert stock into cash (if no credit is given). A value of 26 means that the business converts inventories into cash every 2 weeks. The higher the figure, the better it is for a company's cash flow.

Factors influencing the rate of stock turnover

The main influences on stock turnover are:

■ **The nature of the product.** Perishable products or products that become dated, such as newspapers, have very high rates of stock turnover. In contrast, some products, such as antiques, sell slowly and so have a low rate of stock turnover.

■ **The importance of holding stock.** Some businesses, such as clothes retailers, need to hold high stock levels to encourage shoppers.

■ **The length of the product life cycle/fashion.** Fashionable products are expected to sell quickly and products with very short life cycles (such as computer games) must also have a rapid turnover.

■ **Stock management systems.** Companies that use just-in-time stock control have very low stock levels, so their rate of stock turnover is high.

■ **Quality of management.** Poor market research may lead to inappropriate stock being displayed and therefore low rates of stock turnover being achieved.

■ **The variety of products.** An organisation with 20 varieties of a product will inevitably be holding higher stock levels than an organisation with only one version of a product.

EXAMINER'S VOICE

It is not possible to calculate the inventory or stock turnover figure accurately from published accounts. For a manufacturing company, the cost of goods sold will include production costs in addition to purchase of inventories. Thus 'cost of goods sold' will exaggerate the amount of inventories sold. However, the 'average inventories held' figure may also be an exaggeration, as inventories may be raw materials rather than finished products. These two effects may cancel each other out.

If you are required to calculate and interpret the inventory turnover figure, use the formula provided. However, you may wish to comment on the limitations of this calculation in your overall evaluation.

Based on Tables 4.3 and 4.4, the inventory (stock) turnover figures for Rounded Figures plc for 2009 and 2008 are:

$$2009: \frac{1,150}{60} = 19.2$$

$$2008: \frac{1,050}{50} = 21.0$$

These results suggest that Rounded Figures plc took 365/19.2 = 19.0 days to turn over its inventory (stock) in 2009. In 2008 it took 365/21.0 = 17.4 days. Although the figure has changed slightly from 2008, this change is relatively minor.

Receivables (debtors) days

This ratio shows the number of days that it takes to convert receivables into cash.

$$\text{receivables (debtor) days} = \frac{\text{receivables (debtors)}}{\text{revenue (annual sales)}} \times 365$$

Firms that provide long-term credit for their customers, such as Freemans catalogue, may expect a high figure, but companies that deal mainly in cash transactions, such as Papa John's Pizza, will have a low figure for receivables (debtor) days.

Standards vary between industries, but in general terms a firm will want to have as low a value as possible, meaning that receivables are being paid promptly. Although the finance department will wish for prompt payment, the marketing department may want to offer generous credit facilities to attract customers. Retailers of furniture traditionally offer long credit terms, so high receivables days may be a feature of that trade. Car manufacturers provide garages with credit to encourage them to display a wide range of stocks, leading to high receivables days.

The calculations for Rounded Figures plc based on Tables 4.3 and 4.4 are:

$$2009: \frac{150}{2,500} \times 365 = 21.9 \{22\} \text{ days}$$

$$2008: \frac{140}{2,000} \times 365 = 25.6 \{26\} \text{ days}$$

Conclusion: these figures are reasonable, given the fact that many businesses offer 28 or more days to pay receivables. However, they appear to be high for a business dealing with fresh products that are sold on a daily basis, so the reasons for this should be investigated. Rounded Figures plc will be pleased that the 2009 figure is lower than the 2008 result, because this means its receivables are being turned into cash more quickly in 2009 than in 2008.

Payables (creditors) days

This ratio shows the number of days that it takes to pay back any payables owed by a business. As noted in the calculation of inventory turnover, the cost of sales is the best estimate of what a firm pays to its suppliers. Therefore, this figure is used to represent the total costs of supplies in a year.

$$\text{payables (creditors) days} = \frac{\text{payables (creditors)}}{\text{cost of sales}} \times 365$$

Firms that receive long-term credit from their suppliers may expect a high figure for payables (creditors) days, but companies that pay suppliers in cash will have a low figure.

In general terms, a firm will want to have as high a value as possible, meaning that payables are not being paid quickly. In effect, this means that the business is holding another organisation's money. However, if a business has a high payables days figure because it has not paid a debt on time, this would not be a good sign.

As indicated above, firms will hope for a payables days figure that exceeds their receivables days figure, as this will help cash flow.

The calculations for Rounded Figures plc based on Tables 4.3 and 4.4 are:

$$2009: \frac{300}{1,150} \times 365 = 95.2 \ \{95\} \ \text{days}$$

$$2008: \frac{250}{1,050} \times 365 = 86.9 \ \{87\} \ \text{days}$$

Conclusion: these figures show that Rounded Figures plc has a very high figure for payables days, so it is likely to be able to hold high levels of cash. The company does not appear to be short of cash, so it is probable that these high figures exist because the company's suppliers offer Rounded Figures plc generous credit terms.

Subtracting the 'receivables days' from the 'payables days' gives the following results:

2009: 95 days – 22 days = 73 days

2008: 87 days – 26 days = 61 days

These figures show that Rounded Figures plc is taking approximately 70 days longer to pay its debts than it is taking to receive money owed to it. This means that the business should be able to benefit from possessing high levels of cash (for example, earning interest from the bank and having a healthy cash flow). However, the business needs to be aware of the possible problems it will face if its payables start to demand payment more quickly.

DID YOU KNOW?

The ratio 'payables (or creditors) days' is also known as 'the average age of payables (or creditors)'.

FACT FILE

Sale or return

Some shops purchase inventories on a sale or return basis. This means that they do not have to pay their suppliers until they have sold the product. Consequently, they may have a high payables days figure. However, suppliers that offer these terms tend to charge a higher price to the buyers because it is the supplier that takes the risk if the product is not sold.

PRACTICE EXERCISE 5   Total: 60 marks (60 minutes)

1 Many businesses are now leasing their properties. Why does this reduce the reliability of asset turnover as a measure of financial efficiency? *(4 marks)*

2 How would the introduction of just-in-time stock control affect the value of the inventory (stock) turnover rate of a business? *(4 marks)*

3 Explain two other factors that influence the rate of inventory turnover of a product. *(6 marks)*

4 Explain one benefit of a high rate of inventory turnover. *(4 marks)*

5 Explain one advantage and one disadvantage to a business of having a high value for receivables days. *(6 marks)*

6 Outline one possible benefit and one possible problem to a business whose receivables days are higher than its payables days. *(6 marks)*

7 The following information is extracted from the accounts of DSG International Group plc.

Years ending/as at:	1.5.2008 (£m)	1.5.2004 (£m)
Income statement		
Sales revenue (turnover)	8,546	6,492
Cost of sales	608	1,280
Balance sheet		
Net assets	854	2,308
Receivables	443	507
Payables	2,040	1,542
Inventories (stock)	1,093	793

Based on this information, calculate the following ratios for the year ended 1 May 2008 and the year ended 1 May 2004:

a asset turnover   *(4 marks)*   c receivables days   *(4 marks)*
b inventory turnover   *(4 marks)*   d payables days   *(4 marks)*

8 Based on your answers to question 7, and any other information, compare and discuss the financial efficiency of DSG International Group plc in 2008 and 2004. *(14 marks)*

Shareholders' ratios

Shareholders will judge a business on its ability to reward them for their input into it. This means that shareholders' ratios measure the benefit of a company's activities to its shareholders, rather than other stakeholders. Shareholders' ratios thus have a narrower focus than other ratios. Other stakeholders may not see a 'favourable' shareholders' ratio as a positive sign.

Dividend per share

A dividend is that part of a company's profit that is distributed to shareholders as their reward for holding shares. The term 'earnings' is used to describe the profits available for shareholders (the profit after tax). Usually, companies retain a significant proportion of this profit for future investment or purchase of shares. Thus, only part of the profit is paid as dividends to the shareholders.

The dividend per share is calculated as follows:

$$\text{dividend per share} = \frac{\text{total dividends paid}}{\text{number of ordinary shares issued}}$$

If a business has issued 1 million shares and pays £150,000 in dividends, the dividend per share is: £150,000/1,000,000 = 15p per share.

This ratio is of limited usefulness, as it lacks context. For example, it does not reveal how much the shares cost to buy. A 15p dividend is excellent if the share cost 30p to buy, but it is a very poor return if the share price was £30. The dividend per share is thus used as the first stage of the calculation of the dividend yield (see the next section).

Referring again to Tables 4.3 and 4.4, the dividend per share for Rounded Figures plc in each of the years covered was:

$$2009: \frac{£100,000}{300,000} = 33.3\text{p per share}$$

$$2008: \frac{£200,000}{280,000} = 71.4\text{p per share}$$

This appears to be a significant deterioration, as shareholders received a much smaller dividend in 2009. However, we should remember that Rounded Figures plc made a poorer-quality profit in 2008, with £200,000 profit coming from exceptional items. Furthermore, the business retained more profit in 2009, so this should help the business in future years.

Dividend yield

The dividend yield builds on the dividend per share by expressing it as a percentage of the current market price of the shares.

$$\text{dividend yield (\%)} = \frac{\text{dividend per share}}{\text{market price per share}} \times 100$$

This shows the annual percentage return on the money needed to purchase the share. Its significance is that it can be compared with the percentage return from other investment choices, such as a bank account or other shares. Thus, a dividend yield of 6% might be seen as a good return if banks are paying 3% interest on savings accounts, but it would be a poor return if banks were paying 9% interest.

These calculations ignore the gains or losses that can be made from owning shares. If share prices are increasing, the dividend yield will fall, but owning these shares will be a more attractive proposition. In contrast, a fall in the share price will increase the dividend yield but may be seen as an unfavourable trend by shareholders. If share prices are relatively static, the dividend yield is a more relevant measure. However, it is still limited because it ignores the part of profit that is retained.

In conclusion, dividend yield is a good measure of the short-term rewards from owning shares, but it tends to ignore the long-term consequences.

From Table 4.4 and the earlier calculation of the dividend per share for Rounded Figures plc, the dividend yield was:

$$2009: \frac{33.3p}{225p} \times 100 = 14.8\%$$

$$2008: \frac{71.4p}{200p} \times 100 = 35.7\%$$

The dividend yield was much better in 2008 than 2009, for the reasons indicated in the section on dividend per share. Although shareholders in 2009 are receiving a dividend that has fallen by 38.1p (71.4 – 33.3), the share price has increased by 25p (£2.25 – £2).

PRACTICE EXERCISE 6 — Total: 50 marks (50 minutes)

1 Why is the dividend per share a key ratio for shareholders? (3 marks)

2 Explain two reasons why a company's dividend per share might not be a good measure of the success of the company as a whole. (6 marks)

3 Why would a shareholder use the dividend yield as a way of assessing the benefits of buying shares in a business? (4 marks)

4 Outline one reason why the dividend yield might not be a good guide to whether a potential investor should buy shares in a company. (4 marks)

5 The following information is extracted from the accounts of DSG International Group plc.

	As at: 1.5.2008	1.5.2004
Additional information:		
Dividends paid	£96 million	£143 million
Number of ordinary shares	1,770 million	1,959 million
Share price	70p	155p

a Calculate the dividend per share in 2008 and 2004. (6 marks)
b Calculate the dividend yield in 2008 and 2004. (6 marks)

6 In which year (2004 or 2008) would it have been more advisable for an investor to have purchased shares in DSG International plc? Justify your decision. *(8 marks)*

7 By 21.11.08 the share price of DSG International plc had fallen to 13p.
   a Analyse two possible reasons for this fall. *(8 marks)*
   b Analyse one consequence of this fall. *(5 marks)*

Practice Exercise 7 (below) provides the opportunity to conduct comprehensive ratio analyses of all ten ratios for a particular business.

e EXAMINER'S VOICE

In the BUSS3 examination you will be provided with the formulae for all ten ratios on the AQA A2 business studies specification. These have each been described separately in this chapter. In order to replicate the examination paper, the ten ratios are summarised as an appendix to this chapter. In order to answer the questions in Practice Exercise 7, you are advised to refer to this appendix.

PRACTICE EXERCISE 7   Total: 40 marks (45 minutes)

This is a self-assessment exercise. The answers to the questions below can be found in Case Study 1 towards the end of this chapter.

Doh! Nuts! plc is the main rival of Rounded Figures plc. Although Doh! Nuts! plc has based its reputation on the quality of its doughnuts, it has started to diversify into the market for cream cakes.

Balance sheet for Doh! Nuts! plc, 30 June 2009

	As at:	30.6.09 (£000s)
Non-current assets (fixed assets)		**1,250**
Inventories (stocks)	150	
Receivables (debtors)	25	
Cash and other cash equivalents	25	
Total current assets		**200**
Payables (creditors)	(250)	
Current liabilities	**(250)**	
Net current assets (working capital)		**(50)**
Non-current liabilities (long-term liabilities)		**(600)**
Net assets (net worth)		**600**
Share capital	400	
Reserves	200	
Total equity		600
NB capital employed =		
non-current assets + net current assets		1,200

Income statement for Doh! Nuts! plc

	Year ending: 30.6.09 (£000s)
Revenue	2,000
Cost of sales	(1,200)
Gross profit	**800**
Expenses	(760)
plus (minus) Exceptional items	60
Operating profit	100
Finance income	50
Finance costs	(50)
Profit before tax	**100**
Taxation	(20)
Profit for year	**80**
Earnings per share	£0.20
Additional information:	
Number of shares issued (thousands)	400
Dividends paid (£000s)	80
Share price	£0.50

Based on the balance sheet and income statement, calculate the following ratios for Doh! Nuts! plc for the financial year ending 30 June 2009:

a return on capital employed (%) *(4 marks)*
b current ratio *(4 marks)*
c acid test ratio *(4 marks)*
d gearing (%) *(4 marks)*
e asset turnover *(4 marks)*
f inventory turnover *(4 marks)*
g receivables days *(4 marks)*
h payables days *(4 marks)*
i dividend per share *(4 marks)*
j dividend yield (%) *(4 marks)*

Limitations of ratio analysis

Ratio analysis provides a scientific basis for decision making and is an excellent guide to a firm's current financial position. However, organisations have many different aims and objectives, so financial performance is not the only measure of an organisation's success. Other, non-financial indicators (such as social audits) also have a part to play in assessing an organisation's performance. Ratio analysis should be used alongside these other indicators to assess a firm's success or failure. Some of the problems and limitations of ratio analysis are outlined below.

EXAMINER'S VOICE

This is an important area for evaluative questions. Ratios tend to give a definite view — a company's ratios are either better or worse than desired. Consequently, judgements based on ratios alone will have a limited focus. However, this is not the case if the limitations of ratio analysis are taken into account. Considering actual ratios alongside the reliability of the information, the possible objectives of the business, and the external factors that can influence performance, provides far more opportunities to demonstrate evaluation.

Reliability of information

The reliability of available information limits the usefulness of ratio analysis in several ways:

- The data on which ratios are based may be unreliable.
- Some figures, notably asset valuation, are subjective to some extent. For example, how valuable is a railway line and signalling system to an organisation if it decides to close the route?
- Different accounting methods may be employed. Straight-line depreciation generally provides higher book values for the balance sheet than alternative methods.
- A firm's financial situation changes daily, and it may manipulate its accounts to provide a favourable view on the date on which they are prepared. This practice is known as window dressing.

Historical basis

The historical basis of published accounts affects ratio analysis for the following reasons:

- Accounts indicate where a company has been, rather than where it is going. Past performance is not necessarily a useful guide to the future. A number of former 'blue-chip' companies (firms recognised as excellent performers) have fallen behind rivals in recent years. In 2008 long-established businesses such as Northern Rock, HBOS, Woolworths and MFI got into financial difficulties or went into liquidation.
- Accounts show *what* has happened, rather than *why*, and so they can only serve to point out potential problems.

Comparisons

Ratios rely on comparisons, but they always involve difficulties because no two businesses or divisions face identical circumstances.

Corporate objectives

Ratio analysis only looks at financial measures, and relies on the assumption that maximising profit is the only aim of all firms. It ignores other objectives that may be more important to a business:

- **Reputation.** A profitable company that is seen to be exploiting its customers may suffer a considerable loss of goodwill.

- **Human relations.** A company may experience a high rate of labour turnover and low levels of productivity if it does not meet the needs of its employees.
- **Relationship with suppliers.** Low prices paid for materials can help profits in the short term but might upset suppliers.
- **Product quality.** This may be essential for long-term customer loyalty. Reducing quality as part of a cost-cutting exercise may increase profits in the short term, but in the long run this can lead to a decline in the number of customers.
- **Future profit.** It may pay a company to make decisions that do not lead to, or produce, profit in the short term, in order to create profit for the future. Research and development (R&D) is an example of an activity that may reduce current profit in order to help future profit levels.

External factors

Company performance is very dependent on outside factors. A PESTLE analysis will show the external factors (opportunities and threats) that affect performance. Examples include:

- the stage of the economic cycle (for example, boom or recession)
- government legislation, which may add costs or create markets
- changes in taste — in favour of or against the firm's products
- new technology leading to new products or processes in the market
- the level of competition, which can affect the ability of a firm to make money

It is vital that these and other factors are considered before conclusions are drawn.

Conclusion

Ratios must not be ignored. They are an excellent guide to performance. However, conclusions should be based on the specific circumstances and the problems and limitations involved in ratio analysis should be borne in mind.

PRACTICE EXERCISE 8   Total: 45 marks (45 minutes)

1 For a firm such as Rolls-Royce plc, analyse two factors that may cause the information used in its ratio analysis to be unreliable. *(6 marks)*

2 State the four main types of 'comparison' used in ratio analysis. *(4 marks)*

3 Explain four reasons why comparisons of ratios may provide misleading results. *(12 marks)*

4 Identify two external factors that can affect company performance. Using a particular ratio, show how it might be affected by the two external factors that you have identified. *(6 marks)*

5 Analyse how changes in corporate objectives might influence the ways in which a car manufacturer uses ratio analysis. *(8 marks)*

6 'Ratio analysis is of limited use because it shows the past, not the future.' To what extent is this statement valid? *(9 marks)*

Ratio analysis: choosing the right ratio (or ratios)

Table 4.9 summarises the main purposes of each ratio.

Ratio	Main purpose
Return on capital employed (%)	• To assess whether the business is making a satisfactory level of profit from the capital that it has available to it.
Current ratio	• To see if the business is likely to run short of liquid assets in the short term. • To ascertain whether a cash-flow problem might occur in the short-term.
Acid test ratio	• To see if the business has sufficient liquid assets in the short term, even if it has difficulties in selling its stocks (inventories). • To ascertain whether a cash-flow problem might occur in the short term, especially if the business cannot rely on receiving cash from selling its inventories.
Gearing (%)	• To measure how reliant a business is on borrowed money. • To study the likely impact on the costs of a business if there are changes in interest rates. • To gauge whether a business may be vulnerable from having to repay loans in the next few years.
Asset turnover	• To measure the efficiency of a business in terms of how well it uses its assets to generate sales revenue.
Inventory turnover	• To calculate how many times a year a business is able to sell its stock. • To measure the speed at which a business is able to convert its inventories into sales.
Receivables days	• To discover the time taken for its receivables to pay their debts to the business. • To assess whether individual receivables are possibly going to become bad debts.
Payables days	• To discover the time taken for the business to pay its debts to its payables. • To assess whether the business is in danger of defaulting on the debts it owes.
Dividends per share	• To calculate the direct financial reward that a shareholder will receive from the company every 6 months, in return for owning its shares.
Dividend yield (%)	• To assess the percentage return that a shareholder receives from a share, based on the assumption that the shareholder is considering purchasing shares at the current market price. This return can be compared to current interest rates for savings in a bank.

Table 4.9 Purposes of performance ratios

PRACTICE EXERCISE 9   Total: 20 marks (20 minutes)

Which ratio or ratios would you use to answer each of the following questions?
(Each of the ten AQA ratios should be selected once.)

1 How effective is stock control in a business?   *(2 marks)*

2 Are shareholders likely to be happy with their share of the profit?   *(2 marks)*

3 Is the business likely to be able to avoid a liquidity problem in the short term if it can convert all of its liquid assets into cash?   *(2 marks)*

4 Is the business able to pay its short-term debts if its inventories become unfashionable and difficult to sell? *(2 marks)*

5 Is the business likely to experience a liquidity problem in the long term? *(2 marks)*

6 How successful is the business at generating profit? *(2 marks)*

7 How successful is the business at generating sales revenue? *(2 marks)*

8 How quickly is the business receiving money from customers who buy the goods on credit? *(2 marks)*

9 Would shareholders receive more money from putting their savings somewhere else? *(2 marks)*

10 Are suppliers providing the business with good credit terms? *(2 marks)*

CASE STUDY 1 Rounded Figures versus Doh! Nuts! The battle of the heavyweights

The article below provides a commentary on recent and projected events and factors influencing the cream cake and doughnut markets in the UK.

Item 1: In order to encourage borrowing and spending to overcome economic difficulties facing the UK, the Bank of England is anticipating reducing interest rates to 0% or 1%.

Item 2: A recent medical survey has indicated that doughnuts are much healthier than cream cakes as a means of compensating for the low sugar levels in the diets of some UK citizens.

Item 3: Rounded Figures plc suffered a setback when its main factory was unable to supply the shops with cream cakes for a period of 2 weeks. This closure was a result of a visit by health inspectors, who discovered unhygienic working practices in the factory.

Item 4: Doh! Nuts! plc was recently prosecuted for employing workers at below the minimum wage. In response to this prosecution, the company has modified its recruitment policy to target more 16–18-year-old students, for whom the minimum wage is approximately 25% lower than that of people aged over 18.

Item 5: Shareholders of Doh! Nuts! plc have voted in support of a zero dividend payment in 2010. Any profit made will be donated to Children in Need.

Item 6: The British government has announced a special tax on 'undesirable products'. Cream cakes and doughnuts have both been included in the list of products that will be charged a higher rate of VAT.

Item 7: Rounded Figures plc has confirmed that it will continue to invest in new stores so that it can maintain its recent growth rate of 25% per annum, despite analysts' warnings that the cake market is likely to experience a greater downturn than most other markets.

Table 4.10 summarises the ratio analysis calculations for Rounded Figures plc and Doh! Nuts! Plc for the year ending 30.6.2009.

Table 4.10 Ratio analysis: Rounded Figures and Doh! Nuts!

Ratio	Rounded Figures plc	Doh! Nuts! plc
Return on capital employed (%)	30.0%	8.3%
Current ratio	1.7:1	0.8:1
Acid test ratio	1.5:1	0.2:1
Gearing (%)	18.2%	50.0%
Asset turnover	2.78	3.33
Inventory turnover	19.2	8.0
Receivables days	9 days	5 days
Payables days	95 days	76 days
Dividends per share	33p	20p
Dividend yield (%)	14.8%	40.0%

Questions

Total: 45 marks (50 minutes)

1 Based only on the ratios provided in Table 4.10, evaluate the main reasons why Rounded Figures plc would be seen as a better-performing business than Doh! Nuts! plc.   *(25 marks)*

2 Based on the article, discuss the extent to which the factors (items) described in the case study support your conclusion in question 1.   *(20 marks)*

CASE STUDY 2 The demise of Woolworths?

In August 2008 the interim results of Woolworths plc were published, covering the 6 months between February and August 2008. The accounts were prepared by PricewaterhouseCoopers and concluded with the following damning sentence: 'The data provided indicate the existence of material uncertainties which may cast significant doubt about the company's ability to continue as a going concern.'

The balance sheet in Table 4.11 shows the company's situation as at 2.8.2008 and the income statement in Table 4.12 covers the 6 months prior to that date. The text that follows these accounts summarises some of Woolworths' woes.

Table 4.11 *Balance sheet of Woolworths plc as at 2.8.2008*

		As at: 2.8.08 (£m)
Non-current assets (fixed assets)		**457**
Inventories (stocks)	448	
Receivables (debtors)	289	
Cash and other cash equivalents	<u>53</u>	
Total current assets		**790**
Payables (creditors)	(782)	
Current liabilities		**(782)**
Net current assets (working capital)		**8**
Non-current liabilities (long-term liabilities)		**(230)**
Net assets (net worth)		**235**
Share capital		192
Reserves		<u>43</u>
Total equity		**235**
NB capital employed =		
non-current assets + net current assets		**465**

Table 4.12 *Income statement for Woolworths plc, 26 weeks to 2.8.2008*

	6 months ending: 2.8.08 (£m)
Revenue	1,107
Cost of sales	(855)
Gross profit	**252**
Expenses	(314)
plus (minus) Exceptional items	(20)
Operating profit	**(82)**
Finance income	2
Finance costs	(20)
Profit before tax	**(100)**
Taxation	32 (tax repayment received)
Profit for year	**(68)**
Earnings per share	–£0.05 (–5p)
Additional information:	
Number of shares issued (millions)	1,447
Dividends paid (£ millions)	zero
Share price	£0.03 (3 pence)

In late 2008, a year away from its centenary, Woolworths went into administration. This American company found its way into the hearts of the British shopper. Where else could you buy pick-n-mix sweets, a DVD, a magnifying headlight and a cheese grater? The layout, with the sun lotion, biscuit jars, school bags and calendars close together was part of its charm. Overall, despite its range, Woolworths became heavily reliant on toys and children's clothes for its revenue. It used to cater for everyone but lost direction. Tesco and ASDA offered many of the same goods only more cheaply, and you could buy them with the food shopping.

Ironically, the reason it was so successful nearly 100 years ago was the reason that it got into trouble. Whereas supermarkets benefit from bulk-buying, Woolworths suffered from the variety of different items that it provided. This meant that it did not get the discounts enjoyed by specialist retailers, which could buy vast quantities of a more limited range. Woolworths' poor stock control added to its problems, as stock availability was low in some stores.

Woolworths' profitability had declined in recent years, as shown in Table 4.13.

Table 4.13 *Woolworths' return on capital, 2004 to 30.11.2008*

	2003/04	2004/05	2005/06	2006/07	2007/08
ROCE (%)	13.0	13.7	13.5	5.2	6.4
Capital employed (£m)	584	600	526	509	520

The ROCE showed a significant decline since 2005/06, culminating in the losses experienced since February 2008. The problems were compounded by the low quality of the profit in some cases, as Woolworths made some profit by selling off loss-making stores. High finance costs also meant that the operating profit was much higher than the profit available to shareholders, and it was Woolworths' difficulties in persuading its lenders to continue lending that led to its ultimate demise. This unwillingness to lend money to Woolworths was, in part, caused by the economic downturn in 2008.

Woolworths' liquidity position was worsened further by Camelot's decision to withdraw the right for Woolworths to sell lottery tickets, depriving the business of a regular source of income and, more significantly, taking away from many shoppers a reason for going into Woolworths.

To many observers the demise of Woolworths was inevitable. Some years ago Woolworths' parent company (Kingfisher Group) split the company into separate businesses and this was regarded at the time as an act designed to protect the future of other subsidiaries, such as B&Q, Superdrug and Comet.

Sources: an article by Tom Geoghegan, *BBC News Magazine*; Woolworths plc company reports; and various other sources.

Question

Total: 35 marks (45 minutes)

Based on the text above and the financial data provided (Tables 4.11–4.13), to what extent was it inevitable that Woolworths would fail as a business? Justify your view, using suitable ratios to support your judgement.

(35 marks)

Appendix: formulae for financial ratios — the AQA list

1 Current ratio

current ratio = current assets:current liabilities

2 Acid test ratio

acid test = liquid assets:current liabilities

Liquid assets are current assets – inventories. Therefore:

acid test = current assets – inventories:current liabilities

3 Return on capital employed (ROCE)

$$\text{ROCE (\%)} = \frac{\text{operating profit}}{\text{total equity plus non-current liabilities}} \times 100$$

4 Asset turnover

$$\text{asset turnover} = \frac{\text{revenue}}{\text{net assets}} \quad \text{or} \quad \frac{\text{annual sales turnover}}{\text{net assets}}$$

5 Inventory or stock turnover

$$\text{inventory (stock) turnover} = \frac{\text{cost of goods sold}}{\text{average inventories held}}$$

6 Payables (creditors) days

$$\text{payables'* collection period} = \frac{\text{payables*}}{\text{cost of sale}} \times 365$$

*payables = creditors

7 Receivables (debtors) days

$$\text{receivables'* collection period} = \frac{\text{receivables*}}{\text{revenue}} \times 365$$

*receivables = debtors

8 Gearing

$$\text{gearing (\%)} = \frac{\text{non-current liabilities}}{\text{total equity plus non-current liabilities}} \times 100$$

9 Dividend per share

$$\text{dividend per share (in pence)} = \frac{\text{total dividends}}{\text{number of ordinary shares issued}}$$

10 Dividend yield

$$\text{dividend yield (\%)} = \frac{\text{dividend per share (in pence)}}{\text{market price per share (in pence)}} \times 100$$

Chapter 5

Selecting financial strategies

This chapter examines the selection of financial strategies designed to achieve the goals of an organisation. Four different strategies are scrutinised: raising finance, focusing on the needs of larger organisations; introducing and implementing profit centres; cost minimisation; and allocating capital expenditure. The interrelationship between these strategies and other functions of the business is studied. The chapter also examines the value of these strategies in given circumstances.

Raising finance

This topic was introduced in Chapter 8 of the AS textbook in the context of starting a small business. This section builds on that chapter, focusing on those sources of finance (such as retained profit) that were not relevant or required when considering a business start-up.

Three ways of raising finance that are relevant to a large business — ordinary share capital, bank loans and bank overdrafts — were covered in Chapter 8 of the AS textbook, so only a brief reminder will be provided here.

Classifying sources of finance

Internal or external
Internal sources of finance are ways of raising finance from within the business, such as retained profit or the sale of assets.

External sources of finance are ways of raising finance from outside the business, such as bank loans and debt factoring.

Short term or long term
Short-term finance describes finance that is normally intended for repayment within 12 months. It is usually intended for revenue expenditure.

Long-term finance describes finance that is normally intended for capital expenditure and where repayment, if necessary, is due after 3 years or more.

(Medium-term finance covers the period between short-term and long-term finance).

Internal sources of finance

Trading (retained) profit

Trading profit is a good indicator of the success of a firm, but more importantly it allows the organisation to use the surplus (profit) for future activities. The owners of a business (the shareholders in limited companies) expect a share of the profit as a dividend, but the remaining profit can be retained and used by the business. If this source of finance is used well, the company will succeed and then the shareholders will gain because the share price will rise.

Trading profit is a cheap and flexible form of finance, which can be used for a long-term project such as a new factory or as revenue expenditure to pay daily bills. It is an attractive source for managers because there are no interest charges.

Sale of assets

Selling assets such as a building will allow a business to fund other ventures. A firm usually sells non-current assets for the following reasons:

- The firm is in difficulties and needs cash as a *short-term source of finance* in order to survive a cash-flow crisis. In the long term, however, selling assets will lower the firm's profitability.
- The firm no longer needs the asset (it may be diversifying into other activities). This means that the firm uses the funds as a *long-term* or *medium-term source of finance* in order to expand other, more profitable parts of the business.

> **DID YOU KNOW?**
>
> One of the largest factoring companies (GE Capital) used this method of finance. The management of the company, originally known as General Electric, predicted that financial services would become more profitable than electrical products. So it sold some assets that were not creating profit and, along with some retained profit, it had sufficient funds to set up a division that concentrated on financial services such as factoring. GE Capital now has assets worth more than $425 billion.

> **KEY TERMS**
>
> **trading profit:** the difference between the income received from an organisation's normal activities and the expenditure it incurs in operating.
>
> **retained profit:** the part of a firm's profit that is reinvested in the business rather than distributed to shareholders.
>
> **asset:** any item owned by the firm.

Sale and leaseback

Be aware of the difference between 'sale of an asset' and 'sale and leaseback'. Selling a non-current asset is sensible if the asset is no longer needed (or if the price offered lets the firm move on to more profitable ventures). Sale and leaseback is used if the asset is still needed but the firm wants an immediate injection of cash. The sale gives the firm immediate cash, but the leaseback means that the firm pays regular sums to rent or lease the asset in the future.

ordinary share capital: money given to a company by share-holders in return for a share certificate that gives them part ownership of the company and entitles them to a share of the profits.

loan capital: money received by an organisation in return for the organisation's agreement to pay interest during the period of the loan and to repay the loan within an agreed time.

debenture: a long-term loan made to a business at an agreed fixed percentage rate of interest and repayable on a stated date.

bank loan: a sum of money provided to a firm or an individual by a bank for a specific, agreed purpose.

bank overdraft: when a bank allows an individual or organisation to overspend its current account in the bank up to an agreed (overdraft) limit and for a stated time period.

External sources of finance

Ordinary share capital

For a description of the main features of ordinary share capital and its advantages and disadvantages, refer to pp. 86–87 of the AS textbook.

Loan capital

Three kinds of loan capital are described below.

Debentures are a *long-term source of finance*. Traditionally, debentures were issued for 25 years, but the pace of change in the business world means that firms expect to be able to repay even very large loans much more quickly, so shorter periods are more common. The current rate of interest is another factor. With interest rates (at the time of writing) at their lowest level for half a century, firms are finding long-term debentures very attractive because the interest rate is fixed.

For a description of the main features of **bank loans** and their advantages and disadvantages, refer to pp. 88–89 of the AS textbook.

For a description of the main features of **bank overdrafts** and their advantages and disadvantages, refer to pp. 89–90 of the AS textbook.

Should a business use internal or external sources of finance?

When deciding whether to use internal or external sources, a business will weigh up the following factors:
- the legal structure of the business
- the use of the finance
- the amount required
- the firm's profit levels
- the level of risk
- the views of the owners

If you need an explanation of any of these factors, refer to pp. 94–95 of the AS textbook.

How long is the finance needed for?

When considering sources of finance, the most critical factor is the length of time for which the finance is needed. Finance is used to fund:
- **Capital expenditure.** This is spending on items that can be used time and time again (non-current assets). It may take a long time before these items generate enough revenue to pay for themselves, so a *long-term source of finance* is ideal.

- **Revenue expenditure.** This is spending on current, day-to-day costs, such as the purchase of raw materials and payment of wages. Such expenditure provides a quick return, so the company should rely on a *short-* or *medium-term source of finance*.

> **_e_ EXAMINER'S VOICE**
>
> Raising finance is a popular way of testing analysis and evaluation in the examination. Each source of finance has its own benefits and problems, so analysing the reasons for choosing a particular source (or evaluating/judging the best source or sources) is a good test of your understanding of a business's finances. Always look for clues in the background information on the company and its situation. The owners may want to keep control or may lack security for a loan, so certain sources may not be available.

The interrelationship between raising finance and other functions of a business

Raising finance relates closely to all other functional areas of a business. Because the finance department controls the spending of the other functional areas, and has a duty to manage company finances in the most efficient way possible, the finance department must take a view on the best method of raising the finance required for expenditure by the other departments.

PRACTICE EXERCISE 1   Total: 40 marks (35 minutes)

1 What is the difference between 'sale of assets' and 'sale and leaseback'? *(4 marks)*

2 Explain the difference between internal finance and external finance. *(4 marks)*

3 Explain two benefits of using retained profit as a way of raising finance. *(6 marks)*

4 Identify two sources of short-term finance. *(2 marks)*

5 Distinguish between ordinary share capital and debentures. *(6 marks)*

6 Explain two reasons why a firm might decide to use internal rather than external finance. *(6 marks)*

7 Identify four sources of long-term finance. *(4 marks)*

8 Explain one reason why a firm should choose a short-term source of finance. *(4 marks)*

9 Explain one disadvantage of using the sale of assets as a way of raising finance. *(4 marks)*

Introducing and implementing profit centres

Profit centres

Examples of profit centres are a branch of a retail chain and a particular product within a firm. The sales revenue is easy to calculate and it is possible (but not always easy) to calculate the costs of running that branch or making that product.

In profit centres, it is necessary to identify a person who is responsible for controlling the finances of the centre.

Reasons for profit centres

Organisations use profit centres in order to benefit from delegating power over budgets to managers of the profit centres.

- **They allow a more focused study of a firm's finances.** In the absence of profit centres, a business may be unaware that certain activities are losing money or are working inefficiently, especially if the firm is making a profit overall. Once identified, areas of weakness can be changed.
- **Benchmarking can take place.** The most efficient profit centres can show how efficiency may be improved.
- **Responsibility for a profit centre may help to motivate the individual responsible.** Profit centres may be created deliberately in order to give more staff some level of responsibility. If a more motivated workforce is created, productivity should be improved.

- **Finances may be run more efficiently.** By placing responsibility with the person actually involved in the activity, the firm's finances may be run more efficiently than would be the case if a more remote, senior manager controlled them. Zara lets its shop managers decide what clothes to stock because they know what local customers want more than Zara's senior managers.

Disadvantages of profit centres

Profit centres have the following disadvantages:

- **Allocating costs.** In practice, it may be difficult to allocate costs to a particular division or centre. For example, in a manufacturing company where machinery is used to process a number of different products, it is not easy to calculate the manufacturing costs of each product.
- **Demotivation.** Profit centres may add to the pressure and stress imposed on staff, who may have technical skills that do not include financial management. It may thus demotivate certain staff who want to use their technical ability rather than financial skills, or who simply do not have enough time to cope with the extra work needed.
- **Setting targets.** For specialist areas, the senior managers of the business may lack the detailed knowledge needed to recognise whether a profit centre is being run effectively or ineffectively. Targets may be too easy or too hard.

- **Diseconomies.** If too much financial responsibility is delegated, there may be many profit centre managers all carrying out similar tasks, such as buying materials, on a small, inefficient scale.
- **External changes.** Businesses must be careful when using profit centres to assess the efficiency of the manager responsible for each centre. External factors may make it more difficult (or easier) for the targets to be reached.

> ### e EXAMINER'S VOICE
>
> The idea of profit centres is closely linked to the 'People' function of the A-level course. Profit centres give managers more freedom and allow senior managers to delegate responsibility to junior staff. These policies help to motivate staff.

Cost minimisation

If a company can cut its **direct costs**, such as wage levels or raw material costs, then its profit margin will increase. This means that each product will yield more profit and, assuming that there is no change in demand, this will increase the total profit. In most cases, changes in costs will probably not affect the demand, so this strategy will be successful in improving profits and profitability. However, if the change in costs leads to a decrease in quality or efficiency, the demand for the product may fall. This could happen if costs are being cut because inferior raw materials are being used or if the workers who accept a lower wage are less efficient than those being paid a higher wage.

Similar benefits can be obtained by reducing **overheads**, such as rent, office expenses and machinery costs. Once again, the business must be careful that cutting these costs does not damage sales. For example, a retail outlet may be reluctant to move to lower-rent premises if the location is less accessible to customers. In this case, the savings in costs may be much lower than the decline in sales revenue caused by the unfavourable location.

If the finance department is intending to pursue a strategy of cost minimisation, it must liaise closely with the other functional areas of the company. Cost savings will directly affect the functional area which is targeted to achieve these cost savings. However, there may also be indirect consequences for a functional area arising from cost cutting in a different part of the company. For example, a reduction in the quality of raw materials may be acceptable to the operations department, as lower-quality materials will enable it to meet the lower expenditure budget that it has been allocated. However, the marketing department may now be required to sell products of inferior quality, making it more difficult for it to achieve its revenue budgets.

Similarly, a reduction in marketing expenditure may not help the company if it is not dealt with in a coordinated way. If the marketing department expects a decline in sales levels, this expectation must be relayed to other departments so that they can act appropriately, such as the operations department cutting production levels. Alternatively, it may allow the human resources function to oppose the strategy on the grounds that staff contracts mean that their working hours cannot be cut, so only limited cost savings may result.

Any strategy of cost minimisation must be agreed at strategic management level, as implementation of such a strategy will often have a broader impact than might have been recognised at the functional (departmental) level. There is a danger that cost minimisation will appear to be succeeding at the departmental level but leading to failure at the corporate level.

Allocating capital expenditure

This topic is introduced briefly at this point. However, a detailed analysis of investment appraisal, which examines how decisions on capital expenditure are made, is presented in the next chapter.

Decisions on allocating capital expenditure fit into two categories:
- decisions on whether to introduce capital equipment to replace labour
- investment decisions on whether it is financially viable to put money into a capital project

As with any decision involving expenditure of limited financial resources, it is vital that the finance department liaises with the other functional areas to ensure that they have an input into these decisions. Although there may be a strong financial case for replacing labour with machinery, the human resources function may oppose this on the grounds of its impact on morale and labour productivity. Similarly, the marketing function may oppose this strategy on the grounds of potential damage to the company's reputation as a result of negative publicity arising from its treatment of its workforce. Thus, the strategy in itself might make good financial sense, but its broader impact may be negative.

 EXAMINER'S VOICE

In assessing the value of a given strategy, it is important to assess the impact of the strategy in the particular circumstances of the case study. For example, if the context of the case indicates that the business has a cash-flow problem, then a strategy of raising finance should focus on short-term sources rather than long-term sources. Similarly, if the business operates in a very competitive market in which price is the key element of the marketing mix, cost minimisation may be crucial in enabling the business to be competitive.

PRACTICE EXERCISE 2   Total: 35 marks (30 minutes)

1 What is meant by the term 'profit centre'? *(3 marks)*

2 Explain two possible reasons for setting up a profit centre. *(6 marks)*

3 Why might it be easier for a retailer than a manufacturer to use profit centres? *(6 marks)*

4 Multi-product companies such as Walkers and Nissan often use individual products as profit centres. Explain two difficulties in organising products as profit centres. *(6 marks)*

5 Explain two ways in which a business might attempt a strategy of cost minimisation. *(6 marks)*

6 Examine two reasons why it is important for cost minimisation strategies, and/or decisions on allocating capital expenditure, to be the result of a corporate approach, rather than being planned separately by individual departments. *(8 marks)*

CASE STUDY Shakespeare's bookshop

Will and Anne Shakespeare had purchased their bookshop using the money raised from selling the newsagents shop that they had owned. The couple had been worried about declining newspaper sales and believed that a bookshop would be more profitable.

They had conducted some market research and found that the profitability of bookshops was expanding slightly, whilst many newsagents were being forced out of business. Their decision to open a bookshop had been based on two factors:

- a love of books
- a healthy profit forecast from the small business adviser recommended to them by the bank manager

They were so confident of success that they declined an offer of a bank loan from the bank manager, although they did accept his offer of a £12,000 overdraft limit.

In the first 2 years, Will and Anne struggled to make a profit. However, after the introduction of a number of ideas that enabled them to minimise costs, they were able to overcome this problem. The two most successful strategies introduced were:

- reducing stock levels but guaranteeing 24-hour delivery directly from the supplier's warehouse to the customer's house
- reducing staffing levels so that the shop only employed family members

After 3 years of trading, Will and Anne's bookshop had at last reached their profit target.

Originally, three divisions had been set up, each operating as a profit centre. These divisions were: DVDs, Books, and Newspapers and Magazines.

'DVDs' were Will's responsibility. He concentrated on purchased 'talking books', targeting the elderly and those consumers who enjoyed listening to books while driving.

Anne was responsible for 'Books'. She used her knowledge of the book trade to locate the cheapest suppliers of books. The shop concentrated on new books, but there was an expanding range of second-hand books. Anne enjoyed the challenge of finding first editions, but purchasing these books often led to her exceeding her expenditure targets. However, it did help her to reach her sales targets. Anne was particularly skilled in arranging the stock attractively, to gain maximum sales. Book sales had exceeded their target in every one of the 36 months of trading, even last February when the river Avon had flooded, forcing the shop to close for 2 weeks.

Judith, the couple's daughter, organised 'Newspapers and Magazines'. She decided on the numbers and titles of the newspapers and magazines, and had complete control of the area at the front of the shop. Will and Anne were happy if this division achieved breakeven. In their opinion, its role was to attract people into the shop – once inside, many people also purchased books, particularly the tourists visiting the town.

Hamnet, Judith's twin brother, joined the business a year after it started. There was a lot of unused space in the bookshop and Hamnet's idea of a fourth division, 'The Coffee Bar', seemed like a good idea at the time. Will and Anne set Hamnet a profit target that included a payment towards the building's rent. Hamnet objected because this charge was not included in Judith's target. Will believed that the coffee bar improved the atmosphere and encouraged shoppers to stay longer and buy more.

Anne disagreed, pointing out that the coffee bar meant that there was less space to sell books. As usual, Anne won the argument.

Anne had just bought a large stock of books from a shop that had closed down and was aware that there was no longer enough space in their bookshop. This was going to be a difficult problem to solve, but Anne had suggested the closure of the coffee bar, to free space for more books.

Over tea, the family sat down to consider the issues.

'The number of customers has increased since the opening of the coffee bar,' argued Hamnet.

Anne unexpectedly sided with Hamnet. 'A study of the firm's CCTV footage shows that shoppers using the coffee bar do buy more books.'

'Unfortunately, some read the magazines and then leave them in the coffee bar without paying for them,' Judith added. 'This makes it more difficult for my division to pay its way.'

Will delivered what he considered to be the clinching argument: 'The coffee bar is not making money, even though the business as a whole makes a profit. On the basis of our policy to run each division as a profit centre, I propose that we vote to close the coffee bar. All in favour raise their right hands.'

Will and Anne raised their hands and, after an agonising pause, Judith slowly raised hers too.

'You cannot make a decision like this on the basis of profit centres!' shouted Hamnet, as he stormed out of the room.

Preliminary questions

Total: 20 marks (25 minutes)

1 Will and Anne decided to invest the capital from selling their newsagents into setting up the bookshop. Based on the evidence provided in the case study, how well did they plan this decision? *(6 marks)*

2 Explain one advantage and one disadvantage to Will and Anne from using 'sales of assets' as a way of raising finance for the new bookshop. *(6 marks)*

3 Analyse two possible benefits of setting up profit centres to a business such as Shakespeare's bookshop. *(8 marks)*

Case study questions

Total: 35 marks (45 minutes)

1 Examine the possible reasons why Will and Anne refused the offer of a bank loan but accepted the offer of a bank overdraft. *(10 marks)*

2 Discuss the advantages and disadvantages of the two methods of cost minimisation introduced by Will and Anne. *(12 marks)*

3 To what extent do you agree with Hamnet's view that the use of profit centres by Will and Anne was not an appropriate way to decide whether to close the coffee shop? *(13 marks)*

Chapter 6

Making investment decisions

This chapter introduces the concept of investment decision making. It considers three quantitative methods of investment appraisal: payback, average rate of return and net present value. The calculations of each method and its relative merits as a form of investment appraisal are compared. The chapter also examines the significance of the source of the data and assessment of risk in such decisions. Finally, the qualitative factors that influence investment decisions are scrutinised and their significance is evaluated.

DID YOU KNOW?

Investment appraisal techniques are usually applied to capital investment projects, such as building a new factory, purchasing a new delivery van, relocating an office or installing a new piece of machinery. However, on occasions the techniques described in this chapter can be applied to revenue expenditure, such as putting resources into an advertising campaign or spending money on research and development.

Reasons why businesses invest

Investment or **capital investment** describes the process of purchasing fixed assets, such as new buildings, plant, machinery or office equipment. It considers the buying of any asset that will pay for itself over a period of more than 1 year.

Capital investment is undertaken for two main reasons:
- to replace or renew any assets that have worn out (depreciated) or become obsolescent
- to introduce additional, new assets in order to meet increased demand for the firm's products

KEY TERMS

investment decision making: the process of deciding whether or not to undertake capital investment (the purchase of non-current assets) or major business projects.

How investment can help businesses to reach functional objectives

Although investment decision-making techniques are described as operations management techniques, they can help a business to achieve not only its strategic objectives but also a comprehensive range of functional objectives. Table 6.1 below gives some examples that cover all four functional areas and illustrate how investment decisions can help all areas of the business.

Table 6.1 Examples of how functional objectives can be reached through investment decisions

Functional objective	Example of investment decision assisting this objective
Marketing: increase market share by 4%	Investment decision examining the possibility of opening new outlets or factories
Marketing: improve corporate image	Investment in modern machinery may help to improve the quality of products
Finance: increase ROCE from 10% to 20%	Decision to move to a new factory that allows the business to introduce lean production techniques
Finance: cut costs by 10%	Investment appraisal used to ascertain the most cost-effective way of reducing costs without leading to a loss of sales revenue
People: reduce labour turnover by 15%	Investment in a new training scheme in order to give workers greater responsibility and thus boost morale
People: increase labour productivity	Investment in on-the-job training in order to improve people's technical ability so that machinery can be utilised more efficiently
Operations: identify the ideal location	Investment appraisal in order to discover the 'least cost' site for production of a particular product
Operations: improve customer service	Introduction of a new customer services procedure in order to increase customer satisfaction levels

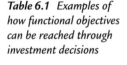

KEY TERM

investment appraisal: a scientific approach to investment decision making, which investigates the expected financial consequences of an investment, in order to assist the company in its choices.

Investment appraisal

Major business projects involve decisions that incorporate more than just capital equipment. Setting up new factories or stores, introducing new products, setting up a research laboratory and relocating to a new country are all examples of major projects which businesses must analyse using rigorous, scientific techniques. Investment appraisal ensures that investment decisions are subject to a rigorous scrutiny before agreement.

Investment appraisal is a *quantitative* (numerical) tool in the decision-making process. Investment appraisal recommendations should be combined with an investigation of *qualitative* factors before a final decision is reached. These qualitative factors are considered later in the chapter.

> **e EXAMINER'S VOICE**
>
> Investment appraisal can be applied to any major business decision. A firm considering a takeover or a new location can assess the financial implications by using investment appraisal. Chapter 14 shows how investment appraisal can be used to make location decisions.

The three investment appraisal techniques examined in this chapter base their recommendations solely on the following financial information:

- the initial cost of the investment
- the net return (revenue minus costs) per annum
- the lifetime of the investment

Methods of investment appraisal

There are three main methods of investment appraisal:

- payback period
- average rate of return, or annual rate of return, or average annual rate of return (ARR)
- net present value (NPV)

Each method provides a numerical calculation of the financial benefits of an investment. This result can be compared with the return required by the business and/or the results of alternative investment decisions.

The following scenario will provide the background information for investment appraisal by each of these methods.

Martin's Motors

Martin's Motors is a small garage on the outskirts of Basingstoke in Hampshire. The business offers servicing of certain makes of car for customers who do not wish to take their cars to the main dealerships.

Martin's key selling points are low overheads and a more flexible and personal service for customers, in comparison with local competitors. Most customers are recommended by friends, but in recent years a number of loyal customers have taken their cars back to the main dealers for their servicing. Martin has discovered that the main reason is the lack of certain technical equipment within his garage, as he is unable to afford the state-of-the-art machinery purchased by the large garages against which he is competing.

A particular weakness is the lack of a machine to recharge (service) the air-conditioning units in his customers' cars. He is looking at purchasing a Viper GT air-conditioning machine for carrying out this task. Martin has financial estimates based on prices in a Viper GT catalogue, comments from other garages, and his own estimates of the number of customers that he has lost through his failure to provide recharging of air-conditioning for his customers. These estimates are outlined below:

Cost to purchase a Viper GT air-conditioning machine: £5,000

Running costs:
| Air-conditioning liquid: | £20 per treatment |
| Wages and other costs: | £5 per treatment |

Price charged to customers: £65 per treatment

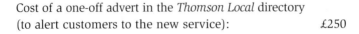

Cost of a one-off advert in the *Thomson Local* directory
(to alert customers to the new service): £250

Anticipated number of customers requesting the treatment:
- Year 1: 60
- Year 2: 45
- Year 3: 39
- Year 4: 34
- Year 5: 30

Martin is expecting to make money by attracting back customers for a full service of their cars. However, he wants to take a pessimistic view, so he is basing his decision on whether the Viper GT will pay for itself by attracting customers who only wish to service their air-conditioning. Any additional revenue is seen as a bonus.

The expected lifetime of the machine is anticipated to be 5 years, although this is probably a pessimistic estimate. As competition for air-conditioning recharging increases, the selling price is expected to fall from £65 to £50 or £60.

Table 6.2 shows the expected revenue, costs and net return on the Viper GT over its expected lifetime, based on the estimated costs, charges and customer numbers. For example, in year 1, revenue is 60 × £65 = £3,900 and costs are 60 × (£20 + £5) = £1,500.

Table 6.2 Expected revenue, costs and return on the Viper GT

Year	Annual revenue (£)	Annual cost (£)	Net return (£)
0*	0	5,250	(5,250)
1	3,900	1,500	2,400
2	2,925	1,125	1,800
3	2,535	975	1,560
4	2,210	850	1,360
5	1,950	750	1,200
Cumulative total	13,520	10,450	3,070

*It is traditional to denote the year in which the initial cost of an investment is incurred as year 0.

Payback

KEY TERMS

payback period: the length of time that it takes for an investment to pay for itself from the net returns provided by that particular investment.

Payback is calculated by adding the annual returns from an investment until the cumulative total equals the initial cost of the investment. The exact time at which this occurs is the payback period. It is often measured in years, but for some investments, months or weeks may be more appropriate. Firms will hope for as short a payback as possible.

An example calculation based on Martin's Motors is shown in Table 6.3.

Year	Annual revenue (£)	Annual cost (£)	Net return (£)	Cumulative returns (£)
0	0	5,250	(5,250)	(5,250)
1	3,900	1,500	2,400	(2,850)
2	2,925	1,125	1,800	(1,050)
3	2,535	975	1,560	510
4	2,210	850	1,360	1,870
5	1,950	750	1,200	3,070
Cumulative total	13,520	10,450	3,070	

Table 6.3 Predicted payback period for a Viper GT air-conditioning system for Martin's Motors

The final column shows the running total of revenues minus costs. When this column reaches zero, payback has been achieved. By the end of year 2, £4,200 of the £5,250 has been repaid. During year 3 the net return is £1,560, leading to a surplus of £510 by the end of year 3. Thus, the payback occurs at some time during the third year.

In payback calculations, it is assumed that costs and income occur at regular intervals throughout the year. Therefore, the £1,560 net return in year 3 is spread evenly over the 52 weeks of the year. This means there are net returns of £1,560/52 = £30 per week. At this rate it will take exactly £1,050/£30 = 35 weeks of year 3 to reach payback. Thus, the payback point is 35 weeks after the end of year 2: that is, 2 years 35 weeks.

An alternative way to calculate the final part is to work out the fraction of the year that elapses before payback is reached. In the above example, £1,050 is still needed to reach payback after the end of year 2. The net return for year 3 is £1,560. Therefore, the payback point is reached 1,050/1,560 of the way through the year. This is 0.673 of a year. Thus the payback period is 2.673 years.

A simpler result is achieved by calculating in weeks:

$$\text{number of weeks before payback is achieved during the third year} = \frac{1,050}{1,560} \times 52 = 35$$

Therefore, the payback period is 2 years 35 weeks.

Average rate of return

Firms want to achieve as high a percentage return as possible. A benchmark that is often used to see if the ARR percentage is satisfactory is the interest rate that the firm must pay on any money borrowed to finance the investment. If the percentage return on the project exceeds the interest rate that the business is paying, the project is financially worthwhile.

An example calculation based on Martin's Motors is shown below:

$$\text{APR }(\%) = \frac{\text{total net return or surplus from a project/no. of years}}{\text{initial cost}} \times 100$$

KEY TERM

average rate of return (ARR): total net returns divided by the expected lifetime of the investment (usually a number of years), expressed as a percentage of the initial cost of the investment.

Calculations for the Viper GT air-conditioning machine:

$$\frac{£3,070/5}{£5,250} \times 100 = \frac{£614}{£5,250} \times 100 = 11.7\%$$

At current interest rates, this ARR would mean that it is financially worthwhile to purchase the air-conditioning equipment.

Net present value

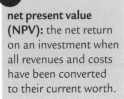

KEY TERM

net present value (NPV): the net return on an investment when all revenues and costs have been converted to their current worth.

Given a choice between £1 now and £1 in the future, a rational individual (or firm) will choose £1 now. Implicitly, this suggests that money today has a greater value than money in the future. This arises because of the **opportunity cost** of the money. For example, £100 received today could be invested at, say, 10% and would be worth £110 in a year's time. Thus, in these circumstances, the **present value** of £110, receivable in 1 year's time, is £100.

The net present value method of investment appraisal takes this factor into consideration.

Any receipts (or payments) in the future are considered to be worth less than the equivalent sum received (or paid) today. In effect, future sums are **discounted** (reduced) by a certain percentage to reflect their lower value. In our example, a 10% discount rate would be appropriate. A commonly used discount rate is the current rate of interest, as this is the opportunity cost of using money for a particular investment. The opportunity cost (next best alternative) is assumed to be the return that the firm could have made by just saving the money involved.

Discounted cash flow

The payback and average rate of return methods assume that the exact timing of the payments and receipts is not important. They ignore the **time value of money**. However, the net present value method of investment appraisal includes this factor in its calculation.

There is no single agreed percentage by which future values should be discounted, as companies face different circumstances. If a company can find a very profitable immediate use for its cash, it will place a much higher value on money in the present (as the opportunity cost of waiting will be the lost opportunity to make a high profit). Paradoxically, a firm suffering from cash-flow problems will deem a high discount rate appropriate: money received in the present may be necessary to keep the business operating. Conversely, a business that is secure but less profitable would consider a low discount rate to be valid.

Whatever the financial situation of a firm, the current market interest rate can be earned if money is received immediately. This acts as a guide to the loss or discount that should be applied to money in the future.

The process of reducing the value of future sums is known as **discounted cash flow**. As time progresses, the 'present' value of a given future sum declines. The higher the discount rate, the lower is the value. Exact values can be determined from a 'present value' table.

Table 6.4 shows the present value of £1, based on four different discount rates.

Table 6.4 *Present value of £1 at selected discount rates*

Year	Discount rate			
	2%	5%	7%	10%
0	1.0	1.0	1.0	1.0
1	0.980	0.952	0.935	0.909
2	0.961	0.907	0.873	0.826
3	0.942	0.864	0.816	0.751
4	0.924	0.823	0.763	0.683
5	0.906	0.784	0.713	0.621

The choice of discount rate may be critical in an investment appraisal. It can be seen that £1 received in 5 years' time is equivalent to £0.784 (78.4p) today, if a discount rate of 5% is applied, but only 62.1p (£0.621) if 10% is used and as much as 90.6 pence (£0.906) if a 2% discount rate is used.

e **EXAMINER'S VOICE**

Do not try to remember discount tables. If you are required to calculate net present value, the discount rates will be provided. However, you may be provided with alternative rates, such as those in Table 6.4, and be required to select an appropriate discount rate based on circumstances (such as a note on current interest rates or the firm's expected percentage return on its investments).

Two example calculations based on Martin's Motors are shown in Tables 6.5 and 6.6.

Table 6.5 *Net present value of a Viper GT air-conditioning system for Martin's Motors, using a 5% discount factor*

Year	Net return (£)	Discount factor (5%)	Present value (£)
0	(5,250)	1.0	(5,250)
1	2,400	0.952	2,284.8
2	1,800	0.907	1,632.6
3	1,560	0.864	1,347.84
4	1,360	0.823	1,119.28
5	1,200	0.784	940.8
Total	**3,070**		**2,075.32**

The net present value of the investment is +£2,075.32. *On financial grounds only*, the project is worthwhile. Net present value gives a definite recommendation. If the NPV is positive, it is financially justified; if the NPV is negative, it is not worthwhile. However, the firm may wish to include other factors in its decision. These will be discussed later.

Note how the actual net return on this investment is +£3,070. However, the net present value is only +£2,075.32. This is because the main costs are incurred in year 0, whereas the returns are in the future when we are assuming that money is less valuable.

Year	Net return (£)	Discount factor (10%)	Present value (£)
0	(5,250)	1.0	(5,250)
1	2,400	0.909	2,181.6
2	1,800	0.826	1,486.8
3	1,560	0.751	1,171.56
4	1,360	0.683	928.88
5	1,200	0.621	745.2
Total	3,070		1,264.04

Table 6.6 *Net present value of a Viper GT air-conditioning system for Martin's Motors, using a 10% discount factor*

Table 6.5 uses a 5% discount factor. If Martin's Motors could earn a 10% return on its money, then a 10% rate might have been selected. Would the project still be worthwhile?

Table 6.6 shows that, at a 10% discount rate, the net present value is +£1,264.04. This is much lower than the net present value at 5% (+£2,075.32), but it is still a positive return and therefore the investment is worthwhile.

FACT FILE

Zero discount

As no discounts are being applied to the first column (the net return), the total of this column (£3,070) is, in effect, the net present value at a 0% discount rate. From 2001 to 2006 interest rates in Japan were held at 0%, in order to encourage spending and discourage saving. It is possible, in some circumstances, for this rate to be appropriate. At the time of writing, UK interest rates have fallen to 1%.

FACT FILE

Investment appraisal in prisons

Investment appraisal can apply to decisions where no revenue is involved. The Home Office is planning to spend £500 million on four huge prisons in the southeast of England so that prisoners can be held closer to their homes, reducing transport costs for the government and for relatives visiting the prisoners.

Traditional, smaller-scale prisons cost the government £21,800 per annum for each prisoner held. These new prisons will reduce annual costs to £15,000 (saving £6,800) per prisoner. The jails will house 6,000 prisoners, giving an annual saving of £40.8 million. This gives a payback period of:

$$\frac{£500m}{£40.8m} = 12.25 \text{ years}$$

This would be a long payback for most private projects. However, for a long-term major government project with no real risk involved, this is an acceptable payback period.

Strengths and weaknesses of investment appraisal methods

The three methods of investment appraisal outlined above use very different approaches in deciding whether an investment is worthwhile. Each method can also be used to compare alternative investments, where a firm has to decide between different projects. The methods have various strengths and weaknesses, as described below.

Payback

Advantages

- The payback period is easy to calculate. If many projects are being considered, this may save valuable time.
- The concept of payback is easy to understand — it is how long it takes to get the money back.
- The payback method emphasises cash flow by focusing only on the time taken to return the money. As a result, it is a particularly relevant approach for organisations that have some cash-flow difficulties.
- By emphasising the speed of return, the payback period is popular with firms operating in markets that are experiencing rapid change because estimates for years in the distant future are going to be less reliable than those for the near future.

Disadvantages

- The calculation of payback ignores any revenues or costs that occur after the point at which payback has been reached. This means that it does not consider the overall net return from a project. As profit is usually considered to be the main aim of most businesses, this is a major weakness. The payback method may lead to a business ignoring the most profitable investment, simply because it takes slightly longer to achieve that profit.
- It is very difficult to establish a target payback time. Some major invest-ments, such as a new factory, will take many years to pay for themselves. However, investment in a marketing campaign or a new recording will pay for itself in months or not at all.
- Payback values future costs and revenues at the same value as current costs and revenues. Thus it does not consider the time value of money in the way that net present value does.
- By focusing on payback, the business may be encouraged towards short-termism. A firm using the payback method would fail to look at the long-term consequences of an investment.

Average rate of return

Advantages

- The result (a percentage calculation) can be easily compared with the next best alternative (the opportunity cost), such as the percentage interest earned from a savings account.

- The average rate of return shows the true profitability of the investment. It is the only method that takes into consideration every item of revenue and expenditure at its face value.
- Percentage returns, such as the average rate of return, are usually understood by non-accountants.

Disadvantages

- The average rate of return is harder and more time consuming to calculate than the payback method, so it may use valuable company time in compiling shortlists of potential investments.
- It considers all income and expenditure as equal in value. Thus, projections a long time into the future are given the same importance as predictions of present costs and incomes.

Net present value

Advantages

- Net present value is the only method that considers the time value of money. By discounting future figures, NPV recognises that people and organisations place a higher value on money paid/received now than in the future.
- As sums of money far into the future are discounted more heavily, this approach reduces the importance of long-term estimates. As long-term estimates are probably the least reliable predictions, NPV helps to make the conclusions more accurate.
- Net present value is the only method that gives a precise answer. A positive NPV means that, on financial grounds, the investment should be undertaken. A negative NPV indicates that the project should be rejected.

Disadvantages

- Net present value is time consuming and more difficult to calculate than the other methods.
- It is more difficult to understand than the other approaches. This may mean that decision-makers distrust any conclusions drawn using this method.
- The calculation of net present value is based on an arbitrary choice of percentage discount rate. Although the method is calculated scientifically, the final conclusion often relies on the discount rate used.

Assessing the risks and uncertainties of investment decisions

For many major projects it is very difficult for a firm to estimate the anticipated costs and revenue. The construction costs for the venues for the Athens Olympics in 2004 were budgeted at £3 billion, but its eventual costs were closer to £4.4 billion. The British Library was budgeted to cost £74 million but the actual cost was £511 million. London's two major millennium projects proved to be unpredictable too. The Millennium Dome was completed on time, but the actual cost of £780 million far exceeded the original estimate of

£399 million. Furthermore, the Dome fell short of its revenue targets. In contrast, the London Eye was not completed on time but has surpassed its expected income levels.

At least the Millennium Dome and the London Eye earned revenue in the year 2000. Portsmouth's millennium project — the Spinnaker Tower — was agreed in 1995 and scheduled for completion in 1999, at a cost of £14 million. Its completion date was in fact October 2005, at a cost of over £35 million. The Spinnaker Tower is an example of three major difficulties that often occur in investment appraisal:

- The tower is a unique piece of architecture, so it was difficult to draw on previous experience to get accurate financial estimates.
- With any major project there is the chance that business logic may not prevail, as the decision-makers may wish to make their mark by providing a grand project.
- Predicting revenue is often very difficult. The more unique the project, the harder it becomes to gauge consumer interest. The Millennium Dome did not attract the revenue that had been forecast, whereas the popularity of the London Eye surpassed even the most optimistic forecasts.

Firms usually take the following actions to allow for risks and uncertainties in their investment appraisals:

- Build in allowances or contingencies in case problems occur. Of course, this can lead to investments being unexpectedly cheaper than the budgeted costs if the project runs smoothly.
- Calculate alternative results. Often three scenarios will be calculated: the expected outcome, the best-case scenario and the worst-case scenario.
- Set more demanding targets, such as a short payback period or a high ARR. By setting a more challenging target, the business is, in effect, allowing for risks and uncertainties.

The other uncertainty that may occur is the market. Most appraisals cover a period of years. Even in stable markets it is difficult to foresee the future. In rapidly changing markets, estimates may be no more than guesswork. Thorough market research, close scrutiny of similar investments in the past, and benchmarking data with other companies are all methods that can reduce the uncertainty.

FACT FILE

Investment decisions and cost escalation

Any organisation must monitor its proposed investments closely and be prepared to modify its decisions if changes occur. In December 2002 the government announced plans for a 2-kilometre tunnel that would take the A303 trunk road away from its current proximity to Stonehenge. The forecast cost of this project was £183 million. Over the next 5 years, the estimated cost of the project increased to £540 million. In December 2007 the government announced that it was abandoning the planned tunnel as the high costs meant that it was no longer feasible on financial grounds.

Evaluating quantitative and qualitative influences on investment decisions

Although each method of investment appraisal can be criticised, investment appraisal in general is still a worthwhile process. It encourages organisations to research and evaluate carefully the possible financial consequences of potential investment decisions. A careful evaluation can help an organisation to avoid expensive mistakes or alert it to projects with tremendous potential.

However, it is vital that decisions are not based solely on quantitative factors. The organisation needs to consider the level of uncertainty in its financial forecasts. Furthermore, it is crucial that qualitative factors are taken into account in its decision making. With a thoughtful blend of quantitative and qualitative analysis, investment appraisal will help an organisation to make sound investment decisions.

Qualitative factors affecting decisions

The qualitative factors to be considered, and their relative importance, vary according to circumstances. Some of the key factors are described briefly below, but these are only an indication of some of the issues that may apply. Every investment project will raise its own issues to consider.

- **The aims of the organisation.** A profit-making firm will emphasise the quantitative (numerical) results of an investment appraisal, and is therefore likely to accept its results. However, a firm that places a high value on social issues might reject a profitable investment that is considered to exploit its workforce or damage the environment.
- **Reliability of the data.** Future costs and incomes rely on the accuracy of market research and an ability to predict external changes. For the more original investments and those of a longer duration, the predictions may be wildly inaccurate, undermining the use of investment appraisal techniques.
- **Risk.** High-return projects often involve high risk. A firm may prefer to choose a project with a lower, but more certain, return.
- **Personnel.** Will the new equipment or method suit the company's staff? The ease of use; the level of training needed; the safety of the machine; the impact on the number of staff employed — these are all factors that should be considered.
- **The economy.** Economic forecasts (for example, predicting a recession or boom) must be considered in the predictions of future costs and revenues.
- **Image.** The firm should consider the influence of a project on its image and public relations. A high-technology project producing a quality product in a prestigious market will be preferred to an equally profitable project that leads to unemployment and damages the environment.
- **Subjective criteria.** All investment decisions are taken by individuals who have their own personal preferences. Sometimes a manager may have a 'gut feeling' that an investment will benefit the business.

PRACTICE EXERCISE 1   Total: 35 marks (40 minutes)

1 Explain what is meant by the term 'investment appraisal'. *(3 marks)*

2 Identify the two main reasons for capital investment. *(2 marks)*

The following table shows the financial details of a new investment.

Year	Income (£)	Costs (£m)	Annual net return (£m)	Present value of £1 at a 5% discount rate
0	0	50	(50)	1.0
1	30	20	10	0.952
2	40	20	20	0.907
3	50	20	30	0.864

3 Calculate the payback period. *(3 marks)*

4 Calculate the average rate of return. *(5 marks)*

5 Calculate the net present value based on a 5% discount rate. *(6 marks)*

6 On the basis of your answers to questions 3, 4 and 5, advise the business on whether it should go ahead with the new investment. Justify your decision. *(4 marks)*

7 Explain two advantages of using the average rate of return method of investment appraisal. *(6 marks)*

8 Explain two problems of using the net present value method of investment appraisal. *(6 marks)*

PRACTICE EXERCISE 2   Total: 25 marks (25 minutes)

1 Explain two reasons why it is difficult to provide reliable forecasts for major investment projects. *(6 marks)*

2 Explain how a business can reduce the risk of inaccurate forecasts. *(6 marks)*

3 Explain two reasons for choosing payback as a method of investment appraisal. *(4 marks)*

4 Explain three qualitative factors that might be considered in assessing an investment. *(9 marks)*

CASE STUDY 1 Maize mazes

Farmers and theme parks, predominantly in the UK and USA, are using maize mazes as tourist attractions. A specialist firm designs a maze and in the spring the maize is planted in accordance with its instructions. Once the maize is fully grown, it forms a maze that can be used from July to September. The following year a revised design can be created to present a new challenge to visitors. Because of the short life span of the maze, the field can be used to cultivate a winter growing crop and generate more profit.

Paul Swaffield, a Dorset farmer, is one individual who has been won over by the idea. The maize maze on his farm brought in 25 times as much revenue as the crop that he usually grew in that field. Furthermore, at the end of the summer the maize was used as cattle feed, providing additional revenue.

Jowett House Farm in Cawthorne, Yorkshire, is a farm that has taken advantage of this new source of revenue. The year 2008 marked its eighth maize maze. The maze is open for 50 days in the summer. The average ticket price is £4 per visitor and the maze is expected to receive an average of 220 visitors per day. However, the vast majority of these visits occur at weekends and heavy rainfall has a big impact on sales revenue.

A typical maize maze costs £25,000 to make, although running costs vary. For a maze such as the one at Cawthorne, where a 'Maze Master Team' is employed to help visitors, the running costs can amount to £120 per day. At the end of the summer, the maize is used to feed the 140 cows in the farm's dairy herd.

(Please note that all the figures in this case study are estimates.)

Questions
Total: 20 marks (25 minutes)

1 Calculate the payback period of the Cawthorne maze, based on the figures in the case study. *(4 marks)*

2 Analyse two additional items of financial data that would have helped you to make the decision on whether to construct a maze at the farm. *(6 marks)*

3 Discuss possible reasons why the average rate of return and net present value methods of investment appraisal are not as suitable as the payback method in assessing the Cawthorne maize project. *(10 marks)*

CASE STUDY 2 The Humbly Grove pipeline

This is a challenging case study based on an unusual industry. It may be worthwhile discussing the nature of the business, and revisiting the ways to calculate each of the methods of investment appraisal, before commencing the questions.

Not all of the UK's oil is found in the North Sea. A number of small-scale, onshore oilfields exist. One such oilfield is situated at Humbly Grove, near Alton in Hampshire.

Oil was discovered there in 1980 and full production at the oilfield began in 1986.

The site is set in a rural area. Many of the 100 jobs created are unique to the business, especially as the firm

employs a relatively high percentage of graduates. The remote setting and effective landscaping of the site mean that relatively few people are aware of its existence.

In its natural state, the oil well is pressurised by the presence of gas overlying the oil. Over time the gas pressure falls, making it more difficult to extract the oil. Star Energy Ltd, the owner of the oil well, responded to this challenge by planning a 25-kilometre gas pipeline that would connect the site to the national gas transmission system.

The pipeline would bring two major benefits to the company. First, it would allow the company to purchase gas from the national gas transmission system. This gas would increase the gas pressure at the existing oil well and increase the economic viability of the oil field. 'Without this project, the field is unlikely to be viable by 2010,' says Star Energy UK onshore managing director Roger Pearson. The pipeline would enable oil extraction to continue until 2020.

Second, it would help Star Energy Ltd to enter the gas storage market. With its oil fields depleting and falling profit levels, the company had identified diversification as a key strategic aim. Gas storage was predicted to be a growth market. The UK has the lowest storage capacity for gas in Europe, largely because it has been self-sufficient in gas supply. However, by 2012 the UK will import 70% of its gas supplies, in contrast to 10% in 2005. The UK government is targeting an increase in UK gas storage capacity to levels similar to France (which can store 35% of its annual consumption). Star Energy would thus be providing a service to a number of stakeholders: the government, its shareholders (the gas can be bought cheaply in the summer and released at peak times in the winter when prices are higher), its workforce (currently 100 people are dependent on the firm restoring its profit levels) and the local community (which will benefit from the wealth and jobs created).

The company has a strong cash-flow situation, but made an operating loss in 2004, after years of profit. Consequently, new profitable ventures were considered to be crucial to the company's long-term future.

The main aim of the company, during construction of the pipeline,

was to minimise environmental damage. Environmentalists had proposed that Star Energy should use some depleted off-shore oil wells for storage rather than Humbly Grove, as these would have less environmental impact. Star Energy argued that these off-shore sites were unviable because of:

- Their initial costs — a minimum of £350 million, and £1,600 million in one case.
- Their low financial viability — ARR returns would be below 8% and payback periods were likely to exceed 8 years.
- The unpredictability of gas prices and the uncertainty in this particular market. Worst-case scenarios showed heavy losses for these projects.

The pipeline would be built to the highest safety standards and the route had been planned to have the least impact on the environment (see Figure 6.1). Eight areas of archaeological potential had been identified and trial digging would lead to slight adjustments to the route if necessary. The route would avoid populated communities but would take away some farmland and require the removal of a number of trees, affecting certain wildlife populations, during the construction process. Some overnight road closures would also take place.

Figure 6.1 Route of the Humbly Grove pipeline

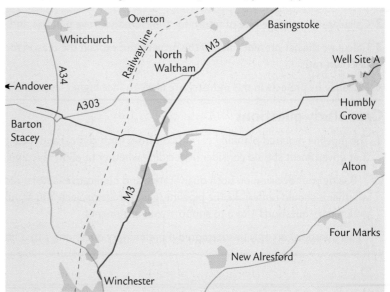

The completion of the pipeline and gas storage facility was scheduled for October 2005. Money was raised from the sale of shares and a long-term loan on which an interest rate of 7% is payable. In total, the construction costs were estimated at £65 million. Income would be received from two sources: the sale of gas and additional oil revenue. The gas and oil revenues and additional costs were estimated to follow the pattern shown in Table 6.7.

Table 6.7 *Estimates of possible changes in gas and oil revenues and extraction costs arising from the pipeline/gas storage project*

Year	Increased revenue (£m)	Increased costs (£m)	Net return (£m)
2005	–	65.0	(65.0)
2006	13.0	1.0	12.0
2007	16.1	1.5	14.6
2008	19.2	2.1	17.1
2009	22.3	2.6	19.7
2010	22.3	2.6	19.7
2011	22.3	2.6	19.7

Given the uncertainty of the gas and oil markets, the company wished to base any investment appraisal on a 6-year lifetime. Table 6.8 provides information on discount rates.

Table 6.8 *Present value of £1 at selected discount rates*

Year	Discount rate		
	5%	7%	10%
0	1.0	1.0	1.0
1	0.952	0.935	0.909
2	0.907	0.873	0.826
3	0.864	0.816	0.751
4	0.823	0.763	0.683
5	0.784	0.713	0.621
6	0.746	0.666	0.564

Currently the company is dependent on oil for 89% of its revenue. As its reserves fall, the empty oil wells will provide an ideal opportunity to diversify, particularly as rival gas storage companies will need to spend large sums to create suitable storage. It is feasible that gas will eventually replace oil as its main source of income.

Sources: adapted from *Humbly Grove News*, published by Star Energy Ltd, 2005 and the Star Energy website, **www.starenergy.co.uk**.

Preliminary questions

Total: 25 marks (35 minutes)

1 Calculate the payback period for the Humbly Grove pipeline and gas storage project. *(4 marks)*

2 Calculate the average rate of return for the Humbly Grove pipeline and gas storage project. *(6 marks)*

3 Calculate the net present value of the project and explain the reason for your choice of discount rate. *(9 marks)*

4 Explain why projects in this industry are likely to face higher levels of risk and uncertainty. *(6 marks)*

Case study questions

Total: 30 marks (35 minutes)

1 The pipeline required planning permission from both central and local government. Discuss the factors that government should consider in deciding whether to allow the pipeline to be constructed. *(12 marks)*

2* Basing your decision on both quantitative and qualitative factors, recommend to Star Energy whether it should undertake the pipeline/gas storage project. You should use your answers to preliminary questions 1 to 3 to support your arguments. *(18 marks)*

*This question can only be attempted if preliminary questions 1 to 3 have been answered.

AQA A2 Business Studies

Financial strategies and accounts

CASE STUDY Mulcahy's

Kathleen and Eddie had set up Mulcahy's Sports, a retailer of sports clothing and equipment, in Bath in 1997.

The store had taken a long time to become a success and this had made them pessimistic about future growth. Ironically, the business started to take off when they took their first holiday after 8 years of running the shop. Kathleen's sister Molly had taken control for a month. During that month the business's main supplier had persuaded Molly to test-market some new fashion sportswear, which proved to be a big hit with the customers.

Molly had provided some excellent feedback to the supplier and this had helped it to develop the range. The supplier was so grateful that it agreed to lend Mulcahy's the money to open up a new shop, with Molly as the manager.

The new shop opened in Bristol in 2006. Kathleen and Eddie were reluctant to leave the Bath store, so they decided to allow Molly to run the Bristol store as a profit centre. The three of them agreed on certain common characteristics, such as the appearance of the two stores and the prices that would be charged for certain stock. Otherwise Molly was left to decide on her own policies, having agreed a profit target with Kathleen and Eddie, based on the profit levels in Bath. Molly would receive 40% of the profit made by the Bristol store.

Within a year the Bristol store had become more profitable than the Bath store, partly because of Molly's skills but also because it was located in a larger city. Molly was given a one-third shareholding in the business as a reward.

The three directors held a meeting to decide on the business's financial objectives. The economy was growing steadily and the market for sportswear and equipment was growing quickly. However, there were a number of competitors in both cities. Mulcahy's had the benefit of a unique range of high-quality products at reasonable prices. However, the business did not have any unique skills and its prices tended to be mid-range. Kathleen and Eddie admitted that they were reluctant to take risks, but Molly's skills at spotting opportunities were seen to be a major strength. Based on these factors they decided to set three main targets:
- achieving an ROCE of 20% per annum
- cutting costs by 5% per annum for the next 3 years
- increasing sales revenue by 20% per annum for the next 3 years

After publication of the 2009 accounts, the directors scrutinised the balance sheet (Appendix 1) and the income statement (Appendix 2) for 2008/09, in order to see whether they had met their targets and whether the business's finances would support future expansion.

Molly was given responsibility for planning any new store development. She immediately started planning a new store to be opened in Cheltenham or Cardiff.

The recession in 2008 and 2009 caused a slowing down in growth, but Molly estimated that sales in the area would pick up again towards the end of 2009. Therefore she went ahead and planned the opening of a new store towards the end of 2009. Cheltenham was a wealthier place than Cardiff, but Cardiff was a bigger market. She drew up data in order to compare the financial implications of opening the two stores. In both cases, Molly wanted to be sure that the store would pay for itself within 4 years of opening. See Appendices 3, 4 and 5.

Molly disagreed with Kathleen and Eddie on the best place to open the store. They preferred Cheltenham because there was more opportunity to charge higher prices and earn higher profit margins. They also had more experience in 'up-market' sports such as skiing and equestrian sports. Molly argued that the business provided much higher-quality sportswear and equipment than most sports shops, but at a reasonable price. She believed that it was better to locate in larger cities, such as Bristol and Cardiff, where there were many more potential customers. (She also lived between Cardiff and Bristol, so they would be more convenient locations for her to visit.)

Although Kathleen and Eddie preferred the Cheltenham option, they did agree with Molly that the new store in Cardiff would create more jobs, which would help the local community. There were also objections in Cheltenham from local residents, who complained that the proposed site would increase parking problems and noise levels in a residential part of the town which had few shops. The Cardiff store would increase costs slightly, as labelling would need to be in Welsh and English.

Both stores would cost £500,000 to set up. The three directors were prepared to get a bank loan, but any borrowing must not allow gearing to rise above 60%. They were also prepared to take no dividend in 2009 so that they could use all of the profit from 2009 to finance the new store. Eddie pointed out that they were holding high levels of liquidity and could use some of the cash that they held.

Appendix 1 *Balance sheet of Mulcahy's Ltd, as at 30 June 2009*

	As at: 30.6.09 (£000s)	
Non-current assets (fixed assets)		1,500
Inventories (stocks	300	
Receivables (debtors)	20	
Cash and other cash equivalents	300	
Total current assets		620
Payables (creditors)	(220)	
Current liabilities		(220)
Net current assets (working capital)		400
Non-current liabilities (long-term liabilities)		(300)
Net assets (net worth)		1,600
Share capital		100
Reserves		1,500
Total equity		1,600
NB capital employed =		
non-current assets + net current assets		1,900

Appendix 2 *Income statements for Mulcahy's Ltd*

	Year ending: 30.6.09 (£000s)
Revenue	3,500
Cost of sales	(1,450)
Gross profit	**2,050**
Expenses	(1,600)
plus (minus) Exceptional items	0
Operating profit (before tax)	**450**
Taxation	(90)
Profit for year	**360**

Appendix 3 *Investment appraisal data for Cardiff store*

Year	Annual revenue (£000s)	Annual cost (£000s)	Net return (£000s)	Cumulative returns (£000s)
0 (2009)	0	500	(500)	(500)
1 (2010)	1,200	1,000	200	(300)
2 (2011)	1,500	1,300	200	(100)
3 (2012)	1,750	1,450	300	200
4 (2013)	2,000	1,640	360	560
Cumulative total	**6,450**	**5,890**	**560**	

Appendix 4 *Present value of £1 at discount rate of 10%**

Year	Discount factor
0	1.0
1	0.909
2	0.826
3	0.751
4	0.683

*This is the discount rate chosen by Mulcahy's.

Appendix 5 *Investment appraisal: calculations of
investment appraisal results for the Cheltenham store*

Payback period:	1 year 11 months
ARR:	12.1%
Net present value:	+ £244,555

Questions

Total: 80 marks (90 minutes)

1 Analyse one internal factor and one external factor that might have influenced Mulcahy's when
setting its financial objectives. *(10 marks)*

2 Discuss the advantages and disadvantages to Mulcahy's of setting up the Bristol store as a
profit centre. *(14 marks)*

3 Using appropriate ratios, evaluate whether Mulcahy's will be able to raise sufficient finance to
fund an investment of £500,000 into a new store in Cardiff or Cheltenham. *(20 marks)*

4 Mulcahy's has decided to open a new store. Using the data in the appendices and information from
the case study, recommend to the board of directors of Mulcahy's whether they should choose to
open the new store in Cardiff or in Cheltenham. *(36 marks)*

Chapter 7

Understanding marketing objectives

This chapter notes how the marketing objectives of a business are derived from the broader corporate objectives. Examples of typical marketing objectives are provided and the internal and external factors that influence them are examined. In showing the process that converts objectives to strategy and tactics, the chapter provides the background to subsequent chapters on marketing strategies and marketing plans.

A firm's marketing aims and objectives are the goals or targets of the marketing function. These must be consistent with the organisation's corporate aims and objectives: that is, with the goals of the organisation as a whole.

In order to achieve their marketing objectives, firms use marketing strategies and tactics. It is therefore possible to place a company's corporate objectives, marketing objectives, marketing strategies and marketing tactics into a hierarchy, as shown in Figure 7.1.

KEY TERMS

marketing aims: the broad, general goals of the marketing function within an organisation.

marketing objectives: the specific, focused targets of the marketing function within an organisation.

marketing strategies: long-term or medium-term plans, devised at senior management level, and designed to achieve the firm's marketing objectives.

marketing tactics: short-term marketing measures adopted to meet the needs of a short-term threat or opportunity.

Figure 7.1 *A marketing hierarchy*

e **EXAMINER'S VOICE**

Marketing objectives are not static. They change as a business develops. They also change in response to both internal and external circumstances.

Corporate objectives
These show the main priorities of the organisation, e.g. to improve profitability by 10% over the next 2 years

Marketing objectives
The marketing department or relevant managers must ensure that the marketing objectives support the achievement of the corporate objectives, e.g. to increase the market share of Brand X by 20% over the next 2 years

Marketing strategies
These strategies must assist the targets, e.g. to increase advertising expenditure on Brand X by 15%

Marketing tactics
Detailed marketing department decisions will also be affected, e.g. the advertisements must be designed to appeal to the market segments that the firm is targeting

This is not just a one-way process. Feedback from staff involved with organising the company's marketing tactics will be used to advise the directors. Feedback from staff can help the senior managers or shareholders to agree more realistic objectives.

Types of marketing objective

Marketing objectives depend on the aims and priorities of an organisation. They can be categorised as follows.

Size

Size can be measured by sales or market share. The objective may be expressed in terms of:

- a specific level of sales volume (e.g. Nestlé trying to maintain KitKat's sales volume of over 4 million bars every day)
- a percentage rise in sales revenue (e.g. Vodafone trying to achieve an 8% rise in sales income in 2008)
- a target percentage market share (e.g. BMW targeting a 6% market share of the UK car market in 2008; Nokia targeting a 40% market share of global sales of mobile phones for 2008)
- market leadership or a certain position in the market (e.g. ASDA and Sainsbury's both aiming to be the second largest supermarket in the UK)
- an increased number of outlets (e.g. Shakeaway aiming to increase its number of shops by offering franchises in certain geographical areas)

Market positioning

This is concerned with a company's appeal to particular market segments. For example:

- rugby league trying to appeal to more market segments by targeting females, spreading its geographical base from its northern roots by awarding franchises to teams in London, Wales and France, and switching the playing season from the winter to the summer, arguably to avoid direct competition with the football season
- Starbucks targeting younger age groups
- Setanta bidding for a variety of football programmes, such as European leagues, selected Premiership games and Blue Square Premier league games in order to attract a particular market segment (young males)

Innovation/increase in product range

For example:

- Ben and Jerry's introducing unusual flavours and names of ice cream in order to maintain its reputation for individuality
- '3' trying to achieve 100% of its sales from third-generation products

- the BBC aiming to increase the availability of its TV and radio programmes through downloading via the internet
- Apple trying to integrate mobile communications more fully through the iPhone

Creation of brand loyalty/goodwill

For example:
- McDonald's aiming to maintain the golden arches as the most widely recognised corporate logo in the world
- Specsavers aiming for a set percentage of 'repeat' customers
- Lush being able to set a premium price in comparison to other soap retailers (partly by refusing to supply other retailers)

Security/survival

For example:
- car retailers trying to survive during an 11% drop in monthly sales of new cars in the UK in July 2008
- Lotto targeting (and achieving) an increase in ticket sales in 2008 after 6 successive years of declining sales
- Dixons moving exclusively to online retailing in order to improve cost effectiveness and competitiveness (and rebranding its high-street stores as Currys)

Reasons for setting marketing objectives

Why do businesses set marketing objectives? The reasons for setting any objectives are the same, regardless of the functional area being considered. These reasons are:
- to act as a focus for decision making and effort
- to provide a yardstick against which success or failure can be measured
- to improve coordination, by giving teams and departments a common purpose
- to improve efficiency, by examining the reasons for success and failure in different areas

Assessing internal influences on marketing objectives

Internal influences are those factors within a business, such as its workforce, resources and financial position.

Corporate objectives

The overall aims of the organisation are a key influence on functional objectives. The marketing department must therefore ensure that its objectives are consistent with the corporate objectives of the business. For example, Harrods has always tried to maintain a reputation for quality as a corporate objective. Consequently, the marketing department must make sure that its marketing objectives are based on quality.

EXAMINER'S VOICE

A business will have a limited range of marketing objectives so that it can focus on its priorities. The list of objectives here should be treated with caution as a typical business will select only a few of them. The final section, in particular, is likely to be used only by a business that is trying to rectify a problem, so it may be unnecessary for many firms.

AQA A2 Business Studies

Finance

A business with a healthy financial background can afford to put more resources into its marketing, and therefore can set more challenging objectives.

Human resources (HR)

Marketing objectives must take into account the size and capabilities of the workforce. A motivated, efficient and productive workforce will affect marketing. Marketing objectives such as higher market share and improved reputation depend on the quality of the human resources within the business.

Operational issues

The operations management of the business is critical if it is seeking to provide products at low cost or of high quality.

Resources available

In the long term, resource availability is closely related to the financial circumstances of the business. A business in a strong financial situation can purchase whatever resources are required to achieve ambitious marketing objectives.

The nature of the product

This factor acts as both an opportunity and a constraint on marketing objectives. The popularity of the product is the key factor. Organisations such as Sony have earned a reputation for high-quality products in areas such as audio systems and games consoles. This leads to considerable word-of-mouth advertising and makes it difficult for competition to enter the market. Consequently, Sony is normally able to target high market share as one of its marketing objectives.

FACT FILE

Green Baby

Jill Barker, founder of Green Baby, set up her first outlet in Islington, North London because 'We were in the kind of area where mothers cared about green issues.' The nature of the product was one that appealed to mothers living in that part of London. This allowed Jill to set marketing objectives that involved high levels of growth and a successful expansion of Green Baby. Having expanded into mail order and supply to other 'green' stores, Green Baby now has a mailing list of 50,000 customers and its products are distributed to 250 stores. It has also expanded from one retail outlet to five outlets, including one in Taiwan. Within 9 years of start-up, the business is estimated to be worth £3 million.

Source: adapted from an article by Anna Shepard in *The Times*, 7 August 2007.

Assessing external influences on marketing objectives

External factors are those outside the business, such as the state of the economy and the actions of competitors.

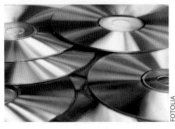

Market factors

The growth or decline of a market will have a major impact on a business's marketing objectives. Organisations such as Facebook can set ambitious growth targets because social networking is becoming more popular, so the market is growing. However, DVD manufacturers, which fairly recently were in a growth market are now more likely to be setting survival targets than ones based on high growth and profits.

Competitors' actions and performance

If the market is highly competitive, such as dairy farming, it is difficult for an individual farmer to achieve a high market share. For this reason, many farmers are now starting to target niche markets, such as sales through farmers' markets, in which there is less direct competition.

Technological change

Technology is a major cause of rapid changes in consumer tastes and markets, and therefore can make it more challenging for a business to set realistic marketing objectives. Businesses that can use technology effectively in their marketing, as Amazon and eBay have, will benefit from increased growth and an ability to set and reach ambitious marketing objectives.

Economic factors

This is a very important influence on marketing objectives for most businesses. Detailed coverage of economic factors is provided in Chapter 21, so the following passage briefly illustrates two examples of their influence.

- **Growth in the economy.** If the economy is growing rapidly, customers will be purchasing more products, and therefore higher targets for sales and prices can be included in the business's marketing objectives.
- **The exchange rate.** If the pound has a high value against the dollar this will encourage UK tourists to visit the USA, allowing businesses to target higher sales levels.

Suppliers

The efficiency, cost effectiveness, quality, reliability and flexibility of suppliers will all influence the ability of businesses to meet the needs of their customers. A supplier that provides cost-effective products of high quality will help a business to achiever higher sales and higher prices.

Other external factors

There are many other external factors that influence the ability of a business to sell its products, and therefore its marketing objectives. Two examples are noted below:

- **Political factors.** Government policies and pressures on issues such as child welfare and obesity have led to the advertising industry introducing voluntary restrictions on advertising during children's television programmes.

■ **Legal factors.** Legal requirements can act as a constraint, as in the case of the ban on cigarette advertising on television. They can also act as an opportunity: for example, the need for greater safety has led to the growth of businesses providing safety equipment and training.

e **EXAMINER'S VOICE**

The factors considered above are a summary of the influences on a business's marketing, and therefore on its marketing objectives. In the examination itself look carefully at the case study and try to pick out the key factors that are relevant to the organisation. This approach will enable you to apply your answer effectively.

GROUP EXERCISE

The corporate objectives of the IT company HP are reproduced in brief below.

Corporate objectives
- Customer loyalty: to provide products of the highest quality and value to customers.
- Profit: to achieve sufficient profit to achieve our other goals and to create value for our shareholders.
- Market leadership: to grow in our chosen fields.
- Growth: to view change in the market as an opportunity to grow and use our profits and ability to develop innovative products.
- Employee commitment: to value their contribution and help them to gain a sense of achievement from their work.
- Leadership capability: to develop leaders at every level.
- Global citizenship: to be an economic, intellectual and social asset to each country and community.

Source: www.hp.com.

Question
Using the five categories of marketing objectives analysed in this chapter, identify suitable marketing objectives to enable HP to achieve its corporate objectives. Give reasons for your choices.

PRACTICE EXERCISE 1   Total: 45 marks (40 minutes)

1 Place the following in the correct order: marketing strategy, marketing objectives, corporate objectives, marketing aims, corporate aims. *(5 marks)*

2 What is the difference between a corporate objective and a marketing objective? *(6 marks)*

3 In Chapter 1 the concept of SMART objectives was introduced. Give six examples of SMART marketing objectives. *(6 marks)*

4 What problem might arise if a firm's marketing department ignored its corporate objectives? *(4 marks)*

5 Analyse two reasons why a printing company would set marketing objectives. *(6 marks)*

6 Identify and explain three internal factors that might influence a fashion retailer's marketing objectives. *(9 marks)*

7 Identify and explain three external factors that might influence a fashion retailer's marketing objectives. *(9 marks)*

PRACTICE EXERCISE 2   Total: 15 marks (15 minutes)

easyCar.com is run in the same way as easyJet. Customers are offered a very basic, low-cost service at a very low price. easyCar.com is an example of how much an organisation's corporate aims can limit its scope for marketing strategies. Its philosophy is based on minimising costs through eliminating unnecessary expenditure. This allows the firm to charge low prices to customers. Marketing costs must also be minimised.

Questions

1 Select two marketing objectives that would be *unsuitable* for easyCar. Explain why you consider them to be unsuitable.   *(6 marks)*

2 Select three marketing objectives that would be *suitable* for easyCar. Analyse why you consider them to be suitable.   *(9 marks)*

CASE STUDY 1   Tesco's marketing objectives

One of Tesco's key corporate objectives over the last 10 years has been sales growth for the company as a whole. In order to achieve this objective, Tesco decided to set the following marketing aims:

- to grow the core UK business
- to become a successful international retailer
- to be as strong in non-food as in food
- to develop retailing services — notably Tesco Personal Finance, Telecoms and tesco.com

Table 7.1 shows certain marketing objectives that Tesco has set in order to achieve its corporate objective of market growth.

As recently as 2004, Tesco chief executive, Terry Leahy, indicated that overseas sales figures would eventually overtake UK sales, but indicated that 'this is some time away'. Despite this recent comment, overseas sales have grown much faster than UK sales and represent 62% of Tesco's total sales. However, targets for overseas store growth were not achieved in Europe and Asia in 2007/08 as external factors made trading conditions more difficult.

Leahy had also played down talk of entry into the US market, saying: 'We've looked at it for 22 years and never made a move. It's a big and competitive market and would be a big effort. Tesco is busy with its present objective and strategy, which is creating a lot of growth. We would need to be sure that we had the spare resources needed to tackle the US market.' Despite these comments, however, Tesco did make a relatively sudden decision to enter the US market, opening 53 stores in 2007/08.

There was a different picture elsewhere. In Asia the number of stores grew but the final total was short

Table 7.1 Tesco's marketing objectives

Marketing objective	Target for 2007/08	Actual level achieved in 2007/08	Target for 2008/09
% growth in sales volume in the UK	2.5%	2.0%	2.0%
% growth in sales value in the UK	4.5%	3.9%	4.5%
% growth in sales value through new stores in the UK	4.8%	2.8%	6.7%
Overall % growth in UK sales value	9.3%	6.7%	11.2%
Number of UK stores	2,106	2,115	2,327
Number of overseas stores	1,716	1,614	2,265
Asia	900	814	1,101
Europe	816	747	961
USA	0	53	203
% growth overall	10%	11%	15%

of the target by 86 stores. A similar pattern emerged in Europe where, despite growth, the number of Tesco's stores was 69 below the target.

Tesco's 53 US stores meant that the number of overseas stores opened only fell short of the target by about 100 stores. Despite financial losses in the USA in the first year of trading, rapid growth in the USA is being targeted for 2008/09, partly because Tesco believes that these additional stores will improve the efficiency of its operations.

Tesco has adopted very different objectives in different countries. In South Korea it has entered a joint venture with a Korean multinational electronics company, focusing on large-scale hypermarkets. In the USA, as with its Japanese operations, it has decided to concentrate on small-scale local retail outlets. In Japan this involved the takeover of an existing chain of Japanese stores; in the USA, Tesco introduced brand-new stores.

Tesco is targeting (and achieving) 25% growth of non-food items — a much higher percentage than its overall growth target. This target is being surpassed in toys, sports goods and electrical products, but financial services and telecommunications are experiencing slow growth.

On the basis of recent market trends, tesco.com is expected to match or surpass its current 30% growth rate.

Sources: www.tesco.com and Tesco annual reports, 2006–08.

Preliminary questions
Total: 25 marks (30 minutes)

1 Analyse why Tesco has chosen to focus on small, local stores in Japan and the USA rather than on larger stores. *(8 marks)*

2 Analyse internal factors that might have influenced Tesco's marketing objectives. *(8 marks)*

3 Examine factors that might cause Tesco to change its marketing objectives suddenly, such as its decision to enter the US market. *(9 marks)*

Case study questions
Total: 30 marks (35 minutes)

1 In 2007/08 Tesco failed to achieve the majority of the marketing objectives shown in Table 7.1. Discuss the possible effects of this failure on the marketing objectives that it decided to set for 2008/09. *(14 marks)*

2 Evaluate the extent to which Tesco is making good progress towards the four marketing aims described in the opening paragraph. *(16 marks)*

CASE STUDY 2 Marketing objectives in practice: Halfords

The main marketing objectives of Halfords in 2007 and 2008 are listed below. Each objective is followed by a brief commentary on Halfords' performance against that marketing objective.

- **Sales growth in all three key categories: car maintenance; car enhancement and leisure.** Growth achieved in all three areas for the twentieth consecutive year, averaging 7.2% and slightly surpassing the target of 7% growth.
- **Retain market leadership in the three key categories.** Market leader in all three categories in 2007/08.
- **Maintain market share for bicycle sales in the UK.** 33% market share achieved.

- **Continue expansion of the number of stores.** Target of 450 stores reached in 2008.
- **Introduce new products that allow customers to purchase with environmental considerations in mind.** Introduction in 2007/08 of a range of car cleaning products under the 'Naturals' brand. These products are water-based and biodegradable.
- **Introduce new brands in growth areas.** New brands have been successfully added to the range, mainly in the areas of satellite navigation systems, in-car digital music, specialist bicycles, and additional ranges of accessories, such as specialist oils.
- **Support product sales with service.** The 'we fit' and 'we repair' services have grown by 13% in 2007 to 1.3 million customers.
- **Improve corporate image, in respect to environmental impact.** Halfords is increasing the use of rail transport, as opposed to road transport, reaching its 2007/08 target of 40% of domestic shipments going by rail. The use of air transport has also been reduced by 64% in a single year.

These examples illustrate how vital it is that businesses review their performance against their objectives on a constant basis. Halfords had a successful year in 2007/08, achieving all of the marketing objectives it had set the previous year. However, as a result of close scrutiny of its marketing achievements it has decided to focus more fully on three areas in which high levels of success were achieved. These are:

- expansion within eastern Europe, especially the Czech Republic
- greater use of mezzanine floors within its super-stores, focusing on its bicycle division (Bike Hut)
- greater emphasis on its fitting and advisory services, in order to create greater customer satisfaction and brand loyalty

Halfords has used its marketing objectives and performance to establish new priorities and objectives for the future, so that it can continue to perform well in its marketing.

Source: Halfords plc annual reports, 2007 and 2008.

Preliminary questions
Total: 10 marks (15 minutes)

1 Analyse why it might not necessarily be beneficial for Halfords to have set marketing objectives that were all achieved with relative ease. *(4 marks)*

2 Identify two possible corporate objectives that might have led to Halfords' marketing objectives. Explain your reasoning. *(6 marks)*

Case study questions
Total: 30 marks (35 minutes)

1 To what extent might Halfords' focus on the three areas in the final paragraph help it to achieve its marketing objectives? *(14 marks)*

2 Discuss the extent to which external factors have influenced Halfords' marketing objectives and its ability to achieve those marketing objectives. *(16 marks)*

Chapter 8

Analysing markets and marketing

In this chapter we look at the reasons for, and value of, analysing markets and the need for methods of forecasting sales. The differences between quantitative forecasting (based on statistical data) and qualitative forecasting (based on human judgement or opinion) are examined. The different methods of forecasting are described, with particular emphasis on trend analysis (moving averages) and extrapolation; test marketing; and correlation. In looking at extrapolation, we identify the importance of trends and show the significance of seasonal variations. The use of information technology and the difficulties associated with particular methods of forecasting and market analysis in general are also discussed.

Analysing the market

Market analysis can be quantitative or qualitative:

- **Quantitative analysis** examines statistical information in order to draw conclusions about the nature of the market (e.g. how much growth is there in a market? who is the market leader?).
- **Qualitative analysis** considers the reasons why certain actions take place (e.g. why are internet sales growing? why is the Ford Focus the most popular car in the UK?).

Reasons for market analysis

Businesses can undertake market analysis either to gather evidence for a new marketing strategy, or to identify sales patterns for their products.

Gathering evidence for devising a new strategy

A business will wish to test the feasibility of a new strategy, such as consolidation and expansion of market share in its existing market, the introduction of a new product, targeting of a new market segment, or diversification into new products and new markets. It is essential that a business has access to any data that can help it to adopt the right strategy as mistakes could prove to be very costly if the strategy is not planned carefully.

> **KEY TERM**
>
> **market analysis:** the study of market conditions to assist a firm's plans.

The evidence gathered should be a mixture of primary and secondary data that enable the business to assess the likely success of any new strategy.

A business should also be gathering data regularly so that it can monitor the current and future success of its existing strategies.

Identifying significant patterns in sales

A business can gain a huge competitive advantage over its rivals by anticipating changes before competitors. Nokia took the decision to move from tyres to mobile phones because it identified changing patterns in the sales of these two products, which suggested that mobile phones would enjoy greater growth than tyre manufacturers.

In the nineteenth century, the founder of Shell recognised that there was greater scope for growth of oil than there was for the business's original product — decorative seashells. This proved to be an excellent decision throughout the twentieth century, but Shell is now diversifying into other products as its sales forecasts suggest that oil will not maintain its previous growth rates.

In order to identify changing patterns of sales, businesses use the quantitative and qualitative forecasting techniques described in this chapter.

The value of market analysis

Market analysis helps a business to understand its existing markets. The data and understanding gathered also allow a business to prepare for the future, by enabling it to forecast sales and other data.

Sales forecasting serves a number of purposes. As with any target, it can be used by the managers of an organisation to:
- measure the performance of an individual or department
- motivate staff by presenting them with a realistic but challenging target
- monitor achievements against targets in order to put into place remedial action if necessary

More specifically, its main use within an organisation is to coordinate the activities of the business and a range of departments:
- Once agreed, the sales forecast allows the senior management to ascertain whether a proposed new business strategy is likely to be successful.
- It helps the operations management or production department to plan its schedules, raw materials and capital equipment needs.
- It helps the HR department in its workforce planning, so that it can identify any potential shortages or surpluses of labour or any training needs.
- It enables the finance department to finalise its cash-flow and profit and loss planning. This ensures that enough funds are available to each department.
- It gives the marketing department itself confirmation of the strategies that it must employ in order to hit the sales targets.

FOTOLIA

e EXAMINER'S VOICE

Sales forecasting is a crucial part of **marketing planning**, which is covered in Chapter 10. However, in the AQA specification, the main quantitative techniques for sales forecasting are detailed in the section 'Analysing markets and marketing'. To avoid repetition, the whole of sales forecasting has been incorporated into this chapter because all of the techniques require analysis of the market.

KEY TERM

sales forecast: a prediction of the level of sales revenue for individual products or for the organisation as a whole.

Quantitative forecasting

Quantitative forecasting usually relies on the assumption that the past will provide an accurate prediction of the future.

Methods of quantitative forecasting

The main methods of quantitative forecasting are:
- test marketing
- analysis of trends/moving averages and extrapolation
- correlation

We will look at each of these in detail.

Forecasting by using test marketing

By launching a product in a limited part of a market, usually a geographical area, a firm can discover customer opinions. For example, Northern Foods tested new flavours of muffins in Sainsbury's stores in order to a compare their popularity with the original flavours. However, test marketing is also used to predict sales. From experience a firm may know that a certain level of sales in test marketing is needed in order to obtain a successful launch of a new product, or that a 'two for the price of one' special offer will usually increase sales by a certain amount.

Once test marketing has taken place, the firm will use the results to make a statistical forecast of future sales. Typically, the firm will take the results from the geographical area in which the test marketing took place and assume that these results will be repeated across the whole country. Thus, if 5% of the region purchased the product, it will be assumed that 5% of the national population will buy it if it is launched nationally.

The benefits of test marketing are as follows:
- The results are a relatively accurate predictor of future popularity, as they are based on actual purchases by customers in the test area.
- Test marketing is a useful way of gauging the popularity of the product without incurring the huge expense of a national launch.

Test marketing has the following drawbacks:
- Fewer firms now employ the technique because it can lead to 'me-too' products (copies) being produced by rivals. Thus test marketing can reduce the time during which a firm benefits from being the only producer.
- In rapidly changing markets, the delay in launching a product nationally may endanger the chances of making a profit from a new launch.
- The 'newness' of the product may encourage people to purchase it once, so the test market may exaggerate its true popularity.
- As firms will want the test market to succeed, they are likely to put a lot of effort into the test marketing, such as providing attractive special offers. This can lead to a very successful start that cannot be maintained once the product is launched nationally.

KEY TERMS

quantitative forecasting: those methods of prediction that are based on statistical information.

test marketing: the introduction of a product to a certain geographical area, in order to assess its likely success or the effectiveness of the marketing methods being used.

Analysis of trends and extrapolation

Predicting future sales using extrapolation

In effect, trend analysis examines the pattern of historic data and assumes that this pattern will continue in the future. If sales of a product have increased at 5% per annum in the recent past, the process of extrapolation will forecast that sales will continue to rise by 5% a year.

DID YOU KNOW?

When choosing the time over which a moving average and trend can be found, you should look for a period during which all seasonal variations occur once. For this reason, many moving averages cover a period of a year (4 quarters or 12 months).

Extrapolation can be carried out visually or by calculation, although the latter method is recommended for greater accuracy.

Figure 8.1 shows the increase in household debt in the UK between 1994 and 2007. A business might wish to forecast future levels of debt, as the amount that people are prepared to borrow is a key factor in consumers' decisions to buy major items, such as houses, vehicles, household appliances (white goods) and furniture.

Visually, it is easy to see how the level of household debt is expected to increase in the future. The line shows that total debt in 2007 was £1,391 billion.

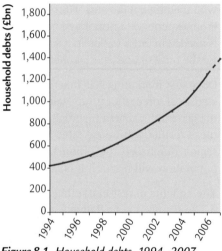

Figure 8.1 Household debts, 1994–2007

Where there is a clear pattern of change (as in Figure 8.1), it is easy to calculate the trend by calculating the average change for a period of time and extrapolating data into the future, on the assumption that this trend will continue. Household debt has been increasing at the rate of 10% per annum in recent years. Based on the 2007 level of £1,391 billion and adding 10% each year, we can predict household debt in the future.

In Figure 8.1, the dashed (extrapolated) line shows that household debt in the future is likely to be as follows:

   2008: £1,530 billion
   2009: £1,683 billion
   2010: £1,851 billion

Table 8.1 shows the number of mobile telephone handsets sold globally between 2001 and 2008.

To forecast sales for 2009 onwards we need to calculate the trend (the average increase per annum). Between 2001 and 2008 (7 years), sales rose from 404 million to 1,230 million, an increase of 826 million. The annual increase is therefore 826 million divided by 7 = 118 million per annum.

Projecting the trend therefore gives us the forecasts for the next 4 years shown in Table 8.2.

Of course, this is only an estimate. Using quantitative analysis, it could be argued that the rate of growth is varying (+91 million per year between 2001 and 2004 but +150 per year between 2004 and 2007 and then only +102 million between 2007 and 2008). Our method takes the annual average of these different increases, so it does not take into account the fact that the rate of growth has generally increased but then fallen slightly.

Qualitatively, it is argued that the global mobile telephone market is reaching maturity. This information would lead us to predict a slowing down of the rate of growth in the next few years.

For these reasons, the actual forecast may be based on a combination of methods.

Table 8.1 Global sales of mobile telephone handsets, 2001–08

Year	Global sales (millions of handsets)
2001	404
2002	479
2003	573
2004	677
2005	835
2006	986
2007	1,128
2008	1,230

Sources: DrKW and Strategic Analytics.

Table 8.2 Sales forecast for mobile telephone handsets, 2009–12

Year	Global sales (millions of handsets)
2008	1,230 (actual sales)
2009	1,230 + 118 = 1,348
2010	1,348 + 118 = 1,466
2011	1,466 + 118 = 1,584
2012	1,584 + 118 = 1,702

e EXAMINER'S VOICE

In an examination, it is vital that you can justify your answer. Therefore it is essential that you use a specific method of forecasting. You may wish to add a comment on its lack of reliability, but make sure that the examiner can see that your answer came from a particular method.

In both of the above examples there was a clear pattern of steady change. However, many sets of statistics have a less clear pattern. There may be an overall fall or rise, interspersed with fluctuations. To predict sales, the trend must be separated from the fluctuations. The techniques for doing this are known as **moving averages** and **seasonal variations**.

KEY TERM

moving averages: statistics used to analyse trends in the recent past so that a firm can predict future sales (through extrapolation).

Predicting future sales based on moving averages and seasonal variations

Moving averages are calculated by combining data over a period of time in such a way that changes caused by fluctuations are eliminated or at least reduced. For example, many data are affected by the seasons of the year. If the trend is based on sets of numbers all representing exactly a year, then any seasonal effect will be eliminated.

KEY TERMS

fluctuations or variations: periods of time when sales are above or below the trend.

Although sales may be increasing at an average rate of 5% per annum, there are periods of time when the rate of growth fluctuates above or below this level of growth. There are three main types of fluctuation:

- **Cyclical.** Sales of most products fluctuate according to the business (trade) cycle, with above average increases in boom periods and below average rises (or even falling sales) in downturns and recessions.
- **Seasonal.** Few products sell consistently throughout the year. It is possible to measure seasonal variations by looking at the level of sales at a particular time of the year, in comparison to the trend figure.
- **Random.** Sales can vary for a wide range of reasons, such as changes in fashion or taste, production difficulties, favourable or adverse publicity, and changes in the weather.

FACT FILE

Predictable fluctuations?

Fluctuations are not always unpredictable. In August 2008 there were dramatic changes in shopping habits while the Beijing Olympics took place. However, market research organisations that use **footfall**, a technique that measures the total number of people in a shopping centre at any one time, were able to draw on experience of previous Olympics to inform retailers of the probable changes in the shopping habits of customers during the tournament. As a consequence, the retailers were more able to cope with the sudden changes to normal shopping patterns that took place. This technique, however, may be less useful in 2012, as interest in the Olympics is expected to be much higher than normal because the main centre is London.

Source: www.footfall.com.

Moving averages allow an organisation to calculate a trend scientifically using a series of calculations designed to eliminate fluctuations within a series of data. The use of moving averages should smooth out the impact of random variations in data and longer-term cyclical factors, and thus highlight the trend. If the fluctuation is cyclical, the moving averages should be based on the span of the business/trade cycle (4 or 5 years). If the fluctuation is caused by seasonal factors, the moving average should be based on a period of exactly 1 year. It is not possible to use this method reliably if the fluctuations are random.

By predicting trends, firms are able to forecast future sales. This information is invaluable in helping to plan production and draw up human resource plans, and is the basis of much financial planning.

FOTOLIA

Table 8.3 shows the UK sales of cheese between the first quarter of 2004 and the fourth quarter of 2007. Although there has been a clear increase in sales, this has not been spread evenly over each quarter. More cheese is sold in the spring and summer for two main reasons:

- Although cheese is an all-year food, it is more traditionally eaten as a cold food and so sales peak in the warmer months (April to September).

AQA A2 Business Studies

- The greater availability of milk-based products in the spring may reduce prices and so increase demand, particularly for cheese that is purchased by companies for use in pre-prepared food products.

In order to predict future sales, it is necessary to calculate:
- the trend (the overall pattern of change in the sales over time)
- seasonal variations (fluctuations in sales caused by the time of year rather than the general trend)

Table 8.3 shows how it is possible to separate these two factors in order to forecast future sales.

Table 8.3 UK sales of cheese, 2004–07

(1) Year	(2) Quarter	(3) Sales (000 tonnes)	(4) Sales: four-quarter total (000 tonnes)	(5) Sales: eight-quarter total (000 tonnes)	(6) Sales trend figures (000 tonnes)	(7) Seasonal variation (000 tonnes)
2004	1	128				
	2	171				
			601			
	3	160		1,220	152.5	+7.5
			619			
	4	142		1,243	155.4	–13.4
			624			
2005	1	146		1,256	157.0	–11.0
			632			
	2	176		1,280	160.0	+16.0
			648			
	3	168		1,305	163.1	+4.9
			657			
	4	158		1,317	164.6	–6.6
			660			
2006	1	155		1,326	165.8	–10.8
			666			
	2	179		1,340	167.5	+11.5
			674			
	3	174		1,356	169.5	+4.5
			682			
	4	166		1,375	171.9	–5.9
			693			
2007	1	163		1,385	173.1	–10.1
			692			
	2	190		1,376	172.0	+18.0
			684			
	3	173				
	4	158				

Source: ONS and DEFRA reports.

Columns 1–3 present the actual sales of cheese in the recent past. Thus, in the first quarter of 2004 cheese sales in the UK totalled 128,000 tonnes; by the fourth quarter of 2007 sales of cheese in the UK were 158,000 tonnes.

If there were no seasonal variation, it would be acceptable to use these two figures (the beginning and end of the time period) in order to calculate the trend. However, the first figure in column 3 represents sales in January, February and March 2004, while the last figure in column 3 gives sales in October, November and December 2007, so we would not be comparing like with like.

This problem is overcome by calculating the four-quarter totals shown in column 4. By adding together four successive quarters, we are covering the whole year and so there is no seasonal effect. This four-quarter figure is excellent for showing the overall trend, as the seasonal variations are eliminated.

However, if we add all the sales for four successive quarters, there is a problem when we try to compare this figure to our quarterly sales. In Table 8.3 the first four quarters are from quarter 1 of 2004 to quarter 4 of 2004. On a graph we would plot this figure halfway through the year — this is the point at which we reach the end of quarter 2 of 2004 and the beginning of quarter 3 of 2004.

To calculate the seasonal variations, we need to compare the trend to the sales figure for a particular quarter. To do this we need to use a process known as **centring**. In this case, the eight-quarter sales figure is used. By adding the first two four-quarter totals, we are in effect adding the following eight figures:

   2004 quarter 1
   2004 quarter 2 (twice)
   2004 quarter 3 (twice) ← midpoint of the data
   2004 quarter 4 (twice)
   2005 quarter 1

This gives us an even spread of data across the calendar year (two figures from quarter 1, two figures from quarter 2, two figures from quarter 3 and two figures from quarter 4), thus overcoming any seasonal variations. The midpoint of these figures is clearly 2004 quarter 3. In other words, the data are centred around 2004 quarter 3.

Column 5 covers eight quarters (equivalent to 2 years) of sales. If we divide the column 5 figures by 8, we get a figure that represents one quarter's sales, shown in column 6. The figures in column 6 represent the trend — these are the sales figures we would expect to achieve having eliminated the effect caused by seasonal variations.

The trend is calculated by working out the average change per quarter. In column 6 we started with a trend figure of 152.5 in quarter 3 of 2004 and ended with a figure of 172 in quarter 2 of 2007. However, as we are starting with the third quarter of the data and ending at the fourteenth quarter, the changes, in effect, span 11 quarters of data.

The trend per quarter is measured by the total change in the trend divided by the change in the number of quarters.

$$\text{trend per quarter} = \frac{172 - 152.5}{11} = \frac{+19.5}{11} = +1.8 \text{ per quarter}$$

It is important to put this back into the units of measurement being used: 1.8 does not seem to be very much, but this means that cheese sales are increasing by 1.8 thousand tonnes (1,800 tonnes) per quarter.

We can now compare column 6 (the figure we would expect if there were no seasonal variation) with column 3 (the actual sales figures achieved). (Note that we cannot do this for the first pair and final pair of quarterly figures.)

seasonal variation = actual sales − trend figure sales

Thus for quarter 3 of 2004 the seasonal variation is:

160 − 152.5 = +7.5 (i.e. +7.5 thousand tonnes, or 7,500 tonnes)

Table 8.4 summarises the seasonal variations.

Seasonal factors are rarely consistent and it can be seen that there are significant differences between the seasonal variations of the quarter 4 figures. For future predictions, the average variation is used. For quarter 1, for example, this is the average of −11.0, −10.8 and −10.1, which is −10.6.

(Technically, a further adjustment can be made to make the total seasonal variations equal to zero, but for sales predictions this is not really necessary. In this example, changing each seasonal variation by −0.4 would give a total of exactly zero for the four quarters.)

Quarter	2004	2005	2006	2007	Average variation
1		−11.0	−10.8	−10.1	−31.9/3 = −10.6
2		+16.0	+11.5	+18.0	+45.5/3 = +15.2
3	+7.5	+4.9	+ 4.5		+16.9/3 = +5.6
4	−13.4	−6.6	−5.9		−25.9/3 = −8.6

Table 8.4 Seasonal variations in UK sales of cheese, 2004–07

Predicting future sales using the trend and seasonal variation

Based on our calculations, we would expect sales to increase by 1.8 (thousand tones) for every quarter, plus or minus the seasonal variation for that quarter.

Table 8.5 shows predicted sales for 2008 and 2009 based on the above calculations.

Table 8.5 Predicted sales for cheese in the UK, 2008–09

(1) Year	(2) Quarter	(3) Predicted trend	(4) Seasonal variations	(5) Predicted sales
2008	1	177.4	−10.6	166.8
	2	179.2	+15.2	194.4
	3	181.0	+5.6	186.6
	4	182.8	−8.6	174.2
2009	1	184.6	−10.6	174.0
	2	186.4	+15.2	201.6
	3	188.2	+5.6	193.8
	4	190.0	−8.6	181.4

Column 3 starts with the final trend figure (172 for quarter 2 of 2007). It then adds the quarterly trend figure of 1.8 to each quarter. Therefore, future trend figures are:
2008 quarter 1: 172 + (3 × 1.8) = 177.4
2008 quarter 2: 172 + (4 × 1.8) = 179.2
2008 quarter 3: 172 + (5 × 1.8) = 181.0 etc.

Column 4 shows the seasonal variations that must be added (or subtracted), as calculated in Table 8.4. For each future quarter 1, we would expect actual sales to be 10.6 below the trend; each quarter 2 will be predicted to be 15.2 above the trend.

Adding columns 3 and 4 gives us the prediction for each quarter (column 5). Although cheese sales are increasing by an average of 1.8 million tonnes for each quarter, it is worth noting that sales are predicted to fall at times because of the seasonal decline in sales in quarters 1 and 4.

DID YOU KNOW?

Centring is needed when there is an even number of sets of figures within a cycle. Thus for most seasonal variations it is essential, as the seasons are measured as either 4 quarters or 12 months. However, for odd-numbered sets of data it is not necessary. If the business cycle is treated as a 5-year cycle, the average of years 1–5 is plotted against the midpoint (year 3), so no further adjustments are needed; similarly, years 2–6 are plotted against year 4.

In the same way, for data measured over the 7 days in a week, any fluctuations can be calculated without centring.

EXAMINER'S VOICE

Calculating moving averages and seasonal variations is a time-consuming task. Consequently, it is very unlikely that you will be asked to carry out such a detailed calculation in the examination. However, it is possible that data might be provided that show a trend and/or seasonal variations that have already been calculated. Alternatively, you may be required to interpret a graph that needs an understanding of the trend and seasonal variations.

The calculations in Tables 8.3 and 8.4 are included to help your understanding of the method involved in calculating the trend and seasonal variations, but an understanding of the end result of these calculations (Table 8.5) should be sufficient to answer most questions that incorporate this topic.

Weaknesses of extrapolation

Extrapolation suffers from a number of weaknesses:

■ It is less reliable if there are fluctuations. Seasonal and cyclical changes are rarely repeated exactly, and random fluctuations are very unpredictable. Many seasonal factors relate to the weather, which is notoriously unpredictable.

■ It assumes that past changes will continue into the future and thus does not take into account changes in the business environment that will influence sales, including changes within the business itself.

■ It ignores qualitative factors, such as changes in tastes and fashion.

Correlation

Correlation can be a useful technique for sales forecasting, as it can show (statistically or graphically) the degree to which factors such as price, the advertising budget or even external factors, such as the proximity of competitors, are linked to sales of a product.

Graphically, the correlation between two sets of data is shown in a scatter diagram or scatter graph. The independent variable (the one causing the other to change) is plotted on the horizontal, x-axis. The dependent variable (the one being influenced) is plotted on the vertical, y-axis. So if we are trying to look at different factors that influence sales of a product, we plot sales on the y-axis and the other factor on the x-axis.

Once the points have been plotted, a line of best fit (or regression line) is added. The line can be drawn graphically 'by eye' but is more accurate if calculated mathematically. (An Excel spreadsheet will construct a scatter graph and will then calculate and add the regression line to any pairs of data that need to be compared.)

The line of best fit (regression line) is used to forecast. For any value of x, a line is drawn vertically until it meets the regression line. From this point, a line is then drawn horizontally to the y-axis in order to read the forecast value of the dependent variable. For example, in Figure 8.2(a) if $x = 20$, we would forecast $y = 4$. In Figure 8.2(b) if $x = 20$, our forecast for y would be 12.

Figure 8.2 show seven different examples of correlation.

Figures 8.2(a), (b) and (c) show **positive correlation**. This means that as x increases in value, the value of y also increases.

Figures 8.2(d), (e) and (f) show **negative correlation**. This means that as x increases in value, the value of y decreases.

Figures 8.2(a) and (d) show **perfect correlation**. All of the points plotted lie on the line of best fit. This means that we would expect 100% accuracy in our predictions. In the business world, it is unlikely that any sets of data would ever be linked as closely as this.

KEY TERM

correlation: a statistical technique used to establish the strength of the relationship between two sets of values.

Figures 8.2(b) and (e) show **strong or high correlation**. The line of best fit is fairly close to the points plotted on the graph, so we could be confident that our forecasts were fairly reliable.

Figure 8.2(c) and (f) show **weak or low correlation**. The line of best fit is not close to all of the points, although there is some link between the sets of data. If we were to use the line of best fit to make forecasts, these forecasts would not be reliable.

Figure 8.2(g) shows **no apparent correlation** between the two sets of data. Forecasts should not be made because there is no detectable link between the two variables.

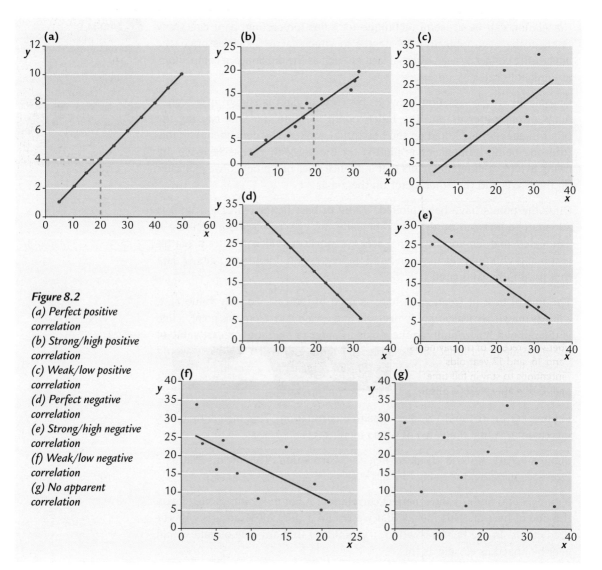

Figure 8.2
(a) Perfect positive correlation
(b) Strong/high positive correlation
(c) Weak/low positive correlation
(d) Perfect negative correlation
(e) Strong/high negative correlation
(f) Weak/low negative correlation
(g) No apparent correlation

AQA A2 Business Studies

Causal links in correlation

It has been said that 'There are lies, damn lies and statistics.' The speaker was probably looking at correlation at the time!

It is highly probable that one set of statistics will correlate with another. After all, over time a set of numbers can go up or down or stay the same. This limited set of alternatives means that it is possible to find apparently close connections between sets of data purely by coincidence. The rise in obesity in the UK correlates very strongly with the increase in medals for the UK in recent Olympics. However, it is unlikely that the two could be connected, at least until sumo wrestling is introduced into the Games.

Before drawing any conclusions that there is a link between two sets of information, it is essential that a **causal link** is discovered. It is logical to expect that more hours of sunshine will cause people to consume more ice cream because of the desire to eat something cool. However, if it was found that more people bought overcoats in the summer, there would be no logic in suggesting that the temperature rise caused this behaviour. Instead we would need to look for other factors (such as shops selling overcoats cheaply at this time to get rid of old stock).

Once a causal link is discovered, correlation can be useful to identify the extent of the link between the two series of data.

FACT FILE

EMA

EMA payments were introduced to encourage students to stay in education after the age of 16.

A survey by the Responsive College Unit (RCU) in 2007 showed a definite correlation between receipt of the payments and 16- and 17-year-olds' intentions to stay in full-time education after their GCSEs.

Not surprisingly, the figure for children staying in education was highest for those students receiving £30 per week, with 7% stating that they would not have continued in education without EMA. For those receiving £20 per week the figure was 4%, and for students receiving £10 per week it was 3%. In all, 16% of students receiving EMA felt that the EMA payments were critical in them being able to complete their course. Two-thirds of all EMA students indicated that EMA, and the bonus system in particular, made them work harder. Throughout the survey, the positive impacts of EMA were strongly linked to the amount of payment received, with those receiving £30 per week reacting more positively than those on £20 or £10.

Source: www.rcu.co.uk.

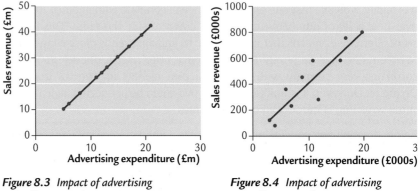

There is a tendency to assume that a company would prefer a high correlation to a low correlation. This may be true for the purpose of forecasting, but accurate forecasts are not everything. Compare Figures 8.3 and 8.4.

Figure 8.3 *Impact of advertising expenditure on sales revenue*

Figure 8.4 *Impact of advertising expenditure on sales revenue*

Figure 8.3 shows perfect positive correlation, indicating that extra advertising is likely to increase sales revenue by an exact amount. In this case, for every extra £1 spent on advertising, sales rise by £2. Although this is high correlation, it is not successful advertising. With all of the other costs involved, it is unlikely that a firm can make a profit if half of the sales revenue is going on advertising.

WHAT DO YOU THINK?

Apply your understanding to the business world. Can you suggest any real-life examples of scatter diagrams that might resemble Figures 8.3 and 8.4?

In contrast, Figure 8.4 shows a much lower level of positive correlation. However, look at the regression line and the scale on the *y*-axis. This shows that every extra £1 spent on advertising is linked to a possible increase in sales revenue of £40. Although the forecast is much less certain, it shows that advertising is probably much more effective in creating extra sales than in the situation described in Figure 8.3.

The regression line (line of best fit) is every bit as important as the level of correlation. Do not ignore its importance.

Limitations of quantitative forecasting

Quantitative forecasting makes sure that businesses scrutinise their predictions carefully and use a scientific form of analysis in their planning. However, there are a number of potential limitations that need to be considered when using it:

- Past trends do not always continue into the future.
- Correlation changes over time. For example, the major influence on sales might change from the price to the amount spent on advertising.
- External influences, such as competitors' actions, consumers' tastes or the stages of the business cycle, can vary over time.
- Corporate objectives may be amended, so that the sales target becomes more or less important.
- Internal policies or actions may change.
- The market research used for forecasts may lack reliability.

- Forecasts become more difficult the further they project into the future.
- Quantitative techniques ignore the special understanding of the market that may be possessed by the staff of a business.

Qualitative forecasting

In business, trends do not tend to follow smooth patterns, so any forecasting techniques based on observing statistics from the past (quantitative forecasting) will have limitations. Qualitative forecasting attempts to overcome these limitations by introducing human understanding.

Methods of qualitative forecasting

The Delphi/Oracle technique

Named after the home of the oracle of ancient Greece, this approach relies on the firm asking individual experts for their views. These expert opinions are then collated into an overall consensus of future events, allowing a more accurate prediction of future sales to be made.

Brainstorming

This method involves all of the individuals concerned with the product or service. A relatively unstructured meeting is conducted in which all ideas are noted and then the more feasible suggestions are considered in depth. Brainstorming tends to be used most often for problem solving, but ideas from brainstorming sessions can be useful in predicting future sales.

Individual hunch

Ultimately, a particular manager will be held responsible for the product or service being considered. Based on his or her own understanding of the market, the manager may feel that sales will increase or decrease at a particular rate, even if other evidence suggests otherwise. As a result, some forecasts will rely on individual hunch, although this hunch may be based on customer feedback or qualitative market research.

Reasons for using qualitative forecasting

Most forecasting is based on a mix of qualitative and quantitative methods. Qualitative forecasting is more likely to be relied on in the following situations:
- When the forecast concerns a new product or business, so there is no previous information on which to base predictions. In these circumstances, people's opinions are the most reliable predictor of the future.
- When there is no clear statistical indication of future sales. It is possible that quantitative methods are unable to produce a reliable forecast.
- When trends have changed, so that it would be unwise to predict on the basis of past statistics.

KEY TERM

qualitative forecasting: methods of prediction that are based on personal opinions. These are often described as 'hunches', but are influenced by the personal knowledge and experiences of the individuals who are involved in the forecasting.

- When the factors influencing sales are not easy to quantify (measure in terms of numbers). Fashion items and the entertainment industry are often difficult to predict, and an experienced manager may be able to deliver a more accurate forecast than any attempt based on statistical data.
- When the character of the individuals is important. For example, if a particular manager is responsible for the forecast, he or she will probably want to make the final decision.

> **_e_ EXAMINER'S VOICE**
>
> Note that all of these reasons for qualitative forecasting are limitations on the use of quantitative forecasting or reasons why a firm would not want to use quantitative forecasting.

Limitations of qualitative forecasting

Qualitative forecasting is subject to the following limitations:
- Experts may be knowledgeable, but it is unlikely that they will understand all aspects of a market.
- Many trends and relationships are broadly consistent over time, so forecasts based on quantitative data are more accurate than hunches or opinions.
- It is easier to persuade a senior manager if your forecast is based on scientific methods.
- Ignoring statistical information may leave a manager open to criticism if predictions turn out to be incorrect. Managers may avoid qualitative forecasting to protect themselves from such criticism.

Conclusion

In general, new businesses (which lack historical data and market research) and managers in small firms (where time might be seen to be crucial and where there are no senior managers to whom the decision-makers must justify their decision) are more likely to use qualitative forecasting.

The implications of incorrect forecasting

Businesses rely on accurate forecasting in their business planning.

If sales are overestimated, there is likely to be a waste of resources as the firm will produce too much. The cost to the firm depends on whether the products are perishable and how expensive they are to store.

Underestimation also causes problems. The opportunity cost of lost sales is high, especially if customer goodwill is undermined.

Conclusion

Although sales forecasts cannot be relied upon, they do give direction and targets for an organisation. Ideally, they should arise from a blend of qualitative and quantitative techniques.

Sales forecasts are more likely to be correct when:

- the product is well established and the market known
- external factors are predictable and there is stability in tastes and competitor actions
- the forecasts are made by, and agreed with, those having day-to-day contact with the market
- the organisation has undertaken detailed and reliable market research
- test marketing and/or backdata give the firm a clear understanding of the market

The use of information technology in analysing markets

Information technology is of particular significance in market analysis because it allows businesses to gather, analyse and distribute a wealth of data, often quickly and cost effectively. Some examples of the ways in which information technology can assist market analysis are noted below:

- An IT-based system can complete quantitative forecasting calculations almost instantaneously, saving time and money for a business.
- The time saved by IT allows a business to compare a number of different strategies, thus improving the quality of planning in the business.
- Organisations are able to link their sales records to other databases, so that every time an item is sold it is registered immediately. Consequently, any sudden changes in trends or patterns of sales can be detected quickly and the necessary action taken.
- Information technology allows firms to improve both internal and external communications, improving efficiency and the firm's understanding of its market.
- The growing use of loyalty cards allows firms to accumulate information on the buying habits of their customers. Organisations can use these data to tailor services or products to customer needs.
- The internet or company intranet allows more data to be stored cheaply and accessed more quickly by a wide range of individuals.

FOTOLIA

PRACTICE EXERCISE 1   Total: 45 marks (40 minutes)

1 Explain the meaning of the term 'market analysis'. *(2 marks)*

2 What is meant by 'sales forecasting'? *(2 marks)*

3 Analyse two possible benefits to a furniture store of using market research for forecasting sales. *(6 marks)*

4 Explain one benefit and one problem of using test marketing as a way of forecasting sales. *(6 marks)*

5 What is meant by the term 'trend'? *(2 marks)*

6 What is meant by a 'moving average'? *(2 marks)*

7 Explain the difference between 'quantitative forecasting' and 'qualitative forecasting'. *(4 marks)*

8 Identify and describe two methods of qualitative forecasting. *(6 marks)*

9 Explain three reasons why a business might use qualitative forecasting. *(9 marks)*

10 Explain two benefits of using information technology for market analysis. *(6 marks)*

PRACTICE EXERCISE 2   Total: 50 marks (60 minutes)

1 The graph shows milk consumption in the UK between 1975 and 2007.

Trends in average household milk consumption in the UK, 1975–2007

  a Extrapolate the lines in the graph in order to forecast consumption levels in 2012 for:
    (i) milk and cream, (ii) whole milk only. Show your workings. *(4 marks)*
  b Calculate the trend for whole milk (the average fall per annum) for the period 1975–2007. Show your workings. *(4 marks)*
  c Sales of whole milk were 0.45 litres per person per week in 2007. Based on your answer to part b, predict the year in which sales of whole milk will fall below 0.2 litres per person per week. Show your workings. *(4 marks)*

2 The table shows the quarterly numbers of air passengers leaving the UK between 2005 and 2008.

Year	Quarter 1	Quarter 2	Quarter 3	Quarter 4
2005			27.6	20.1
2006	18.3	24.6	28.4	20.8
2007	19.1	24.9	29.7	21.7
2008	19.8	25.0		

Quarterly numbers of air passengers leaving UK airports (millions), 2005–08

Source: Office for National Statistics.

  a Plot these figures on a graph. *(6 marks)*
  b Using moving averages, calculate the trend. *(8 marks)*
  c Calculate the seasonal variations for each quarter. *(6 marks)*
  d Use these calculations to forecast air passenger numbers for quarters 1 and 2 of 2009. *(6 marks)*
  e Use the graph or your calculations to predict when the trend will rise above 25 million passengers per quarter. *(3 marks)*
  f Explain three reasons why your forecast in part e may prove to be incorrect. *(9 marks)*

PRACTICE EXERCISE 3

1 Look at the seven charts in Figure 8.2. Ignore Figures 8.2(a) and (d), which show perfect correlation. If the y-axis measures sales of a type of washing powder, identify an independent variable that would show high positive correlation (as in Figure 8.2(b)). Then identify a different independent variable that would show a low positive correlation (as in Figure 8.2(c)), and so on for Figures 8.2(e), (f) and (g). *(5 marks)*

2 Briefly justify each of your answers to question 1. *(10 marks)*

PRACTICE EXERCISE 4

Study the data on Unilever's ice cream sales in the case study below and then answer the following questions.

1 Statistically, are ice cream sales more strongly correlated to the average temperature or hours of sunshine? Briefly explain your answer. *(4 marks)*

2 Study Figure 8.5. If the weather forecast indicates an average temperature of 4°C, what will be the forecast revenue from ice cream sales? *(2 marks)*

3 Study Figure 8.5. If the weather forecast indicates an average temperature of 16°C, what will be the forecast revenue from ice cream sales? *(2 marks)*

4 For every 1°C that the temperature rises, calculate the forecast increase in sales revenue for Wall's ice cream. *(2 marks)*

5 Study Figure 8.6. If the weather forecast indicates monthly sunshine of 50 hours, what will be the forecast revenue from ice cream sales? *(2 marks)*

6 Study Figure 8.6. If the weather forecast indicates monthly sunshine of 150 hours, what will be the forecast revenue from ice cream sales? *(2 marks)*

7 For every extra hour of sunshine, calculate the forecast increase in sales revenue for Wall's ice cream. *(2 marks)*

8 Identify two other factors that would have a positive correlation with ice cream sales. *(2 marks)*

9 Identify two factors that would have a negative correlation with ice cream sales. *(2 marks)*

CASE STUDY The influence of the weather on sales

Sales levels of many products are influenced by the weather. A business that is able to establish this correlation is likely to be more exact in its forecasts than firms that are unaware of the link. Research by the French insurance giant AXA has found that beer sales increase by 3.2% for every 1°C rise in temperature. The research has even identified variations across the country: the 3.2% average conceals regional variations between 1.2% in the northeast and 5.2% on the south coast.

Of course, this assumes that weather forecasts are correct. The Met Office claims that predictions are becoming more accurate. Today's 72-hour forecasts match the accuracy of the 24-hour forecasts of the previous decade and the number of accurate forecasts is continuing to rise as a greater understanding of weather patterns is established.

Sales figures also depend on the efficiency of firms' operations management. The bad weather in the summer of 2008 saw a large increase in late bookings of holidays. Two of the main beneficiaries were Croatia and Tunisia, where the tourist industries were able to adapt quickly to meet increases in demand of 150% and 95% respectively.

Following record-breaking temperatures in 2006, businesses were well prepared for a sweltering summer in 2007. Unfortunately, the weather had other plans. In recent years, Nestlé, Boots and ASDA have identified poor weather conditions as a key cause of failure to meet growth targets. However, sales of weatherproof clothing, such as raincoats, have benefited from recent poor weather. In the spring of 2008, Burberry reported a 20% increase in sales of its raincoats due to poor weather.

The weather can also influence shopping habits. Heavy rainfall in 2008 boosted internet sales at the expense of traditional stores. In 2008 sales of electrical products increased by 100% as fewer people visited shopping centres.

So how important is the weather to a traditional ice cream maker such as Unilever, which owns brands such as Wall's? People expect ice cream sales to depend on the weather, but is there statistical proof of this link?

Table 8.6 shows the sales of Unilever's ice cream and weather information over a period of 2 years between August 2006 and July 2008. This information is plotted graphically in Figures 8.5 and Figure 8.6.

Table 8.6 *Sales of Unilever's ice cream compared to weather conditions*

Year	Month	Average temperature (°C)	Sales of Unilever's ice cream (£m)	Hours of sunshine
2006	August	15.4	144	319
2006	September	15.3	144	287
2006	October	11.5	89	204
2006	November	11.0	76	185
2006	December	5.9	40	114
2007	January	6.4	51	121
2007	February	5.7	66	129
2007	March	6.8	137	144
2007	April	10.5	200	204
2007	May	11.0	180	243
2007	June	13.8	136	311
2007	July	14.8	166	332
2007	August	14.8	178	350
2007	September	12.8	133	288
2007	October	10.1	104	211
2007	November	10.7	57	177
2007	December	4.8	43	111
2008	January	5.7	39	118
2008	February	5.4	107	112
2008	March	5.6	111	140
2008	April	7.3	154	170
2008	May	12.4	209	253
2008	June	12.9	180	303
2008	July	15.7	175	330

Sources: Unilever and the Met Office.

Figure 8.5 *Correlation between sales of Unilever's ice cream and temperature, 2006–08*

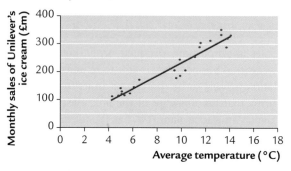

Figure 8.6 Correlation between sales of Unilever's ice cream and hours of sunshine, 2006–08

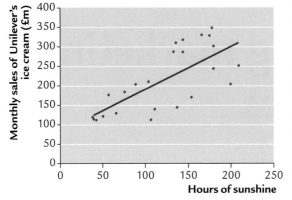

For trend analysis purposes, the data provided in Table 8.6 have been put into quarterly data and extended to cover the period between October 2005 and September 2008. The results are shown in Table 8.7.

Table 8.7 Quarterly sales of Unilever ice cream (£m), 2006–08

Year	Quarter 1	Quarter 2	Quarter 3	Quarter 4
2005				512
2006	411	775	936	503
2007	394	758	970	499
2008	370	726	943	

Question

Total: 30 marks (35 minutes)

Study the data in Tables 8.6 and 8.7 and in Figures 8.5 and 8.6.

Analyse how Unilever might use this information to forecast its ice cream sales and evaluate how useful this information would be to Unilever in producing an accurate forecast. *(30 marks)*

Chapter 9

Selecting marketing strategies

This chapter investigates how businesses select their marketing strategies. Porter's generic strategies model is used to compare the choice between low-cost and differentiation strategies. Ansoff's matrix is then utilised to examine market penetration, product development, market development and diversification as marketing strategies. The chapter shows how to assess the effectiveness of these alternative marketing strategies and concludes by examining the methods, benefits and risks involved in entering international markets.

Two different strategic approaches to marketing will be considered in this chapter:
- Porter's generic strategies
- Ansoff's matrix

Porter's generic strategies: low cost versus differentiation

If a successful firm's winning formula is easy to copy, its superior returns will not last long. Rivals will offer either a better price or a better product, and profitability will be driven downwards. Only if the winning formula is 'special' in some way, and difficult to imitate, will superior profitability be sustainable. A formula of this kind represents a competitive advantage.

Every business strategy needs to find a basis for competitive advantage that can be defended against the forces of competition. This means that business strategy must involve the analysis of **Porter's five competitive forces**. Five forces analysis considers the following factors:
- new entrants
- substitute products
- the power of buyers
- the power of sellers
- the level of competition between firms

Thus, if customers can see acceptable alternatives from new entrants or existing competitors, or if suppliers can find alternative markets, the firm's competitive advantage will be weak. However, if the firm is a major buyer of its materials, or if there is limited competition in the market, then the firm's advantage will be strong.

Relevant questions for a firm to consider include: Is this an attractive industry in which to compete? How can we protect ourselves from the threat of these forces? How can we build our competitive advantage so that it will be resilient in the face of such threats? Successful companies build highly distinctive products and services for which there is no ready substitute. The perils of a business strategy that ignores competition may seem obvious, but established companies such as Marks and Spencer, Sainsbury's and WH Smith have lost ground over recent years as a result of complacency and a failure to maintain competitive advantage.

Michael Porter's work suggests that firms that achieve 'sustainable competitive advantage' do so through one of three generic strategies — cost leadership, differentiation and focus (see Figure 9.1) — each of which is explained below.

Figure 9.1 Porter's generic strategies

		Strategic advantage	
		Low producer cost	High customer value
Strategic target	Mainstream market	Cost leadership	Differentiation
	Niche market	Focused cost leadership	Focused differentiation

Cost leadership

By pursuing a strategy of cost leadership, a firm sets out to become the lowest-cost producer in its industry. It does this by producing on a large scale and gaining economies of scale. Its products will tend to be standard and mass produced.

The key to success with this strategy is to achieve the lowest costs in the industry, but with prices that are close to the industry average. A problem with this strategy occurs if customers perceive the quality/value of products to be lower than that of competitors, which may then force the company to reduce prices and thus profits. Moreover, if competitors are able to reduce their costs to match the firm's levels, cost leadership will be lost.

A low-cost strategy may arise because a business identifies an opportunity to reduce costs. This may result from a number of sources:
- the introduction of a new method of production
- discovery of a new source of supply that is cheaper than that available to competitors
- new technology allowing a business to cut costs
- a new method of distribution that lowers costs of transportation or rental payments
- improvements in productivity that reduce unit costs

However, it is likely that competitors will be able to copy these ideas in the medium term. *Permanent* cost leadership is difficult to achieve but it may be created by:

- A patent on the process that allows a business to reduce unit costs.
- Achievement of economies of scale by the business as a result of its scale.
- Creating barriers to entry that prevent competition from eroding its market.

Examples of firms following this strategy are B&Q, Wilkinson and ASDA.

KINGFISHER PLC MEDIA CENTRE

Differentiation

In order to compete in a mass market, a firm needs to make sure that its product is different from competitors' products. If consumers value this difference, it will benefit the firm in two ways:

- increased sales volume
- greater scope for charging a higher price

Differentiation, also known as **value leadership**, can be based on a number of characteristics, such as:

- superior performance
- product durability
- after-sales service
- design, branding and packaging to improve the attractiveness of a product
- clever promotional and advertising campaigns to boost brand image and sales
- different distribution methods

WHAT DO YOU THINK?

Are Nike sportswear and trainers of better quality than their competitors, or are they just marketed more effectively? Is their success due to their distribution and their ability to get shelf space in shops?

Avon cosmetics differentiated itself by selling cosmetics directly to the customer; Amazon differentiated itself through internet selling, without the use of a traditional shop outlet.

Pursuing a policy of differentiation can add value by creating a unique selling point/proposition (USP). This may be real, such as a different design or different components, or it may be based on image and branding.

The key to success with this strategy is to try to reduce costs in areas that do not affect the uniqueness of the product and to identify the features that add value to the product without leading to significant increases in costs. Examples of firms following this strategy are Next, BMW and Thorntons.

Focus

Cost leadership and differentiation have so far been applied to firms in mainstream mass markets. Porter also identified the comparable approaches of firms operating in niche markets, where a strategy of focus on one or more market segments is applied. This focus may depend on cost leadership or on differentiation, and is the basis of success for most smaller and medium-sized enterprises.

By pursuing focus as a strategy, a firm picks a segment of the market that is poorly served by the main players in the industry and then adopts either a cost leader strategy or a differentiation strategy to target the segment or niche.

Porter suggests that a firm must make a conscious choice about the type of competitive advantage it seeks to develop. If it fails to choose one of these strategies, it risks being stuck in the middle, trying to be all things to all people, and ends up with no competitive strategy at all (see Figure 9.2).

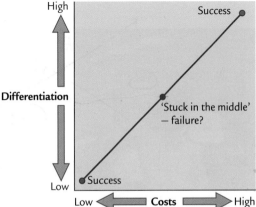

Figure 9.2 *Porter's generic strategies and firms that are 'stuck in the middle'*

 YOU KNOW?

Not all commentators agree with Porter's view that a company must make a choice about the type of generic strategy to pursue. But it is interesting to note that, while Sainsbury's was still the UK's number one supermarket, Porter argued against its compromise strategy of 'Good Food Costs Less at Sainsbury's'. Since then, Sainsbury's has been struggling and it is now in third place.

PRACTICE EXERCISE 1   Total: 25 marks (25 minutes)

1 Identify Porter's five forces.   (5 marks)

2 Selecting any company that you have studied, explain how its competitiveness has been affected by two of Porter's five forces.   (6 marks)

3 Porter's generic strategies model is a tool for assisting business to identify strategic options. Explain his three recommended strategies.   (9 marks)

4 Why does Porter suggest that 'being stuck in the middle' of the generic strategies model is likely to lead to failure?   (5 marks)

CASE STUDY 1 Ryanair and Starbucks

Ryanair

In the early 1990s, the Ryan family was considering closing down the loss-making Irish airline, Ryanair. As a last resort, a new young chief executive, Michael O'Leary, was hired and sent to the USA to see how Southwest Airlines was becoming a rising star. O'Leary learned well, and returned to Ireland convinced that the Southwest Airlines approach was right — focus solely on minimising costs in order to deliver the lowest possible price, and set up routes going directly from point to point, so that people do not need to change flights.

O'Leary, as a graduate of business studies, understood that the underlying strategy was to take Ryanair out of the centre ground of the Ireland–UK market. Instead it would be positioned as the lowest-cost operator in a niche market. From then on, every aspect of the Ryanair operation was geared to minimising costs — to provide enormous pricing flexibility. The success of this approach is shown in a few figures. Whereas British Airways and low-cost easyJet need a capacity utilisation level of 75–80% to break even on a flight, Ryanair needs less than 55% — yet Ryanair's actual utilisation rates are above 80%.

O'Leary set about the task of building up Ryanair's position in a number of ways:
- Extreme minimisation of overhead costs; staff work in cramped surroundings and are expected to work extremely hard.

- Minimising aircraft costs (depreciation and interest charges) by purchasing second-hand Boeings.
- Minimising maintenance costs by buying just one model (the Boeing 731), so that stocks of spares are minimised and the maintenance staff know the planes backwards and can therefore service and repair them quickly.
- Minimising landing charges: that is, the price that airports charge to allow a plane to land and to 'rent' time on the ground at the stand, waiting to take off again. Ryanair pioneered the use of secondary airports, flying from Stansted to unheard-of airports such as Alghero (Sardinia) and Dinard (Brittany). Airports keen to build business were willing to offer cheap deals to an airline that could bring in so many passengers.
- 'Sweating' the key asset — the planes — by ensuring that they operate many more times per day than rivals. The key is the turnaround time. Ryanair takes little more than 20 minutes to get passengers off the plane, clean it, refuel it and get new passengers seated. So the plane spends the maximum time in the air — earning revenue.
- 'Sweating' the staff. A Ryanair pilot flies around 80–90 hours per month — twice the British Airways equivalent. Cabin crew are similarly hard-worked. For example, during a 6-month period Ryanair flew 24 million passengers with 2,000 staff; in the same time, Lufthansa flew twice as many passengers, but with more than 30,000 staff. Ryanair has achieved this partly through ruthless treatment of unions; the compensation is that it pays well and gives staff share options that have proved very valuable as its share price has risen.

Ryanair's marketing mix has also been rooted in cost minimisation. O'Leary learned from Southwest Airlines that low airline prices are newsworthy — they can be showbusiness. So Ryanair launched by painting its telephone ticket sales number in huge letters on the planes, refused to sell through travel agents (saving 10–15%) and relied on news reports of its unprecedented low prices and word-of-mouth advertising from customers.

O'Leary's other ace was to follow Richard Branson's example by manipulating the media. He staged stunts such as an 'attack' on easyJet's Luton headquarters. O'Leary hired a tank, dressed himself and other staff in army uniform, and drove up to the easyJet HQ waving banners saying 'Ryanair blasts 50% off easyJet's fares'. The newspapers and television cameras lapped up the story, giving Ryanair masses of free promotion.

The basic marketing rule for airlines has always been to encourage repeat business by looking after the passengers. Ryanair, by contrast, lays down rules that it will not break, such as 'no refunds'. If you are booked on to a Ryanair flight and are rushed into hospital that morning, don't waste time asking for a refund.

Part of the company's cost-cutting approach is that there is no customer service section at all. Bizarrely, O'Leary even created some terrible publicity by reneging on a promise that his one millionth customer would have free flights for life. Yet despite tut-tuts from the media, investors recognised that O'Leary's passion for cost cutting could be good news, while customers were reminded again that Ryanair means low costs and low fares.

British Airways (BA) and the other main European airlines have been left gasping as the Ryanair strategy (copied by other low-cost airlines) has stripped their scheduled services of passengers. Ryanair has a much stronger balance sheet than BA, meaning that there is no possible threat from a price war or even from excessively rapid growth. Ryanair's low-cost strategy has worked during periods of economic growth, because it has helped to make a former luxury (air travel) more widely available. Early signs are that it is coping well with the economic downturn in 2008, as customers are switching away from the more expensive airlines.

Source: adapted from Ian Marcousé, 'Strategic marketing', *Business Review*, November 2003.

Starbucks

Starbucks recorded the first quarterly loss in its 15-year history in the UK in June 2008 — a loss of $6.7 million in contrast to a $158 million profit in the same quarter in 2007. Similar problems in the USA and Australia have led Starbucks to re-examine its marketing strategies in the last year.

Starbucks' rapid growth, from its foundation as a coffee bar in Seattle, USA, was a classic example of differentiation. Starbucks' strength lay in delighting customers with little touches that differentiated it from its rivals, such as free Wi-Fi, comfy seats, newspapers to read, cheerful welcomes and great tunes. These touches created a sense of occasion when customers visited Starbucks, encouraging repeat custom and brand loyalty.

Starbucks has become a victim of its own success. It has widened high-street interest in the coffee shop and, in doing so, has helped to increase consumer interest in coffee. Its place at the high-quality end of the coffee market is being displaced by more specialist coffee shops focusing on the quality of the coffee, rather than the wide range of differentiated 'touches' provided by Starbucks. High-quality coffee customers are looking towards some of the new competitors entering the market.

The atmosphere of Starbucks has been copied by many of the new competitors, but as it has grown Starbucks has found it difficult to maintain the consistency and quality of its stores.

Warwick Cairns, head of strategy at Brandhouse, believes that Starbucks must find new ways to regain the excitement felt by customers when it was first established.

Ben Kay, head of planning at RKCR/Y&R, believes that any strategy must focus on the uniqueness of Starbucks as a 'place'.

Management at Starbucks believe that there are other aspects to include in a new marketing strategy, in order to maintain the company's differentiation. With reference to Kay's view on 'place', it has recently opened Europe's first drive-through coffee store in Cardiff and is seeking to expand quickly through the use of franchises in places such as Center Parcs and the University of Surrey. It is also considering responding to health concerns related to the calorie content of some of its products, particularly its focus on large sizes of milky drinks. Until recently, Starbucks has relied on word-of-mouth advertising. For the first time it is now running a national advertising campaign to promote its Vivanno range of products.

Source: adapted from an article by Jeremy Lee in *Marketing*, 13 August 2008.

Questions

Total: 45 marks (55 minutes)

1 Evaluate the effectiveness of Ryanair's low-cost marketing strategy in achieving its objectives. *(16 marks)*

2 To what extent have Starbucks' recent difficulties been the result of its inability to retain its level of differentiation from other markets? *(14 marks)*

3 Using Ryanair and Starbucks as examples, discuss the extent to which Porter's five competitive forces can influence a firm's ability to achieve a competitive marketing advantage through low cost or differentiation. *(15 marks)*

Ansoff's matrix

Ansoff's matrix is another decision-making tool for marketing planning and developing a suitable marketing strategy. It was created by Igor Ansoff and first published in his article 'Strategies for diversification' in the *Harvard Business Review* in 1957. Ansoff's matrix provides a useful framework for analysing a range of strategic options in relation to risks and rewards.

EXAMINER'S VOICE

In looking at the strategic options available in Ansoff's matrix, draw upon your understanding across all of the functional areas and external influences. Try to take an integrative view of business when using Ansoff's matrix.

Ansoff's matrix consists of four cells that provide a company with a range of options or strategic choices, each with a different degree of risk attached (see Figure 9.3). We will examine each of these choices in turn.

Figure 9.3
Ansoff's matrix

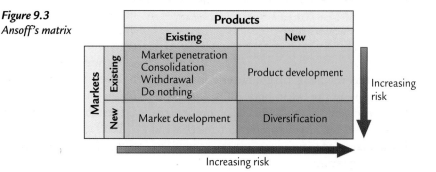

Existing products, existing markets

In this situation, the company has the choice of whether to penetrate the market further, consolidate its present position, withdraw from the market altogether or simply do nothing. Providing existing products in existing markets is a low-risk strategy because the firm is working in areas in which it has both knowledge and experience.

■ **Market penetration** — promoting growth in existing markets with existing products. Several different tactics can be employed: increasing brand loyalty in order to reduce customers' purchases of substitute products; encouraging customers to use the product more often, and therefore make more frequent purchases; or encouraging customers to use more of the product on each occasion — for example, by promoting the sale of larger packs. In highly competitive markets, taking customers from rivals may result in short-term gains, but competitors are likely to fight back. As a strategy, market penetration has its limits and once the market approaches saturation, another strategy must be pursued if a firm is to continue to grow.

FACT FILE

Classic toys: a case of market penetration

Makers of traditional toys such as teddy bears and board games (e.g. Monopoly) have been facing tough competition in a world where children are more interested in playing computer games than spending their time with a more 'passive' toy or taking hours playing a time-consuming game.

Both types of organisation have used marketing strategies that fit into Ansoff's matrix. Teddy bear makers such as Deans, Merrythought and Steiff have started to market nostalgia more aggressively and to aim their products at grandparents, who are buying more toys for their grandchildren. For Christmas 2008 Merrythought released a Teddy Roosevelt bear, celebrating the US president to whom the interest in teddy bears is attributed.

There is now a niche market among adults for 'collections' of bears, particularly from manufacturers with a long tradition, such as Deans and Steiff. Some toys, such as Hornby Trains, are targeted directly at the older consumer. 'People are retiring earlier, going back to their old hobbies and renewing their interest in toy trains and Scalextric sets. They are the ones with the disposable income.'

Source: adapted from *Business Review*, April 2005 and company websites.

■ **Consolidation** — concentrating activities on those areas where the firm has established a competitive advantage or competence, and focusing its attention on maintaining its market share. If this strategy is prompted by falling profits, then some form of retrenchment, such as redundancies or the sale of assets, might be needed.

■ **Withdrawal** — through the sale of all or part of the business. This might be appropriate if there is an irreversible decline in demand or the firm cannot match new competitors.

■ **Doing nothing** — that is, continuing with the existing strategy. This might be appropriate in the short term when the environment is static or the firm is waiting to see how a situation develops, but it is not realistic or beneficial in the long term.

Existing products, new markets

Here the strategy of **market development** is followed to extend a product's market into new areas. Examples are seeking new geographical territories, promoting new uses for the existing product, or entering new market segments. The development of new markets for the product is a good strategy if a firm's core competencies are related more to the product than to its experience with a specific market segment. Market development is more risky than market penetration because the firm will not be familiar with the needs and wants of the new market.

FACT FILE

Market development at Starbucks

Opened in Seattle in 1971, Starbucks now has more than 7,500 stores located in over 31 countries. In the USA, it has ten times the number of stores of its nearest competitor, and this market has now reached saturation point. In terms of Ansoff's matrix, Starbucks has pursued a strategy of market development and its growth has been based on a number of factors. It has a powerful brand name that is recognised around the world and it has sought to ensure customer satisfaction by speeding up service and introducing a range of new drinks. But the main reason for the company's growth has been its ability to repeat a winning formula throughout the world, with stores from Chile to China and Hong Kong to Hawaii. However, it has pulled out of the coffee bar market in Israel and has also struggled in Japan. The economic downturn in 2008 led to store closures in many different countries.

FACT FILE

Market development at Costa Coffee and Caffè Nero

Costa Coffee and Caffè Nero have also built their success around a strategy of market development. Costa Coffee has developed a successful store model, with Costa stores in partner outlets, such as Homebase, WH Smith and Abbey. Meanwhile, Caffè Nero has expanded by opening stores in suburban high streets and city centres and inside department stores, such as Selfridges. Opening coffee shops within existing retail outlets is a good way of keeping overhead costs down — particularly the cost of city-centre rents — in order to remain competitive.

New products, existing markets

Here a **product development** strategy is followed, which may involve substantial modifications or additions to a product range in order to maintain a competitive position. This strategy is particularly useful in competitive markets where firms need to maintain product differentiation. In some instances, products are changed completely, while in other cases, 'spin-offs' are developed, such as Mars Ice Cream and KitKat Kubes.

This strategy might need extensive research and development funding, but the company has the advantage of operating from the security of its established customers. Product development is appropriate if a firm's strengths are related to its customers rather than a specific product. Like market development, product development is more risky than simply trying to increase market share.

New products, new markets

The strategy of launching new products in new markets is known as **diversification**. It is a high-risk strategy because it requires both product and market development and may be outside the core competencies of the firm. Despite this, it may be the right choice if high risks are balanced by the chance of a high rate of return. Diversification could take place by means of organic growth, or it could involve a move into new but related markets by vertical or horizontal integration, or into new and unrelated markets by conglomerate integration. Nokia moved from being a producer of car tyres in the early 1990s to become a major player in the mobile phone market 10 years later.

Assessing the effectiveness of marketing strategies

Ultimately, the effectiveness of marketing strategies will be judged by the extent to which the achievements of the marketing function match its objectives. However, it is only possible to recognise whether the marketing objectives have been achieved after the marketing strategy or strategies have been implemented.

In order to gain some understanding of the potential effectiveness of a given marketing strategy, a business may use Porter's generic strategies model or Ansoff's matrix.

Porter's generic strategies

This model can be used to assess the possible effectiveness of a strategy involving low cost, differentiation or focus. In each case the model will be used to examine the following features of the strategy:

- whether the strategy provides a significant advantage to the business, through a much lower level of costs in comparison to competitors, clear differentiation from competitors' products, or a successful focus not enjoyed by rivals in the niche market
- whether the strategy can be maintained over a long period of time, so that there will be sufficient time in which the business can reap its reward
- whether the strategy appeals to sufficient numbers of customers to allow the business to reach its targets

Ansoff's matrix

This model can be used to assess the degree of risk involved in a particular marketing strategy. In general terms, market penetration or consolidation is the least risky option when considering the four quadrants of Ansoff's matrix.

Product development and market development increase the level of risk facing a business, and diversification (that is, new products in new markets) is considered to be the most risky strategy of all.

However, Ansoff's matrix can oversimplify the level of risk. Diversification into a new market with similar features to an existing market, and selling a new product that is slightly modified from the original, may not present a huge risk for a business.

e EXAMINER'S VOICE

Use Ansoff's matrix to assess the degree of risk in a particular marketing strategy, but be prepared to modify your assessment of the risk involved in accordance with the situation in the case study. For example, while Ansoff suggests that product development and market development are of similar levels of risk, it will depend on the level of development. For example, Nokia's move from tyres to mobile phones was a much more significant (and riskier) example of product development than its decisions to update models of mobile phones. Similarly, in international marketing there will usually be less risk for a UK-based business that moves into markets in Europe and the USA than there would be for the same business trying to market its products in China or Bolivia.

Ansoff's matrix is a useful tool for deciding on strategic direction, but it does not take account of what competitors are doing or what they are planning for the future; nor does it take account of how competitors will react to the selected strategy, and in what timescale.

e EXAMINER'S VOICE

When analysing possible marketing strategies in a Unit 3 (BUSS3) case study, use Ansoff's matrix if one or more of the four strategies is being implemented. This will show your ability to analyse strategic situations in a theoretical way.

The methods, benefits and risks involved in international markets

With increased globalisation and improved communications through improved transport links and the development of the internet, more and more businesses are seeking market development outside their country of origin.

This can be implemented in a number of different ways. The choice of method or methods will depend on the circumstances of the individual business.

Methods of expanding into international markets

Exporting

This takes place when a business manufactures the products in its own country but sells them abroad. For many businesses this is the least risky strategy, as it incurs relatively few additional costs. Furthermore, if the business is unable to sell its products in international markets, it can always consolidate by selling the same products in its country of origin (unless the product has been modified to suit the needs of the overseas market).

The vast majority of UK exports are services rather than goods. With technological advancement many of these services, such as banking and insurance, can be provided through the internet at similar costs to their provision for the domestic market. This has allowed many UK businesses to move into export markets at very little cost.

A major disadvantage of exporting is that control of the marketing often passes out of the hands of the company making the product, as invariably it is selling its product to an agent or retailer based in the other country. Businesses may wish to avoid this difficulty by setting up a base overseas.

Setting up a base overseas

In the last few decades there has been a rapid expansion in the number of global businesses that keep greater control of their international activities by having bases in many different countries. Overseas bases can be formed in one of two ways:

- **Organic growth by funding the establishment of an overseas factory or outlet.** In the motor industry, this strategy has been used often by Japanese manufacturers such as Honda, Nissan and Toyota, which have set up factories in countries such as the UK.
- **The takeover of a foreign business.** An example is the Bank of Santander entering and expanding in the UK through the takeover of Abbey, Alliance and Leicester, and Bradford and Bingley's branch network.

For many businesses, setting up a base overseas not only saves transport costs, but also avoids tariff barriers (such as taxes on imports) imposed by free-trade areas like the European Union, because the goods are manufactured in the country in which they are sold.

Joint ventures

Joint ventures occur when two or more companies agree to act as one organisation in launching a product or providing a service. Joint ventures are becoming particularly popular with businesses trying to enter emerging markets, such as India and China. Businesses in emerging markets may lack the technology and financial resources but possess a much greater understanding of local market conditions. In these circumstances, a joint venture can prove to be a very effective combination of strengths. However, joint ownership of a new business by two existing businesses can lead to conflict and communication problems.

Virgin Mobile has entered a joint venture with Indian conglomerate Tata. Tata's car division has also entered into a joint venture with car manufacturer Fiat, to make cars in India.

Franchising

If a business wishes to retain some control of its international marketing, while limiting its financial commitment, franchising offers a good solution. Firms such as McDonald's and Papa John's Pizza have used franchising to assist rapid expansion.

Franchising reduces risk to the franchisor because, if the business gets into difficulties in another country, it is the franchisee who suffers most of the financial loss. However, a badly managed franchise may damage the reputation of the franchisor, so there is a risk involved.

Licensing

Licensing normally applies to manufacturing industries. Permission to make a product in a certain country is given in the form of a licence granted by the original manufacturer to a manufacturer in another country. Licensing is particularly useful for businesses in which both the cost of transportation and the cost of establishing a foreign base would be high. Brewers such as Carlsberg frequently use licences in order to sell their products in other countries. High transport costs and potential quality problems arising from long-distance transport make licensing an ideal solution in these circumstances.

Methods of international marketing are also discussed in Chapter 21, which considers the globalisation of markets and the development of emerging markets, and hence discusses a number of the issues raised in this section.

Benefits to a business from international marketing

There are many advantages to be gained by a business from international marketing. Some of the key benefits are explained below.

Achieving growth

Many businesses find that it becomes difficult to sustain growth in the domestic market. This may be due to the level of competition or the existence of only a limited customer base. In some cases, further expansion can be limited by a government's competition policy. For example, in the UK the government has made it clear to Tesco that it will not be allowed to grow by purchasing another supermarket. In part this has led to Tesco seeking expansion in overseas markets. This reflects the market development strategy in Ansoff's matrix.

See Chapter 21 for more details of Tesco's overseas expansion.

Boosting profitability

Increased growth achieved through international marketing will help to increase a business's profit. Furthermore, a company's products or services may provide greater opportunity for profitability because of the nature of a particular overseas market. For example, car prices in the UK have traditionally been higher than those in most of Europe. This market feature has encouraged Japanese car manufacturers to target the UK car market in order to boost their profitability.

Spreading risks

Although moving into an international market can be seen to be a risky proposition, it may also reduce a firm's dependence on a single market. British tobacco companies such as BAT adopted a policy of market development when they recognised that lung cancer fears were likely to lead to a decline in UK demand for tobacco products. BAT has recently set up a joint venture with the world's largest tobacco company, China National Tobacco Corporation (CNTC), both to help it access the Chinese market and to provide a Chinese manufacturing base.

Helping international competitiveness

Countries with large domestic markets, such as China and India — each with populations in excess of 1 billion people — provide their industries with great potential growth. This enables companies from these countries to achieve greater economies of scale (see Chapter 12), and this in turn enables them to lower their costs and improve their competitiveness. A UK firm trying to match these economies of scale will need to spread into other countries so that it can produce on a very large scale and lower its unit costs.

Improving understanding of markets

Many businesses use international marketing to increase their understanding of developments in both products and markets. Ideas from other countries can be used to introduce new products and to recognise global changes in consumer tastes.

Risks to a business from international marketing

There are many risks to a business from international marketing. Some of the key risks are explained below.

Cultural, social and language factors

A business must recognise cultural differences when dealing with people from other businesses and when trying to appeal to customers in other countries.

Social factors may also have a major impact on the business, especially if a product is targeted at a particular market segment. For example, the structure of family life, the roles of males and females, lifestyles of different age groups and religious beliefs can all vary considerably between countries.

The most prominent cultural difference is that of language. UK firms are fortunate that English is a widely accepted business language.

HSBC has run a very successful advertising campaign focusing on and highlighting the significance of cultural differences between countries.

Legislation

While the UK has similar laws to other EU countries, there can be considerable differences in legislation for a business that is seeking to market its products beyond the European Union. Major differences in legislation may involve factors such as laws on advertising, laws on product safety and laws related to environmental considerations. A UK business must ensure that it complies with this legislation.

Business practice

There are cultural differences within business practice. A business must be aware of mannerisms, forms of greeting, the acceptability or unacceptability of gifts and more functional factors such as acceptable credit terms. A lack of awareness of business etiquette may lead to the loss of a contract.

Economic factors

International marketing can be influenced greatly by changes in economic variables, such as economic growth and exchange rates. Exchange rates, in particular, have had a huge impact on the profitability of international marketing.

In 2008 the value of the pound (sterling) fell from $1.99 to $1.47. For businesses trading in Europe, the value of sterling fell from €1.37 to €1.05. Both of these changes meant that UK exports to the USA and Europe were a lot cheaper to buy in those markets. Consequently, a firm may have decided that international marketing was not worthwhile in January 2008 because of the high exchange rate, only to find that it had missed many opportunities brought about by the dramatic fall in sterling. However, UK businesses exporting to South Korea would have found it more difficult because the pound gained value against the South Korean Won, rising in value from 1,850 Won to 1,940 Won in 2008.

Economic factors are covered in detail in Chapter 21.

Operational factors

International marketing involves complexities that do not occur in domestic markets. Challenges facing the business include international laws relating to exporting and importing, documentation required by foreign governments and the physical transportation of products over much greater distances. In many cases, businesses will choose to use intermediaries to provide these services, although this will lead to some loss of control in the management of the international marketing process.

Political factors

A business undertaking international marketing will normally seek advice from UK authorities, to establish the level of political risk involved in transactions in a certain country. On a practical basis, it is unlikely that the business will be able to get insurance for transactions in countries that represent a political risk, such as Somalia. Most international marketing by UK businesses tends to be in countries with which the UK has strong political links.

FACT FILE

Risks of international marketing

The risks outlined in this chapter may outweigh the benefits of international marketing to a particular business. Many UK retailers, such as Sainsbury's and Marks and Spencer, have experienced difficulties in international marketing that have led to overseas activities being closed or sold off because of losses being made. In extreme cases, such as Baring Brothers, the losses of the overseas division of the business have been so great that it has led to the collapse of the business. This is not just an issue for UK businesses. C&A is a highly successful Dutch retailer that has successfully expanded throughout Europe. However, after enjoying success in the UK market, it started to struggle. After 5 years of losses, it eventually closed its UK branches in 2000.

PRACTICE EXERCISE 2   Total: 45 marks (45 minutes)

1 Identify the four options available to a business that is following a strategy of 'existing product/existing market'. *(4 marks)*

2 Distinguish between the market development and product development strategies in Ansoff's matrix. *(4 marks)*

3 Explain one benefit of the diversification strategy in Ansoff's matrix. *(4 marks)*

4 Which strategic option from Ansoff's matrix is a risk-averse firm likely to follow and why? *(5 marks)*

5 Explain one weakness of Ansoff's matrix in helping a firm to develop a successful strategy. *(4 marks)*

6 Analyse three methods that a coffee bar business might use in order to market internationally. *(9 marks)*

7 Explain two benefits to a car manufacturer from international marketing. *(6 marks)*

8 Explain three risks to a car manufacturer from international marketing. *(9 marks)*

CASE STUDY 2 Stagecoach: a brief history

Stagecoach was founded by Brian Souter and his sister, Ann Gloag, in Perth, Scotland, in 1980. The business started with just two buses.

1980s: transport deregulation

Stagecoach was one of the first companies to take advantage of transport deregulation in the UK in 1980, and in the early years of the decade it operated coach services in Scotland, as well as longer-distance links to London.

The Transport Act of 1985 deregulated bus services, which had previously been owned and operated by councils and local transport authorities. In the late 1980s, Stagecoach borrowed heavily and bought a number of former National Bus Company businesses, including Hampshire, Cumberland, United Counties, East Midlands, Ribble and Southdown.

Stagecoach was one of the first major transport operators to expand overseas and this period saw it run its first services outside the UK after buying UTM, the major bus company in Malawi.

Early 1990s: expansion in the UK and overseas

Expansion continued at a rapid pace in the early 1990s as Stagecoach bought further bus operations in Scotland and England.

Stagecoach continued to develop its overseas portfolio, adding to its operations in Africa and moving into New Zealand in 1992.

The flotation of Stagecoach on the London Stock Exchange in 1993 valued the company at £134 million, and provided a basis for the company to grow significantly in the mid- to late 1990s.

Major overseas bus operations were bought in Portugal, Sweden and later Hong Kong. Stagecoach has since exited all of its overseas markets except North America.

Mid-1990s: diversifying into rail

After the UK network was privatised in 1995, Stagecoach put in bids for all 25 rail franchises. Its founder, Brian Souter, was described by Richard Branson as 'a maverick, like me' because of his willingness to take risks. Two of the 25 bids were successful and, as a result, Stagecoach took over South West Trains, the UK's biggest rail franchise. It was also successful in winning the UK's smallest railway, Island Line, on the Isle of Wight.

In 1996, Stagecoach bought Porterbrook, a company that leases trains and rolling stock to rail franchises, but it sold this business to Abbey (Santander) Bank in 2000, making over £100 million profit from the deal.

In 1997 it moved into trams, purchasing Sheffield Supertram. Within 6 months, the company had announced a tie-up with Sir Richard Branson's Virgin Group as it took a 49% stake in Virgin Rail Group, the operator of the Cross Country and West Coast inter-city rail franchises.

For a few years, Stagecoach also had an interest in air travel after buying Prestwick International Airport in 1998. This business was later sold.

Late 1990s: new markets in Asia and North America

The year 1998 was one of the busiest periods for acquisitions in the company's history, as it added bus operations and ferries in Auckland to the New Zealand business and purchased Citybus in Hong Kong — businesses that were later sold.

However, Stagecoach's biggest deal took place in North America the following year with the purchase of Coach USA, the largest bus and coach operator in the States, which also included services in Canada.

STAGECOACH GROUP PLC

From 2000: new millennium, a new approach

Stagecoach is now focused on market consolidation and market penetration in the UK and USA, with smaller complementary acquisitions.

In 2005, Stagecoach sold its New Zealand operations in order to fund the acquisition of other UK bus companies. Overall Stagecoach had experienced mixed fortunes in its overseas activities and this decision left North America as its only remaining international operation.

Stagecoach Group was awarded the new East Midlands rail franchise in June 2007 and it became the UK's biggest tram operator in July 2007 when it took over the contract to operate and maintain the Manchester Metrolink tram network.

The company's focus is now on innovations within its existing products and markets. In 2003 it introduced the UK's first web-based low-cost inter-city travel service, megabus.com, which now serves more than 30 major cities across the UK. It has also piloted demand-responsive taxibus services. Recent projects have focused on introducing biodiesel buses, fuelled by cooking oil, in order to reduce carbon emissions. In April 2008, Stagecoach launched Scotland's first carbon-neutral bus network.

Market share information for Stagecoach's UK bus and UK rail services are provided in Figure 9.4. It should be noted that Stagecoach owns 49% of Virgin Rail Group, which has a 10.8% market share. Although its market share in the USA is only 1%, it is a significant transport provider in a country with 5,000 operators, where the average market share per operator is only 0.02%.

Source: www.stagecoachplc.com.

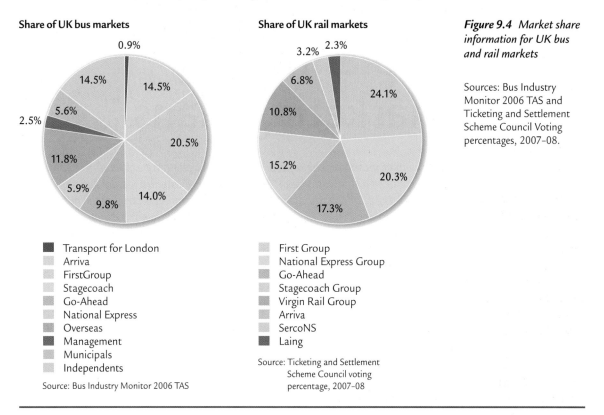

Share of UK bus markets

Transport for London
Arriva
FirstGroup
Stagecoach
Go-Ahead
National Express
Overseas
Management
Municipals
Independents

Source: Bus Industry Monitor 2006 TAS

Share of UK rail markets

First Group
National Express Group
Go-Ahead
Stagecoach Group
Virgin Rail Group
Arriva
SercoNS
Laing

Source: Ticketing and Settlement Scheme Council voting percentage, 2007–08

Figure 9.4 *Market share information for UK bus and rail markets*

Sources: Bus Industry Monitor 2006 TAS and Ticketing and Settlement Scheme Council Voting percentages, 2007–08.

Questions

Total: 40 marks (50 minutes)

1 Analyse the possible reasons why Stagecoach decided to sell most of its overseas activities.   *(10 marks)*

2 In the mid-1990s, Richard Branson described Brian Souter, the co-founder of Stagecoach, as a risk-taker. Using Ansoff's matrix, evaluate the extent to which Stagecoach's strategy from 1980 to the mid-1990s supports Richard Branson's opinion. Justify your view.   *(15 marks)*

3 To what extent has Stagecoach's marketing strategy changed since 1995, in terms of the level of risk being taken?   *(15 marks)*

CHAPTER 10
Developing and implementing marketing plans

This chapter introduces the concept of marketing planning and outlines the main components of a marketing plan. The internal and external factors that influence the marketing plan are examined. Particular consideration is given to the marketing budget, the methods used to set it and the factors that influence the budget allocated to marketing. The chapter concludes by looking at the reasons for marketing plans and the issues involved in implementing them.

KEY TERM

marketing plan:
a statement of the organisation's current marketing position and future strategies, and a detailed examination of the tactics that it will use to achieve its objectives.

Components of a marketing plan

The main components of a marketing plan are outlined below. Some of the components of the marketing plan have been dealt with in earlier chapters. A brief cross-reference will be provided in these instances.

A SWOT analysis

This is an audit of the factors that influence the marketing of a business. In effect, it looks at internal strengths and weaknesses and external opportunities and threats. In order to carry out this audit, the business would conduct market research.

SWOT analysis also assesses the internal and external influences on the business, so that these factors are taken into consideration when finalising the marketing plan. These internal and external influences are dealt with later in this chapter.

Forecasting sales and market analysis

Using information gained from its market research, the business will analyse the market and make sales forecasts. These forecasts will advise a business of the expected outcomes of its marketing plan. The forecasts will also show the possible alternative outcomes if circumstances become more favourable or adverse. In this way, the business can also assess the possible risks of pursuing the strategies that are agreed through the marketing plan.

Setting SMART marketing objectives

These marketing objectives will be based on the market research and the SWOT analysis that the business has conducted. The objectives will also take into consideration the capabilities of the other functional areas of the organisation, such as the operations and human resources departments.

Agreeing marketing strategies

Once the marketing objectives have been set, marketing strategies, such as low cost, product development or diversification, will be established in order to meet these objectives.

Allocating a marketing budget

In order to finance the actions agreed in the marketing plan, a marketing budget must be agreed. The different methods that can be used to set a marketing budget are described later in this chapter.

Implementing marketing tactics through the marketing mix

Once the marketing strategy has been agreed, the marketing department will plan a marketing mix that fits into the overall strategy. Different marketing strategies tend to emphasise different elements of the marketing mix. For example:

- **Low cost/cost leadership.** This strategy tends to require a marketing mix that emphasises low *price*.
- **Differentiation or focus.** Strategies of differentiation or focus require individualised products, in which case *product* is the most critical element of the marketing mix. In order to ensure that the public is aware of this differentiation, emphasis is also placed on *promotion*, to ensure that the public is aware of the product's USP.

- **Market penetration or consolidation.** In order to increase sales within an existing market, the business needs to examine all four aspects of the marketing mix, unless one aspect of the marketing mix is perceived to be weaker than the other three Ps.
- **Product development.** This strategy requires clear emphasis on the *product* element of the marketing mix.
- **Market development.** The main feature of market development is the *place* in which the product or service will be sold.
- **Diversification.** Moving into a new market requires emphasis on both *product* and *place*. Although these are two critical elements of the marketing mix, in order to get the product recognised *price* must be competitive and any new development requires considerable *promotion* in order to make people aware of the product.

Control and review

Once the plan has been finalised, there is a continuous process of control and review to monitor progress against the marketing objectives established in the plan. The control and review process ensures that there is complete integration of all elements of the plan. For example, failure to achieve a marketing objective will require a review to discover the reasons. This review may uncover a poor choice of strategy, or a correct strategy accompanied by an unsuccessful application of the marketing mix. It may be that internal or external factors have changed, making the initial marketing objectives much more challenging (or easier to achieve) than was originally thought. In some cases this may mean a change of marketing objective, if the original objective was unrealistic.

 EXAMINER'S VOICE

In effect, the marketing plan brings together all aspects of a business's marketing. In order to gain a thorough understanding of the marketing plan, you are advised to revisit earlier marketing chapters. This section has been kept relatively brief to avoid excessive repetition of topics that have been covered elsewhere.

Assessing internal and external influences on marketing plans

Internal influences on the marketing plan

Any business must ensure that each of its functional areas works cooperatively with other areas. When compiling its marketing plan, a business must liaise closely with the other departments within the organisation to ensure that each department is working towards the same goals and adopting consistent strategies. The sections below provide some examples of ways in which the marketing plan is influenced by the other business functions.

The marketing plan and operational issues

The marketing objectives must be consistent with the production department's approach. If the marketing plan is aiming to create an upmarket, quality image, it is vital that the operations department can manufacture products of a high enough quality to meet this requirement. High-quality after-sales service will also be necessary if this target is to be achieved, especially if the marketing department has emphasised this as a key element of its plan.

The marketing plan and finance

Similar cooperation is needed between finance and marketing. If the marketing plan is ambitious, it may be necessary to curtail certain marketing activities if there is insufficient funding. The finance department must also allocate sufficient money to each department that is supporting the marketing effort. Ultimately, the marketing budget and all other budgets must be agreed with the finance department.

The marketing plan and human resource management (HRM)

Successful marketing strategies need people to deliver them. Consequently, HRM and marketing need to coordinate their activities. Staff in the marketing department must be recruited effectively, and the workforce planning of the business is essential if each department is to have the right number of suitably qualified staff with the required skills. Customer service training is a specific example of human resource activities that will influence the marketing plan and its operation.

Although each functional area has to compete with the other areas of the business for resources, ultimately they are all striving to achieve the same (corporate) objectives. The Fact File on the Co-op provides an example of a marketing plan that depends for its success on cooperation between marketing, operations, finance and HRM.

EXAMINER'S VOICE

When answering questions on marketing planning, you should look for evidence of approaches that have been successful or unsuccessful and use any reasons behind this in your answer.

FACT FILE

Marketing planning at the Co-op

The Co-op is an example of a business that has developed an integrated marketing plan in order to target a large niche market — the UK's 2 million blind and partially sighted people. The Co-op pioneered the use of Braille on packaging for certain medicines and it has extended Braille labelling to over 300 own-brand products.

The Co-op has signed up to the Guide Dogs for the Blind Association's high-street charter and is relying on word-of-mouth advertising — a strategy based on the close-knit network of blind people. Financially, the Co-op is guaranteeing that prices will be the same as its usual own-brand range, in keeping with its stance on ethical and socially responsible behaviour. To assist blind and partially sighted people, the supermarket has planned the layout of its stores to ease access for blind customers. It has also trained its staff on the new labelling and on the charter, which advises shops on ways to assist blind people, such as offering explanations of store layout, store guides and helping to pack their shopping.

External influences on the marketing plan

When compiling its marketing plan, a business must be aware of factors outside the business that may affect the details of the plan. Some of the key external factors that influence marketing objectives were introduced in Chapter 7. The same factors will tend to influence the other elements of the marketing plan. A brief comment on some external factors is noted below.

Market factors

The marketing plan needs to include details of the market research required to understand the market in which the business is seeking to target customers.

Competitors' actions

Flexibility needs to be incorporated into the marketing plan, so that the business can respond to any changes in the marketing strategy adopted by major competitors.

Technological change

This factor has developed most businesses' understanding of their markets, through mechanisms such as loyalty cards and electronic point-of-sale (EPOS). This enables businesses to plan more accurately.

Suppliers

It is vital that the marketing plan takes into consideration the capability of its suppliers to provide whatever the business believes can be sold. For this reason, many businesses deliberately source supplies of vital materials from a variety of different businesses, rather than relying on one major supplier.

Political factors

In most cases, political factors are relatively long-term changes. Businesses involved in international marketing, in particular, need to be aware of any political developments that might influence their target markets, so that the marketing plan can be amended, if necessary.

Social factors

Social changes mean that businesses must adapt to new circumstances. For example, in recent years the internet has overtaken television as the main medium for advertising.

Legal factors

Changes in legislation may be a threat to a business because, in order to comply with the legislation, costs of production may increase. However, a business that monitors proposed legal changes can benefit by adapting its marketing strategy ahead of its competitors.

Environmental factors

Environmental considerations are of growing importance and most businesses will be adapting their marketing plans so that they can demonstrate to consumers that they produce environmentally friendly products in an efficient manner.

The marketing budget

Methods of setting the marketing budget

KEY TERM

marketing budget: the amount of money that a firm allocates to spend on marketing activities. This money may be used for activities such as advertising and sales promotions.

The most common approaches to setting a marketing budget are described below.

Budgeting according to marketing objectives

The more ambitious the objectives, the greater the budget that is allocated.

> **e EXAMINER'S VOICE**
>
> Don't confuse the marketing budget (which plans expenditure on marketing activities) with the sales budget (which is a revenue budget that details expected income from sales).

AQA A2 Business Studies

Budgeting according to competitors' spending

In order to stay competitive, a business may have to match the spending of its rivals.

Marketing budget as a percentage of sales revenue

Although this is less scientific, it is commonly used because it is seen to be fair. If a firm matches the national average by spending just under 2% of its sales revenue on advertising, then a product with sales of £100 million per annum will be given a budget of just under £2 million and one with sales of £100,000 will receive almost £2,000.

Zero budgeting/budgeting based on expected outcomes

In effect, this method allocates a budget on the strength of the case presented by the budget manager. It is ideal for marketing budgets, as the dynamic nature of marketing means that a budget can be quickly agreed to suit a sudden event.

Budgeting according to last year's budget allocation

Although it is less scientific than the other methods, it is common practice for budgets to be set according to last year's allocation plus an allowance for inflation. The logic behind this approach is that, if it was suitable last year, it will be suitable this year.

Factors influencing the size of the marketing budget

Some of the factors affecting the size of the marketing budget were dealt with in the previous section. The overall size of the budget will depend on:
- the marketing objectives
- the actions of competitors and the usual level of advertising for that industry
- the benefits to be gained from the spending
- last year's allocation

In addition, the marketing budget will be influenced by the following factors.

The organisation's financial situation

If an organisation is experiencing losses or cash-flow problems, it will tend to look more closely at any budget allocations.

The cost of advertising in particular media

To some extent, the marketing budget is influenced by the cost of advertising in the media that the organisation wishes to use. Traditionally, television advertising is more expensive than other media, and if a firm feels that television advertising is essential, its budget must be set so that it can afford to use this medium.

The nature of the market

A monopoly may have less need to spend money on marketing, although monopolists do need to advertise in order to increase consumer awareness and prevent consumers moving to different products or services.

Consumer expectations

In some markets, consumers anticipate that marketers will communicate with them in certain ways and through certain media. For example, many supermarkets offer price reductions on petrol as a reward for expenditure in the store. Any supermarket not making this offer may alienate consumers.

The level of change in the market

In a static market, businesses can rely on long-established reputations to sell products. However, in more dynamic markets, consumers need more information and persuasion in order to keep buying, so a larger budget is required.

The potential return compared with other activities

Marketing is in competition with other functions for the finances in a business. Large budgets should be allocated to the departments that will use the money most effectively.

The benefits of marketing planning

Firms use marketing planning for the following reasons:

- It provides a clear sense of direction. By emphasising the need to set objectives, it helps to ensure that people involved in the decision-making process are aiming towards the same goals.
- This may also motivate staff if they are given responsibility for an element of the plan.
- Decisions are based on business logic, involving comparisons between alternative strategic approaches. This makes it less likely that a decision will be made without its pros and cons being examined first.
- It is probable (but not certain) that more than one person will be involved in the process. This will reduce the possibility of bias.
- The plan arises from a consideration of all functions of a business. This makes managers think strategically and forces them to coordinate marketing actions with the activities of other departments.
- Departmental plans such as the marketing plan allow senior managers to compare alternative demands for resources. This enables the firm to allocate resources to the activities that are likely to benefit the business to the greatest extent.
- Managers can assess efficiency by comparing actual outcomes with the plan and discovering the reasons for any differences.
- Continual review of the marketing plan enables the firm to remain aware of any developments in the marketplace, allowing it to stay ahead of competitors.
- Finally, an individual manager may prefer a carefully planned approach, so that he or she can justify the decision if things go wrong. It is easier to defend a policy that has been developed on the basis of good planning (and in cooperation with other managers) than one that is based solely on one person's opinion.

Issues in implementing marketing plans

The usefulness of market planning will be limited if:

- it takes up excessive time in both the planning and reviewing stages, and thus becomes a brake on progress
- there are constant changes in the market, leading to an inability to assess the effectiveness of the planning process
- there is a lack of coordination between the different functional plans and the corporate plan
- the plans are too ambitious or complicated
- managers and employees only pay lip service to the plan and do not implement the strategies agreed
- review of progress against the plan seldom takes place or lacks regularity
- the plan remains rigid despite significant changes in circumstances, such as a recession or a high turnover of staff

A good plan needs to be disciplined and focused but must allow some flexibility where changes make elements of the original plan meaningless.

FACT FILE

HMV

Not all marketing plans are focused on growth and expansion. HMV, which also owns Waterstone's bookshops, operates in two declining markets:

- records
- books

The HMV marketing plan is a long-term strategy to shift into expanding markets. According to its 2008 annual report: 'We continue to plan and adapt for structural change taking place in our markets by refocusing our mix of products to higher growth categories, improving the communication with our customers and enhancing our store environments.'

The main element of this strategy has been for HMV stores to reduce emphasis on CDs and focus more on DVDs and games console-related products.

HMV has also recognised that it needs to provide a more interactive environment for its customers. 'We invite our customers to "Get Closer" to the content we sell.' For example, in Waterstone's the environment has encouraged customers to read books while in-store. In addition, marketing campaigns have been targeted around the key seasonal gifting periods, such as Christmas.

In its HMV stores, the company embarked on successful trials of a 'next generation' store format, featuring a social hub providing access to entertainment websites, multi-player games zones and transactional kiosks. All product lines in the trial outperformed the rest of the chain, leading to a decision to convert another 10–15 stores and to use the new format for any new stores opened.

In 2008, games and technology represented 21% of HMV's sales, up from 14% in 2007. This was a result of HMV achieving a 42% increase in sales of games and technology. Similar growth is targeted for 2009 and 2010.

HMV has also focused on online sales, which coincidentally also grew by 42% in 2008.

HMV has acquired seven entertainment stores and various related trademarks from the administrator of Fopp. These stores provide a differentiated customer base and offer scope for some more future store openings.

A different strategy has been employed at Waterstone's, with emphasis on brand loyalty through a loyalty card. The stores are also stocking DVDs in order to compensate for declining book sales. New technology is also providing electronic books that store a huge number of novels. Waterstone's is also piloting new technology that allows a book to be printed and bound in store. If successful, these changes will reduce the physical stock levels that bookshops need to hold.

Source: HMV company reports.

PRACTICE EXERCISE
Total: 45 marks (45 minutes)

1 What is meant by the term 'marketing plan'? *(3 marks)*

2 Identify five components of a marketing plan. *(5 marks)*

3 Explain two internal factors that might influence the marketing plan. *(6 marks)*

4 Explain two external factors that might influence the marketing plan. *(6 marks)*

5 What is meant by the term 'marketing budget'? *(3 marks)*

6 Analyse two factors that might influence the size of the marketing budget that WH Smith plc would allocate to its magazines section. *(8 marks)*

7 Outline two advantages of marketing planning. *(6 marks)*

8 Explain two situations in which a marketing plan might not be very useful to an organisation. *(8 marks)*

CASE STUDY Marks and Spencer's marketing plan

The importance of flexibility in marketing plans is exemplified by Marks and Spencer plc.

The financial year 2003/04 was a bad one for Marks and Spencer, which suffered a 10% fall in sales of its clothing. The new Autograph range had failed to inspire customers. The products received excellent reviews, but the prices, many in excess of £100, were too high for Marks and Spencer customers.

Marks and Spencer responded by lowering the price, a tactic that revived the brand. It also shifted its target market. In order to attract back its main customer segment, it recruited George Davies, the man behind ASDA's 'George' range of clothing. Davies introduced a new brand for women, Per Una, which was less fashion-led but also much cheaper. The Per Una range was

introduced in September 2001 and was (and is still) targeted at 30- and 40-somethings. After early success, Marks and Spencer decided to target the teenage market. It launched another new range, Per Una Due, aimed at teenage girls seeking high-quality fashion clothes. The new range featured styles such as shorter skirts and boob tubes.

Marks and Spencer was hoping to appeal to mothers and daughters. A spokesperson for Marks and Spencer explained: 'There is scope for mothers and daughters to shop together. The mothers can buy Per Una and the daughters can buy Per Una Due. Marks and Spencer hopes that the mothers will be attracted by the quality, which is better than rivals such as Topshop. The company also expects the daughters to enjoy the new "boutique"-style layout of its shops. To keep the clothing fashionable, Per Una Due stock will be completely replaced every 8 weeks. M&S also used text messaging to promote the Per Una Due range.

The Per Una Due range was introduced into 65 stores in May 2004. Close monitoring of sales, and comparisons with stores that were not offering the new range, allowed Marks and Spencer to determine that this new strategy was not successful, as daughters were reluctant to use Marks and Spencer for fashion clothing.

In November 2004, Marks and Spencer announced that it was abandoning the Per Una Due range in order to focus on its traditional market of women aged over 30.

New objectives were set to increase market share in women's wear (currently M&S has a market share of 11.1%) and lingerie, where it enjoys a market share of 24.8%. In addition, M&S would concentrate on reviving its 'menswear' and 'kidswear' divisions. In 2008, despite difficult trading conditions, M&S was able to increase its market share in menswear from 10.3% to 10.5% and its market share in children's clothing from 4.5% to 4.8%.

Using market research and techniques such as SWOT analysis, Marks and Spencer has recognised that its reputation is growing in both its 'home' and 'food' divisions. Its marketing plan has focused mainly on consolidation in its traditional, clothing markets.

However, growth is targeted in the 'home' division. The 8% growth achieved in 2008 has been assisted by a strategy of product development, with the introduction of electrical brands such as Sony being a particularly notable change.

In terms of sales revenue, the 'food' division is the major success story and M&S has already achieved one element of its long-term objectives — a 5% market share of the UK food market. A key element of M&S's marketing strategy is to expand the 'Simply Food' stores, which concentrate only on food sales. M&S has targeted train stations and motorway services for many of these stores, with 64 of its 98 'Simply Food' stores being based at BP service stations. Another long-term objective relates to online sales through the internet. M&S's objective is to reach online sales of £500 million by 2010/11. In 2008 it reached online sales of £220 million, which means that it is on target to achieve its long-term objective. Online sales have also enabled M&S to reach new customers. Its Big and Tall range is not stocked in most stores because of limited demand, but is popular amongst online purchasers.

Source: adapted from an article by Jess Cartney-Morley in the *Guardian*, 5 May 2004, and Marks and Spencer annual reports 2005 to 2008.

Questions

Total: 35 marks (45 minutes)

1 Using Ansoff's matrix, evaluate the main marketing strategies that Marks and Spencer has adopted in recent years.

(*15 marks*)

2 Based on your understanding of business studies and the evidence in the case study, evaluate the extent to which Marks and Spencer has benefited from its marketing planning.

(*20 marks*)

Marketing strategies

CASE STUDY Carters Clothing

Carters was established in Bradford in 1988. It specialised in selling high-quality men's clothing. Over time its focus on quality and individually tailored clothing meant that it started to appeal more to middle-aged men, rather than younger men looking for fashionable clothing.

In 1988 the firm's founder, Rick Carter, set three main marketing objectives for the business:
- increase sales by £100,000 per annum
- increase market share in Bradford by 2% per annum among males aged 35 and over
- maintain a reputation for high-quality clothing

The business started to expand quickly in 1995 when Rick's younger brother, Andy, and his wife, Ying, joined the business. They both had a flair for fashionable clothing and started introducing items that appealed to younger males. Word-of-mouth advertising led to a rapid increase in sales and within 2 years the majority of customers were aged 25 and under. Ying also attempted to introduce women's clothing to the store, but its image as a men's shop meant that this was not a successful strategy.

In 1998 the Carters decided to use the high profits that they had been earning to expand.

Andy developed a marketing plan and carried out primary and secondary research in the local area, something that Rick had tended to neglect. Each department in a store and each store would operate as a profit centre, with managers being given responsibility for their own marketing budgets. A 'Carters' image based on quality and fashion at reasonably competitive prices was developed. All stock was purchased centrally, but branch and department managers were given the authority to decide on the exact items that they stocked. Three major new marketing objectives were agreed in 1998:

- open a new store every year for the next 5 years
- increase market share among under-25-year-old males by 2.5% per annum for the next 5 years
- maintain its existing market share among males over 35

Carters Clothing became a plc and within 5 years new stores had been opened in Leeds, Sheffield, Nottingham, Derby, Leicester, Hull and Doncaster. At this point, Carters chose to focus on consolidation and expanding its market share in the area, rather than opening new stores. All of these new stores proved to be very successful, particularly among the younger male market segment. However, Rick was concerned that the original customer base was being neglected. In contrast, Ying believed that the business should be seeking to expand into female clothing and accessories, as this market provided greater potential for growth.

In 2008 the Carters were approached by IPEG, an international private equity group that wanted to put money into the business. IPEG suggested that Carters should be split into three separate divisions, each running shops specialising in:
- clothing for men aged 35 and over — these shops would keep the Carters name
- clothing for younger men — these shops would be named Style
- fashionable female clothing — the female shops would be called Ipeg

IPEG had considerable experience of operating female clothes shops in the USA and male clothes shops in Germany, and wanted all three divisions to open shops in the USA and Germany. IPEG believed that the German market was similar to the UK market, so further market research would not be needed. However, the US market would require some primary market research to assess whether Carters, Style and Ipeg would be successful.

The expansion programme would be funded by IPEG in the form of loans and a 40% shareholding in Carters Clothing plc.

IPEG conducted some market research (see Appendices 1–4 below). Using this information and Carters' and IPEG's understanding of the market for clothing, new marketing objectives were agreed in 2008. These were:
- reach a 22% market share of clothing in the eight UK cities in which it has been established by 2013
- open nine new stores in the USA and nine new stores in Germany within 3 years
- achieve 200% growth in sales revenue by 2013

Appendix 1 Carter's market share data

Year	Market share of men's clothing in cities with a Carters store (%)
1998	11.6
1999	12.0
2000	12.5
2001	13.0
2002	13.6
2003	14.2
2004	14.5
2005	15.2
2006	16.1
2007	17.2
2008	18.6

Appendix 2 Results of test market in the USA

Factor	Actual (%)	Target (%)
% of male customers aged 35 and over 'very interested' in purchasing clothes from Carters	12	17
% of male customers aged 25 and under 'very interested' in purchasing clothes from Carters	28	17
% of female customers 'very interested' in purchasing clothes from Carters	12	10
% of male customers aged 35 and over who prefer 'Carters' men's fashions to those provided in existing men's stores in Boston	14	17
% of male customers aged 25 and under who prefer 'Style's' men's fashions to those provided in existing men's stores in Boston	32	17
% of female customers who prefer the 'Ipeg' female fashions to those provided in existing female stores in Boston	15	10
% of all customers who stated that the company's clothes represented 'good value for money'	56	50

Appendix 3 Market research results from Bradford store

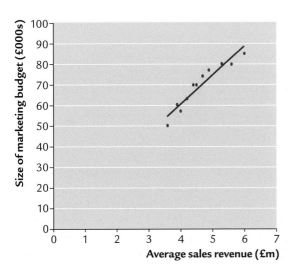

Appendix 4 Market research results from Bradford store

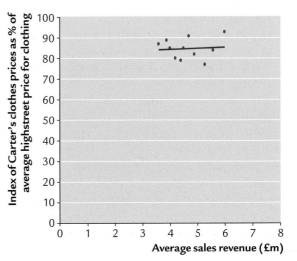

Questions

Total: 80 marks (Time: 1 hour 45 minutes)

1 Examine the possible reasons why Carters changed its marketing objectives between 1988 and 1998. *(10 marks)*

2 Consider the marketing plan that Andy developed in 1998. Discuss the problems that Carters might have experienced in implementing this marketing plan. *(13 marks)*

3 Evaluate the extent to which the marketing strategy introduced in 1998 was more risky than the marketing strategy introduced in 1988. *(17 marks)*

4 Using the data in Appendices 1–4, and any other information from the case study, evaluate whether the business is likely to achieve the new marketing objectives that were agreed between Carters and IPEG in 2008. *(40 marks)*

Chapter 11

Understanding operational objectives

This chapter examines how the operational objectives or targets of a business are linked to its corporate objectives. Examples of typical operational objectives are provided and the internal and external factors that influence them are studied. This chapter provides the foundation for subsequent chapters that study operations management strategies.

An operations management hierarchy

A firm's operational aims and objectives are the goals or targets of the operations management department or function. These aims and objectives need to be consistent with the organisation's corporate aims and objectives to ensure that a consistent set of objectives are being pursued by each department.

> ***e*** **EXAMINER'S VOICE**
>
> While 'finance', 'marketing' and 'human resources' are terms widely used in business, the operations management function can be described by many different terms: 'production department', 'manufacturing function' and 'logistics' are some of the ways in which the management of operations may be described.

As noted in earlier chapters, there is a hierarchy of aims, objectives, strategies and tactics. The hierarchy is the same in operations management as it is in all the other functional areas:
- corporate aims
- corporate objectives
- operational aims
- operational objectives
- operational strategies
- operational tactics

KEY TERMS

operations management aims: the broad, general goals of the operations management function within an organisation.

operations management objectives: the specific, focused targets of the operations management function within an organisation.

operations management strategies: long-term or medium-term plans, devised at senior management level, and designed to achieve the firm's operations management objectives.

operations management tactics: short-term operations management measures adopted to meet the needs of a short-term threat or opportunity.

Types of operational objective

Operations objectives can be classified in the ways outlined below:

Quality targets

Listed below are some examples of quality targets. Businesses will use those that suit their needs (or are most appropriate to their customers).

- **Customer satisfaction ratings.** A survey of customers can reveal customer opinions on a numerical scale (e.g. 1 to 10) or using qualitative measures (e.g. excellent – very good – good etc.). A typical operational objective is to beat last year's rating or to score a higher level of satisfaction than a rival. For example, in 2007 Waitrose came top of the Comparisat 'customer satisfaction' survey with an average weighting of 8.75, narrowly ahead of ASDA, which scored 8.64. However, customer satisfaction ratings were collected for specific aspects of the business as well as for the business as a whole. In Waitrose's case, it scored 8.9 for product quality but only 6.8 for value for money. For a company like Waitrose, whose aims are more focused on providing quality and good customer service, these specific measures can be more useful than general measures of customer satisfaction.
- **Customer complaints.** This measures the number of customers who complain or calculates them as a percentage of the total number of customers. Organisations with many branches or departments can use this measure as a way of comparing the quality of its different branches or departments.
- **Scrap rate (%).** This calculates the number of items rejected during the production process as a percentage of the number of units produced. The business sets a particular percentage scrap rate, such as 0.5%, as its target, the aim being to record a rate below this figure.
- **Punctuality.** This calculates the degree to which a business delivers its products (or provides its services) on time. It is often measured as a percentage:

$$\text{punctuality} = \frac{\text{deliveries on time}}{\text{total deliveries}} \times 100$$

This measure is used by many businesses, especially those involved in transporting goods (e.g. haulage firms) or customers (e.g. rail franchises).

FACT FILE

Is the train on time?

An example of a punctuality target is a joint target shared by National Express and Network Rail, to ensure that 90% of all train journeys arrive on time. In the first half of 2008, the rate of punctuality was 90.2%. This led to a target of 91% being set for 2009.

At this time First Great Western had the least punctual train service. Only 79.7% of its trains arrived on time during the 3 months reviewed. The most punctual operator was Chiltern Railways with 95.6% punctuality.

These figures compare favourably with BAA's performance at Heathrow airport. In the first 3 months of 2008, only 56% of flights were punctual.

Cost targets

Cost targets can come in different forms. Commonly used cost targets for businesses include:

■ **Reducing unit costs.** This is likely to be the primary aim of most businesses in terms of cost targets. Low unit costs enable a business either to keep prices low or to enjoy a higher profit margin by keeping prices at their same level. The most recent Competition Commission report on supermarkets (2007) suggested that supermarkets have used their superior bargaining power to keep down the costs of buying products such as milk and food.

■ **Reducing fixed costs.** Although most cost targets are expressed in terms of unit costs, a business might focus on cutting fixed costs. This allows a more specific focus and is often a more manageable target than a broader, unit cost reduction. Reducing fixed costs is a common aim for businesses that have recently merged or been taken over. Santander cited this as one of the main reasons for its bid to buy Alliance and Leicester Bank. Santander owns Abbey and has calculated that it can make considerable savings by merging branches of these two UK banks. It is setting a target to cut costs by £180 million by 2011.

■ **Reducing variable costs per unit.** Manufacturers and retailers constantly strive to find cheaper sources of supply or cheaper ways of manufacturing. By cutting labour and raw material costs, a business can reduce its variable costs per unit. This target can also be achieved by improving labour productivity because this means that employees' wages are spread over a higher level of output.

Volume targets

Volume targets will be closely related to the corporate aims of the business. Typical targets include:

■ **Number of items to be produced.** Nintendo recognised that the Wii is a very popular product and that it had been unable to produce sufficient units to satisfy demand. Consequently, it increased its production volume target for manufacturing from 10 million units per year to 21 million units per year between 2007 and 2008. For the financial year ending 2009, the annual volume target was increased to 25 million Wiis.

■ **Targets in individual markets.** BAT is targeting much higher volume growth overseas than it is in the UK.

■ **Percentage growth targets.** Often targets are set in terms of a particular percentage growth in output. This may vary between different parts of the organisation. In the UK, Tesco is targeting faster growth for convenience stores than for its supermarkets.

■ **Volume in comparison to other branches or organisations.** In order to compare the relative efficiency of different branches or factories, a business may set volume targets relative to those achieved in other branches or factories.

Innovation

Innovation and research and development allow businesses to gain a unique selling point. Therefore they are sometimes crucial in creating products that enable businesses to achieve high added value. Innovation targets include:

- **Spending a certain amount on research and development.** It is impossible to guarantee success from research and development, so businesses often target a certain level of expenditure on it, in the hope that this will lead to successful innovation. For example, in 2007 the Bosch Group set itself (and achieved) an objective to spend over $3.4 billion on research and development
- **Targeting research and development expenditure as a percentage of sales.** Research and development expenditure varies considerably between industries. Lilly Industries, a pharmaceutical company, has an objective of spending 19% of its annual sales on research and development as pharmaceuticals are an R&D intensive industry.
- **Achieving a certain number of patents.** The number of patents registered by a business is, to some extent, a measure of the success of research and development within that business. For example, the Bosch Group has an objective of registering 14 patents per day (over 3,000 each year).
- **Developing a particular innovation.** Invariably, businesses have a particular objective in mind for the innovation process. Currently, Toyota is one of the leading companies developing hybrid cars that can operate on different sources of power. Microsoft is developing a new system known as 'Midori'. This is based on the internet and is intended eventually to replace the Windows operating system.
- **Innovation to extend product ranges.** Many retailers focus their innovation on new styles and brands. Debenhams has developed 25 'Designers at Debenhams' ranges and 55 own-brand ranges in order to provide a choice of innovative, value-for-money products.

FOTOLIA

Efficiency

This describes the effectiveness of the production or operations process. In order to stay competitive, it is important that these processes operate well. Some examples of efficiency objectives are:

- **Labour productivity.** This is calculated by the formula:

$$\text{labour productivity} = \frac{\text{output}}{\text{number of workers employed}}$$

An increase in this figure indicates that each worker is becoming more productive and efficient.

- **Output per hour (or a measure of production over a given time period).** This is a more relevant measure of efficiency on, say, a car production line. This statistic can be compared to competitors and to the company's own performance in previous years to see if efficiency is being maintained or improved. Honda has an objective of producing a Honda Civic every 90 seconds (or 40 cars per hour) at its Swindon factory.

- **Reducing stockholding.** Retailers and manufacturers are constantly trying to save money by reducing the scale of their warehouses and the level of their stocks. Honda's target between 2005 and 2007 was to cut its level of stockholding from 1.5 days' worth of stock to 1 day's worth. It actually achieved 0.7 days.
- **Just-in-time delivery.** One of Honda's major suppliers is TDG, which delivers 20% of the components used in its Swindon factory. One of TDG's objectives is to deliver any component within 24 hours of request.
- **Speed of response and action objectives.** Office environments, such as call centres, also have targets for speed of response. Three examples of such objectives are the time taken to pick up the telephone (e.g. within 15 seconds or by the fifth ring), the number of calls answered per hour (e.g. 15 calls per hour) and the percentage of problems solved through the first call (e.g. 80% of calls).

FOTOLIA

Environmental targets

Environmental targets are becoming a much more important aspect of operations management. Typical targets are:

- reducing water pollution by a certain level or percentage
- reducing the business's carbon footprint or reducing carbon dioxide emissions
- reducing noise levels
- reducing the use of energy
- minimising waste products or materials
- increasing levels of recycling
- making products that can be easily and largely recycled
- achieving self-sufficiency in energy use
- reducing the use of non-renewable inputs
- replacing resources that have been extracted or used

Environmental issues and their impact on business are considered in much more detail in Chapter 23.

Reasons for setting operations management objectives

Why does a business set objectives for its operations management function? The reasons for setting objectives are the same, regardless of the functional area being considered. These reasons are:

- to act as a focus for decision making and effort
- to provide a yardstick against which success or failure can be measured
- to improve coordination, by giving teams and departments a common purpose
- to improve efficiency, by examining the reasons for success and failure in different areas

_e_ EXAMINER'S VOICE

The factors influencing operations management objectives are broadly the same as those affecting the objectives of the marketing, finance and human resources departments. These factors have been covered in some detail in Chapters 2 and 7. Consequently, only a brief summary is provided here.

Assessing internal influences on operations management objectives

Internal factors affecting operational objectives are those within the business, such as its workforce, resources and financial position.

Corporate objectives

The operations department must ensure that its objectives are consistent with the corporate objectives of the business. For example, Beaverbrooks has always tried to maintain a reputation for quality as a corporate objective, so it limits its jewellery to more expensive stones. In contrast, one of FW Hinds' corporate objectives is to provide affordable jewellery, and therefore its operations function must ensure a wider range of cheaper jewellery for its customers.

Finance

Operations management objectives rely on considerable expenditure on capital equipment or research and development. Therefore, a healthy financial situation is necessary.

Human resources (HR)

The skills, training and motivation of a business's human resources will have a major impact on operational objectives. If there are weaknesses in human resources, less ambitious objectives will need to be set.

Resources available

If the business is well resourced with state-of-the-art machinery and equipment, well-known brands, and a good reputation for quality and customer service, then it is much easier for it to produce high-quality products cost effectively.

The nature of the product

Some products are well suited to mass production, while others are more appropriate for individual methods of production. The type of product can also influence the ease with which high quality and good customer service can be achieved. The impact of the product and its manufacturing process on the environment will also vary according to the nature of the product. All of these factors need to be taken into account when the business is setting its operational objectives.

Assessing external influences on operational objectives

External factors are those outside the business, such as the state of the economy and the actions of competitors. These are considered in detail in Chapters 21 to 25, but a brief summary of their impact on operations management is provided below.

Market factors

The growth or decline of a market will have a major impact on a business's operations management objectives. If demand changes, the business may need to modify its production levels. If sales are declining, it may need to introduce new products to replace those in decline.

Competitors' actions and performance

Competitors' actions may influence a business, by encouraging it to introduce new products that are proving successful for the competitor. Alternatively, it may confirm that a type of product is in decline throughout the market.

Technological change

Technology has a major impact on a business's costs, the level of quality of its products, the ways in which waste can be reduced and levels of productivity within the business. These four factors are key performance targets for the operations management function of most businesses, and therefore technological change is, arguably, the most important factor for many businesses when it comes to deciding on its operational objectives.

The impact of technology on operations management is described in detail in Chapter 27 of the AS textbook.

Economic factors

Interest rates are one economic factor that has a major impact on operations management targets. The effectiveness of operations management is heavily dependent on capital investment, and if interest rates increase, this can have a negative effect on the success of the operations management function in two different ways:

- It can increase costs by increasing the rate of interest that has to be paid on any loans, therefore reducing the profitability of the investments.
- It may reduce sales levels as people cannot afford the repayments on loans and so cut back on their purchases.

Political factors

Operations management departments are often responsible for targets related to minimising production costs. This can bring them into conflict with politicians, who may disagree with the methods used to reduce costs, especially if this involves potential exploitation of workers or unsafe working conditions in factories.

Legal factors

Because of the potential for health and safety risks, the operations management function is heavily controlled by legislation.

Environmental factors

As a result of environmental factors, firms are now much more closely controlled in terms of the products that they can produce, the ingredients and raw materials that they use, and the manufacturing processes that take place in their factories.

Suppliers

Most businesses work closely with suppliers to ensure flexibility, high quality and relatively low-cost materials. A supplier that delivers these three factors can help a business to achieve its operations management targets, as they will help it to compete effectively with competitors.

PRACTICE EXERCISE   **Total: 50 marks (55 minutes)**

1 State an alternative name for an operations management department. *(2 marks)*

2 Cost reductions are often a priority for an operations management department. Identify one other department of a business that would also see cost reduction as one of its objectives. *(2 marks)*

3 Identify two different ways in which innovation can be measured as an operations management objective. *(2 marks)*

4 Explain why a business might set 'volume' targets for individual branches, as well as for the company as a whole. *(6 marks)*

5 Reducing stock levels is often an operational objective. Outline one advantage and one disadvantage of setting such an objective. *(8 marks)*

The table contains data on the performance of the operations management function of Fine Furniture plc.

Operations management performance of Fine Furniture plc, 2009

Measure of performance	Data for Fine Furniture plc	Performance of closest competitor
Customer satisfaction rating (max. = 10)	8.4	6.9
Customer complaints	1.2%	5.9%
Wastage/scrap rate	5.6%	2.8%
Punctuality of orders	95%	90%
Weekly output (items)	180	280
Number of workers	30	40
Weekly production costs	£32,400	£42,000

Fine Furniture plc's operational objectives for 2009 were as follows:
- unit costs = £175 per item
- labour productivity = 6.5 items per worker per week
- customer satisfaction rating = 7.5
- customer complaints = 2%
- punctuality of orders = 92%

Based on the data in the table and the operational objectives listed above, answer questions 6 and 7.

6 To what extent did Fine Furniture plc achieve its operational objectives?   *(15 marks)*

7 Fine Furniture plc is looking for advice on the operational objectives that it should set for 2010. In the light of your answer to question 6 and the performance of Fine Furniture's main competitor, modify the targets set for the five operational objectives. Explain the reasoning behind your thinking for each of these five targets.   *(15 marks)*

CASE STUDY   Operations at Toyota

In the UK, Toyota manufactures cars in Burnaston, Derbyshire and engines in Flintshire, north Wales. The majority of these cars and engines are exported from the UK: for example, 80% of Toyota cars manufactured in the UK are for export to Europe. Both of these factories opened in 1992.

As with any manufacturer, operations management plays a key role in Toyota's overall performance. Toyota's operational objectives can be categorised into four different areas:

- production targets
- productive efficiency
- quality and safety
- environmental objectives

Production targets

- Toyota aims to produce approximately 275,000 vehicles per annum in the UK.
- Over 340,000 engines are produced in north Wales.
- Capacity utilisation to exceed 90% — a target that was achieved in 2007.
- Toyota aims to produce 20% of the cars manufactured in the UK.

Productive efficiency and suppliers

- Toyota aims for its production to be localised (sited close to the customers). Efficiency is gained through its key production principles of standardisation, just-in-time and kaizen (continuous improvement).
- Cost savings: Toyota has targeted cost savings of £900 million from its purchasing of materials.
- Suppliers are selected on the basis of fair competition and local sourcing.
- Toyota's overall aim is to provide customers with the highest-quality vehicles at the lowest possible cost, in a timely manner and with the shortest possible lead times.

Quality

- Toyota is introducing a new, more efficient petrol engine in 2009, following an £88 million investment.
- Toyota uses a system of total quality management (TQM), where each member of the production line is responsible for the quality of their work. Each member (worker) has an objective: never to pass on poor quality to the next member. Each member can stop the production process if anything unusual is seen.

- Toyota achieved its target of receiving the Royal Society for the Prevention of Accidents (RoSPA) award for health and safety for the seventh consecutive year. In fact, it exceeded this target, as its overall performance was recognised by RoSPA as the best in the UK's entire manufacturing sector.

Environmental objectives

Toyota's philosophy is to minimise the environmental impact of its vehicles and their manufacturing process. The company's broad aims are based on the five Rs:

- **Refine** — no CFCs and use water-based paints where possible.
- **Reduce** the use of natural resources (i.e. water, gas and electricity).
- **Reuse** — 99.9% of packaging should be reused.
- **Recycle** as much material as possible.
- **Retrieve energy** — for example, exhaust gases are used to reheat other production processes.

The Toyota philosophy is continually to reduce its environmental impact. The UK plant is targeted for innovation, in order to achieve 'sustainable plant' activities and minimise its environmental impact. Its achievements since the plant opened in 1992 are to reduce its environmental impact as follows:

- energy use per vehicle — over 70%
- water use per vehicle — over 75%
- volatile organic compound emissions — 70% plus
- waste generated per vehicle — 60% plus

Toyota achieved its objectives and gained 'Big Tick awards' from 'Business in the Community' for its environmental leadership and for achieving each of the four targets identified above. In 2004 it achieved a target of zero waste to landfill sites, the first UK car manufacturer to achieve this environmental target.

Toyota's objective of being environmentally friendly also includes a tree planting programme which has led to 350,000 trees on its site.

Preliminary questions

Total: 30 marks (35 minutes)

1 State one other production target that Toyota might use and explain one reason for its use. *(4 marks)*

2 Examine why high capacity utilisation is one of Toyota's objectives. *(5 marks)*

3 Analyse two possible reasons why Toyota produces as much as 20% of the total production of cars in the UK. *(6 marks)*

4 One of Toyota's operational objectives is that: 'Suppliers are selected on the basis of fair competition and local sourcing.' Analyse the benefits of achieving this objective. *(8 marks)*

5 Explain why the achievement of quality is a key objective for Toyota. *(7 marks)*

Case study questions

Total: 30 marks (35 minutes)

1 Toyota's operational objectives place a very high priority on environmental objectives. To what extent do you believe that this emphasis on environmental objectives is helpful to Toyota's competitiveness as a car manufacturer? *(15 marks)*

2 Toyota's operational objectives are influenced by both internal and external factors. Do you consider internal or external factors to be the more important influence on Toyota's operational objectives? Justify your view. *(15 marks)*

Chapter 12

Operational strategies: scale and resource mix

In this chapter we look at the concepts of economies of scale and diseconomies of scale, and show how a business uses its understanding of these concepts in order to choose the right scale of production. The second part of the chapter examines the concepts of labour intensity and capital intensity, and explains how these concepts enable businesses to choose the optimal mix of resources.

Choosing the right scale of production

What are the benefits and problems of large-scale enterprises? As a business expands, it experiences economies of scale and diseconomies of scale.

KEY TERMS

economies of scale: the advantages that an organisation gains due to an increase in size. These cause an increase in productive efficiency (a decrease in the average cost per unit of production).

diseconomies of scale: the disadvantages that an organisation experiences due to an increase in size. These cause a decrease in productive efficiency (an increase in the average cost per unit of production).

Economies of scale

Fixed costs, such as the depreciation of machinery and administrative expenses, must be paid, regardless of the number of units that an organisation produces and sells. This enables large firms that utilise their equipment effectively to produce at much lower costs per unit.

Variable costs, such as labour and raw materials, can be combined more effectively in a large firm, also leading to a saving in unit costs.

Internal economies of scale (often abbreviated to **economies of scale**) can be classified under a number of headings. Three examples of economies are outlined below.

EXAMINER'S VOICE

Remember that, as output increases, the total costs will also increase. It is the average cost (unit cost) that falls as output rises, when economies of scale are being achieved.

Technical economies

- Modern equipment that will improve efficiency can be installed. This should lower unit costs and improve the quality and reliability of the product or service.
- Mass production (flow) techniques can be employed to improve productivity.
- Highly trained technicians can be employed to improve the reliability of the production process.
- Large-scale transportation can reduce distribution costs per unit.
- The purchase of computer systems can improve efficiency in both production and administration.
- Improvements in communication systems using new technology can enhance customer service and the working environment, improving the company's operations and its reputation.

> **DID YOU KNOW?**
>
> Technical economies of scale are particularly important in mass production industries such as textiles and cars. Small firms in these markets need to compete on factors other than price because they cannot match the low costs obtained by the largest firms.

Specialisation economies

- Large firms can afford to employ specialists with particular skills. In smaller organisations, staff tend to take on a wider variety of tasks, and specialist skills, when needed, are bought from outside at a relatively high price.
- Production techniques can be adapted to encourage division of labour (specialisation) in large firms.
- A small firm is unlikely to be able to pay a high enough salary to attract the best staff, so larger firms should be more efficient. Training to improve specialist skills is also easier in large firms.
- If staff are able to specialise, they are likely to become even more skilled in their role, again increasing the efficiency of the firm.

> **DID YOU KNOW?**
>
> In recent years, Tesco has removed control of distribution (transportation) from many of its suppliers and taken control itself. Tesco used to pay suppliers a price that included delivery to its stores or warehouses, but it found that smaller suppliers were too small to benefit from cheap transport. Tesco now uses its specialisation in transportation to save money. It buys the supplies at the factory gate price (FGP), picks up the goods from the factory and delivers the goods itself. Over two-thirds of Tesco's supplies are now purchased in this way, with only the very large suppliers delivering directly to Tesco. Tesco's huge buying power also means that it can buy additional transport cheaply at short notice, giving it a competitive and flexible system.

Purchasing economies

- Large firms can buy in bulk. This reduces costs because suppliers can produce in large quantities and thus lower their own costs.
- Suppliers may offer greater discounts in order to guarantee a contract with a large customer. In October 2008, Tesco and ASDA decided to focus on low-price competition, in response to rising unemployment and negative economic growth. To support Tesco's aim, it met with its suppliers and told them that it expected them to accept lower prices and/or give Tesco a longer credit period. B&Q was able to cut its costs by 4% by bargaining with suppliers, and having specialist purchasing departments.

e EXAMINER'S VOICE

There are many economies of scale. Because the AQA Business Studies specification is concerned with the principle rather than with details, it is only necessary to recognise the three economies of scale described above (technical, specialisation and purchasing). However, unit costs can also fall because of other economies, as outlined below.

Marketing economies

Large firms can use more expensive media that reach more customers in a more persuasive way. This can both increase the effectiveness of the advertising and reduce unit costs. Large firms can also do more market research, so that they understand markets more fully than smaller competitors.

Financial economies

Because they are considered to be safer, large companies should be able to get loans more easily and at lower rates of interest. They will find it easier to access funds through other sources, such as retained profits and shareholders.

Research and development economies

Large companies can afford to devote more money to innovation and research and development. This expenditure should enable a business to discover new products or to find easier ways to produce goods.

Social and welfare economies

Larger companies are able to provide social facilities such as sports clubs, canteens and relaxation areas. Welfare facilities such as medical care, health insurance and pension funds may also improve conditions for staff. These benefits will make it easier to recruit workers and should improve morale among existing staff, leading to a more highly motivated workforce with lower levels of absenteeism and a lower rate of labour turnover.

Managerial and administrative economies

Large companies can employ the best managers and adopt more cost-effective administration procedures. These economies should reduce the overheads of the business and thus improve its competitiveness.

FACT FILE

TV advertising now cheaper

Advertising on television has fallen in price according to new research from media buyer Zenith Optimedia.

The company said television advertising has fallen by almost a third in real terms over the last decade, as a result of three main factors:

- declining demand for terrestrial airtime
- financial pressure on marketing budgets
- the increased popularity of internet advertising

Researchers have calculated that 30 seconds of television advertising now costs just £4.81 per thousand adults. Allowing for inflation, this is 29% cheaper than the peak year of 2000. In contrast, radio advertising typically costs £2.80 per thousand adults.

However, a report by accountants PriceWaterhouseCoopers suggests that there are still many benefits from television advertising. The report found that when a company reduces its share of television advertising, there is a 78% chance this will damage brand awareness.

Source: adapted from an article by Rowena Mason in the *Daily Telegraph*, 11 November 2008.

Diseconomies of scale

As organisations grow, they may suffer disadvantages that lead to a lowering of efficiency and higher unit costs of production. These are known as **diseconomies of scale** or **internal diseconomies of scale**. Some examples are given below.

Coordination diseconomies

- There may be a loss of control by management as an organisation becomes more complex, particularly if the organisation becomes more geographically spread or management experiences an increasing workload.
- Individuals are less likely to follow organisational policies if the level of control is reduced. This happens in larger organisations because managers have larger spans of control and there are more levels of hierarchy.
- Large firms often have more rigid and inflexible policies. These are imposed to limit the loss of control described above but reduce the ability to respond quickly to changing customer needs.

Communication diseconomies

- Too many levels of hierarchy in a business can reduce the effectiveness of communication. Messages can be distorted (as in Chinese whispers) and it is possible that communications do not reach everyone.
- Difficulties also occur as spans of control widen. It becomes much more difficult for managers to meet with subordinates.
- In large firms, inappropriate methods of communication are likely to be used, as standardised, large-scale approaches are more common.
- Employees who do not receive, or are not involved in, communications may feel unvalued and demotivated.

Motivation diseconomies

- It is more difficult to assess the needs of many individuals. Even if motivational methods are used, it is less likely that the managers will know the best approach for each subordinate.
- In large firms there may be less time for recognition and reward.
- Large hierarchies create feelings of distance between decision makers and employees.
- Large firms often have the financial wealth to introduce schemes to motivate employees, but they can lack the management time to provide recognition.

These problems occur in firms of all sizes. They are only diseconomies of scale if they have been caused by the large size of the organisation rather than by other factors, such as poor management.

Other diseconomies of scale

Other diseconomies of scale include the following:

- **Technical diseconomies.** Production on a very large scale can become difficult to organise.
- **Excessive bureaucracy.** As organisations grow, the number of levels of management increases and this may slow down decision making.
- **Staff problems.** Industrial relations problems and higher staff turnover and absences may result from the factors described above.
- **Less flexibility.** This means that firms may not continue to meet the changing needs of their customers.

FACT FILE

Scale of production in the car industry

The huge size of some car plants led to diseconomies of scale in the 1970s. Poor coordination meant huge wastage of materials and poor quality control. The difficulties in communication and the boring nature of jobs led to many days lost through absenteeism or disputes between workers and managers. These problems have been reduced by modifying jobs and giving workers more responsibility. Car manufacturers have also reduced the size of individual factories.

Car manufacturers need to find a balance between economies and diseconomies of scale. Professor Garel Rees at the Centre for Automotive Industry Research believes that car firms need to make 3 million cars a year to be cost-competitive. He forecasts that firms, such as MG Rover, Fiat and even Peugeot Citroën, are unlikely to survive unless they merge with other manufacturers.

FACT FILE

Economies of scale in further education

A number of mergers between colleges have taken place in the last 10 years. This led to a government project to find out whether the creation of larger colleges led to economies of scale.

In the context of further education provision, the report identified the following potential **economies of scale**:

- **Technical economies.** If class sizes increase, the costs of the teacher, classroom and materials would remain the same, and other costs might increase only slightly. Therefore the more efficient use of resources and equipment means that average cost of the course falls as student numbers rise.
- **Managerial economies.** Larger colleges benefit from having specialist managers and being able to attract more expert staff.
- **Marketing economies.** Some costs associated with publicity and promotion are the same regardless of size: for example, average advertising costs fall as size increases.
- **Purchasing economies.** Larger colleges may be able to achieve savings through bulk buying.
- **Financial economies.** Larger colleges may be able to exploit improved access to capital funds and better terms from financial organisations.
- **Risk-bearing economies.** Larger colleges may be able to adapt to changes in policy, local labour markets or their curriculum.

The report also pointed out the **diseconomies of scale** facing very large colleges in terms of communication and coordination, particularly those colleges operating on multiple sites.

The report examined the connection between unit costs and the quality of the education received, as measured by Ofsted inspections. It concluded: 'There is no relationship between college size and financial health. There is no evidence to suggest a relationship between quality and scale.'

Source: report by Laura Payne for the Department for Innovation, Universities and Skills, October 2008.

Table 12.1 Economies and diseconomies of scale

Units of output	Fixed costs (£)	Variable costs (£)	Total costs (£)	Average (unit) costs (£)
0	240	0	240	–
1	240	200	440	440
2	240	340	580	290
3	240	420	660	220
4	240	476	716	179
5	240	520	760	152
6	240	570	810	135
7	240	642	882	126
8	240	736	976	122
9	240	849	1,089	121
10	240	1,000	1,240	124
11	240	1,201	1,441	131
12	240	1,476	1,716	143

Economies and diseconomies of scale and unit costs

Table 12.1 quantifies the effect of both economies of scale and diseconomies of scale. It shows how, initially, the unit (average) costs of production fall as the company increases its output. This occurs for three main reasons:

- The fixed costs stay the same (and so fixed costs per unit fall) as output rises.
- Variable costs increase at a slower rate because division of labour enables the organisation to combine its factors of production more efficiently.
- The firm can benefit from the economies of scale described earlier.

However, once the output rises beyond 9 units, diseconomies of scale outweigh economies of scale. Although economies such as bulk buying may be helping to lower unit costs, problems such as coordination are having a larger impact and so, overall, the unit costs are beginning to rise.

Firms use information on economies and diseconomies of scale in order to plan their most efficient size, but exact guidelines cannot be established and opinions change over time. Thirty years ago, the emphasis was on large-scale operations to get the benefits of economies of scale; in the last 25 years, however, greater flexibility has been demanded, so many firms have demerged or split themselves into smaller operations to avoid diseconomies of scale. For example, Racal, the company that created Vodafone, viewed any operation with more than 800 staff as too large and had a policy of splitting any division that exceeded this size. This led to Vodafone being split away from Racal Tacticom, the division that dealt with mobile communications for military purposes.

Choosing the optimal mix of resources: capital and labour intensity

Chapter 3 of the AS textbook looked at the resources used by a business to produce outputs through the transformation process. The four resources used, known as the **factors of production**, are:

- enterprise
- labour
- land
- capital

Enterprise and land tend to be unique. However, labour and capital are often interchangeable, so a business must decide whether its transformation process or production methods will be predominantly based on the use of capital or the use of labour.

Factors influencing the choice between capital-intensive and labour-intensive production

A business will weigh up a number of factors before deciding whether to use capital- or labour-intensive production. The most significant factors are as follows.

The method of production
In general, mass production on a large scale, such as at a car plant, requires capital equipment. Machinery can produce more quickly and consistently than a human being. Consequently, large-scale production usually means that a firm will choose capital-intensive production methods.

In contrast, if products are specifically designed for the consumer, then labour-intensive methods are more likely. The success of the business will depend more on the workers than on machinery.

The skills and efficiency of the factors of production
A business that depends on the skills of its workers (such as a hairdresser's or a theatre company) is more likely to use labour-intensive methods. However, if machinery or other forms of capital can greatly lower unit costs, or produce a more consistent, high-quality product, then capital-intensive methods will be employed.

KEY TERMS

capital-intensive production: methods of production that use a high level of capital equipment in comparison to other inputs, such as labour. A fully automated factory (e.g. a Fiat car plant) and a nuclear power station are examples of capital-intensive production.

labour-intensive production: methods of production that use high levels of labour in comparison to capital equipment. Many service industries, such as retailing, restaurants and call centres, use a large number of people in comparison to equipment.

The relative costs of labour and capital

Labour is relatively expensive in western Europe as compared to other parts of the world. As a result, firms that operate in this area will benefit from replacing labour with capital equipment. Ever fewer people in western Europe are now employed on production lines, as firms have automated production (replaced workers with machinery). In other parts of the world, labour is much cheaper to use and so production lines are more labour intensive. This situation has led to multinational corporations moving production from western Europe to other parts of the world.

Another consideration is the reliability of labour and capital. Industrial relations problems in industries such as car manufacturing led firms to decide that capital-intensive production methods were more cost effective because disruptions to production were very expensive. Conversely, unreliable equipment may encourage firms to choose labour-intensive production.

The size and financial position of a business

Capital equipment is expensive to buy. It may not be possible for small businesses or firms with cash-flow difficulties to purchase the equipment needed for capital-intensive methods. As a consequence, these firms will choose labour-intensive production.

The product or service

The more standardised a product, the greater are the advantages of capital-intensive production because machinery can produce vast quantities at low unit costs.

The customer

If customers want personal contact, this may limit the scope for capital intensity. The banking industry has lowered its costs by automating many of its processes, but many of its customers prefer the more sociable nature of a branch to the automated cashpoint. NatWest has used its 'labour intensity' as a selling point in its marketing campaigns.

 FILE

Portakabin Ltd

Portakabin Ltd uses a mixture of capital- and labour-intensive methods. Capital intensity is used to provide the basic structure and standard fittings for a building. At the same time, capital-intensive methods are used to lay the foundations for the new building at the customer's site. The items are then delivered to the site, where more labour-intensive methods are used to add the special internal features required by the customer.

FACT FILE

Computer games — from labour intensive to capital intensive

Ian Higgins, former chief executive of Empire Interactive, a games publisher and developer, says that when the company was founded in 1987 its first game cost £4,000 to produce. By 2008 new generation games titles were costing between £4 million and £6 million to develop. Production has changed from being labour intensive to capital intensive.

'The rise in costs has been driven by technology,' according to Higgins. 'You used to be able to produce a game with a couple of people — a programmer and an artist. These days you need a team of 20, 30 or even 40. That includes programmers, artists, sound engineers, producers and so on.' However, it is the need for more sophisticated capital in the form of new technology that has been the main feature of the changes in the industry. Although a new game requires 10 to 20 times as many people, the overall costs have risen by a multiple of 1,000 to 1,500. These vast changes reflect the much greater emphasis on state-of-the-art capital equipment

Despite potential diseconomies of scale, large firms can gain from technological economies of scale. They also have stronger bargaining power when dealing with retailers.

In 2000 there were over 300 computer games publishers in the UK, but the need for high technology and cost effectiveness means that individuals with bright ideas are excluded from the market, unless they can get employment with a publisher.

The research organisation Screen Digest has compared the market share needed by a single game to reach breakeven over the last 15 years. Table 12.2 shows the results of this research.

Table 12.2 Analysis of required breakeven market share of worldwide computer games market

Year	1993	1998	2003	2008
Size of market ($m)	9,108	14,997	18,471	23,901
Wholesale market ($m)	4,910	8,085	9,959	12,886
Development spend ($m)	982	1,617	1,992	2,577
Typical development budget per game ($m)	1.125	2.25	5.0	8.0
Breakeven market share	0.11%	0.14%	0.25%	0.31%

The need to spend $8 million to develop a game has led to the removal of small firms from this market, and even some large businesses are thinking twice before committing $8 million to an investment that has an increasingly high risk of failure.

Sources: Empire Interactive; Screen Digest.

PRACTICE EXERCISE   Total: 50 marks (50 minutes)

1 Distinguish between internal economies of scale and internal diseconomies of scale.   *(4 marks)*

2 At what level of output is the company in Table 12.1 at maximum productive efficiency?   *(2 marks)*

3 Using Table 12.1, calculate the fixed costs per unit at the following levels of output:
   a 4 units   *(2 marks)*
   b 12 units   *(2 marks)*

4 Analyse two possible economies of scale that might occur in a national newspaper publisher, or another firm of which you have knowledge. *(10 marks)*

5 Analyse two possible diseconomies of scale that might occur in a national newspaper publisher, or the firm that you chose in question 4. *(10 marks)*

6 Distinguish between labour-intensive production and capital-intensive production. *(4 marks)*

7 Explain two factors that would influence a farmer when deciding whether to use labour-intensive production or capital-intensive production. *(6 marks)*

8 Read the Fact File on computer games. To what extent was it inevitable that firms providing computer games would change from being labour intensive to capital intensive? *(10 marks)*

CASE STUDY The Wal-Mart effect

TOPFOTO

'The Wal-Mart effect touches the lives of literally every American every day. Wal-Mart reshapes the economic life of the towns and cities where it opens stores; it also reshapes the economic life of the United States — a single company that steadily, silently, purposefully moves the largest economy in history. Wal-Mart has become the most powerful, most influential company in the world. Who knew shopping would turn out to be so important?' (from Charles Fishman, *The Wal-Mart Effect*)

In his book Charles Fishman describes how Wal-Mart changes prices in the global economy. It forces competitors to reduce prices to stay in business and forces suppliers to reduce prices. Wal-Mart's selling, general and administrative costs are maintained at an unheard-of level of only 17.5% of sales, giving the retail giant the opportunity to charge customers the lowest possible price. 'Save Money. Live Better' is Wal-Mart's new slogan as it has attempted to re-create its image.

Purchasing economies of scale can have a huge impact on costs. ASDA used to pay $14 per metre for 50,000 metres of material to make men's jeans. After the company was taken over by Wal-Mart, purchasing rose to 6 million metres per annum and the price fell to $4.77 per metre. ASDA also benefited from technical economies when the Wal-Mart takeover took place. Analysts at Deutsche Bank estimated that ASDA saved £150 million when it linked into the Wal-Mart IT system.

One of the reasons that Wal-Mart and other dominant players have such bargaining power is because they concentrate buying in just a few firms' hands and they buy in huge volumes. Bain and Company research in the USA, for example, studied 38 publicly traded companies that sell more than 10% of their product through Wal-Mart. The companies included American Greetings (13% of sales to Wal-Mart), Atari (26%), Clorox (27%), Del Monte (29%), Kimberly-Clark (13%), Hasbro (21%), Leapfrog Enterprises (28%) and Revlon (21%).

In the USA, Wal-Mart claims such a huge share of sales in some markets that many companies simply have no choice but to woo the giant. Wal-Mart holds 36% of the market for dog food, 32% for disposable nappies, 30% for film, 26% for toothpaste, and 21% for pain remedies. Wal-Mart is the place where consumers buy 32% of their wireless phone handsets, 37% of their DVDs, and 22% of consumer electronics. Every supplier knows the rule of thumb: to the volume leader goes the bargaining power.

However, Wal-Mart, the world's largest retailer, admitted its one-size-fits-all business model had failed in Germany, as it announced its withdrawal from the country at a cost of $1 billion (£540 million), selling its 85 loss-making German superstores to its rival Metro at significantly less than the value of the assets.

Ironically, this failure was attributed to a lack of economies of scale. Although Wal-Mart is currently the world's largest company, its limited scale of operations in Germany meant that it could not compete with the low prices of German supermarkets such as Lidl and Aldi.

The humiliating retreat means that Wal-Mart's sole remaining European outpost is in the UK, where it owns ASDA. It will also serve as yet another warning to ambitious retail executives — not least Sir Terry Leahy at Tesco — that dominance in one market is not always easy to replicate overseas.

Wal-Mart's business model, which has been increasingly criticised even in the USA, involves driving down the prices of groceries and other general merchandise through putting pressure on suppliers and keeping out unions.

But in Germany, where domestic 'value retailers' already dominate the grocery market, it found customers were turned off by the early designs of its stores, by a too-narrow range of produce, and by the famous 'greeters', who welcome shoppers to the store and are instructed to smile when within a certain distance of a customer. It also became embroiled in labour disputes that led to strikes.

Robert Buchanan, a retail analyst at the US brokerage AG Edwards, said that he was pleased Wal-Mart had decided to cut its losses. 'They sent a lot of people over who didn't know the German market, so it makes sense to focus on countries where they have had more success,' he said.

Wal-Mart bought into Germany 8 years ago, but its vice-chairman, Michael Duke, said the German market was already highly competitive and Wal-Mart had proved unable to generate the economies of scale it needed to drive prices below those of competitors. The company also blamed high unemployment and weak consumer spending in Germany for making the market even harder to crack.

'As we focus our efforts on where we can have the greatest impact on our growth and return on investment strategies, it has become increasingly clear that in Germany's business environment it would be difficult for us to obtain the scale and results we desire,' Mr Duke said.

The retreat from Germany is Wal-Mart's second international capitulation this year, after it sold its South Korean stores in May. There is speculation that it may also sell out of Argentina. However, this is becoming less likely as Wal-Mart announced in December 2008 that it is buying a large shareholding in D&S in Chile — a supermarket that has a 32% market share in the country. This suggests that Wal-Mart is learning from its European lesson. In Germany its market share peaked at 13%, meaning that it did not have the scale or infrastructure to match its German competitors. Wal-Mart's infrastructure in South and Central America is much stronger, given that it already operates stores in Argentina, Brazil, Costa Rica, El Salvador, Guatemala, Honduras, Mexico, Nicaragua and Puerto Rico.

The company has 2,700 stores in 14 countries outside the USA, representing 40% of the group's total stores but only 20% of its revenues. Lee Scott, the chief executive, has promised expansion abroad as the company reaches saturation in the USA.

A spokeswoman reaffirmed Wal-Mart's commitment to ASDA, saying the business had clawed back some market share in recent months, reaching 17.3%. It has managed to hold off Sainsbury's, which came within a whisker of regaining the number two spot earlier this year. However, ASDA, which has missed sales and profit targets in the past year, has not lived up to Wal-Mart's hopes. The US group's dream of mounting a challenge to Tesco's market leadership petered out when it was barred from bidding for Safeway in 2003 by the competition authorities. However, the well-established brand name of ASDA and the higher profit margins of UK supermarkets, in comparison to their German equivalents, have encouraged Wal-Mart to maintain its efforts to penetrate the UK market.

Sources: Charles Fishman, *The Wal-Mart Effect*; an article by William Marquand in *BNET*, 11 December 2006; and various newspaper articles in 2008.

Preliminary questions

Total: 15 marks (20 minutes)

1 Briefly analyse why Wal-Mart has enjoyed more success in the UK than in Germany. *(7 marks)*

2 Why might Wal-Mart be more successful in Chile than in Europe? *(8 marks)*

Case study questions

Total: 30 marks (40 minutes)

1 Generally, businesses become more capital-intensive as they grow. Wal-Mart has recently become the world's largest business. Wal-Mart is recognised as a labour-intensive business. Discuss the reasons for the apparent contradictions between these three statements. *(15 marks)*

2 Using the information in the case study and your understanding of business, evaluate the significance of economies and diseconomies of scale in accounting for Wal-Mart's success in the USA and its failure in Germany. *(15 marks)*

Chapter 13

Operational strategies: innovation

This chapter introduces the concepts of innovation and research and development, and identifies those business activities that fall within these descriptions. The benefits of, and reasons for, innovation and R&D are investigated. These factors are contrasted with the risks and problems associated with innovation and R&D. The methods by which a business can improve the likelihood of successful innovation are then examined. The need to integrate innovation with other business functions is investigated through an examination of its links with other functional areas. The chapter concludes by looking at the factors that influence levels of spending on innovation and R&D.

What is innovation?

The government department responsible for innovation is the Department for Innovation, Universities and Skills (DIUS). The department conducts an innovation survey every 2 years. In its latest innovation survey in 2007, it defines a business as 'innovation active' if it is engaged in any of the following:

- introduction of a new or significantly improved product (good or service)
- introduction of a new process for making or supplying a product
- expenditure in areas such as research and development, linked to innovation activities
- training or the acquisition of external knowledge that is linked to innovation activities
- introduction of new machinery and equipment for the purpose of innovation activities

Based on the definition above, 64% of UK enterprises surveyed were 'innovation active'.

It can be seen that research and development is an element of innovation, as the latter term incorporates a variety of activities, one of which is research and development. For this reason, the benefits and problems associated with innovation will, by and large, also apply to research and development, and vice versa.

KEY TERMS

innovation: the successful exploitation of new ideas. Innovation enables businesses to compete effectively in an increasingly competitive global environment.

research and development (R&D): the scientific investigation necessary to discover new products or manufacturing processes, and the procedures necessary to ensure that these new products and processes are suited to the needs of the market.

EXAMINER'S VOICE

Do not confuse research and development with market research. Market research involves finding out what consumers want and developing a product to meet that need. R&D, which often starts in a laboratory, means that the product or process is invented or discovered and then its commercial applications are investigated. As a consequence, products developed from market research are often described as 'market led', while those arising from R&D are 'product led'.

The DIUS also recognises an additional form of innovation: **strategic innovation**. Strategic innovation takes place when a business undertakes major changes in its management practices, business structure, organisational structure or marketing strategy in order to improve its competitiveness.

Table 13.1 shows the percentage of UK businesses that fall into these categories of innovator.

Table 13.1 Main types of innovation in the UK

Type of innovation	Percentage of UK businesses*
Innovation active	**64**
of which:	
Product innovator	22
Product innovator — goods	14
Product innovator — services	18
Process innovator	12
Innovation-related expenditure, such as research and development	55
Strategic innovator	**31**

*Figures and sub-totals do not add up to 100% because organisations may fit into more than one category.

Source: DIUS, *Persistence and Change in Innovation*, December 2008

Innovation activities

As indicated earlier, a variety of activities are recognised by the DIUS as examples of innovation. Figure 13.1 provides a more detailed breakdown of the main innovation activities by type.

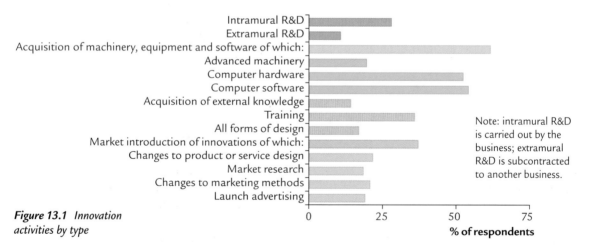

Note: intramural R&D is carried out by the business; extramural R&D is subcontracted to another business.

Figure 13.1 Innovation activities by type

Figure 13.1 shows that the category 'acquisition of machinery, equipment and software' is dominated by computer hardware and software manufacturers. The category 'market introduction of innovations', however, shows a more even spread across the four sub-categories indicated. Comparisons with previous years reveal that more firms are active in applying design to the market than previously.

Benefits and purposes of innovation and R&D

Innovation and R&D are carried out for a variety of purposes:

- **Improve quality.** Innovation and R&D may help a business to develop higher-quality products that will be more attractive to consumers, leading to increased sales and a better reputation.
- **Enter new markets.** Innovation can help businesses to enter new markets. It is a key element of product portfolio planning and enables firms to identify opportunities in new markets through a combination of product-based and market-based innovation.
- **Increase value added.** Innovation and R&D help firms to develop products or services that have a unique selling point (USP), allowing a business to achieve a higher degree of product differentiation. Products with a USP usually sell in higher quantities and their uniqueness tends to lead to more inelastic demand, allowing the organisation to increase price and so earn a higher profit margin. In addition, if innovation or R&D uncovers a new invention, this can be patented, giving the business a guaranteed monopoly of manufacture for a number of years. Analysis by the UK and US governments shows a high correlation between the increase in sales achieved by a business, its level of R&D spending and the number of patents that the company acquires. This in turn allows a business to achieve higher value added.
- **Increase product range.** Innovation and R&D can allow a business to update its product range continually and stay ahead of competitors. In rapidly changing, technologically advanced industries, innovation is vital in presenting new products to the market. In addition, innovation enables firms to balance their product portfolio through the creation of new growth products to take over from those that have reached the decline stage of the product life cycle.
- **Reduce costs.** Innovation is often designed to improve processes: that is, to improve the efficiency of production methods. Innovative ways of producing goods reduce the average cost of production and help competitiveness.
- **Improve flexibility.** Greater flexibility is now an expectation of most customers, particularly in b2b (business-to-business) marketing. As a consequence, a great deal of innovation is designed to find ways of enabling a business to adapt quickly to changing circumstances.
- **Increase capacity.** High capacity utilisation helps a business to maintain a reputation for good customer service while controlling its fixed costs. In 2007, 30% of firms surveyed cited the need to increase capacity as a reason for innovation.
- **Meet regulations.** Innovation enables a business to respond to changes in UK and EU laws that necessitate changes to businesses' products and production methods. UK businesses expanding beyond the EU may need to make changes in accordance with the legislation of the countries in which they are trading.
- **Reduce environmental impact.** The environment is considered to be a stakeholder of any business, so a business may innovate in order to reduce any negative environmental effects of its activities.

Although it would not be a reason for innovation, a business's human resources management may benefit. The opportunity to create new products and ideas provides a stimulating working environment and therefore motivates employees. This may improve labour productivity, reduce turnover and make it easier for a business to recruit workers.

Table 13.2 summarises the main purposes and benefits of innovation for UK firms.

Reason for innovation	% of firms stating that this factor is of 'high' importance
Improve quality	53
Enter new markets	48
Increase value added	45
Increase product range	43
Reduce costs	37
Improve flexibility	30
Increase capacity	30
Meet regulations	30
Reduce environmental impact	25

Table 13.2
Main purposes and benefits of innovation for UK firms

Source: DIUS, *Persistence and Change in Innovation*, December 2008

Problems of innovation and R&D

Although innovation and R&D bring many benefits, businesses need to be aware of the risks and potential pitfalls.

- **Uncertainty.** There is no guarantee that innovation and R&D expenditure will lead to new products and processes. Some projects, such as research into the common cold, have still not generated successful outcomes. The level of uncertainty in R&D in particular makes it much more difficult to justify the high levels of spending that are often needed.
- **Operational difficulties.** These are common with new products, processes and ideas. Companies often suffer setbacks when new products are released or innovative processes introduced, particularly if they are in a hurry to release them and have had to rush their testing processes. In industries where product safety is vital, a hasty action can destroy a firm's reputation and the trust of its customers.
- **Competition.** Innovation spending may encourage rivals to undertake similar activities. This will merely lead to increased costs for both firms, but with no competitive advantage being gained.
- **Generic products.** In industries such as pharmaceuticals, there is a growing tendency towards generic products. These 'copies' are produced cheaply as soon as the patent expires. In industries where patent protection is more difficult to achieve, this can negate the benefits of innovation and R&D. A company may spend millions developing an innovative product, only for a rival to market a similar product at a much cheaper price because the rival has not had to spend so much money on R&D.

In the UK government's most recent survey, the main factors limiting innovation were:

- innovation costs
- economic risks
- costs of finance
- government regulations
- availability of finance
- market dominated by established businesses
- uncertain demand

However, no single factor was identified as a problem by more than 12% of the companies surveyed.

How to improve the chances of successful innovation

Innovation will always involve risk because there are no guaranteed results. However, a firm can improve the likelihood of its innovation and R&D being successful by taking the following actions:

- **Protection.** Make sure that any results are protected as soon as possible and in as many countries as possible through the use of copyrights, trademarks and patents. This protection will give the firm sole ownership of the idea and will also give it time to refine the product.
- **Early planning.** Plan projects early rather than late. A business should be aware of its existing products, particularly those that are approaching (but not yet in) the decline stage of their life cycles. At this point, the business should undertake innovation so that it always has a product in the maturity stage of the product life cycle.
- **Developing a supportive culture.** Create a business culture that is supportive of innovation and encourage all employees to use their initiative. Quality circles are a classic Japanese approach to development, encouraging lots of small changes rather than relying on a major discovery. This culture must include the management of finance. In times of difficulty, innovation and R&D are often the first areas of spending to be cut because of the uncertainty of returns. However, successful innovation and R&D can be the ideal way to overcome problems.
- **Maintaining secrecy.** Attempt to maintain high levels of secrecy so that ideas cannot be copied. This will often involve signing confidentiality agreements with suppliers and other business partners.
- **Remembering the consumer.** Pay careful attention to the attractiveness of the idea to consumers. Many inventions have not been developed further by their inventors because they did not recognise the potential or were unable to persuade consumers to buy the product.

> **DID YOU KNOW?**
>
> Have you ever dreamed of owning Harry Potter's invisibility cloak but thought it was a technical impossibility? Think again. Scientists in Japan have developed an invisibility cloak.
>
> The cloak has cameras built into the back and front of the garment. The material acts as a screen and the image from the cameras at the front of the cloak is projected on to the rear of the cloak and vice versa.
>
> The only problem is that passers-by see a disembodied head. The scientists are working on an invisibility balaclava to overcome this problem.
>
> Unfortunately, commercial applications have not yet been identified.

FILE

R&D for tea

Even the humble cup of tea is subject to rigorous research. Unilever, producer of PG Tips, undertook a major R&D programme investigating the ideal teabag shape for optimum infusion of the tea. This R&D led to the introduction of the pyramid teabag — a process that took 4 years to complete.

On 14 May 2008 Unilever, the world's biggest tea company, opened its global R&D Centre of Excellence for Drinks at the Colworth Science Park in the UK. Unilever has an annual R&D budget of €50 million.

Unilever's R&D capabilities in drinks to date have supported the rise of Lipton to become the world's number one tea brand (and the world's second largest branded beverage) and that of PG tips, the UK's number one tea brand, with innovations like the pyramid teabag, Ready-To-Drink teas, tea products for slimmers, and natural leaf tea that brews in cold water, so that consumers can make fresh ice tea without having to wait hours for it to cool down. Other drinks innovations based on these R&D capabilities include Flora cholesterol-lowering milk and yoghurt drinks, Knorr Vie fruit and vegetable mini-drinks and the soy-based fruit juice Adez.

Source: Unilever website: www.unilever.com.

R&D spending in UK businesses

The importance of science and technology has been recognised by the Department for Business, Enterprise and Regulatory Reform (DBERR). DBERR publishes an annual survey — the R&D Scoreboard — in which it examines the role of R&D in improving UK business efficiency.

Some 40% of R&D in the UK is undertaken by the pharmaceutical and biotech sectors. However, in recent years a major increase in R&D has taken place in computer software.

Overall, the UK still lags behind countries such as the USA in terms of R&D spending. The UK's major firms invest only 2% of their sales revenue in R&D, compared with 5% for similar firms in the USA. GlaxoSmithKline, in seventh place globally, is the only UK business in the world's top 25 R&D spenders.

Table 13.3
Annual R&D
spending, 2007

UK top 5	R&D spending (£bn)	International top five	R&D spending (£bn)
GlaxoSmithKline	3.5	Pfizer	3.9
AstraZeneca	2.0	Ford	3.7
BAE Systems	1.2	Johnson and Johnson	3.6
BT	1.1	Microsoft	3.6
Unilever	0.6	DaimlerChrysler	3.5

Source: DBERR R&D Scoreboard, 2007

FACT FILE

R&D at Apple

The Apple iPod is a product that arose from R&D. However, rather than rest on its laurels, Apple has increased the iPod's capacity from 5 gigabytes to 10 and then on to 120, and introduced a smaller model. Meanwhile, while its competitors were still trying to catch up with the iPod, it launched the iPhone.

Apple recognises that good product design is important. Innovation and R&D can deliver a well-designed product and can provide a number of benefits, such as:

- improving the durability and reliability of the product
- improving the appearance of the product and making it more fashionable
- enhancing the convenience of use for consumers
- allowing a firm to keep within the law by modifying products to meet new legislation, such as the need for more environmentally friendly products
- reducing the cost of manufacture by modifying production processes or designing a product that is easier to make

DID YOU KNOW?

Formula 1 racing is very R&D intensive, as car manufacturers use their racing cars to test advanced techniques and equipment. In 2008 Toyota had the biggest budget for Formula 1, spending £445.6 million.

Other big spenders were McLaren $433.3m, Ferrari $414.9m, Honda $398.1m and Renault $393.8m. Toyota sees all of this money as spending on 'innovation', of which over 72% ($313 million) was spent on activities defined as R&D.

The belief that economic downturn hits innovation is borne out by Honda's decision to withdraw from Formula 1 racing in 2009. Other teams are planning to cut their budgets.

The implications of innovation for other functional areas

Finance

Innovation tends to be an expensive undertaking. For this reason the finance department must be aware of, and in agreement with, any plans for new innovation. It is almost certain that new sources of finance will be needed to support the innovation process.

The finance department will carry out investment appraisal in order to assess the likely results of innovation. If an innovation or R&D project is approved by the finance department, there are still major repercussions for cash flow. In some industries, such as motor vehicles and pharmaceuticals, it can take as much as 8 years of innovation before a product is launched. However, these returns can be very impressive. In 2008 AstraZeneca made a profit of £9 billion from sales of £29 billion because many of its products are protected by patents.

Operational strategies

Marketing

The marketing department will be affected in two ways. First, market research will be needed to ascertain whether the innovation project is likely to appeal to customers. Second, innovation is often linked to the product life cycle, so the innovation and marketing functions must cooperate. The marketing department's experience will help a firm to ascertain the normal time that it takes to modify a product or develop and release a new one. With this information, firms can plan the timing of extension strategies and new product launches.

Figure 13.2 shows the link between R&D and extension strategies. The company forecasts that, at point A, sales of its existing product will reach the decline stage of the product life cycle. The dotted line AB shows the forecast sales of the original product. Careful timing of an R&D programme will allow the firm to create a modified version of the product that will revitalise sales, keeping the product in the maturity stage. The line AC shows the sales of the modified product.

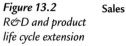

Figure 13.2
R&D and product
life cycle extension

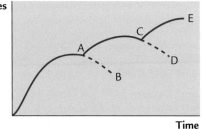

Again, at C a further modification is introduced in order to prevent sales falling (as shown by the line CD). This modification again prolongs the maturity stage of the product life cycle, allowing sales to grow from C to E.

Human resource management

Typically, the role of HRM in the innovation process has been to recruit and train suitable employees and then to ensure that the business retains their services. Successful innovation can also lead to the growth of a business and this may require additional recruitment and training. In its workforce planning, the HR department must ensure that the impact of innovation and research and development are taken into consideration.

Recently, much greater emphasis has been placed on the creative aspects of the innovation process, focusing on activities such as restructuring the organisation, instilling a corporate culture that supports innovation and creativity, introducing greater flexibility, and changing processes as well as the goods and services provided.

These changes require much greater involvement from HRM, in providing training and creating more autonomy within the workforce so that ideas for change can be provided by the workforce itself.

AQA A2 Business Studies

How much should an organisation spend on innovation and R&D?

The UK government believes that the UK is not spending enough on innovation and R&D. However, for individual organisations, the need for innovation varies considerably. The main factors that influence the need for innovation spending are as follows:

- **The nature of the product.** Technically advanced industries offer scope for firms to improve through innovation and research and development. Among the most highly developed economies in the world, there is a consistent pattern of high innovation spending in industries involved in the production of cars, pharmaceuticals and biotechnology, computer hardware and software, electronics and chemicals. In 2008, these industries accounted for approximately 80% of the world's R&D spending.

- **Competition.** The need to keep ahead of rivals is often identified as the driving force behind innovation. UK businesses that export have a much greater tendency to spend money on innovation because they face higher levels of competition than firms that do not need to match overseas competitors.
- **The market.** Ultimately, innovation succeeds only if the firm provides products that are wanted by consumers. If customer tastes are continually changing, such as in computer software, the need for innovation is increased. In more static markets, such as furniture, there is less need for innovation.

The factors above identify the main influences on the need to spend money on innovation. The following factors are significant in determining *how much* is actually spent:

- **Company finance.** Innovation is expensive and cannot guarantee results. In times of financial difficulty, it is often cut back; in times of plenty, it may be generously funded.
- **Company culture.** Risk-taking firms are much more likely to involve themselves in innovation. Another aspect of culture is whether the business takes a long-term or short-term view of its future. Innovation rarely brings in profit in the short term, so it is not going to be encouraged in a business seeking immediate returns.
- **Chances of success.** Ultimately, innovation involves risk. Research into the common cold has not increased in line with other pharmaceutical research because organisations are not optimistic that they will find a cure.
- **Efficiency of innovation.** Although innovation is subject to chance, businesses can take steps to improve the effectiveness of their innovation. GlaxoSmithKline is an example of a business that is introducing changes in its approach rather than in its overall spending levels. Thus, an effective programme of innovation may actually lead to a fall in the expenditure needed to achieve a firm's targets.

FACT FILE

Wiggly Wrigglers

Wiggly Wrigglers started in 1990 when Heather Gorringe, a farmer's wife from Herefordshire, decided to use worms to create compost from kitchen waste. Heather's creativity has created a £2 million business that has diversified into 700 natural products. Wiggly Wrigglers' core values mean that it focuses on providing natural products, sourcing supplies and labour from the local area. However, as with any innovative business, Wiggly Wrigglers has seized opportunities as they arise. Although it is focused on environmentally friendly products, it has embraced new technology too. Online orders enable the business to monitor changing tastes and ensure delivery of products within 48 hours. The company has also introduced podcasts, reaching 3,000 listeners every week.

Source: Wiggly Wrigglers website.

FOTOLIA

PRACTICE EXERCISE   Total: 50 marks (50 minutes)

1 Distinguish between the terms 'innovation' and 'research and development'.   *(6 marks)*

2 Identify five different types of innovation.   *(5 marks)*

3 Analyse three benefits of innovation for a car manufacturer, such as Ford.   *(9 marks)*

4 Analyse two problems that a car manufacturer, such as Ford, might experience in its innovation and research and development.   *(6 marks)*

5 Explain two actions that a firm can take in order to improve the chances of success for its research and development.   *(6 marks)*

6 Identify three UK industries that are major investors in research and development.   *(3 marks)*

7 Explain two problems that might occur if innovation is not linked to other functional areas of the business.   *(6 marks)*

8 Explain three factors that influence the level of innovation in a business.   *(9 marks)*

CASE STUDY 1 Small business innovation: Martek Marine Ltd

Martek is a world leader in providing marine safety and environmental monitoring systems, most notably an engine efficiency optimisation system that allows ship owners to make significant fuel savings and reduce vessel downtime. It was established in 2000 with £6,000 capital. In 8 years it has grown to reach a turnover of £6 million a year.

The challenge for Martek was to improve its human and technical support, as the market required 24-hour service throughout the world. The solution was based on communications technology — the company adopted a teleworking strategy with staff being provided with access to the company's communication network from home. Offices were also opened in the USA and in Singapore, 8 hours behind and 8 hours ahead of Greenwich Mean Time respectively. This enabled Martek to provide a 24-hour service effectively.

Another key element was the human resource strategy — Martek needed to recruit, train and encourage the right staff to work in a dynamic and empowered working environment. Martek's focus on technology and the achievement of work–life balance (staff in all three offices work, in effect, from 9 to 5 in their respective countries) has paid dividends in terms of staff retention, which is almost 100%. The managing director, Paul Luen, believes that the single biggest indicator of the success of its approach is its labour productivity — its 32 workers achieve an annual sales turnover of £6 million. 'This is between two and four times greater than our competitors in our sector.'

Preliminary questions
Total: 10 marks (15 minutes)

1 Calculate the productivity of labour at Martek Marine Ltd, based on its annual sales revenue. *(2 marks)*

2 Analyse two ways in which technology has assisted innovation at Martek Marine Ltd. *(8 marks)*

Case study question
Total: 15 marks (20 minutes)

To what extent does Martek's background show the importance of integrating R&D with the other functional areas of the business, such as marketing, finance and HRM? *(15 marks)*

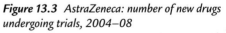

CASE STUDY 2 Innovation through research and development at AstraZeneca

AstraZeneca is one of the world's leading pharmaceutical companies and the UK's second biggest spender on research and development.

The company focuses on six therapy areas. It has a broad product portfolio including many world-leading products such as Arimidex (cancer), Crestor (cardiovascular), Nexium (gastrointestinal disease), Seroquel (schizophrenia and bipolar disorder) and Symbicort (asthma and chronic obstructive pulmonary disease).

The company's R&D takes place in eight countries but is mainly concentrated in Sweden, the UK and the USA. Its employee base is worldwide with over 67,000 employees (55% in Europe, 30% in the Americas and

15% in Asia, Africa and Australasia). Production takes place in 20 different countries.

Since the start of the millennium, AstraZeneca has increased its R&D efforts even more. As a result, the number of drugs under development (in the 'pipeline') has grown steadily (see Figure 13.3).

Figure 13.3 AstraZeneca: number of new drugs undergoing trials, 2004–08

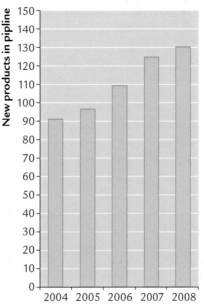

However, not all of these drugs will become government-approved treatments, although AstraZeneca's success rates are above average for pharmaceutical firms. In 2007, the company's R&D introduced 36 new drugs into its pipeline and succeeded in producing 24 products that were accepted for human use.

People are naturally cautious about new drugs, so pharmaceutical companies face greater risks than firms in other industries. In 2007, AstraZeneca was hit by four drug failures at a late stage of development, when early signs had suggested success.

However, these risks can be offset by successes. In April 2008, independent monitors put an early halt to a 15,000-patient study of AstraZeneca's Crestor because early findings were so conclusive that the drug significantly reduced the risk of heart problems.

The company hopes that the success of the trial will allow Crestor to be used more widely and that the findings will give it a marketing advantage over its competitors. Crestor was also helped by adverse publicity concerning two competitor products, which led to a recommendation to the medical profession that the competitors' drugs should be offered to fewer patients.

These two pieces of news encouraged analysts to forecast annual sales of $5.5 billion by 2012. Currently, sales are $2.8 billion and growing at a rate of 33% per annum.

However, it is not all good news. AstraZeneca is facing legal challenges that could allow generic copies on to the market. The market for cholesterol-lowering drugs has been changed since the earliest products lost patent protection and cheap generic versions became available.

Sources: AstraZeneca website and an article by Steven Foley in the *Independent*, 1 April 2008.

Preliminary questions
Total: 20 marks (25 minutes)

1 Analyse two types of risk that AstraZeneca might experience through its R&D activities. *(10 marks)*

2 Examine the reasons why a company such as AstraZeneca focuses its research and development in eight countries and yet has production bases in 20 different countries. *(10 marks)*

Case study question
Total: 20 marks (25 minutes)

On the basis of the evidence provided, evaluate whether AstraZeneca has benefited from its decision to put more resources into research and development (R&D) in the twenty-first century. *(20 marks)*

Chapter 14

Operational strategies: location

This chapter discusses the factors that influence business decisions on location and relocation. Different methods of decision making about location are considered, including the quantitative technique of investment appraisal. In addition, qualitative factors are considered. The benefits of optimal location are noted and the advantages and disadvantages of multi-site locations are examined. The chapter concludes by studying the concept of 'offshoring' and the issues that relate to international location.

The main factors influencing business location

In Chapter 9 of the AS textbook, the main factors influencing the location of a business start up were discussed. A brief summary of the key factors is provided below. Each factor concludes with a note specific to its relevance for large-scale businesses.

Technology

Technology has allowed businesses to be more flexible, operating from a much wider choice of locations. In particular, technology has encouraged the use of tele-working, where employees work from home. For large businesses considering international location, it is vital to consider how advanced the technology is in the country in which location is planned. Many businesses, such as call centres, have located in the emerging economies of eastern Europe, China and India because of their increased levels of technological development.

Costs of factors of production

In order to improve their competitiveness, business will take into consideration any costs affected by location. The main costs involved are land costs (rent), transport costs and labour costs (wages). In the case of wages, it is the labour costs per unit that are most important: if wages in a particular location are 50% higher, this is still a good location if labour productivity is 80% higher.

The target for most businesses is to locate at the **least-cost site**: this is the business location that allows a firm to minimise its unit costs. As a consequence, more businesses are relocating their manufacturing to emerging economies, such as China and Russia.

Operational strategies

Infrastructure

This is the network of utilities, such as transport links, telecommunications systems and health and education facilities, which ensure that there is a good infrastructure to support the activities of a given business. When considering relocation, large businesses will need to be aware of the quality of the infrastructure in comparison to its existing location. For emerging economies in particular, the local infrastructure can pose difficulties.

Qualitative factors

The personal preferences of directors or owners can influence location decisions. The owner may wish to locate the business close to his or her own home, or in a place that has good local facilities, such as cinemas, gyms or a picturesque location.

> **e EXAMINER'S VOICE**
>
> These were considered to be the main factors influencing the location of a business start-up in Unit 1 of the AS course. In the A2 specification, the focus is on large, nationally based businesses that are considering relocation, multi-site locations and/or international locations. As a consequence, other factors need to be added to the above list.

Factors influencing location decisions involving expansion and/or relocation

Resources

The location of **raw materials** is the crucial influence for most primary industries. Extractive industries such as mining and quarrying must locate where the materials are found. However, the costs of extraction and transport to the market may determine whether it is economically worthwhile to operate at all.

Heavy industries — notably iron and steel — usually locate in close proximity to their raw material supplies. During the manufacturing process, a significant percentage of the raw materials is wasted. As a result, the final product weighs much less than the raw materials. Therefore, it is cheaper to distribute the finished product to the market than it is to move the raw materials to the place of manufacture. For these **bulk-reducing** or **weight-losing industries**, the least-cost site tends to be close to the raw materials.

For some industries, such as brewing and soft drinks, the ready accessibility of water means that the final product is bulkier to transport than the raw materials. These **bulk-increasing** or **weight-gaining industries** tend to locate closer to the market than the raw materials.

The location of suppliers is still a key factor influencing business location. A manufacturer will reap the benefits of a location that is close to its suppliers, particularly if it is using just-in-time methods.

The market

For retailers and other service industries, the market is the most important influence on location. As the UK's economy is predominantly based on **tertiary production** (the provision of services), this makes the market a crucial factor in determining the location of many UK firms. Customers expect convenience and easy access, so firms such as electrical retailers, hairdressers and restaurants see this factor as particularly important.

Organisations save transport costs if they locate close to their market. A company supplying raw materials to a manufacturer may find that transport costs represent a large percentage of the final costs. In this case, proximity to the customer may be a key factor.

As just-in-time production grows in popularity among manufacturers, the ability to transport goods quickly becomes a key factor in the choice of suppliers, so the latter will seek to locate close to their customers.

FACT FILE

Virtual markets

For many businesses in sectors such as retailing and financial services, proximity to the customer is still vital, but it is no longer an influence on location. In these businesses, the marketplace is via a telephone line or an internet connection. As a result, local branches are not needed. In the financial services industry, this means that the service is provided through a call centre. The location of a call centre is more likely to be influenced by cost factors such as wage rates, as its geographical situation no longer affects its proximity to the market.

Government intervention

Member countries of the European Union (EU) must regulate their regional policy within the guidelines established by the European Commission. Assistance can only be provided in specific areas. In England, these are the Assisted Areas (see Figure 14.1); the National Assembly for Wales and the Scottish Parliament provide similar schemes of regional assistance.

KEY TERM

Assisted Areas: parts of the UK that have relatively low levels of economic activity and high and persistent unemployment.

The financial assistance provided usually takes the form of a grant. The government pays for a certain percentage of the cost of capital investment, with higher percentage grants available to smaller firms.
- Firms in areas designated as Article 87(3)(a), such as Cornwall, are entitled to a maximum grant of 30–50% of the cost of capital investment.

Figure 14.1
Assisted Areas in the UK, 2007–13

■ 87(3)(a) coverage
□ 87(3)(a) coverage (See Note)
■ 87(3)(c) coverage

Note: Highlands & Islands will have 87(3)(a) coverage until 31 Decemeber 2010, at which point this status will be reviewed by the European Commission. Northern Ireland will have full 87(3)(c) coverage.

FOTOLIA

- Firms in areas designated as Article 87(3)(c) are entitled to a maximum grant of 15–35% of the cost of capital investment.

The European Commission restricts aid according to certain criteria:
- Only certain sectors of the economy qualify, such as iron and steel, coal, synthetic fibres, vehicles, and agriculture and fisheries.
- The project must not lead to overcapacity in its industry.
- The investment must create jobs or introduce new technology, and any jobs must not just be transferred from another Assisted Area. Consequently, local services such as retailing would not qualify.

In England, for grants in excess of £2 million, firms must apply to the DBERR.

The UK's regional policy has been most successful in encouraging foreign multinational businesses to locate in areas of high unemployment. Multinational corporations such as Nissan, locating in Sunderland, have helped to regenerate areas that were suffering from high unemployment. To date, the UK has attracted more foreign multinationals than any other EU member country. Government research in 2004 estimated that regional policy cost, on average, £6,840 for each job.

Industrial inertia

Industrial inertia is another factor that can influence location. Once established, firms may be reluctant to relocate elsewhere. One reason for this is that established firms can benefit from external economies of scale.

The main external economies of scale are:
- a labour supply with the skills needed by firms in that industry
- specialist training facilities in the region
- an infrastructure that is geared towards the needs of that industry, such as specialist transport facilities
- suppliers and customers based locally
- the reputation of the area, which may help to sell the product or allow the firm to charge a premium price

KEY TERMS

industrial inertia: the tendency for firms to remain where they are, even though the original reasons for location no longer apply.

external economies of scale: the benefits gained by a firm as a result of the concentration of an industry in one location.

e **EXAMINER'S VOICE**

Do not confuse *external* economies of scale with *internal* economies of scale.

Internal economies of scale (often referred to as just 'economies of scale') are the advantages that an organisation gains due to an increase in the size of the organisation. Internal economies of scale are explained in Chapter 12.

External economies of scale are benefits to a firm from being part of a large industry that is concentrated in a particular area or region. External economies therefore depend on the scale of the industry, rather than of individual firms within it. Thus a small financial services company will benefit from being located in London because of the concentration of financial services organisations in that location.

Businesses should also be aware of the problems arising from a concentration of firms in an area. These are known as external diseconomies of scale.

The main external diseconomies are congestion, pollution and a potential shortage of resources in the area. All of these factors cost a firm in terms of time and money.

KEY TERM

external diseconomies of scale: the disadvantages arising from the concentration of an industry in one location.

- **Congestion.** The concentration of firms in an area increases travelling times and expenses. Where delivery times are an essential factor, this may reduce the competitiveness of an organisation because transport costs will increase and delivery may become unreliable.
- **Pollution.** The social costs created in these areas may be considered excessive by firms that place a high value on their impact on society. Local councils may impose additional costs on firms in order to alleviate this problem.
- **Shortages of resources.** In particular, the cost of land and skilled labour will be inflated by the competition among firms to acquire these resources.

On balance, firms usually find that the external economies of scale outweigh the external diseconomies of scale. This encourages firms to remain in their original location.

In addition, relocation can be disruptive to a firm. Even though, in the long term, a new location may offer lower costs, the short-term inconvenience may be considerable and endanger the future of the organisation.

Other factors that will be considered by a firm if it already has a base and is considering relocation elsewhere are:
- loss of skills developed in the existing workforce
- lower morale and productivity prior to the relocation, as a result of some staff probably losing their jobs
- the break-up of working groups
- finding new suppliers and customers
- the cost of relocation
- redundancy payments
- transitional difficulties while adjusting to the new location and processes
- potential damage to the firm's image caused by these changes

These problems need to be set against the benefits gained from the new location.

Methods of making location decisions

This section shows how decisions on location can be taken using quantitative methods.

Location decisions using investment appraisal

Investment appraisal is necessary to see if a location decision provides a quick payback, yields a high average rate of return (ARR) percentage or gives a positive net present value (NPV). An example of the use of investment appraisal in deciding on location is set out below.

Example

Magnifico is considering the opening of a new store in Liverpool. The expected initial costs (year 0) are £800,000, as shown in Table 14.1. Future revenue and annual costs for the first 5 years of the store are also shown.

Table 14.1
Forecasts revenue and costs of the new Magnifico store

Year	Revenue (£000s)	Costs (£000s)	Net return (£000s)
0	0	800	(800)
1	550	350	200
2	750	450	300
3	900	540	360
4	950	560	390
5	950	560	390
Total	**4,100**	**3,260**	**840**

Magnifico's targets for its new stores are as follows:
- payback — less than 3 years
- average rate of return — greater than 12%
- net present value — positive, based on a 10% discount rate

A new store must achieve all three of these targets in order to be opened. Any revenue or costs after year 5 are ignored.

For detailed information on how to complete the calculations for investment appraisal, see Chapter 6.

$$\text{payback period} = 2 \text{ years} + \frac{300}{360} = 2 \text{ years 10 months}$$

$$\text{annual return} = \frac{£840,000}{5 \text{ years}} = £168,000 \text{ per annum}$$

Table 14.2
Net present value of the new Magnifico store

$$\text{average rate of return} = \frac{£168,000}{£800,000} \times 100 = 21\%$$

Table 14.2 shows the net present value of the new Magnifico store.

Year	Revenue (£000s)	Costs (£000s)	Net return (£000s)	Discount factor (10%)	Present value (£000s)
0	0	800	(800)	1.0	(800)
1	550	350	200	0.909	181.8
2	750	450	300	0.826	247.8
3	900	540	360	0.751	270.4
4	950	560	390	0.683	266.4
5	950	560	390	0.621	242.2
Total	**4,100**	**3,260**	**840**		**408.6**

Table 14.3 summarises the decisions on location using investment appraisal.

Method of investment appraisal	Target	Forecast result	Decision (YES/NO)
Payback period	<3 years	2 years 10 months	YES
Average rate of return (%)	>12%	21%	YES
Net present value	>£0	+£408,600	YES
Overall decision			**YES**

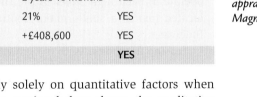

Table 14.3
Summary of investment appraisals of new Magnifico store

However, a business should not rely solely on quantitative factors when deciding on a business location. The section below shows the qualitative factors that should also be considered before the final decision is taken.

Location decisions using qualitative factors

Ultimately, all business decisions are taken by individuals, often without access to perfect forecasts of the implications of the different choices available. Consequently, directors may base their choices on factors other than business criteria. For example, The Body Shop is located in Sussex because Anita Roddick lived there at the time that she set up the business. Similarly, production of the BMW Mini is based in Cowley, Oxford because its original founder — William Morris — lived there. Other qualitative factors include:

- accessibility to leisure facilities
- types of leisure facility (e.g. indoor versus outdoor)
- quality of life
- accessibility to good transport links for personal use
- geographical attractiveness, such as coastal location or access to natural landscape
- convenience of access to other places
- availability of housing
- opportunity to make a difference to a local community

Benefits of optimal location

The optimal location is the best location for a specific business. There is growing recognition that multi-site locations may be preferable to a single location. This issue will be discussed later in this chapter.

Location decisions are primarily taken with the purpose of finding the least-cost site, although a number of other benefits can arise from a good choice of location:

- **Improving competitiveness.** If the business is aiming for a low-cost marketing strategy or is operating in a very competitive market, the least-cost site can greatly assist its marketing strategy. In times of economic difficulty, a low-cost location can also help a businesses to survive.
- **Providing a unique selling point.** Some businesses use their location to enhance their image. Cities such as Paris and Milan are attractive locations for fashion houses because of their image, although they are not the least-cost location.

EXAMINER'S VOICE

These are just some examples of qualitative factors. If an examination question requires you to consider qualitative factors, look for 'non-quantifiable' factors within the case study. There may also be reference to 'inertia' factors that can be instrumental in persuading the business to stay where it is.

- **Increasing access to customers.** Many business locations are chosen because they give consumers easy access to the business. This is particularly crucial for multi-site locations in businesses such as retailing. A retailer that can operate in each high street in the UK will achieve greater sales than one located just in a single major centre such as Oxford Street, London or Bluewater.
- **Increasing flexibility.** With the growth of lean production (see Chapter 15) it is becoming more imperative for suppliers to locate close to the businesses requiring their products or services. For example, when Honda located in Swindon, many suppliers of car components also chose to locate in the area so that they could respond quickly to Honda's requests for additional components. For companies involved in lean production, time is very important.

Multi-site locations

For many businesses, there is not an ideal location. If a business wants to be close to its customers, this may involve a number of different business locations.

The key advantages and disadvantages of multi-site or single-site locations are closely linked to the factors already studied when investigating business location. Consequently, the sections below will only cover the key points briefly.

Advantages of multi-site locations

A business will choose multi-site locations in order to reap one or more of the following benefits:

- **Lower costs.** Where transport costs are high, it can be cheaper to locate close to the market. For a global brand this will involve multi-site locations in many different countries.
- **Improved market focus.** Many multinational businesses use multi-site locations to enable them to understand local markets more fully. This practice — known as 'glocalisation' — combines the benefits of being a global organisation with the local knowledge needed to serve regional or national customer bases.
- **Avoidance of trade barriers.** Many countries or groups of countries, such as the EU, impose tariffs (taxes) on foreign imports. By locating in a country or within a trading area, a company can avoid these tariffs.
- **Increased flexibility.** Proximity to a market in a particular country can enable a business to react more quickly to changes in that marketplace.
- **Overcoming cultural barriers.** By setting up bases in a number of countries, a business is able to understand a country's culture more fully.
- **Regional specialisation.** Many areas of the world have particular specialisations and skills. By operating in different locations around the world, businesses can benefit from local specialisation and so improve their efficiency.

Disadvantages of multi-site locations

There are several problems associated with multi-site locations. These are outlined below:

- **Globalisation.** A disadvantage of multi-site locations is that local people may perceive that another country's culture is being imposed on their own. A company that has been accused of this is Coca-Cola. This has led to some competitor products, such as Zam Zam Cola and Evoca Cola, being launched, targeted at the Muslim market for soft drinks.
- **Increased unit costs.** It is possible that unit costs will be increased rather than decreased by multi-site locations. Single-site locations provide the opportunity to achieve huge economies of scale. By setting up in many locations, it is possible that some of these economies will be lost.
- **Increased risk.** Where multi-site locations are chosen in order to target many markets, the business strategy can be seen as one of market development. According to Ansoff's matrix (see Chapter 9), this can lead to increased risks because the business will have less understanding of the new markets it is targeting.
- **Loss of control.** Other diseconomies of scale that can arise from multi-site locations are difficulties in coordinating and communicating. The loss of control arising from difficulties in managing a branch or division in a different country can outweigh the benefits outlined earlier.
- **Cultural differences.** Although multi-site locations can bring benefits to the marketing department, they can often present major challenges to operations and human resources management because of different working practices and traditions in the working environment.

Issues relating to international location

In making worldwide decisions on location, organisations will consider all of the factors discussed previously in this chapter, as these apply to nations as well as to regions. In addition, a business might wish to consider the political and economic stability of the country in which it is planning to locate, and examine exchange rates to see if there are financial gains to be made from location decisions. Government legislation on employment may also influence location. Countries with more flexible working practices and/or fewer restrictions on levels of pay may be attractive to some firms.

Three factors of particular importance in international location decisions are described below.

Global markets

The UK has a population of 61 million. This has enabled UK firms to expand considerably just by focusing on the domestic market. With 61 million potential customers, firms in the UK can produce on a large scale, achieving high economies of scale. This leads to lower costs of production and greater

KEY TERMS

offshoring: where companies outsource business activities overseas, largely because labour and facility costs are much cheaper there.

outsourcing: where companies give responsibility for some of their activities, such as IT support, catering or manufacturing processes, to other businesses.

Table 14.4 *World's leading economies by GDP ($ trillion), 2007*

	Country	GDP
1	USA	13.8
2	China	7.0
3	Japan	4.3
4	India	3.0
5	Germany	2.8
6	UK	2.2
7	Russia	2.1
8	France	2.1
9	Brazil	1.8
10	Italy	1.8

Source: IMF report, October 2008.

efficiency for the firm. It gives UK firms an advantage in comparison with firms from smaller countries such as Holland, but they remain at a disadvantage in relation to firms from larger economies such as Japan.

The world has a rapidly increasing human population, currently totalling 6,750 million people. With 20% of the world's population living in China and 17% in India, firms are encouraged to locate there, particularly as the population of Asia as a whole is expanding rapidly.

For individual multinational firms, the size of a market is a major factor in deciding on location. Countries with a high gross domestic product, or open access to a free trade area such as the EU, enable these firms to produce on a large scale and transport their goods without trade barriers. Table 14.4 shows the world's largest markets. Despite its population China is still, economically and financially, a much smaller market than the USA.

Cost reduction

Many firms locate internationally in order to achieve cost reductions. Western economies, in particular, can benefit from much lower wage and land costs by relocating to countries in eastern Europe or Asian countries such as India and China. Over 60% of UK businesses that move abroad indicate that cost reduction is the main motivation for relocating internationally.

International locations can also make it easier to target large markets where economies of scale can be achieved. For example, Samsung is a Korean company that has been able to achieve massive economies of scale by becoming a worldwide brand. This improves its global competitiveness.

 KEY **TERMS**

trade barriers: methods of restricting trade (usually used to limit the level of imports into a particular country).

protectionism: a decision by a country or countries to place restrictions on trade between nations, in order to help (protect) domestic firms competing with foreign companies.

DID **YOU KNOW?**
- 30% of UK companies do part of their manufacturing abroad.
- 10% have more than half of their production abroad.
- One in three companies say that they are planning to increase the proportion of foreign production.
- 62% of businesses say that cost is the main reason for moving abroad.

Source: Engineering Employers' Federation.

Avoidance of trade barriers

One of the main reasons why companies choose to locate abroad is to avoid protection.

The most common forms of protection are:
- quotas (a limit on the number of imports allowed)
- tariffs (taxes) on imports from other countries, to make imports more expensive
- subsidies on domestic products, allowing these firms to keep their prices low

These approaches 'protect' domestic producers from outside competition. Quotas achieve this by physically preventing more than a certain quantity of imports. Tariffs and subsidies are used to help domestic producers match the prices of external firms.

The World Trade Organization (WTO) is a global organisation that promotes free trade (trade without protection) to increase efficiency globally. More significantly, a number of 'free trade' areas have been formed, such as the European Union (EU), NAFTA (based in North America) and APEC (Asia and the Pacific). These areas are groups of countries that have agreed to remove restrictions on trade between member countries.

These areas tend to adopt policies of protectionism against non-member countries. As a consequence, businesses try to locate operations in countries within these areas, so that they can have free access to the other countries in the free trade area. For example, many US, Japanese and Korean companies have set up bases in the UK so that they can access the EU market.

FACT FILE

Into India

In April 2008, Capital One, the US credit card provider, announced that it was cutting its British workforce by 40% after announcing plans to lay off 750 workers in Nottingham. The company said that the jobs would be moved from its UK call centres and account servicing division and transferred to India and other countries. In May 2008, Lloyds TSB announced that it would be 'offshoring' about 450 IT positions, including permanent and contractor jobs, to its technical delivery unit in India. In addition to lower costs, India has a vast pool of software engineering. India benefits from time zones too. Engineers in India can carry out work on IT systems while the USA and Europe sleep.

FACT FILE

Out of India

Offshoring is not all one-way traffic. Encouraged by the availability of finance and long cultural ties between the two countries, some Indian financial services firms have located in the UK. In 2008 the India Infrastructure Finance Company UK (IIFC UK) set up London operations to raise foreign currency, equipment and expertise for Indian infrastructure projects.

'London's broad range of world-class services makes it an ideal destination for Indian businesses,' said Palaniappan Chidambaram, India's finance minister.

The move follows the Punjab National Bank's decision in 2007 to locate the international headquarters of its global business arm in the UK. Similarly, Indian bank ICICI has decided that its UK subsidiary will be responsible for financing its global operations.

Operational strategies

WHAT DO YOU THINK?

In 2007 DaimlerChrysler introduced new working conditions for many of its German workforce. These changes involved longer working hours (rising from 35 to 40 hours per week), for the same level of pay. The company has threatened to move around 6,000 jobs from its Sindelfingen plant, which produces the Mercedes C-Class, to South Africa, where wages are much lower.

In the past, public opinion in Germany supported workers' demands, arguing that workers should benefit from Germany's wealth. However, an opinion poll shows that the German people are beginning to believe that the working week should be increased from 35 to 40 hours, in order to improve competitiveness.

This development followed Siemens' success in persuading 8,000 workers to increase their working week from 35 to 40 hours. Siemens had threatened to move production to Hungary.

Should European companies move jobs from western Europe to low-wage countries?

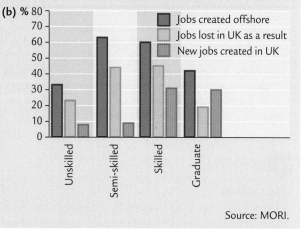

© DAIMLERCHRYSLER MEDIASERVICES

FACT FILE

UK offshoring

UK companies are moving a variety of activities 'offshore'. Figure 14.2 shows the nature of jobs that are relocating to other countries and the effects that this 'offshoring' is having on UK employment.

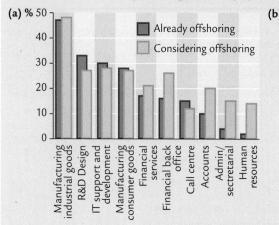

Figure 14.2 (a) UK companies relocating 'offshore' or considering such a move (b) The effects of offshoring on UK employment.

Source: MORI.

FACT FILE

UK production at Rolls-Royce

One company that plans to keep a firm base in the UK is Rolls-Royce. The company's management thought about moving one of its manufacturing plants from Glasgow to the Czech Republic. John Cheffins, chief operating officer, says: 'The simple assumption that low wages will give you a low-cost product just isn't true.' New technology, a skilled workforce and flexible work contracts, including a policy of single status, have all helped to increase productivity simply by moving to a new factory in Glasgow. Staff have an average salary in excess of £28,000, but the skills that they possess are critical to the success of the firm's products. Over 60% of Rolls-Royce's workforce of 35,000 employees are based in the UK, despite recent job cuts.

PRACTICE EXERCISE 1   Total: 40 marks (40 minutes)

1 What is meant by the term 'least-cost site'?   *(2 marks)*

2 Explain the significance of the term 'weight losing' or 'bulk
   reducing' with reference to the location of industry.   *(4 marks)*

3 What is the meaning of the term 'Assisted Area'?   *(3 marks)*

4 Examine two issues that a components manufacturer might
   consider when *relocating* a business. Which would *not* be
   considered when a business decides on its first location.   *(6 marks)*

5 Analyse three factors that might influence the international
   location of a frozen food producer.   *(9 marks)*

6 What is industrial inertia?   *(2 marks)*

7 Explain the difference between internal economies of scale and
   external economies of scale.   *(5 marks)*

8 How do trade barriers influence international location decisions? *(4 marks)*

9 Identify five factors that might be seen as qualitative influences
   on a decision about where to locate a business.   *(5 marks)*

PRACTICE EXERCISE 2   Total: 30 marks (40 minutes)

1 A furniture manufacturer is planning to relocate its factory to Hungary. It has gathered together the
   information shown in the following tables.

Forecast revenue and costs of the new factory

Year	Revenue (£m)	Costs (£m)	Net return (£m)
0	0	25	(25)
1	27	21	6
2	32	22	10
3	29	17	12
Total	**88**	**85**	**3**

Present value of £1 at selected discount rates

Year	Discount rate			
	2%	5%	7%	10%
0	1.0	1.0	1.0	1.0
1	0.980	0.952	0.935	0.909
2	0.961	0.907	0.873	0.826
3	0.942	0.864	0.816	0.751

a Calculate:
   (i) the payback period   *(3 marks)*
   (ii) the average rate of return (ARR)   *(5 marks)*
   (iii) the net present value (NPV), using an appropriate discount rate *(7 marks)*
b Briefly justify the discount rate that you have used in **a(iii)**. *(3 marks)*
c Based on your answers, recommend whether the new factory should be opened. *(2 marks)*

2 Analyse three qualitative factors that the furniture manufacturer might take into account
   when choosing whether to relocate its factory to Hungary.   *(10 marks)*

CASE STUDY Call centres

The financial services sector has led the trend for UK call centres, or contact centres, to relocate. Currently, UK call centres employ almost 930,000 workers. Despite the impression given in the media, the call centre industry in the UK is still growing, with 17% more jobs in the last 4 years. Furthermore, the Indian industry is still only one-third of the scale of that in the UK, with 312,500 call centre employees, although it is growing quickly. Most of the high-profile decisions to relocate to countries such as India have come from finance companies.

Among the businesses that have decided to locate their call (or contact) centres in India are Prudential, Abbey, HSBC, GE Capital and American Express. The Prudential transferred 850 jobs from its call centre in Reading to Mumbai (formerly Bombay) in India. The new call centre costs the Prudential £6 million a year. This represents a large saving as call centre wages in India average £2,250 compared with about £12,950 in the UK. Overall, the Prudential estimates that an equivalent centre in the UK would have cost £12 million a year to run. (This is a greater cost saving than usual. On average, call centre costs in India are 35–40% lower than in the UK, with nearly all of the savings coming from lower wage levels.) The transfer is estimated to have cost Prudential £10 million.

Other financial organisations that have moved work from the UK to India include Abbey, Lloyds and HSBC. However, other destinations are becoming more popular, with more offshoring to Malaysia and China now taking place, on the grounds of cost. Ironically, in 2007, 11 large Indian manufacturers signed contracts offshoring $5 billion of manufacturing from India to China because of the cost savings available. In 2007 IBM was one of only two large-scale UK based companies that offshored activities to India, with more offshoring taking place in Malaysia and China. Indian businesses are seeking to attract more technologically advanced businesses, such as IT and R&D. R&D offshoring to India has tripled in the last 4 years.

For UK businesses that use an overseas agent, rather than their own set-up, the payback period for offshoring can be as little as 3 months. However, companies must also keep up quality. Customers value most highly a prompt answer, with the telephone call completed quickly and the problem solved at the first attempt.

Rival firms adopt most changes in the banking industry quickly, but on the issue of call centres the banks are polarising into two camps. Organisations such as HBOS, Nationwide, Alliance and Leicester and the Cooperative Bank have all ruled out going abroad. Nationwide's chief executive, Philip Williamson, says that he receives letters from new customers stating that they are switching accounts into his organisation because their previous bank has transferred jobs overseas. He says: 'There is a view that the quality of service in India is not as good. A number of companies [such as Shop Direct] have transferred jobs back to the UK.'

A particular problem in both countries has been the high rate of labour turnover, which in India has reached 50%. Indian call centres are also experiencing recruitment difficulties, blamed primarily on anti-social hours and abusive customers and absence rates of 11%. In the UK, surveys suggest that it costs £2,444 to replace a person who leaves. Furthermore, new agents are only 16% as effective as experienced ones during the early period of their service.

Trade unions are also taking a firmer view on call centres. Bernadette Fisher, national officer of the financial services trade union UNIFI, described Lloyds TSB's decision to move 1,500 jobs to India as 'a callous move. It shows no respect for staff, customers or local communities'. The union is also critical of decisions taken by other financial organisations and is threatening to take industrial action.

Evidence from the UK government confirms this view, to some extent. Table 14.5 summarises some of the key comparisons made in the government's study of call (contact) centres.

Table 14.5 *A comparison of UK and Indian call (contact) centres, 2004*

Feature	UK	India
Total cost of operations (index)	100	65
Average wage (new operators)	£12,945	£1,502
Labour turnover (%)	15%	29%
Office rents (per square metre)	£303	£62
Average speed to answer telephone	15 seconds	7 seconds
Perception of suitable accent	100%	70%
Proportion of problems solved through first call	87%	60%
Number of calls answered per operator per hour	15	12
Proportion of call centres using two or more quality assurance methods	81%	66%

Note: more recent surveys by Mckinsey in August 2008 and www.cca.org.uk suggest that the key comparisons in this survey, such as relative costs and the quality of customer service, still apply in 2008, although labour turnover is now much higher in both countries — 23% in the UK and 50% in India.

Source: Department of Trade and Industry, 2004.

A study by the World Bank also highlights India as a greater trading risk for international businesses. Table 14.6 shows the key features included in its study of comparative risk.

Table 14.6 *Comparative trading risk*

International preferred location score	UK	India
Contract enforcement	3	2
Ease of business entry	1	7
Insurance industry sophistication	1	4
Political and economic stability	1	6
Business English proficiency	1	1
Corruption	1	5
Average	1.3	4.2

1 = most favourable rating;
7 = least favourable rating.

Source: World Bank.

Sources: Nick Heath, 'UK contact centres up there with the world's priciest', silico.com, 20 June 2008; data from Customer Contact Association at www.cca.org.uk; and *The UK Contact Centre Industry: A Study* (DTI, May 2004).

Preliminary questions

Total: 20 marks (25 minutes)

1 What is meant by the term 'offshoring'? *(3 marks)*

2 Study the second paragraph, concerning the Prudential's decision to relocate from Reading to Mumbai in India.

   a Calculate the payback period for this relocation decision. *(3 marks)*

   b Calculate the average rate of return (%) for this decision, over a 4-year period. *(5 marks)*

3 Analyse the possible reasons why more call centres are beginning to locate in China and Malaysia rather than India. *(9 marks)*

Case study questions

Total: 35 marks (45 minutes)

1* Evaluate the limitations, for the Prudential, of relying solely on the calculations in **2a** and **b** in order to decide on whether to relocate. *(15 marks)*

2 Discuss the main issues that a financial services business needs to examine when deciding whether to locate a call centre in the UK or India. *(20 marks)*

*It is advisable but not essential to have answered questions 2a and b from the Preliminary questions before attempting this question.

Chapter 15

Operational strategies: lean production

KEY TERM

time-based management: an approach that recognises the importance of time and seeks to reduce the level of 'unproductive' time within an organisation. This leads to quicker response times, faster new product development and reductions in waste, culminating in greater efficiency.

This chapter begins by looking at the need for effective management of time. Critical path analysis is described and the construction of critical path networks is shown. These diagrams are interpreted in the context of critical and non-critical activities, and discussion of CPA leads on to an assessment of the value of network/critical path analysis. The section concludes by examining the benefits and limitations of its use as a technique. Lean production is then introduced, leading on to an examination of the main lean production techniques. This section focuses on just-in-time production and kaizen as methods of assisting businesses to make the best use of their resources.

The effective management of time

Time-based management

In some organisations, time is used as a selling point — the ability of the firm to respond to a customer request can give firms a competitive advantage.

The AA, RAC and other motoring organisations see quick response times as a means of improving customer loyalty. They pay particular attention to the needs of female motorists and families, who might be considered to be in need of a more rapid response.

More specific applications of time-based management can be seen in the form of reduced lead times or shorter product development times.

Reduced lead times

The **lead time** is the time taken between an order being received and the final product or service being delivered to or provided for the customer. Critical path analysis shows how, when all the areas involved in a project are planned together, the time taken to complete the project can be reduced.

AQA A2 Business Studies

Shorter product development times

Constant changes in customer demands and the high failure rate of new products mean that companies which can produce new products quickly are able to stay competitive. Continual market research enables firms to identify potential trends and so change their product range.

Flexible production methods can also allow firms to modify their products quickly in response to the market. Information technology has helped businesses to modify and adapt their processes very quickly.

The end result of these two methods is that the new product is brought to the market or the customer's order is met more quickly. The firm can therefore beat its competitors in the race to provide the newest version of a product or the fastest delivery of a product or service.

Critical path analysis

Background

The roots of critical path analysis (CPA) lie in aircraft use. During the Second World War, the US Air Force recognised that an aircraft on the ground was both ineffective as a fighting weapon and more vulnerable to attack. Consequently, critical path analysis techniques were employed to ensure that planes were serviced and overhauled as quickly as possible.

Ironically, one of the latest converts to CPA is the airline industry. Southwest Airlines in the USA and Ryanair in Europe have used CPA to excellent effect to reduce the turnaround time on a plane (the time between it touching down and taking off again) to 25 minutes — half the time of rivals such as British Airways. This increases the number of journeys that a plane can make.

Critical path analysis is widely used in industries such as construction, in which it is possible to operate a range of activities in parallel. By mapping out the network of different activities, the firm is able to see which activities can run concurrently (at the same time) in order to save time and thus complete complex projects as quickly as possible. CPA also allows a business to identify those activities that cannot be delayed without holding up the overall project.

KEY TERMS

network analysis: a method of planning business operations in order to identify the most efficient way of completing an integrated task or project. The main form of network analysis is critical path analysis.

critical path analysis: the process of planning the sequence of activities in a project in order to discover the most efficient and quickest way of completing it.

critical path: the sequence of activities in a project that must be completed within a designated time in order to prevent any delay in overall completion of the project.

critical activity: any activity on the critical path.

Features of critical path analysis

Networks in critical path analysis are constructed in a specific way (see Figure 15.1). The features of a network are identified below:

■ **Nodes.** These are circles representing a point in time, identified by the completion or start of an activity. Nodes are split into three. The left half of the node contains the **number of the node**. This serves to provide a unique identity for each node. The right half of the node is split into two. The top segment shows the **earliest start time (EST)** that an activity can commence, and depends on the completion of the previous activity. For the opening activity or activities the EST is always zero. The bottom segment shows the **latest finish time (LFT)** of the previous activity, or can be seen to represent the **latest start time (LST)** at which the next activity can commence without delaying the overall project.

■ **Activities.** These are events or tasks that consume time and are shown as lines that link the nodes on the network diagram. Most network diagrams show activities moving from left to right, but for clarity, arrows are usually shown on the lines to indicate the sequence of activities. A letter (or description of the activity) is placed above the line that represents that activity.

■ **Duration.** This is the length of time that it takes to complete an activity. Depending on the nature of the project, the duration may be measured in months, weeks, days or minutes. The duration is shown as a number below the line that represents that activity.

■ **Prerequisite.** This is the activity (or activities) that must be completed before our selected activity can commence. For example, 'reading the questions' should be a prerequisite of 'starting to answer questions in an examination', and 'getting dressed' should be a prerequisite of 'catching the bus in the morning'.

■ **Dummies.** These are activities that do not consume time, but are incorporated into a network to show the true sequence of events. (Dummy nodes and activities may also be used to show more clearly the ESTs and LSTs/LFTs of non-critical activities.)

e EXAMINER'S VOICE

There is no direct reference to the use of 'dummies' in the AQA specification and no examination questions to date have required their use. Consequently, their use is not featured in any of the example networks in this book.

Similarly, because the AQA specification refers to the latest finish time (LFT) rather than latest start time (LST) of an activity, any examples in this book will use latest finish times (LFTs).

Figure 15.1 *Features of critical path analysis*

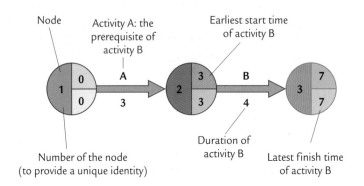

Constructing a critical path network

Table 15.1 shows a series of activities that form a network. This table lays out the logic behind the sequence of activities that make up a project.

Activity	Duration (days)	Prerequisite(s)
A	6	–
B	7	A
C	5	A
D	3	C
E	8	C
F	4	B, D
G	2	E, F

Table 15.1
Activities in a network

Once a table of this type has been constructed, the network is laid out by following the approach outlined below.

1 Draw a node (circle) to represent the start of the network. (All networks must start and end at a single node.) See node 1 (the first node on the left) in Figure 15.2. Number each node as it is drawn.

2 Identify any activities that have no prerequisite. Draw lines from left to right, starting from the original node, for the activities that have no prerequisite. Do not draw any nodes at the right-hand end of these activity lines at this stage. See activity A in Figure 15.2.

3 Identify the activity line by placing a description of it immediately above the line in the diagram (either the letter or activity description). See activity A in Figure 15.2.

4 Put the duration of the activity immediately under the line. Activity A is represented by a 6, showing that it takes 6 days to complete.

5 Move on to the first activity that has a prerequisite (activity B in this example). Place a node (circle) at the end of the line that represents the prerequisite activity, as this activity must be completed before the next activity can begin. Draw a line starting at the node that you have just drawn to represent the new activity (see activity B in Figure 15.2). Do not place a circle at the end of this node at this stage. If a new activity has two or more prerequisites, the lines representing these prerequisite activities must be drawn in such a way that they both lead into the same node. This node therefore represents the point of time at which both of the prerequisites have been completed and the new activity can begin. See activities F and G in Figure 15.2 for examples.

6 Repeat stages 3 to 5 for activity B.

7 Continue this process until every activity has been completed. (At this point there will be at least one line that has not been completed by a node.)

8 As all of the network's activities have now been plotted, bring any remaining lines together into a final node. This node represents the completion of the project that has been planned by the network. See node 6, the last node on the right, in Figure 15.2.

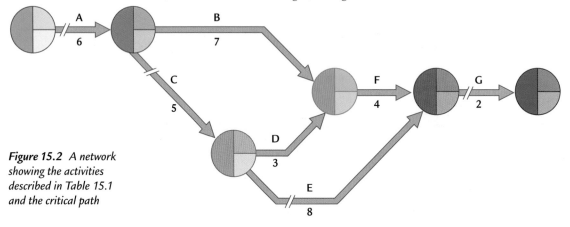

Figure 15.2 *A network showing the activities described in Table 15.1 and the critical path*

Completing the earliest start times

Once the outline diagram has been completed, work forward (from left to right) to calculate the earliest start times (ESTs). The EST in the first node (the EST of activity A) is shown as a zero.

For subsequent activities, the EST is found by adding the sum of the durations of activities on the path that leads up to the node that represents the start time of that activity. For example, the EST in node 3 is 6 + 5 = 11 (see Figure 15.3). Thus both D and E cannot start before day 11 because activity A takes 6 days and activity C takes 5 days to complete.

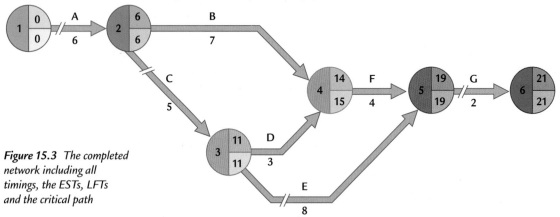

Figure 15.3 *The completed network including all timings, the ESTs, LFTs and the critical path*

If there is more than one path to a node, the highest total is taken as the EST. For example, activity F cannot begin until A and then B are completed (6 + 7 = 13 days). However, activity F also cannot start until activities A, C and D have been completed. These three activities take 6 + 5 + 3 = 14 days to complete. Therefore, the EST for activity F is 14 days rather than 13 days.

Insert the EST in the top right-hand corner of the node at the start point of that activity. The EST in the final node represents the earliest completion time for the project.

Completing the latest finish times (LFTs)
Once the ESTs have been completed, work backwards from right to left to calculate the latest finish times (LFTs). The LFT in the final node must equal the EST because a final activity must be on the critical path. Place the LFT in the bottom right-hand quadrant.

Moving from right to left, deduct the duration of the activity in order to calculate the LFT of the previous activity. Keep moving from right to left inserting the LFTs in the bottom right-hand quadrants. For example, the LFT for activity F, shown in node 5, is 19. This figure is calculated by taking the LFT in node 6, 21, and deducting the 2 days that it will take to complete activity G: $21 - 2 = 19$.

Be cautious where there are nodes that lead on to more than one activity. For example, the bottom right-hand sector of node 2 shows the number 6. This is because by working backwards from right to left on the path G to E to C, we arrive at a figure of 6 as the LFT for activity A ($21 - 2 - 8 - 5 = 6$). Thus the LFT shown in node 2 is 6. However, by moving backwards from right to left along the path G to F to B we also arrive at node 2. The calculation for the LFT via this path is $21 - 2 - 4 - 7 = 8$. *If there is more than one path working backwards to a node, the lowest total is taken as the LFT.* In effect, the digit 6 in the bottom right-hand quadrant of node 2 means that the latest finish time for activity A is 6 days, if activity C is to be started on time. However, it is possible to start activity B on day 8 without delaying the overall project.

Plotting the critical path
The critical path is the sequence of activities that cannot be delayed without delaying the overall completion of the project. It is represented by those activities that:
- have LFTs identical to their ESTs
- represent the longest path between the nodes

In Figure 15.3 the sequence A–C–E–G represents the critical path. For these critical activities, the ESTs and LFTs in each node are the same.

Non-critical activities are those that can be delayed without extending the completion time of the project. In Figure 15.3, these are activities B, D and F. Although both node 2 and node 3 show identical ESTs and LFTs, these arise because activities C and E are both on the critical path. We have seen already, by working back from right to left, that activity B can be delayed by 2 days without delaying the overall completion of the project. Similarly, activity D can be delayed by 1 day because the working-back process gives a figure of 12 for node 3.

In Figure 15.3, the critical path is shown by the symbol //. This is common practice, but the critical path may be shown in other ways, such as through the use of a highlighter or colour.

We can therefore see that, although individually the seven activities in Table 15.1 take a total of 35 days, by careful planning the project can be completed in 21 days.

Float times

Table 15.2 Float times

The float times can be derived from the network and are set out in Table 15.2.

Activity	Total float (days)
A*	0
B	2
C*	0
D	1
E*	0
F	1
G*	0

*Critical activity.

> **KEY TERMS**
>
> **float time:** the amount of time that non-critical activities within a project can be delayed without affecting the deadline for completion of the project as a whole.
>
> **total float for an activity:** the number of days that an activity can be delayed without delaying the project, measured by the formula:
>
> total float for an activity = LFT – EST – duration of the activity
>
> Thus activity D can be delayed by 15 – 11 – 3 = 1 day, without delaying the project.

Constructing a critical path network from descriptive information

In real life, managers will not be given a table of activities with their prerequisites neatly defined. The first step in compiling a real network is to work out the logic behind the project in order to identify sequences of events.

The following activities represent the steps needed to introduce a new product that has just completed its design stage:
A Brief advertising agencies — 1 day
B Await ideas from agencies — 15 days
C Select advertising agency — 2 days
D Prepare advertising materials for launch — 40 days
E Order new production machinery — 3 days
F Await delivery of machinery — 20 days
G Install machinery — 12 days
H Production run for initial launch — 15 days
I Recruit production workers — 21 days
J Off-the-job training of production workers — 6 days
K Launch product — 1 day

Activities A to D form a logical sequence of events in the marketing department, with A being the first stage. Activities E to H are the sequence of production department activities, with activity E being able to start at the beginning of the network. Activities I and J are human resource management roles. Activity I can start at the beginning of the project and is the prerequisite of activity J. However, J must be completed before activity H, as this stage requires trained workers. Once all the marketing and production activities have been completed, the final activity (K) can take place.

The sequence of events based on the logic described above is shown in Table 15.3.

Activity	Duration (days)	Prerequisite(s)
A	1	–
B	15	A
C	2	B
D	40	C
E	3	–
F	20	E
G	12	F
H	15	G, J
I	21	–
J	6	I
K	1	D, H

Table 15.3
Network of activities needed to launch a new product

Figure 15.4 shows the network based on these data. The critical path is A–B–C–D–K.

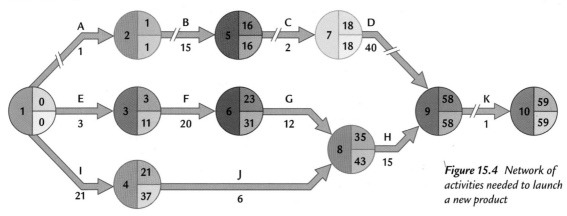

Figure 15.4 Network of activities needed to launch a new product

e EXAMINER'S VOICE

Note that, although the sequence of events in the network may not change, the critical path can change because it is dependent on the timings of the activities. For example, in Figure 15.4 an increase in the duration of F from 20 days to 30 days will lead to a change in the critical path (from A–B–C–D–K to E–F–G–H–K). Overall, the duration of the project will increase from 59 days to 61 days.

Benefits of critical path analysis

Use of critical path analysis brings many advantages to a business, if the system operates smoothly.

- Critical path analysis allows a business to improve the efficiency of its resources. If the business can reduce the time taken to complete a project, it can translate these savings in time into cost savings. In turn, this will increase the competitiveness of the business, particularly if cost or speed of completion is a vital factor in the eyes of the customers.
- The process lets a business know precisely when activities are scheduled to take place. This assists the business in its resource planning and stock ordering. This should improve the efficiency of resources, such as labour, as it enables the business to make sure that the use of labour corresponds to the available supply.
- If necessary, the business can use CPA to investigate changes in resources or sequencing that would improve efficiency. For example, additional resources can be transferred from a non-critical activity to one on the critical path. This will reduce the time taken on the critical path and therefore reduce the overall duration of the project.
- CPA can be used to help control and review. Monitoring of progress against the original plan will identify any delays and allow the business to take steps to rectify the problem.
- Critical path analysis forces managers to engage in detailed planning. This helps the business to reduce the risk of delays.
- The business's relationships with its customers can be improved, as CPA can provide detailed information on the schedule for completion of a project.
- During the operation of the project, CPA can be used to calculate the likely impact of any delays that are unavoidable.

FACT FILE

Critical path analysis at Unilever

Unilever is a company that has benefited from using CPA to obtain an integrated view of its projects. A network constructed to plan the release of a new food product shows that, at different stages of the network, the critical path activities are, on the whole, marketing department responsibilities. However, at particular points of time, production, packaging and distribution activities are on the critical path. Consequently, Unilever managers know when it is most vital to monitor the progress of particular departments.

- Critical path analysis helps the firm to estimate the minimum time within which it is possible to complete a project (through identifying the critical path).
- By identifying the (critical) activities that cannot be delayed without delaying the completion of the project, CPA gives a firm the opportunity to focus its attention on the more 'important' tasks.

- The network helps the organisation to calculate the extent to which other (non-critical) activities can be delayed. This reduces the possibility of a project failing because the delay in a non-critical activity suddenly becomes significant and causes that activity to be on the critical path.
- Critical path analysis allows a firm to plan when it needs particular resources. This means that the firm can avoid holding unnecessary stock.

Problems of using critical path analysis

Although critical path analysis is a useful tool, its use can lead to difficulties:

- It can encourage rigidity. On paper, CPA works best with fixed times for each activity and a fixed sequence of activities. This may encourage managers to see these timings and this sequence as unchangeable, so they may miss opportunities to reduce the overall time of a project by failing to identify the scope for flexibility.
- As every activity in a network is strictly timetabled, it can lead to greater inefficiency if a crucial activity is delayed. This can happen in projects such as the construction of a building, where subcontractors and suppliers will plan their workloads around the original network. Any delay can lead to the project coming to a halt because, for example, the crane hire company has agreed to hire the crane to another company or the electricians are working on another firm's building.

- Complex activities may be difficult to represent accurately on a network. (In practice, businesses use computer modelling to construct highly complex networks, but these need to be understood by the manager.)
- CPA relies on estimates of the expected duration of activities. If these are inaccurate, the whole process may break down. As major projects are often one-offs, it is possible that the firm has no experience in this field. Consequently, the probability of producing an accurate forecast of timings is low.
- CPA encourages businesses to focus on the speed of completion of a project, rather than other elements such as quality and flexibility to meet customers' needs.

ⓔ EXAMINER'S VOICE

Although most networks are large-scale projects, it is not possible to include a complex network in an examination. Any requirements to interpret a network will therefore involve a fairly small-scale project. The minimum mark for a Unit 3 AQA question is 10 marks, so remember that critical path analysis is not just about drawing diagrams. Make sure that, for a particular project, you can present relevant arguments on the benefits of CPA and the limitations to its usefulness.

CPA diagrams may also be used in appendices to a case study. In these situations you may be required to understand whether the critical path network shows that a project can be completed within a certain deadline, or whether a delay might mean that a deadline is missed.

PRACTICE EXERCISE 1 — Total: 35 marks (30 minutes)

1 What is meant by the term 'network analysis'? *(3 marks)*

2 What is meant by the term 'critical path'? *(3 marks)*

3 In a network, what is represented by:
   a a node (circle)? *(2 marks)*   b a line? *(2 marks)*

4 Distinguish between the EST and the LST. *(3 marks)*

5 What is a prerequisite? *(2 marks)*

6 What is meant by the term 'float'? *(2 marks)*

7 Explain three advantages to a business of using critical path analysis. *(9 marks)*

8 Explain three problems that may arise as a result of using critical path analysis. *(9 marks)*

PRACTICE EXERCISE 2 — Total: 45 marks (50 minutes)

The table shows a network of activities.

Activity	Duration (days)	Prerequisite(s)
A	5	–
B	4	–
C	5	A
D	8	B
E	3	D
F	3	D
G	6	C, E
H	5	F

1 a Draw a fully labelled network diagram of the activities described in the table, including the numbered nodes, the duration of each activity, the earliest start times (ESTs) and the latest finish times (LFTs). *(12 marks)*
   b Show the critical path. *(2 marks)*

2 Based on the original network in each case, describe how the critical path and overall duration of the project will be affected by the following changes in the duration of individual activities:
   a Activity F increases from 3 days to 6 days. *(3 marks)*
   b Activity D decreases from 8 days to 4 days. *(3 marks)*
   c Activity C increases from 5 days to 12 days. *(3 marks)*

The following diagram shows a sample network. Questions 3 and 4 are based on this network.

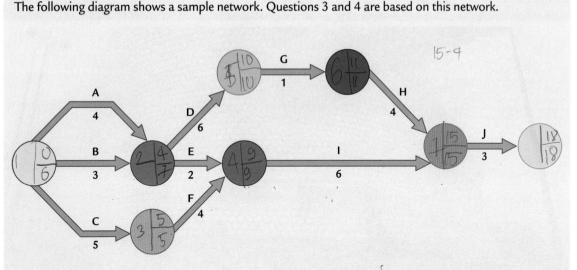

15-4

3 Complete the nodes, showing the earliest start times (ESTs) and latest finish times (LFTs), and show the critical path.   *(6 marks)*

4 Copy the table below and complete the prerequisites column, based on the network shown in the diagram in question 3.

(6 marks)

Activity	Duration (days)	Prerequisite(s)
A	4	
B	3	
C	5	
D	6	
E	2	
F	4	
G	1	
H	4	
I	6	
J	3	

5 Complete a network and show the critical path for the following project:

Ingredients are mixed for 15 minutes and then weighed (1 minute). At the same time, the container is cleaned for 5 minutes and labelled (2 minutes) before being transported to the production line (6 minutes).

Once all of the above processes have been completed, the ingredients are placed in the container (7 minutes). The finished product is then simultaneously checked for defects (2 minutes) while being placed on a conveyor belt that puts the containers into boxes of a dozen products (4 minutes). The finished products then take 3 minutes to be loaded on to pallets, ready for delivery.   *(10 marks)*

CASE STUDY 1 Critical path analysis at Balfour Beatty

TOPFOTO

The construction industry is a major user of critical path analysis. In order to improve efficiency, construction firms use CPA to plan the most efficient method of construction and to monitor progress.

Balfour Beatty is a major construction company that uses CPA. In one project, the use of CPA enabled the company to design and build a new road within the budget of £35 million considerably quicker than customer expectations. The customer requested completion in 124 weeks, but through careful planning using CPA, Balfour Beatty was able to plan the project for completion in 79 weeks.

Moreover, through close supervision and teamwork with its subcontractors, the company was able to take advantage of favourable external factors and complete the project 9.5 weeks earlier than its own estimate, despite some changes that increased the scope of the project.

Construction companies face particular problems in planning projects because they rely on other companies (subcontractors) to complete certain tasks. Furthermore, expensive earth-moving equipment is hired and any delays (or even improvements) in the schedule can make it difficult to acquire resources at the time they are needed. For this reason, companies tend to build large margins of error into their project timings.

A further complication that is often faced by construction companies is the need to keep existing facilities open. New roads or shopping centres can cause tremendous disruption to existing businesses. Most contracts now reward construction companies for planning projects that minimise disruption to existing facilities.

A project in which this was an important element was the construction of Birmingham's Bull Ring Shopping Centre. Balfour Beatty was involved in this project, supporting the main contractor, Sir Robert McAlpine.

The following list gives the estimated timings of certain key aspects of the completion of the Bull Ring between 2000 and 2003:

A Demolition of old Bull Ring – 8 months
B Planning of new Bull Ring – 6 months
C Agreement reached with key retailers – 4 months
D Construction of West Mall – 25 months
E Construction of East Mall – 23 months
F Construction of 'flagship' stores – 18 months
G Food Court constructed – 5 months
H External work on Rotunda – 4 months
I Completion of works – 1 month

These are represented in the critical path network shown in Figure 15.5.

AQA A2 Business Studies

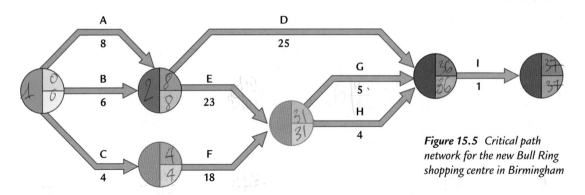

Figure 15.5 Critical path network for the new Bull Ring shopping centre in Birmingham

Sources: Highways Agency website, www.highways.gov.uk; Balfour Beatty website, www.balfourbeatty.com; Bull Ring website, www.bullring.co.uk.

Preliminary questions   Total: 15 marks (25 minutes)

1 Copy and complete the network for the construction of the new Bull Ring and use your completed diagram and timings to identify the following:
   a the earliest start time for activity G   (2 marks)
   b the latest finish time for activity H   (2 marks)
   c the 'float' time for activity F   (2 marks)
   d the critical path   (2 marks)
   e the prerequisites of activity E   (2 marks)

2 Based on your network, briefly indicate the implications of a delay of 6 months in the completion of activity D.   (5 marks)

Case study questions   Total: 30 marks (35 minutes)

1 Discuss the benefits to Balfour Beatty of using critical path analysis in order to plan its construction projects.   (15 marks)

2 Evaluate the main difficulties faced by Balfour Beatty and other construction companies in their use of CPA to plan their projects.   (15 marks)

Lean production

Methods of lean production

This section looks at two of the main elements of lean production:
- just-in-time production
- continuous improvement (kaizen) and the principles of gradual change and staff involvement in change

KEY TERM

lean production: production based on the range of waste-saving measures inspired by Japanese manufacturing companies.

KEY TERM

just-in-time:
a Japanese philosophy that organises operations so that items of stock (inventory) arrive just at the time they are needed for production or sale. The ultimate aim is to eliminate the need for stock, although in practice this is not always ideal.

DID YOU KNOW?

The move to flexible production is being driven by consumers. Companies such as Dell have led the way in providing fast, customised products for consumers. In the travel industry, the fastest-growing sector is the provision of tailor-made holidays built around the requirements of the individual customer.

Just-in-time

Purposes of just-in-time

The main aim of just-in-time is to reduce waste by eliminating the need for high levels of stock. This can enable a business to reduce costs by cutting warehouse space and staffing costs linked to the warehouse. Lower stock levels also reduce the losses to a firm caused by pilferage (theft), damage during storage, or products perishing or becoming obsolete (out-of-date).

Just-in-time techniques also save time, as stock can be delivered straight to the production line or shelves, ready for use, saving on the time spent moving them from the 'goods in' area to the warehouse and then on to the production line or shelf. The space saved makes the production line more compact, reducing distances between different stages of production, and avoiding some of the problems of stock cluttering up the factory that can be commonplace in factories not using just-in-time methods.

Just-in-time also aims to provide flexibility for customers. Companies with zero stock levels are more willing to respond to changes in customer tastes, as they will not suffer from unsold stock if there is a sudden shift to the production of new goods.

A central business aim is to 'add value'. Stock in a warehouse is not adding value to the business; it only adds value when it forms part of the finished product. Just-in-time places stock straight on to the production line, where it immediately adds value.

Just-in-time methods are often described as a system based on 'pull' rather than 'push'. Traditionally, businesses made products which were 'pushed' through the production process in the hope that they would then sell in the marketplace. The driving force behind the decision to manufacture was the firm's desire to sell a product. Just-in-time is linked to customers' needs instead. Customers place an order, which leads to the product being made. The product is 'pulled' through the production process by the desire of the customer to have a particular design on a particular date. The push system led to stocks of finished products waiting to be sold. The pull system means that there is a customer waiting for the finished product, eliminating the need for high stock levels.

Requirements of a just-in-time system

To operate efficiently, just-in-time requires careful planning and organisation. For it to work a firm needs:

- **Excellent communications and high levels of cooperation and flexibility from suppliers.** Ironically, to guarantee just-in-time deliveries to their customers, some suppliers need to keep high levels of stock in case of problems.
- **Reliable and flexible employees** who are prepared to modify their workloads to cope with sudden increases in activity. Many organisations have needed to agree new contracts and working conditions with their employees, as rigid job descriptions prevented the success of just-in-time methods. Workforces have also changed to include more short-term or part-time workers, who can help a business to cope with sudden changes in workload.
- **A flexible approach to managing workers,** so that employees see tangible benefits (such as financial rewards or time off) from their greater flexibility. A benefit that has suited both employees and employers has been increased training to allow workers to become multi-skilled (able to do a wide range of jobs). This has increased job opportunities for workers and flexibility for the organisation.
- **Suitable equipment** so that machinery can be adapted quickly to changing needs. Many production lines can be changed in this way. For example, to change their production, cinemas only need to insert a different film, so they can plan their schedules on a short-term basis according to customer demand. Car manufacturers can modify the fittings, colours and components of a particular model of car so that six different versions of a model are completed in sequence. These are then driven straight on to the transporter, for delivery to the garage whose customers ordered those styles of car.

Just-in-time and people

Just-in-time links closely to people management. Greater responsibility is placed on individual employees. Many factories give authority to production-line workers to stop the production line if they detect that a delivery of new stock is likely to endanger the quality of the finished product.

Flexibility is also key. Workers in the factories of suppliers must be prepared to complete a job at short notice, if an organisation wants an immediate delivery. Similarly, workers at the organisation must react quickly to sudden changes in the requirements of their customers. Multi-skilling and job enrichment have become essential features of organisations, so that the workforce has the ability and authority to meet urgent requests from customers without having to consult with and involve other staff or managers. It is also possible that well-trained, highly-skilled staff will be able to anticipate changes in the market and prepare the business in a proactive manner, rather than constantly reacting to changes after they have happened.

kaizen (or continuous improvement): a policy of implementing small, incremental changes in order to achieve better quality and/or greater efficiency. These changes are invariably suggested by employees and emanate from a corporate culture that encourages employees to identify potential improvements.

Kaizen at Toyota

In January 2009, middle managers at Toyota came up with an idea that would help to fight the threat of recession. They suggested that all Toyota middle managers should buy a new Toyota car.

Japanese companies like Toyota get an average of over 20 written suggestions per annum from each employee. In the UK, the average is estimated to be one idea every 6 years.

Table 15.4 Features of lean production compared to traditional (mass) production

Continuous improvement (kaizen)

Kaizen can operate through individuals or by using **kaizen groups** or **quality circles** — groups designated to identify potential productivity and quality improvements. It is considered to be a cost-effective means of steady improvement because all employees of an organisation support its aims.

The key features of kaizen are as follows:

■ It relies on many small steps, rather than on fewer, more significant changes, such as happen with research and development.
■ It uses everyday ideas from ordinary workers rather than major technological or dramatic innovative changes.
■ It usually focuses on methods rather than outcomes, assuming that improved methods and approaches will guarantee a more effective outcome.
■ It employs the talents of the workforce rather than requiring expensive equipment, and encourages staff to use their talents to seek improvements.

Kaizen is based on two main principles:

■ **Gradual change.** Kaizen relies on many small changes rather than sudden leaps. Britain's industrial revolution in the nineteenth century was characterised by a number of dramatic leaps forward, caused by major inventions or innovations. In contrast, the kaizen approach concentrates on finding lots of small improvements. Over time, the sheer volume of improvements leads to major advances.
■ **Staff suggestions.** Because continuous improvement relies on staff identifying ways in which efficiency can be improved, it is more likely to be successful if staff are given opportunities and encouraged to express their opinions. It also works better if the workforce is more educated and skilled, and thus able to recognise potential weaknesses in the firm's existing approach.

Table 15.4 summarises the main features of lean production, contrasting it with the features of more traditional (mass production) methods.

Lean production	Mass production
Short lead times	Longer lead times
Minimal stock levels	High stock levels
'Right first time' quality	Quality inspection of finished product
Elimination of unnecessary processes	No close scrutiny of unnecessary processes
High levels of worker responsibility	Low levels of worker responsibility
Multi-skilled workers	Specialist or unskilled workers
Excellent two-way communications	One-way communications
Frequent, small deliveries from suppliers	Fewer, large-scale deliveries from suppliers

Benefits of lean production

Lean production has been widely adopted because it creates a variety of advantages for firms. These include:

- increased productivity as better methods are identified by staff and greater flexibility prevents bottlenecks and idle time on the production line
- a more motivated workforce as a result of their greater skills and more interesting jobs, with greater chances of recognition and responsibility
- increased worker participation in decision making leading to better, more informed ideas and methods
- reduced waste and stockholding costs, improving firms' cash-flow positions
- higher quality and a greater variety of goods and services that are continuously improved for the customers' benefit

FACT FILE

Inflexibility in the market for foreign holidays

In July 2008 a large number of campsites in the UK were fully booked as the exchange rate made overseas holidays less attractive. However, continued rain led to many people deciding to book last-minute holidays abroad. Resorts in Croatia and Tunisia experienced over 100% increases in late bookings because they had spare capacity, but in some traditional destinations tour operators had cut back on holiday bookings. They were unable to respond to the sudden increase in demand by UK tourists, as hotels had been booked by operators from other countries.

EXAMINER'S VOICE

The topics of people in organisations and operations management are closely linked. The whole process of lean production is focused on giving employees more autonomy and responsibility, particularly for product quality and control over their own work situation. Rotation of job roles provides variety and less likelihood of boredom or monotony. Project teams lead to improved communications, which can lead to improvements in motivation. These factors are linked in with Herzberg's motivators, the higher-level needs in Maslow's hierarchy and Mayo's human relations school of motivation.

Why do some firms use traditional methods?

Lean production does not always guarantee benefits. Many firms choose more traditional production methods so that they can benefit from bulk buying. If demand is predictable, they will know how much to produce and may not need any flexibility. Moreover, unexpected demand is not always dealt with more efficiently by using flexible methods.

Lean production at easyCar

An example of a business that employs lean production techniques is easyCar. Its goal is to simplify the product that it offers and pass the benefits on to customers in the form of lower prices.

- Customers are expected to return the car in a clean condition (or pay a charge for cleaning set by easyCar).
- In the past, an empty-to-empty fuel policy was used, to save on staff costs for refuelling (although this is now full-to-empty at many branches).
- 90% utilisation of cars is targeted.

- Only one type of car is stocked at each branch.
- Customers must make their own way to and from the easyCar base — no delivery or collection is arranged.
- A free mileage level may be set — additional charges can be made if these limits are exceeded.
- Bookings are made through the company website or a call centre.
- Cancellations are not usually refunded.
- Marketing costs are reduced by displaying the company name on each car.

Source: easyCar website (www.easycar.com).

PRACTICE EXERCISE 3   Total: 20 marks (20 minutes)

1 Study the Fact File on easyCar and identify the characteristic of lean production that the company uses most often. Justify your choice. *(7 marks)*

2 Explain the meaning of the phrase 'time-based management'. *(3 marks)*

3 What is a kaizen group? *(4 marks)*

4 Select any organisation of your choice and explain how kaizen (continuous improvement) could be used to improve its profitability. *(6 marks)*

CASE STUDY 2   A comparison between Marks and Spencer and Zara

Marks and Spencer represents the traditional, large-scale approach to fashion retailing. Zara, a Spanish company, is an example of lean production in this trade.

Marks and Spencer buys in large quantities and enjoys the benefits of economies of scale. However, because it is 'pushing' garments into the stores, it is taking a risk

that its idea of this year's fashion may differ from its customers' views. For this reason, Marks and Spencer has been most successful in providing high-quality items where fashion has been less important (such as socks). If fashion changes quickly, Marks and Spencer struggles because its high-quality, high-price strategy becomes irrelevant. Marks and Spencer tried to change into a more fashion-focused store, but has met resistance from both existing and potential customers. Its strategy of targeting the teenage fashion market was withdrawn within 6 months.

In contrast, Zara's approach is based on speed and economy. Zara's designers are crucial to the company's success. They must decide on the stock to be produced, although this is mainly choosing which items to copy from the popular designer items in fashion shows and celebrity events, and then simplifying them so that they can be made quickly and cheaply. This is a demanding role, as designers need to combine a sense of fashion with considerable understanding of the manufacturing process. Design time is minimised and production and distribution take about 5 days. A few copies of each item are delivered to each store, in a limited range of sizes and colours. The decisions on whether to order further stock are made by shop managers, who can identify which items are selling well. Thus there is less risk of unsold stock — a major problem for Marks and Spencer.

For Zara quality is low, but with new stocks in the shops every 2–3 weeks it is unlikely that the garments will be worn long enough for quality to become a problem. Zara has also found that customers visit its stores more frequently, because they know that a completely new batch of stock will have arrived. In addition to empowering the designers and shop managers, Zara has given more independence to its workshops, which deliver directly to the shops in most cases. The differences in approach between Zara and Marks and Spencer are summarised in Table 15.5.

Zara has been flattered by the number of businesses benchmarking against the company. Visits from senior managers of businesses such as Marks and Spencer are a testament to the success of Zara's approach to fashion retailing. From its formation in La Coruña in Spain in 1975, Zara has grown to become an international business with over 4,100 stores in 71 different countries, including 63 Zara fashion stores in the UK, although its parent company Inditex has a further 25 stores in the UK. In 2007/08 Zara overtook Gap to become the world's biggest fashion retailer.

Sources: various, including www.inditex.com and www.marksandspencer.com.

Table 15.5 The fashion cycle at Marks and Spencer and Zara

Marks and Spencer	Zara
Fashion cycle (12 months)	**Fashion cycle (2–3 weeks)**
design (anticipating customer tastes)	copy designs from fashion shows or celebrities
↓	↓
purchase raw materials	manufacture (emphasising speed rather than quality)
↓	↓
manufacture (emphasising quality of garment)	distribute limited numbers and sell
↓	↓
distribute	further distribution and sale, pulled by demand from shops
↓	↓
sell	replace with new stock
↓	
discount (if stock is not selling)	

Preliminary questions

Total: 20 marks (25 minutes)

1 Explain two benefits to Marks and Spencer arising from its approach to large-scale retailing. *(6 marks)*

2 Explain why Marks and Spencer's approach is more suited to socks than to fashion items. *(6 marks)*

3 Zara's supply of clothing operates on a 'just-in-time' basis. Analyse two factors that might lead to problems in using this approach. *(8 marks)*

Case study questions

Total: 30 marks (40 minutes)

1 To what extent is the success of Zara's operations management dependent on its strategy of empowering some of its key employees? *(10 marks)*

2 Evaluate the advantages and disadvantages to Zara of its shorter product development times. *(20 marks)*

CASE STUDY 3 Herman Miller

Herman Miller is a supplier of office furniture that has successfully introduced lean production. Traditionally, Herman Miller supplied large businesses, but it recognised that small businesses were likely to become a growth area for office furniture. Smaller businesses were more concerned about price and speed of delivery, and less worried about choice of colours and fabrics.

The office furniture industry was conditioned to accept delays. An average order would be planned to take 8 weeks, but the company still delivered a third of all orders late. This led to late delivery payments from customers and reduced customer loyalty. A lot of effort had to be made finding new customers because repeat orders were relatively low as a result of poor customer service.

Stockholding was also costly. Herman Miller held high levels of stock, just in case they were needed by customers. However, whole orders were invariably postponed because one important item of furniture was out of stock. This poor stock control meant that high stock levels invariably did not help to speed up delivery of an order. The processing of a customer request for furniture normally went through three stages:

1 **From initial contact with the customer to the placing of the order.** This process took up to 3 months as Herman Miller tried to finalise the exact needs of the customer and then had to identify the manufacturer whose products would meet the customer's requirements. The process concluded with a costing of the customer's order based on the manufacturer's costings.

2 **From order to delivery of the furniture.** The manufacturer would receive the order from Herman Miller, and within 4–8 weeks the manufacturer would deliver the goods to a Herman Miller warehouse.

3 **From warehouse to installation.** Herman Miller would collect the items from the warehouse, deliver them to the customer's building and install them on site.

Herman Miller decided to introduce a new system based on lean production.

As a result, sales staff were able to use a laptop to show a three-dimensional view of the office layout from any angle and change it to include or exclude different items of furniture. This helped customers to plan layouts and furnishing that met their specific needs much more effectively. The costs of any changes to the order could also be calculated on the laptop. This reduced stage 1 from up to 3 months to 1 or 2 days, as data on manufacturers' products and their costs were included in the database.

Using the laptop, the order could be sent directly to the furniture manufacturer. Previously, these manufacturers had been reluctant to begin production because amendments were often made, but now the orders were final, so manufacturers no longer delayed production. The average time to manufacture the furniture (stage 2) fell to only 2 weeks.

The expense of warehousing has also been eliminated. With definite completion dates now agreed, the manufacturers deliver directly to the customers. Consequently, stage 3 became installation of the furniture, eliminating the cost of warehousing completely.

In the 5 years following the introduction of Herman Miller's new lean production system, late deliveries fell from 33% of all orders to 0.3%, even though planned delivery times to customers fell from 8 weeks to 2 weeks.

Staff morale has increased dramatically. The irregular and unpredictable arrival of furniture under the old system meant that, in the past, Herman Miller used a very structured authoritarian approach to the installation and fitting of the furniture. The certainty that all of the furniture will now be delivered has enabled Herman Miller to adopt cell production techniques. Each team of fitters is given responsibility for deciding on the best approach to take, and teamwork methods are employed. With more and more jobs being one-off orders, customised to the specific layout and requirements of the customer, greater variety and responsibility have been added to the office fitters' jobs. Individuals or teams are now responsible for the quality of the installation.

The higher level of enthusiasm among the workforce has led Herman Miller to consider the introduction of kaizen groups.

In the first 5 years after the new lean production system was introduced, customer satisfaction levels increased, annual sales growth was 25% per annum, stock levels were halved and profit margins increased.

Source: adapted from the MMC Views website, www.mmc.com.

Preliminary questions   Total: 15 marks (20 minutes)

1 Explain why a high level of enthusiasm would be helpful if kaizen groups were introduced
   by Herman Miller.   *(7 marks)*

2 Analyse two features of the new lean production system that allowed Herman Miller to
   improve efficiency.   *(8 marks)*

Case study questions   Total: 30 marks (40 minutes)

1 Evaluate the importance of time-based management to Herman Miller.   *(15 marks)*

2 The introduction of lean production led to higher staff morale at Herman Miller.
   Discuss the main reasons for this improvement in morale.   *(15 marks)*

Operational strategies

CASE STUDY Metov's

Metov's Plastics had grown steadily since opening its first factory in Liverpool. At first, Pavlo Metov's business had struggled to compete with its competitors, but when Pavlo patented a new process for finishing the plastics products, the level of profitability grew rapidly.

Initially these profits came about from cheaper manufacturing costs. However, Pavlo realised that the process could help many manufacturers that were not in direct competition with Metov's Plastics. As a result, the company licensed the process to a number of other businesses. With this new revenue source, Pavlo was able to focus on some of his business's weaknesses:

- The marketing budget was expanded so that more market research could be undertaken, in order to assist the firm's understanding of its market. This led to a series of highly successful advertising campaigns, which produced major increases in sales revenue. As the business expanded, Metov's Plastics was able to use a wider range of media, enabling it to reach more potential customers in a cost-effective way.
- R&D spending was increased, leading to a number of new products that Metov's plastics patented. In addition to increasing sales volume, these patents helped the company to increase its prices and profit margins.
- The company's ICT system was upgraded so that more advanced software could be utilised. This enabled the company to plan projects more effectively using network analysis. It also improved communication within the business.

Most of Metov's customers were small- to medium-scale enterprises that used the plastics to manufacture finished products. Initially these businesses were attracted to Metov's Plastics by Metov's ability to offer low prices and consistent quality. However, as more and more of these businesses adopted lean production methods, speed of delivery and the flexibility to meet changing needs became the top priority. Metov's adopted a 24-hour, round-the-clock shift system so that it could meet customer orders within a matter of hours. However, although it could manufacture the products quickly, distribution times caused problems.

Liverpool had been chosen as the location of the factory because of its access to imported raw materials. It also provided good access to the northwest of England, where most of Metov's early customers were located. However, as Metov's business expanded, a growing number of customers were based in other parts of the UK.

Pavlo had been concerned that production at the Liverpool factory had been getting too high, almost reaching the factory's capacity of 10.2 million units per year. The business had experienced difficulties in extending its premises, so some technical diseconomies had occurred. The operations management team had redesigned the factory in order to increase the levels of production possible, but the space was very constrained. This had led to a growing number of accidents and inefficiencies, as stocks of particular products were difficult to access because of the congestion in the factory.

Furthermore, a number of customers complained about missing orders and poor communications. These communication problems had also led to some industrial disputes, as the workforce representatives argued that their thoughts and ideas were being ignored by management. Middle managers had also complained about their lack of involvement in decision making. The workers had gone on strike for 2 days — this coincided with two large orders from customers that had not been delivered on time. The two customers had not returned to Metov's Plastics again and Pavlo himself blamed the workforce for this loss of two important customers.

The finance department had produced figures showing production levels and unit costs over the last 6 years, which confirmed Pavlo's suspicions that the factory was becoming less efficient as the business expanded. (These figures are shown in Appendix 1.)

The directors met and agreed that a second factory should be built in a separate location. As Metov's Plastics expanded, a growing number of its orders were coming from overseas — particularly from companies based in France, Italy and Spain. In the UK, the main customer base was now situated in the southeast and Midlands.

In autumn 2008 the directors agreed to open a new factory at one of two separate sites:

- an existing, empty factory unit in Dover in Kent, which could be easily adapted to Metov's Plastics' needs
- a brand-new factory unit in Cadiz, in Spain

Details of the financial background to these two factories is provided in Appendix 2. Details of other information related to the two factories are provided in Appendix 3.*

*References to customers in appendices 2 and 3 apply only to those customers whose orders will be met from the new factory. Once the new factory is opened, Metov's Plastics' plan is to produce 8 million units a year in the Liverpool factory and the remaining units in either Cadiz or Dover. Sales are expected to increase by 1.5 million units a year for each of the next 5 years, with sales of 17.5 million units forecast for 2013.

Pavlo had calculated that, based on predicted orders, it would be a 'disaster' if a new factory could not be opened within 28 weeks. However, two major orders were due for completion in 20 weeks' time and in 24 weeks' time. Failure to meet these two orders on time would not be a 'disaster', but would lead to financial losses of £1 million and £2 million respectively.

The company had appointed a consultant in Spain who estimates that the factory in Cadiz could be opened in exactly 26 weeks' time. For the Dover factory, the Operations Management Team had provided information in the form of a network, in order to calculate the critical path. Details are shown in Appendix 4.

Appendix 1 Unit costs in the Liverpool Factory, 2003–08

Year	Output (millions of units)	Unit (average) costs (£ per unit)
2003	4.0	£5.27
2004	6.0	£4.75
2005	8.0	£4.40
2006	9.0	£4.40
2007	9.5	£4.47
2008	10.0	£4.67

Appendix 2 Financial data relating to the two proposed factories (forecasts)

Factor	Cadiz, Spain	Dover, England
Forecast average costs of production (£ per unit)	£4.33	£4.85
Distribution costs per unit, 2009 — based on existing customer base	£1.45	£0.45
Distribution costs per unit, 2013 — based on planned expansion into France, Italy and Spain	£0.77	£0.88
Cost of setting up factory	£14 million	£9 million
Annual running costs of factory	£6 million per annum	£8 million per annum

Appendix 3 *Other information relating to the two proposed factories (forecasts)*

Factor	Cadiz, Spain	Dover, England
Factory capacity (millions of units)	9.0	5.0
Shift system	9 a.m. to 5 p.m.	24 hours a day
Average lead time from order to delivery	48 hours	24 hours
Quality of finished products: minimum = 1; maximum = 10 (industry average = 7.8)	7.3	8.4
Wastage (%)	0.5%	2.5%
% of materials recyclable	85%	90%
Energy efficiency	High	Low
Carbon footprint	Zero	Low

Appendix 4 *Critical path analysis: setting up the new factory in Dover, Kent*

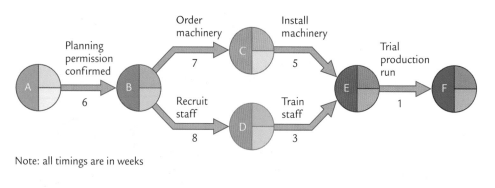

Note: all timings are in weeks

Questions
Total: 80 marks (1 hour 45 minutes)

1 Examine the ways in which Metov's Plastics benefited from the use of lean production techniques such as time management and CPA. *(10 marks)*

2 Discuss whether the economies of scale enjoyed by Metov's Plastics in its Liverpool factory outweighed the diseconomies of scale that it experienced. *(16 marks)*

3 To what extent did Metov's Plastics' policy of innovation help the company to grow? *(16 marks)*

4 Using the data in appendices 1 to 4, and any other information from the case study, evaluate whether the business should choose to open its new factory in Cadiz, Spain or Dover, England. *(38 marks)*

Chapter 16

Understanding HR objectives and strategies

This chapter begins by explaining what human resource management (HRM) is and why the human resource management approach has replaced the traditional personnel management approach. It then considers human resource (HR) objectives and assesses the internal and external factors that influence them. Finally it examines HR strategies, focusing on 'hard' and 'soft' strategies and the strengths and weaknesses of each.

Human resource management

Human resource management (HRM) is the strategic process of making the most efficient use of an organisation's employees. People are a vital resource for modern businesses, and planning their use must be part of strategic management if a business is to compete in global markets. HRM views activities relating to the workforce as integrated and vital in helping the organisation to achieve its corporate objectives. Thus, policies relating to recruitment, pay and appraisal should be formulated as part of a coordinated human resource strategy.

Since the 1980s, HRM has tended to replace personnel management in describing the function within business that focuses on the selection, appraisal, development and reward of people.

Personnel management regarded activities such as planning the workforce, recruitment and selection, training, appraisal, monitoring performance, and motivation and rewards as separate tasks to be done when necessary and in response to demand: in other words, it was *reactive*. HRM, on the other hand, regards all of these activities as being linked and integrated with all other areas and functions of the business and its development: that is, it is *proactive*.

> **KEY TERM**
>
> **human resource management:** the management of people at work in order to assist the organisation in achieving its objectives.

Horizontal and vertical matching

Each individual policy adopted in the management of people, such as recruitment, training and payment systems, should fit with every other policy used. This is the principle of horizontal matching. For example, an attempt to introduce flexible working needs to be considered in relation to the introduction of appropriate payment systems, training methods and appraisal systems.

Figure 16.1 HRM policies and horizontal matching

Source: adapted from C. J. Fombrun, N. M. Tichy and M. A. Devanna, *Strategic Human Resource Management*, John Wiley, 1984.

Figure 16.1 illustrates how all of the policies adopted by HRM fit together, and demonstrates horizontal matching. For example, individuals are selected, they perform their tasks and they are appraised. Appraisal leads to reward and payment, which in turn has an effect on performance. Appraisal also leads to training and development, which in turn affects performance and can lead to selection for a more senior position.

HRM policies should fit with the overall strategic position of an organisation. This means that how people are managed is determined largely by the goals the company has set itself, and that employees are organised to ensure that these goals are met. This is achieved by vertical matching between HRM policies and outcomes, and the corporate objectives and long-term direction of the company as a whole. Thus a company that is attempting to expand significantly may consider moving towards a more decentralised structure and will need an HR strategy that takes account of this in relation to the staff it recruits and promotes, and in relation to training and payment systems.

Figure 16.2 illustrates the idea of vertical matching. It demonstrates how the approach of HRM is integrated into the long-term competitive position of the firm by linking the individual HRM policies and outcomes developed in Figure 16.1 with the goals of the organisation as a whole.

Figure 16.2 HRM and vertical matching

Personnel functions

The fundamental difference between HRM and personnel management relates to the overall approach or philosophy adopted rather than to the activities undertaken. These activities remain the same whether undertaken by the personnel department or the HR department or by delegation to other departments, and can be considered as part of the *personnel function* of the organisation. The key activities covered by the personnel function are:

- human resource or workforce planning
- recruitment and selection
- training and development
- appraisal
- consultation

- collective bargaining
- wage and salary systems
- fringe benefits
- disciplinary and grievance procedures
- health and safety issues
- employment legislation

HR objectives

HR objectives will be determined by an organisation's overall corporate objectives, but regardless of these, all organisations are likely to pursue the following:

- **Matching workforce skills and the size and location of the workforce to the requirements of the business.** Thus, if a new plant is to be opened or new technology is being introduced, the HR function will need to ensure that sufficient employees are recruited and/or trained to meet the business's needs. One SMART HR target in this case might be 'the new factory, which will be fully operational by 1 February 2010, is fully staffed by 2 January 2010 and staff at manager and supervisor level are in post by 1 November 2009'. (Workforce planning is considered in more detail in Chapter 17.)
- **Minimising labour costs.** This will be an HR objective for all businesses in order to ensure they are operating efficiently, but it will be a particularly important objective when a business is suffering from financial problems. A SMART version of this objective might be 'to reduce overall staffing costs by 10% within the next 2 years'. This would then be translated into detailed strategies and more detailed short-term targets: for example, cutting back on the recruitment of new staff, removing a layer of management and delegating their responsibilities to a lower level in the organisation's hierarchy, and limiting wage increases to below the rate of inflation.
- **Making full use of the workforce's potential.** This will ensure that the productive efficiency of the workforce is maximised, and by improving motivation, it is likely to lead to greater productivity, reduced labour turnover and reduced absenteeism. Such an objective might be met by detailed strategies to involve the workforce more fully in decision making or by introducing job enrichment programmes (covered in detail in the AS textbook).
- **Maintaining good employer/employee relations.** Without good employer/employee relations, an organisation is unlikely to achieve maximum levels of productivity and is unlikely to have a committed, satisfied and motivated workforce. Effective employer/employee relations are considered in detail in Chapter 19.

e **EXAMINER'S VOICE**

Remember that, where possible, objectives should always be SMART, i.e. specific, measurable, agreed, realistic and time-bound.

FACT FILE

Employee commitment and leadership capability at HP

As mentioned in Chapter 1 (p. 3), corporate objectives at HP (Hewlett-Packard) include 'employee commitment' and 'leadership capability'. They are listed in full below.

Employee commitment

To help HP employees share in the company's success that they make possible; to provide people with employment opportunities based on performance; to create with them a safe, exciting and inclusive work environment that values their diversity and recognises individual contributions; and to help them gain a sense of satisfaction and accomplishment from their work.

Leadership capability

To develop leaders at every level who are accountable for achieving business results and exemplifying our values.

GROUP EXERCISE

Develop SMART HR objectives that might assist HP in achieving the corporate objectives listed in the fact file.

Factors influencing HR objectives

Both internal and external factors can influence HR objectives. **Internal factors** include:

- **Financial constraints.** These may, for example, affect HR objectives relating to the provision of staff training and development.
- **Corporate culture.** The impact of financial constraints on HR objectives may not be as severe if the corporate culture is such that HRM has a high profile in the organisation and human resources are recognised as a valuable asset that needs to be trained and developed
- **Organisational structure.** If the organisational structure becomes flatter or if delayering takes place, this may influence HR objectives in relation to motivation and communication.
- **Trade unions and the relationship between employers and employees.** These may influence HR objectives concerned with the introduction of change, such as flexible working practices.
- **New technology.** This may influence HR objectives by affecting the amount and type of labour required, training requirements and workers' motivation.
- **Overall performance of the business.** How the business develops or expands may influence HR objectives — for example, if unprofitable areas are closed down or the focus of the business changes.

External factors include:

- **Political factors.** For example, a change in government can lead to significant change in the attitude to trade unions and the amount of power they are able to wield in the workplace. The Conservative government in the 1980s,

led by prime minister Margaret Thatcher, took a very firm stance with trade unions. As a result, and via legislation, many of the freedoms they had previously enjoyed in relation to strike action and picketing were curtailed. These changes had a major impact on HR objectives in relation to employer/employee relations.

- **Economic factors.** For example, changes in the market and the economy may lead to changes in the demand for a firm's products and services, which are likely to cause changes in both the number and type of employees it requires.
- **Social factors.** For example, organisations have had to revise their HR objectives to take account of the increased emphasis on work–life balance and make moves towards more flexible working.
- **Technological factors.** For example, HR objectives must encompass the need to ensure that relevant staff are well trained in the use of computers, but also that full account is taken of their health and safety if they are sitting at a computer for most of the day.
- **Legislation.** HR objectives will be influenced by the presence, or introduction, of a range of employment-related legislation, including equal opportunities legislation, conditions of employment and industrial relations legislation. This will apply, for example, to objectives related to the recruitment and selection of employees, and to their training and promotion.

- **Actions of competitors.** These may influence HR objectives: for example, if there is a shortage of skills in a particular area, poaching of workers by competitors may occur and salaries may be forced up.
- **Structure of the population.** Factors such as the UK's ageing population and the future requirement for people to work beyond the traditional retirement age of 60/65 may influence HR objectives over the long term.

e **EXAMINER'S VOICE**

Note that many of the external factors noted above are structured around the PESTLE concept, which has been referred to in earlier chapters and will be considered in detail in Chapter 21.

HR strategies

There are two distinct types of approach or strategy to achieve an organisation's HR objectives. These are known as hard and soft HR strategies.

Hard HR strategy

In this approach, the aim is to utilise employees as efficiently as possible by directing them. A hard HR strategy treats employees simply as another resource, like raw materials or fixed capital. Just like any other resource, employees need to be monitored, used efficiently and have their costs controlled, in order to achieve the strategic objectives of the organisation. This approach sees HRM as essentially a control mechanism.

KEY TERMS

hard HR strategy: this strategy treats employees as a resource, just like any other resource, to be monitored and used in an efficient manner in order to achieve the strategic objectives of the organisation.

soft HR strategy: this strategy views employees as valuable assets, a major source of competitive advantage and of vital importance in achieving strategic objectives.

The style of management in organisations using a hard HR strategy is likely to be authoritarian or autocratic, and because the approach requires that authority is kept in the hands of a few, it is likely to involve a centralised rather than a decentralised organisational structure. This type of HR strategy includes workforce planning, analysing the current and future demand for and supply of employees, and predicting labour turnover.

Soft HR strategy

A soft HR strategy focuses on motivational issues, organisational culture, leadership approaches and industrial relations. As it is essentially a strategy for the personal development of all staff, soft HRM is likely to be associated with a democratic management style. With this approach, managers will wish to pass authority throughout the organisation and are likely to favour delegation and decentralisation rather than centralisation. Equally, because firms that embrace a soft HR approach recognise that they will benefit from employees' ideas, they are likely to encourage high levels of employee participation.

EXAMINER'S VOICE

Refer back to F. W. Taylor, one of the motivation theorists studied at AS. He viewed employees as a resource and believed that managers should manage and that workers should be told what to do and be paid according to their output — an approach that is not dissimilar to the hard HR approach.

Strengths and weakness of hard and soft HR strategies

Whether a company adopts a hard or soft HR approach depends largely on the history and culture of the firm, the approach and attitudes of managers and their management style, their relationship with recognised trade unions, the skills and attitudes of staff, and the level of employee participation in decision making.

Today, employees are likely to react more favourably to the soft HR approach than to the hard HR approach. As employees become increasingly educated and skilled, they begin to expect greater involvement in business decision making. This is encouraged by trends in industrial relations in the workplace, such as the partnership approach that is being adopted by some organisations and their recognised trade unions, requirements for European works councils and the EU Information and Consultation Directive (see Chapter 19).

The benefits of effective HR strategies for a firm are huge, including more motivated and committed staff, who contribute more ideas and exhibit greater loyalty. These factors, in turn, are likely to lead to lower labour turnover, less absenteeism and greater productivity, all of which can be used as indicators of effective HRM within an organisation.

PRACTICE EXERCISE 1   Total: 50 marks (45 minutes)

1 Explain the difference between human resource management and personnel management.   *(6 marks)*

2 What is horizontal matching in relation to human resource management?   *(4 marks)*

3 What is vertical matching in relation to human resource management?   *(4 marks)*

4 List four activities covered by the personnel function in an organisation.   *(4 marks)*

5 Explain how HR objectives are related to corporate objectives.   *(2 marks)*

6 Outline four HR objectives that are likely to be common to most organisations.   *(8 marks)*

7 Identify and explain two internal factors that might influence the HR objectives of an organisation.   *(6 marks)*

8 Identify and explain two external factors that might influence the HR objectives of an organisation.   *(6 marks)*

9 Distinguish between 'hard' and 'soft' HR strategies.   *(6 marks)*

10 What are the relative strengths of the soft HR strategy compared to the hard HR strategy?   *(4 marks)*

PRACTICE EXERCISE 2   Total: 20 marks (25 minutes)

Each of the following two situations corresponds to either the personnel management approach or the human resource management approach.

Situation A

Mike works in an engineering firm where most of his time is taken up with recruitment, training and development, and disciplinary issues. He has an assistant who does most of the interviewing along with managers from the relevant departments that require staff. Mike handles most of the disciplinary and grievance work. The disciplinary procedures mean that the appropriate departmental managers issue a first warning, but Mike is responsible for any subsequent warnings and further action. This action is taken in the presence of the departmental manager and also the trade union representative.

Mike spends a great deal of his time negotiating and consulting with the trade union representatives on a range of issues related to pay and conditions. In addition, he and his assistant meet with individual workers to discuss their particular problems. Mike or his assistant visits each departmental manager daily to discuss any problems and to obtain information about absenteeism. They also use these visits as an opportunity to talk to the workers and to deal with their problems.

Mike has no clear objectives, other than to ensure that there are sufficient and appropriately qualified staff in the firm and that there are no employee-related problems.

Situation B

Amanda works in an insurance company and has a number of assistants. The aim of the insurance company is to provide its customers with quality advice and service at competitive prices. Amanda's boss is a director of the company and is mainly concerned with strategic issues and how their work fits in with the broad corporate objectives. Amanda's department has its own set of objectives. These include reducing the levels of labour turnover and absenteeism for the company as a whole by 10% within the next year. Because of the competitive nature of the industry, they are also looking at ways of restructuring how people work in order to improve efficiency. Amanda and her staff spend much of their time considering these issues, assessing current policies and practices, coming up with proposals, and involving employees in designing and evaluating them.

Most of Amanda's time is spent with either her own staff or other departmental managers. She monitors absentee rates, labour turnover rates and a range of other personnel indicators on spreadsheets that are updated daily on her computer. Amanda's department provides advice to departmental managers, coordinates recruitment advertising and provides the associated paperwork and correspondence, but leaves responsibility for interviewing, appraising, disciplining and dismissing employees etc. to departmental managers and their staff.

Questions

1 Consider which of the two situations above matches the personnel management approach and which one matches the HRM approach. Justify your choices. *(8 marks)*

2 Using the information in the two scenarios, suggest how the corporate objectives of an organisation might be converted into HR objectives. *(4 marks)*

3 Which of the above scenarios suggests a hard or a soft HR strategy? Justify your response. *(8 marks)*

CASE STUDY Halfords

Halfords is the UK's leading retailer, on the basis of turnover, in each of the key product markets in which it operates:

- car maintenance (including car parts, servicing consumables such as oil, workshop tools and body repair equipment)
- car enhancement (including in-car entertainment systems, cleaning products, accessories, interior and exterior car styling products, navigation systems and alloy wheels)
- leisure (including cycles and cycle accessories and roof boxes, cycle carriers, child car seats and outdoor leisure equipment)

Halfords' store portfolio comprises approximately 430 stores across the UK. Its directors believe that Halfords

differentiates itself from its competitors through its national store portfolio, its broad product range, competitive pricing (achieved through scale of purchasing power), customer service offerings performed in-store by staff (e.g. fitting and repair services) and its strong brands.

The main HR objectives of Halfords in 2007 and 2008 are listed below. Each objective is followed by a brief commentary on Halfords' performance against that HR objective.

- **Ensure that employees have market-leading knowledge of a wide choice of products.** The success of staff training programmes is confirmed by results of customer satisfaction surveys. Halfords now employs specialists as follows: 750 capable of hardwired technology fitting, 2,000 trained to fit child seats professionally and safely, 1,500 trained to deliver satellite navigation systems and 800 fully trained bicycle mechanics.

- **Achieve a high level of safety training.** Staff are trained to provide training for customers in the use of their products, particularly for children's cycles. Occupational safety targets are based on the industry benchmark. The annual injury incident rate remains below the benchmark.
- **Increase the involvement of employees in the company.** Over 2,400 employees now have a personal stake through share ownership and share incentive schemes.
- **Practise ethical trading.** Halfords endeavours to ensure that its suppliers' workforces are not exploited.
- **Reward employees for their efforts.** A quarterly bonus scheme has been introduced for all staff, based on group, team and individual measures.

Preliminary questions
Total: 30 marks (35 minutes)

1 a Identify two other HR objectives that Halfords might have set. *(2 marks)*
  b Briefly explain why these would have been good objectives for Halfords to set. *(4 marks)*

2 Explain one internal factor that might have influenced Halfords' HR objectives. *(3 marks)*

3 Explain two external factors that might influence Halfords' HR objectives. *(6 marks)*

4 Consider why Halfords' HR objectives might be constrained by its financial objectives. *(6 marks)*

5 Identify three possible corporate objectives that might have determined Halfords' HR objectives. Explain your reasoning. *(9 marks)*

Case study questions
Total: 40 marks (50 minutes)

1 Consider whether Halfords' HR objectives are SMART? *(10 marks)*

2 Discuss the extent to which internal and external factors might have influenced Halfords' HR objectives and its ability to achieve those objectives. *(15 marks)*

3 In achieving its HR objectives, assess whether Halfords' HR strategy is likely to have been hard or soft, and why the particular strategy is likely to have been selected. *(15 marks)*

Chapter 17

Developing and implementing workforce plans

This chapter looks at the stages of workforce planning and the components of workforce plans. It also assesses the internal and external influences on workforce plans. Issues in implementing workforce plans are considered and, finally, the value of using workforce plans is discussed. The focus is on workforce planning as an integrated process, taking into account production, marketing and corporate plans.

Workforce plans

Workforce planning is one of the central activities of human resource management and helps organisations to foresee change, to identify trends and to implement human resource policies. It is an important part of the overall strategic plan and should be centralised to ensure a whole-company view.

Efficient workforce planning requires managers to question the existing employment structure at every opportunity: for example, when an employee leaves the firm, when an employee is promoted internally, when there is an increase in workload or when a new product or new technology is developed that requires employees with different skills.

KEY TERM

workforce planning: the method by which a business forecasts how many and what type of employees it needs now and in the future, and matches up the right type of employees to the needs of the business.

e **EXAMINER'S VOICE**

'Workforce planning' is a widely misunderstood term. It is specifically about matching the numbers of employees and the skills of the employees to a company's needs. In case studies, look for evidence of planning, or lack of it.

FACT FILE

Workforce planning at British Gas Services (BGS)

By predicting how much the UK market for domestic gas engineering services will grow, BGS is able to decide how many additional engineers it will need in the future. The company makes detailed forecasts of its demand for engineers for 1 year in advance and makes more general estimates for a further 2 years into the future. Its workforce requirements are influenced by demand from two different sources: contract customers who have service agreements with the company; and customers who call for one-off assistance if they have a specific problem. Demand for both of these services has grown and, as a consequence, BGS's need for engineers has increased and it has had to recruit more staff.

Stages in workforce planning

Workforce planning involves a number of stages to ensure that the right people are in the right place at the right time in order to meet the organisation's objectives. These stages are summarised in the workforce planning cycle (Figure 17.1) and explained in more detail below:

- **Setting objectives.** This involves setting HR objectives based on the corporate objectives of the organisation and converting these HR objectives into human resource requirements.
- **Forecasting the future demand for labour.** This should be done for the short term (e.g. to cover sick leave or maternity leave), medium term and long term (e.g. to meet future growth or expansion overseas). Forecasts should be constantly reviewed and updated. Forecasting should provide estimates of the size and nature of the workforce required, including how many workers are needed, what type of workers are needed, in which location they are needed and when they are needed.
- **Assessing the current workforce.** This involves identifying how many workers there are, what type (e.g. full time or part time), and their characteristics in relation to age, length of service, qualifications, staff turnover rates and reasons, promotion patterns and retirement rates. To do this effectively requires an organisation to keep detailed and up-to-date personnel records on an ongoing basis.
- **Identifying the shortfall or oversupply between the workforce needed in the future and the current workforce.** The organisation needs to compare the future demand for skills and staff with the organisation's current workforce, and estimate the changes required in the existing supply of labour in the short, medium and long term, taking into account potential labour turnover and retirement. These changes need to be fully costed to determine whether the organisation can afford them.
- **Reviewing the internal and external supply of labour in relation to the organisation's future requirements.** This involves estimating the future state of the labour market and the availability of staff with the skills and attributes that the firm needs in the short, medium and long term.
- **Developing strategies to fill the gaps or reduce the oversupply of labour.** These will form the basis of workforce plans for the short, medium and long term.

Figure 17.1 Workforce planning cycle

DID YOU KNOW?

Skills gaps occur when employers believe that members of their existing workforce need additional skills in order to meet changing demands.

Skills shortages occur when employers cannot find enough appropriate people to fill vacant positions in their workforce.

KEY TERM

workforce plans:
plans of action that
result from the process
of workforce planning.

Components of workforce plans

Workforce plans are the culmination of the workforce planning process described above. Appropriate plans should be drawn up for the short, medium and long term. Plans should include the background analysis involved in the various stages of the workforce planning process and a detailed plan of action involving recruitment and training, and possibly redeployment or transfers and redundancies, in order to match the current workforce with the desired one.

By analysing the current workforce and the future demand for labour, an organisation can draw up workforce plans that relate to both the internal and external supply of labour.

Example: overcoming a labour shortage

Where there are shortages in the supply of labour, this might be overcome by a workforce plan that involves:

- **outsourcing** — the transfer of internal activity to a third party (see p. 267)
- introducing **training programmes** or retraining existing employees to ensure that there are appropriately qualified staff
- increasing **mechanisation/automation** to reduce the need for staff
- offering **better terms and conditions** of employment to attract more or better applicants
- **rescheduling work or increasing overtime** in order to meet changes in demand in the short term

Assessing internal and external influences on workforce plans

Workforce plans require constant review and update to take account of both internal and external influences that may affect both the demand for and supply of labour. These influences can be internal or external.

Internal influences on workforce plans

Internal influences on an organisation's workforce plans include the following:

- **The organisation's corporate or strategic plan, including its corporate objectives.** It is vital that workforce planning, which ensures that human resources are sufficient to facilitate the meeting of overall corporate objectives, is recognised as a part of the strategic planning process. Changes in corporate objectives — for example, as a result of a change in ownership — are likely to lead to changes in workforce plans.
- **The organisation's marketing and production plans, including its marketing and production objectives.** For example, innovation and technological developments may require employees with different skills. Expansion abroad may require marketing staff with the ability to speak a number of different languages. Workforce planning needs to ensure that sufficient workers, in relation to skill and job level, are available to meet the requirements of the marketing and production departments.

- **The financial position of the organisation.** The budget available for recruitment and training will determine whether the organisation is able to fund the requirements of the workforce plan and thus enable the organisation to meet its objectives.
- **The internal labour supply.** This is influenced by: internal promotional opportunities; training and development opportunities; changing employment conditions, such as flexible working or job rotation; retirement and staff turnover; and legal requirements that, for example, influence redundancy.
- **Other internal factors.** These include the organisation of work (whether cell production and teamwork or traditional production-line work), and motivational and other issues that result in changes to labour turnover.

External influences on workforce plans

External influences on an organisation's workforce plans include:

- **Market conditions.** These may cause demand for products to change. For example, an increase in competition may cause demand to fall, thus leaving the firm with too many employees. Unless demand is expected to pick up, the firm may have to consider issuing redundancy notices. Similarly, a firm may face a sudden huge increase in demand for its products because a competitor has gone out of business. In such a situation, it may be faced with a sudden shortage of staff.
- **The labour market and demographic trends.** These will influence the supply of labour from which an organisation can recruit its staff. For example, fewer young people may be available for full-time work if the government achieves its target of getting 50% of all young people into higher education. On the other hand, there may be more people over 60 available for work as a result of changes to pensions and retirement dates. The migration of workers from other countries, such as eastern Europe, may increase the supply of workers who are prepared to work for lower wages than British workers. Similarly, the concentration of particular skills may change; there may be insufficient people available with the skills required by the organisation, and the wages they demand may increase as a consequence. In such a situation, a firm may decide that it is more efficient to train its own staff than to recruit trained staff from outside.

- **The state of the economy and government policy.** These factors may affect the demand for products and services, the number of workers available and the level of wages and salaries that must be paid. The costs of labour may suddenly increase, as they did for some organisations when the government introduced the minimum wage.
- **Legislation.** Workforce plans may also be affected by changes in the law: for example, by legislation requiring an organisation to ensure that it meets stringent equal opportunities and health and safety requirements.
- **Local factors.** Travel to work patterns, the availability of housing and amenities, local unemployment rates and the cost of living all influence an organisation's ability to attract workers.

FACT FILE

Workforce planning for National Health Service dentists

Table 17.1 illustrates a stage in national workforce planning for dentistry in the NHS by identifying a range of factors and how they affect the supply of, and demand for, dental services in the future.

Table 17.1 Factors influencing the supply of, and demand for, dental services

Demand factors	Estimated effect on demand
Increasing proportion of the elderly in the population	Increase in demand
Increasing number of individuals who have natural teeth	Increase in demand
Increasing number of more complex treatments available	Increase in demand
Increasing public expectations of dental treatments/services	Increase in demand
Increasing proportion of children with untreated decay	Increase in demand
Reduction in oral disease	Reduction in demand
Technological changes	Increase/reduction in demand
Supply factors	**Estimated effect on supply**
Predicted decline in number of registered dentists	Reduction in supply
Increased early retirement and part-time working	Reduction in supply
Increased availability of dentists from overseas	Increase in supply
Reduction in UK dental graduates	Reduction in supply
Loss of dental workforce to other countries	Reduction in supply
Increase in non-NHS working	Reduction in supply
Working Time Directive, conditions of service (e.g. maternity leave)	Reduction in supply
Dissatisfaction with working conditions	Reduction in supply

GROUP EXERCISE

On the basis of the information in Table 17.1, identify possible strategies that the government might consider in order to ensure that sufficient dentists are available in the NHS in the future.

 EXAMINER'S VOICE

Ensure that you recognise the integrated nature of business studies and avoid looking at individual topics in isolation from the rest of your business studies specification. For example, there are clear links between workforce planning and marketing and production because producing the workforce plan requires a detailed review of the plans of the marketing and production areas of a business.

Issues in implementing workforce plans

Issues involved in implementing workforce plans include:

- **Employer/employee relations.** In order to maintain good employer/employee relations, effective workforce planning involves consultation with employees and their representatives so that the final plan is accepted throughout a business and can be implemented successfully.
- **Corporate image.** Successful implementation of a well-thought-out and widely accepted workforce plan will enhance the corporate image of the organisation. On the other hand, a plan that is imposed and that is not acceptable to employees or their representatives is likely to lead to industrial unrest and have a negative impact on an organisation's corporate image.
- **Cost.** Sufficient financial resources need to be guaranteed so that the workforce plan can be implemented fully.
- **Training.** Ensuring the successful implementation of a workforce plan usually requires extensive training and development activities, including the induction and training of new staff and the retraining or updating of current staff.

The value of using workforce plans

The benefits of effective workforce planning are significant, in that it ensures that an organisation has a sufficient and appropriately skilled workforce to meet its objectives. On a practical level, it enables an organisation to avoid labour shortages and thus to ensure that production continues. This means that customer demand is met on time, with products in sufficient quantity and of the right quality. Workforce planning therefore allows an organisation to compete more effectively in the market.

Without effective workforce planning that takes into account appropriate forecasting of future trends, problems might occur. For example, there could be problems in recruiting and selecting appropriately skilled individuals, or staff could be inadequately trained for new processes that are introduced. Morale and motivation problems might occur if existing workers are expected to cover staff shortages. This in turn might lead to high levels of stress, more absenteeism and higher labour turnover, and increased costs for the business, which in the longer term may affect demand and competitiveness.

Without workforce planning, managers will simply react to events when they occur rather than being prepared for them, which may lead to hasty and poor-quality decision making when it comes to staffing.

Firms undergoing continual change may find workforce planning more difficult. However, such firms still need to recruit the right number of employees and ensure that staff have the right skills and attitudes. If anything, workforce planning is likely to be even more important for firms operating in markets that are constantly changing than in other markets, since few firms can afford either to have too many staff or to be short of staff at critical moments.

> **DID YOU KNOW?**
>
> The government's definition of the workforce planning process is 'activity that improves the level and application of skills, so as to achieve greater success for individuals and employers, and, ultimately, enhanced sectoral and national competitiveness'.

PRACTICE EXERCISE   Total: 60 marks (55 minutes)

1 Define the term 'workforce planning' and explain its value to a business. *(8 marks)*

2 Identify four stages involved in workforce planning. *(4 marks)*

3 What are the main components of a workforce plan? *(4 marks)*

4 State and explain two factors that might influence the internal supply of labour in a firm. *(6 marks)*

5 Identify and explain one local factor that might influence the external supply of labour to a firm. *(4 marks)*

6 Identify and explain two national factors that might influence the external supply of labour to a firm. *(6 marks)*

7 Outsourcing is one method of overcoming a shortage in the supply of labour. Explain the term 'outsourcing' in this context. *(6 marks)*

8 Identify and explain two other methods of overcoming a shortage in the supply of labour to a firm and therefore achieving labour targets. *(8 marks)*

9 Identify and explain two internal and two external influences on workforce plans. *(8 marks)*

10 Identify two possible long-term consequences for a firm that does not have a workforce plan. *(6 marks)*

CASE STUDY 1 Workforce planning at Cameco

Managers at Cameco, the world's largest uranium producer, based in Saskatchewan, Canada, recognised that their growth strategies would be adversely affected if they weren't able to attract the right employees. The global labour shortage of mining professionals, particularly engineers, was making it difficult to move forward with long-term projects. The management consultancy, Deloitte, was engaged to work with Cameco's HR team to develop a workforce plan to deal with the situation.

Traditionally in Cameco's asset-intensive business, people were often the last component considered in the planning process. However, in the changing labour market, where the pool of skilled workers is smaller and more companies are competing for the same skills, this was no longer acceptable. As a result of its work with Deloitte, the emphasis was placed on identifying Cameco's critical workforce segments (i.e. those people who provide a disproportionate amount of value to the organisation, have the most valuable skills, and are generally the hardest to replace). They were identified as geologists, geo-scientists, mining engineers and environmental engineers.

Cameco and Deloitte started with the overall business plan and the corporate objectives. By taking this approach, a deeper understanding of the business and its needs was possible. Following some qualitative and quantitative data gathering, gaps in the supply and demand of talent were identified. Through regular workforce planning, the HR department was able to monitor projected changes resulting from both internal and external influences to ensure that appropriate staffing numbers and skills were maintained.

Because of workforce planning, Cameco is now more strategic with regard to recruitment. HR representatives are now more involved in the business planning phases, contributing valuable information and proactive solutions that are useful and crucial to the business.

The HR contribution has become truly strategic, helping to secure future projects through both recruiting and retention strategies.

Source: adapted from 'The HR opportunity: achieving value through strategic workforce planning', **www.deloitte.com**.

Preliminary questions

Total: 40 marks (45 minutes)

1 Explain how a firm such as Cameco might anticipate its changing labour market needs in advance. *(6 marks)*

2 Consider how Cameco might benefit from producing a workforce plan. *(6 marks)*

3 Explain how Cameco's corporate objectives are likely to influence its HR objectives and its workforce plans. *(8 marks)*

4 Identify ways in which Cameco might fill the gaps between its demand for labour and the supply of labour. *(8 marks)*

5 **a** Identify and explain two internal influences on Cameco's workforce plans. *(6 marks)*
  b Identify and explain two external influences on Cameco's workforce plans. *(6 marks)*

Case study questions

Total: 40 marks (50 minutes)

1 Analyse the issues Cameco is likely to face in implementing its workforce plans. *(10 marks)*

2 To what extent does workforce planning enable Cameco to achieve its corporate objectives? *(15 marks)*

3 Discuss the major internal and external influences that are likely to require Cameco to review its workforce plans constantly to ensure it can meet its objectives. *(15 marks)*

CASE STUDY 2 West Yorkshire Sports Partnership

West Yorkshire's population is just over 2 million. Its characteristics include a growing minority ethnic population of 11.4% and a 16–18-year-old cohort estimated at 89,760. According to the Sport Industry Research Centre at Sheffield Hallam University (SHU), sport generates £2.5 billion in annual turnover in the region, 1.5% of the region's economy. Around 508,000 people participate in organised sports clubs, and residents in the region spend £1.2 billion annually on sports-related goods and services, around 3% of total household spending

Increased participation in sport and physical activity by children, young people and adults will lead to increased demand for leisure opportunities. With this demand comes the need for an enlarged workforce with ever more sophisticated skills, knowledge and competence. There is a need, therefore, to ensure that

FOTOLIA

the sport and active recreation sector in West Yorkshire has the right people in sport with the right skills, by continually raising its profile as a professional sector with initiatives to help up-skill the workforce, increase employability and encourage continuous professional development.

The agreed vision for the West Yorkshire Sports Partnership (WYSP) is *'For West Yorkshire to have a well-motivated and highly skilled workforce (paid and unpaid) that will drive the development of sport during the next decade.'*

The WYSP team undertook an audit that established agreed workforce development plan objectives. The audit involved a cross-section of the WYSP that was representative of the various sub-sectors. In addition to this audit, Sheffield Hallam University was commissioned to carry out a survey across the sector. The results obtained by the survey provided quantitative data to support the more qualitative forecast obtained through the WYSP audit.

The next step in the planning process involved analysing the results of the WYSP audit and the SHU survey. This was communicated to partners via a workforce development planning day. The planning day outlined the current position, but focused mainly on discussing the implications of the research findings, establishing an agreement of where the WYSP wanted to be in terms of workforce development and discussing how the vision would be achieved in each sub-sector.

As a result of the workforce development planning day, draft 3-year plans were drawn up alongside 1-year action plans for each sub-sector. These plans were fed into a consultation process with the WYSP and all comments were fed back into the plans.

A monitoring process was put in place to allow the WYSP to assess the success of the workforce development plan and to enable the partnership to improve the process continually and make it easier each time it is completed. The WYSP evaluates the success of the workforce development plan so that it can begin the cycle again every year, having taken into account any changes that need to be made to the process.

Source: adapted from **www.westyorkshiresport.co.uk**.

Preliminary questions

Total: 30 marks (35 minutes)

1 What is the purpose of a workforce development plan for an organisation like WYSP? *(4 marks)*

2 What is the relationship between WYSP's vision and its workforce development plans? *(6 marks)*

3 What does the information suggest are the important stages in the workforce development planning process? *(8 marks)*

4 Explain how an organisation such as WYSP might gather information about its future workforce needs. *(6 marks)*

5 Explain two major external influences on WYSP's workforce development plan. *(6 marks)*

Case study questions

Total: 40 marks (50 minutes)

1 Consider how useful monitoring and evaluation of the workforce development plan might be for WYSP. *(10 marks)*

2 To what extent can internal and external influences have both positive and negative effects on the workforce development plan of WYSP? *(15 marks)*

3 Assess the value of constructing a workforce development plan and the possible consequences of not having such a plan for an organisation like WYSP. *(15 marks)*

Chapter 18

Competitive organisational structures

This chapter considers the factors determining the choice of organisational structures. Methods of adapting organisation structures to improve competitiveness are discussed, including centralisation and decentralisation, functional and matrix organisational structures, delayering and flexible workforces. In relation to the last of these, core and peripheral workers, outsourcing and home working are reviewed.

EXAMINER'S VOICE

Before reading this chapter, review Chapter 19 in the AS textbook as this chapter builds directly on many of the issues considered there.

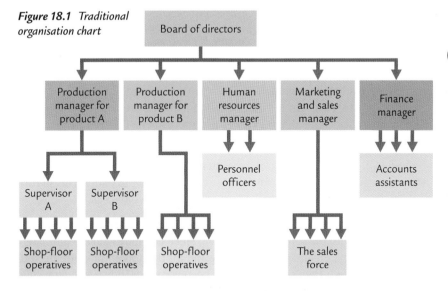

Figure 18.1 *Traditional organisation chart*

KEY TERMS

organisational structure: the relationship between different people and functions in an organisation — both vertically, from shop-floor workers through supervisors and managers to directors, and horizontally between different functions and people at the same level.

organisation chart: a diagram showing the lines of authority and layers of hierarchy in an organisation. Figure 18.1 provides an example of a traditional organisation chart.

Factors determining the choice of organisation structure

The structure of an organisation will be influenced by many factors including:

■ **The size of the organisation.** The larger the organisation, the more complex its structure is likely to be and the more layers of hierarchy, divisions or departments it is likely to have.

- **The nature of the organisation.** The firm's structure will depend on whether it is in the manufacturing or service sector, national or multinational, single product or multi-product, and on whether it is in an area where tight control, safety or security issues are paramount.
- **The culture and attitudes of senior management.** The structure will be affected by whether the management style is autocratic and controlling, or democratic and participative.
- **The skill and experience of its workforce.** The nature of the workforce — whether the majority of workers do low-skilled, repetitive jobs, or whether they are highly skilled, each doing very different jobs — will also influence a firm's organisational structure.
- **The dynamic, or ever-changing, external environment.** This will influence the effectiveness of any existing structure. For example, the increasing emphasis on work–life balance is leading to greater flexibility in how firms deploy their staff; a recession or credit crunch may mean a firm needs to reduce costs, perhaps by delayering its organisation (i.e. removing a layer of management); a successful takeover bid may lead to a complete restructuring of the organisation.

Accountability and responsibility

Whatever organisational structure is chosen, it is essential that accountability and responsibility are clear.

When a company's management structure is clear, as shown by its **organisation chart**, staff should know what authority has been given to them and by whom. According to Herzberg, achievement and recognition of that achievement will produce motivation. Recognition of achievement is more likely if the lines of accountability are clear. On the other hand, if mistakes are made, it is essential to know how they came about, in order to correct them. This can be identified more easily if the lines of accountability are clear.

In some instances, clear lines of accountability can be seen as a threat that deters managers from taking decisions in case they turn out badly. This in turn may make them overcautious, to the detriment of the business.

Although authority is delegated lower down the hierarchy, responsibility should remain with the senior management, since it is they who are ultimately responsible for the organisation's strategy and for the appointment of the staff

involved. There have been occasions, however, when chief executives have refused to accept responsibility for actions taken by their subordinates or when, because of the nature of the organisation, it was very difficult to identify where responsibility and accountability lay. The rail accidents that have occurred since British Rail was privatised are classic examples of such incidents, where lines of authority and responsibility have not been clear.

KEY TERM

accountability: the extent to which a named individual is held responsible for the success or failure of a particular policy, project or piece of work.

TOPFOTO

Centralisation versus decentralisation

On the one hand, organisations desire stability, uniformity and centralised control. However, they also recognise the differences in regional characteristics, customers and products, and the fact that individuals tend to identify more readily with smaller work groups than with the whole organisation, and desire more authority and involvement in decision making. How these considerations are balanced influences whether an organisation has a centralised or a decentralised structure.

DID YOU KNOW?

Successful organisations develop and adapt their structures to the dynamic environment in which they operate. Supermarkets centralise decisions on shop layout (because the head office researches the best layouts), but decentralise recruitment of workers because local conditions in the labour market are different between areas. They also devolve decision making about products and promotions to local branch managers — which means that each branch provides slightly different stock and promotions — to suit the local market.

KEY TERMS

centralisation and decentralisation: the degree to which authority is delegated within an organisation. A centralised structure has a greater degree of central control, while a decentralised structure involves a greater degree of delegated authority to the regions or to subordinates.

Centralised structures

Organisations that keep their decision-making power firmly at the top of the hierarchy, rather than delegating decisions to local levels or lower down the hierarchy, have a centralised decision-making structure. Burger King and other fast-food chains are examples of organisations with centralised structures. You can recognise this because the meal, service and décor are exactly the same regardless of which branch you enter.

Advantages of centralisation

- Consistent policies on marketing and production mean greater control and standardisation of procedures.
- Decisions can be made quickly without the need to consult with all branches or sections.
- Every branch of a retail business is identical, meaning that customers know exactly what to expect.
- It enables tight financial control, the efficient use of resources and lower overheads.
- The corporate view can be clearly emphasised.
- Strong centralised leadership is useful in times of crisis.

Disadvantages of centralisation

- The manager of a local branch may have far better knowledge about customers' needs, but has little input into the decision-making process.
- The lack of decision-making powers of managers in local branches may adversely affect their motivation.
- It can lead to inflexibility and inappropriate decisions at local level and may also lengthen the whole decision-making process.

Decentralised structures

A decentralised structure is where the power and authority to make decisions is delegated from head office to management in the local branches or lower down the hierarchy of a business. This delegation should be backed up by financial resources. Decentralisation involves less uniformity in how things are done, as decisions are likely to be made in relation to local circumstances and opportunities.

Advantages of decentralisation

- It can empower local managers, encouraging them to be more innovative, thus improving their job satisfaction.
- Their local knowledge may have beneficial effects on sales and promotions may be targeted more accurately.
- It reduces the volume of day-to-day communication between head office and local branches.
- Senior managers should have more time to consider long-term strategy rather than day-to-day issues.
- Flexibility should improve as an organisation becomes more responsive to changing customer demands.
- All these changes should enhance motivation and in turn improve performance and reduce labour turnover.

Disadvantages of decentralisation

- Customers may not like the reduction in uniformity of branches.
- By focusing on local issues, local managers may not see the big picture and hence may miss an opportunity or trend that would have been picked up more effectively in a centralised structure.

DID YOU KNOW?

In a survey of 450 large and medium-sized European companies, well over half had decentralised decision-making structures. The leadership style at the top tends to be more democratic in a decentralised company.

KEY TERM

functional organisational structure: the traditional management structure consisting of a different department for each of the main functions of the business (e.g. marketing, production, finance and personnel).

Functional versus matrix organisational structures

Functional organisational structure

A traditional functional organisational structure is illustrated in Figure 18.1. This structure could be adapted and used for businesses that organise themselves according to geographical regions or product brands. Figure 18.2 shows some organisational charts based on brands and regions.

A functional organisation is based on a hierarchy in which each department operates separately under the leadership of those above it. Coordination between the different functions must occur at the top, as each division in effect operates as a separate organisation. This is therefore a relatively inflexible type of structure.

(a) Based on geographical region

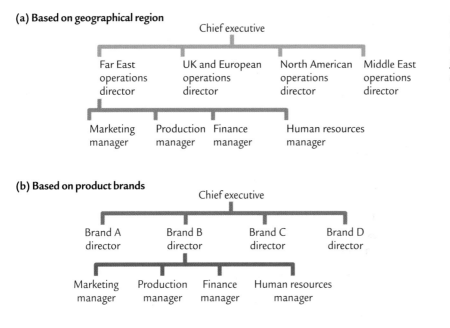

Figure 18.2
Functional organisation charts based on geographical region and product brands

(b) Based on product brands

Matrix organisational structure

A matrix organisational structure tends to be used alongside a functional organisational structure, not instead of it. Employees involved in a project team will report to the team leader on issues linked to the project, but will also be answerable to their departmental manager for their other roles. An example of matrix management is a new product development team that includes an engineer, a marketing manager, a designer and an accountant, as shown in Table 18.1. In higher education, business schools are often organised on matrix management lines. For example, the staff who contribute to teaching on a BA in Business Management will be coordinated by a specific course tutor, but will also belong to their own specialist academic divisions, where they will have a line manager (see Table 18.2).

KEY TERM

matrix organisational structure: a flexible organisational structure in which tasks are managed in a way that cuts across traditional departmental boundaries.

Table 18.1 New product development team: matrix management

	Engineering department	Marketing department	Design department	Finance department
New product team manager	The new product team manager takes staff from each of the above departments to form the new product development team			

Table 18.2 A university business school

	Academic divisions					
	Accounting and finance	Economics	HRM	Marketing	Operations management	Strategy
Course tutor for BA in Business Management	The course tutor takes staff from each of the above divisions to form the course lecturing team					

Advantages of a matrix organisational structure

- It ensures that projects are better coordinated.
- It gives people in different departments the opportunity to use their abilities and share their knowledge.
- This in turn prevents a single view — for example, about costs — dominating the decision-making process.
- It may lead to greater motivation.
- It allows for the possibility of synergy.

Disadvantages of a matrix organisational structure

- It means that each team member can end up with two bosses — their departmental boss and the project leader.
- Since there is usually little coordination between departmental heads and project leaders, individuals may suffer if both bosses make heavy demands on them.
- Lines of accountability may be unclear.

e EXAMINER'S VOICE

Think about the implications of changes in organisational structure for management and workers, communication, efficiency, morale and costs.

DID YOU KNOW?

Synergy occurs when the whole is greater than the sum of its parts, i.e. when more advantages occur as a result of experts from different departments working together rather than working separately.

FACT FILE

Phileas Fogg

The Phileas Fogg brand, part of the large United Biscuits (UB) group, was relaunched in 2002. This required a new approach to marketing and innovation. To facilitate these changes, patterns of working were changed. Individuals responsible for new product development were put into what the company called 'cross-functional teams'. These were teams of workers with a range of different but relevant specialisms, including specialists in market research, production, design and financial management. Such an approach is very similar to the matrix management approach explained above. The result of this change was that new products were developed and introduced in record time.

MIKE GOLDWATER/ALAMY

e EXAMINER'S VOICE

Always remember to apply your knowledge. Think about the particular business you are being asked about, and relate your knowledge to that business — don't just trot out textbook knowledge without giving it context. For example, if you are considering a small, family-run private limited company, your answers about organisational structure will be very different from if you are analysing a large multinational plc.

AQA A2 Business Studies

Delayering

In a dynamic environment, businesses need to be able to respond quickly and effectively to changes. A very tall management structure is unlikely to be as responsive as a flatter structure. Many organisations have realised that the way to ensure they respond swiftly to change is to flatten or shorten their management structure by delayering — removing layers from the hierarchy. This leads to a flatter hierarchical structure with a wider span of control.

> **KEY TERMS**
>
> **delayering:** the removal of one or more layers of hierarchy from the management structure of an organisation.

The advantages and disadvantages of delayering are similar to those for a flat hierarchical structure with a wide span of control. (A detailed consideration of this was provided in Chapter 19 of the AS textbook.) However, delayering is often done in order to cut costs by making people redundant. A real problem with this kind of delayering is that the organisation loses many of its very experienced managers and thus what is sometimes called its 'corporate memory'. This means the knowledge of its history, past events, situations and contacts — much of which can be extremely valuable in dealing with the present.

> **EXAMINER'S VOICE**
>
> To help you analyse issues, think about the advantages and disadvantages of different structures and try to see how these link with the strengths and weaknesses of the business being studied.

Flexible workforces

In a dynamic business environment, organisations need to have structures that can respond quickly to changes taking place in the external environment. One approach is to introduce more flexible workforce structures that allow organisations to expand or reduce capacity quickly and easily. Flexible workforce approaches include core and peripheral workers, outsourcing and home-working, each of which is considered below.

Core versus peripheral workers

An example of a flexible workforce approach is to employ a core of permanent, full-time, salaried workers supported by other peripheral, temporary or part-time workers. The activities and responsibilities of core workers are central to the organisation and such workers are likely to be fully committed to the aims and objectives of the organisation. Peripheral workers, on the other hand, are likely to be engaged in activities that are additional to the main purpose of the organisation. Their jobs are less secure and they are less likely to be committed to the organisation's aims and objectives.

Figure 18.3
The shamrock organisation

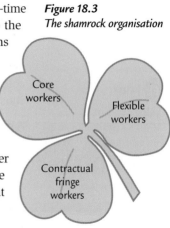

The shamrock organisation

Charles Handy, in *The Age of Unreason* (1990), developed this idea further and suggested that modern firms would increasingly be composed of three elements: the core, the contractual fringe and the flexible or contingent workforce. He called this the 'shamrock organisation' (see Figure 18.3).

The core

The core includes the professional, permanent employees who are essential to the organisation's continuity and have detailed knowledge of the organisation and its aims. They have the skills to move the company's core capabilities forward. They have to work hard and give commitment, but, typically, are very well paid.

The contractual fringe

There has been a strong trend for organisations to outsource their non-critical work to independent contractors, so that the organisation can concentrate on its core competences.

Handy suggests that the contractual fringe element of the shamrock is made up of both individuals and organisations of self-employed professionals or technicians. These independent contractors are project experts who may be used, for example, for advertising, R&D, computing, catering and mailing services. They are rewarded with fees rather than with salaries or wages. Their contribution to the organisation is measured in output rather than in hours, in results rather than in time. Management chooses not to add these people to its permanent payroll and benefits plan, thus achieving a significant cost saving.

The flexible or contingent workforce

The third element of Handy's shamrock organisation is the flexible workforce, sometimes known as the contingent workforce. This comprises part-time, temporary and seasonal workers, who are often young and female. These people are brought in from outside to do individual, low-level, temporary tasks. Some may desire more permanent jobs; others (such as women with young families) may not, desiring only a job to supplement the family income, and with some outlet for meeting people.

The growth of flexibility

It is possible to argue that the three-level organisational structure described by Handy has always existed: firms have always, to some degree, been a mixture of permanent staff working with independent contractors and contingent, temporary workers. But what Handy has identified is the scale of the phenomenon today. The shamrock organisation is here to stay for the foreseeable future, and so are the 'portfolio people' with their 'portfolio careers' that constitute the contractual fringe.

A portfolio career might consist of different working arrangements at different times. It typically includes periods of employment obtained through short-term contracts, but it could equally involve a permanent part-time job combined with short-term project or freelance work. Having a self-managed portfolio career is a cumulative process and replaces the traditional idea of promotion and progression within one organisation.

KEY TERM

portfolio career: a career in which income is derived from a variety of sources – perhaps a number of jobs, or a job and a business.

AQA A2 Business Studies

For many firms, this emphasis on being responsive to the external environment has led to a decline in the size of the core group of workers. Handy suggested that for many organisations, the 'permanent' core of highly skilled employed staff might amount to only 20% of the total activity, the remainder being accounted for by external suppliers, contractors and the self-employed. Over the last 30 years, this core component of the large organisation has typically declined as a result of a refocusing on core competences and the 'downsizing' efforts that have accompanied this in a world of tougher international competition. Almost all functions other than those directly concerned with the organisation's primary business activity begin to take on a support role and are therefore candidates for outsourcing. This includes the bulk of the operations, administration, finance, personnel, legal, property and IT functions.

FACT FILE

Perils of the periphery

Some commentators suggest that the approach of using temporary workers (the peripheral or flexible workforce), which provides a cushion of 'disposable workers' in the case of an economic slowdown or cancellation of non-core projects, seems reasonable in principle. However, experience suggests that temporary workers cause tensions and jealousies with permanent employees during the good times because of the different terms under which they work and their lack of commitment to the company. Then when the temporary/flexible workforce is no longer required and is 'disposed of', the permanent employees feel just as exposed as if permanent employees were being cut. These findings emerged from the Watson Wyatt's human capital index (HCI) research, which suggested that companies avoiding the 'disposable worker' approach deliver more shareholder value.

Outsourcing

The most usual method of achieving a flexible workforce structure is by subcontracting work to other firms — now more commonly known as outsourcing. Outsourcing gives a firm the opportunity to use expertise not otherwise available in the organisation, to offload low-level administrative work, to free employees to undertake more interesting work and to reduce costs.

KEY TERMS

outsourcing: using sources outside a business to undertake functions that used to be done internally by a section of the business itself. These sources include marketing consultants, call centres, and production and assembly plants. Outsourcing is linked to the issue of 'downsizing'.

downsizing: reducing the size of a firm to make it more responsive to market conditions — for example, by removing 'back room' activities such as office functions and call centres or the production and assembly of parts, which are then contracted out to other agencies.

Areas of work that are commonly outsourced include: recruitment, especially the initial stages of dealing with enquiries and applications, and carrying out standard assessment; training; and payroll activities. Such activities can then be increased or decreased at short notice, according to demand, without the need for expensive recruitment and selection processes or the difficult and expensive process of redundancies.

FACT FILE

The Natural History Museum

The Natural History Museum is one of London's top tourist attractions and one of the world's foremost resources for natural science, with magnificent collections and groundbreaking research expertise.

The museum outsources all of its payroll needs, including the monthly payroll run, the production of payslips, making statutory payments, and expertise to ensure ongoing compliance with legislation and tax changes. David Williams, personnel services manager at the Natural History Museum, is clear about why the museum prefers an outsourced arrangement: 'We simply couldn't make a financial case for running an internal payroll team. Our team of three in the personnel department is able to handle some of the tasks, such as gathering information about starters, leavers and so on. But we are able to access a fully managed payroll service that makes sense financially and avoids the need to allocate management resources to an internal solution.'

Source: www.noa.co.uk (National Outsourcing Association), 18 September 2008.

Homeworking

Advances in technology and the growing availability of broadband mean that many people can work very effectively from home. There are now increasing opportunities to use audio and video conferencing for meetings, seminars and online training — which all combine to make flexible working increasingly attractive to employers and employees. As well as market research, design and software development, many other occupations can be based away from the office.

By working from home, employees remove the need to travel, in itself a great saving in time, making them more productive, less stressed and happier, especially if they have family commitments. This can motivate staff by giving them more independence and responsibility and, at the same time, reducing the impact of Herzberg's hygiene factors. Employees who are given the option of working flexibly are likely to be more committed to their employer and are less likely to take time off work due to sickness or stress. However, although such flexibility is likely to improve employees' work–life balance, some tele-workers find it difficult to separate work from leisure, which is a major factor in causing stress.

Organisations can reduce their costs significantly if workers are based at home rather than in an office, but projections that the typical office will cease to exist are probably unrealistic, as many teleworkers find that they miss

KEY TERM

teleworking: people working from home and other locations, and keeping in contact through information and communications technology (ICT).

the social aspects of working alongside colleagues. In addition, for the majority of organisations, some journeys are unavoidable and there will probably always be a need for face-to-face meetings with colleagues.

The growing use of flexible workforce structures, and of homeworking in particular, has a significant impact on management and on HR departments. For example, managers need to be properly trained in how to manage home-workers because different skills are required. HR departments need to ensure that all their policies are as robust for those employees who do not work regularly in an office as they are for those who do.

The impact of a more flexible workforce structure on organisations

Research suggests a number of factors that are critical to the success of a flexible staffing structure in an organisation. These include:

- **Work activities that are clearly different for core and peripheral groups.** If an organisation requires labour flexibility to achieve its business goals, management must clearly define the nature of 'core' and 'peripheral' activities within its operation.
- **Human resources policies and practices that are distinct for each group and that reinforce the different flexibility objectives.** These distinctions include policies and practices in relation to employee autonomy and decision making, remuneration, performance management and training.
- **Ongoing monitoring of staffing plans to accommodate changing business and employee needs.** Change is a reality. A staffing strategy requires constant monitoring and adjustment to changes in the environment to ensure optimal utilisation of capital and human resources.

Advantages of a flexible workforce structure include the following:
- The organisation is able to respond more quickly to market conditions by expanding or contracting capacity.
- It can make more efficient use of resources by directing them to the organisation's priorities or strengths.
- It is able to cut down on costs — particularly labour, which for most businesses is their major cost.
- It can make more use of specialists.

Disadvantages of a flexible workforce structure include the following:
- Such an approach is likely to require a culture change for firms, which might be problematic in the short term.
- Organisations will be dependent on other organisations and agencies outside their direct control.
- In the short term, if employees are laid off, this is likely to have a negative effect on workforce motivation and hence productivity. In the longer term, the peripheral workforce may be less motivated than the core workers.
- By downsizing and focusing on core activities, there may be less opportunity for future expansion as workers' skills and experience will be lost.

EXAMINER'S VOICE

Always try to relate these ideas to your knowledge of motivation theories. For example, consider the issue of job security in relation to Maslow's hierarchy of human needs.

FILE

Benefits of flexibility for employers

A recent survey by YouGov asked 1,000 company directors for their views on flexible working. Three-quarters of directors thought that their employees were more productive or at least as productive when working flexibly and at home. They ranked the benefits as follows:

- improved staff motivation
- increased productivity
- improved client service
- reduced absenteeism
- improved company resilience against transport problems
- better-quality job applicants
- improved candidate perception of company

PRACTICE EXERCISE   Total: 60 marks (55 minutes)

1 Explain two factors that might influence the structure of an organisation. *(6 marks)*

2 Distinguish between authority and responsibility. *(4 marks)*

3 Distinguish between centralised organisational structures and decentralised organisational structures. *(4 marks)*

4 a Explain one advantage and one disadvantage of a centralised organisational structure. *(6 marks)*
  b Explain one advantage and one disadvantage of a decentralised organisational structure. *(6 marks)*

5 Distinguish between a functional management structure and a matrix management structure. *(4 marks)*

6 Explain one advantage and one disadvantage of a matrix management structure. *(6 marks)*

7 Define the term 'delayering' and explain two possible reasons for delayering an organisation. *(6 marks)*

8 Distinguish between core and peripheral workers in an organisation. *(4 marks)*

9 Explain the term 'outsourcing' and why a business might outsource some of its activities. *(6 marks)*

10 Explain two advantages and two disadvantages to a business of moving to a more flexible workforce structure. *(8 marks)*

CASE STUDY 1 United Biscuits

In early 2001, United Biscuits (UB) changed its organisational structure from a geographical to a product-based structure, supported by common shared services that work across the biscuits and snacks products. This has given the business greater alignment and common purpose and direction.

Previously, the structure was based on three separate divisions with total responsibility for all activities in the UK, France and Benelux respectively. (Benelux is a name used to describe a combination of Belgium, the Netherlands and Luxembourg.) In contrast, the new structure is based on individual products, with managers responsible for a particular product across the whole of western Europe.

As a starting point, UB rationalised its commercial and corporate business premises, moving from three offices to a single cost-efficient head office in Hayes, Middlesex, as well as reorganising its regional offices in France and Benelux.

This is a company with enormous growth potential. Introducing the new structure has helped to release that potential. UB is concentrating on creating an organisational structure that will allow it to grow.

The first phase of this work aimed to release £65 million costs from across the business by the end of 2002, to be reinvested in marketing and technological innovation. This was to be achieved in part through centralising service functions, restructuring sites across the UK and Europe, and rationalising manufacturing capacity.

One of the most visible examples of the change came in September 2002 when the management of UB was brought under one roof with the biscuit and snacks business. The new headquarters, based in Hayes, became a physical expression of the 'one company, one vision' that UB encourages.

Centralising various human resource services led to increased efficiencies within the group. This process

was made possible by the organisational change introduced, moving from a geographical to a product-based structure. The company now has centralised buying, finance, information technology and human resource management services, avoiding the duplication that existed when each geographical part of the business had its own services and systems.

By 2003, this activity had released £30 million, putting UB in a strong position to compete in this market and achieve its growth targets.

Source: adapted from United Biscuits' Annual Review, 2003.

Preliminary questions   Total: 25 marks (30 minutes)

1 What is meant by the term 'organisational structure'?   (3 marks)

2 Explain the nature of the change to organisational structure that took place at United Biscuits.   (5 marks)

3 How might the change in United Biscuits' organisational structure have released millions of pounds to be spent elsewhere?   (5 marks)

4 Excluding cost savings, explain one other advantage of changing the structure from a geographical base to a product base.   (4 marks)

5 Analyse two possible disadvantages that might have arisen from the policy of centralisation at United Biscuits.   (8 marks)

Case study questions   Total: 40 marks (50 minutes)

1 Analyse the reasons why United Biscuits felt that the new organisational structure would be more likely to allow it to grow.   (10 marks)

2 To what extent might centralisation have helped United Biscuits achieve its aim of 'one company, one vision'?   (15 marks)

3 Discuss how adapting its organisational structure was likely to improve the competitiveness of United Biscuits.   (15 marks)

CASE STUDY 2 BT — before and after

This case study consists of two parts. The first extract is a letter written by someone who was an employee of BT in the 1990s, while the second extract describes the more recent organisation of BT and its flexible workforce.

Letter from an employee

Dear Sir

Back in 1994, I worked for a near 200,000-strong organisation called British Telecom. How many of those people-factory, monolithic bureaucracies are around today? I was one of 20,000 managers, all of whom were just cogs in a wheel, following the same routine, nine-to-five office life, and doing whatever was in the procedures manual.

Six years later, having left BT, I was leading a team of people that had a business plan, but otherwise no rules or procedures. The entire team was home-based, and we had as many relationships and partnerships outside of the organisation as within. We worked hard, motivated by both significant bonus and share-save schemes, but mainly because we felt more empowered and could make a difference at an individual level. Work had become more challenging and rewarding.

I recall Handy predicting the 'shamrock organisation' as one that would have three layers. First, there would be the small core of key employees who develop the organisation, then the 'contractual fringe', comprising contractor and partner organisations that would be paid by results, and finally the flexible workforce, often freelance agents, who would be employed as and when required. This is the exact model for my organisation, a management consultancy, where we have outsourced IT, accounting and many marketing functions, and provide as much work for our partner (freelance) consultants as our own staff.

Is there an organisation that has not outsourced functions or is not using freelance support in some capacity?

Source: letter to *Personnel Today*, 30 November 2004.

Flexible working

An important aim of BT is to ensure that its workforce best delivers its telecommunications, internet and IT services locally, nationally and internationally to millions of diverse and increasingly demanding customers. It recognises that technology alone is no longer able to offer competitive advantage and that the quality of its workforce — the way they behave with customers and their motivation — is the only sustainable differentiator in today's markets.

BT has harnessed communications technology to transform the way it runs, moving from a more static, site-based workforce to an 'eBT' of employees who work flexibly and/or from home. Equipping people with access to the information necessary to do their jobs seems obvious, but prior to 'eBT' much of the information was not available to people where they were working. Often engineers had to leave customer premises to find the information they needed, wasting time and decreasing customer satisfaction. Providing employees with online, real-time access to information and training not only increased productivity, it also increased sales and customer satisfaction, and enabled flexible working. BT now has:

- over 9,000 home workers
- nearly 500 job sharers
- over 5,000 part-time workers

BT has used its own technological products and services to effect this change. For example:

- BT broadband is used by employees at home, in the office, on customer premises or while travelling.
- 70% of BT's training is delivered online (253,000 course completions in the last year) to employees at work or home.

BT has changed processes and attitudes to enable flexibility. Managers are encouraged to agree flexible working requests, performance focus has shifted to outputs, and extensive information and support facilities are provided through BT's intranet site.

Benefits from the move to a more flexible workforce include:

- A more talented workforce. Surveys show that people want to work for companies with a sound work–life balance ethos.
- A more diverse workforce. Flexible working attracts and retains people often under-represented in the UK workforce, such as disabled people, lone parents and carers.
- A more flexible and responsive workforce.
- Improved retention: 98% of women return to BT after maternity leave, and flexible working over the last 2 years has helped retain 1,000 people
- Reduced absenteeism. BT homeworkers average just 3 days sick absence a year, and the rate of absenteeism is 20% below the UK average

- Increased productivity. Over 9,000 BT employees now work from home with productivity gains of 15–31%, and home-based call centre operators handle 20% more calls than site-based colleagues.
- Happier customers. Flexible working helps BT respond to customer demand 24/7 and customer dissatisfaction is down 22%.
- Reduced costs. The annual cost to support an office-based worker in central London is around £18,000 but it costs less than £3,000 a year to support a homeworker; on average each homeworker saves BT £6,000 a year and improved retention saves £5 million a year on recruitment and induction.

Source: www.employersforwork-lifebalance.org.uk, April 2005.

Preliminary questions
Total: 45 marks (50 minutes)

1 Distinguish between the core and peripheral employees in an organisation. *(4 marks)*

2 How does Charles Handy split the peripheral employees in an organisation? *(3 marks)*

3 Explain the terms 'flexible workforce', 'outsourcing' and 'homeworking' in the context of BT and the writer's management consultancy. *(9 marks)*

4 Explain two benefits of having a flexible approach to workforce structure to:
   a the letter writer's organisation
   b BT *(12 marks)*

5 Explain two problems that such a structure might cause the organisations. *(6 marks)*

6 Explain the advantages for employees of BT of the more flexible workforce structure. *(5 marks)*

7 Explain two concerns that employees might have about such an approach to workforce structure. *(6 marks)*

Case study questions
Total: 40 marks (50 minutes)

1 Using illustrations from motivation theories you are familiar with, consider how the move towards a more flexible workforce structure, for both the letter writer's management consultancy and BT, might affect the motivation of both firms' employees. *(10 marks)*

2 To what extent is a move towards a more flexible workforce structure as beneficial for a small organisation, such as the letter writer's management consultancy business, as it is for a large organisation, such as BT? *(15 marks)*

3 Discuss the extent to which a more flexible workforce structure is likely to have a beneficial impact on both organisations and their employees. *(15 marks)*

Chapter 19
Effective employer/ employee relations

This chapter looks at how organisations manage communications with employees. It considers the importance of communication in employer/employee relations and barriers to effective communication. It identifies methods of employee representation, including works councils, employee groups and trade unions, and the advantages and disadvantages of employee representation. The different forms of industrial action are identified and methods of avoiding and resolving industrial disputes are considered.

The importance of communication in employer/employee relations

Effective communication with employees offers organisations a number of benefits:

- **Implementing change.** It makes it easier to implement change because employees and other stakeholders understand and recognise the need for it. Taking into account the opinions of employees is also likely to encourage greater commitment to the change process.
- **Motivation.** Effective communication encourages a more motivated workforce and develops commitment to the business from employees at all levels of the organisation. Motivational theories recognise the importance of effective communication in raising morale. Just as good communication can increase employee motivation, well-motivated employees are likely to communicate more readily with management by suggesting ideas, listening to advice and contributing their opinions, and to be more willing to participate in decision making.

e EXAMINER'S VOICE

Wherever possible, make use of the knowledge you gained in your AS studies and, in particular, your knowledge of motivation theories. For example, good communication is likely to mean that employees are praised for their efforts, which might, in accordance with Maslow's hierarchy of human needs, meet their ego needs, and effective feedback is one of Herzberg's motivators. Similarly, good communication can help to make employees feel involved and meet their social needs.

- **Achieving objectives.** Good communication helps to ensure that the business is well coordinated and that all employees pursue the same corporate objectives. It is important that employees understand the objectives of their organisation, how their own job contributes to meeting these objectives and how well they are performing their job and hence contributing to the success of the organisation.
- **Improving competitiveness.** It allows the organisation to be more competitive by improving efficiency and identifying opportunities.

> **𝑒 EXAMINER'S VOICE**
>
> Refer back to Chapter 19 of the AS textbook to recap your understanding of communication in a business context.

Barriers to effective communication

Effective communication takes place if a message is received and understood by the receiver. A number of barriers might prevent this from happening. Barriers to communication occur as a result of noise. The term 'noise' in this context is broader than the general meaning of noise as a physical sound.

> **KEY TERM**
>
> **noise:** anything that can interfere with the receipt of a message, including physical problems or aspects of attitude or culture that get in the way of the communication.

Physical problems might include noisy environments that make conversation impractical, or geographical distance that causes a manager in, for example, an outlet in the north of England to be less well informed than one in London, where the head office is based.

> **DID YOU KNOW?**
>
> One of Elton Mayo's findings was that the informal groups to which workers belong exert significant influence over their attitudes.

Attitudes

How employees perceive other people can affect how they interpret the messages that are sent. Employees are more likely to have confidence in people they trust, and hence are likely to be more receptive to any communication they receive from them, even if such communication includes bad news.

In a similar way, stereotyping can influence the effectiveness of any communication and how one person interprets a message from another. For example, if male employees view a female manager as less rational or less able than a male manager, their initial reaction might be to have less respect for her authority. Thus they will treat any communications from her less seriously than they might treat communications from a male manager.

Intermediaries

The greater the number of intermediaries, and therefore the longer the chain of command, the less effective the communication system is likely to be. As Figure 19.1 illustrates, if employee J wants to communicate with manager A, the message has to go via intermediaries F, C and B. This will slow the message down and may lead to it becoming distorted. Even worse, F, C or B may either forget to forward it or decide it is not worth passing on.

In contrast to this, delayering has been a feature of many organisations. This means that fewer intermediaries exist. In such a situation, managers have much wider spans of control and effective communication is vital to ensure the efficient running of the organisation.

Lack of a common language or sense of purpose

The skills of the sender and the receiver should be appropriate for the message. For example, if communication is to be effective, the sender must have the ability to send an appropriate message and the receiver must have the ability to understand it.

Similarly, if jargon is to be used, it must be clearly understood by the recipient.

The terms understood by a certain group of people may be meaningless to those who do not have this technical or specialist knowledge. For example, technical information about a product that is not understood by the marketing department may result in misleading advertising and poor sales.

Modern-day organisations possess multinational workforces operating globally. This increasing internationalisation has brought new cultural challenges to many organisations. The ability of companies to interact successfully with people of different cultures is dependent on their capacity to understand their own cultural make-up as well as that of their counterparts.

Communication and large organisations

Communication often becomes more difficult as organisations grow. Poor communication leads to diseconomies of scale because of reduced motivation, weak coordination and control difficulties. Inadequate understanding of corporate objectives, different languages and cultures, different time zones and too many intermediaries all make effective communication much more difficult for larger businesses, especially multinationals. These firms are likely to place much greater reliance on technological communication, which may improve speed and efficiency, but means that the benefits of face-to-face communication are not as evident.

Communication overload

More communication does not necessarily mean better communication. It can lead to communication (or information) overload and adversely affect decision making.

Figure 19.1
Communication channel with intermediaries

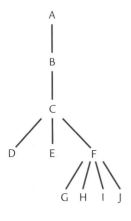

KEY TERMS

intermediaries: individuals or groups within official communication channels through whom messages must be passed in order to reach the intended receivers.

jargon: a word or phrase that has a technical or specialised meaning.

communication overload: when an individual becomes swamped by the sheer volume of communication and information.

Communication overload might apply to managers wanting to be kept fully informed of the activities of all their subordinates. As a result, they may miss key issues, fail to respond to urgent requests and generally become less effective in their role. At the same time, they may come under great stress as a result of their inability to cope. E-mail, which benefits an organisation because of its speed, immediacy and convenience, often adds to this problem of communication overload. The solution is to encourage managers to delegate more widely, reducing the need for so much upward communication.

Many layers of hierarchy

As firms grow in size, they tend to add more layers of hierarchy. This in turn means that communication becomes more difficult, as messages moving from the top of the organisation to the bottom have to go through more intermediaries. This slows down the decision-making process and makes it more likely that messages will get distorted or confused. It also means that communication from the bottom to the top of the organisation is more likely to be discouraged.

One possible solution to the inevitable problems of communication associated with large organisations is decentralisation. Decentralisation reduces the volume of day-to-day communication between head office and the branches, and thus gives senior managers more time to consider long-term strategy, while empowering local managers and encouraging them to be more innovative and motivated.

EXAMINER'S VOICE

If you are not confident about your knowledge of the benefits and problems of delegation, refer back to Chapter 19 of the AS textbook.

EXAMINER'S VOICE

If you are not confident about your knowledge of the benefits and problems of decentralised organisations, refer back to Chapter 18.

FACT FILE

Communication at Beaverbrooks

Beaverbrooks, the jewellery retailer chain, has been in the top five in *The Sunday Times 100 Best Companies to Work For* in each of the last 4 years. Employees say their managers regularly express appreciation when they do a good job, talk openly and honestly with them, trust their judgement and care about them as individuals. Staff are impressed that Mark Adlestone, the chain's managing director, knows everybody by name and staff feel comfortable enough to phone him personally with any concerns. In fact, employees are encouraged to have direct contact with any executive by phone or e-mail. One employee says: 'I feel I have an input in how things change and feel that, if necessary, I could approach the company director about anything, personal or professional.'

Source: *The Sunday Times 100 Best Companies to Work For*, 2004, 2005 and 2007.

PRACTICE EXERCISE 1   Total: 40 marks (35 minutes)

1 Explain three benefits to a firm of good communication with its employees.   *(9 marks)*

2 Explain two problems that a firm might encounter if it has poor communication with its employees.   *(6 marks)*

3 In the context of barriers to communication, what does the term 'noise' mean?   *(3 marks)*

4 In what way can attitudes influence the effectiveness of communication in both a negative and positive manner?   *(4 marks)*

5 Explain how the number of intermediaries can affect the quality of communication.   *(3 marks)*

6 What is communication (or information) overload?   *(3 marks)*

7 Explain how communication overload can create problems for a business.   *(3 marks)*

8 Explain one way in which such problems can be reduced.   *(3 marks)*

9 Why might a large organisation with many layers of hierarchy experience less effective communication?   *(3 marks)*

10 In what way might a more decentralised structure improve communication for large firms?   *(3 marks)*

CASE STUDY 1 Mushroom management: don't keep your workforce in the dark

Ragbags is a producer of fine leather handbags. It has grown from a single small factory in Leeds to a much larger manufacturer with six new production sites throughout the UK and a headquarters based at its original site in Leeds. It sells its products to upmarket department stores and leather retailers only.

Initially the owner and managing director, Joe Watts, managed the small factory well. His approach was somewhat paternalistic, but he knew everyone and made a point of having an 'open door' policy as far as staff were concerned. All staff, regardless of their position, knew they could see him personally to raise issues and make suggestions about any aspect of their work.

As the company grew, the organisation adopted a more formal structure, with more layers between senior management and

the workforce. The organisation chart for the growing organisation is shown in Figure 19.2.

The new structure meant that some directors were never seen at any one site for months at a time. In addition, issues that staff at one site might be concerned with were never communicated to other sites and there was a general feeling among staff of being left in the dark. Increasingly, employees spent tea breaks moaning

Figure 19.2 Ragbags: organisation chart

AQA A2 Business Studies

to each other and talking about looking for new jobs. Despite this general feeling of unhappiness, so far there had been no adverse effects on productivity rates and production levels.

Robina Smith was appointed to the business manager's post, which was a new appointment with responsibility for all administrative staff and procedures across all sites. Each of the six new sites had an administrative supervisor answerable to her. Robina saw her role as that of a strategic manager and did not feel that 'meeting the troops', as she put it, was an essential part of this — and anyway she thought that it could be done much better by the administrative supervisors. She did, however, believe in communicating with all her staff and she did this regularly — always by e-mail. Every week, staff received endless e-mails from her about new policies and procedures she was introducing. Many of these e-mails people just ignored because they knew the policies and procedures would never work.

The administrative supervisors were a bit put out by Robina's approach. They could tell that she was highly efficient and really keen to change and update their working practices, but they felt that it should be they who communicated changes to their staff. The six of them were required to travel to Leeds once a month for a meeting with Robina but had no other opportunity to meet each other or her. It was often difficult to raise issues of concern at these meetings because the agenda, set by Robina, was very tightly structured and the meetings always kept to time.

Production staff were increasingly unhappy about the way their shift-working system was developing. A new system had been introduced recently, but although there had been consultation with the unions and general agreement that it would benefit the company and the workforce, staff did not feel that anyone had really talked it through with them. The production managers at the six sites were in the same position as the administrative supervisors, meeting once per month with the production director at headquarters (HQ). However, they did talk to each other a lot on the phone and correspond by e-mail, mostly complaining to each other about the lack of involvement of senior management in the operations of the six sites and the failure of anyone at senior management level to take their views and the views of their workers into account.

Joe Watts, the MD, had little idea of the discontent at the various sites. As far as he was concerned, the company was prospering, sales were high and growing, and profitability was excellent. He was currently setting up talks with a group of businesses in Japan to discuss the possibility of selling the company's products in department stores over there. The company had recently invested a significant amount of money in improving its ICT, including its communication systems, and all the directors had talked very positively about the beneficial impact of this in terms of communication with the different sites.

It came as something of a surprise to Joe when he met Bill Sykes, one of the production managers, by chance at HQ. Bill had been with the company from the start and Joe knew that he was a first-rate production manager who was loyal and hard working. Bill had come to HQ for one of his monthly production meetings. They got chatting and Joe learned that Bill was leaving at the end of the month. Joe assumed that Bill had got a promotion and congratulated him on 'moving up the ladder', as he put it. Bill said that it was not a promotion, just a sideways move to another firm. Joe got worried. He reasoned that unless it is to do with their personal circumstances, most people do not move sideways to another company unless they are unhappy with their present job. 'Quite honestly Joe, we feel — I feel — that I'm kept in the dark most of the time, and I don't like it so I'm going! The staff don't like it either, but they have no way of telling you.'

Joe decided that he needed to raise this at the next day's senior management meeting. As far as he knew, none of the directors was aware of any problems — which meant the problem was even more serious...

Questions

1 Examine the communication problems facing Ragbags as it has grown from a single-site producer to a multi-site producer. *(10 marks)*

2 Discuss the possible solutions that might be discussed at Ragbags' senior management meeting. *(15 marks)*

3 To what extent are effective communications vital in maintaining good employer/employee relations at Ragbags? *(15 marks)*

KEY TERMS

employee participation: a general term referring to the extent to which employees are involved in the decision-making process.

industrial democracy: when employees have the opportunity to be involved in and to influence decision making. It can take the following forms: worker directors, who are elected to the board of directors by employees from the factory floor; works councils, which are discussed in detail below; and workers' cooperatives, where a firm's workers own a majority of its shares, such as in the John Lewis Partnership.

Employee representation

All organisations involve employees in decision making to some extent. In very small organisations, this may simply involve employers providing their employees with information and asking for their views. In larger organisations, informing and consulting employees is essential in order to maintain good employer/employee relations and is also a legal requirement. Employee representation may take many forms, including trade unions, works councils and other employee groups.

Employee representation is also known as employee participation and industrial democracy.

e EXAMINER'S VOICE

Refer back to your AS work on Mayo's study of the Western Electric factory at Hawthorne and Maslow's hierarchy of human needs (see Chapter 22 of the AS textbook) to ensure that you can relate these ideas to motivation theory.

Employee representation and motivation

Theories of motivation suggest that employees are happier if they feel involved, if they have a part to play in the organisation they work for and if their views are valued by management. In addition, workers have much to offer their employers in terms of their knowledge, ideas and insights into processes with which they are familiar. Thus, more involvement of employees can improve motivation, which in turn may result in lower labour turnover and, often, more innovation and more effective problem solving, all of which lead to increased productivity.

Employee representation and decision making

Problems can arise from employee representation, as involving more people in decision making may slow the whole process down. However, this is not necessarily a bad thing if it causes firms to review situations from different perspectives and therefore make more informed decisions.

Representation also means that people come together with very different points of view and conflicting objectives, which may lead to difficulties in arriving at a consensus in decision making. Managers may resent the power and influence of workers and the amount of information they are provided with. Workers, on the other hand, may feel that they do not have enough power or are not provided with enough information.

Finally, representation can be costly in relation to setting up the process and both the actual and opportunity cost of the time that workers are involved in meetings.

Types of employee representation

Works councils

Works councils are committees of management and workforce representatives that meet to discuss company-wide issues such as training, investment and working practices. Excluded from the agenda is bargaining over issues such as wages, terms of employment and productivity levels, which are left to trade union negotiations. The role of the works council is essentially in looking ahead at the company's plans and in providing an opportunity to consult and gain ideas or improvements from the shop floor. A weakness of this process is that, because a works council includes representatives from the whole firm, it usually lacks the focus of a localised quality circle or improvement group.

The European Works Council Directive requires that large companies operating in two or more EU countries must set up European works councils. The directive aims to 'improve the right to information and to consultation of employees'.

A European works council (EWC) usually meets once a year and is made up of at least one elected representative from each country plus representatives of central management. Areas for discussion include corporate structure, the economic and financial situation, investment, the employment situation, health and safety, cutbacks and closures, acquisitions and new working practices. Single-country issues, including pay and conditions, are not discussed. Most commentators agree that the process is worthwhile and encourages two-way communication.

FACT FILE

The EU Information and Consultation Directive

Introduced in April 2005, the EU Information and Consultation Directive gives employees in organisations with 50-plus staff the right to be informed about the business's economic situation and prospects. In effect, the workforce must be notified of all changes that could affect the nature of staff's employment, such as work organisation, contractual relations, redundancies, mergers and takeovers. The law includes a requirement to hold ballots to elect staff representatives, and gives staff rights to information and consultation. Companies that fail to comply face fines of up to £75,000. In the UK, the requirement for national works councils came into force in April 2008.

Other methods of encouraging employee participation and representation include employee groups, such as improvement groups, quality circles and autonomous groups, worker directors, suggestions schemes and a democratic style of management, which encourages employees to contribute to decision making.

KEY TERMS

worker directors: employees of a company who sit on its board of directors, are involved in decision making at this level and represent the views and interests of the workforce.

trade union: a pressure group that represents the interests of people at work.

negotiation (also known as **collective bargaining**): where union representatives in a particular organisation discuss with management the issues that affect employees working in that organisation.

DID YOU KNOW?

Job satisfaction, and therefore motivation, can be enhanced if employees work together in groups in order to achieve common goals. Giving employees more responsibility provides them with a sense of purpose and thus improves morale and possibly productivity. **Autonomous work groups** are teams of people who are given a high level of responsibility for their own work. This might include organising and scheduling their own work, making decisions about the allocation of tasks and, in some cases, recruiting new members of staff.

Trade unions

Modern trade unions tend to be categorised according to whether they have more open or more restricted recruitment policies. The latter tend to recruit employees with certain skills, such as Equity (actors) and the National Union of Teachers.

More open recruitment policies tend to be associated with larger unions that seek membership regardless of their members' jobs or industries (for example, Unite) or those that recruit from a wide variety of related industries, such as the public service industries (e.g. UNISON). Problems that arise for unions with such large, open recruitment policies include the difficulty of taking account of the needs of different groups of members and the conflict that can result when unions are accused of 'poaching' members from other areas.

What do trade unions do and how do they benefit employees?

The main functions that trade unions provide for their members are **negotiation** and **representation**.

There are often differences of opinion between management and trade union members in relation to issues in the workplace. Negotiation involves the process of finding a solution to these differences. In many organisations, trade unions are formally 'recognised' by the employer, meaning that there is a formal agreement between the trade union and the organisation, giving the trade union the right to negotiate with the employer.

Trade unions also represent individual union members when they have problems at work. If employees feel they are being unfairly treated, they can ask their trade union representative to help sort out their difficulties with management. If the problems cannot be resolved amicably, they may go to an industrial tribunal, at which individual union members can ask their trade unions to represent them.

Trade unions also offer their members legal representation — for example, helping them to get financial compensation for work-related injuries.

In addition to the two main functions of negotiation and representation, trade unions provide information, advice and member services. For example, they can advise on a range of issues, such as employment rights and health and safety issues.

More generally, individual employees have very little power to influence decisions that are made about their jobs. In relation to negotiating pay and conditions, they are in a very weak position compared with a large employer. By joining together with other workers in a trade union, there is more chance of having a voice and therefore having influence. By collective bargaining with employers on behalf of their members, trade unions are able to improve the lot of their members at work in relation to issues such as rates of pay, work facilities, working conditions, bonuses and targets, job security, contracts, redundancy, dismissal, grievance procedures, job descriptions and job specifications.

> **KEY TERM**
>
> **collective bargaining:** the process whereby workers' representatives meet with employers to discuss and negotiate employment-related issues.

Do trade unions benefit employers?

Media reporting tends to suggest that trade unions are something of an irritation to employers, disrupting their operations and preventing them achieving their objectives. However, in general, trade unions benefit employers as well as employees.

- They provide a valuable communication link between senior management and the workforce that has not been filtered by middle managers.
- The presence of a trade union means that management can avoid what would be very time-consuming bargaining and negotiation with each individual employee in relation to their pay and conditions.
- A strong union may encourage management to take workers' needs seriously and may thus improve employee morale, which in turn may have a positive influence on productivity.
- The presence of a trade union may ease situations that could cause difficulty for a firm, such as relocation, retraining for new technology, downsizing and redundancy, and renegotiation of employment conditions and contracts. Trade union officials can be consulted at an early stage of the decision-making process, which may make the workforce more confident that management is acting properly and thoughtfully.

How have trade unions changed in recent years?

Trade union membership has declined over the last three decades. In 1979, 13.3 million people were members of trade unions, while in autumn 2008, 6.5 million UK workers belonged to trade unions. The proportion of union members in the workforce, known as union density, has also been declining.

union density: the proportion of all employees who are union members:

$$\text{union density} = \frac{\text{actual union membership}}{\text{potential union membership}} \times 100$$

Reasons for the fall in union membership over the last 30 years include:

- a dramatic fall in the number of jobs in manufacturing industries, where union membership was traditionally high (e.g. shipbuilding, steel and mining)
- the privatisation of major utilities, reducing the number of employees in the public sector
- a fall in traditional, permanent, full-time employment and an increase in flexible working, including part-time workers, temporary staff and home workers, who are less likely to join unions or be covered by employment legislation
- an increase in the proportion of the workforce employed by small businesses, many employing fewer than ten workers, where it is often difficult for unions to organise
- legislation that makes it more difficult for unions to operate and keep their members
- improved employment rights for individuals and greater employee participation in the workplace, causing people to feel that unions are less necessary
- a fall in the number of collective bargaining agreements and an increase in deals between individual employees and management

The overall decline in trade union membership has reduced the power of trade unions generally. However, this may not be the case in particular industries, where union density may be high — for example, among tube train drivers and postal workers.

Industrial disputes and industrial action

industrial dispute: a disagreement between management and the trade union representing the employees, which is serious enough for industrial action to result.

industrial action: measures taken by employees to halt or slow production or disrupt services in order to put pressure on management during an industrial dispute (e.g. a strike, overtime ban, work-to-rule or go-slow).

Most collective bargaining takes place quietly, away from media attention and with agreements being reached quickly and amicably by the union and the employer. However, disagreements can occur. In this case, an industrial dispute might result. An industrial dispute might be resolved by successful conciliation or arbitration. If this does not occur, the union may ballot its members on whether to take industrial action.

TOPOFTO

Strikes are only called as a last resort since both sides have a lot to lose: employers lose sales revenue because of interruptions to production or services, while employees lose their wages and salaries and may find that their jobs are at risk.

Work-to-rules, go-slows and overtime bans are similar in their impact on employees and the firm:

- In a **work-to-rule**, the workforce applies the employer's own rules and procedure 'to the letter', thus stopping overtime and many forms of participation and communication that are accepted practice. This behaviour cannot be criticised by the employer and may lead to considerable delay. Staff may prefer to work-to-rule rather than go on strike, since they are able to draw their basic pay.
- A **go-slow** loses employees any bonuses, but ensures that they receive their basic pay. If conducted at a time of high demand, a go-slow could be successful in applying considerable pressure upon an employer.
- An **overtime ban** can only be effective if a significant proportion of work in a key section is done on overtime. This is only likely to occur in seasonal production peaks.

Table 19.1 identifies the factors that influence the success of industrial action and the possible problems and benefits for employees and employers.

KEY TERMS

strike: a form of industrial action involving the complete withdrawal of labour by employees.

work-to-rule: a form of industrial action in which employees refuse to undertake any work that is outside the precise terms of their employment contract.

go-slow: a form of industrial action in which employees keep on working, but at the absolute minimum pace required to avoid being subject to legitimate disciplinary action.

overtime ban: a form of industrial action that attempts to disrupt the employer while keeping employees' basic wages unaffected.

Table 19.1 Industrial action

Factors that influence the success of industrial action	Problems of industrial action for employers	Problems of industrial action for employees	Benefits of industrial action
• Nature and strength of union	• Lost production, reduced revenue and lower profits	• Reduced or lost earnings	• Resolves ongoing grievances and improves the atmosphere
• Workforce concentration (e.g. lots of union members in one firm compared with a few members in many firms)	• Continuing poor relationships and grievances with employees, that lead to poor motivation and communication	• Closure of the business and redundancies	• Often leads to new rules about which all agree (e.g. regarding rates of pay or the need to consult)
• Management tactics (e.g. if stocks are available to meet demand during a strike)	• Shifts management's focus away from strategic planning for the future	• Stress and friction between levels of the hierarchy	• Leads to greater understanding of employer/employee positions
• Economic and legal climate	• Harms the firm's reputation with its customers	• If unsuccessful, workers are in a weaker position	
• Public support		• Support from the public may decline if action affects them	
		• Must conform to legislation or be liable for damages	

Employers can also take industrial action by withdrawing overtime, introducing a lockout (i.e. closing the factory and not allowing employees in to continue working), changing standard and piecework rates, closing the business and dismissing workers.

As Figures 19.3 and 19.4 illustrate, times have changed and industrial unrest in the form of days lost and stoppages (industrial action that involves employees stopping work) are much less frequent today. The main causes of disputes have not changed, however, and pay still dominates. Figure 19.5 shows the principal causes of working days lost in 2006: 73% of working days lost were due to disputes over pay and 22% were due to redundancy. In comparison, working conditions accounted for 2% of working days lost, and hours worked and discipline both accounted for 1%.

Figure 19.3
Working days lost in the UK, 1987–2006

Source: Office for National Statistics.

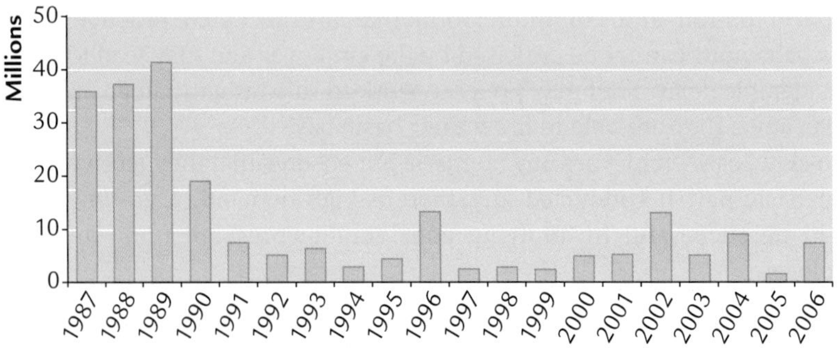

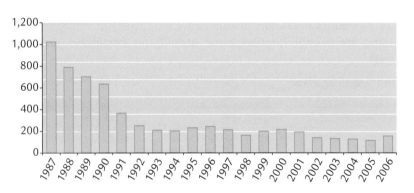

Figure 19.4
Stoppages in progress in the UK, 1987–2006

Source: Office for National Statistics.

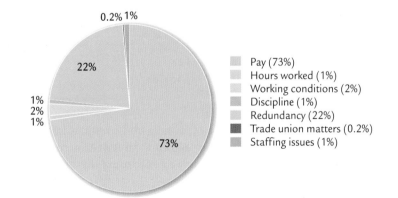

Figure 19.5
Principal causes of disputes leading to working days lost in the UK, 2006

Source: Office for National Statistics.

Pay (73%)
Hours worked (1%)
Working conditions (2%)
Discipline (1%)
Redundancy (22%)
Trade union matters (0.2%)
Staffing issues (1%)

Methods of avoiding and resolving industrial disputes

Single-union and no-strike agreements

The introduction of a single-union agreement removes the potential disruption caused by inter-union disputes and reduces the time spent on negotiations. Single-union agreements have sometimes added no-strike agreements.

> **FACT FILE**
>
> **Single-union agreement at Nissan**
>
> In February 1984, Nissan and the UK government signed an agreement to build a car plant in Sunderland in the northeast of England. The region had recently undergone a period of industrial decline, with the closure of shipyards and coalmines. The high unemployment this caused meant that Nissan had a large, eager, manufacturing-skilled workforce to draw upon.
>
> One of Nissan's more controversial demands was that the plant be single-union. This was unprecedented in UK industry at the time. In April 1985, an agreement was reached with the Amalgamated Engineering Union (AEU). Critics argued that this meant the plant workforce would be weakly represented. Nissan argued that, as a result of the single-union agreement, its workforce would be much more flexible than at other plants. In support of Nissan, not a single day has been lost due to industrial disputes at the factory.

> **KEY TERMS**
>
> **single-union agreement:** the recognition by a firm of only one trade union for collective bargaining purposes.
>
> **no-strike agreement:** a contract, signed as part of a firm's negotiation and disputes procedure, which prevents the trade unions in a particular firm from calling a strike.

The Advisory, Conciliation and Arbitration Service

The Advisory, Conciliation and Arbitration Service (ACAS) was founded in 1975. It aims to improve organisations and working life through better employment relations. It is a non-governmental body that is fully independent, impartial and confidential. It is governed by a council made up of leading figures from business, trade unions and academia.

ACAS only becomes involved if both sides (employers and employees or their trade union representatives) believe that ACAS can help them make progress in the dispute. Once involved, representatives from ACAS will discuss the dispute with both sides and all will agree on how best ACAS can help. The role of ACAS can involve:

- sorting out the issues
- finding common ground between the two sides
- giving people the space to calm down and see the problems from the other side too (sometimes this means taking the dispute out of the media spotlight)
- having meetings with each side separately and together to discuss and explore the issues, and then starting to negotiate a solution
- repairing relationships and building trust

As an independent and neutral party, ACAS provides mediation, conciliation and arbitration services. Mediation and conciliation are where it tries to bring both sides of a dispute together to reconcile their differences and reach an agreement. Arbitration is where both sides agree that ACAS will review the evidence and arrive at a decision, which they will accept.

Although ACAS helps to solve high-profile labour disputes, such as the Royal Mail and London Underground train drivers' disputes, much of its work is focused on individual complaints to employment tribunals. These are passed to ACAS and, at present, 75% are settled or withdrawn at the ACAS stage, so preventing the need for an industrial tribunal hearing.

Another growth area is in solving employment issues before they become problems at all. ACAS advisers give guidance on topics such as discipline and dismissal, contracts, layoffs, short-time working, redundancy, holidays and holiday pay, wages, maternity provisions, working-time regulations, grievance procedures and paternity rights. They also promote good practice at training sessions and work in individual companies with employer, employee and trade union groups in partnership to find lasting solutions in the workplace.

A number of other organisations contribute to the avoidance or resolution of industrial disputes, including the TUC, employers' associations and the CBI, each of which is discussed below.

> **DID YOU KNOW?**
>
> The approach that ACAS takes is: 'Don't get angry — get curious.' Its advice for a first step towards a solution in any kind of dispute is to find out why people are taking the positions they are and why they are angry.

The Trades Union Congress

Formed in 1868, the Trades Union Congress (TUC) is the national organisation that represents trade unions in the UK. It has 58 affiliated (member) unions representing nearly 6.5 million working people. Trade unions join the TUC because they know that they can be stronger and more effective if they work together with other unions to protect the rights of working people.

The role of the TUC in relation to avoidance or resolution of industrial disputes includes:

- bringing the UK's unions together to draw up common policies
- lobbying the government to implement policies that will benefit people at work
- helping unions avoid clashes with each other

Employers' associations

Just as trade unions represent employees, so employers' associations represent the views and interests of companies within a sector or industry — for example, the Engineering Employers' Federation. They are especially useful for small firms negotiating with large trade unions. Like trade unions, they are financed by members' subscriptions. Their functions in relation to avoidance or resolution of industrial disputes include:

- providing advice to employers about collective bargaining
- acting as a pressure group influencing government policy in areas of interest to the sector or industry they represent
- providing a negotiating team that can agree minimum pay and conditions with trade unions throughout the industry

The Confederation of British Industry (CBI) was formed in 1965. It performs a similar role to the TUC. It is the main employers' association and includes most of the country's leading firms as members. Its main functions are to:

- lobby the government in order to influence legislation and economic policies favoured by the private sector
- promote the image of industry as a worthwhile career
- provide its members with well-researched reports, such as the CBI's Quarterly Survey of Economic Trends

The CBI works with the TUC on consultative bodies such as ACAS.

Improving industrial relations

Successful industrial relations result when both employers and trade unions compromise and recognise each other's objectives and needs.

According to the TUC, a strong sense of worker participation in decisions, often coordinated through trade unions, seems in recent years to have enhanced business performance. One study reported that organisations that had strong employee involvement were growing four to five times as quickly as those that did not. Other research has suggested a link between employee representation and productivity.

It would be simplistic, however, to suggest that strong employee representation is, by itself, a benefit to businesses. The common factor in successful organisations has been a management team that is highly committed to including employees. This has given rise to the concept of partnership, where unions and employees work together with an open-minded management to generate positive change and growth for the business (see the Thames Water case study overleaf).

KEY TERM

industrial relations: the atmosphere prevailing between an organisation's management and its workforce representatives (i.e. the trade unions).

PRACTICE EXERCISE 2   Total: 50 marks (45 minutes)

1 Explain the term 'employee representation'.   *(3 marks)*

2 Explain one advantage and one disadvantage of employee representation for a business.   *(6 marks)*

3 a What is a works council?   *(3 marks)*
   b Under what circumstances must a business set up a European works council?   *(3 marks)*

4 What is a trade union?   *(3 marks)*

5 Explain three functions that trade unions carry out on behalf of their members.   *(9 marks)*

6 Explain two benefits of trade unions for employers.   *(6 marks)*

7 a What is an industrial dispute?   *(3 marks)*
   b Identify three forms of industrial action that trade union members might take during an industrial dispute.   *(3 marks)*

8 Why might industrial action have an adverse impact on employees?   *(4 marks)*

9 What do the terms 'mediation' (or 'conciliation') and 'arbitration' mean in relation to avoiding or resolving industrial disputes?   *(5 marks)*

10 Identify two other methods that might be used to avoid or resolve industrial disputes.   *(2 marks)*

CASE STUDY 2   Thames Water

A good example of the benefits that a partnership approach can bring is demonstrated by Thames Water. The company recognises four unions, and operates in a highly regulated environment. By 1999 it was coming under heavy pressure from the Competition Commission and shareholders simultaneously. The unions suggested that the way forward might be a partnership agreement. As discussions about this progressed, both sides realised that greater employee involvement might be a route by which changes to archaic working practices could be brought about. The central concept is a 'Partnership Forum' with seven directors and seven elected representatives, but the real heart of the partnership is changed approaches throughout the business in terms of the way decisions are taken, which have brought benefits to employees and business alike.

Pay negotiations

One example is the annual round of pay negotiations. In the past this had tended to be a prolonged process of offer and counter-offer, with neither side prepared to divulge key information. As a result, the negotiations were felt to be antagonistic. The most recent round of pay negotiations was very different. The partnership approach meant that the key information was known to both management and unions as a result of their shared approach to decision making on a day-to-day basis. Negotiations that had previously taken months were concluded in 2 days.

New shift system

Another example is a change in the shift system, which had previously created an annual £1 million overtime bill. Thames Water had attempted to change the system in the past, but with no success due to a complex system of local agreements and precedents. For the first time, shift workers (assisted by union representatives and managers) took part in the discussions about possible changes. Over a 3-month period, a new system was agreed that was expected to save Thames Water £380,000 a year, but also gave employees more say over the hours that they worked.

Thus, in both cases, effective employee involvement, facilitated by constructive union support, has brought substantial business benefits as well as helping to improve terms and conditions for employees.

Source: adapted from Simon Harrison, 'Employee–employer relations in the UK', *Business Review*, November 2003.

Preliminary questions   Total: 40 marks (45 minutes)

1 Explain two methods of employee representation in place at Thames Water.   *(6 marks)*

2 Explain the term 'negotiation'.   *(4 marks)*

3 Employees at Thames Water belong to one of four trade unions. Explain three possible benefits to employees of belonging to a trade union.   *(9 marks)*

4 The case study suggests that in the past pay negotiation were antagonistic. If they had resulted in industrial disputes, identify and explain three possible actions trade unions might have taken against employers.   *(9 marks)*

5 What does the case study suggest are the benefits of employee representation to:
   a employees of Thames Water   *(6 marks)*
   b Thames Water itself?   *(6 marks)*

Case study questions   Total: 30 marks (40 minutes)

1 'Trade unions are no longer necessary given the increasing emphasis on employee participation and the recent EU Information and Consultation Directive.' Discuss this statement in the context of Thames Water.   *(15 marks)*

2 To what extent has the partnership approach between the trade unions and Thames Water effectively avoided or resolved potential industrial disputes?   *(15 marks)*

Human resource strategies

CASE STUDY FirstClass Solutions

FirstClass Solutions is a business consultancy that provides strategic advice to small and medium-sized businesses. It works with companies wishing to implement change, draw up contingency plans or deal with crises, and its work covers all functional areas. Thus it might work with a business on organising the relocation of its factory or advise on dealing with the media following a major problem. Unfortunately, as good as its work is with other companies, it has not focused much on its own problems.

The business has six offices throughout the UK. Each office employs 60–70 staff, including administrative, marketing, operations and finance staff and the consultants. The business has grown rapidly over the last 3 years. Its objective is to continue to grow and to grab as much of the market as it can, which means accepting almost any work that comes its way. There is some disagreement about this among the board of directors. Some feel that it would be much better to focus their activities and to specialise in the management of change so that they can build a strong reputation and possibly expand into the international market.

The director of human resources (HR) left recently following months of problems with his approach and the impact of this on the morale of staff. He was known to take a 'hard' approach to HR. Although this had seemed right at the time, it became increasingly obvious that the HR strategy at FirstClass Solutions was not working and was in fact leading to a range of problems. A complete overhaul of HR provision was needed and the first step was to appoint a new director of HR who could successfully introduce a 'soft HR strategy' into the organisation.

The situation was not helped by the severe recession in the economy in the early part of the year, when unemployment seemed to increase every week and interest rates fell to unusually low figures. In some respects, FirstClass Solutions might have prospered in this environment — businesses were closing or contracting and there was lots of 'managing change', but few businesses had the money to spend on expensive consultants. Thus FirstClass had to face its own round of redundancies — for the first time in its existence — and it was the consultants who were hit hardest, with 10 or 15 being laid off in each office. This had massive repercussions on the morale of the entire workforce. Most were not in any type of trade union and there were no formal means of representation within the organisation. That and the 'hard' approach of the previous director of HR combined to produce a pretty awful environment to work in.

The managing director pondered all these issues as he waited for the other directors, including the new director of HR, to arrive for what he hoped might be a turning point. He had given the new director of HR a month to assess the current state of the business from an HR perspective and to come up with a series of preliminary recommendations. Today was the day she would present these to the board.

Her opening slide included the following points:
- HR objectives
- Internal and external influences on HR objectives
- Hard/soft strategies
- Workforce planning
- Organisational structure

The board listened to her presentation with keen interest. At present, the company had no formal HR objectives. Thus the HR department simply responded but was never proactive. The new director was already implementing changes in order to introduce a 'soft' HR strategy. This would take time and would involve difficulties, not least the need to change the culture of the organisation and its approach to HR. Workforce planning was needed in order to ensure that the current and future requirements of the business were properly reflected in it workforce.

The structure of the organisation was called into question. Why six regional offices? There is a huge central office in London with plenty of unused space. Why not centralise activities, which would reduce the need for middle managers and office-based staff – all of which would reduce costs and streamline activities. Why did consultants have to be office-based? Why did they all have to be employed full time? Consultants could work from home, travelling to clients as appropriate and calling into the central office for meetings. In place of full-time, permanent consultants, core and peripheral staff could be employed to ensure that staffing closely met business needs. It was no surprise that morale was poor: communications were ineffective; there was no employee representation; and employees had no voice in the decision-making process.

She ended by issuing charts illustrating the present organisational structure (Appendix 1), the reorganised structure (Appendix 2) and sheets summarising the implications of the changes (Appendices 3 and 4) and saying that more detailed cost and revenue estimates would be available in a week's time.

The director of HR sat down. The board of directors looked at each other. The managing director thanked the new director and said: 'If we implement these recommendations, it will mean major changes to FirstClass Solutions — particularly in relation to organisational restructuring and the move to flexible working. I'd like to reconvene this meeting for next week when the more detailed estimates will be available. That should give us all time to think through the implications for the company.'

Appendix 1
The present organisational structure

The London office   Managing director

Director of finance	Director of marketing	Director of HR	Director of operations	Director of professional services
Finance manager	Marketing manager	HR manager	Operations manager	Professional services manager
Finance officers (5)	Marketing officers (5)	HR officers (5)	Operations officers (5)	Consultants (39)

Each of the five regional branches   Branch manager

Finance manager	Marketing manager	HR manager	Operations manager	Professional services manager
Finance officers (5)	Marketing officers (5)	HR officers (5)	Operations officers (5)	Consultants (39)

Appendix 2
The organisational structure suggested by the new director of HR

Managing director

Director of finance	Director of marketing	Director of HR	Director of operations	Director of professional services
Finance manager	Marketing manager	HR manager	Operations manager	Core consultants (employed on a full-time permanent basis) (60)
Finance officers (10)	Marketing officers (10)	HR officers (10)	Operations officers (10)	Peripheral consultants (175)

Appendix 3 *Staffing at FirstClass Solutions*

	Before reorganisation	After reorganisation
Senior management	6	6
Middle management	35	4
Core consultants	234	60
Peripheral consultants	0	175
Finance office staff	30	10
Marketing office staff	30	10
HR office staff	30	10
Operations office staff	30	10
Total	**395**	**285**

Appendix 4 *Summary of implications of reorganisation*

Cost of rent and utilities	Fall of approx. 80%
Cost of salaries:	• Middle management: fall of approx. 90% • Office staff: fall of approx. 60% • Core consultants: fall of approx. 70%
Fees of peripheral consultants	Difficult to quantify at this stage as the figure will relate directly to the level of work in any year, but initially suggest equivalent to the fall in core consultants' salaries
Costs of reducing the workforce	• All: early retirement bonuses and enhanced pension rights for everyone over 58 or redundancy payments in line with contractual requirements • Office staff: costs of relocation for those moving to the London office • Consultants: those taking up peripheral consultant roles will maintain their current salary for 1 year
Cost of training	• All: to ensure organisational and cultural changes are fully embedded • Middle managers: to ensure they understand their new national remit • Core consultants: to provide them with the skills to manage the work of a group
Selection for new posts	Internal recruitment: • 4 middle managers from existing middle managers • 20 additional London-based office staff from existing regional office staff • 60 core consultants from existing consultants External recruitment: • Only where we fail to recruit internally
Changes in roles and responsibilities	• Middle managers: increase in span of control • Core consultants: significant change as they become responsible for the performance of teams of peripheral consultants

Questions

Total 80 marks (1 hour 45 minutes)

1 Examine the issues FirstClass Solutions might face in implementing workforce plans. *(10 marks)*

2 Discuss the importance of FirstClass Solutions having HR objectives and how such objectives might be influenced by internal and external factors. *(15 marks)*

3 To what extent is a 'soft' HR strategy likely to bring more benefits to FirstClass Solutions than the previous 'hard' HR strategy? *(15 marks)*

4 Consider the suggested change to the organisational structure and the proposal to introduce more flexible working. Using the information available to you and your knowledge of these areas, make a justified recommendation on whether or not this would be a good move for FirstClass Solutions. *(40 marks)*

Unit 4

The business environment and managing change

Chapter 20

Understanding mission, aims and objectives

EXAMINER'S VOICE

Refer back to Chapter 1 for an introduction to the use of objectives and strategies in business, and to Chapters 2, 7, 11 and 16 for introductory references to functional objectives and strategies.

KEY TERM

mission statement: a qualitative statement of an organisation's aims. It uses language intended to motivate employees and convince customers, suppliers and those outside the firm of its sincerity and commitment.

This chapter considers mission statements, and corporate aims and objectives. It explains the purpose and nature of corporate strategies and their relationship to aims and objectives. It identifies differing stakeholder perspectives and discusses the potential for conflict and the pressure that stakeholders may bring to decision making.

Mission statements

Before an organisation can start to address the task of planning and setting objectives, it must have a clear understanding of its overall purpose. This is expressed as a mission and is communicated via a mission statement. The mission of an organisation is its essential purpose, and the mission statement a means of communicating to key stakeholders (for example, shareholders, employees, suppliers and customers) what the company is doing and what it ought to be doing. It should set out clearly the primary purpose of the organisation, its values and distinctive features, and provide a rationale for its strategic plan. It should be presented in as clear, concise and memorable a way as possible.

Disney's vision or mission statement (the two terms can be used interchangeably) is 'to make people happy'. The mission of 3M, the inventors and producers of Post-It Notes, seems appropriate: 'to solve unsolved problems innovatively'. Bill Gates has said that the Microsoft Mission is: 'Taking the internet, combining it with great software and turning that into the most powerful tool of all time'. British Airways, from describing itself as 'the world's favourite airline' now defines itself as 'the undisputed leader in world travel'. Other examples are BT, which aims 'to provide world-class telecommunications and information products and services...', and ASDA, which intends 'to be the UK's best-value retailer exceeding customer needs always'.

BT MEDIA IMAGE LIBRARY

Why use a mission statement?

If a company is small, employing, say, 100 people, all the employees are likely to know exactly what the business does and will have a reasonable idea of what its goals are. In a small company, everyone is involved, but in a large company, employing thousands or even tens of thousands of people, this is not the case. An organisation such as a large public limited company may have a varied range of activities, with plants and offices in different locations. There is no reason to expect a manager from a manufacturing division in Scotland to share a sense of mission with the board of directors, who are hundreds of miles away in the head office in London, or with the human resource manager of a retailing division in the USA. So, for a large, diversified company, a mission statement is useful for defining what the company is trying to do in a way that all staff can understand and identify with.

Factors to consider in producing a mission statement

One difficulty with drawing up a mission statement for a large organisation is that it can tend to ignore parts of the business. How, for example, do you write a single-sentence mission statement for a supermarket that is also a bank? To counter this, some companies produce mission lists, while others produce mission booklets. While these tend to cover all of a company's activities, they are less memorable than a single sentence.

In general, when producing a mission statement, a company should start from the top and get everyone involved in thinking about what the statement is going to be. Once the statement is defined and understood by senior management, it needs to be disseminated effectively throughout the organisation, ensuring that everyone within the company understands what the organisation is doing and what it wants to do. The statement can then be communicated to other stakeholders, such as customers and suppliers.

Once a mission statement has been written and communicated effectively in a company, it needs to be continually monitored and altered as the nature of the business and its goals change. Over 20 years ago, Microsoft supplied the operating system for a major mainframe provider; its early vision was 'a computer on every desk and in every home'. Today, its range of activities has grown to encompass the internet and related technologies and its mission now is: 'helping our customers realise their full potential'.

Problems with mission statements

- Some mission statements have been criticised for containing idealistic values that have no meaning in practice and are simply part of a public relations (PR) strategy. This criticism has arisen because many mission statements fail to show how the high ideals they express are to be put into practice.
- Some mission statements fail to have any impact on company performance because they do not provide a clear signal as to how the purpose, values and strategy should guide employees' standards and behaviour.

DID YOU KNOW?

McDonald's mission statement is: to be the world's best quick service restaurant experience. Being the best means providing outstanding quality, service, cleanliness, and value, so that we make every customer in every restaurant smile.'

- Mission statements do not necessarily add value and can do serious harm if, for example, employees recognise that the values and behaviour standards mentioned in the statement are different from their own. When a high-profile petroleum company issued a mission statement that included an appeal for a balanced home and work life, many of the hardest workers in the company started to ridicule the document.
- Mission statements need to match what is actually happening in the company and should be checked for any hidden meanings or negative implications before being placed into the public domain. This was clearly not the case when the former British Rail, noted for delays and cancellations of train services, launched its 'We're getting there' mission statement.

DID YOU KNOW?

Scott Adams, in his office satire *The Dilbert Principle*, describes mission statements as 'long, awkward sentences that demonstrate management's inability to think clearly'.

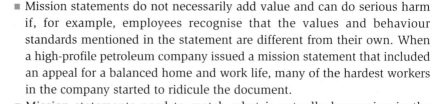

e EXAMINER'S VOICE

Remember that mission statements can sometimes be more about PR than meaningful statements of an organisation's actual aims.

KEY TERM

corporate aims: the long-term intentions of a business.

corporate objectives: targets that must be achieved in order to meet the stated aims of the business.

Corporate aims and objectives

Corporate aims

Corporate aims are often provided in the form of a mission statement and give a general focus from which more specific objectives can be set. Aims determine the way in which an organisation will develop. They provide a common purpose for everyone to identify with and work towards, and a collective view that helps to build team spirit and encourage commitment. They are not usually stated in numerical terms.

Corporate objectives

Corporate objectives are medium- to long-term targets that give a sense of direction to the whole organisation. They act as a focus for decision making and effort, and as a yardstick against which success or failure can be measured. They also encourage a sense of common purpose among the workforce. A sense of common purpose makes it much easier to coordinate actions and to create a team spirit, which in turn is likely to lead to improvements in efficiency and a more productive and motivated staff. Corporate objectives govern the targets for each division or department of the business (as discussed in more detail in Chapters 2, 7, 11 and 16).

It is important to distinguish between an organisation's mission, its corporate aims and objectives. Figure 20.1 presents a hierarchy indicating the order in which they might be set and thus how they influence each other.

Figure 20.1 The hierarchy of objective setting within an organisation

Mission statement

Corporate aims

Corporate objectives

Functional/departmental objectives

Key corporate aims and objectives

Aims and objectives vary from firm to firm, depending on the size of the business and the legal structure. For example, a corner shop may simply aim to survive, whereas a multinational organisation may be more interested in its corporate image and the possibility of diversifying. Aims and objectives can be concerned with any of the following:

- **Survival.** This is a key objective for most small or new firms, especially if they are operating in highly competitive markets, and it is an even more significant objective during periods of uncertainty and recession.
- **Profit.** Profit maximisation is often cited as the most important objective, but in practice firms are more likely to aim for a satisfactory level of profit. Financial objectives will always be influenced by the business environment. For example, the level of competition, the existence of spare capacity, the stage of the business cycle and the demand for the product all affect the chances of making a profit.
- **Growth.** This could relate to increasing market share, turnover, number of outlets or number of business areas, and can be achieved by growth of the existing business or by takeovers of other businesses. Growth is less likely to be an important objective for small businesses that value their independence. External factors are also likely to influence the attainment of objectives related to growth.
- **Diversification.** A firm might wish to diversify in order to spread risk by reducing its dependency on a single market or product.
- **Market standing.** Depending on the organisation, this might involve being seen as the most innovative and progressive organisation or the leader in technology or the best retailer. It is linked to corporate image and an organisation's reputation. Achieving an appropriate corporate image is likely to assist with the achievement of other objectives, such as growth and profit. The nature of this objective will vary according to the target market. For example, a different corporate image will benefit the company if the target market requires products that are 'cheap and cheerful' than if the target market is influenced by an exclusive image and high prices.
- **Meeting the needs of other stakeholders.** To an extent, the above objectives benefit owners or shareholders. However, organisations also place a high value on considering the needs of other stakeholder groups, such as customers, workers and the local community, which in turn will enhance the company's reputation. For example, Tesco's aims and objectives (see Case Study 1) are clearly related to satisfying customer and staff needs.

DID YOU KNOW?

Small businesses are unlikely to write down their aims and objectives, or even consider them formally, although they are likely to be tacitly understood. Even if aims and objectives are not written down, it is still important for employees to know what the business is striving to achieve and to share the vision.

Other examples of corporate aims and objectives include: maximising shareholder wealth; maximising sales revenue; focusing on the firm's core capabilities rather than venturing into risky diversification; social and environmental responsibility; adding value; and enhancing reputation through continuous technological innovation.

Long-term and short-term corporate objectives

Decisions about objectives need to be made in the context of a firm's overall aims. In practice, however, objectives are constantly modified in response to changes in the market and the external environment, and in relation to present levels of achievement and future opportunities. Thus, short-term objectives may vary from the longer-term objectives and aims for a number of reasons. For example:

- A financial crisis is likely to encourage a firm to focus on short-term survival rather than, say, growth or market share. This does not mean that its long-term aims and objectives in relation to growth or market share have changed, but clearly in the very short term, contingency plans and alternative strategies may be required.
- A firm may have a long-term objective of improving profitability, but in the short term profitability might be sacrificed in order to try to eliminate a competitor. For example, in the short term, a firm might use very low pricing (sometimes known as **destroyer** or **predatory pricing**) in order to force a competitor from the market. This might mean losses being sustained in the short term in order to pursue growth and increase market share, which in turn should improve long-term profitability.
- In a recession, emphasis is likely to be placed on survival, whereas over the longer term and in a boom, the potential for high profits may encourage other objectives, such as helping the environment or local community, or diversification.
- Changes in government policy may force a company to adopt different short-term priorities. For example, an increase or decrease in interest rates can have a significant impact on the borrowing costs of a business, and depending on the market it operates in, on consumer demand for its products. (Interest rates and their impact on business are discussed in detail in Chapter 21.)
- Negative publicity from a faulty product or an environmental disaster will cause a firm to focus on improving its image in the short term in order to re-establish itself in the market, regardless of its longer-term objectives. See the Fact File on Bernard Matthews (opposite) for an example of this. The Bernard Matthews website acknowledges that the company has not always made the best decisions but argues that it has listened to its customers and made significant improvements to its products in order to ensure that it meets their needs.

FACT FILE

Negative publicity at Bernard Matthews

Bernard Matthews has suffered from negative publicity on a number of occasions in recent years. For example:

- In January 2005, 'Turkey Twizzlers' were singled out for criticism by the chef Jamie Oliver in his television series *Jamie's School Dinners*. The product became an emblem of the mass-produced, processed food that Oliver wanted to remove from schools. In the wake of the programme, several major catering organisations announced that they would no longer serve Turkey Twizzlers in schools. Bernard Matthews discontinued the product in 2005.
- Bernard Matthews received further bad publicity in January 2007, when the first ever case of industrial avian flu occurred at one of Bernard Matthews' turkey farms in Suffolk. Operationally, Bernard Matthews was well prepared for such a crisis and

its prompt management meant that the timescale for culling the turkeys on its farm was reduced from the government's projected 5–15 days to just over 2 days. It was suspected that the source of the infection was turkeys imported from Hungary; however, despite rigorous inspection, this remains unconfirmed. Bernard Matthews stopped importing turkey meat from Hungary in February 2007.

Source: adapted from information on Bernard Matthews' website, www.bernardmatthewsfarms.com.

There is no single corporate aim or objective to which every firm should aspire or that guarantees success. However, as long as clear objectives are derived from sound aims, and as long as these objectives are pursued with realistic and well-resourced strategies, business success is much more likely.

EXAMINER'S VOICE

In practice, many of the terms introduced in this chapter are used interchangeably. Some companies refer to their 'vision' or 'core purpose' or 'values' rather than mission; others use the terms 'aims' and 'mission' interchangeably. A goal is another term for an objective and in many cases the term 'aims' is substituted for 'objectives'. The term 'targets' is often used instead of objectives, although in other situations the term 'targets' is used for narrow, very specifically focused objectives, often at the level of department, team or even individual.

The important concept for you to understand is that there is a hierarchy with broad corporate aims or goals at the top, which are then translated into more specific but still company-wide objectives, which are in turn translated into specific functional or departmental objectives (for marketing, production, operations, finance and human resources).

Corporate strategies

Corporate strategies are the general approaches that a company uses and the policies and plans it develops in order to achieve its corporate aims and objectives. Just as corporate aims and objectives are translated into more detailed functional objectives, corporate strategies are translated into more detailed functional strategies.

Corporate strategies are planned by the board of directors but have an impact at functional levels within the firm. They involve decisions about broad issues such as what precise market the business is in, who its competitors are, and how it intends to compete. Corporate strategies may also involve decisions on whether to diversify into new products and new markets.

In a multi-product firm, corporate strategy will be concerned with how the various products fit together and contribute to the overall success of the business. If one of its corporate objectives is to increase market share, the firm's corporate strategies will focus on how this will be achieved, which might involve decisions on whether to expand, for example, into America or into Europe. If a corporate objective is to improve profitability and cut costs, a corporate strategy might be to outsource much of its backroom administrative activities to countries where labour is much cheaper. If the company has been hit by falling demand or a need to improve efficiency in order to compete more effectively, corporate strategies might involve reorganisation from a functional to a matrix structure or from a geographical to a product-based structure.

KEY TERM

stakeholder:
an individual or group with a direct interest in the activities and performance of an organisation.

TOPFOTO

Differing stakeholder perspectives

The main stakeholders in a business are its shareholders, its staff, its customers, its suppliers, the financiers, the local community and the government. Figure 20.2 illustrates the stakeholder groups that might have an interest in a football club such as Manchester United. Stakeholders may be either internal or external to an organisation. On certain issues, stakeholders may share common concerns, while on others they may not. Stakeholders exert their influence over the organisation through the position they hold and the means available to them. Successful modern businesses must prove as effective at managing their stakeholders as they are at managing their market or financial position.

Figure 20.2 Manchester United: its stakeholder groups

EXAMINER'S VOICE

Depending on their relationship with the organisation, stakeholders can be divided into two categories:

- internal stakeholders — owners, shareholders, employees, managers etc.
- external stakeholders — customers, competitors, suppliers, central and local government agencies, pressure groups, bankers, trade associations, the local community etc.

Think about the implications of this division when analysing stakeholder issues.

Shareholder versus stakeholder approaches

The traditional view: the shareholder approach

Traditionally, firms were established by their owners to meet the needs of those owners. Business aims and objectives were therefore dominated by the needs of the shareholders (the owners). Today this view assumes that management is responsible solely to the owners of the organisation (i.e. the shareholders), who employ the managers to run the company on their behalf. Thus everything managers do should be in the direct interest of shareholders, and their aim should be to maximise shareholder value by striving for short-term rewards, such as profit and dividends.

The alternative view: the stakeholder approach

Over time, a number of organisations have taken a different view by giving prominence to the needs of other groups of stakeholders. For example, the John Lewis Partnership meets the needs of employees and the Cooperative Society aims to satisfy the needs of its customers. Firms have also been encouraged by government and pressure groups to meet the wider needs of society by taking into account the externalities arising from their decisions. This approach emphasises the need to meet, or at least to consider, the objectives of wider groups of individuals who have an interest in the business. It takes the view that firms benefit from cooperation with their stakeholder groups and from incorporating their needs into the decision-making process.

> **DID YOU KNOW?**
>
> Externalities are those costs and benefits that occur as a result of a firm's activities, but which are not taken into account in its income statement. For example, pollution and congestion may be caused by a firm's activities, but the costs are borne by the local community and not by the firm.

'Win–lose' or 'win–win'

Because a firm may not be able to meet the needs of all stakeholder groups, it has to set priorities and is therefore likely to encounter conflict. For example, if it helps the local community, fewer funds will be available for shareholders. Conversely, if more rewards are directed towards the owners (shareholders), less are available for employees. This analysis takes a 'win–lose' approach to the situation: that is, it views the company as having a fixed pot of benefits to share out among all groups; if one group gains more, another gains less.

An alternative approach is that of 'win–win'. According to this analysis, a firm can, by its actions, cause the pot of benefits to grow and thus all groups to gain more. For example, better conditions and rewards for employees, although reducing rewards for shareholders in the short run, may increase them in the long run. This occurs because increased staff loyalty and motivation result in better-quality work, which in turn increases consumer loyalty and enhances the firm's reputation. This leads to less marketing expenditure in order to achieve the same or a higher level of sales, and therefore profit. Social responsibility might therefore make good business sense.

> **_e_ EXAMINER'S VOICE**
>
> Remember that limited resources and opportunity costs are fundamental issues to consider when discussing the stakeholder and shareholder approaches.

What stakeholders want

The things that stakeholders may look for from an organisation are called **stakeholder expectations**. As an organisation's survival depends, to a great extent, on support from its stakeholders, how and to what extent it can satisfy their demands is crucial. What makes the task difficult to accomplish is the fact that, on some occasions, different groups of stakeholders share common interests, while on other occasions their interests conflict.

Common interests

All stakeholders in an organisation, except its direct competitors, have much to gain from a prosperous business. Some stakeholders, such as shareholders and employees, have a direct interest in the business, while others, such as suppliers and buyers, have their own business interests tied to that particular organisation. The closure of a car manufacturing firm affects not only the employees of that firm but also the suppliers of parts, the dealers and small servicing outlets specialising in the cars made in that factory.

The shareholders who have invested money in the business naturally expect a good return on their investment in both the short and the long term. If the business fails, they stand to lose some or all of their money.

The directors and managers may lose the privileges associated with their present position if the business fails, and may be forced to look for alternative employment. Moreover, with a change of job come the problems and costs associated with having to relocate their homes and families.

The desire to see the business prosper is also likely to be strong among the other employees, whose job security and livelihood are dependent on the success of the organisation. The closure of a large factory can often be detrimental to the families affected and the local economy.

Conflicting interests

In the business world, however, there are many situations where conflicts of interest can arise. For instance, the directors of a public limited company are appointed to manage, coordinate and make profit. If they fail at any of these, they may be voted out by the shareholders at the next annual general meeting. The nature of their job requires them to adopt a view on what is going on both inside and outside the organisation.

Unlike the managers, most employees of the firm are there to carry out specific tasks. It is often difficult for them to see things from the management's point of view. This does not mean that management is always right and the employees are always wrong, but it does present a potential source of conflict.

Even within a particular stakeholder group, there may be conflicting aims. For example, some customers will favour low prices, while others will favour quality.

Table 20.1 summarises the possible aims of each stakeholder group in relation to the activities of the firm. All stakeholders are concerned that the firm they are associated with has a good corporate image. However, the table illustrates the possibilities for conflict between the aims of different groups of stakeholders.

DID YOU KNOW?

If a business is failing, short-term profits and survival are likely to become the most important objectives regardless of its obligations to other stakeholder groups.

Stakeholder group	Aims
Shareholders	Shareholders may want the firm to achieve high profit levels either by keeping costs low or by charging high prices. High profits will in turn allow high dividends to be paid. Shareholders may also wish the firm to achieve a positive corporate image and long-term growth in order to create favourable conditions that will encourage share prices to rise.
Employees	Employees may want job security, good working conditions, high levels of pay, promotional opportunities and job enrichment.
Customers	Customers may want the firm to provide high-quality products and services at low prices, and to offer a good service and a wide choice.
Suppliers	Suppliers may want the firm to provide regular orders, prompt payment and steady growth, leading to more orders in the future.
Local community	The local community may want the firm to provide local employment opportunities and to behave in a socially responsible manner, safeguarding the environment and accepting the full social costs associated with its activities.
Government	The government may want the firm to make efficient use of its resources, to provide employment and training, and to comply with legislation on consumer protection, competition policy, employment, and health and safety.

Table 20.1 The aims of different groups of stakeholders

DID YOU KNOW?

Social costs are the internal or financial costs plus the external costs of an activity. For example, the social costs of operating a particular plant include not only the financial or internal costs involved but also the costs of pollution and congestion that might be imposed on the local environment as a result of its activities.

EXAMINER'S VOICE

Make sure that you understand the difference between stakeholders and shareholders. Shareholders are those people who provide a share of the capital needed to run a business in exchange for part-ownership; thus shareholders are stakeholders in the business. However, there are a lot of other stakeholder groups with an interest in the business apart from shareholders.

PRACTICE EXERCISE 1   Total: 30 marks (25 minutes)

1 What is a mission statement?   *(3 marks)*

2 Explain one advantage for an organisation of having an effective mission statement.   *(3 marks)*

3 Distinguish between corporate aims and corporate objectives.   *(4 marks)*

4 Explain the hierarchy of objective setting in an organisation and the reason for this.   *(6 marks)*

5 Explain two reasons why short-term objectives are likely to differ from longer-term objectives. *(6 marks)*

6 Explain the term 'corporate strategies'. *(3 marks)*

7 What is the relationship between the corporate strategies of a business and its corporate aims and objectives? *(5 marks)*

PRACTICE EXERCISE 2   Total: 45 marks (40 minutes)

1 Distinguish between the terms 'shareholder' and 'stakeholder'. *(5 marks)*

2 Explain the traditional shareholder approach in relation to the objectives of a business. *(4 marks)*

3 Explain the alternative stakeholder approach in relation to the objectives of a business. *(4 marks)*

4 What are externalities? *(4 marks)*

5 What is meant by the 'win–lose' approach to meeting stakeholder needs? *(3 marks)*

6 How can a 'win–win' approach be applied to meeting stakeholder needs? *(3 marks)*

7 Consider the extent to which different stakeholder groups have aims in common. *(9 marks)*

8 Identify and explain two examples of conflicting stakeholder aims. *(6 marks)*

9 Identify three examples of internal stakeholders and four examples of external stakeholders. *(7 marks)*

CASE STUDY 1   Tesco plc

Tesco is the UK's biggest supermarket retailer with a market share (in December 2008) of 30.9%. Because, originally, its profits were almost entirely dependent on the food market in the UK, it had to pursue a policy of diversification in order to grow and to spread its risks. The market for supermarkets in the UK is close to saturation and Tesco probably has almost as many stores as it wants in the UK. If it simply opened more stores, it would be in danger of cannibalising the sales of its existing stores. So in order to continue to grow, it needed to expand overseas and/or into other markets in the UK. It has done both. It has expanded abroad by opening stores in the USA, Thailand, India and Korea. In addition to this, it has moved into faster-growing non-food markets such as toiletries, household goods, music, clothing, mobile phones and financial services.

Mission statement

'Tesco is one of Britain's leading food retailers. The company owes its success to its emphasis on meeting changing customer needs through service and innovation, while maintaining its commitment to value and quality.'

Aim

'To increase value for customers continually and to earn their lifetime loyalty.'

Objectives

1 'To understand our customers better than any of our competitors do.'

2 'To earn the respect of our staff for these values and to appreciate their contribution to achieving them.'

3 'To be energetic and innovative and to take risks in making life better for our customers.'

4 'To recognise that we have brilliant people working for us and to use this strength to make our customers' shopping enjoyable in a way that no competitor can.'

5 'To use intelligence, scale and technology to deliver unbeatable value to customers in everything we do.'

Each of these five objectives is then broken down into more specific targets. For example, objective 1 includes 'To reduce customer complaints by 5% over a 3-year period'; objective 4 includes 'To increase the return to staff from profit-sharing on a year by year basis' and 'To ensure that all staff are involved in on-going training and development with a view to increasing their professional competence levels.'

Tesco operates a management tool called a steering wheel (Figure 20.3) which enables the company to balance the needs of all its stakeholders. This brings together Tesco's resources and ensures that all staff have a common focus — on customers, people, operations, finance and the community. The steering wheel is based on the philosophy that if Tesco looks after its customers well and operates efficiently and effectively, its shareholders' interests will always be best served in terms of growth in sales and profits.

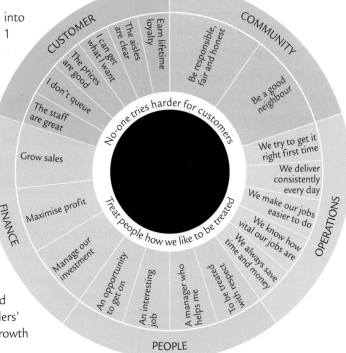

Figure 20.3 Tesco's steering wheel

Tesco's strategy

Tesco's strategy is shown in Figure 20.4 and comprises the following elements:

- **Core UK.** The UK is Tesco's biggest market and the core of its business. It aims to provide all its customers with excellent value and choice. In 2008, improvements in competitors' performance and consumers who were more cautious in their spending made growth harder. However, with strong productivity, strong product mix and careful cost control, Tesco delivered good results.
- **International.** Tesco is an international retailer that aims to provide local customers with what they want, wherever it operates. Its overseas business had an excellent year, contributing over half of the growth in profit in the year.
- **Retailing services.** Tesco has expanded into retailing services, aiming to bring simplicity and value to complex markets. These services performed well in 2008, with sales in its online businesses up over 30%, Tesco Mobile moving into profitability and Tesco Personal Finance getting back to a faster rate of growth.

- **Non-food.** Tesco's aim is to be as strong in non-food as in food. This means offering the same quality, range, price and service for customers in non-food items as it does in its food business. Tesco's non-food sales grew by 12% to £11.8 billion in 2008, accounting for 23% of its total sales.
- **Community.** Community was added as the fifth part of Tesco's strategy in 2008. Tesco recognises that in order to operate effectively, it must ensure that its operations meet environmental standards.

Figure 20.4
Tesco's strategy

Source: adapted from information on Tesco's website (www.tesco.com)

Preliminary questions
Total: 30 marks (35 minutes)

1 Rewrite two of Tesco's five objectives so that they meet the SMART criteria. *(6 marks)*

2 What are the likely benefits to a company such as Tesco of having detailed aims and objectives? *(8 marks)*

3 If Tesco's main corporate objective was to grow, identify what the case study suggests were the corporate strategies to bring this about. *(4 marks)*

4 Briefly explain how diversifying abroad might have affected Tesco's short-term objectives. *(6 marks)*

5 Explain the following statement: 'if Tesco looks after its customers well and operates efficiently and effectively, its shareholders' interests will always be best served'. *(6 marks)*

Case study questions

Total: 40 marks (50 minutes)

1 Analyse Tesco's corporate strategies and their relationship with its corporate aims and objectives. *(10 marks)*

2 To what extent is it clear that Tesco's objectives are based on its corporate aims? *(15 marks)*

3 Assess the potential for conflict among Tesco's stakeholders and how effectively its 'steering wheel' approach might reduce any conflict between customers and shareholders. *(15 marks)*

CASE STUDY 2 Greggs

Mission statement

- We aim to become Europe's finest retail baker, growing, highly profitable and operating with integrity for the benefit of our people, customers, shareholders and communities.

- We believe that the key to this is making sure that customers have a really enjoyable experience whenever they visit our shops. We want our customers to love their local Greggs for irresistible baker-fresh food, great prices, great service and great people.

- Ultimately, it's great people who will deliver this great customer experience so we focus on making sure that Greggs is a great place to work. In doing so we refer to the following principles:

Our culture: we are achievers, working hard together in a friendly and informal way, where everyone matters.

Our values: we will be enthusiastic and supportive in all that we do, open, honest and appreciative, treating everyone with fairness, consideration and respect.

Our communities: we will be responsible neighbours, supporting our local communities, continually improving our standards and reducing our impact on the environment.

Over the years Greggs has evolved from a traditional high-street baker into the leading UK specialist retailer of sandwiches, savouries and other bakery products for the takeaway food market. It has been transformed from a single Newcastle bake shop into the UK's largest bakery chain, with more than 1,400 outlets.

The development of Greggs has been characterised by a number of pivotal moments. The first of these was expanding beyond its home territory of Newcastle where it had about 20 shops. According to Ian Gregg, the founder of the business: 'The real point of the decision was to move out of having just one bakery, one business site in Tyneside. It was a difficult decision. It would have had its attractions to stay in one area and build up a business focused on excellence.'

The second pivotal moment was floating the company in 1984 to fund long-term expansion and a move into the fast-growing market for takeaway sandwiches and savouries, such as sausage rolls and pasties, which have driven the group's performance against a declining bakery market.

In the past, analysts commented on the company's cavalier attitude towards investors, in a strategy that

put shareholders third in line behind employees and customers. Ian Gregg, in 2003, was unapologetic about this stance, which he said reflected the values and sense of responsibility that underpinned the business: 'We will not seek to maximise shareholder value in the short term. We take a lot of flak about it, but if the profit of the business is the last thing on the page, we try to get the focus on the lines higher up. If you get these right then everyone benefits.'

Source: adapted from various sources, including www.greggs.co.uk and an article in the *Financial Times*, 4 January 2003.

Preliminary questions   Total: 25 marks (30 minutes)

1 Using the information about Greggs in the case study, identify what appear to be the company's main corporate objectives.   *(4 marks)*

2 What does the text suggest are the main corporate strategies and how do these link with the corporate aims and objectives?   *(8 marks)*

3 Explain the meaning of the following sentence: 'We will not seek to maximise shareholder value in the short term.'   *(3 marks)*

4 Greggs appears to take a stakeholder rather than a shareholder approach to the business. Distinguish between these two approaches and explain what evidence there is to support this view. *(10 marks)*

Case study questions   Total: 40 marks (50 minutes)

1 Analyse how Greggs' corporate strategies are linked to its corporate aims and objectives and, ultimately, to its mission.   *(10 marks)*

2 Assess the possible long-term benefits to Greggs of a 'strategy that puts shareholders third in line behind employees and customers'.   *(15 marks)*

3 Discuss those aspects of Greggs in which there is likely to be conflict between the aims of different stakeholders.   *(15 marks)*

Chapter 21

The relationship between businesses and the economic environment

This chapter explains the key macroeconomic variables that affect business organisations and identifies trends in these variables. It assesses how changes to the macroeconomic variables might affect business organisations and evaluates the strategies businesses might deploy in response. The key macroeconomic variables reviewed include: the business cycle, economic growth, interest rates, exchange rates, inflation and unemployment. The chapter also assesses the effects of the globalisation of markets and developments in emerging markets on business organisations and the strategies that businesses might deploy in response.

Business and its external environment

Although business studies is concerned with the internal operations of a business, it is also vital to understand and appreciate that all business takes place within a much wider context than the business itself. This is illustrated in Figure 21.1.

Figure 21.1 *The business and its environment*

First, a business operates within a competitive environment. The nature of this competition varies from industry to industry. The number of competitors, for example, dictates the extent to which a business can raise or lower its prices, and the amount of advertising it is likely to undertake. (The competitive environment is considered in detail in Chapter 25.)

Second, a business operates within a general business environment. This involves the broader influences that affect all businesses, including issues such as the impact of changes in government policy on business, how legislation influences business behaviour and the extent to which technological change and environmental considerations affect the type of products that are demanded and the way in which they are produced.

PESTLE analysis

The use of PESTLE analysis enables all the different influences in the general business environment to be classified into six categories. Table 21.1 summarises some of the issues that could be considered in each category.

KEY TERM

PESTLE analysis: a framework for assessing the likely impact of the political, economic, social, technological, legal and environmental factors in the external environment of a business. (This framework is also known as PEST analysis, with the legal element being included in the analysis of the political environment, and the environmental element in the social environment.)

Table 21.1 PESTLE analysis

PESTLE category	Examples of issues in each category that might affect business
Political factors	• government economic policies • government social policies • the extent of government intervention
Economic factors	• the business cycle • interest rates • exchange rates • the level of inflation • the level of unemployment • membership of the EU
Social factors	• ethical issues • the impact of pressure groups • the influence of different stakeholders • changing lifestyles
Technological factors	• new products • new processes • the impact of change • the costs of change
Legal factors	• legislation
Environmental factors	• environmental issues

This and the next three chapters consider the issues identified here, i.e. the economic environment (this chapter), the political and legal environment (Chapter 22), the social and environmental environment (Chapter 23), the technological environment (Chapter 24).

EXAMINER'S VOICE

In order to provide a context and background to the discussion of macroeconomic factors, some explanation is provided about the determinants of such factors. However, the AQA specification does not require candidates to have knowledge of the determinants of macroeconomic factors.

Macroeconomics

The study of macroeconomics is concerned with the total (or aggregate) level of spending (or demand) in the economy, the total or aggregate level of production (or supply) in the economy, national employment and unemployment levels, the general level of prices, and the rate of interest and the exchange rate. It is, in effect, concerned with making the most efficient use of an economy's resources.

FACT FILE

Index numbers

Many pieces of information, particularly sales records and economic data, are presented as index numbers. The use of index numbers simplifies comparisons between the different items over time. To demonstrate this, consider which of the products in Table 21.2 has experienced the fastest rate of growth in sales.

	Year			Change from 2006 to 2008
	2006	2007	2008	
Product A	150	285	345	+195
Product B	600	780	990	+390
Product C	250	225	215	−35
Product D	40	70	120	+80
Product E	80	100	128	+48

Table 21.2 Volume of product sales (units)

Sales of product C have declined, so it is clear that this has been the most disappointing product.

Sales of product B have increased by the greatest number, but does this mean that it has performed better than product A?

Product A has more than doubled its sales in the 2 years, but product B has less than doubled its sales. In this respect, product A has performed better than product B if the firm's main objective is growth.

Index numbers are used to make it easier to compare numbers that would otherwise be difficult to compare. They are constructed as follows:
- A base year is selected. The sales volume (or value) in this year is given an index number of 100 (a figure from which it is easy to calculate percentage changes).
- Figures in later years are calculated as a percentage of the base-year figure.
- The index number is calculated as follows:

$$\text{index number} = \frac{\text{actual sales volume in selected year}}{\text{actual sales volume in base year}} \times 100$$

Thus sales of product A were 150 units in 2006 and 285 units in 2007. The index number for 2007 is thus:

$$\frac{285}{150} \times 100 = 190$$

KEY TERMS

macroeconomics: the study of the whole economy.

microeconomics: the study of the individual parts of the economy.

gross domestic product (GDP): the total value of a country's output over the course of a year.

gross national product (GNP): the total value of a country's output over the course of a year plus net income from abroad (i.e. income earned on overseas investment less the income paid to foreigners investing in the UK economy). The growth in real GNP per head of population is the main measure of economic growth.

consumer durables: goods that are owned by households, but which are not instantly consumed by them (e.g. cars, computers, televisions, refrigerators and washing machines).

stock: raw materials, components, work-in-progress, finished goods.

capital (or investment) goods: items that are purchased by firms because they help them to produce goods.

Similarly, the index number for product A in 2008 is:

$$\frac{345}{150} \times 100 = 230$$

This shows the percentage growth in sales between the base year and the year being studied. For product A, growth between 2006 and 2008 has been from 100 to 230, an increase of 130. As a percentage, this is:

$$\frac{130}{100} \times 100 = 130\%$$

Completing the calculations for all of the products in years 2006, 2007 and 2008 gives the results detailed in Table 21.3.

	Year			
	2006	2007	2008	
Product A	100	190	230	*Table 21.3* *Index number of* *product sales*
Product B	100	130	165	
Product C	100	90	86	
Product D	100	175	300	
Product E	100	125	160	
Base year (2006) = 100.				

At a glance it can be seen that product A has grown much faster than product B. It also shows that product D has had the fastest growth rate, and that the growth rate of product E is only slightly less than that of product B (although it was much less in terms of volume).

Index numbers are used where it is more important to compare percentage growth rates than the actual volume of change. They can be used to calculate and compare information on the business cycle, exchange rates, inflation and unemployment.

The circular flow of income

The circular flow of income (Figure 21.2) illustrates the interrelationship between the main parts of the macroeconomy — that is, between producers (firms), consumers (households), the government and other countries.

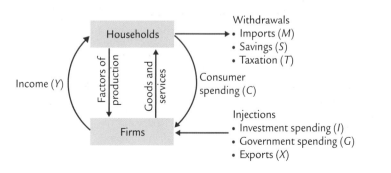

Figure 21.2 A simple circular flow of income

Firms receive revenue or consumer spending (C) in exchange for the goods and services that they provide. This revenue is used to pay incomes (Y) to workers and to other factors of production, in return for their contribution to the production of the goods and services available for sale.

The income of households (Y) is either spent on consumer goods and services that are produced by UK firms (C) or withdrawn from the circular flow. Income withdrawn from the circular flow is used to buy imported goods from abroad (M), is saved (S) or is paid to the government as taxation (T).

The revenue received by firms comes either from consumer spending (C), or from injections. Injections include investment spending by other firms (I) (e.g. when they purchase capital goods such as a JCB digger or a lorry), government spending (G) (e.g. paying for the building of a new school or hospital) or export sales abroad (X).

The business cycle

Some firms are more vulnerable to changes in the business cycle and GDP than others. Indeed, some are often known as cyclical businesses because demand for their products fluctuates very closely in line with the business cycle.

The extent to which a business is affected by the business cycle depends on the income elasticity of demand for the firm's products: that is, how much demand for products is influenced by changes in income. For example, the construction industry and firms producing machine tools and heavy capital equipment are all very sensitive to changes in GDP, the demand for their products being highly income elastic. In a boom period, when incomes are high and rising, demand for consumer goods is high and this in turn generates a high demand for capital goods. Similarly, high incomes create more demand for house building. On the other hand, the demand for products that are relatively income inelastic (i.e. whose demand does not change much when income levels change), such as flour, soap and paper, is unlikely to be much affected by the business cycle.

INGRAM

KEY TERM

business (or trade) cycle: the regular pattern of ups and downs in demand and output within an economy, or of gross domestic product (GDP) growth over time. It is characterised by four main phases: boom, recession (or downturn), slump and recovery (or upturn) (see Figure 21.3).

e EXAMINER'S VOICE

The concept of income elasticity of demand is not on the AQA specification but it is an important concept, particularly when analysing the impact of the economic environment on business. Income elasticity of demand is the extent to which demand for a product or service changes as a result of a change in income. If demand for a product or service changes proportionately more than the change in income, demand is said to be income elastic. If demand for a product or service changes proportionately less than the change in income, demand is said to be income inelastic.

Luxury and high-value goods and services tend to be income elastic: for example, as incomes fell during the recession at the end of 2008, sales of cars fell dramatically and by a greater proportion than the fall in income levels. Essential and low-value goods and services tend to be income inelastic: for example, a rise or fall in income is unlikely to affect the purchase of potatoes or boxes of matches.

e EXAMINER'S VOICE

Remember that normal or luxury goods are those for which demand increases as incomes rise and vice versa — for example, fillet steak and other high-quality meat products. Inferior goods are those for which demand falls as incomes rise and vice versa — for example, Spam and other inferior meat products.

FACT FILE

Times must be hard – Americans are buying Spam again

In times of trouble the United States has historically turned to a tin of pink processed meat to see it through – and so it is again that sales of Spam (spicy ham and pork) are soaring as the recession bites. They have shot up by more than 10% in the past 3 months and the Hormel Foods Corporation has had to introduce a double shift at its factory in Austin, Minnesota, 7 days a week, to keep up with demand.

Spam costs only about $2.40 (£1.65) for a 12-ounce tin and keeps for ever. Hungry consumers, desperate to cut back on spending but keen to put meat on the table, have been buying the product that 'helped win the Second World War'.

Spam was invented during the Great Depression of the 1930s by Jay Hormel, the son of the founder of the company. It is a brick of ham, pork, sugar, salt, water, potato starch and a hint of sodium nitrite 'to help Spam keep its gorgeous pink color'. Hormel Foods told *The Times* that the good value of the product made it appealing in uncertain economic times.

Source: adapted from an article in *The Times*, 6 December 2008.

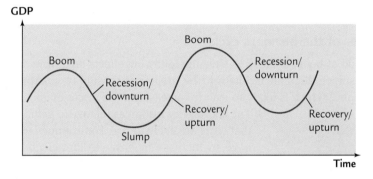

Figure 21.3
The business cycle

The length and magnitude of each stage of the business cycle varies. Some are short-lived, lasting only a few months, while others are as long as 3–4 years. This is illustrated in Figure 21.4.

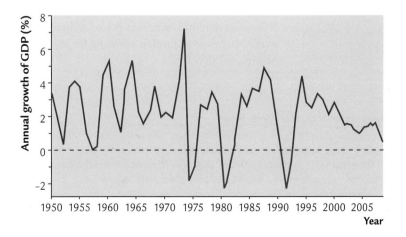

Figure 21.4
Trends in the business cycles in the UK, 1950–2008

Possible causes of the business cycle

■ Changes in business confidence, which lead to changes in the level of investment in fixed assets. Usually a business replaces fixed assets that have worn out, but mostly it uses existing fixed assets. If a business believes that its sales are going to increase, it will buy more fixed assets and, overall, this could mean a large increase in orders to the producer of the fixed assets. The opposite applies if confidence is low, as a business will cancel orders to replace assets that have worn out.

■ Periods of stock building and then de-stocking. Again, these depend on the confidence of a business in its ability to sell the stock.

■ Irregular patterns of expenditure on consumer durables, such as cars, washing machines and televisions. These are influenced by the level of interest rates and consumer confidence in the economy, and by the need to replace old items.

■ Confidence in the banking sector and its ability to make sound decisions about whom to lend money to. When banks have insufficient funds to meet the demands of their depositors, they are more likely to call in loans. This has a knock-on effect on business and consumers. The most recent recession saw the collapse of a number of high-profile banks.

Phases of the business cycle

A period of **boom** is likely to have the following effects on a firm:

■ Consumer demand is likely to be greater than supply, creating excess demand, which is likely to lead to increases in the prices of goods.

■ The shortage of resources relative to demand means that costs are likely to rise. For example, wages may have to increase in order to attract and/or keep skilled workers, which may in turn lead firms to increase their prices.

■ Increased demand may result in firms utilising their production capacity to the full. Such high capacity utilisation may lead firms to consider expansion plans in order to increase output and meet demand.

■ Increased demand and high prices may result in an overall increase in profits, allowing for high retained profits and dividends.

DID YOU KNOW?

De-stocking is where a business attempts to reduce its stock-holding by cutting orders of materials or by cutting production levels. This is usually undertaken by businesses at the beginning of a recession when orders begin to fall.

KEY TERM

boom: period characterised by high levels of consumer demand, business confidence, profits and investment at the same time as rising costs, increasing prices and full capacity.

FACT FILE

Business cycle for capital goods firms

Firms producing capital goods such as machinery and plant tend to suffer most in a recession because other firms cut back on their orders dramatically if they expect to sell fewer items. However, in a boom they benefit most because businesses must buy new equipment etc. in order to keep pace with new demand. In effect, these industries are more likely to experience dramatic changes than businesses producing consumer goods, especially essential products such as food.

FACT FILE

Recession hits the UK

In January 2008, BT said it was shedding a total of 10,000 jobs. The company had already cut 4,000 jobs and a further 6,000 would go by March. A hiring freeze means that BT is aiming to achieve the cuts largely by natural turnover, by a reduction in contract workers and voluntary redundancy schemes.

Taken in isolation, BT's job cull is alarming. But factor in the 4,200 British jobs axed earlier this week by household names such as Virgin Media and GlaxoSmithKline, add the 1,000 job cuts announced by ITV, tot up redundancies at Vodafone and estimate the tens of thousands of positions being axed at small companies and the outlook becomes bleak.

Source: adapted from an article in *The Times*, 14 January 2008.

KEY TERM

recession (or downturn): period characterised by falling levels of consumer demand, output, profit and business confidence, little investment, spare capacity and rising levels of unemployment.

e **EXAMINER'S VOICE**

Remember, when analysing the impact of a particular phase of the business cycle on a firm, to consider the organisation and its products. If a firm is producing and selling inferior goods, for example, it may find that it benefits during a recession as incomes fall. Don't ignore the context of the case study.

DID YOU KNOW?

The official definition of recession is a fall in GDP for two consecutive quarters.

Some of the implications of a **recession** are as follows:
- Falling demand and therefore excess stock may lead to reduced prices.
- Falling demand and reductions in output may lead to low profits or even losses being made and workers being laid off. On the other hand, firms producing inferior goods may benefit, as consumers switch from luxury items to low-priced alternatives.
- Liquidations or business closures, as a result of falling demand and losses, may result in fewer suppliers of certain products and fewer customers for other products.
- As business struggles with falling demand and individuals feel the effects of lower incomes, firms are likely to experience an increase in bad debts. To address this issue, firms may need to introduce tighter credit control procedures, which may lead to less trade.
- A strong balance sheet, sufficient liquidity and low gearing are important requirements for survival during a recession. High unemployment will lead to a drop in demand for some goods and a switch in demand to other (e.g. inferior) goods. This may lead firms facing falling demand to search for new markets. Indeed, one way to survive a recession for a producer of consumer goods is to diversify the product range. In this way the business is not too dependent for its profits on those products that are likely to experience wide variations in demand over the course of the business cycle.
- Low investment due to falling demand may lead to a decline in the output of firms producing capital goods.
- In order to survive during a recession, businesses need to operate as efficiently as possible. As a result, those that do survive may emerge stronger and better able to compete during the subsequent recovery stage.

WHAT DO YOU THINK?

Nannies

The telephone at Bright Beginning Childcare Agency in York has been ringing non-stop with calls from parents who need nannies because they have to return to work. Profits are up and the business is growing. The daycare centre and the nanny agency have seen a big increase in the number of people looking for part-time care.

Plumbers

Nick Chapman, a plumber, said: 'People are putting things on hold until they can see some light — their priority is to pay the mortgage.' Mr Chapman still has his job but is aware that thousands of people in the construction and property industries have lost theirs as people resort to DIY. 'It's better for me than for carpenters and decorators. People are wary of trying plumbing but they say any fool can paint.'

Cobblers

Martin Middleton, who runs the Greenmarket Cobbler business in Newcastle upon Tyne, said: 'People will always wear shoes.' Less expected, however, was the 40% increase in business as a result of the recession. 'City types used to spend £90 on a pair of shoes, wear them until they "died" and then throw them in the bin. Now, people are more willing to be seen having their shoes repaired.'

It is usually assumed that recession will have a negative effect on business. Why do you think the recession has had a positive impact on each of these businesses?

Source: adapted from an article in *The Times*, 26 October 2008.

EXAMINER'S VOICE

Notice how the analysis of the effects of a recession tends to be circular. For example, falling demand leads to reductions in output, which results in redundancies and more unemployment, which leads to falling income, which leads to falling demand...

KEY TERMS

slump: period characterised by very low levels of consumer demand, investment and business confidence, an increasing number of businesses failing and high unemployment.

recovery (or upturn): period characterised by slowly rising levels of consumer demand, rising investment, patchy but increasing business confidence and falling levels of unemployment.

'**Slump**' is a rather vague term, sometimes used interchangeably with depression; essentially it means a very severe recession. A full-scale depression is much rarer — an example is the Great Depression of the 1930s.

A slump has the following implications:

- The lack of demand means that firms are content to charge low prices, concentrating on sales volume rather than sales revenue. It is possible that deflation (falling prices) may occur across the whole economy.
- The low level of demand means that factories are likely to close, leading to large-scale unemployment.

Some of the implications of a **recovery** are as follows:

- Increasing demand for consumer goods may lead to increased profits and to new businesses starting up.
- The pace of recovery will vary between firms. Some will benefit from the increasingly favourable conditions almost immediately; others will need to await the completion of capital investment before they begin to benefit.

- Business confidence is growing, which may mean more investment in fixed assets and more borrowing.
- To meet the increasing demand, existing spare production capacity will be used. However, one of the characteristics of a recovery is that shortages, which are almost inevitable as recovery kicks in, may lead to increased costs and potential bottlenecks.

Business confidence

Business confidence can be a key influence on the business cycle. Many commentators believe that a high level of business confidence can become a self-fulfilling prophecy — an optimistic outlook leads to higher levels of investment spending and stock building, which in turn cause the economy to grow. For this reason, governments often try to describe the economy in positive terms so that confidence will increase.

Figure 21.5 Company liquidations

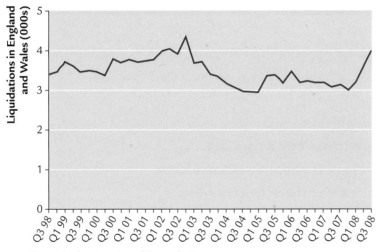

Source: Insolvency Service and Companies House.

Evaluating business strategies in response to changes in the business cycle

The strategies a business might use in response to changes in the business cycle will depend on which phase of the cycle the economy is in. For example, during a recession, many businesses will suffer declining demand. As a result they will wish to reduce production and improve efficiency. For many, this will mean laying off workers in order to reduce costs and survive. Although this may be an appropriate strategy in the short term, in the longer term, losing experienced staff could become problematic, especially when demand begins to improve and experienced workers are difficult to find. The Fact File on JCB suggests an alternative approach that is likely to retain the goodwill of the workforce and benefit the business in the longer term.

DID YOU KNOW?

Business confidence is measured regularly by the CBI's Quarterly Survey. The government's Insolvency Service publishes data on company liquidations: that is, on the number of businesses that stop trading because of financial difficulties. These are used as a means of analysing business confidence.

Figure 21.5 shows the trend in liquidations (or insolvencies) between 1998 and 2008. It reflects the ups and downs of the business cycle during this time. For example, during the economic recession in the third quarter of 2008, liquidations showed an increase of 10.5% on the previous quarter and an increase of 26.3% on the same period in 2007.

FACT FILE

JCB

As growth slowed to its weakest level in $2^1/_2$ years, most economists predicted unemployment to be 2 million by the end of the year.

Like many firms producing capital goods, JCB, maker of bright yellow diggers for muddy building sites, needs to cut jobs as a result of the recession. However, it has come up with a more positive approach. In negotiation with the trade union, about 2,500 staff have agreed to a 4-day week and a £50-a-week pay cut. It is an unusual deal. Wages are usually assumed to be 'sticky' and resistance to cuts is normally severe, yet Keith Hodgkinson, of the GMB union, declared: 'I am delighted we have been able to save 350 jobs.'

Source: adapted from an article in the *Independent*, 24 October 2008.

PRACTICE EXERCISE 1   Total: 50 marks (45 minutes)

1 What is macroeconomics?   *(3 marks)*

2 Draw the circular flow of income and explain the interrelationship between households and firms. *(6 marks)*

3 Explain how any one of the three 'withdrawals' takes money out of the circular flow. *(3 marks)*

4 Explain the term 'business cycle'.   *(3 marks)*

5 Why might demand and output in the economy as a whole fluctuate in a cyclical manner? *(5 marks)*

6 Explain the causes of the recession phase of the business cycle.   *(6 marks)*

7 Analyse the effects of the boom phase of the business cycle on business.   *(8 marks)*

8 Compare the different implications of a recession for a firm selling:
a an inferior good   *(4 marks)*   **b** a luxury product   *(4 marks)*

9 Business confidence is a major factor in influencing the business cycle. Why is this the case and how might it be measured? *(8 marks)*

PRACTICE EXERCISE 2   Total: 30 marks (35 minutes)

Refer to Figure 21.4 and answer the following questions.

1 What evidence is there to suggest that the current government's strategy is aiming to reduce the fluctuations in the business cycle? *(5 marks)*

2 Analyse the possible business opportunities available to a clothing retailer during an upturn or recovery in the business cycle. *(10 marks)*

3 Evaluate the implications for a manufacturer of kitchen equipment of the unpredictability of the length of the business cycle over the period covered in the graph. *(15 marks)*

Economic growth

Essentially, economic growth is the extent to which the volume of goods and services being produced increases over time. If the value of a country's GDP increases by 6% in a year, but the inflation rate is 2%, the increase in actual output of goods and services is approximately 4%. This is the increase in real GDP. Real GDP is a better measure of whether a country is getting wealthier than GDP measured in money. Figures for economic growth are thus based on the percentage increase in real GDP. The growth in real GDP per capita (i.e. per head of population) is the main measure of economic growth and measures the growth in average income per person adjusted for inflation.

Measuring GDP

The value of a country's economic activity (GDP) can be measured in three ways:

- The **income method** involves totalling all the income earned in an economy — rent, wages and salaries, interest and profit.
- The **output method** involves totalling the value of all goods (whether these are consumer or capital goods) and services produced in an economy.
- The **expenditure method** involves totalling all spending by consumers, businesses and government plus the balance of export less import spending.

> **DID YOU KNOW?**
>
> Each method gives the same result because it is just a different way of looking at the value of economic activity. For example, from a simplified point of view, if everything that is produced is sold, the total value of output will be the same as the total value of expenditure, and the total expenditure becomes the income of all the factors of production used to create the goods.

The trend in UK annual economic growth as measured by changes in GDP is illustrated in Figure 21.6.

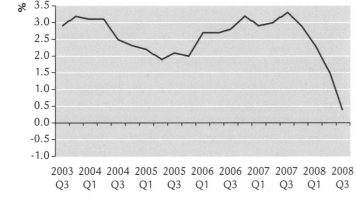

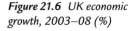
Source: **www.statistics.gov.uk**.

KEY TERMS

economic growth: an increase in the level of economic activity or real gross domestic product (GDP).

gross domestic product (GDP): the total value of a country's output over the course of a year.

Figure 21.6 UK economic growth, 2003–08 (%)

The level of economic growth in an economy is influenced by a number of factors. These include:

- **The exploitation of valuable natural resources.** For example, the extraction and sale of oil in the Middle East and in the North Sea has significantly increased economic growth in these areas.
- **A well-educated and highly skilled labour force.** This improves productivity and generates economic growth.
- **Increasing investment and new technology.** This enables firms to keep pace with other countries and so create economic growth.
- **Government policy.** Governments can adopt policies aimed at encouraging economic growth (see Chapter 22).

Evaluating business responses to changes in the rate of economic growth

The effects of economic growth on business depend on whether the rate of economic growth is rapid, slowing down or actually decreasing. This reflects the various phases of the business cycle. For more detail on this, refer back to the section on the implications of the business cycle.

Impact on sales

With higher levels of real GDP, real incomes in the economy are higher, which in turn is likely to lead to higher retail sales. Higher growth rates are usually recorded for non-food items than for food items. This is probably because many food items are income inelastic and therefore, despite higher consumer incomes, sales in these areas are less positively affected. In contrast, firms producing or selling income-elastic goods and services, such as DVD players, mobile phones and wide-screen televisions, are likely to see sales improve more significantly as real GDP increases. From a strategic point of view, this illustrates the need for businesses to consider the possibility of having some income-elastic products or services in their portfolio.

EXAMINER'S VOICE

Notice how often elasticity — whether price elasticity of demand or income elasticity of demand — is relevant to the analysis of data on sales.

Impact on corporate profits

Higher incomes lead to greater demand for goods and services, which provides opportunities for firms to generate higher profits. Not only are sales likely to increase, but in many cases higher demand should provide more opportunities to raise prices as well, helping to boost profit margins. There appears to be some correlation between the UK's economic growth rates (Figure 21.6) and company profitability, as indicated in Table 21.4. With higher profits, share prices are likely to increase and investor confidence should improve, which in turn means that firms should find it easier to raise further funds.

Year	Total	Manufacturing	Services
2002	12.1	6.6	15.4
2003	12.8	7.0	15.6
2004	13.0	10.0	17.8
2005	13.1	7.4	17.0
2006	13.6	6.5	18.1
2007	14.2	6.3	19.1
2008	14.4	5.1	16.2

Table 21.4 Net rate of return by private, non-financial corporations, 2002–08 (%)

Source: **www.statistics.gov.uk**.

Table 21.4 illustrates a clear distinction between the profitability of different sectors of the economy. Despite overall UK corporate profitability improving, the weaknesses in the manufacturing sector are clearly apparent. Manufacturing is suffering the effects of intense international competitive pressure, most notably from lower-wage, industrialising economies, such as China.

Impact on investment

Higher demand for goods and services means that firms are more likely to invest in expanding their operations — for example, seeking larger premises or extensions to existing facilities, or planning to install extra machinery and equipment. Increasing demand is likely to be accompanied by rising share prices, which will make it easier for firms to raise funds, and higher profitability, which will mean more retained profits are available for reinvestment.

Impact on employment

Businesses seeking to expand production may initially choose to make their existing labour force work harder, by offering overtime to employees, and only recruit more workers once they are convinced that the increase in demand for their products or services is sustainable.

If businesses intent on expansion cannot find sufficient skilled employees to meet their demands, it may prevent such firms from growing as quickly as desired and may act as a brake on the rate of economic growth in the UK.

Skills shortages can lead to higher wages, which present further problems. For example, if average earnings increase, firms will be faced with rising input costs due to rising wage rates. This leaves them with a dilemma: should they absorb the higher wage costs and squeeze their own profit margins, or should they pass these higher costs on to consumers in the form of higher prices?

DID YOU KNOW?

Retained profit is very important as a means of financing investment, traditionally providing between 60 and 70% of the funding used for business investment.

DID YOU KNOW?

Just as labour is likely to become more expensive in a fast-growing economy, so firms will find that other resources become scarce and their prices rise. For example, the cost of land and premises is likely to increase significantly, adding to a firm's costs and possibly leading to higher prices.

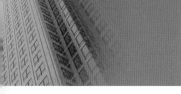

Impact on business strategy

The impact of economic growth suggests that certain business strategies are better suited to an environment of economic growth.

- **Expansion.** Rapid company expansion is more easily achieved during this period, as a firm may be able to expand production and sales without having to gain sales from rivals. However, expansion and a rapidly growing business can bring their own problems and test a firm's ability to cope in terms of organisational structure, personnel, technology, production capacity and finance.
- **New products.** Economic growth provides new opportunities for firms to update or extend the range of products and services they offer. Thus, strategies based around launching new products have a greater chance of success, as rising consumer incomes lead to greater demand for new products and more willingness on the part of consumers to try them.
- **Repositioning.** Firms intent on repositioning and changing their appeal may also find this policy easier during a period of rising economic prosperity. With higher incomes, consumers are more willing to consider new trends and fashions, which in turn are likely to shorten product life cycles. This has encouraged some companies to redefine their image as well as their product offerings, in effect repositioning their brands in the market.

FACT FILE

Brand repositioning at McDonald's

In March 2004, McDonald's announced a new strategy of offering healthier alternatives to its high-carbohydrate, high-fat range of burgers and fries. It announced the introduction of 'Salads Plus', along with a new range of healthy yoghurts, garden greens, quorn sandwiches and fresh fruit.

In effect, McDonald's was deliberately attempting to tap into the healthy eating trend, appealing to consumers' awareness about the perceived health benefits of certain food groups. The timing of the strategy was important. McDonald's was more likely to gain trial purchases of its new range of products during periods of economic prosperity, as consumers are prepared to be more adventurous.

Source: adapted from Andrew Boden, 'Economic growth', *Business Review*, September 2004.

𝑒 EXAMINER'S VOICE

This analysis suggests that timing the introduction of appropriate business strategies is critical. In order to enable them successfully to schedule their strategic plans well into the future, many firms invest in economic forecasting.

In general, economic growth provides favourable trading conditions and new business opportunities. It means growth and possibly new markets for existing products and market opportunities for new products. High levels of income and spending may even encourage the introduction of what might otherwise have been seen as risky products or business ventures. Economic growth also offers more security and certainty to firms and therefore provides them with more confidence in planning for the future.

Effects of economic growth on the environment

Economic growth and increased wealth do not necessarily produce an increase in welfare and can have serious consequences for the environment. For example, economic growth can result in serious negative externalities, such as pollution, congestion and harm to the environment. This is often apparent in developing countries that undergo rapid industrialisation and also in regional areas that are subject to heavy concentrations of industry. It is important, therefore, to have sufficient regulation and safeguards in place to minimise such externalities. In the long term, many commentators suggest that it will be impossible to sustain present rates of economic growth, as the world's resources are not inexhaustible.

DID YOU KNOW?

The level of economic activity differs not only internationally between countries, but also between regions within a particular country and between specific areas within a particular region. This has consequences for firms operating in different parts of the country as well as for firms that operate internationally.

PRACTICE EXERCISE 3   Total: 30 marks (25 minutes)

1 Define the term 'economic growth'. *(2 marks)*

2 State three ways in which GDP can be measured. *(3 marks)*

3 Identify two determinants of economic growth. *(2 marks)*

4 Explain two possible adverse effects that economic growth may have on the environment. *(6 marks)*

5 Explain the possible impact of economic growth on the sales of goods with income-elastic demand. *(5 marks)*

6 Explain how investment in capital goods might be affected by a period of strong economic growth. *(3 marks)*

7 Why might skills shortages occur during periods of economic growth? *(3 marks)*

8 Explain two strategies that companies might adopt to benefit from a period of sustained economic growth. *(6 marks)*

CASE STUDY 1   UK growth is forecast to trail rivals

The UK economy is set to trail behind key EU competitor countries over the next 15 years, with its growth outstripped by the Irish Republic, Spain, France and Portugal, startling new projections suggest.

The UK's annual growth between 2006 and the end of the next decade is set to average only 1.9%, according to the long-term projections (see Table 21.5). This would leave the UK lagging behind the USA with average growth of 3.1%, Spain (2.8%) and France (2.3%).

In a league of 32 nations, the UK's forecast growth performance places it in 21st place. Over 15 years, one result would be that Spain's standard of living, measured by national income per head, would leapfrog the UK's. By 2020, the UK's GDP per head is expected to put it 19th in the ranking of global living standards, with Spain in 17th place. The USA takes first place with GDP per head almost twice that projected for the UK, and with Ireland not far behind the USA (see Figure 21.7).

Table 21.5 Forecast average annual GDP growth, 2006–20

	Growth % per year		Growth % per year
India	5.5	Norway	2.1
Malaysia	5.4	New Zealand	2.1
China	5.2	Austria	2.1
Thailand	4.5	Portugal	2.0
Turkey	4.1	**UK**	**1.9**
Irish Republic	3.8	Sweden	1.8
Indonesia	3.5	Greece	1.7
South Korea	3.3	Denmark	1.7
Mexico	3.2	Italy	1.6
Chile	3.1	Belgium	1.5
USA	3.1	Germany	1.5
Argentina	3.0	Finland	1.3
Spain	2.8	Netherlands	1.3
Brazil	2.8	Australia	1.3
Canada	2.4	Japan	1.3
France	2.3	Switzerland	0.7

Source: Deutsche Bank, *Global Growth Centres 2020*.

Globally, the forecast shows India as the fastest-growing economy up to 2020, with Malaysia pipping China for second place. Slowing population growth in China is expected to just prevent it eclipsing the USA as the world's largest economy by 2020. By then, the UK is forecast to be the seventh largest world economy, behind the USA, China, Japan, India, Germany and France.

Source: Deutsche Bank, *Global Growth Centres 2020*.

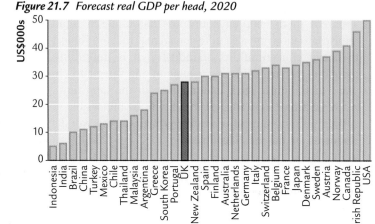

Figure 21.7 Forecast real GDP per head, 2020

Questions

Total: 30 marks (40 minutes)

1 Discuss the possible implications of the global GDP projections made by Deutsche Bank for a UK company that operates in both domestic and international markets. *(14 marks)*

2 Discuss appropriate long-term strategies for a business to deal with these projections. *(16 marks)*

CASE STUDY 2 Topps Tiles' expansion strategy

Topps Tiles is the UK's biggest tile and wood floor covering specialist group. It started trading in Manchester in 1963. Following a period of growth, it was floated on the stock market in 1997. It has grown from just 54 stores at flotation to 250 stores today, with another 20 stores opening each year. For the same period, turnover has jumped from £24.4 million to £207.9 million and pre-tax profit has leapt from £2.5 million to £37.8 million.

Tops Tiles is taking advantage of the fact that its products are highly income elastic, and have flourished in popularity as rising incomes have propelled the home improvement boom. Over the past decade, it is estimated that the average semi-detached house has doubled the number of tiles used, partly fuelled by the trend to have bigger kitchens and more bathrooms. Thus, Topps Tiles is successfully penetrating the same market with its products and gaining market share, at the same time as rival operators should also be benefiting from higher sales. Topps Tiles has been able to grow at a faster rate than that of the whole market, without necessarily poaching rival firms' customers.

Source: adapted from Andrew Boden, 'Economic growth', *Business Review*, September 2004 and www.toppstiles.co.uk.

Questions

Total: 30 marks (40 minutes)

1 Consider the possible reasons why Topps Tiles was able to grow quickly without getting involved in hostile competitive strategies. *(6 marks)*

2 To what extent might the timing of expansionary strategies have been of vital importance to the success of Topps Tiles? *(12 marks)*

3 Evaluate how a recession, such as that which began in winter 2008, might affect Topps Tiles' expansion strategies. *(12 marks)*

Interest rates

A firm that is considering an investment project will take into account whether the financial return from the project exceeds the interest that must be paid if the money to fund the investment is borrowed. It will also consider the interest that could be earned elsewhere if the firm's own funds are used to fund the investment project.

Interest rates are also an important tool of government economic policy. By influencing the cost of borrowing and the reward for lending, the government can influence spending in the economy and therefore the rate of inflation, the level of employment, the rate of exchange of pounds sterling and the level of exports and imports.

KEY TERM

interest rates: the cost of borrowing money and the return for lending money. They also measure the **opportunity cost**, to both individuals and firms, of spending money rather than saving it and receiving interest.

DID YOU KNOW?

Opportunity cost measures cost in terms of the next best alternative forgone. For example, the cost of an evening spent revising could be the missed opportunity of attending a concert or of earning money by working in a supermarket.

***e* EXAMINER'S VOICE**

Opportunity cost is an excellent concept to use when analysing a range of issues. Make sure that you understand its meaning and can apply it to different situations.

Who sets interest rates?

Since 1997, the control of interest rates has been the responsibility of the Monetary Policy Committee (MPC), headed by the governor of the Bank of England. The MPC is responsible for maintaining price stability in the UK. It meets monthly to consider interest rate changes and is free to decide the level of interest rates necessary to meet the target for inflation set by the government, which is currently 2% or less.

More recently, and as a result of falling demand in 2008 and 2009, there has been increased pressure to use the rate of interest as a tool to boost the level of total demand in the economy and thus to reduce the potential impact of recession on the level of employment and business confidence.

Since 2000, interest rates in the UK have been relatively low, as shown in Table 21.6 and Figure 21.8.

Year	2000	2001	2002	2003	2004	2005	2006	2007	2008
Interest rates	6.0	4.0	4.0	3.75	4.75	4.5	5.0	5.5	2.0

Table 21.6 Trends in UK interest rates (%)

Source: HM Treasury website, **www.hm-treasury.gov.uk**.

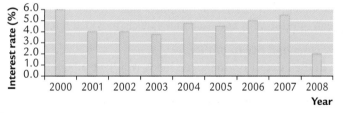

Figure 21.8 Trends in UK interest rates (%)

Implications of changes to the rate of interest

If interest rates fall, there are likely to be the following effects on business.

Increase in demand for consumer goods

The demand for consumer goods is likely to increase for a number of reasons:

- Saving money is less attractive because less interest is received. This may mean that people prefer to spend rather than save, causing demand for consumer goods to increase.
- The cost of goods bought on credit will fall. In particular, this will affect expensive, durable items such as cars, furniture and electrical goods, and luxuries such as holidays, which tend to be income elastic. People may be encouraged to purchase things that were previously considered too expensive, or to buy replacements more frequently, or to purchase more of a particular item.
- Variable-rate mortgage payments and other loan repayments will fall, meaning that homeowners will have more discretionary income, which they may spend on more consumer goods.

Increase in demand for capital goods

Because it becomes cheaper to purchase expensive capital equipment on credit, the demand for capital (investment) goods may increase. Thus firms might bring forward planned future investment or actually increase the level of investment. This is because the return on projects is likely to exceed interest payments that must be made on borrowed funds or that could be received by investing the firm's own funds elsewhere. This results in a rise in demand for capital goods, such as machinery, as firms become more confident.

Fall in export prices and rise in import prices

If interest rates fall, this will lead to a fall in the value of the pound, which in turn will lead to a fall in export prices and a rise in import prices. Assuming that demand for both exports and imports is price elastic, this is likely to lead to a rise in demand for UK goods at home and abroad because domestic goods are priced more competitively than imported goods, and UK exports are priced more competitively than other products sold abroad. (More detail on the link between interest rates and exchange rates is provided later in this chapter.)

Fall in costs and rise in profits

A fall in the interest payments on loans will have a beneficial effect on firms that are **highly geared**. (Highly geared firms are those with a high proportion of their capital employed in the form of long-term loans.) Interest payments are part of fixed costs, so fixed costs for these firms will fall. This in turn will reduce unit costs and the breakeven point. It may also make it possible to introduce price cuts and therefore adopt a more competitive strategy in the market. Alternatively, it can have potentially favourable effects on profits. As unit costs fall, there will be a rise in profit margins unless price is reduced.

As a result of a fall in interest rates, the overall increase in demand, for both consumer and capital goods, may lead firms to consider expanding production. As a consequence, more employees may be needed, leading to increased competition in the labour market. This in turn might create skill shortages in certain areas, resulting in increasing wage costs. Overall, the increasing demand for goods and the possible increasing wage demands may be inflationary. (The impact of inflation on business is considered later in this chapter.) Equally, the rise in demand for both consumer and capital goods may increase the rate of economic growth, which, as we have seen, can have further effects on business.

If interest rates rise, the opposite effects will occur.

Interest rates and their influence on exchange rates

When interest rates in the UK are high, relative to interest rates in other countries, it becomes more attractive to invest in the UK. As a result, capital from abroad (known as **foreign investment**) flows into the UK in order to take advantage of the attractive interest rates. Investment in the UK can only take place in pounds sterling, so there is an increase in the demand for pounds and an increase in the price, or the **exchange rate**, of pounds. Figure 21.9 summarises this process.

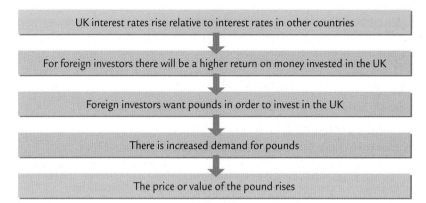

Figure 21.9 The effect of an increase in interest rates on the exchange rate

As exchange rates rise, export prices rise and exports become less competitive. If demand for exports is price elastic, export sales tend to fall as buyers turn to cheaper substitutes. At the same time, import prices fall and imports become more competitive. If demand for imports is price elastic, purchases of imports tend to rise as buyers are attracted by their relatively cheap price. The resulting fall in demand for exports and increase in demand for imports creates downward pressure on output and employment in the UK.

The opposite effects occur when interest rates are low, relative to interest rates in other countries.

The impact on firms of changes in exchange rates is discussed later in this chapter.

DID YOU KNOW?

The exchange rate for the pound is the price of the pound in terms of other currencies. Just as demand and supply can influence the price of goods and services, so they can also influence the price of the pound.

 **EXAMINER'S VOICE**

Note how interrelated so many of the macroeconomics issues are. Ensure that you understand the links and can analyse them clearly and fully.

Evaluating business strategies in response to changes in interest rates

The strategies that might be deployed by a business in response to changes in interest rates will depend on whether the rate of interest is rising or falling, on the nature of the goods or services that are provided by the business and on what else is happening within the economy. For example, when interest rates fall, the cost of borrowing falls and demand may increase. Firms may decide to increase production in order to meet demand. However, whether this is a suitable strategy depends on the nature of the firm's products or services, and in particular on whether they are income elastic or inelastic. It also depends on what else is happening in the economy. For example, as a result of the recession towards the end of 2008, the fact that interest rates were falling had no effect on consumer spending.

PRACTICE EXERCISE 4   Total: 40 marks (35 minutes)

1 Explain the term 'interest rates'.   *(3 marks)*

2 How are interest rates set in the UK?   *(3 marks)*

3 Identify and explain three different ways in which a fall in interest
  rates is likely to affect demand for consumer goods.   *(9 marks)*

4 Explain how a rise in interest rates is likely to affect demand for
  capital goods.   *(4 marks)*

5 Explain how a change in interest rates might affect profit margins.   *(4 marks)*

6 How could profit margins be maintained if interest rates cause
  unit costs to rise?   *(4 marks)*

7 If interest rates fall, what is likely to happen to the value of
  the pound?   *(4 marks)*

8 Explain the likely impact of the trend in interest rates since 2000 on
  a motor manufacturer that sells its vehicles in the UK and abroad.   *(9 marks)*

Exchange rates

There are exchange rates for pounds sterling against all other currencies, although the ones most commonly quoted are the rates against the euro, the US dollar, the Japanese yen and also a 'basket of currencies' (an average of a number of major currencies).

KEY TERM

exchange rate: the price of one country's currency in terms of another.

Trends in the annual average exchange rates of the pound against the euro and the dollar since 2000 are given in Table 21.7 and Figure 21.10.

Exchange rate	2000	2001	2002	2003	2004	2005	2006	2007	2008
€s to the £	1.64	1.61	1.59	1.44	1.47	1.46	1.47	1.46	1.20
$s to the £	1.51	1.44	1.50	1.63	1.83	1.82	1.84	2.00	1.53

Table 21.7 Trends in the €/£ and $/£ exchange rates

Source: **www.statistics.gov.uk**.

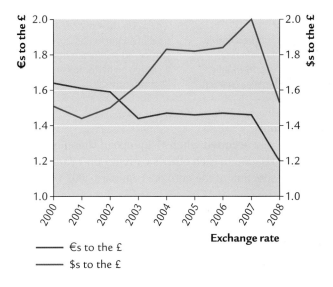

Figure 21.10 Trends in the €/£ and $/£ exchange rates, 2000–08

Exchange rate policies

Exchange rate policies are strategies that the government can adopt in order to determine the exchange rate of the country's currency.

KEY TERM

flexible/freely floating/fluctuating exchange rates: the demand for, and the supply of, the currency determine the exchange rate.

Free/floating exchange rates

As with any 'product', if lots of people want (demand) it, the price will go up. On the other hand, if there is too much available (being supplied), then the price will fall as it is easy to obtain. The demand for pounds comes from those who wish to buy UK goods and services (i.e. from UK exports) or invest in the UK. The supply of pounds comes from those who need foreign currency in order to purchase foreign goods and services (i.e. from imports to the UK) or invest abroad. Thus the exchange rate is influenced by the level of demand for exports and imports and the level of foreign investment.

FACT FILE

Exchange rate uncertainty

Because UK exchange rates are determined by supply and demand for the pound sterling, the rate can change from day to day. Firms that are exporting and importing on a regular basis find fluctuations in exchange rates a source of considerable uncertainty, making it difficult for them to predict the volume of overseas sales or the price they will receive from these transactions. Such uncertainty affects a firm's ability to plan ahead effectively. In some instances, it can be enough to stop firms developing export markets, especially at times when the exchange rate is rising rapidly, since the loss of competitiveness quickly erodes profit margins. To overcome some of this uncertainty, firms can make use of **futures contracts**, which are a form of insurance that enables them to buy currency in advance at a guaranteed fixed rate. This reduces the level of uncertainty and risk but is expensive and may reduce profits.

On a more practical level, for an exporting firm, unpredictable exchange rate changes create administrative and marketing problems, such as the costs and inconvenience of continually updating pricing and advertising literature for overseas markets.

DID YOU KNOW?

The foreign exchange market is a good example of **perfect competition** (see Chapter 34 of the AS textbook). The products are identical: for example, one dollar is exactly the same as another dollar. There are many buyers and sellers, all of whom are too small to influence the price on their own. Everyone buying and selling a particular currency knows the price, so sellers are unlikely to try to charge higher or lower prices than their competitors.

KEY TERM

fixed exchange rates: the government decides to fix the value of its currency permanently in relation to other currencies.

Fixed exchange rates

A fixed exchange rate occurred when 11 European Union countries fixed their exchange rates in relation to each other's currency on 1 January 1999 in preparation for the introduction of the euro on 1 January 2002 (see Chapter 22).

The UK has a free exchange rate system, although if the exchange rate of sterling rises too high or falls too low, the government may request the Bank of England to intervene and 'manage' the exchange rate, by buying or selling pounds, until it reaches an acceptable level.

Causes of changes in exchange rates

An *increase* in the exchange rate can result from any of the following:
- An increase in exports increases the demand for the currency.
- A reduction in imports decreases the supply of the currency.
- High interest rates attract savings from abroad and therefore increase demand for the currency.
- If speculators expect a currency to increase in value in the future, this is likely to cause an increase in the demand for the currency now. Then, when its value does rise, speculators will sell the currency and make a profit.
- If foreign multinationals wish to invest in a country, they will need to buy its currency, which in turn will increase the demand for it.
- The government may buy the currency in order to support its value.

A *decrease* in the exchange rate is caused by the opposite factors.

FACT FILE

Exchange rate plunge has many Brits staying home

Legions of British shoppers used to delight in popping across the Atlantic Ocean for bargain iPods, Levis and Abercrombie and Fitch gear when the pound was worth $2 — but they are cutting back now that it has plunged to $1.50. Many Brits, still smarting over the pound's rapid descent, are expected to stay much closer to home this holiday season, experts say. A Travelodge UK study of 3,000 Brits this month found that 50% fewer shoppers will head to the USA for a December shopping trip.

Sean Tipton, a spokesman for the Association of British Travel Agents, said the plummeting pound is the culprit. 'America is more exchange-rate sensitive than any other destination for us,' Tipton said.

Source: adapted from an article on www.nydailynews.com, 23 November 2008.

EXAMINER'S VOICE

Price elasticity of demand is an important concept in this area, so ensure that you understand the concept and the implications of different elasticities for a firm's revenue.

Implications for business of changes in exchange rates

The level of, and changes in, exchange rates affect businesses in different ways depending on whether they are:

- businesses that export their goods to consumers in other countries
- businesses that sell their goods in the UK, competing against foreign imports
- businesses that purchase imported fuel, raw materials and components to use in the production of their own goods

EXAMINER'S VOICE

Consider the relevance of each of these three perspectives when analysing the effects of changes in exchange rates.

Assuming that profit margins remain the same, an increase in the exchange rate may increase the price at which exports are sold abroad and reduce the price charged for imports in the UK. This in turn will affect revenue, competitiveness and profitability. The extent to which the changing prices of exports and imports will affect export sales and the purchase of imports depends on the price elasticity of demand.

- If the price elasticity of demand for exports is inelastic, an increase in their price, due to a rise in the exchange rate, will have little effect on sales. Although it is likely to increase revenue substantially in terms of the foreign currency, when converted back to pounds sterling there will be a minimal effect.
- If, on the other hand, the price elasticity of demand for exports is elastic, an increase in export prices is likely to lead to a significant fall in sales volume and in sales revenue.
- If the demand for imports is price elastic and their price falls due to a rise in the exchange rate, consumers are likely to purchase more of them, possibly substituting them for domestically produced goods. This will mean a reduction in demand for UK goods.
- If, on the other hand, the price elasticity of demand for imports is inelastic — often the case where firms purchase imported raw materials and components — the reduction in price will cause their costs to fall, which could lead them to reduce the price of their finished products or simply increase their profit margins.

The above analysis assumes that firms prefer to maintain their profit margins at the same level. If this were not the case — for example, if a firm were prepared to absorb the rise in the exchange rate and reduce its profit margins — it could leave prices unchanged.

It is, however, important to note that the levels of export sales and import purchases are influenced not only by exchange rates, but also by a range of other factors, including reputation and quality, after-sales service, the reliability, design and desirability of the product, the overall packaging provided and payment terms. In order to determine the most appropriate strategy, firms need to assess the price elasticity of demand for their products and whether price or other factors are the most important influences on sales.

> **e EXAMINER'S VOICE**
>
> Remember that many firms have a competitive advantage based on factors other than price. If a firm has a unique selling proposition, this may override any adverse effects due to changes in the exchange rate or prices.

Impact of exchange rate changes on exporters

Examples 1 and 2 show the impact of changes in exchange rates on a UK car exporter.

Example 1: the effect of a change in the exchange rate on the price and competitiveness of an exporter

The figures used here are for illustration only and are not intended to reflect the actual value of the currencies involved. In this example, profit margins per unit remain fixed at £2,000 but the selling price abroad changes as the exchange rate changes.

Currently £1 = €1.60.

In the UK a car costs £8,000 to produce.

It sells for £10,000 in the UK.

At the current exchange rate, it sells for €16,000 (10,000 × 1.60) in Spain.

Similar models in Spain sell for €17,000.

Therefore, the UK car is competitively priced.

If the value of the pound rises to £1 = €1.75, the UK car now sells for €17,500 (10,000 × €1.75) in Spain.

Therefore the UK car is no longer competitively priced.

If the value of the pound falls to £1 = €1.50, the UK car now sells for €15,000 (10,000 × 1.50) in Spain.

Therefore the UK car is very competitively priced.

Thus it can be seen that in this situation a *rise* in the value of the pound leads to a *less competitive* export price, while a *fall* in the value of the pound leads to a *more competitive* export price.

Example 2: the effect of a change in the exchange rate on the profitability of an exporter

In this example, selling price abroad remains fixed at $20,000, but profit margins change as the exchange rate changes.

Currently £1 = $2.00.

In the UK a car costs £8,000 to produce.

It sells for $20,000 in the USA (£10,000).

Therefore profit margin per car is £2,000.

If the value of the pound rises to £1 = $2.5, the revenue per car ($20,000) is now equivalent to £8,000.

Therefore the profit margin per car is zero.

If the value of the pound falls to £1 = $1.6, the revenue per car ($20,000) is now equivalent to £12,500.

Therefore the profit margin per car is £4,500.

In this situation, the *rise* in the value of the pound leads to a *smaller profit margin*, while a *fall* in the value of the pound leads to a *larger profit margin*.

Impact of exchange rate changes on importers

In both examples 1 and 2, the best result for the exporter is brought about by a fall in the exchange rate. But what effect will exchange rate movements have on an importer of raw materials? This is shown in Example 3.

Example 3: the effect of a change in the exchange rate on an importer of raw materials

Currently £1 = €1.60.

An importer buys 1,000 units of raw materials from France at a cost of €32,000 or €32 each. At the current exchange rate this is a total of £20,000.

If the value of the pound rises to £1 = €2, the UK importer will now need to exchange only £16,000 in order to get the €32,000 to buy the raw materials.

If the value of the pound falls to £1 = €1.28, the UK importer will now need to exchange £25,000 in order to get the €32,000 to buy the raw materials.

Therefore, the *rise* in the exchange rate has made it cheaper for the importer to buy raw materials and the *fall* in the exchange rate has made it dearer for the importer to buy raw materials.

FACT FILE

Sterling's plunge hurts small business

The dramatic fall in the value of sterling in October 2008 (it plunged to a 5-year low against the dollar) is adding to the financial pressures faced by thousands of small businesses that deal overseas. About a fifth of the UK's export and import business is carried out by small and medium-sized firms, which represents overseas trade worth £141 billion.

A weak pound is usually good news for exporters, but the worldwide slowdown has hit demand in the markets. The slump in sterling against the dollar and the euro has affected profit margins, as buying goods and services from abroad has become more expensive.

SMEs (small and medium-sized enterprises) are losing nearly £900 million a year because they are failing to protect themselves against currency fluctuations. Up to 50% of all import and export business undertaken by smaller firms is unprotected against movements in the exchange rate.

Instead, firms buy or sell currency at the market rate at the time that money is received or has to be paid, leaving them financially exposed.

There are ways to reduce the risk of losing money through currency fluctuations. The simplest way is by taking out a 'forward contract', also known as hedging. This is an agreement that allows firms to buy or sell a currency at a fixed rate on or before a certain date, up to a year ahead, limiting their potential losses if exchange rates move sharply.

James Moore, 35, runs an independent car hire brokerage in Essex, which does a lot of business in the USA. For the past 4 years he has bought forward contracts for dollars and sterling. As a result, James, whose firm employs 23 people and has a turnover of £12 million, estimates that he has avoided potential losses of up to £1 million.

Source: adapted from an article in the *Financial Mail*, 2 November 2008.

Evaluating business strategies in response to changes in exchange rates

The strategies a business might deploy in response to changes in exchange rates will depend on whether exchange rates are rising or falling and what market the business operates in.

For a business that exports its goods to consumers in other countries, a rising exchange rate for the pound means that it must understand how higher prices will affect sales. If sales are likely to fall because foreign buyers switch to competing substitutes whose price has remained the same, it may be better to accept lower profit margins. Staying competitive when the exchange rate is rising is very difficult. Most big businesses want a stable, and low, exchange rate if export markets are important to them.

For a business that exports its goods to consumers in other countries, a falling exchange rate for the pound is a bonus. The value of its product in pounds will rise if the foreign currency price stays the same. It has a choice: it could leave prices the same and accept a higher profit margin, or it could cut the price in the hope of higher sales. The best strategy depends on the price elasticity of demand for its product. A high elasticity — greater than 1 — means that a price cut will bring a disproportionately large increase in sales.

For a business that sells its goods in the UK in competition with foreign imports, a rising exchange rate for the pound will put it under added pressure to improve its efficiency. It may consider increasing investment in labour-saving machinery and reducing the workforce. It may introduce new technologies and organisational strategies. It will increase its marketing efforts. The fight will be on just to maintain competitiveness.

For a business that purchases imported fuel, raw material and components to use in the production of its own goods, staying competitive is more complicated, especially if it then exports its final product, since it will need to think through each of these perspectives when deciding on its strategy.

Thus, for any firm, a decision to enter an export market is influenced by the potential exchange rate risk. A firm that is over-reliant on one foreign currency because a majority of its sales go to one country could find a rise in the value of the pound to be crippling. On the other hand, for many businesses, selling abroad is absolutely essential if they wish to expand their markets.

Firms in European countries that have adopted the euro, and which trade with other countries in the eurozone, encounter no such risk and have a great advantage over outsiders. (The euro is considered in more detail in Chapter 22.)

PRACTICE EXERCISE 5   Total: 50 marks (45 minutes)

1 What is an exchange rate?   (2 marks)

2 Explain the meaning of the term 'freely floating exchange rate'.   (3 marks)

3 State and explain three reasons why a currency might increase
   in value.   (9 marks)

4 List two reasons that might cause a currency to fall in value.   (2 marks)

5 When the exchange rate rises:
   a How might a firm ensure that its prices abroad do not rise?   (3 marks)
   b Why would a firm not always choose to take the action that
      you have chosen in part a?   (3 marks)

6 What is the effect of a fall in the exchange rate on the price of
   exports and of imports?   (6 marks)

7 If a firm is dependent on imported raw materials, what will be the possible
   impact of a fall in the exchange rate on its costs and pricing?   (4 marks)

8 Why might fluctuating exchange rates cause difficulties for a firm
   involved in exporting or importing?   (4 marks)

9 At an exchange rate of £1 = $1.50, a firm sells 10,000 units abroad at
   a price equivalent to £6.00. If the exchange rate rises to £1 = $2, what
   effect might this have on its sales revenue? Explain your answer. (5 marks)

10 The exchange rate of a currency rises by 10%. Consider how an
   exporter of goods with an elastic demand might be affected
   differently from an exporter of goods with an inelastic demand.   (9 marks)

PRACTICE EXERCISE 6   Total: 50 marks (45 minutes)

Study Table 21.8 and answer the questions below.

Year	US dollar	Japanese yen	Euro
2003	1.63	189.34	1.44
2004	1.83	198.10	1.47
2005	1.82	200.14	1.46
2006	1.84	214.33	1.47
2007	2.00	235.63	1.46
2008	1.53	148.63	1.20

Table 21.8
Sterling exchange rates,
2003–08

Source:
www.statistics.gov.uk.

1 Describe the changing value of the pound sterling against the three currencies given
   in Table 21.8.   *(6 marks)*

2 If a component purchased from Japan in 2003 cost 17,000 yen, how much would that have
   been in sterling? Assume that the Japanese supplier did not alter the yen price of the
   component between 2003 and 2008. What would its sterling price have been in 2008? *(6 marks)*

3 Assume that in 2003, the price of a particular product in the UK was £500. What would
   its price have been in euros? Assume that the sterling price of the product did not change
   between 2003 and 2008. What would its euro price have been in 2008?   *(6 marks)*

4 Compare and contrast the impact of the exchange rate changes shown on the following firms:
   a a UK business that exports to Germany and to the USA   *(6 marks)*
   b a UK business that imports from Japan and from the USA   *(6 marks)*
   c a UK business that sells its products worldwide on the basis of quality and service
      rather than price   *(5 marks)*

5 Discuss the possible impact of the changes in exchange rate shown in the table on a firm
   that imports essential components for production from Japan and sells its finished products
   mainly in Europe.   *(15 marks)*

KEY TERMS

inflation: an increase
in the general level
of prices within an
economy. Inflation also
means that there is a
fall in the purchasing
power of money.

deflation: a decrease
in the general level of
prices within an
economy or a rise in
the purchasing power
of money.

Inflation

Trends in the annual average rates of inflation since 2000 are given in Table 21.9.

Table 21.9 Trends in the annual UK rate of inflation (CPI)

	2000	2001	2002	2003	2004	2005	2006	2007	2008
Inflation (%)	0.8	1.2	1.3	1.4	1.3	2.1	2.3	2.3	4.9

Source: **www.statistics.gov.uk**.

It is important to be able to distinguish between **real** and **money or nominal
values**. Real income broadly measures what you can buy with your income.
If prices increase by 2% over a year (in other words, the cost of living rises
by 2%) and your money or nominal income also increases by 2% over the
same period, then your real income (i.e. what you can buy with your income)

has remained the same. Thus real income increases only if the nominal or money value of income rises by more than the rate of inflation over the same period. If money income rises by 10% and prices rise by 3%, then real income has risen, since you can now buy more with your income. But if money income rises by 2% and prices rise by 5%, then real income has fallen, since you can now buy less with your income.

> ### *e* EXAMINER'S VOICE
>
> 'Real' as opposed to 'money' changes should always be considered when analysing changes in the value of variables quoted in money terms. These variables include income, output, the amount of government expenditure and marketing budgets. Always consider the rate of inflation and how this has affected any increase or decrease in the value of those variables.

> ### DID YOU KNOW?
>
> The chancellor of the exchequer sets the inflation target for the UK, which currently stands at 2.0% (CPI). The Bank of England's Monetary Policy Committee (MPC) is required to set interest rates in order to keep the rate of inflation at or below the target rate.

Measuring inflation

Until 2003 inflation in the UK was only measured by the **retail price index (RPI)**. This shows changes in the price of the average person's shopping basket. It is calculated using a weighted average of each month's price changes.

In Europe a different measure of inflation is used, known as the **harmonised index of consumer prices (HICP)** or the **consumer price index (CPI)**. This was introduced in the UK in December 2003. In general, the CPI (HICP) tends to be approximately 0.5–0.75 percentage points below the RPIX, but this can vary. The CPI gives a more accurate view of inflationary pressures. In the UK, the term 'CPI' has been adopted rather than the term 'HICP', which is favoured on the Continent, but they both measure inflation in the same way.

Causes of inflation

In general, the causes of inflation can be divided into two types: **cost-push** and **demand-pull**. In addition, expectations can also play a role in generating inflation.

Cost-push inflation could be due to trade unions achieving wage increases that are greater than productivity increases, or it could be due to a massive increase in the price of an essential fuel, such as oil.

Just as an increase in demand for a particular product might lead to an increase in its price unless there is a corresponding increase in supply, so **demand-pull inflation** can be explained as a situation when aggregate (or total) demand in the economy increases without a corresponding increase in aggregate supply in the economy. This leads to an increase in the general level of prices because aggregate supply cannot increase beyond the point where firms are working at full capacity.

As a result of **inflationary expectations**, people expect a period of rising inflation to continue into the future. For example, if the rate of inflation has risen from 1% 2 years ago, to 2% last year and then to 3% this year, people are likely to expect

> ### KEY TERMS
>
> **cost-push inflation:** occurs when there is an increase in the costs of production (including wages, raw materials, fuel, taxation and interest rates) that forces firms to increase their prices in order to protect their profit margins.
>
> **demand-pull inflation:** the process by which prices rise because there is excess demand in the economy.

KEY TERM

inflationary expectations: views about what will happen to the rate of inflation in the future.

inflation to be 4% next year. If this is the case, they are likely to try to negotiate a pay rise of 4% in order to avoid a fall in their real income if inflation does rise to 4%. If they are successful, this will add to costs and will help bring about a 4% rate of inflation.

In practice, the causes of inflation are difficult to disentangle. As prices rise, for whatever reason, people negotiate wage increases to maintain their standard of living, anticipating future levels of inflation and thereby helping those levels to come about. An **inflationary spiral** is the way in which price rises in one sector of the economy cause price increases in another, in a continuous upward spiral. Pay increases become price rises, which in turn lead to demand for further pay increases, which cause further price rises, and so on.

> ### *e* EXAMINER'S VOICE
>
> Don't make the mistake of thinking that a fall in the inflation rate means a fall in prices. It simply means a slowing down of the rate at which prices are rising. Falling prices (or **deflation**) can only occur if the inflation rate is negative — which, at the time of writing in 2009, has not happened in the UK since the 1930s.

> ### DID YOU KNOW?
>
> While deflation might sound welcome, in fact it can be devastating to borrowers, banks and businesses. The Great Depression in the 1930s was accompanied by deflation of 10% per year, reflecting the widespread lack of demand. As prices fall, consumers and businesses become less willing to spend and invest, thus worsening the economic downturn.
>
> A sustained drop in prices hurts in two ways. First, because consumers and businesses anticipate prices will continue to fall, they are likely to cut back on present spending and investment, as they wait for prices to fall even lower. As spending dries up, the economy starts to shrink. As GDP shrinks, so do the companies providing those goods and services for consumers. As companies shrink or go out of business, unemployment rises. Out-of-work consumers have less money to spend, which cuts deeper into the economy. Once the cycle takes hold, it is very difficult to stop.

KEY TERM

hyperinflation: a situation where the value of money decreases so fast that people lose confidence in it.

During hyperinflationary periods, people start to barter or to make use of other commodities, such as gold, which have their own intrinsic value, or to use an internationally dependable foreign currency such as the US dollar. There is no precise level of inflation that means it is hyperinflation. It is more the case that price rises become so rapid and uncontrollable that confidence in the currency is lost and people are reluctant to enter into transactions with it.

Hyperinflation has severe consequences for society because it not only affects people's willingness to enter into transactions, but also leads to a major redistribution of income in favour of those with debts and with non-financial assets, and against those dependent on fixed incomes, such as pensioners and those relying on their savings.

DID YOU KNOW?

The best-known example of hyperinflation occurred in Germany in the 1920s, when prices were rising every day and paper money rapidly became worthless. By 1923 the annual rate of inflation had reached 7,000,000,000,000%, and in 1924 the German currency was replaced by a new currency. More recently, Zimbabwe has experienced chronic inflation. Inflation reached 624% in 2004 and 1,730% in 2006. The Reserve Bank of Zimbabwe revalued the currency in August 2006 at a rate of 1,000 old Zimbabwean dollars to 1 revalued Zimbabwean dollar. In June 2007, inflation reached 11,000%. Zimbabwe's annual inflation was 231,000,000% in July 2008, i.e. prices were doubling every 17.3 days. In August 2008, the Zimbabwe dollar was redenominated by removing 10 zeroes. ZWD 10 billion became 1 dollar after the redenomination. At the beginning of November 2008, the inflation rate was calculated to be at 516 quintillion per cent (516,000,000,000,000,000,000%). In January 2009, the Zimbabwe government introduced a range of trillion dollar bank notes; 100 trillion Zimbabwean dollars is estimated to be worth about £22.

Effects of inflation on business

Some of the effects of inflation can be positive for individual firms or consumers, but in general the effects are negative.

- Inflation tends to encourage borrowing if interest rates are less than the rate of inflation. For highly geared firms and those with heavy borrowing, inflation reduces the real value of the sum they owe, making it easier to repay the loan towards the end of its life. For example, if a firm borrowed a large sum of money 10 years ago, and if inflation has been increasing such that the average price level is double what it was then, it is likely that the firm's income or revenue has also doubled in this period, so the loan will be much easier to repay towards the end of the 10-year period.

- As inflation rises, so do property prices and the price of stock. Thus balance sheets tend to look healthier as rising property and stock values boost reserves.

- A firm will find it easier to increase the price of its own products when prices are rising generally, because cost increases can be passed on to the consumer more easily.

- Higher prices may mean lower sales, depending on the price elasticity of demand for particular products.

- The producers of major brands that tend to sell at premium prices may suffer as inflation makes consumers more aware of the prices of different products. This increased price sensitivity on the part of consumers may lead them to switch brands towards more competitively priced items. As a result, brand owners will either cut their price premiums or greatly increase their advertising expenditure in order to try to regain customer interest and loyalty.

- Just as consumers become more aware of prices, so workers become far more concerned about the level of their real wages because, unless they obtain a pay rise at least as high as the rate of inflation, their real income will fall. Therefore industrial action often increases in inflationary periods as workers and trade unions negotiate hard for pay increases. As a consequence, industrial relations tend to deteriorate.

- Suppliers may increase prices for the goods and services they supply, adding further to a firm's costs and putting more pressure on the firm to increase its own prices.
- If inflation in the UK is relatively higher than inflation in other countries, the international competitiveness of UK firms may be reduced.
- As the future is uncertain, forecasts of sales revenue and profits will become very difficult to make, and planning will be less reliable. As forecasting is subject to greater uncertainty, firms will begin to want higher forecast average rates of return on any investments that they undertake.
- If the Monetary Policy Committee (MPC) of the Bank of England (the institution that sets interest rates) takes action to reduce inflation by increasing interest rates, this is likely to reduce demand and sales, which will have an adverse effect on business.
- When prices are changing quickly, businesses find it more difficult to keep track of competitors' pricing strategies.
- Cash flow is squeezed as the costs of new materials and equipment rise.

Possible effects of a low rate of inflation

A low level of inflation, as experienced in the UK over recent years (see Table 21.8), can have a number of effects on business strategy:

- Interest rates are likely to be low if the rate of inflation is low, which will benefit most businesses.
- A low rate of inflation relative to other countries is likely to mean that firms become more competitive in their export markets and in their domestic markets against imports.
- In general, low levels of inflation create more certainty in the economy, which means that business is able to plan ahead because prices can be predicted more easily.
- Marketing and administrative costs will be lower, as there will be fewer price adjustments to, for example, price lists and advertising information.
- The fact that there is more certainty about short-term pricing decisions means that there should be more time available for long-term strategic decision making.
- Efficient firms survive and inefficient firms disappear. Continually rising prices mean that poorly performing firms can record increasing sales and profits in nominal terms. However, low inflation means that such firms cannot disguise poor sales performance and cannot easily raise prices to cover their own inefficiency.

Evaluating business strategies in response to changes in the level of prices

When evaluating the strategies a business might deploy in response to changes in the level of prices, it is important to consider whether inflation or deflation is occurring and, in the case of inflation, whether this is a low or a high rate. It is also important to consider the nature of the business and the products or services it offers. For example, a luxury product with a high status and popular brand, and for which price is not a major factor in determining demand, may be able to maintain its high price even during a period of deflation. However, products in highly competitive markets, where price competition is of crucial importance in maintaining demand, are likely to be involved in extensive price cutting during a period of deflation.

During inflationary periods, it is usual for workers to try to maintain their real income by pushing for wage increases at least in line with price increases. In such situations, firms are generally able to pass on cost increases without affecting the demand for their products. However, when deflation occurs and prices are falling, a major issue is that wages tend to be 'sticky' and may not fall in line with general costs and prices. Strategies will also depend on what is happening to the price of the firm's supplies and the prices of its competitors both at home and abroad.

PRACTICE EXERCISE 7   Total: 30 marks (25 minutes)

1 Explain the term 'inflation'.   (3 marks)

2 Distinguish between cost-push and demand-pull inflation.   (6 marks)

3 If the rate of inflation in 2007 was 2.1% and my annual salary in 2008 increased by 2.5%, was I better off? Explain your answer.   (4 marks)

4 Explain why inflationary expectations are likely to cause inflation.   (5 marks)

5 Explain one benefit that inflation might have for firms and individuals.   (3 marks)

6 Identify and explain three adverse effects of inflation on a firm.   (9 marks)

PRACTICE EXERCISE 8   Total: 40 marks (45 minutes)

1 Table 21.10 gives inflation rates for selected countries between 2006 and 2008.

Country	2006	2007	2008
USA	3.2	2.9	5.3
UK	2.3	2.3	4.9
France	1.7	1.5	3.2
Germany	1.6	2.3	3.0
Japan	0.3	0.0	2.2
Australia	3.3	2.4	5.1

Table 21.10 Consumer price inflation rates for selected countries, 2006–08 (%)

a Explain what the rates of inflation quoted for Japan indicate about price levels in that country.   (4 marks)

b As a UK company trading in all of these countries, discuss the possible implications of their differing inflation rates for the competitiveness of your product.   (14 marks)

2 Refer to Table 21.9.

  a Consider the likely impact of inflation on a firm producing consumer durables such as televisions and other electrical goods between 2000 and 2008. *(8 marks)*

  b Inflation in the UK has been low and stable in recent years. To what extent might a firm be adversely affected by such low inflation? *(14 marks)*

KEY TERMS

unemployment: the number of jobless people who want to work, are available to work, and are actively seeking employment.

structural unemployment: long-term unemployment resulting from a change in demand, supply or technology in the economy, which produces a fundamental decline in an industry.

cyclical unemployment: unemployment resulting from an economic downturn or recession in the business cycle.

Unemployment

Unemployment levels since 2000 have been low. In June 2001, unemployment in the UK went below 1 million for the first time since 1975. Trends in annual average rates of unemployment since 2000 are given in Table 21.11.

Table 21.11 *Annual UK rates of unemployment (%)*

2000	2001	2002	2003	2004	2005	2006	2007	2008
4.0	3.0	3.0	3.0	2.8	4.7	5.5	5.3	5.8

Source: **www.statistics.gov.uk**.

Types of unemployment

Structural unemployment

Structural unemployment is often concentrated in regions that have been heavily dependent on certain industries. For example: Wales (coal), the northeast (shipbuilding), Lancashire and Yorkshire (textiles).

DID YOU KNOW?

Technological unemployment (where people are replaced by machinery or technology) can be included as part of structural unemployment or can be treated as a separate type of unemployment.

Cyclical unemployment

Cyclical unemployment can be expected to last for as long as the recession itself, which might be for 1–2 years. Figure 21.11 illustrates that, like economic growth, unemployment tends to follow a cyclical pattern.

Figure 21.11
Unemployment in the UK, 1980–2008

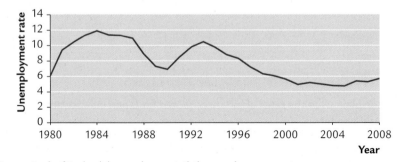

Source: Bank of England data and **www.statistics.gov.uk**.

The impact of cyclical unemployment will vary according to individual firms and their products, but might include the following:

- In theory, the sales of luxury products will decline significantly as income declines, whereas firms selling inferior goods may gain increased sales as people cut back on luxuries.
- Firms selling products in a growing market may be able to ride out the effects of recession, but on the other hand, firms selling products with low profit margins may suffer as price becomes a more important element of the marketing mix.
- Capital goods firms and construction firms are likely to experience the greatest problems as business confidence falls and there is less demand for their products.

Seasonal unemployment

Seasonal unemployment tends to be of a temporary nature and disappears in the next 'season'. For example, people working in the tourism industry and in the building and construction industry are often laid off during the winter when there is less demand for their service.

Frictional unemployment

Frictional unemployment is also known as 'search' unemployment and occurs in the time between losing one job and finding another when people are temporarily unemployed. Government can reduce frictional unemployment by improving the quality of service in job centres, so that people who are newly unemployed are able to find work more quickly.

Implications of unemployment for business and how business might respond

Both high and low levels of unemployment can affect a firm's business strategy.

Implications of high levels of unemployment

- Consumer incomes fall, leading to lower sales. This not only reduces revenue and profits but may, in the extreme, lead to redundancies as firms decide to reduce production levels in line with the lower sales. This analysis applies most significantly to firms that produce income-elastic products: that is, luxury products. Firms that produce normal goods will experience a fall in sales that is similar to the fall in incomes in the economy. Firms that produce income-inelastic products, such as food, will find that, despite falling consumer incomes, demand for their products remains more or less the same. Those producing inferior goods may find that low incomes actually lead to a *higher* demand for their products.
- Workers have less bargaining power as alternative jobs are harder to find, which is likely to mean less pressure to increase wage levels. This is reinforced by the fact that, as jobs are scarce, people may be more willing to work for lower wages in order to get a job. In turn, this will lead to lower costs and possibly reduced prices, enabling firms to cope better with the decline in demand.

FOTOLIA

e **EXAMINER'S VOICE**

The classic phrase 'On balance I think...' will not earn any evaluation marks unless the reasons for this thinking are explained in your answer.

- As demand falls, cost-saving strategies may be introduced. Some of these may lead to increased efficiency, but others may be short-sighted, bringing short-term benefits but creating greater problems in the longer term. For example, a firm may decide to reduce its commitment to the training and development of its workforce in order to make cost savings, but in the longer term it may find that this strategy leads to a lack of essential skills and expertise. Similarly, a firm may decide that significant cost savings can be made by delayering the organisation, but may find that as this entails much wider spans of control, it creates longer-term difficulties in relation to management and coordination.

- The reduction in demand is likely to lead to cutbacks or delays in investment projects. This, in turn, may lead to a further decline in employment both in the firms that are reducing investment spending and in other sectors of industry that produce capital goods: for example, producers of heavy machinery and construction firms.

- The reduction in demand and the need to make cost savings by cutting back on the workforce and investment may cause businesses to consider **rationalisation** as a strategy. Essentially, this means reorganising the business in order to increase its efficiency. The term is used when major savings are required, involving cutbacks in fixed overhead costs that enable the firm to reduce its breakeven point. Rationalisation can be achieved in a number of different ways. For example, it could involve delayering or, in a multi-site business, it could involve closing a factory or the administrative or finance departments in each site and creating a single, centralised department. Alternatively, it could involve outsourcing the work, which will inevitably lead to redundancies. Ultimately, the reduction in demand may eventually lead to takeovers and mergers.

- Because more skilled and experienced people are available for work, businesses may benefit from reduced training needs.

EXAMINER'S VOICE

Ensure that your knowledge of income elasticity of demand and of normal and inferior goods is secure, and that you can apply your knowledge in this context.

DID YOU KNOW?

Minimum wage legislation limits the extent to which firms can push down wages during a period of high unemployment.

EXAMINER'S VOICE

'On the other hand' is a useful phrase to remember when analysing business issues. Most situations have a whole range of different consequences and businesses can choose from a range of different strategies to deal with them. For example, the above analysis suggests that, as a result of unemployment and the need to reduce costs, a firm might cut training and suffer long-term adverse effects. An alternative analysis might suggest that, because of high levels of unemployment, more skilled and experienced people are available for work. Thus, businesses might benefit from reduced training needs, which in turn reduces costs and the short-term fall in productivity that is inevitable while new employees are being trained.

Implications of low levels of unemployment

- More people in employment mean that consumers as a whole have more income, and therefore that more spending will take place. This will significantly increase the sales of income-elastic (luxury) goods.

■ As more people become employed, the labour market is said to 'tighten': that is, fewer people are looking for work. This makes it more difficult for firms to recruit suitably skilled or qualified individuals. The existing workforce and potential applicants have more bargaining power, and firms may be forced to increase wages for existing workers and to offer substantially higher wages in order to attract new workers.

Evaluating business strategies in response to changes in the level of unemployment

The strategies a business might deploy during a period when the economy is experiencing rising unemployment will depend on the nature of its business and how efficient it is. Rising unemployment will mean falling levels of incomes and thus falling levels of general demand for goods and services. The appropriateness of a firm's business strategy at this time will depend on whether it provides income-elastic or inelastic goods: that is, whether the products it offers for sale are normal, luxury or inferior goods. At the same time as revenue is likely to be falling, the business needs to be implementing strategies to cut costs so that, although profit margins will be falling, sufficient resources are available to sustain the business during the downturn and to ensure that it is ready to build business again when the economy looks more promising.

An important factor to consider is that strategies put in place to deal with problems that face a business in the short term do not have a negative effect on the business in the long term. Thus, responding to falling revenue by making huge numbers of workers redundant or selling off sites may solve the short-term problem of falling demand, but it may mean that when the recovery comes, the business has insufficient experienced workers or insufficient productive capacity to meet demand.

PRACTICE EXERCISE 9	Total: 30 marks (25 minutes)

1 Explain the term 'structural unemployment'. *(3 marks)*

2 Give three examples of structural unemployment. *(3 marks)*

3 Explain the term 'cyclical unemployment'. *(2 marks)*

4 Explain the term 'seasonal unemployment' and give one example of it. *(4 marks)*

5 Explain the term 'frictional unemployment'. *(3 marks)*

6 Identify and explain three adverse effects of unemployment on businesses. *(9 marks)*

7 Identify and explain two possible benefits to firms of the presence of unemployment. *(6 marks)*

PRACTICE EXERCISE 10   Total: 30 marks (35 minutes)

1 Refer back to Figure 21.11. Describe the extent to which the pattern of unemployment reflects the business cycles shown in Figure 21.4. *(8 marks)*

2 This diagram shows the pattern of regional unemployment in the UK in 2008.

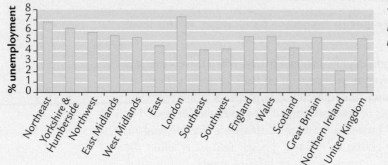

Table 21.12
Regional unemployment in the UK, 2008

Source: www.statistics.gov.uk.

a Briefly explain why there are differences in levels of unemployment between different regions of the UK. *(6 marks)*

b Analyse the possible impact of these unemployment data on two different firms, one of which produces and sells its products in the southeast of England while the other produces and sells its products in the northeast of England. *(8 marks)*

c The UK has experienced relatively low rates of unemployment in recent years. Analyse the possible problems resulting from this for a firm operating in the financial services industry. Assume that the firm requires highly skilled and well-qualified staff. *(8 marks)*

KEY TERM

globalisation:
the process enabling financial and investment markets to operate internationally, largely as a result of deregulation and improved communications

Globalisation of markets

The pace, scope and scale of globalisation have accelerated dramatically in the last 25 years for two main reasons:

- Modern communication and the rapid spread of information technology (IT) are changing the way companies, whether manufacturing or service providers, organise their activities. Such developments allow, for example, for the British service sector to deal with its customers through a call centre in India, or for a sportswear manufacturer to design its products in Europe, make them in southeast Asia and sell them in the USA.
- Trade has increased, made easier by international agreements to lower tariff and non-tariff barriers on the export of manufactured goods, especially to rich countries.

More and more global production is carried out by big multinational companies that operate across international borders, locating manufacturing plants overseas in order to capitalise on cheaper labour costs or to be closer to their markets. Some multinationals, like Apple, have become 'virtual firms', outsourcing most of their production to other companies, mainly in Asia.

AQA A2 Business Studies

The threats to Western manufacturing industry caused by increasing globalisation of markets are also felt by the service sector, with many service sector jobs under threat as global companies try to save money by outsourcing functions that were once done internally. What China has become to manufacturing, India has become to the new world of business process outsourcing (BPO) — which includes everything from payroll to billing to IT support. India is the world's leading exporter of IT services and almost every major international company in the IT industry now has a huge presence in India.

WHAT DO YOU THINK?

Some commentators argue that the spread of globalisation, free markets and free trade into the developing world is the best way to beat poverty. Others argue passionately that globalisation is the cause of low-paid sweatshop workers, GM seed being pressed on developing world farmers, the sale of state-owned industry to qualify for loans from international aid organisations, and the increasing dominance of US and European corporate culture across the globe. Where do you stand on the issue of globalisation?

Influences on international competitiveness

 KEY TERM

International competitiveness may be based on price competition and/or non-price competition. In general, businesses seek to improve their competitiveness in order to secure a larger market. The more competitive a firm is in relation to its international rivals, the larger will be its potential global market share.

international competitiveness: the ability of firms to sell their products successfully both abroad in export markets and at home in competition against imports.

Firms seek to compete in international markets for a variety of reasons. These include:

- avoiding the risks of operating in a single market
- taking advantage of economies of scale and increasing profits
- a desire to increase market share
- a need to compete against international firms in order to safeguard domestic markets

In addition, reductions in trading barriers in the European Union and internationally, and the opening up of extensive markets in eastern Europe, India and China, have increased competition in world markets and therefore have increased the need for UK firms to be internationally competitive.

Internal factors that influence international competitiveness

Being internationally competitive involves considering factors that are internal to the firm, such as production, human resource management and marketing issues. A firm needs to consider how to improve its efficiency and productivity in order to reduce unit costs and increase the quality of its products. This could mean introducing more capital-intensive means of production and new technology, and generally ensuring that the production process is as efficient as possible in order to increase the rate of productivity. The higher the rate of productivity, the lower unit costs are likely to be and therefore the lower the price that can be charged for the product.

Increasing efficiency could also mean improving the skills of the workforce by training and development, and more generally ensuring that the organisation of human resources is effective and that HRM strategies are linked closely to the needs of the firm.

International competitiveness also involves increasing marketing efforts, ensuring that strategies are appropriate to each of the overseas markets in which the firm intends to operate. To be successful internationally requires that a firm competes with the best companies in the world. Benchmarking against such companies should allow a firm to improve and enhance its procedures and strategies, and therefore its performance.

External factors that influence international competitiveness

A firm must also take account of the external business environment. Factors to consider include the inflation rate in the UK compared with the rate in the other countries with which it intends to trade, phases of the business cycle in the UK and other countries, the degree of trade protection in the form of import controls, and the levels of exchange rates.

This analysis is further complicated for firms that export their finished goods abroad and use imported raw materials and components in the production of these items. In such a situation, it is important to consider all of the different possible outcomes that might affect a firm.

In general, the influences on a firm's international competitiveness include the exchange rate, unit costs, the price and quality of the product, prompt delivery and after-sales service. The level of the foreign exchange rate is often seen as the

BMW GROUP PRESS CLUB

crucial factor in the success of companies competing internationally, but successful exporting countries and companies appear to perform well despite high and rising exchange rates, suggesting that the price of goods is not necessarily the main determinant of competitiveness. Germany and Japan, for instance, have thrived through well-designed, high-quality products such as BMWs and Sony televisions, for which consumers are willing to pay a price premium.

PRACTICE EXERCISE 11   Total: 40 marks (35 minutes)

1 Explain the term 'globalisation'. *(3 marks)*

2 Identify and explain two factors that have led to the increasing globalisation of markets. *(6 marks)*

3 Why might increasing globalisation create threats to both manufacturing and service sector businesses in the UK? *(6 marks)*

4 Explain the term 'international competitiveness'. *(3 marks)*

5 Identify two reasons why a firm might wish to compete in international markets. *(2 marks)*

6 Explain two internal factors that might influence the international competitiveness of firms. *(6 marks)*

7 Explain two external factors that might influence the international competitiveness of firms. *(6 marks)*

8 How might a fall in the value of the exchange rate influence a country's international competitiveness? *(4 marks)*

9 How is knowledge of price elasticity of demand useful to your answer to question 8? *(4 marks)*

CASE STUDY 3 Clarks left with a sole survivor after closure

In April 2005, C. and J. Clark, the shoemaker, closed its last big UK plant. Clarks, a private limited company, which once had more than 20 UK factories, has cut tens of thousands of manufacturing jobs since the early 1980s, and its shoes are now made in China, India, Vietnam, Romania, Brazil and Portugal.

In its prime, Clarks was one of the UK's biggest manufacturers, exporting shoes throughout the Commonwealth. The company employed tens of thousands of people in factories across the West Country. However, in the early 1980s, competition from cheap imports took its toll, sales began to fall and profits slumped, leaving Clarks vulnerable to takeover.

After deciding to stay private, Clarks set about aggressively cutting costs by closing factories and shifting production to cheaper overseas locations. Once costs were under control, Clarks set about giving itself a younger, 'trendier' image. It had been best known for children's shoes, but the image lost favour and the brand became associated with dull, chunky designs. With its aim to reduce the age of the typical Clarks buyer from the late 50s to 35–45, it embarked on multimillion-pound advertising campaigns, including 'Act your shoe size, not your age' and 'Enjoy every step', and a revamping and rebranding of its stores.

The company still employs about 1,200 people at its headquarters in Street, near Glastonbury. Shoemaking ended there in 1992 and most of the head office jobs are in distribution, IT, accounts and marketing. Former factory buildings were sold and turned into Clarks Village, a collection of shops and restaurants.

Clarks traces its history to 1825 when Quaker brothers, Cyrus and James Clark, began making shoes in Street. By the 1850s, Clarks employed a third of the population of Street. Products such as the Desert Boot and Clarks Wallabee heralded the company's golden years in the 1960s and 1970s.

Today, new technology, state-of-the-art facilities and a strong commitment to its product means that Clarks is now the number one shoe brand in the UK. With continuing growth in North America, western and eastern Europe, India and China, it is also the world's largest casual and smart shoe company and the fourth largest footwear company in the world.

Questions
Total: 30 marks (40 minutes)

1 Evaluate the possible reasons for Clarks's loss of international competitiveness. *(15 marks)*

2 In response to the increasing globalisation of markets, to what extent have the strategies that Clarks has pursued been the most appropriate? *(15 marks)*

The development of emerging markets

As well as India and China, eastern Europe is a good example of an emerging market. The fall of the communist regimes in the late 1980s and early 1990s and the absorption of 12 such countries into the EU since then have had the following implications for UK business:

- Eastern Europe's population is a major new market.
- There are market opportunities for new products and well-established branded products. For example, supermarkets and companies operating in mature markets such as those for chocolate and detergents have seen huge potential for whoever can establish their brand name first.
- Production costs in eastern Europe are lower, with cheaper labour and land rents plus less stringent government controls.
- The introduction of capitalism and the market system in eastern Europe means new competition.

Figure 21.13
Who's growing faster?

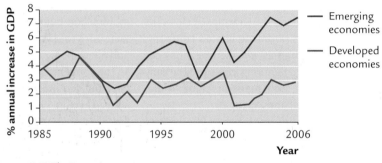

Source: IMF/*The Economist.*

Eastern Europe represents a huge opportunity for UK business, but the transition from an emerging market to a fully developed one does not take place overnight and results in a range of problems:

- The markets in eastern Europe are not wealthy ones, with the average income being approximately one-third of that in the countries of the original EU. This means that eastern European consumers have relatively little income to spend on the products of EU firms.
- The political systems of many central and eastern European states are still immature and can be unstable, leading to unpredictable decision making and sudden changes in trading conditions.
- High inflation can be a problem. Where this affects confidence in the currency, it may lead to transactions being made in other currencies with more stable values and internationally acceptable status, such as the dollar.
- There may be problems in raising finance in countries where the banking system needs developing or where there is no stock market.
- Relatively poor infrastructure, in terms of transport and communication systems, can be problematic.
- Markets may be less well developed than in western Europe.

PRACTICE EXERCISE 12   Total: 15 marks (10 minutes)

1 Explain the term 'emerging markets'.   *(3 marks)*

2 Explain two possible benefits of emerging markets, such as those in eastern Europe,
   for UK business.   *(6 marks)*

3 Explain two possible problems for UK firms attempting to enter emerging markets in
   eastern Europe.   *(6 marks)*

CASE STUDY 4 Emerging markets tempt Tesco

Tesco, the UK's largest supermarket chain, with approximately 31% of the UK grocery market, has to look beyond the UK if it is to grow further.

It currently operates in 13 countries. Tesco began a rapid expansion in the late 1990s into emerging markets, focusing on eastern Europe and southeast Asia. These areas have relatively undeveloped grocery retail markets but ones that are changing rapidly, offering Tesco major opportunities. Tesco has managed to become among the top retailers in many of the countries in which it operates, giving its business a secure basis. Tesco entered the USA in autumn 2007, and is currently trying to break into India.

The potential offered by the retail food sector in India is huge. However, the country's stringent rules on foreign direct investment (FDI) have barred multinationals from entering in a manner of their choosing. For example, Tesco would have preferred to enter the Indian retail food sector by starting up or acquiring a consumer retailer. Instead, Tesco has entered into an agreement with the huge Indian Tata group, which will see Tesco provide backroom support for the expansion of Tata's Star Bazaar hypermarket chain. Tesco will also open its own wholesale cash-and-carry business to provide a range of fresh food, grocery and non-food products to small retailers, restaurants and other business owners. This deal provides a platform for future growth and an opportunity to learn about the market, and enables Tesco to establish a supply chain in the country. By entering the wholesale market and forming links with Tata, Tesco is setting the stage for future growth into the consumer retail market.

TESCO PLC IMAGE LIBRARY

Although the majority of Tesco's stores are still in the UK, its large-format hypermarkets overseas mean that only around a third of Tesco's floorspace is actually in the UK. Even so, Tesco's average floorspace has been falling in many countries in the past 2 years or so, as it diversifies into smaller-format stores in countries like the Czech Republic, Poland and South Korea. Tesco estimates that within a decade, over half of its annual revenue will be generated outside the UK — it is currently around a quarter.

Emerging markets are likely to attract even greater interest in the future as retailers enter a new phase of globalisation. A spokesperson for the Institute of Grocery Distribution (IGD) commented: 'The next few years are likely to be challenging for the leading global retailers, yet all are well placed to achieve further growth, particularly internationally. Scale alone will

not determine who will win in today's global trading environment. Global retailers must also show increased simplicity, greater efficiency, flexibility and strong brand positioning to succeed. Emerging markets will not be immune to the global economic slowdown, but the pace of growth will continue to outstrip that of the developed world. We estimate that in grocery, retail markets in China and India will each grow at a compound annual rate of 13.2% between 2008 and 2012, exceeding any other country in the top ten.'

Source: adapted from information on **www.igd.com**.

Preliminary questions
Total: 25 marks (30 minutes)

1 Explain why Tesco needs to consider expansion abroad if it wishes to grow further. *(6 marks)*

2 Identify three emerging markets in which Tesco has a presence. *(3 marks)*

3 From the case study, identify what Tesco's ultimate objective appears to be in relation to its development in India. *(4 marks)*

4 Explain what the case study suggests are Tesco's strategies for achieving this objective. *(6 marks)*

5 The case study suggests that all markets will be affected by the 'global economic slowdown' but that emerging markets will do better than markets in the 'developed world'. Explain why this is likely to be the case. *(6 marks)*

Case study questions
Total: 40 marks (50 minutes)

1 Using Tesco as an example, analyse the potential link between the increasing globalisation of markets and the existence of emerging markets. *(10 marks)*

2 Discuss the benefits to Tesco of establishing supermarkets in emerging markets rather than in western Europe or North America. *(15 marks)*

3 To what extent might Tesco's current developments in India contribute to its longer-term objectives of establishing itself as a consumer retailer in the Indian market? *(15 marks)*

CASE STUDY 5 Harewood Ltd

Tessa Harewood opened the newspapers excitedly. Following the takeover of T. J. Laing Ltd, she was now the chief executive of the UK's fifth-largest sports goods supplier.

It was a gamble. Harewood Ltd had built up a tremendous reputation for its sportswear, and sales were growing fast, helped by Tessa's decision to move all of the production of its sportswear to India. However, Tessa found it difficult to foresee a time when Harewood Ltd could displace some of the major international sportswear suppliers. On that basis the takeover made good sense.

T. J. Laing specialised in equipment manufacturing. However, the company had been plagued by problems. The fitness equipment was manufactured in a factory in Birmingham, but more and more competitors had moved production to Asia or eastern Europe, where wage costs were lower. T. J. Laing had responded by specialising in the higher-quality, technically sophisticated end of the market, but the current recession had hit sales of these products significantly.

The other division of T. J. Laing was racquet production. Production of racquets was based

AQA A2 Business Studies

in China, but difficulties with quality and delivery had led to heavy financial losses.

Year 1

Tessa's first action was to start producing racquets in two more places. Harewood Ltd opened a new factory in Portugal. In Birmingham, Tessa used some of the spare capacity in the fitness equipment factory to produce racquets. Only 30% of racquet production was left in China, with 60% in Portugal. After delivery costs had been allowed for, the production in Portugal was only slightly dearer than China. The remaining 10% was manufactured in Birmingham — mainly the more expensive racquets — but there was also scope to produce other racquets just-in-time, to meet sudden orders or shortages in the UK.

Gradually sales in all products improved, as the UK came out of the recession that had started just before the takeover. Sportswear recovered most strongly in the UK, but by the end of the year fitness equipment sales there were still at their lowest level for 3 years. Tessa was pleased that the business was not reliant on UK sales for the majority of its revenue from fitness equipment. The sales in Italy and France accounted for 65% of the company's sales of fitness equipment and the T. J. Laing brand name was very strong in those two countries. Tessa's long-term strategy was to use the T. J. Laing brand name and reputation to sell its sportswear in Italy and France.

Year 2

As the business cycle moved from recession to recovery, sportswear sales grew quickly, but it took much longer for the fitness equipment sales to pick up. However, by the end of the year, the growth in orders for fitness equipment was so high that Harewood was forced to subcontract manufacturing to other companies in order to keep up with demand.

In the economy, borrowing had reached record levels. A mixture of major construction projects in the public sector and high consumer spending in the private sector led to a sudden rise in inflation. Tessa was not worried overall, but did have concerns that this would have a negative effect on some products. People did not seem to be too concerned about price when buying fitness equipment and most racquets, but some of the sportswear goods were price elastic in demand. By the end of the year, the company was achieving record profits and Tessa's main problem was finding ways of meeting the huge increase in demand for fitness equipment.

Year 3

The new factory in Wolverhampton opened at the beginning of the year. Cyclical unemployment was low in the economy. However, the Midlands had been hit by high levels of structural unemployment in the metal manufacturing industry. As a consequence, it was relatively easy for Harewood Ltd to find both a suitable site and the necessary skilled labour to produce fitness equipment.

Sales (and prices) continued to grow. The announcement of a 1.5% increase in interest rates in April took Tessa by surprise. Harewood Ltd had borrowed all of the money needed to open the new factory, hoping to benefit from the low interest rates at the time. All the same, the firm's cash flow was strong and all three product areas were producing high profits.

Tessa had expected some slowing in the rate of growth of sales, but she was shocked to see the order book at the end of June. Orders from shops for sportswear were down by 2% and racquet sales had fallen by 5%, but the biggest shock was fitness equipment — orders had decreased by 20%. Tessa wondered whether she had been too hasty in agreeing to the new factory.

The increase in interest rates also coincided with an increase in the value of the pound against other currencies. Tessa wondered whether this was good news or bad news for Harewood Ltd.

Tessa was not the only person surprised by developments. By July the economy had lurched from a strong recovery back into a downturn. In August the Bank of England announced a reduction of 1% in interest rates. By the end of the year, another cut (of 0.5%) had been made and the threat of a recession seemed to have disappeared.

At the end of the year, Tessa was thinking about her new year's resolutions. She decided that from now on she would seek a clearer picture of future macro-economic changes before making any strategic decisions.

On 31 December she looked at the newspapers carefully. The *Guardian* had presented a summary of the current (year 3) data, with its predictions for the next 2 years (years 4 and 5). This is shown in Table 21.10.

Table 21.10 The UK economy: current and forecast macroeconomic variables

Year	Change in GDP (%)	Unemployment (%)	Inflation (% change in CPI)	Value of the pound against other currencies (index)	Average interest rates (%)
Year 3 (actual)	+1.2	5.6	1.4	100	4.5
Year 4 (forecast)	+2.0	5.5	1.6	98	4.0
Year 5 (forecast)	+4.0	4.4	2.0	90	5.0

Preliminary questions

Total: 45 marks (50 minutes)

1 Define the terms 'recession' and 'recovery' in relation to the business cycle. *(6 marks)*

2 Outline two different ways in which the business cycle has influenced Harewood Ltd. *(6 marks)*

3 Explain why Tessa believed that inflation would not have the same effect on all of Harewood Ltd's products. *(6 marks)*

4 Why are the sales of goods that are price elastic likely to suffer during a period of high inflation? *(5 marks)*

5 Distinguish between cyclical and structural unemployment. *(4 marks)*

6 Consider two ways in which a rise in interest rates might affect Harewood Ltd. *(6 marks)*

7 Explain how a rise in the value of the pound might affect Harewood Ltd. *(6 marks)*

8 Identify and explain two problems for Harewood Ltd of operating in global markets. *(6 marks)*

Case study questions

Total: 40 marks (50 minutes)

1 Consider the implications for Harewood Ltd of the sudden and unpredictable fluctuations of the business cycle during years 1 to 3 and evaluate the strategies it has taken in response. *(10 marks)*

2 To what extent are the globalisation of markets and emerging markets influencing the performance of Harewood Ltd? *(15 marks)*

3 Assess the extent to which the success of Harewood Ltd has been influenced by changes in the economic environment and how the forecast changes in macroeconomic variables are likely to affect the business in the future. *(15 marks)*

Chapter 22

The relationship between businesses and the political and legal environment

This chapter assesses the effects on business of: government intervention in the economy; government economic policies; political decisions affecting trade and access to markets; and the impact of legislation relating to businesses. In relation to government intervention, consideration is given to the provision of products by the government, government regulation and legislation and other forms of intervention, such as tax and subsidy. In relation to government economic policies, monetary policy, fiscal policy and supply-side policies are considered. Political decisions affecting trade and access to markets include the enlargement of the European Union and moves towards greater freedom of trade. The chapter includes a consideration of the scope and impact of the following areas of legislation relating to business: employment, consumer protection, environmental protection and health and safety.

Government intervention in the economy and its effects on business

In general, governments seek to have some control over the business environment in order to achieve a range of economic objectives and to establish an ordered, predictable and equitable (fair) environment. The range of policies used to achieve these objectives includes the provision of products and services by government, economic policies such as monetary and fiscal policy, regulation and legislation, and other forms of intervention such as taxes and subsidies.

EXAMINER'S VOICE

Remember that the issues considered in this chapter should be viewed as part of the external environment of a business. When analysing or evaluating the external environment facing a business, ensure that you make use of the PESTLE framework discussed in Chapter 21. This will encourage you to think about other aspects of the external environment, not just the political and legal environment, which are the focus of this chapter.

KEY TERM

government intervention: policy based on the belief that government should exert a strong influence on the economy, rather than allowing market forces to dictate conditions.

The use of such policies is described as government intervention. Depending on the political values of the government, it may wish to introduce more or less government intervention and leave more or less business decision making to market forces. A complete lack of government intervention is known as a laissez-faire approach.

Examples of intervention that have an effect on businesses are:

- economic policies (e.g. monetary and fiscal, which are considered later in this chapter)
- support for new firms and rescue packages for large manufacturing industries
- regional policies (e.g. the provision, via the EU, of funding to help regenerate areas of high unemployment and social deprivation)
- policies to influence the exchange rate (considered in Chapter 21)
- legislation to provide protection for consumers and workers (considered later in this chapter)
- competition policies (considered later in this chapter)

Support for new firms was considered in the AS textbook in the section 'Starting a business'. Whether a government provides rescue packages for businesses that are struggling will usually depend on how important the business is to the economy and what impact its closure is likely to have on employment both regionally and nationally.

FACT FILE

Government rescue package for the banking industry

On 8 October 2008, the chancellor of the exchequer unveiled a £500 billion rescue package for Britain's battered banking industry. The plan will see the taxpayer take large stakes in the major banks in return for a massive injection of money to prop up their shattered balance sheets. The part-nationalisation comes as a last-ditch effort to prevent the banks from a catastrophic collapse, following another day of hammering on the stock market.

The Treasury announced that the following banks had confirmed they would seek government help under the scheme: Abbey, Barclays, HBOS, HSBC Bank plc, Lloyds TSB, Nationwide Building Society, Royal Bank of Scotland (RBS) and Standard Chartered.

Source: adapted from an article on www.telegraph.co.uk.

KEY TERM

laissez-faire: policy based on the belief that the free market will maximise business efficiency and consumer satisfaction; government therefore tries to avoid interfering in the running of business or any other part of the economy.

The extent to which governments intervene in the economy varies from country to country and also changes over time. For example, most eastern European countries, under their previous communist regimes, were extremely interventionist in their approach but have become more laissez-faire as a result of political changes. In the UK, the trend towards privatisation and deregulation in the 1980s and 1990s was a move towards a more laissez-faire approach.

AQA A2 Business Studies

Most governments in the developed world provide a range of what are considered to be essential products and services, including education, health and housing. The politics of the government of the day will determine the degree of intervention in the economy and hence whether a more extensive range of products and services are provided by, or controlled by, government. For example, before 1979 in the UK a range of vital industries, known as **nationalised industries**, were under government control. These included coal, steel and the railways, and hence these products and services were provided by government.

The election of a Conservative government, led by Margaret Thatcher, in 1979 had a huge impact on the economy and the business environment, and significantly changed business conditions. The changes placed a much greater emphasis on the market with the introduction of an extensive policy of **privatisation and deregulation**, and legislation to reduce the power of trade unions and 'free up the labour market'. Despite the election of a Labour government in 1997, there has been no return to the more interventionist government policy of Labour governments prior to 1979.

Privatisation

The process of privatisation can be viewed as a way of reducing intervention in the economy. A wave of privatisations took place in the UK during the 1980s and 1990s. Examples are:

- contracting out of services, such as refuse collection, which were previously run by government or local authorities, to private sector organisations
- deregulation or the removal of restrictions that prevent competition — for example, in the provision of bus services
- the transfer of nationalised industries such as British Telecom (BT), British Gas, British Airways and British Rail into public limited companies, by the sale of shares to the public
- the sale of government-owned assets

> **KEY TERM**
>
> **privatisation:** when state-run industries and state-owned assets are returned or sold to the private sector.

Privatised organisations are owned by shareholders rather than the government, and are therefore likely to pursue different objectives from those of nationalised industries or public-sector organisations. In favour of privatisation is the fact that the introduction of competition and the reduction in bureaucracy is likely to improve efficiency. In addition, competition will provide consumers with more choice. The impact of privatisation depends on how much competition is created and how well regulated the industry is. Recognising the need for regulation, the government established regulatory bodies (watchdogs), such as Ofgem (gas and electricity), Ofwat (water) and Ofcom (communications), to prevent privatised monopolies exploiting their markets. These watchdogs have responsibility for:

- monitoring behaviour and pricing
- setting performance standards
- allowing or forbidding new entrants to the industry

FACT FILE

Nationalised industries

The opposite of privatisation is nationalisation, which describes the transfer of firms and industries from the private sector to the public sector. Interestingly, most of the nationalised industries that were privatised in the 1980s — for example, the railways, steelmaking and coalmining — were originally failing private sector industries that were nationalised after the end of the Second World War.

When a whole industry is taken into public ownership, it usually becomes a monopoly. Monopolies face little pressure to stay efficient and may allow their costs to rise more than if they faced strong competition. The losses of nationalised industries are carried by the government and ultimately by the taxpayer.

More than 60 years later, in 2008, the government has intervened again to rescue the banking sector from near collapse by part-nationalising it via a huge injection of cash (see the Fact File on p. 358).

PRACTICE EXERCISE 1   Total: 35 marks (30 minutes)

1 Distinguish between interventionist and laissez-faire approaches
   to government policy.   (6 marks)

2 Identify and explain two examples of government intervention
   that have an effect on business.   (6 marks)

3 Distinguish between nationalisation and privatisation in relation
   to government policy.   (6 marks)

4 Give two examples of privatisation.   (2 marks)

5 Explain, with examples, how the privatised businesses that were
   previously nationalised industries are regulated.   (6 marks)

6 Explain two arguments in favour of privatisation.   (6 marks)

7 Explain one argument against privatisation.   (3 marks)

Government economic policies and their effects on business

Economic policy involves efforts by the government to control the economy in order to achieve its objectives. Key economic objectives that most governments try to achieve are:

- encouraging economic growth
- controlling and reducing inflation
- maintaining a satisfactory level of employment
- achieving a satisfactory balance of payments
- maintaining a stable exchange rate

Table 22.1 illustrates the UK's achievement in each of these areas over the last 5 years.

	2004	2005	2006	2007	2008
Economic growth (%)	2.3	2.0	3.0	3.0	0.3
Inflation (CPI) (%)	1.3	2.1	2.3	2.3	4.9
Unemployment (%)	2.8	4.7	5.5	5.3	5.8
Current account* (£bn)	−25.2	−32.6	−45.0	−39.5	−36.0
Exchange rate (€/£)	1.47	1.46	1.47	1.46	1.20
Exchange rate ($/£)	1.83	1.82	1.84	2.00	1.53

Table 22.1 UK economic indicators, 2004–08

*See the Did You Know? box for an explanation of this term.
Source: **www.statistics.gov.uk**.

DID YOU KNOW?

The balance of payments is a record of transactions between one country and the rest of the world. It records exports and imports as well as transfers of income and assets.

An important part of the balance of payments is the **current account**, which includes:
- trade in goods (also known as the **balance of trade** or the **visible balance**), which records exports of goods minus imports of goods
- trade in services (or the **invisible balance**), which records exports of services minus imports of services
- the balance of income going to and coming from abroad, such as interest, profits and dividends, together with transfers such as UK government payments to the EU or gifts

The current balance shown in Table 22.1 is the total of the current account. Traditionally, the UK has a deficit on its trade in goods, which is compensated for by a surplus on its trade in services. However, as can be seen in Table 22.1, this has not been the case in recent years.

A major problem in managing the economy is the degree of trade-off between these economic objectives. For example, in a boom, GDP and the level of employment will both be growing. But inflation will also be accelerating and the generally high level of demand may suck in more imports. On the other hand, during a recession, inflation will usually slow down and exports may rise as businesses seek foreign markets, but growth will be sluggish and unemployment is likely to rise.

Macroeconomic policy is the government's attempt to influence the level of demand in the economy as a whole: that is, in the macroeconomy. It works primarily through **monetary policy** (such as the impact of interest rates) and **fiscal policy** (that is, the impact of government tax and expenditure changes). The choice of economic policies depends on the priorities of the government of the day and the particular objectives it wishes to pursue. Since the 1990s, most governments, regardless of their politics, have been concerned to keep inflation down.

A major problem in using economic policy is timing. By the time the government has identified the problem and decided on appropriate policies, the original problem may either have disappeared or have got a lot worse.

Thus, in thinking about the effect of economic policies, and particularly macroeconomic policies, it should always be remembered that such policies will work with a time lag or delay.

Monetary policy

KEY TERM

monetary policy:
controlling the money supply and the rate of interest in order to influence the level of spending and demand in the economy.

In recent years, the emphasis of economic policy has been on controlling interest rates. Interest rates can be changed more easily and more quickly than rates of taxation, with decisions about interest rates being made each month by the Monetary Policy Committee of the Bank of England. In addition, in comparison with taxation and government spending, which can be targeted to influence particular groups, interest rates have a blanket effect on the economy. In fact, a single change in interest rates has a complex array of effects on the economy.

e EXAMINER'S VOICE

Refer back to Chapter 21 to ensure that you understand the possible implications of a change in interest rates.

Initial changes in monetary policy have multiplier effects on business and the economy. For example, increasing interest rates to stop inflation from rising may throw the economy into recession. Falling demand will cause businesses to cut production. People may be made redundant and their incomes will then fall. They will spend less, which will cause demand to fall further in a downward spiral. Before long, the problem of inflation will give way to unemployment and slow or non-existent economic growth. Interest rates then need to fall in order to encourage spending; taxes need to fall and government spending needs to rise.

Fiscal policy

e EXAMINER'S VOICE

Remember that interest rates have a significant impact on the exchange rate.

Taxation allows the government to raise revenue and to influence demand by placing a charge on goods, services or income. It is a withdrawal of money from the economy, in that it tends to reduce total spending and demand. In contrast, government expenditure is an injection of money into the economy and thus tends to increase total spending and demand.

KEY TERM

fiscal policy:
the use of taxation and government expenditure to influence the economy.

DID YOU KNOW?

Government expenditure includes subsidies, i.e. financial assistance provided by government to business. Subsidies are usually paid to support businesses that might otherwise fail (for example, motor manufacturers in 2009), or to encourage business activity that would otherwise not take place (for example, to encourage businesses to set up in areas of high unemployment).

e EXAMINER'S VOICE

Injections and withdrawals are part of the circular flow of income that was discussed in Chapter 21.

There are two main categories of taxation: **direct taxation** and **indirect taxation**.

Direct taxes are taxes on incomes or profits. Households pay income tax, while businesses pay corporation tax. Direct taxes are usually levied as a proportion of income or profit, so as more income or profit is earned, proportionately more tax is paid.

Indirect taxes are taxes on spending. Value added tax (VAT), at the rate of 15%, is charged on almost every product and service sold, with the supplier paying this 15% VAT to the government. Petrol, cigarettes and alcohol all have an additional tax, known as excise duty, imposed upon them by the chancellor of the exchequer.

WHAT DO YOU THINK?

In 1978, the highest rate of UK income tax was 83%, levied on income above £24,000 a year. For people on the highest incomes, for every additional £1 they earned above £24,000, the government took 83p in income tax, leaving them with 17p. What might be the justification for such a rate, and what impact is it likely to have?

DID YOU KNOW?

Taxes can be proportional, progressive or regressive:
- A **proportional tax** is one that takes the same proportion of someone's income regardless of how much they earn.
- A **progressive tax** takes a larger proportion of someone's income the more they earn. Income tax is an example of a progressive tax because the rate levied on the lowest income levels is less than that levied on higher incomes. In 2008, the rates were 20% and 40%.
- A **regressive tax** is one that takes a larger proportion of someone's income the less they earn. Flat-rate taxes, such as VAT, are regressive. For example, an individual earning £1,500 per month who purchases a television costing £400, on which £60 of VAT is added, is paying 4% of their monthly income in VAT. On the other hand, someone earning £6,000 per month who purchases the same product is paying only 1% of his or her monthly income in VAT.

FACT FILE

A reduction in VAT

On 1 December 2008, the government reduced the rate of VAT from 17.5% to 15% in order to boost consumer spending and alleviate the effects of recession. 15% VAT is the lowest rate allowed under EU law. The rate is expected to revert to 17.5% on 1 January 2010. In the case of alcohol, tobacco and petrol, the reduction in VAT is offset by a rise in excise duty.

FACT FILE

Taxation on cigarettes

Tax is levied on cigarettes in three ways: specific excise duty of approximately £100 per 1,000 cigarettes; an 'ad valorem' excise duty of 22% of the total retail price; and VAT at 15% of the price including the other taxes. On a typical pack of 20 cigarettes, the total tax burden of about £4.33 accounts for 76% of the recommended retail price (RRP) of £5.66, and on some of the least expensive brands the total tax burden accounts for up to 90% of the RRP.

Fiscal policy is also known as **budgetary policy** and is the responsibility of the chancellor of the exchequer.
- A **budget surplus** is where taxation is greater than government spending. Thus, more money is being withdrawn from the circular flow than is being injected into it. As a result, overall spending and demand in the economy will be reduced, leading to a fall in economic activity.
- A **budget deficit** is where government spending is greater than taxation. It means that overall spending and demand are likely to increase, leading to a rise in economic activity.

- A **balanced budget** is when taxation is equal to government spending. Overall spending and demand in the economy remain unchanged, although specific industries and areas may see changes in economic activity.

Initial changes in fiscal policy, such as a change in tax rates or a change in government expenditure, have further **multiplier effects** on business and the economy. For example, an increase in indirect taxation may lead to an increase in the price of goods and a subsequent reduction in demand. This may in turn lead to a cutback in production and, in the extreme, redundancies, triggering a further fall in demand. An increase in income tax will reduce disposable income and thus lower demand.

Governments use fiscal policy in various ways. For example, in a recession, government could try to boost demand in the economy by reducing taxes because this should leave firms and households with more money and so encourage spending. This is why the government reduced the rate of VAT by 2.5 percentage points in autumn 2008. Alternatively, government spending could be increased, which will, in turn, increase demand for goods and services.

The impact of an increase in taxation depends on how much it has been increased, which taxes have been increased and whether consumers and firms are sensitive to such changes and react as expected. Taxes cannot be changed as often or as easily as interest rates, since tax changes are usually announced in the annual budget statement produced by the chancellor of the exchequer. However, compared with interest rates, taxation and government spending can provide the flexibility to target certain products or affect certain types of behaviour more specifically. In this sense, changes in tax and government expenditure can be a very effective way of influencing demand.

Because a tax increase effectively reduces the spending power of taxpayers, it can be used selectively to target particular groups of people or types of spending. For example:
- to increase incentives for people to set up their own businesses, corporation tax for small firms could be reduced
- to encourage consumer spending, the rate of VAT can be reduced, leading to a reduction in prices
- to deter people from using leaded petrol and thus to reduce environmental pollution, excise duty on leaded petrol can be increased, making it more expensive
- to redistribute wealth from the well-off to the less well-off, higher rates of income tax could be increased and the bottom rate could be reduced or the starting point for paying it increased

Impact of monetary and fiscal policies on the economy and business

Tracking through the business cycle illustrates how both fiscal and monetary policies affect the economy and business.

During a period of recession, growth can be encouraged by allowing demand to increase. Keeping interest rates down, reducing taxes and increasing government expenditure will all have this effect:

- Low interest rates encourage investment and consumer spending.
- Tax cuts give people more spending power.
- Government spending has multiplier implications throughout the economy. For example, the building of a new hospital involves the employment of builders and eventually of medical staff, who have incomes that they will spend in the local economy. Suppliers of raw materials will receive additional demand that may have favourable effects on their financial position, and so on.

When the economy is booming, symptoms of 'overheating' may start to appear, such as high inflation and shortages of skilled labour. Governments, faced with accelerating inflation and rising imports, want to reduce the rate at which demand is growing. They will focus on how to reduce the level of demand by restricting consumer and government spending. Reducing the level of demand to cut inflationary pressures can be done by increasing interest rates and/or increasing taxes and/or reducing government expenditure.

Of course, reduced demand and a cut in the level of spending will eventually lead to a reduction in investment, which may lead to reduced productivity and competitiveness, and also to unemployment.

Other economic policies

In addition to fiscal and monetary policy, government can introduce other economic policies depending on the economic circumstances:

Supply-side policies

Monetary and fiscal policies are known as **demand-side policies** because they influence the overall level of demand in the economy. Since the early 1980s, most governments have been strongly in favour of encouraging markets to work efficiently at a micro level. Policies to encourage this have become collectively known as **supply-side policies**. Most supply-side policies focus on particular parts of the economy rather than the economy as whole. Their underlying objective is to make markets work in ways that optimise the level of output. Examples are measures that allow the labour market to function efficiently by reducing the power of trade unions and improving incentives for people to find and retain jobs. In addition, measures have been introduced to raise the efficiency of business by improving access to education and training, by increasing competition, and by privatisation and deregulation (discussed earlier in this chapter).

Protectionism

This is the extent to which the government uses controls to restrict the amount of imports entering the country. The UK's position on this is determined by its membership of the EU, which has a policy of free trade among member countries and a common external tariff barrier for goods and services coming from non-member countries (see Fact File on protectionism on p. 374).

PRACTICE EXERCISE 2   30 marks (25 minutes)

1 List three of the government's main economic objectives. *(3 marks)*

2 Distinguish between the use of fiscal policy and monetary policy in attempting to influence the level of demand in the economy. *(6 marks)*

3 Explain three ways in which a rise in interest rates might affect a business. *(9 marks)*

4 Explain how a rise in the rates of income tax, corporation tax and VAT might affect a business. *(9 marks)*

5 What is meant by the term 'supply-side policies'? *(3 marks)*

CASE STUDY 1   Economic policies to improve the economy

Early in November 2008, the Bank of England's Monetary Policy Committee reduced interest rates to 3%. The Governor of the Bank of England, Mervyn King, warned that monetary policy alone would not be a sufficient response to the economic downturn and that fiscal measures would also be necessary.

In November 2008, the chancellor of the exchequer announced a £20 billion fiscal stimulus for the economy. This included a temporary reduction in the main rate of VAT from 17.5% to 15% to take effect from 1 December 2008 until 1 January 2010. Mervyn King said that it would be difficult to assess how well this fiscal stimulus was working until later in 2009:

'One of the impacts of the temporary cut in VAT is likely to be that during the second half of 2009 there will be a lot of advertisements saying buy now before VAT goes back up again in January 2010.' Commentators have mixed views on the potential for the cut in the rate of VAT to encourage consumer spending, particularly because firms are already engaged in very heavy discounting to encourage consumers to buy their products.

In early December 2008, the Monetary Policy Committee announced a further cut in interest rates to 2%.

Source: adapted from various items on www.telegraph.co.uk.

Preliminary questions   Total: 20 marks (25 minutes)

1 Outline two different ways in which a reduction in the rate of interest to 2% is likely to have a favourable impact on a business of your choice. *(6 marks)*

2 Explain how a reduction in interest rates and a reduction in the rate of VAT are together expected to stimulate the level of demand in the economy. *(6 marks)*

3 Consider how a reduction in income tax and in corporation tax might affect business. *(8 marks)*

Case study questions   Total: 40 marks (50 minutes)

1 Analyse the likely impact of a reduction in VAT and a reduction in interest rates on UK retailers of price- and income-elastic goods and services during a recession. *(10 marks)*

2 Assess the possible responses of a business selling price- and income-elastic goods and services to a reduction in VAT and a reduction in interest rates. *(15 marks)*

3 Discuss the range of economic policies available to a government and suggest what actions it might take in response to a recession. *(15 marks)*

CASE STUDY 2 The car industry

April 2005

Almost 5,000 MG Rover workers were made redundant and a further 2,000 manufacturing jobs at component suppliers were lost, following the collapse of the car maker, which was losing £25 million a month.

If a similar situation had arisen in the 1960s and 1970s, with the closure of a major car factory, then either a Labour or Conservative government would have intervened with subsidies to keep production going. That was done by the Wilson (Labour), Heath (Conservative), Callaghan (Labour) and Thatcher (Conservative) governments in various sectors. The results were almost universally bad in the medium to long term, as most of the jobs were eventually lost and taxpayers paid out billions of pounds.

But governments no longer pretend they can guarantee specific jobs and in this case there appeared to have been a general acceptance that there was no easy alternative on offer. So when the crunch came, the government accepted that closure could not be avoided and concentrated on helping to cushion the immediate pain, while assisting with retraining schemes and helping to create jobs in a new industrial park.

The closure of Rover was an example of how far UK industry and government policy had changed over the last 30 years.

December 2008

The UK recession in late 2008 has led to a significant fall in demand for cars. As a result, ministers are set to unveil a limited aid package as fears grow over tens of thousands of job losses in the industry.

Senior car-industry executives told the *Sunday Times* that they feared the worst if substantial aid was not forthcoming before Christmas. 'There will have to be layoffs and there is a real danger of the collapse of component makers, who are finding it more and more difficult to get funding,' said one. The GMB trade union fears that at least 25% of all car-making jobs will be lost in the economic downturn if help from the government is not forthcoming. The UK car industry has an annual turnover of about £50 billion and car making directly employs some 190,000 people, but the industry as whole, once the components and retail sector are taken into account, indirectly supports 850,000 jobs.

Source: adapted from articles in *The Times*, 16 April 2005 and at www.timesonline.co.uk.

Questions   Total: 40 marks (50 minutes)

1 On the basis of the information in the case study, outline the supply-side policies that appear to have been used in relation to the car industry.   *(10 marks)*

2 With reference to the car industry, to what extent is government intervention in the economy a good thing?   *(15 marks)*

3 Discuss the range of economic policies available to government and how successful these might be in averting the potential collapse of the car industry suggested in the December 2008 article.   *(15 marks)*

Political decisions affecting trade and access to markets and their effects on business

The European Union

A vision of a new Europe began to emerge at the conclusion of the Second World War in 1945. The objective was to unite the economies of Europe and thereby overcome long-established national rivalries.

In 1957, Belgium, the Netherlands, Luxembourg, Italy, France and West Germany signed the Treaty of Rome, which established the European Economic Community (EEC). The six members of the EEC formed a **free trade area** with no trade barriers between member states, and a **customs union** in the form of a common external tariff barrier that was levied on goods and services from non-member countries. The six members enjoyed strong economic growth, which encouraged the UK, Ireland (Eire) and Denmark to join this free trade area in 1973.

The next stage of development was a **common market** with the free movement of all factors of production across national boundaries. In 1986, an agreement between member states of the common market, which by then was known as the European Community (EC), committed them to the creation of a **single market** by the end of 1992.

Key elements of the single market were:
- the creation of common technical standards for EU products
- the harmonisation of VAT and excise duties, ending tax advantages resulting from locating in a particular EU country
- the free movement of people — EU citizens are allowed to travel, reside, study and work wherever they wish in the European Union
- a reduction in customs posts and the paperwork necessary for trade within the EU
- the free movement of capital, making it possible to invest money anywhere in the EU
- the ending of duty-free sales within the EU in 1999

The Maastricht Treaty was signed by all the member states and took effect on 1 November 1993. This treaty created the European Union with the aim of developing even greater unity between member countries and, particularly, introducing **monetary union** and a **single European currency**. By 1995, there were 15 members of the EU after Austria, Finland, Greece, Portugal, Spain and Sweden had joined.

In May 2004, the EU was expanded to 25 member states when ten new countries joined, mainly from eastern Europe. These new members were Cyprus, the Czech Republic, Estonia, Hungary, Latvia, Lithuania, Malta, Poland, Slovakia and Slovenia. In 2007, Bulgaria and Romania joined the EU, making a total of 27 member countries. Figure 22.1 shows the 27 members of the enlarged EU.

Figure 22.1
The 27 members of the European Union

Implications of the EU for business

In general terms, the value to a British firm of the UK being a member of the EU depends on the extent to which the firm trades with other member countries and with countries outside the EU, such as the USA. General benefits for British firms of the UK's membership are that it is easier to trade within the EU because there are no barriers, and that firms have access to more customers, bringing opportunities for economies of scale. On the other hand, the UK cannot use protectionist policies such as tariffs on imports against firms from other EU countries, UK firms are subject to EU legislation and the UK has to impose tariffs against firms from countries outside the EU.

Positive implications of the EU for UK business

Membership of the EU offers the following benefits to businesses in the UK:

- There is access to a market of 495 million people, which is bigger than Japan and the USA put together.
- The large market provides opportunities for economies of scale, lower costs and increased specialisation.
- More competition may lead to improved efficiency and therefore lower costs.
- More intense competition can encourage innovation.
- There are opportunities for more European mergers and joint ventures, resulting in synergy and improved efficiency.
- There is encouragement for inward investment from non-EU countries, which increases employment, income and opportunities for supplier industries. The UK has been a major recipient of this, with firms like Toyota in Derby and Nissan in Sunderland establishing themselves within the external tariff wall.
- There is greater mobility of labour, giving firms a wider labour force to draw on.
- With firms more able to invest anywhere in the EU, there is greater mobility of capital.
- The free movement of factors of production makes it possible for existing EU (and UK) businesses to move to new EU countries where costs are substantially lower. Some firms, such as Volkswagen, have already made the move east.

FACT FILE

Foreign workers

With the UK experiencing a labour market skills shortage in some areas, there were several instances of UK employers deliberately seeking to take advantage of EU enlargement to solve their recruitment difficulties. For example, BUPA Care Homes recruited carers from Poland, the Czech Republic and Lithuania, while First Group, the UK's largest bus operator, recruited drivers from Poland.

Negative implications of the EU for UK business

The UK's membership of the EU presents the following difficulties for firms in the UK:

- There is an increase in legislation and the need to meet common technical standards.
- There is increased competition both in Europe and in the domestic market.
- Labour and capital may be attracted to other European countries.
- Low wage rates in countries such as Poland, where average salaries are only 18% of the EU average, will make these new EU members fierce competitors for jobs, and they may attract inward investment that might previously have come to the UK.

FACT FILE

UK investment in Slovakia

The UK is the sixth largest investor in Slovakia. One major investment was the acquisition by Tesco of seven department stores in 1996, and the more recent major development of a chain of hypermarkets. Tesco is now the top retailer in Slovakia, and one of the main employers in the country. Other major UK investors are Shell, Provident Financial, CP Holdings and Tate & Lyle. Next, Mothercare and Accessorize are among the established and well-known franchises that have recently opened stores in the capital, Bratislava.

Source: Foreign and Commonwealth Office website, www.fco.gov.uk.

FACT FILE

The Social Chapter

The Social Chapter is an element of the Maastricht Treaty signed by the 12 members of the EU in 1992. The intention of the Social Chapter is to harmonise working conditions throughout the EU and to ensure that all workers are guaranteed the basic rights to:

- join a trade union
- take industrial action
- be consulted and informed about company plans
- equal treatment for men and women
- a minimum wage and a maximum working week of 48 hours
- a minimum of 4 weeks' paid holiday per year

In addition, the Social Chapter contains provisions relating to redundancies and seeks to encourage employee participation and consultation (see the Fact File on the Information and Consultation Directive on p. 281). Table 22.2 illustrates the main business arguments for and against the Social Chapter. In 1997, the UK adopted the provisions of the Social Chapter.

Table 22.2 The Social Chapter: for and against

Arguments in favour of the Social Chapter	Arguments against the Social Chapter
• Better worker motivation, improving efficiency and productivity.	• Rising labour costs as a result of reduced working hours and increasing pay rates.
• Improved industrial relations as a result of increased participation and consultation.	• Higher costs make it more difficult to compete against non-EU producers.
• If all EU countries sign the Social Chapter, there will be a level playing field and none will be at a disadvantage.	• Firms will be affected differently; some countries have a tradition of shorter working weeks and higher pay.

WHAT DO YOU THINK?

Countries outside the EU do not guarantee the rights included in the EU's Social Chapter. Many EU-based multinationals choose to locate in countries like India and China rather than the countries of the EU. Is this morally right?

The single European currency: the euro

On 1 January 1999, the euro was introduced as the single European currency. On that date, the currencies of the 11 countries adopting the euro were fixed permanently to each other. Greece adopted the euro in 2001. At the same time as the single currency was introduced, the European Central Bank took control of interest rates across those countries that had adopted the euro (known as the eurozone).

Today, the euro is used by more than 320 million Europeans in 16 countries of the EU. These countries are: Austria, Belgium, Cyprus, Finland, France, Germany, Greece, Ireland, Italy, Luxembourg, Malta, Netherlands, Portugal, Slovakia, Slovenia and Spain. Slovakia was the latest EU country to join the euro on 1 January 2009). Lithuania is expected to join the euro in 2010 and Estonia in 2011. Original members of the EU that decided not to convert to the euro include the UK, Denmark and Sweden. Other newer EU member countries are working toward becoming part of the eurozone.

If the UK were to adopt the euro, there would be some short-term problems such as the transition costs of new electronic tills, computer software and staff training. However, a single currency and a common interest rate would make trading with the EU much easier and cheaper. UK business might benefit in several ways:

- There would be no exchange rate **transaction costs**, i.e. commission charges when exchanging pounds for euros.
- There would be no uncertainty due to exchange rate changes (e.g. in relation to export earnings or costs of imported raw materials). This is likely to encourage trade and make financial forecasting more accurate.
- There would be no need to use expensive futures contracts to insure against exchange rate changes.
- There would be price transparency, making it easier for consumers and producers to compare prices within the eurozone.
- A single currency and common interest rates might encourage firms to operate in a wider market, with expansion bringing the benefits of economies of scale.
- New and improved sources of supply, previously considered too risky, might become viable once exchange rate fluctuations no longer occurred.
- Investment from the rest of the world might increase as a single currency makes trade with a large market simple and relatively cheap. There have been occasional comments from the chief executives of some multinational companies operating in the UK that they would prefer to be located within the eurozone.

FACT FILE

How advantageous is the euro?

In 2000, Toyota insisted that its UK suppliers put their invoices in euros. This removed Toyota's exchange rate risk and passed it on to the suppliers, which incurred costs in one currency (pounds) and received revenue in another currency (euros).

Despite these benefits, it must be remembered that at least 40% of the UK's overseas trade is conducted outside the EU. This means that there are many firms which, if the UK adopted the euro, would not benefit from the reduced costs of trade with Europe, and which would still face exchange rate issues when they traded with countries outside the eurozone.

The impact of political change in central and eastern Europe

The fall of the communist governments in central and eastern Europe (CEE) in the late 1980s and the 1990s had major implications for businesses in the UK and the rest of Europe. In most cases, the new governments wanted to replace the old centrally planned systems, which were thought to be inefficient, with market-based systems. As a result, many of these countries have undertaken huge privatisation policies and, in the early years of this process, recruited experts from the UK and other western economies to advise on the transfer of assets from the public to the private sector. Opportunities and constraints in these new emerging markets were discussed in Chapter 21.

In many cases, governments are keen to attract western European businesses to locate in these economies and do this by providing tax advantages and government funding. For example, in Estonia some company taxes have been as low as 0% in order to attract foreign investment, and in Slovakia, government subsidies of over £200 million were provided to US Steel when it located in the country.

Businesses in the EU have sought to take advantage of the CEE markets in a number of ways:

- **Joint ventures** — where EU firms contribute cash, machinery and management skills, while the host country provides land, buildings and labour. As wages and rents are lower, and in some cases controls on production and pollution are less stringent, EU firms gain a low-cost means of production and access to a relatively untapped market.
- **Technical cooperation**, which allows some co-production, short of a formal joint venture. Such agreements might encompass joint assembly of products or the creation of assembly plants in the host countries near to potential markets, as with Volvo cars in Hungary. This reduces production costs for Western producers, while offering eastern firms technical expertise.
- **Selling technology and expertise** to producers in CEE countries, often in the form of licences to produce particular products. For example, Coca-Cola has granted a licence to allow manufacture in Bulgaria, which provides a cheap method of extending its market.

Moves towards greater freedom of trade

As noted earlier, the European Union is an example of a **free trade area**, that is, a group of countries that agree to trade with each other without erecting any barriers to trade. This encourages competition between firms in the different member countries and, as a result, fosters greater efficiency in the delivery of goods and services and lower prices for consumers.

As well as the EU, there are other free trade areas in the world, including ASEAN (Association of Southeast Asian Nations), AFTZ (African Free Trade Zone), NAFTA (North American Free Trade Agreement) and SAFTA (South Asia Free Trade Area). In addition to these well-defined areas of free trade, there are ongoing developments globally towards greater freedom of trade. The World Trade Organization (WTO) is a group of over 153 countries that are committed to the encouragement of free and fair international trade through the elimination of trade barriers. It aims to ensure that 'trade flows as smoothly, predictably and freely as possible'.

FACT FILE

Protectionism

Import controls, or protectionist policies, are used to limit the number of overseas goods entering domestic markets. Import controls take a number of different forms.

Tariffs

Tariffs are taxes imposed on imported goods. In general, the imposition of tariffs leads to an increase in the price of the imported good and, depending on price elasticity of demand, is likely to lead to a reduction in demand, making cheaper domestic goods more attractive to consumers. Import tariffs are banned between members of the EU, but a common external tariff is imposed on imports from non-EU countries.

Two types of tariff can be levied:
- an ad valorem tax, which is a percentage added to the price of the imported good, such as 10% added to the price of all imported goods, regardless of whether they are priced at £10 or £1,000
- a specific duty added to the price of the imported good, such as £2 per item added to the price of all imported goods, regardless of whether the good is valued at £10 or £1,000

Quotas

Quotas are a form of import protection that limits the sales of foreign goods to a specified quantity (e.g. 1 million pairs of shoes), value (e.g. £50 million worth of products) or market share (e.g. no more than 10% of the total market for the good).

Non-tariff barriers

Non-tariff barriers are more subtle controls that are imposed by governments because they wish to restrict imports without being seen to do so, perhaps because it would be contrary to international regulation under the World Trade Organization. Such barriers may take several forms, including:
- constantly changing technical regulations, which make compliance difficult for importers
- forcing importers to use specified points of entry where documentation is dealt with only slowly
- introducing regulations that favour domestic production — for example, packaging and labels that conform to local language requirements

Embargos

An embargo is an order forbidding trade with a particular country, perhaps imposed by the United Nations against a country that has broken international laws or conventions.

PRACTICE EXERCISE 3   Total: 45 marks (40 minutes)

1 How many countries make up the European Union (EU)? *(1 mark)*

2 Identify and explain three benefits of the EU for UK businesses. *(9 marks)*

3 Explain the significance of a free trade area and a customs union, such as that provided by the EU, for a business, based in the UK, that buys its supplies from businesses outside Europe and sells its products within the EU. *(9 marks)*

4 Outline why a UK business might benefit if the UK were to adopt the euro. *(5 marks)*

5 What is a joint venture? *(3 marks)*

6 Explain one advantage and one constraint for UK firms that wish to do business in CEE countries. *(6 marks)*

7 Distinguish between ad valorem and specific duty tariffs. *(4 marks)*

8 What is a quota in relation to import controls? *(3 marks)*

9 Give two examples of non-tariff barriers, excluding quotas. *(2 marks)*

10 State the purpose of the World Trade Organization. *(3 marks)*

CASE STUDY 3 Slovakia

A report from the World Bank in 2004 suggested that Slovakia was one of the countries that had improved its business climate the most during 2003. It had cut the time needed to start a business, revamped labour laws, reduced red tape and made it easier for firms to collect debts. As a result, growth had picked up and the black economy had shrunk.

Helping to drive the reform in Slovakia, as well as in a number of other European nations, was the lure of European Union membership. One of the ten new entrants that joined in May 2004, Slovakia needed to bring its domestic regulation in line with EU standards and ensure that companies were prepared for the increase in competition that was likely to follow once a member of the EU: foreign companies rushing to take advantage of its low labour costs and well-educated workforce.

Among the pioneering foreign firms that established themselves in Slovakia were the American giant US Steel and the German car-maker Volkswagen. Both played a major role in transforming Slovakia's image abroad.

US STEEL KOSICE 2005

Volkswagen established a plant in Slovakia in 1991, turning a decaying and obsolete Skoda car parts factory near Bratislava into a huge, state-of-the-art production line, employing 8,000 people. The company now accounts for over 25% of Slovakia's exports.

Its success prompted its rivals Peugeot Citroën and Hyundai to start setting up their own factories there. Slovakia's economic fortunes are now so closely tied up with those of the automotive sector that some analysts are becoming concerned. If there is a slowdown in the industry, Slovakia could be badly hit.

US Steel bought its plant in 1999, after the collapse of the state-owned Eastern Slovakian Iron Works. The deal included government subsidies worth £240 million over 10 years. In exchange, US Steel agreed to safeguard the jobs of the 16,000 workers it inherited in the deal. The company is now the largest employer in Slovakia, and in a region where unemployment exceeds 20%, its presence is vital.

It is clear that both Volkswagen and US Steel enjoy the benefits of very low labour costs and low taxes in Slovakia, as well as growing markets in eastern Europe. But there are strong signs that both firms take their responsibilities seriously, and believe that their interests are best served by Slovakia's increased prosperity.

Volkswagen has deliberately recruited from outside the relatively wealthy Bratislava region, bussing in workers every day from less prosperous areas up to 200 kilometres away. It has also chosen to take on a great many younger workers, aged between 20 and 35.

US Steel, as the dominant economic force in the eastern region, also takes an interest in general welfare. It sponsors badly needed educational and infrastructural projects throughout the region. It has also spent significant amounts of money reducing the pollution caused by the plant's ageing mills, investing heavily in new and more efficient technologies. All this has helped win the companies a degree of popular support in Slovakia.

There is no doubt that US Steel and Volkswagen have done well out of their investments in Slovakia. Both companies say their plants are now very profitable. In return, there is equally no doubt that their presence helped to tip the balance in favour of Slovakia's entry into the EU — and has provided a lead that other foreign companies are now eagerly following.

Source: adapted from a range of articles over a period of time in the press and at www.bbc.co.uk.

Questions

Total: 30 marks (40 minutes)

1 Discuss the opportunities and constraints that political changes in Slovakia and other central and eastern European countries might offer to a UK manufacturer of car components. *(15 marks)*

2 The EU now has 27 member countries, including Slovakia. To what extent is this enlarged membership beneficial to a UK motor manufacturer that sells it products in the UK, in Europe and to the rest of the world? *(15 marks)*

EXAMINER'S VOICE

The AQA A2 Business Studies specification suggests that 'a broad understanding' of the scope of legislation and its impact on business is 'all that is required'. Thus although detailed knowledge of particular pieces of legislation is not required for the examination, explanations of relevant legislation are given here in order to provide background understanding of the issues involved.

The impact of legislation relating to businesses

In general, legislation and regulations are intended to protect those with weaker bargaining power: for example, individual employees working in, or individual customers purchasing from, large firms. In turn, the impact of legislation reduces the possibility of a firm exploiting its customers or its employees through unfair practices.

Regulations enable businesses to operate in an environment that ensures a level playing field: where companies must publish their accounts, where creditors have legal rights if debts are not paid, and so on. Legislation, whether related to employment, consumers, the environment, health and safety or competition issues, assists this process. Laws ensure that employees are treated fairly, that consumers receive a fair deal, that firms pay due attention to the impact of their actions on the environment, that products meet health and safety standards and that competition between firms is fair. In this sense, regulation and legislation ensure a more ordered and predictable environment, and one that is fairer for all parties concerned.

> **DID YOU KNOW?**
>
> The legal system of the European Union takes priority over national legislation. EU regulations are directly binding on all member states without the need for national legislation to put them in place.
>
>
>
> European Union directives are instructions from the EU to member countries. These usually require each country to pass legislation through its own parliament so that there is 'harmonisation' (i.e. the same laws in each country). In practice, different countries do not always pass identical laws, as interpretation may vary.

Employment legislation

Employment legislation falls into two broad categories: individual employment law, which aims to ensure that employees and employers act fairly in dealing with each other; and collective labour law, which aims to control industrial relations and trade union activity.

Individual employment law

Race Relations Acts, 1968 and 1976

These make it unlawful to discriminate in the workplace against any person on grounds of colour, race, ethnic or national origin. Specifically, the Acts make it unlawful to refuse employment, training or promotion on these grounds, or to select someone for dismissal on grounds of race. The Commission for Racial Equality (CRE) was given the responsibility to ensure the effective implementation of the Race Relations Act, 1976. Its key duties are to work towards the elimination of discrimination and to promote equality of opportunity.

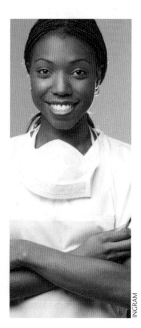

Equal Pay Act, 1970

This requires employers to provide equal pay and conditions for those doing the same jobs, or work of equivalent difficulty. This has had some effect in narrowing the pay gap between men and women, although it was not until the European Union's Equal Pay Directive of 1975 that the principle of equal pay being given for work of equal value was firmly established. This regulation, for example, enabled shop workers to claim successfully that operating cash-tills (a job performed mainly by women) is as valuable and demanding as working in a warehouse (performed mainly by men). Despite many successes, however, women's pay currently remains significantly below that of men. In 2008, the average weekly wage for women was approximately 77% of that for men.

Sex Discrimination Acts, 1975 and 1986

The 1975 Act forbade discrimination in the workplace against either sex in relation to recruitment, terms and conditions, and access to training or promotion. It also set up the Equal Opportunities Commission to promote the ideas and practices required to eliminate sex discrimination in education, advertising and employment. Despite the existence of this Act, the difficulty of obtaining legal proof of discrimination has meant that discrimination still persists. As with other issues of social responsibility, the passing of laws cannot provide a substitute for ethical behaviour.

The 1986 Act enables a common retirement date to be imposed on men and women. This is to be 65.

FACT FILE

Sex discrimination in practice

A former human resources manager for manufacturing company Barco, who claimed her job was worth the same as the male financial controllers, received £19,000 compensation in an out-of-court settlement. Her case was supported by the Equal Opportunities Commission (EOC).

Avril Johnson, who had worked for Barco for more than 9 years, was paid £8,000 less than the financial controller. She also missed out on the annual bonus he received, was allocated fewer share options, and was the only member of the management team not to be given a mobile phone. She resigned in August 2002 after failing to resolve her complaints with her employer. She claimed unfair dismissal, alleging that Barco had tried to demote her role to that of an HR administrator.

Julie Mellor, then chair of the EOC, said: 'Employers need to be confident that there are good reasons for any differences between the pay of people in comparable jobs. The best way to make absolutely sure that your pay system is fair is to carry out an equal pay review. In some cases a review might uncover the fact that jobs usually done by women have historically been undervalued, leading to lower rates of pay than for jobs traditionally done by men. If you want to be an employer of choice, you need to be able to prove you pay fairly.'

Source: EOC website, www.eoc.org.uk.

FACT FILE

The Equality and Human Rights Commission

Prior to October 2007, there were three separate equality commissions: the Commission for Racial Equality, the Disability Rights Commission and the Equal Opportunities Commission. On 1 October 2007, these three equality commissions merged into a new Equality and Human Rights Commission.

Disability Discrimination Act, 1995

This forbids employers from treating those employees with disabilities less favourably than others. It requires employers to make reasonable adjustments in order to provide working conditions and an environment that helps to overcome the practical difficulties of disability.

AQA A2 Business Studies

Age discrimination

The Employment Equality (Age) Regulations 2006 Amendment Regulations, 2008, came into force on 6 April 2008. This made it unlawful for an employer to discriminate against someone on the grounds of age. Age discrimination legislation provides for a default retirement age of 65. Compulsory retirement ages below 65 are unlawful unless objectively justified. In addition, employees have the right to request to work beyond that age and employers have a duty to consider such requests.

Collective labour law

Employment Relations Acts, 1999 and 2004

The 1999 Act increased employee rights in relation to union membership and claims for unfair dismissal. Among its key measures were:

- reducing the employment qualifying period for those claiming unfair dismissal from 2 years to 1 year
- requiring an employer to recognise a union if 50% or more of the workforce are members
- introducing rights to 3 months' leave for mothers and fathers when a baby is born

The 2004 Act improved and modernised the 1999 Act.

Employment Act, 2008

This Act brings together, strengthens, simplifies and clarifies key aspects of UK employment law relating to dispute resolution in the workplace, the enforcement of the national minimum wage and trade union membership. In particular, it brings together both elements of the government's employment relations strategy — increasing protection for vulnerable workers and lightening the load for law-abiding businesses.

Employment tribunals

Employment tribunals are informal courtrooms where legal disputes between employees and employers can be settled. The main areas of dispute covered by the tribunals are: unfair dismissal; workplace discrimination on grounds of sex, race or disability; the national minimum wage; and working time. Each tribunal comprises three members — a legally trained chairperson plus one employer and one employee representative. The worker with the complaint against the employer can present his or her own case at little or no cost, but may be put at a disadvantage if the employer has hired a top lawyer.

Implications of employment legislation for business

- **Impact on disruption.** Fewer working days are now lost due to strikes or industrial action.
- **Additional costs.** These might be incurred in order to comply with the legislation, such as providing more rights for individual workers.

- **Influence on efficiency and productivity.** Equal opportunities legislation is likely to ensure that the 'best' candidates are recruited.
- **Influence on motivation.** Motivation will be improved if the relationship between employees and employers is clearly stated and understood by all parties.

Consumer protection legislation

This aims to safeguard consumers from exploitation or exposure to unsafe products or services. Legislation in this area is overseen by the Office of Fair Training (OFT).

Weights and Measures Acts, 1963 and 1985

This legislation makes it illegal to sell goods below their stated weights or volume, and provides an enforcement procedure through trading standards officers and the Office of Fair Trading. The 1985 Act allowed metric measures to be used.

Trade Descriptions Act, 1968

This prohibits false or misleading descriptions of a product's contents, effects or price. This affects packaging, advertising and promotional material. Advertising must be truthful and accurate.

Consumer Credit Act, 1974

This provides the regulations covering the purchase of goods on credit. It is intended to prevent consumers signing unfair contracts and to ensure that purchasers know exactly what interest rate they are to be charged for the credit they receive. The legislation limits the giving of credit to licensed brokers or organisations.

All advertising or display materials quoting credit terms must also state the annualised percentage rate (APR) of interest.

Sale of Goods Acts, 1979 and 1994

These lay down the contract implied by the purchase of an item. They specify that goods must be of 'merchantable quality': that is, fit for the purpose for which they were purchased, and as described.

Food Safety Act, 1990

This controls the safety of food products and incorporates and strengthens the Food Act of 1984. The Food Safety Act is a wide-ranging law that brought food sources — and, by implication, farmers and growers — under food safety legislation for the first time. It made it an offence to sell food that is not of the 'nature or substance or quality' demanded by the purchaser. Other key features are that:

- premises selling food must register with the local authority
- those handling food must receive appropriate training
- enforcement officers can issue an improvement notice or, in extreme cases, an emergency prohibition notice

Consumer Protection from Unfair Trading Regulations, 2008

These enable the UK to implement the EU's Unfair Commercial Practices Directive on unfair commercial practices. As well as a duty not to trade unfairly and to avoid misleading statements or omissions, there is also a duty on businesses not to conduct aggressive sales practices, such as harassment, coercion and undue influence. A spokesman from the National Consumer Council said: 'These new laws represent a big boost to consumer protection, particularly for vulnerable people who are targeted by rogue traders.'

Implications of consumer protection legislation for business

- **Increased costs of production.** Complying with the legislation may raise costs, which may affect price and profit margins. However, these should be balanced against the possible fines that might be incurred if an expensive legal case were successfully brought against a firm that was not complying with legislation.
- **Improved quality.** Complying with the legislation may improve the quality of a product or service, which in turn may enhance a firm's reputation and strengthen consumer loyalty.
- **Less waste.** Improved quality may also lead to potential savings in relation to rejects and returns.
- **Impact on UK competitiveness.** Higher costs of compliance need to be set against possibly higher quality of products and services.

Environmental protection legislation

Environmental Protection Act, 1990

This Act was introduced to prevent the pollution from emissions to air, land or water from scheduled processes. Authorisation to operate the relevant processes must be obtained from the enforcing authority, such as HM Inspectorate of Pollution or the local authority.

Environment Act, 1995

This Act set up the Environment Agency and the National Park authorities. It also required the secretary of state to prepare a national air quality strategy and a national waste strategy, and to improve the protection of hedgerows.

The Waste and Emissions Trading Act, 2003

This Act makes provision about waste and penalties for non-compliance with schemes for the trading of emissions quotas.

EU directives have been produced on a range of environmental issues including the collection, transport, recovery and disposal of waste, and air quality.

Climate Change Act, 2008

Two key aims underpin this Act: to improve carbon management and help the transition towards a low carbon economy in the UK; and to demonstrate strong UK leadership internationally, signalling that the UK is committed to taking its share of responsibility for reducing global emissions. A key provision is the introduction of legally binding targets for greenhouse gas and carbon dioxide emissions.

Implications of environmental protection legislation for business

- **Additional costs.** As with most legislation, in order to meet the requirements of environmental protection legislation, business costs inevitably increase.
- **Impact on corporate standing.** Business has a major role to play in helping to protect and enhance the environment, and sound environmental management of its processes and products can be regarded as a core business issue that can help promote a company's products and services and improve its corporate standing.

Health and safety legislation

The aim of health and safety legislation is to provide a safe working environment for employees. The key piece of legislation in this area is the Health and Safety at Work Act (HASAW), 1974.

Health and Safety at Work Act, 1974

This Act imposes on employers a duty 'to ensure, as far as is reasonably practicable, the health, safety and welfare at work' of all staff. 'Reasonably practicable' in this context indicates that the risks must be weighed against the costs of prevention.

In addition to the HASAW Act of 1974, a number of European Union directives control working hours, the lifting of heavy weights, the use of computer screens and the rights of pregnant workers.

Implications of health and safety legislation for business

- **Additional costs.** For example, the introduction of safety measures, training and the employment of safety staff will increase costs and therefore might affect profit margins and prices.
- **Influence on a firm's reputation.** For example, a lack of safety could damage sales and hence profit levels. Equally, a good safety record could have a beneficial effect on recruitment, since potential employees will want to work for a firm with a good safety record.
- **Influence on the motivation of employees.** For example, security in the work environment is recognised as one of Herzberg's hygiene factors, which are likely to prevent demotivation (see Chapter 22 of the AS textbook).

Competition policy

Competition policy involves the use of legislation and regulation to ensure that all businesses are able to compete fairly with each other, and to limit the power of firms to take advantage of monopolies, mergers and restrictive practices. Competition should lead to better-quality, cheaper products and to increasing international competitiveness. Key legislation in this area includes the following.

DID YOU KNOW?

NetRegs is a website that aims to help small and medium-sized businesses understand and comply with current and forthcoming environmental legislation.

EXAMINER'S VOICE

The AQA A2 Business Studies specification does not specifically include consideration of competition policy legislation, but it has been included here for the sake of completeness and background.

Fair Trading Act, 1973

This set up the Office of Fair Trading which has three main duties:

- to consider whether takeover bids should be investigated by the Competition Commission on the grounds of being against the public interest
- to investigate suspected anti-competitive practices, such as market-sharing agreements where firms agree not to compete with each other in areas of the market
- to investigate existing monopolies

Competition Act, 1998

This legislation reformed and strengthened UK competition law by prohibiting anti-competitive behaviour and raising substantially the fines that could be imposed on offending companies. It brought UK competition law into line with European Union law. Responsibility for applying and enforcing the Act rests with the Office of Fair Trading. Key features of the Act include:

- prohibiting anti-competitive agreements such as cartels (agreements among companies to limit competition)
- prohibiting the abuse of a dominant market position (e.g. abuse by limiting production, by refusing supply, by restricting new technical development or by full-line forcing — forcing retailers to take the whole of a product range rather than a single item)
- allowing fines of up to 10% of UK turnover
- introducing the Competition Commission

The Competition Commission

This government-funded organisation oversees and enforces laws that attempt to eliminate anti-competitive business practices in the UK, oversees proposed mergers and checks that, where monopolies do exist, they are not against the public interest.

Enterprise Act, 2002

The main provisions of this Act are:

- more transparent and accountable decision making by competition authorities
- criminal sanctions to deter cartels
- greater opportunities for victims of anti-competitive behaviour to gain redress
- strengthening consumer protection measures

Implications of competition policy for business

- **Lower prices.** There are likely to be lower prices for customers as a result of legislation improving the competitiveness of markets.
- **Lower profit margins.** Complying with competition laws will not usually add to business costs, but may prevent a business making the profit it could have made if it had adopted anti-competitive tactics.
- **'Fair' competition.** There will be greater incentives for firms to seek competitive advantage through 'fair' rather than 'unfair competition'.
- **Benefits to small firms.** Perhaps the main benefits of competition policy accrue to smaller firms, which will be more able to compete in the market.

 **EXAMINER'S VOICE**

When considering the impact of specific areas of legislation, or legislation in general, try to weigh up the arguments: that is, evaluate. There will always be constraints and additional costs or administrative burdens imposed on business in complying with legislation, but there will also be benefits for individual firms and consumers and for the wider business community.

PRACTICE EXERCISE 4   Total: 45 marks (40 minutes)

1 Explain the general purpose of legislation from the point of view of a small business, an employee of a business and a consumer. *(9 marks)*

2 Explain two advantages and one disadvantage to a business of employment legislation. *(9 marks)*

3 Explain two advantages and one disadvantage to a business of consumer protection legislation. *(9 marks)*

4 Explain one advantage and one disadvantage to a business of environmental protection legislation. *(6 marks)*

5 Explain one advantage and one disadvantage to a business of health and safety legislation. *(6 marks)*

6 Explain two implications for a business of competition policy legislation. *(6 marks)*

ESSAY QUESTIONS   Total: 40 marks (50 minutes)

Answer one of the following questions:

1 It is often suggested that government intervention, in the form of legislation, creates a level playing field for business. Is this true and is it desirable? Justify your answer. (You may choose to answer this question by reference to a specific area of legislation, such as employment, consumer protection, environmental, health and safety or competition policy, or by reference to legislation in general.) *(40 marks)*

2 To what extent are businesses able to anticipate changes to the political and legal environment they face or must they simply respond to changes as they occur? *(40 marks)*

Chapter 23

The relationship between businesses and the social environment

This chapter assesses the effects on business of changes in the social environment (including demographic and environmental issues) and the changing nature of the ethical environment with which a business is faced. It includes an evaluation of the responses of business to the changing social environment. Consideration is given to the actions that businesses can take to demonstrate corporate social responsibility and whether these reflect genuine values or are just a form of public relations.

The social environment: demographic issues

The major issues in relation to recent demographic change in the UK include:
- the increasingly diverse racial and religious distribution of the population
- immigration — for example, from eastern Europe
- the ageing population

Demographic changes influence two important aspects of business: employees, and markets or customers. Demographic change can be perceived as either an opportunity or a threat, and the response of a business to such change will largely determine which of these it is. The following examples illustrate how the three aspects of demographic change identified above can be used as opportunities for business:
- A business can benefit from HR policies that promote diversity and equality by achieving better recruitment and retention, better information and planning, and better staff morale and performance. ACAS suggests that 'Businesses that take a positive approach to diversity generally are likely to do better than their competitors. Research shows that organisations with high-quality HR systems — in which equality plays its part — deliver better products and services and ultimately better shareholder value.'

EXAMINER'S VOICE

Remember that the issues considered in this chapter should be viewed as part of the external environment of a business. When analysing or evaluating the external environment facing a business, ensure that you make use of the PESTLE framework discussed in Chapter 21. This will encourage you to think about other aspects of the external environment, not just those issues covered in this chapter.

KEY TERM

demographics: the characteristics of human populations and population groups, including elements such as age, ethnicity, gender, religion and sexual orientation.

■ By valuing all staff, regardless of age group, religion and ethnic background, any investment in training provided for employees is more likely to be rewarded with greater loyalty and ultimately a greater return on that investment.

■ If a business is regarded as a diverse, ethical and intelligent employer, it will become more attractive to potential customers and investors, and is more likely to attract a more diverse customer base and to provide a better, more tailored service to them.

■ A diverse workforce in terms of age and ethnicity might provide ideas for products and services which a more homogeneous workforce could miss. Equally, a workforce that is diverse in terms of age, faith and ethnicity might provide a greater understanding of markets that may be segmented on the basis of these factors. An ethnically diverse workforce might also provide more natural links to market opportunities abroad, through linguistic skills, cultural knowledge and knowledge of foreign markets.

■ A business that is attractive to older workers is likely to be able to retain and benefit from the knowledge and experience of older staff and, statistically, older staff are less likely to take time off sick.

■ The business benefits of a mixed-age workforce are now widely recognised. There is clear evidence that both staff turnover and absenteeism are reduced and that motivation and commitment are improved in organisations employing people of all ages.

The social environment: environmental issues

Business and external costs

KEY TERM

externalities: the environmental effects of a firm's activities, which may be positive, such as job creation or providing a pleasing landscape around the factory; or negative, such as polluting the atmosphere with fumes or congesting the roads with lorries.

Negative externalities are also known as **external costs**. They are costs imposed on society by a firm. The firm does not pay for these costs, which are borne by the public, other organisations or the government. Essentially, therefore, firms fail to pay for the full cost of their actions and make private profit at the cost of social welfare.

Individuals also create external costs. For example, by travelling to work by car rather than bus, an individual creates higher levels of pollution and congestion.

Cost–benefit analysis is a method used in making decisions about large-scale investment projects, such as new roads or airports, which are likely to have an impact on the environment. This method involves costing all aspects of a project and weighing up the financial and external costs and benefits. Only if the benefits outweigh the costs should the firm consider going ahead with the project.

In a market economy, because the external costs that a firm creates do not directly affect the profit of that firm, there is no direct incentive for the firm to minimise them. This is a form of market failure that requires government intervention in order to influence the behaviour of firms and individuals.

Types of intervention include:

- legislation to ban or control certain activities
- licences that allow a certain level of activity to be undertaken
- taxation to make the polluter pay and encourage firms and individuals to select options that have less impact on the environment (Case Study 1 provides an example of environmental taxation)
- fines to penalise those who carry out undesirable actions

The extent to which a firm is concerned about the external costs it creates depends on the degree of government intervention in this area, pressure group action and the extent to which the firm takes its environmental responsibilities seriously.

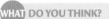

WHAT DO YOU THINK?

Should passengers have to pay for the pollution they generate by flying?

> *e* **EXAMINER'S VOICE**
>
> The key issue in analysing questions on this subject is to consider both costs and benefits. In many cases, a particular course of action that may have environmental benefits may also have other external costs, such as unemployment.

The opportunities provided by environmental responsibility

Taking account of environmental responsibilities can be beneficial for business as well as for the environment.

WHAT DO YOU THINK?

Is it right to make 500 workers redundant because the factory they work in is polluting the environment? It is important not to ignore one side of the argument in favour of another.

- **Marketing opportunities.** A good reputation in relation to environmental issues can act as a positive marketing tool that encourages consumers to choose one brand over another. As a result, many firms have spent time and money building up a 'green' image as an integral part of their marketing strategy. Examples are the Co-operative Bank and The Body Shop. In addition to increased sales and possibly stronger brand loyalty, a 'green' firm may be able to charge a higher price for its products. Many different products, from shampoos to coffee to banks, trade on the environment as a unique selling point. However, the increasing significance of the whole area of **corporate social responsibility (CSR)**, which includes social and environmental responsibility, suggests that, eventually, a 'green' image will not be a unique characteristic of certain products, but a requirement for all.
- **Financial opportunities.** Firms may find it easier to gain finance if they are able to point to a solid record of helping rather than damaging the environment. There are now a number of banks, most notably the Co-operative Bank, that will not invest in firms with a proven reputation for damaging the environment.
- **Human resource opportunities.** A reputation for damaging the environment can have adverse effects on employees' perceptions of a firm and its products, leading to a demotivated workforce and adversely affecting the ability of the firm to attract high-quality applicants. An organisation that is keen to improve its overall environmental reputation and performance needs its employees to be committed and to behave in a way that is consistent with the firm's environmental stance. This commitment is likely to come from good communication and training.

Production dilemmas

Business faces dilemmas about low-cost production versus environmentally responsible production. For example, firms have choices about whether to use finite resources such as coal and oil, or to use renewable resources. In many cases, the finite resources are cheaper, but their continued use will deplete supplies and may also cause additional environmental damage.

Another environmental choice involves waste and by-products generated by production processes. Gases may be released from large chimneys into the environment, liquid waste may be pumped into rivers and solid waste is likely to be taken away and buried in landfill sites. Each of these methods of disposal is harmful to the environment. The safe disposal of waste is often expensive and the alternative — changing methods of production in order to reduce waste — may be even more costly. Although governments may tax or fine firms that pollute the environment, it might be cheaper for a firm to pay the fines and continue polluting than to find a better way to dispose of its waste.

FACT FILE

Electrical waste

The electrical goods scrapheap has been growing at 6 million tonnes a year. The Waste Electrical and Electronic Equipment Directive (WEEE), which came into force in January 2007, requires manufacturers to recycle all unwanted electronic appliances. The legislation aims both to reduce the amount of electrical and electronic equipment being produced and to encourage everyone to reuse, recycle and recover it. Manufacturers estimate that new products may increase in price as a result of these additional responsibilities. However, it is hoped that the new requirements will give companies an incentive to design more environmentally friendly products.

WHAT DO YOU THINK?

Should firms operate at the lowest cost or should they operate at the most environmentally responsible level, regardless of costs?

KEY TERM

contingency planning: planning for unexpected, often unwelcome events in order to minimise their risks and costs.

Environmental responsibility and contingency planning

The aim of contingency planning is to minimise the risks and costs of an environmental disaster, such as a leakage or spillage of dangerous substances, by limiting its immediate impact and its long-term consequences for the company in terms of reputation and demand. Many large companies have environmental policies aimed at minimising any damage that their activities might cause to the environment. If a firm is prepared, it should be in a better position to manage any crisis that occurs. The Fact File below indicates how Severn Trent, the water, waste and utility services group, tries to anticipate and manage climate change in order to minimise the potential risks and costs to the business. Contingency planning is considered in detail in Chapter 27.

If an environmental disaster occurs, the firm's image will be under serious threat. Successful public relations will often form a vital part of the management of the crisis. This means that the firm needs to communicate with its consumers, directly and clearly: for instance, using a wave of informative advertising designed to get a clear message across. This can be an expensive solution, since the advertising will undoubtedly be required to reach as many consumers as possible, as quickly as possible. Alternatively, traditional public relations methods, such as press releases and press conferences, can be used. These involve few costs, but leave the message in the hands of the journalists. So it is vital that the firm manages its press releases and press conferences as clearly and openly as possible.

FACT FILE

Contingency planning at Severn Trent

Severn Trent, the water, waste and utility services company, sees global warming as a reality that it must tackle today if its business is to prosper tomorrow. The reason it is taking climate change seriously now is that it expects to be one of the first companies to be affected by it. Climate change is by far the most important environmental issue for the company. The probability of extreme drought or flooding occurring in any given year is rising. Drier summers put more pressure on its water resources, and wetter winters mean flooding, which threatens sewerage systems. The company must also take account of factors such as how higher temperatures affect the rate at which waste degrades and produces landfill gas.

Anticipating and managing the effects of climate change helps minimise the risks and costs to the business. It is also trying to limit the impact of its activities on global warming by developing and generating renewable energy — for example, by capturing and using methane gas from landfill sites — and optimising the energy efficiency of its operations.

Source: adapted from *The Sunday Times, Companies that Count*, 2005.

Environmental audits

An environmental audit is an organisation's key to environmentally responsible behaviour. It:

- identifies the ways in which the business interacts with the environment
- establishes priorities in tackling environmental issues
- establishes policies and procedures
- identifies responsibilities
- commits the organisation to train staff on environmental matters
- establishes standards of monitoring performance

KEY TERM

environmental audit: an independent check on a firm's polluting activities, such as emissions, wastage levels and recycling.

FACT FILE

Environmental management systems

An environmental management system (EMS) enables a business to monitor and control its use of resources and the impact of its products and services on the environment. Many companies find that an effective EMS improves efficiency and can reduce the costs of waste, raw materials, process energy and heating.

ISO 14001 is the international standard for the establishment and operation of an EMS and many larger companies are now insisting that their entire supply chain is accredited to this standard. For example, all Nokia's suppliers must meet environmental and ethical requirements and have in place an EMS in line with ISO 14001.

Pressure groups

Pressure groups include single-issue groups, such as a group against the construction of a particular road or building project, and those with ongoing concerns, such as Greenpeace, trade unions and the consumers' association, Which? Pressure group activity usually aims to change legislation, the actions of businesses or public opinion.

 KEY TERM

pressure group: an organisation formed by people with a common interest or shared goal, who join together to further their interests or achieve their goals by putting pressure on the general public, governments or businesses.

Responses to pressure group activity

- **Companies agree to change.** In some situations, companies might actually agree with pressure groups and introduce the changes demanded. Such a decision might be motivated by genuine ethically, socially or environmentally responsible beliefs, by a desire to protect the image of the company, or simply by a wish to avoid the costs that might be incurred in doing battle with a pressure group. A compromise might be reached, following negotiations between the company in question and representatives of the pressure group.
- **Companies resist pressure group demands.** Companies may launch a PR campaign to counter and discredit a pressure group's claims. The fact that companies usually have far greater financial resources at their disposal than pressure groups means that this response might be successful. Alternatively, trade associations often have good access to government and might engage in lobbying in order to ensure that a pressure group campaigning for changes in the law is defeated.
- **The government imposes change by passing new laws.** If pressure group activities are successful, the government could require firms to change their operations. For example, in the case of tobacco companies, it might mean a ban on advertising on television and in other media, while in the case of a chemical company, it might involve technical requirements to reduce emissions.
- **The public changes its approach.** Pressure group activity might persuade people to change their approach to the consumption or disposal of certain products, or the pollution that accompanies certain activities.

Pressure groups as stakeholders

If a pressure group is accepted as a valid stakeholder by a business, it is likely to have more impact. In order for it to become a valid stakeholder, the pressure group must persuade the business that it represents the views of people affected by the actions of the business. If a pressure group succeeds in gaining acceptance as a stakeholder, it is in the interests of the business to listen to its views.

FILE

The *Greener Electronics Guide*

The *Greener Electronics Guide*, compiled by Greenpeace, aims to persuade the electronics industry to take responsibility for the entire lifecycle of its products, to face up to the problems of e-waste and to take on the challenge of tackling climate change. First launched in 2006, the guide ranks the leaders of mobile phone, computer, television and games console markets according to their policies and practices on toxic chemicals, recycling and energy.

The guide has been a key driving force in getting many companies to make significant improvements to their environmental policies. Nokia is in the lead, followed by Samsung. Fujitsu Siemens Computers is in third place, having finally set late 2010 as its deadline for eliminating toxic chemicals from across its product range. Languishing at the bottom of the rankings are Sharp, Microsoft and Nintendo.

Source: adapted from information on www.greenpeace.org.

FACT FILE

GE crop campaign

'In a victory for activists and consumers across Europe, who lobbied for tougher legislation and boycotted genetically engineered (GE) products, Bayer CropScience, a German company authorised to plant a herbicide-resistant variety of maize, said regulations on how and where the crop could be planted would make it "economically non-viable". It was this crop that was pulled up by Greenpeace UK activists in 1999. The activists were acquitted of charges of criminal damage when the court agreed they were acting in the interest of protecting the environment.' (31 March 2004)

'Thanks to years of pressure from environmental groups, we can celebrate a victory for the environment following the announcement by Monsanto that it would suspend further development of its GE wheat. Monsanto stated that it was deferring all further efforts to introduce the crop.' (11 May 2004)

Source: adapted from information on www.greenpeace.org.

PRACTICE EXERCISE 1   Total: 45 marks (40 minutes)

1 How do external costs differ from other costs? *(6 marks)*

2 Explain the meaning of 'cost–benefit analysis'. *(3 marks)*

3 Identify two examples of investment projects for which cost–benefit analysis might be used. *(2 marks)*

4 Explain two ways in which acting in an environmentally responsible way might benefit a firm. *(6 marks)*

5 Explain two problems that a firm might face as a result of acting in an environmentally responsible way. *(6 marks)*

6 What is contingency planning? *(3 marks)*

7 How might effective PR minimise the impact of an environmental disaster for a firm? *(4 marks)*

8 State three ways in which government could encourage business to reduce pollution. *(3 marks)*

9 What is an environmental audit? *(3 marks)*

10 Explain three possible responses that a business might make to pressure group activity. *(9 marks)*

CASE STUDY 1 Air travel and the environment

In 2003, a government report suggested that airline passengers might be forced to pay higher fares because they were not covering the cost of the environmental damage done by their flights.

Passengers on long-haul flights were likely to see the sharpest increases in fares if the government imposed a green tax on air travel.

The government report calculated that a Boeing 747 travelling 3,700 miles, the distance from London to Miami, would emit 171 tonnes of carbon. The cost of the environmental damage caused by the flight was put at £12,000. The cost per passenger would therefore be £40, based on British Airways' records at the time of selling 300 seats on a 400-seat 747. The report also measured the climate change costs of the 8 tonnes of carbon emitted by a Boeing 737 flying 600 miles, the distance from London to Nice. Each passenger would pay about £4, based on an average of 135 seats sold on the aircraft.

The report concluded: 'Full environmental costs are not currently factored into the prices paid by those who benefit from aviation. Hence there is a case for the government to intervene.'

The report considered the cost of air pollution and noise caused by aviation, but concluded that these were negligible compared with carbon emissions.

The aviation industry argued that it already contributed some £800 million a year in air passenger tax. However, the Treasury made clear that the air passenger tax is not an environmental tax.

Mike Toms, BAA's planning director at the time, said that a new charging structure was needed that more closely reflected the environmental cost of each flight and gave the industry an incentive to purchase quieter, less polluting aircraft. 'We are not arguing that taxes should be used to stop people flying, but we would want people to fly in the most environmentally efficient way,' he said.

A 2007 survey into consumer attitudes to flying, by the Department for Transport (DFT), revealed that despite growing publicity around the impact of aviation on climate change, consumers rank cost as a significantly more important factor than environmental damage when it comes to reasons not to fly.

About 22% of respondents said they planned to take more flights than the previous year. Despite claiming that environmental issues will not deter them from flying, about 66% of respondents agreed that air travel does harm the environment.

In a move that runs contrary to the push towards budget airlines and lower fares, about 40% of people said that they would be prepared to pay more for flights to compensate for the environmental effects. Of this group, 29% said they would be prepared to pay up to 20% more for the price of a ticket.

A spokesman for British Airways said the airline was the first to offer customers the chance to offset their flight emissions and has designed its scheme to make it more user-friendly: 'Aviation is playing its full part in controlling its carbon dioxide emissions, but its share of global emissions is small – less than 2%. Road transport contributes six times more and power generation 16 times more.'

Source: adapted from articles in *The Times*, 15 March 2003 and www.computing.co.uk.

Questions
Total: 50 marks (60 minutes)

1 Consider the possible impact on airlines of a move to charge passengers prices that reflect environmental as well as general business costs. *(10 marks)*

2 To what extent is there conflict between the objectives of the following stakeholder groups – the industry, the consumer and the government – in relation to the aviation industry and environmental concerns, and how might this conflict be resolved? *(40 marks)*

The ethical environment

Ethics are the set of moral values held by an individual or group. An organisation may make a decision that it believes to be morally right rather than one that suits the needs of some of its stakeholders. Thus a decision made on ethical grounds might reject the most profitable solution for an organisation in favour of one of greater benefit to society as a whole, or to particular groups of stakeholders. Such ethical decision making is likely to distinguish a business that is behaving ethically from one focused on profit.

Ethical dilemmas

Firms are frequently presented with ethical dilemmas when making decisions. Typical ethical dilemmas facing businesses are as follows:
- Should an advertising agency accept a cigarette manufacturer as a client?
- Should a producer of chemicals sell to an overseas buyer that it suspects will be using the goods to produce chemical weapons?
- Should a firm relocate to a country paying lower wages?
- Should a firm always pay suppliers on time or should it delay as long as possible?
- Should a manufacturer of military aircraft sell to a foreign government suspected of using force to maintain power?
- Should a firm try to minimise its production costs and prices by using environmentally polluting processes?

Possible ethical stances

Organisations may take different stances in relation to ethics, including any of the following:
- **Viewing shareholders' or owners' short-term interests as their only responsibility.** These organisations are likely to meet only their minimum obligations in relation to other stakeholder groups and to the wider environment.
- **Recognising that well-managed relationships with other stakeholders bring long-term benefits to shareholders or owners.** The approach of such organisations is not dissimilar to the previous stance, but in addition they realise that expenditure on welfare and other provision is sensible, while not seeing it as an ethical duty.
- **Including the interests and expectations of stakeholders in their mission.** Organisations with this stance are likely to go beyond their minimum obligations. For example, they might avoid selling anti-social products or making products in a manner that is considered unethical, and would be prepared to accept reductions in profitability for the social good.
- **Taking an ideological approach and placing financial considerations secondary.** The extent to which this stance is viable depends on how accountable the organisation is to its shareholders or owners. It is probably easier for a private, family-owned organisation to be run in this way.

EXAMINER'S VOICE

Don't confuse ethical behaviour with behaviour that is within the law. Behaving in an ethical way is more than behaving according to the law.

KEY TERM

business ethics: the moral principles that should underpin decision making. Ethical behaviour involves actions and decisions that are seen to be morally correct (i.e. match the moral values or principles of the decision-makers).

Ethical codes

The focus of the code will depend on the business concerned. Banks may concentrate on honesty, food manufacturers on the healthiness of their products, and chemical firms on pollution control. A typical ethical code might include sections on:

- personal integrity in dealing with suppliers and in handling the firm's resources
- corporate integrity, such as forbidding collusion with competitors and predatory pricing
- environmental responsibility, highlighting a duty to minimise pollution emission and maximise recycling
- social responsibility to provide products of genuine value that are promoted with honesty and dignity

Critics of ethical codes, like critics of social responsibility, believe the codes to be no more than public relations exercises rather than genuine attempts to change behaviour. The proof of their effectiveness can, of course, only be measured by how firms actually behave, not by what they write or say.

KEY TERM

ethical code: an instruction from an organisation to its employees to indicate how they should react to situations relating to moral values.

DID YOU KNOW?

The arguments for and against ethical behaviour by business are similar to those for and against corporate social responsibility, which is discussed later in this chapter.

FACT FILE

Ethics at Texas Instruments

Texas Instruments (TI) prides itself on its ethical stance and is seen as a benchmark against which other firms can measure themselves. Since 1987 it has had a specific office dealing with ethics and an ethics director.

The company's approach to ethics is clearly and simply summed up as:

know what's right   value what's right   do what's right

All employees are given a business card that carries TI's 'Ethics Quick Test':
- Is the action legal?
- Does it comply with our values?
- If you do it, will you feel bad?
- How will it look in the newspaper?
- If you know it's wrong, don't do it.
- If you're not sure, ask.
- Keep asking until you get an answer.

Source: www.texasinstruments.com.

FACT FILE

Codes of ethics

The Institute of Business Ethics sets out a methodology for developing and implementing a code of ethics, indicating the issues that need to be incorporated. These range from environmental responsibility, whistle-blowing and data protection to conflicts of interest, bribery and gifts.

Ethical investment

The Co-operative Bank is an example of an ethical investor. It will only invest in firms that:

- do not finance weapons deals to oppressive governments
- do not make products involving tobacco, the fur trade, animal testing or exploitative factory farming
- act responsibly toward the environment
- are good employers

KEY TERM

ethical investment: stock market investment based on a restricted list of firms that are seen as ethically sound.

e EXAMINER'S VOICE

Because this area is value laden, ensure that you provide well-argued points in your answers to questions on ethics and avoid the temptation to make value judgements and assertions that are unsupported by argument or evidence.

Advantages of ethical behaviour

As consumers become better informed and better educated about products, processes and companies, they demand products and services that do not pollute, exploit or harm. In order to be successful, companies need to respond positively to these demands.

Ethical behaviour can give companies a clear competitive advantage on which marketing activities can be based. Indeed, some companies have developed their ethical behaviour into a unique selling point and base their marketing campaigns on these perceived differences: for example, by creating a caring image through its marketing, The Body Shop hopes to gain increased sales.

Firms that adopt ethical practices may also experience benefits in relation to their workforce. They may expect to recruit staff who are better qualified and more highly motivated. Employees can be expected to respond positively to working for a business with a positive ethical image. Equally, employees may be less likely to leave. All of these factors can help to reduce the employment costs incurred by the business.

Problems with ethical positions

Adopting an ethical stance can, however, cause problems:

- **Effect on profit.** An ethical choice can incur extra costs: for example, buying renewable resources from a less developed country or continuing extensive testing of a product before releasing it.
- **What is ethical?** People have different views on what is ethical and these views change over time. For example, in the past, few shops opened on Sundays because it was against many people's religious beliefs and was considered unethical. Now many firms open on Sundays and many would open for longer if legislation did not limit their opening time to 6 hours.

- **Communication of ethics within an organisation.** In large organisations, it may be difficult to inform staff of the ethical policy or ethical code and to monitor adherence to it. At Texas Instruments (TI) (see the Fact File on p. 394) an ethics booklet is issued to every employee. This booklet was first published in 1961 when TI's founders felt that the company was getting too large and the marketplace too complex to have ethical standards passed on simply by word of mouth. The booklet has been revised regularly to take into account expanding world markets, marketplace complexities, changing government regulations, and business growth and modifications.
- **Delegation and empowerment.** As empowered workers take more decisions, it becomes harder to maintain a consistent company policy on ethical behaviour.

Reviewing a firm's ethical position

A number of elements should be considered when reviewing a company's ethical position.

- **Individuals.** Each individual working in a business has his or her own set of personal standards, which is derived from their upbringing, education and background. In a business, decisions are made by individuals or by groups of individuals who inevitably bring to the decision their own ideas of what is right and wrong.
- **Corporate culture.** Corporate culture is the set of unwritten rules that affect the attitudes and management style of a business (see Chapter 29). If, for example, managers are seen to be ruthless in their pursuit of profit, and if such behaviour helps determine who will earn promotion, then workers lower down the organisation are more likely to adopt a similar approach, even if this is against their own judgement.
- **Public standards.** Businesses operate in an environment that affects everything they do and the results they achieve. A public outcry against a particular type of activity will force a business to look at itself and decide if it needs to change its stance. If a high-profile firm, such as Nike or Gap, is accused of using child labour, other firms that produce in similar circumstances are likely to review their own operations and perhaps change to a more acceptable method of operation. Similarly, the accounting scandals surrounding Enron, WorldCom and Bernard Madoff (see Fact File opposite) will have caused many firms to take a closer look at their own accounting policies.
- **Competitors.** Within a marketplace, businesses can attempt to create a unique selling proposition for their product by emphasising their ethical stance. A successful campaign like this can force other firms to review their operations. In the early 1980s, The Body Shop single-handedly created a market niche for environmentally friendly cosmetics that had not been tested on animals. Similarly, the Co-operative Bank has gained a reputation for its position on ethical investments.

FACT FILE

The Madoff scandal

In December 2008, the financial services world was rocked by a fraud of spectacular dimensions. One of the most highly regarded hedge fund managers, Bernard Madoff, allegedly cheated his hedge fund and investment banking business out of an estimated $50 billion. (Hedge funds work by allowing investors to deposit a set amount for a defined period. Usually there is a 'lock-in' for about 6 or 12 months, during which time investors cannot withdraw their money but can monitor how their investment is performing.)

In Madoff's case, it appeared to investors and the market that his hedge fund was successful. Investors were receiving up to 12% in promised returns and this, combined with Madoff's reputation as a highly respected businessman, gave investors a sense of security. But the truth was that Madoff was misrepresenting the success of his hedge fund and sending out paper copies of his trading records that showed false returns. His fund was not profitable at all, but Madoff was using money from new investors to pay current investors, thus maintaining the image of a successful fund.

While the financial markets were buoyant, no one noticed because investors were getting their money. However, as the financial markets dried up, the number of new investors declined and Madoff could not pay his old investors and, as a result, the fraud was uncovered.

Ethics, business culture and delegation

Organisations have cultures and codes of behaviour that affect attitudes, decision making and management style. If there is any conflict between the ethical position of the organisation and the moral values of the individuals it employs, then delegated decision making may not reflect the ethical position of the organisation.

The potential for this problem to arise can be minimised if the culture of the organisation is one in which all employees understand the firm's ethical position and take responsibility for ensuring that their actions and decisions reflect this. Changing business cultures is not easy to achieve and investment in effective training and communication is important in order to ensure that all staff behave in an agreed ethical manner and that delegated activities are performed on an agreed ethical basis. Of course, it may be that employees actually have higher standards than their managers.

There is considerable evidence to suggest that creating an ethical culture within a business can improve employee motivation and becomes part of a wider policy of employee empowerment.

Ethics or public relations?

Public relations usually involves obtaining favourable publicity via the press, television or radio. Unlike advertising, it is not paid for and there is no control over its content. When a business behaves ethically, it may be good for PR.

KEY TERM

public relations (PR): activities to boost the public profile of an organisation.

Indeed, some commentators suggest cynically that good PR is the main reason for ethical behaviour — it can help to enhance the image of a business and is likely to generate more goodwill. This in turn might lead to improved sales and may eventually boost the company's share value.

WHAT DO YOU THINK?

If a firm reconsiders its decisions in response to public opinion and/or media pressure, is it acting more ethically or just responding to pressure?

e EXAMINER'S VOICE

Business ethics is an important aspect of the specification and is an area where you are often required to demonstrate the skill of evaluation. As this topic considers many different values, ensure that you provide well-argued points in your answers to questions about ethics, and avoid the temptation to make value judgements and assertions that are unsupported by argument or evidence.

GROUP EXERCISE

Discuss each of the ten actions below and rank them in order, with the most ethical behaviour first and the least ethical last. Justify your choices to the rest of the class.

1 In order to prevent an epidemic, a drugs company releases a new drug before it has been thoroughly tested.

2 In order to increase public awareness of child poverty, a charity publishes unpleasant images of children that upset members of the public.

3 An animal rights pressure group frees animals that are being used for experiments on the effects of cosmetics.

4 A recycling plant dumps toxic waste in a deep trench in the middle of the Atlantic.

5 An armaments manufacturer saves 1,000 jobs by supplying arms to North Korea.

6 An animal rights pressure group frees animals that are being used for experiments that will save human lives.

7 A supermarket decides that it will open as normal on Christmas Day.

8 A farmer tips slurry into the river that adjoins his farm, killing all of the fish downstream for 10 kilometres.

9 In order to reduce its production costs, a sportswear business moves production of its trainers to a country that employs child labour.

10 A cigarette manufacturer aims its latest campaign at schoolchildren by concentrating on poster sites next to schools.

PRACTICE EXERCISE 2   Total: 55 marks (50 minutes)

1 What is meant by the term 'ethical behaviour'?   *(4 marks)*

2 Explain two examples of ethical dilemmas that might occur in business.   *(6 marks)*

3 Explain the purpose of an ethical code.   *(4 marks)*

4 What does 'ethical investment' mean?   *(3 marks)*

5 State and explain two factors that might affect the ability of a firm to adopt an ethical stance.   *(6 marks)*

6 Outline two benefits to a business of operating in an ethical manner.   *(6 marks)*

7 Explain two possible disadvantages to a firm of operating in an ethical manner.   *(6 marks)*

8 Explain the potential conflict between ethics and delegated decision making.   *(4 marks)*

9 How might a business minimise this conflict between ethics and delegated decision making?   *(4 marks)*

10 How might business culture influence the extent to which an organisation operates in an ethical manner?   *(4 marks)*

11 Define 'public relations' and explain how it differs from advertising.   *(5 marks)*

12 Give three examples of favourable public relations that you have read or seen recently.   *(3 marks)*

CASE STUDY 2   The Co-operative Bank plc

The Co-operative Bank has a long history as one of the UK's most innovative banks and a reputation as a leader in corporate social responsibility. The company is recognised for its strong ethical investment policy statement, its social auditing practices and its ethical marketing strategies. The bank's eight-point ethical investment policy outlines the company's position on socially responsible investing, including its decisions not to finance weapons deals to oppressive governments, and not to invest in companies involved in tobacco, the fur trade, animal testing or exploitative factory farming. According to its chief executive, the Co-operative Bank's ethical and ecological policies, which it frequently strengthens and revises based on extensive customer input, are inextricably linked to its business success; its ethical policies are the most frequently cited reason why customers choose the bank.

The company has also been a pioneer in the area of stakeholder relations and social reporting, producing a 'Partnership Report' each year since 1997 that measures the impact and identifies improvements that the company could make in social responsibility areas such as customer satisfaction, ecological sustainability, workplace practices, community involvement and ethics. The report includes the statement of an outside auditor who assessed the report. Through its ethical marketing campaign, the Co-operative Bank has contributed millions of pounds to various causes, including fair trade and living wages, environmental protection, the acceptance of diversity and bans on the financing of landmines.

Source: adapted from information on
www.co-operativebank.co.uk.

Question

Some financial organisations lend money according to customers' financial strength rather than their ethical behaviour, and some have transferred operations, such as call centres, to low-wage countries. Discuss the advantages and disadvantages to the Co-operative Bank of its approach to ethical issues, in comparison to that of its competitors.

(40 marks)

CASE STUDY 3 **Ethics and farming**

Ethics is an increasingly important issue in relation to the farming industry. There are a number of reasons for this trend:

- There have been changes in the scale and methods of farming that have raised the profile of ethical issues. For example, intensive production methods have raised serious ethical concerns about rearing animals under 'factory farming' conditions, or growing crops intensively using the latest biotechnology.
- Businesses have seen various changes in the use of technology, many of which have raised the profile of ethical issues. Examples are the increasing use of antibiotics, genetically modified (GM) material, fertilisers and agrochemicals, as well as 'hi-tech' machinery and equipment.
- At the same time, the power of consumers, pressure groups and the media has increased, with the internet now providing huge amounts of information on every topic. Thus, issues related to intensive production and new technology are highlighted more fully and immediately.

One of the major ethical dilemmas in the farming industry is the choice between organic and intensive methods of farming.

- Organic farming involves integrating animal and crop production in an economically and environmentally sustainable system, and placing priority on animal welfare. It also involves minimal use of chemicals, including pesticides, fertilisers and herbicides, and a ban on GM inputs and antibiotics. Such conditions may be desirable for the production of food, but organically produced products are more expensive than intensively farmed equivalents.
- Intensive farming uses mass production techniques to increase productivity and therefore profits for farmers, wholesalers and retailers, and to reduce prices for consumers. It uses environmental control to raise production, and antibiotics to prevent disease and increase growth rates. For example, battery hens are kept in cages with no room to behave normally — they cannot stretch, flap their wings or bathe in dust. Because the environment (including lighting, ventilation and heating) is controlled, more eggs are produced than under organic or free-range systems, where hens are not so enclosed or permanently housed. Intensive farming may be ethically undesirable for the production of food, but the products produced in such a manner are less expensive than organic products.

Questions

1 Most ethical discussion centres on the behaviour of businesses, including producers, wholesalers and retailers. To what extent does the consumer have an ethical responsibility to purchase organic food? *(15 marks)*

2 Pressure from the government, the media and the public has resulted in a substantial change in business practices in the farming industry. If this pressure leads to improved and environmentally friendly farming practices, does it matter whether it is due to market forces or ethical considerations? Justify your answer.

(15 marks)

Corporate social responsibility

Business for Social Responsibility (BSR), an organisation that helps companies achieve commercial success in ways that respect ethical values, people, communities and the environment, defines corporate social responsibility as 'achieving commercial success in ways that honour ethical values and respect people, communities, and the natural environment'. It also says that corporate social responsibility means addressing the legal, ethical, commercial and other expectations that society has for business, and making decisions that balance the claims of all key stakeholders fairly.

KEY TERM

corporate social responsibility (CSR): the duties of an organisation towards employees, customers, society and the environment.

DID YOU KNOW?

There is historical evidence of firms accepting social responsibilities. For example, in the nineteenth century, religiously motivated firms such as Cadbury in Birmingham and Rowntree in York (chocolate and confectionery manufacturers, respectively) and Titus Salt, a woollen mill owner in Saltaire, Bradford, treated their workforce with respect, providing good working conditions, education, housing and a pleasant communal environment.

e EXAMINER'S VOICE

This is an area of business studies that is value laden. People and firms have very different views of what corporate social responsibility means and whether firms should meet their social responsibilities. Ensure that when you answer questions on this topic you provide soundly analysed and balanced arguments rather than making assertions of the 'I think...' variety.

Why should firms accept their social responsibility?

Accepting social responsibility offers benefits to both society and businesses.

Benefits for society
- Problems such as unemployment and pollution are likely to be reduced.
- The quality of life is likely to be improved, as decisions will be based on what is best for society rather than what is best for an individual firm.
- Society's long-term needs are likely to be considered, rather than simply the short-term needs of a business.
- Life and business activity will be easier if everyone involved is working together for the common good, rather than if one group is trying to exploit another for its own benefit.
- It can be argued that it is simply the right thing to do and that firms have a duty to be concerned with the wider impact of their activities.

Benefits for firms
- **Improved financial performance.** A recent US study showed that the overall financial performance of companies gaining awards in a league table for business ethics and citizenship was significantly better than that of other companies.

- **Reduced operating costs.** Some CSR initiatives can reduce operating costs. For example, many initiatives aimed at improving environmental performance — such as reducing gas emissions that contribute to global warming or reducing the use of agricultural chemicals — also lower costs. Many recycling initiatives cut waste-disposal costs and generate income by selling recycled materials.

- **Enhanced brand image and reputation.** Customers are often drawn to brands and companies with good reputations in CSR-related areas. A company considered socially responsible can benefit both from its enhanced reputation with the public and from its reputation within the business community, increasing the company's ability to attract capital and trading partners.

- **Increased sales and customer loyalty.** A number of studies have suggested that there is a large and growing market for the products and services of companies perceived to be socially responsible.

- **Increased ability to attract and retain employees.** Companies perceived to have strong CSR commitments often find it easier to recruit and retain employees, resulting in a reduction in staff turnover and associated recruitment and training costs, because employees feel happier working in such a business.

- **Access to capital.** The growth of socially responsible or ethical investing (e.g. the Co-operative Bank) means that companies with strong CSR performance have increased access to capital.

FACT FILE

What's the carbon footprint of your product?

Businesses can now assess the carbon footprint of their goods and services and play a greater part in fighting climate change. A new standard launched by BSI (British Standards) called PAS 2050 is a consistent way of counting the greenhouse gas emissions embedded in goods and services throughout their entire life cycle — from sourcing raw materials, through to manufacture, distribution, use and disposal.

The aim of the new standard is to help businesses move beyond managing the emissions that their own processes create and to look at opportunities for reducing emissions in the design and supplying of products. This will then help businesses make goods or services which are less carbon intensive and ultimately develop new products with lower carbon footprints. Examples include Boots, which has redesigned its logistics network so that its Botanics shampoo can be delivered direct to stores, reducing road miles and packaging and the carbon footprint of making the product by 10%. Innocent helped one of its suppliers to increase the amount of waste materials being recycled throughout its factory. In the first month, waste to landfill was reduced by 15% and within 6 months the reduction reached 54%.

What's your **carbon footprint?**

FOTOLIA

What are the arguments against firms accepting their social responsibilities?

A case can also be made that firms should not accept their social responsibilities:

- Efficient use of resources is likely to be reduced if businesses are restricted in how they can produce and where they can locate. This might lead to higher prices.
- Socially responsible policies can be costly to introduce. International competitiveness will be reduced if other countries do not consider externalities and social responsibility, and therefore produce more cheaply.
- Stakeholder groups tend to have differing objectives (as shown in Table 23.1) and they are therefore unlikely to agree on what is socially responsible behaviour.
- Social responsibility may be just a passing fashion and no one can be sure of the value to firms of being socially responsible.
- If the economy is generally doing well, managers feel able to look at intangibles such as social responsibility. During a recession, however, they will look more at profits and survival, even if this means taking little or no notice of social responsibility.
- If something is important to society at large, it can be argued that the government should pass laws to ensure that everyone acts responsibly.
- It can be argued that social responsibility is just an extension of firms being market orientated. In other words, because consumers want firms to act this way, firms respond in order to maximise their profits. According to this view, firms are cynically using the idea of social responsibility as a method of marketing their products, and will use the idea only for as long as it allows them to extend the product life cycle.

Stakeholders	Objectives
Employees	Secure, reasonably paid employment
Customers	Good-quality, safe products at a competitive price
Suppliers	Fair prices to be paid, regular custom and prompt payment
Owners	Good profit, leading to increases in share prices and/or dividends
Government/society	Efficient use of resources and consideration of the environment and society's needs
Local community	Employment and wealth creation without the imposition of major external costs

Table 23.1
Stakeholder objectives

DID YOU KNOW?

A key factor in any firm's attitude towards its social responsibilities is probably the time span of its objectives. For example, a get-rich-quick kitchen or window installation firm will have an approach to issues of social responsibility that is very different from an established family business that has been around for generations.

Social responsibility in practice

Examples of activities that would be viewed as socially responsible are:

- using sustainable sources of raw materials
- ensuring that suppliers operate responsibly — for example, avoiding the use of child labour
- operating an extensive health and safety policy above the legal requirements, thereby protecting the wellbeing of employees
- engaging in a continuous process of environmental management and monitoring the effects of production on the environment
- trading ethically and taking account of moral issues

Conclusion

Although there is evidence that accepting social responsibility provides direct benefits to firms, in general the benefits tend to accrue to society as a whole or to the local community. In this sense, firms that accept their social responsibility create external benefits for society (or positive externalities). But equally, if society and/or the local community improves in terms of wealth, standard of living and quality of life, then in the longer term business will also benefit.

Social auditing

Purpose of social auditing

Businesses are becoming more aware of the need to try to meet the expectations of different groups of stakeholders. The various stakeholder groups tend to have different objectives (see Table 23.1) and it may never be possible to reconcile all of these different objectives. Social auditing goes some way towards assisting businesses to address this issue and to meet their social responsibilities.

The process of social auditing is part of the move towards more scrutiny of business practices and increased availability of information for stakeholders, whether employees, consumers, pressure groups, the local community or the government. Social audits are much broader than environmental audits, which tend to investigate the impact of a business on the local environment and which are part of a social audit.

KEY TERM

social auditing (or corporate social responsibility reporting): the process by which a business attempts to assess the impact of the entire range of its activities on stakeholders and society in general.

FACT FILE

Business in the Community

Business in the Community (BIC) was formed over 20 years ago when a group of UK companies decided to improve the way that business affects society. It now has 750 member companies, including 72 of the companies making up the FTSE100, and a further 2,000 businesses participate in its programmes and campaigns.

In 1996, it created the Corporate Responsibility Index to help companies benchmark their environmental management and performance. In 2008, the top five companies in the index were Accenture (accountants and consultants), BAA (transport), Barclays (banks), BHP Billiton (mining), and Bradford and Bingley (banks).

DID YOU KNOW?

Most companies include a concise summary of their corporate responsibility performance in their annual report, backed up by a much more detailed report available online.

Implementation of social auditing

Social auditing, or corporate social responsibility reporting, involves the following stages:

- identifying social objectives and ethical values
- defining stakeholders
- establishing social performance indicators
- measuring performance, keeping records and preparing social accounts
- submitting accounts to independent audit and publishing the result

DID YOU KNOW?

The role of an independent auditor is to form a view, on the basis of detailed and systematic investigation, as to whether the statements and claims made in the corporate social responsibility report are trustworthy and adequately supported by evidence. In doing this, they seek to apply the following three tests:

- **Materiality.** Is the information relevant to stakeholders' concerns and interests and will it help them make informed judgements about the company's performance?
- **Completeness.** Does the information provide sufficient evidence that the company understands all its significant social, economic and environmental impacts?
- **Responsiveness.** Does the report demonstrate the company's responses and commitment to improving its performance?

Non-financial measures of efficiency

A social audit results in the production of a set of social accounts that attempt to evaluate performance against a set of non-financial criteria. Just as financial ratios allow a firm to judge and compare financial management and performance over time and within and between companies, social ratios can be used to examine how well a company is performing in relation to a range of 'social' issues.

BIC suggests that an audit might be divided into four sections, each of which explores a particular area of responsibility that a business needs to consider.

The workplace
In this area, a business should consider:

- how well it is treating its employees and how well it values them
- how well it monitors health and safety-related accidents, and the strategies it has in place to reduce accidents
- the range of salaries in the organisation
- whether it is respecting human rights
- the extent to which it is employing individuals from minority ethnic groups

The marketplace

Here a business should consider:

- the extent to which it is responding to its customers' needs
- the extent to which it trades with ethically sound suppliers

The environment

Here a business should consider:

- the extent to which it is using renewable raw materials and recycling inputs
- how effectively it is monitoring the pollution and emissions it creates and the waste it generates
- whether it is setting targets in this area and the extent to which it is reaching them
- whether it is talking to pressure groups

The community

In this area, a business needs to consider the extent to which it is communicating with, helping and giving something back to the community.

DID YOU KNOW?

Research suggests that graduates and, in particular, post-graduates with MBA (master of business administration) degrees favour companies that are able to demonstrate high levels of social responsibility.

FACT FILE

The 'ethics' of cigarettes

British American Tobacco (BAT), the major cigarette manufacturer, produces CSR reports. The anti-smoking group ASH calls the whole idea laughable. BAT's CSR report defines targets for reducing energy use, water consumption, carbon dioxide emissions and waste production, and commits itself to enlightened employment practices. This is at odds with what many see as BAT's ruthless marketing to entice young people to smoke, as illustrated by the situation when BAT employees were caught on television handing out packets of Benson and Hedges to teenage volleyball players in the Gambia. BAT helped to draw up the International Tobacco Products Marketing Standards, intended to bring worldwide marketing in line with UK restrictions. However, it does not fund, for example, anti-smoking campaigns among the young.

The value of social audits

Social auditing or CSR reporting, if done seriously and effectively, is beneficial both for business and for stakeholders.

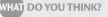
WHAT DO YOU THINK?

How useful is a social audit? Can a company such as BAT, which produces an arguably lethal product, be socially responsible? Can an organisation such as BAT reconcile its business interests with people's health?

A social audit provides information to all the stakeholders of a business about the extent to which it is meeting its non-financial objectives. Evidence suggests that consumers increasingly prefer to purchase their goods and services from 'responsible' businesses. Social audits enable consumers to be more informed about which firms to purchase from and which firms to avoid. They enable pressure groups to gain access to valuable information, which may inform their campaign against a particular firm or minimise their complaints against it. They also assist government in monitoring the behaviour of firms and identifying the need for legislation or regulation in certain sectors of business.

A social audit provides employees with information about the non-financial performance of the whole organisation rather than simply the department or office they work in. It ensures that senior management has a complete view of the impact of the firm's activities on all of its stakeholders, thus identifying areas for improvement and encouraging more informed decision making. This is particularly important for large organisations and multinational companies, such as BP, which have businesses in many different locations worldwide.

By opening up its activities to public scrutiny, a social audit might deter future criticism of a firm, which in turn might reduce the actions of pressure groups. This is more likely to be the case if the social audit is carried out by independent consultants or is independently scrutinised and published in full.

Of course, undertaking social audits may highlight areas that need improving and that will incur high costs. Firms may be reluctant to pursue developments that will incur these costs, but pressure from stakeholders and more responsible competitors is likely to mean that, eventually, they will have no choice.

FACT FILE

Hard issues

'Issues that many managers think are soft for business, such as environment, diversity, human rights and community, are now hard for business,' says David Grayson, a director of Business in the Community (BIC). 'They are hard to ignore, hard to manage, and very hard for businesses that get them wrong. However, managed well, these issues can be a source of competitive advantage.'

PRACTICE EXERCISE 3   Total: 70 marks (60 minutes)

1 Explain the term 'corporate social responsibility'. (3 marks)

2 Explain two examples of a firm acting in a socially responsible manner in relation to:
   a its employees   (6 marks)   b its customers   (6 marks)

3 Identify two stakeholders (other than employees and customers) and for each, explain a company action that could be seen as socially responsible in relation to the particular stakeholder. (8 marks)

4 Explain two benefits to a business of accepting its social responsibility. (6 marks)

5 Explain two arguments against firms accepting their social responsibility. (6 marks)

6 Why might it be difficult for a firm to act in a socially responsible way towards all its stakeholders? (6 marks)

7 Define the term 'social cost' and give two examples. (5 marks)

8 Distinguish between negative and positive externalities. (5 marks)

9 Explain the term 'market failure' in relation to this topic. (4 marks)

10 Assess the difficulties that an organisation might face if it were required to produce a social audit of its activities. (15 marks)

CASE STUDY 4 Corporate social responsibility at Starbucks and B&Q

Starbucks Coffee Co.

Starbucks defines corporate social responsibility (CSR) as conducting business in ways that produce social, environmental and economic benefits for the communities in which it operates. Starbucks has been widely recognised for its commitment to numerous stakeholders, including coffee growers, the environment, employees and communities, while simultaneously achieving rapid financial growth. The company has a senior vice president of CSR who provides strategic development of policies, strategies, processes and tools to link corporate social responsibility with business success.

Since 1998, Starbucks has supported Conservation International's (CI's) Conservation Coffee programme, which encourages sustainable agriculture practices and the protection of biodiversity through the production of shade-grown coffee and the institution of coffee-purchasing guidelines. The programme has resulted in a 60% price premium being paid to farmers and a 220% increase in the coffee-growing land preserved as tropical forests.

The company has been praised for its generous employee benefits and its commitment, unusual in the industry, to provide full benefits for both full- and part-time employees. Starbucks also has a number of programmes to help benefit the communities in which it has stores, as well as in the developing economies where its coffee is grown, harvested and processed.

B&Q

B&Q is a do-it-yourself retailer. It operates nearly 1,400 stores in 16 countries. About 22% of B&Q's turnover is timber and timber-related products, and the company has worked to lessen its impact on forests and other environments since 1991. B&Q has monitored its suppliers' social and environmental practices, sourcing 99% of wood-based products from independently certified, well-managed forests, becoming a model to other companies and encouraging change in its business partners. B&Q also managed to reduce environmental impact at its stores by minimising packaging, increasing recycling and improving energy efficiency and waste management.

More recently, B&Q has adopted a more holistic approach to corporate social responsibility through the theme of 'being a better neighbour': 'We believe sustainable development is about improving the quality of life for all the people we touch. This can only be achieved by striving to be a better neighbour, whether it is to our store or global trading neighbourhoods.'

The company has found that close monitoring of its suppliers and their sources helps to ensure healthy working conditions, maintain good environmental practices and increase its profits through improved brand loyalty and reduced costs. B&Q also aims to employ people of all backgrounds, particularly older workers, and tries to meet the needs of all customers, including the disabled. B&Q has awarded thousands of Better Community grants to local store-run community projects.

Source: adapted from information on **www.bsr.org.uk**

Questions

Total: 25 marks (35 minutes)

1 Analyse how stakeholders benefit from Starbucks' and B&Q's socially responsible approach. *(10 marks)*

2 To what extent might it be argued that Starbucks' and B&Q's approach to social responsibility is simply another strategy for increasing consumer demand and consumer loyalty? *(15 marks)*

ESSAY QUESTIONS   Total: 40 marks (50 minutes)

Answer one of the following questions:

1 To what extent do social and ethical decisions depend on other factors such as the market
   and competition?   *(40 marks)*

2 Discuss the actions a business might take to demonstrate corporate social responsibility,
   and evaluate whether these reflect genuine values or are just a form of public relations.   *(40 marks)*

3 Assess the effects on a business of changes in the social environment and the changing nature
   of the ethical environment it is faced with, and evaluate possible responses it might make.   *(40 marks)*

Chapter 24

The relationship between businesses and the technological environment

EXAMINER'S VOICE

Remember that the issues considered in this chapter should be viewed as part of the external environment of a business. When analysing or evaluating the external environment facing a business, ensure that you make use of the PESTLE framework discussed in Chapter 21. This will encourage you to think about other aspects of the external environment, not just the techno-logical environment.

KEY TERMS

technological change: adapting new applications of practical or mechanical sciences to industry and commerce.

information technology: the creation, storing and communication of information using microelectronics, computers and telecommunications.

This chapter considers the relationship between businesses and the technological environment. It assesses the effects of technological change on business and evaluates the response of businesses to such change. In particular, it focuses on the impact of technological change in relation to marketing opportunities, business culture and the processes and systems used within business.

Technological change

Technological change occurs in all sectors of business. Examples in the primary sector are: specialist machinery such as combine harvesters, mining equipment, deep-sea oil rigs and computerised fish-locating equipment; genetically modified crops, fertiliser and pesticides. Examples in the secondary sector include: production-line equipment such as robotics and computer-aided manufacture (CAM); computer-aided design (CAD); research and development; stock control; and packaging. Examples in the tertiary sector include: communications; financial records and services (e.g. automated teller machines); logistics design and transport; internet shopping; and barcodes.

Technological change and information technology are reshaping the global economy, making the location of a business irrelevant, levelling the playing field on which business operates and eliminating barriers to participation. New business models involving integrated customer and supply chains, global product development and servicing all rely on information technology to create new ways of working. Used effectively, information technology enables organisations to make dramatic leaps in productivity and to redefine competition within whole sectors. Tesco, as the largest online supermarket retailer, and lastminute.com are excellent examples.

𝑒 EXAMINER'S VOICE

The impact of technology and technological change is covered in many areas at both AS and A2. For example, in Chapter 18 of this book detailed consideration was given to the impact of technological change in allowing for a more flexible workforce, and in Chapter 27 of the AS textbook, the use of technology in operations management was considered.

The innovations resulting from the use of new technology can be split into three main types:

- **processes** — advancements in manufacturing technology and automation
- **products** — new product opportunities using microelectronic technology such as fax machines, electronic games and mobile phones
- **communication links** — developments in information technology

Benefits of technological change

Technological change offers several benefits:

- **Improved efficiency and reduced waste.** Cost-effective use of resources benefits consumers and firms, and in the long term resources last longer, thus benefiting society in general.
- **Better products and services.** Consumers benefit from more choice, and if this leads to more demand, company profits are likely to increase.
- **New products and materials.** Needs and wants that were previously not satisfied can be provided for, as with the invention of the dishwasher and the bread maker.
- **Advances in communication.** Company efficiency is increased and consumer needs are met more directly.
- **Improved working environment.** Employees work in safer conditions and there are a greater number of jobs that are less physically demanding and more interesting.
- **Wealth creation.** Higher living standards are achieved.

Problems in introducing new technology

The introduction of new technology is associated with the following problems:

- **The cost of keeping up to date with the latest technology.** The need to remain up to date in order to stay ahead of or level with competitors can lead to very high replacement costs that occur on a regular basis.
- **Knowing what new technology to buy and when to buy it.** In rapidly changing markets, an investment in technology that is becoming outdated can be a very expensive mistake.
- **Industrial relations between employers and employees.** As technology replaces jobs, there is a danger of resistance by workers and trade unions, and a consequent lowering of morale.

■ **Personnel issues.** As technological change occurs, new skills are required and this has implications for recruitment, retention and training, and their associated costs.

New technology and competition

The ability of firms to benefit from new technology depends on the competition they face. The following analysis demonstrates the possible costs and benefits of new technology to business in relation to both products and processes.

New products

Price skimming can be introduced because consumers are often prepared to pay premium prices for unique products in the short term before competitors catch up. The high profits that result from such price skimming can be retained if a patent is gained that prevents competitors from copying the product. However, it is likely that copycat or 'me too' products will emerge that reduce the original uniqueness of the product.

Firms might use the period before competition catches up to develop their next unique product. In monopoly markets, a lack of competition allows companies to continue to make high profits, thus limiting the incentive for them to introduce new, improved products. In some industries, the high cost of new technology acts as a barrier to entry, allowing existing organisations to maintain high profits in the long run.

New processes

New technology can improve the efficiency of processes, which may help a company to increase its profit margins in the short term. However, in a competitive market, this advantage will soon disappear. New firms will begin to adopt these processes and prices will begin to fall, causing profit margins to fall. In the longer run, if prices fall and if demand is price elastic, profits may rise as a result of greater sales volume. Labour costs can also be reduced, which may be particularly important if companies in high-wage economies are to remain competitive.

e EXAMINER'S VOICE

Remember that in any situation where prices are likely to change, price elasticity of demand may be relevant and could be used as part of your analysis.

Issues to consider when introducing new technology

■ The adoption of any new technology will be influenced by existing technology. For example, is the new technology compatible with the existing technology? Can the changeover from existing to new technology be managed effectively and efficiently?

■ The reaction of the workforce to new technology is important, since their cooperation will be essential.

■ In any given situation, there needs to be a reasoned judgement balancing the benefits of new technology (usually new markets and customers) against the problems created by new technology (usually personnel and operational issues).

- Potential short-term difficulties caused by the changeover must also be considered, such as possible cutbacks in production while old technology is being replaced.
- Finance is a major concern. It is likely that new technology will impose huge financial costs in the short term, but it may generate huge financial benefits in the long term.
- The reliability of forecasts and projections of costs, revenues, markets and technological developments need to be considered, since it is impossible to be totally sure of the impact of change. Firms need to be aware of, and have contingency plans for, when actual figures start to become significantly different from forecast figures.
- The use of IT within an organisation tends to reflect the prevailing management style and culture. A supermarket chain might collect vast quantities of data at shop-floor level and then transmit this to head office for analysis of the popularity of particular product lines etc. In this way, those at the top of the management hierarchy are pulling information up and then passing decisions back down to local branches. A leadership with a more democratic approach might use computer networks to allow such information to flow more freely around the branches, which might empower local branch managers with the information needed for sound decision making.

INGRAM

𝒆 EXAMINER'S VOICE

The impact and effect of technological change is viewed differently by different stakeholders, so remember when answering evaluative questions on this area to be aware of the arguments from differing points of view. Read the question carefully to make sure that you are answering it relevantly: for example, it may want a specific stakeholder's view.

PRACTICE EXERCISE   Total: 40 marks (35 minutes)

1 Give two examples of technological change:
  a in the primary sector of industry   (2 marks)
  b in the secondary sector   (2 marks)
  c in the tertiary sector   (2 marks)

2 What is meant by technological change or innovation in processes?   (3 marks)

3 What is meant by technological change or innovation in products?   (3 marks)

4 Explain two benefits to consumers of the use of new technology.   (6 marks)

5 Explain two benefits to firms of the use of new technology.   (6 marks)

6 Explain two problems for business of introducing new technology.   (6 marks)

7 Consider the main factors that might encourage a business that makes and installs kitchens to introduce new technology.   (10 marks)

CASE STUDY Improving business performance with barcode technology

One of the reasons for Tesco's success has been its investment in IT and particularly in barcode technology. By minimising the stock level of every item, shelf space is freed up, which allows it to expand its range of non-food items.

ISBN 0-86003-376-7

9 780860 033769

Minimum stock levels mean it must replenish continuously, which it does by capturing in-store product data. As well as scanning barcodes at checkouts, staff monitor stock with handheld computers, which they use to scan barcodes on the shelves and check the quantity. Tesco's responsive supply chain then keeps the deliveries coming.

Even small companies can use barcodes to cut errors. A retailer asked its supplier of artificial flowers to put a barcode label on each bloom. Eighteen months later the three to five complaints the supplier used to receive every day (such as 'you sent five yellow and two white when I ordered two yellow and five white') had fallen to three a year — the packer scanned the barcodes before boxing the order and hence eliminated most of the errors. This simple system paid for itself in weeks by cutting the cost of errors.

Food processors include barcodes in their pack designs. An in-line scanning system detects rogue items and stops the line, thus reducing the risk of loading the wrong material into the packaging machine. A well-known jam maker uses such a system to inspect 230 jars a minute to prevent raspberry jam going out as strawberry jam.

An engine manufacturer, with a £40 million annual turnover and a 350-strong workforce, used to check all of its stock manually. With over 25,000 stock locations, this was a very slow process. And even when the physical stock check had been completed, it would take up to 2 weeks for staff to input the data manually into an in-house computerised stock record. The solution was to barcode products and locations, and introduce handheld computers for counting purposes. The benefits gained through this application were impressive. Payback was immediate. Man-hours were saved, costs were reduced and stock control procedures improved.

Source: adapted from information on www.codeway.com.

Questions

Total: 30 marks (40 minutes)

1 Using the information in the article, assess whether a small company should be as involved in technological developments as its larger rivals. *(15 marks)*

2 The article seems to suggest that there are many benefits from adopting technology such as barcodes, and few, if any, costs. To what extent is this always true in relation to the introduction of new technology in business? *(15 marks)*

Chapter 25

The relationship between businesses and the competitive environment

This chapter assesses the effects on business of changes in the competitive structure in which it operates, and evaluates business responses to the changing competitive environment. Changes in competitive structure that are considered include the emergence of new competitors, the development of dominant businesses (for example, through takeover or merger) and changes in the buying power of customers and/or the selling power of suppliers.

Competition

In chapter 21, it was stated that businesses operate within a competitive environment that varies from industry to industry. Some businesses operate in highly competitive markets with many firm all jostling for position, others operate in markets where only a few firms exist.

Almost all business operates in competition with other businesses, whether this is Sainsbury's competing with Asda for customers at a local, national and international level or two local hairdressers competing for clients in a single town. Competition is usually between firms supplying the same products, but it can be broader. For example, British Gas competes not just with other suppliers in the gas provision market but also with the suppliers of other types of fuel, including coal, electricity and oil. Similarly, the *Guardian* competes not just with other newspapers but also with other news sources, including internet sites, radio and television. The managing director of Waterman Pens is famously quoted as saying: 'We are not in the market for pens, but executive gifts.' Thus he redefined the company's competitors as Dunhill and Rolex, rather than Parker and Bic.

Competition is generally regarded as being positive, bringing benefits in particular to customers. The advantages of competition are based on the fact that, in order to gain market share, firms need to offer the cheapest or the best-quality products to customers. This requires them to operate as efficiently as possible, in as cost-effective a way as possible, while at the same time improving the quality of products and services as much as possible.

There are however, some disadvantages of competition:

- Where competition is based solely on price, product quality might be sacrificed because resources that are devoted to competing with other firms, such as the huge amounts spent on advertising and packaging, could be directed to producing cheaper or better products.
- Competition between firms means that, inevitably, some businesses will be forced out of the market, with the economic and human consequences of redundancy and unemployment.
- The competitive process tends to mean that successful businesses gradually take over, or merge with, unsuccessful ones. This in turn leads to the existence of a smaller number of larger and larger businesses. This has happened, for example, in the supermarket sector.

The competitive structure

Some businesses operate in very competitive markets, where there are many small firms, each selling only a tiny proportion of the total market sales. Other businesses operate in markets that tend to be dominated by a few large firms, each selling a significant proportion of the total market sales.

Chapter 34 of the AS textbook discussed the different market structures in detail, including monopoly, oligopoly, monopolistic competition and perfect competition. Review the contents of Chapter 34 in order to ensure that you are familiar with these different market structures, their characteristics and how they influence the behaviour of firms that operate in them. Table 25.1 summarises their characteristics and how they influence the behaviour of firms that operate in them.

Table 25.1 Market conditions

Characteristic	Perfect competition	Monopolistic competition	Oligopoly	Monopoly
Number and size of firms	Many and small	Many and small	Few and large	One, in theory*
Nature of product	Identical	Differentiated	Differentiated	Unique
Examples	Foreign exchange market, stock market, fruit and vegetable market	Hairdressers, plumbers, cafés and insurance companies	Supermarkets, banks and motor vehicle manufacturers	Nationalised industries (pre-1980s), Royal Mail (for letters)
Barriers to entry	None; it is easy to enter or leave the market	None; it is easy to enter or leave the market	High barriers to entry	High barriers to entry
Effect on business	• Price takers • Cost efficiency needed for survival • No real scope for marketing • Very low profit margins	• Some control over price • Cost efficiency is important unless the firm has a strong USP • Benefits from marketing • Low profit margins	• Non-price competition • High overheads • High profit margins but aim to achieve USP through branding • High spending on promotion • Collusion can occur between firms	• Price setter • Can become complacent • Power depends on importance of the product and its alternatives • High profit margins

*In theory, a monopoly is a single producer; in practice, a monopoly is a firm with a market share of 25% or more.

The banking industry

The banking industry is an oligopoly market. The merger between Lloyds TSB and HBOS was finalised in January 2009. The newly named Lloyds Banking Group will control about 25% of British customers' personal bank accounts and about 28% of the mortgage market. In order to permit the merger of HBOS and Lloyds TSB, competition law was set aside by the UK government because it was felt that the deal would help maintain the stability of the banking sector. The Treasury is to own 43.4% of the merged bank. There have been worries that the bank could limit choice for consumers. At the end of 2008, the Office of Fair Trading said there could be a 'substantial lessening of competition' in personal current accounts, bank services for smaller firms and the mortgage market as a result of the transaction.

From the customers' point of view, does it matter that there has been 'a substantial lessening of competition' in the banking market?

An alternative way of analysing market conditions is to draw on Michael Porter's idea of competitive forces. Porter's model identified five features of markets that determine how a successful firm might cope with its competitors. This is also discussed in chapter 34 of the AS textbook, so review the discussion there before continuing with this chapter. Figure 25.1 summarises Porter's five competitive forces.

Figure 25.1 Porter's five competitive forces

Changes in the competitive structure in which a business operates may occur for a number of reasons and in each case, a business needs to be able to respond appropriately to the changing environment in which it finds itself. The following changes in competitive structure are those identified in the AQA specification.

1 The emergence of new competitors

This can occur because a new business enters the industry. In very competitive markets, such as those that can be described as monopolistic competition, new competitors enter all the time. For example, a new hairdresser or a new café might set up on the high street. In order to compete, existing businesses will need to ensure that their product or service is of an appropriate quality, is priced and promoted appropriately and has its own USP. In some industries, barriers to entry prevent or deter new firms from entering. They thus enable existing firms to continue relatively unchallenged and, in effect, protect them from new entrants and allow them to earn higher profits than they might in a more competitive environment. This is the case in monopoly or oligopoly markets such as car manufacturers, supermarkets and banks.

Barriers to entry include:

- the high capital costs required to set up a new business in markets in which existing firms are monopolies
- possible patents that allow existing firms to 'monopolise' the market legally
- the loyalty of customers to existing firms
- the need to achieve large economies of scale quickly in order to be able to charge a competitive price
- government policy and regulation
- access to resources and distribution channels

Car manufacturing, for example, involves huge capital investment in manufacturing equipment, compliance with safety and emission rules and regulation, access to parts suppliers, development of a network of car dealerships and a huge marketing campaign to establish a new car brand with consumers.

New and often unexpected or, non-traditional, competitors can emerge and completely change the nature of a market. For example, supermarkets now sell perfume, books, electrical equipment and mobile phones — often massively undercutting the more traditional sources of such products. This illustrates the need for a business always to be considering the threat of competition from all sources and how to respond.

Existing businesses may try to protect themselves against new competitors' products by introducing exclusive distribution agreements or by the use of strong branding, trade marks, patents and other psychological and legal barriers against substitutes.

2 The development of dominant businesses

From being a relatively small player in a market, a business can develop into a dominant business as a result of a takeover or a merger. (Mergers and takeovers are discussed in detail in chapter 26.) This can have a significant impact on the competitive forces for existing firms that are now faced with a more powerful competitor. For example, in 2003, Morrisons, a medium sized but fast-growing supermarket chain, took over Safeway and became a much more significant competitor for Asda, Sainsbury's and Tesco.

3 Changes in the buying power of customers

The power of customers is related to their ability to influence the price that they pay. The extent to which an individual customer has power over a business will depend on whether they are one among many customers or one of only a small number of customers. In the case of the former, the value of any one customer's purchases is likely to be very small and hence is unlikely to have any influence over a business's behaviour. If, however, the value of a customer's purchases are huge, that customer is likely to be very influential. For example, if a small pig farm sells all of its own sausages to a major supermarket, it will be in a highly vulnerable position if the supermarket insists on reducing the price it pays for supplies or demands a longer credit period.

In addition to the actual number of customers, the economic climate can influence the buying power of customers. Recession and deflationary periods, such as in 2008/09, give customers stronger buying power and put them in control. For example, businesses that are the customers of other businesses may choose to renegotiate contracts with their suppliers every 6 months rather than entering traditional longer-term agreements lasting 2 to 3 years.

Improvements in ICT have an influence on the power of customers. The internet and general access to information mean that customers today are much more aware, much better informed and much more prepared, for example, to switch energy suppliers, phone networks or mortgage firms more regularly if it means getting a better deal.

4 Changes in the selling power of suppliers

The power of suppliers is related to their ability to influence the prices they will receive for their supplies. The more concentrated and controlled the source of supply, the more power an individual supplier is likely to wield in the market. This will be determined by whether the resources a business requires are purchased from a small firm for which there are many alternative competing suppliers or from a large firm that is the only source of the supply. The latter will be able to influence the price to a greater extent. Suppliers can group together in order to wield more power. They can join together as a cartel, such as OPEC (the Oil Producing and Exporting Countries) to try to influence prices to their own advantage. (Note that in most developed countries cartels are illegal.) Sometimes suppliers engage in secret collusion. For example, in 2005, a group of independent schools in the UK was found guilty of secretly colluding on the setting of school fees.

An example of an industry facing a powerful supplier is the personal computer making industry, which is supplied by the, almost monopoly-like, operating system supplier, Microsoft. In the example above, where the small pig farmer is in a vulnerable position because his main customer is a large supermarket, the converse is that if the large supermarket is supplied by a range of small farmers and many of its other products come from a huge range of small suppliers, all of which are competing with each other for the supermarket contract, the power of these suppliers is likely to be weak.

Because such changes can have a significant impact on the success of a business, it is vital that any business understands fully the competitive environment in which it operates. This means it should have good information: about the market in which it operates; the number and size of competitors; the nature of the product and the quality of substitute products produced by its competitors; how easy it is for a new firm to set up in the industry; whether it has control over the price it charges (for example is it a price setter or a price taker?); how important price and non-price competition are; how many and how powerful its suppliers are; and how many and how powerful its customers are.

By constantly assessing the changes that are taking place in its competitive environment, a business is able to introduce strategies that help it to create the right conditions for establishing a competitive advantage over its rivals. If, for example, a new competitor emerges in the market, a business might try to diversify into other markets or consider merging with or taking over another business in order to establish itself as a dominant business in the market. If a supplier has too much power over a business, one possibility is for the business to find alternative sources of supply. Equally, if a business currently sells to a single buyer, its strategy might be to find more buyers in order to reduce the power of any one buyer.

Concentration ratios

The level of competition in a market is indicated by how many firms are operating in it — the more firms, the more competitive the market. However, it could be that although many firms are operating in a market, the market is dominated by just a few firms that each have a significant market share. For example, an industry with 500 firms in it might at first glance appear very competitive, but if the largest five firms have 90% of the market, the market is likely to be oligopolistic. Similarly, if the largest three firms in an industry have 60% of the total market share compared to another industry in which the largest five firms have 10% of the total market share, the former industry would be considered heavily concentrated compared to the latter.

A method of identifying this is to use concentration ratios. A 5-firm concentration ratio identifies the total market share of the five largest firms in an industry, while a 4-firm concentration ratio gives the market share of the largest four firms in an industry. The 5-firm concentration ratio for the supermarket industry is approximately 80%; the five firms are Tesco (with a market share of about 32%), ASDA (17%), Sainsbury's (16%), Morrisons (11%) and Waitrose (4%).

Market structures can be classified by their concentration ratios. For example:
- A perfectly competitive market will give a very low concentration ratio.
- A monopolistically competitive market will usually have a 4-firm concentration ratio of less than 40%.
- An oligopolistic market will usually have a 4-firm concentration ratio of above 60%. An example is the car industry.
- A monopoly market will have a 4-firm concentration ratio of almost 100%. (In practice, a monopolist is deemed to have as little as 25% of the market.)

Table 25.2 gives the 5-firm concentration ratios for a range of industries.

Table 25.2 Five-firm concentration ratios

Industrial sector	Market share of the largest five firms in the industry (%)
Tobacco products	99
Confectionary	81
Soft drinks and mineral waters	75
Motor vehicles	63
Wood and wood products	9
Furniture	5
Clothing	4

Fair versus unfair competition

The more competitive the market, the less opportunity there is for profit as firms try to cut costs and prices in order to attract customers. Where there is little competition but a strong demand, **supernormal profits** may be made: that is, profits well above what could be 'reasonably expected'. Such profits are often a sign of unfair competition.

Examples of unfair competition include:

- monopolies charging high prices because of a lack of competition
- oligopolies agreeing to restrict supply or fix high prices (e.g. supermarkets and independent schools have been accused of colluding to set high prices or fees)
- producers only supplying retailers that promise not to stock rival products or that agree to stock the whole range of a supplier's products
- predatory pricing by large firms (i.e. undercutting the prices charged by a small firm in order to force it out of the market)

In practice, it is often difficult to establish immediately whether competition is fair or unfair. A company may offer lower prices because its costs are lower (fair competition), but if it eliminates competition and then increases its prices, this is unfair competition. If unfair competition is likely to be 'against the interests of consumers', it is possible that the Competition Commission will intervene.

KEY TERMS

fair competition: where firms compete on equal terms in a way that offers consumers the best choice of products and prices.

unfair competition: where firms do not compete fairly, but act in a way that restricts consumer choice in the short or long run.

WHAT DO YOU THINK?

The granting of a patent generally guarantees a monopoly for 20 years. Is this unfair? If people demand a particular product and are prepared to pay high prices for it, is it unfair for a company to charge them a high price? Does your answer depend on the nature of the product and whether it is a basic necessity or a luxury?

DID YOU KNOW?

Market conditions can be linked with most marketing strategies and tactics. For example, the marketing mix may need to be adapted to the market situation (e.g. non-price competition for oligopolies), and the length of the product life cycle may depend on the level of competition. Similarly, links can be made with operational issues. For example, economies of scale are more accessible for monopolists than for firms in very competitive situations, but are not so likely if there is spare capacity.

PRACTICE EXERCISE 1   Total: 50 marks (45 minutes)

1 Briefly explain the main characteristics of each of the following:
   a monopoly *(3 marks)*   c monopolistic competition *(3 marks)*
   b oligopoly *(3 marks)*   d perfect competition *(3 marks)*

2 Identify Porter's five competitive forces. *(5 marks)*

3 Identify and explain four possible changes in competitive structure *(12 marks)*

4 Distinguish between a heavily concentrated industry and a lightly concentrated industry. *(6 marks)*

5 If the 5-firm ratio for soft drinks and mineral waters is 75%, what does this mean? *(3 marks)*

6 Distinguish between fair and unfair competition. *(5 marks)*

7 Explain one example of unfair competition. *(3 marks)*

8 Why is it difficult to assess whether competition is unfair? *(4 marks)*

PRACTICE EXERCISE 2   Total: 20 marks (20 minutes)

1 Using the data in Table 25.2, identify and briefly explain the market structure that is likely to be present in:
   a the tobacco products industry *(3 marks)*
   b the furniture industry *(3 marks)*

2 Using your knowledge and understanding of the motor vehicle and clothing industries, discuss the reasons why the motor vehicle industry is so highly concentrated compared to the clothing industry. *(14 marks)*

CASE STUDY The jewellery and watch market

The jewellery and watch market is highly competitive in terms of both supply and retail. Recent years have seen the emergence of several luxury-goods and high-fashion conglomerates* in the market, which possess strong brands that are supported by substantial financial resources. However, this has had the effect of over-crowding — particularly in the watches sector — and is putting pressure on the small and medium-sized operations that make up the majority of the UK industry.

This overcrowding has led to excess capacity in the industry as the number of manufacturers and retailers has increased at a faster rate than the demand for watches and jewellery. Analysts predict that some smaller firms will be forced out of the industry eventually, unless they can find a niche market for their products. The high-fashion conglomerates are able to purchase the more expensive locations in the high street and can afford to spend much more money on advertising in order to promote their brands and achieve brand loyalty.

Overall, jewellery and watches have gained from their repositioning, over a number of years, into the fashion market. This has led to consumers owning and buying a wider range of pieces, from costume jewellery to precious items. At the same time, it has opened up the market to a number of new players and brands, including fashion and retail clothing labels. There has also been an increase in the number of retailers offering both fashion and real jewellery pieces.

Major developments in the market have included the successful introduction of branded jewellery ranges. As specialist retail jewellers have endeavoured to differentiate themselves from mixed retailers and other competitors, branding has been a key part of the package, with exclusive ranges and designs playing an important role. The market has also gained increasing transparency, owing to the development of online sales.

The jewellery and watch market comprises a wide range of suppliers and retailers. Global brands operating within this market are of great importance, as they invest in promotion and development.

Women are the major buyers in the UK market and are more likely than men to buy either watches or jewellery. While the majority of women's purchases are for themselves, male buyers tend to buy jewellery as a gift. The men's jewellery market is continuing to develop, driven by younger consumers.

The market has gained from a rise in consumer spending since the end of the 1990s. However, it has had to compete for its share of spending against a wide range of products and services, from home electronics to holidays. More recently, a downturn in the property market and a recession have dampened demand for luxuries and non-essentials such as jewellery and watches. The volume market seems most exposed, as consumers cut back on their spending and retailers respond with price cuts, although lighter-weight pieces or those containing less precious metal or gems may offer a compromise. At the other end of the market, consumers may be more likely to revert to the traditional tendency of regarding jewellery as an investment buy.

*A conglomerate is a firm that has joined with another firm in a different line of business to create a larger company.

Source: adapted from information on www.keynote.co.uk.

Questions
Total: 25 marks (35 minutes)

1 Analyse the market conditions for the jewellery and watch industry using Porter's five forces model. *(10 marks)*

2 To what extent might the traditional small jewellery and watch operators be considered to be suffering from unfair competition from 'luxury-goods and high-fashion conglomerates'? *(15 marks)*

ESSAY QUESTION
Total: 40 marks (50 minutes)

Using a relevant business example, assess the effects on the business of changes in the competitive structure in which it operates, and evaluate its responses to this changing competitive environment. *(40 marks)*

e EXAMINER'S VOICE

The integrated case study on assessing changes in the business environment, which follows on the next page, is not an example of a Unit 4 examination paper — its purpose is to encourage you to consider the external environment in total (i.e. the issues covered in chapters 21 to 25), how it might influence a major industry and how such an industry might respond.

Assessing changes in the business environment

CASE STUDY External influences and the car industry

The global picture

'The current economic climate is having an unprecedented impact on the car industry. The combination of evaporating consumer confidence combined with significant restrictions on available finance and credit, and overcapacity have created the car industry's "perfect storm"' (KPMG spokesperson).

The global car industry now has the capacity to make 94 million vehicles each year — an overcapacity of about 34 million, or the output of about 100 plants, based on current sales. In other industries, merger and acquisition activity has removed excess capacity, but not in the car industry. As a result, over the next year or so car-makers are likely to close down factories and lay off thousands of workers. The challenge for the industry will be to cut production now without losing the ability to increase it when people start buying cars again.

On the one hand, Japanese car-makers are closing production plants at home, where sales have slipped, but in North America, they are only slowing production, cutting contract workers, and postponing plans to open more factories because they are keen to grab market share once the US economy improves. The so-called Big Three American manufacturers (General Motors, Ford and Chrysler) do not have the same opportunities, and for them the probable cuts at home are likely to be significant. To become profitable, according to experts, US car-makers will need to close at least a dozen of their 53 factories in North America in the next few years.

Nowhere is there greater overcapacity than in China, where local companies are likely to absorb much of the pain as the weakest players close and large state-owned companies gobble up the stronger ones. That could be good news for foreign makers and their joint-venture partners. General Motors may be closing plants at home, but not in China, where it is much easier to lay off workers and rehire them when things pick up. Toyota is actually expanding its Chinese operations. As in China, the global downturn has hammered car-makers in Russia and eastern Europe. Multinational car companies, which have grabbed about three-quarters of the Russian market, are hurting too but are reluctant to pull back for fear of losing out in the longer run.

Supporting this picture, the key findings of KPMG's 2009 survey of executives in global automotive industry include the following:

- The profitability of the car industry will decrease between 2009 and 2013 and there will be increasing risk of company insolvencies or bankruptcies.
- Overcapacity of 11–20% is expected in the next 5 years and high costs and declining demand will drive restructuring — including more mergers and acquisitions and alliances.
- Prospects in emerging markets are being scaled back, as consumers are hit by rapid credit contraction. However, demand for cars in emerging markets is still expected to grow faster than in all other regions. In addition to China and India, the biggest potential growth is expected in central and eastern Europe.
- Technology and innovation are keys to the future of the industry — with fuel efficiency, advanced fuel technologies and environmental pressures considered the most important trends.
- Consumers are becoming increasingly price sensitive. Lower fuel consumption will be the most important criteria in the next 5 years and affordability of vehicles is likely to be more important than quality.

- Chinese and Indian car brands are expected to significantly expand their market share between 2009 and 2013, while US manufacturers (GM, Ford and Chrysler) are expected to lose market share.

The UK picture

The UK is the third largest car market in the EU. Over 850,000 people are employed by the UK motor industry, which has a manufacturing turnover of £51 billion and exports 75% of its manufactured vehicles.

The car industry is influenced by the business cycle because it produces durable goods, which are very sensitive to changes in income. As a result of the downturn in 2008, new car sales fell to their lowest level for 12 years. All parts of the market were hit, from Rolls-Royce and Bentley at the top end to the Nissan Micra at the other. Ford and Aston Martin sent staff home for an extended Christmas 2008 break, as plants closed temporarily in order to save money. Vauxhall offered workers sabbaticals of up to 9 months on reduced pay, while Honda axed its Formula One racing team to lower costs. Nissan announced plans to cut a quarter of its 5,000-strong workforce at its Sunderland plant. It said the reduction was necessary to 'safeguard our long-term future' and 'ensure we are in a strong and viable position once business conditions return to normal'. These are 'extraordinary circumstances, not of our making'.

The chief executive of the Society of Motor Manufacturers and Traders (SMMT) said the announcement from Nissan emphasised how much the industry needed government support. 'Swift action is necessary to limit the extent of the damage and ensure we retain valuable industrial capability,' Lord Mandelson, the business secretary, said: 'This is a highly skilled workforce that has many of the skills that UK industry will need as conditions globally improve.' At the time of writing, no firm decision had been made by the government about whether it will provide aid. Interestingly, many of the country's largest car plants are based in Labour constituencies, including the Nissan HQ, leading to concerns among MPs about the impact of substantial job losses on the local electorate.

One of the few success stories of 2008 was the Smart car, which recorded a sales increase of more than 43%

to 7,526. Among the big losers were Aston Martin and Bentley, which saw sales down by more than a quarter in 2008, and Land Rover, where sales fell 30%. A Ford spokesman said the number of small cars the company had sold had risen.

The slump in car sales has been good news for those wanting to buy a new car, with dealers knocking thousands of pounds off vehicles in a desperate attempt to shift stock. Some of the biggest bargains involved 4x4s and other large cars that are deemed 'environmentally unfriendly' and which face the threat of increased taxation by the government. Over the past decade, car and fuel taxation and excise duties have been structured so as to encourage motorists to drive more environmentally friendly vehicles. In the 2008 Budget, plans were announced to increase vehicle excise duty on cars with high carbon dioxide emissions and to apply this increased rate retrospectively to cars registered before March 2006. It is estimated that the proposed changes will affect 1.2 million motorists and cost them a total of £260 million.

The SMMT, reporting on environmental factors in its annual 'Sustainability Report', accepts the evidence of global warming and that increasing levels of carbon dioxide in the atmosphere, caused by non-natural sources, are to blame. As a result, improvements have been made in the environmental credentials of cars and their production sites. For example, from production sites across the UK, energy use and carbon dioxide emissions per vehicle produced, water use and waste to landfill have all been significantly reduced, and from products, average new car carbon dioxide emissions have dropped, thanks to investment in alternative fuel technologies.

Sources: adapted from information on www.businessweek.com, www.kpmg.co.uk and www.smmt.co.uk.

Appendix 1 UK economic growth, 2003–08 (%)

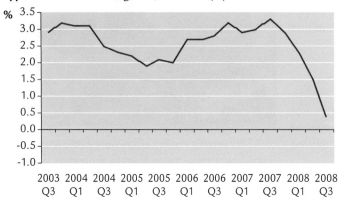

Source: www.statistics.gov.uk.

Appendix 2 New car registrations

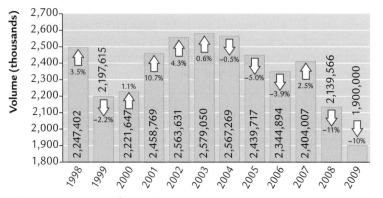

Source: www.smmt.co.uk.

Percentage change in new car registrations, May–November 2008

Month	Month-on-month
May	–3.5%
June	–6.1%
July	–13.0%
August	–18.6%
September	–21.2%
October	–23.0%
November	–36.8%

Source: www.smmt.co.uk.

Appendix 3 Five-firm concentration ratio in the UK car industry (car production in the UK), 2007

Car-makers	Volume	% market share
Largest five producers:		
Nissan	353,718	23.1%
Toyota	277,825	18.1%
Honda	237,772	15.5%
BMW (MINI)	237,709	15.5%
Land Rover	232,548	15.2%
5-firm concentration ratio	1,339,572	87.5%
Total car production	1,534,567	

Source: www.smmt.co.uk.

Appendix 4 *Carbon dioxide emissions in the car industry*

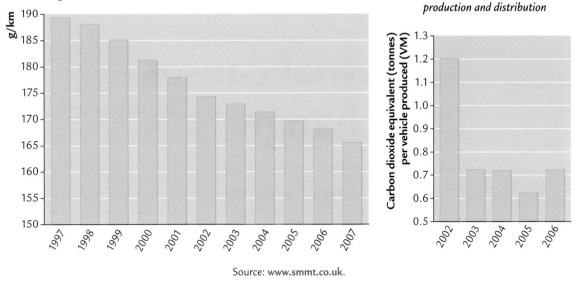

UK average new car carbon dioxide emissions

Carbon dioxide emissions from production and distribution

Source: www.smmt.co.uk.

Questions
Total: 80 marks (1 hour 45 minutes)

Section A

Answer one of the following questions, both of which are related to the text and the data:

1 Using the information in the case study and the data in the appendices, evaluate the opportunities and threats in the external environment facing the car industry in the UK. *(40 marks)*

2 In light of the situation described in the case study and appendices, analyse the situation facing Nissan (or any of the other main producers) and advise it on the most appropriate strategies to introduce. *(40 marks)*

Section B

Answer one of the following essay questions:

1 Discuss how emerging markets might contribute to any improvements in the future performance of the car industry. *(40 marks)*

2 Assess the impact of the business cycle on the car industry and the effectiveness of its response to the downturn. *(40 marks)*

3 Discuss the impact of environmental issues on car production and how well producers are responding to such issues. *(40 marks)*

Chapter 26

Internal causes of change

This chapter considers internal causes of change. It focuses in particular on changes in organisational size, which may come about due to mergers, takeovers, organic growth and retrenchment. It also considers internal change as a result of new owners and leaders and as a result of poor business performance.

Change in organisational size

Reasons for the growth of firms

Growth is usually seen as a natural development for a company. It can provide benefits and opportunities for a business and for its stakeholders. At a basic level, growth enables a company to reach breakeven and make profit. It provides more opportunities for a company to take advantage of economies of scale, and a growing and dynamic company is more likely to remain competitive. Growth by diversification allows a company to spread risks, and a large company with plenty of assets and diversified activities will find it easier to cope with recession and fluctuations in the business cycle.

Growth is an important objective, and is sometimes the only way to ensure that a firm survives. Growth can be achieved either internally or externally. The choice of which type of growth is best suited to a particular organisation depends on a trade-off between the costs involved, the level of risk and the speed of each method of development.

Internal or organic growth

Internal growth may be pursued by a firm for a number of reasons: for example, when its product is in the early stage of its life cycle and is not yet fully established in the marketplace, or when its product is highly technical and the firm needs to gain experience of dealing with it, ensuring that any problems can be ironed out. If the costs of growth need to be spread over time, internal growth is likely to be pursued. For many firms, internal growth is the best option because there are no suitable acquisitions available.

KEY TERM

internal (or organic) growth: when a firm expands its existing capacity or range of activities by extending its premises or building new factories from its own resources, rather than by integration with another firm.

Finance for the investment and expansion accompanying this type of growth usually comes from the retained profit resulting from existing activities, from borrowing or by attracting new investors. As a result, this process of growth tends to be relatively slow, but less risky than external growth.

External growth

External growth tends to be via the integration of two or more companies and can occur by **merger** or **takeover** (usually known as **acquisition**). Mergers occur when two businesses believe and jointly agree that they can increase their combined profit, or achieve other objectives, by merging their businesses. Takeovers or acquisitions are accomplished by the acquiring firm offering cash or shares (or both) to the shareholders (i.e. the owners) of the firm that is being taken over. External growth is usually the fastest way to achieve growth, but given the problems of integrating two separate organisations, it can be risky.

Takeovers can be hostile or friendly. A hostile takeover is where the attention of the predator company (the company wishing to take over the other company) is not welcome. The company being targeted recommends that its shareholders do not accept the bid, as was the case in the  unsuccessful bids in 2004 by Philip Green, owner of BHS, for Marks and Spencer. In contrast, a friendly or recommended takeover is where the company being targeted welcomes the takeover and recommends shareholders to accept the bid.

External growth, whether by merger or takeover, friendly or hostile, can be classified into three broad types of integration — vertical, horizontal and conglomerate — each of which is discussed below.

Vertical integration

Vertical integration can occur by one firm integrating *backwards*. A manufacturer might integrate with the supplier of its raw materials or components: for example, a car assembler owning a component supplier or an oil distribution company owning oil wells. On the other hand, vertical integration can also occur by one firm integrating *forwards*: for example, where a manufacturer integrates with a retailer that sells its finished product.

KEY TERMS

integration: the coming together of two or more businesses via a merger or takeover.

merger: where two or more firms agree to come together under one board of directors.

takeover (or acquisition): where one firm buys a majority shareholding in another firm and therefore assumes full management control.

KEY TERM

vertical integration: the coming together of firms in the same industry but at different stages of the production process.

FOTOLIA

An example of a firm using vertical integration is BP, which has grown by integrating with firms at all points in the chain of production, from oil exploration, extraction and refining, to distribution and retailing via petrol stations. A further example is American Apparel, a fashion retailer and manufacturer that actually advertises itself as a vertically integrated industrial company. The brand is based in Los Angeles, where from a single building it controls the dyeing, finishing, designing, sewing, cutting, marketing and distribution of the company's product. The company shoots and distributes its own advertisements, often using its own employees as subjects. It also owns and operates each of its retail locations as opposed to franchising. According to its management, the vertically integrated model allows the company to design, cut, distribute and sell an item globally in the span of a week.

Backward vertical integration means that the resulting organisation is in a position to control the supplies of raw materials and components in terms of price, quality and reliability, while forward vertical integration means that it is able to control the marketing and sale of products to the final consumer. In both cases, integration:

- enables internal planning and coordination of processes to overcome the uncertainty of dealing with external suppliers and retailers
- facilitates cost savings in both technical and marketing areas
- builds barriers to entry for new competitors
- enables the resulting organisation to absorb the profit margins of suppliers and/or retailers

In practice, mergers or takeovers designed to achieve vertical integration are relatively few in number; the vast majority are designed to achieve horizontal integration.

Horizontal integration

Firms involved in horizontal integration are usually potential competitors, such as Lloyds TSB and HBOS, Wal-Mart and ASDA, and Morrisons and Safeway. Horizontal integration is likely to create significant economies of scale, resulting in lower unit costs because duplicate and/or competing facilities can be closed down. However, diseconomies are possible if the integration results in poor communications and coordination.

Horizontal integration reduces the amount of competition in the market and thus means that the resulting organisation has an increased market share. But if, as a result of the takeover, market share is likely to reach or exceed 25%, it might be referred to the Competition Commission, which may either ban the takeover or set various conditions.

KEY TERM

horizontal integration: the coming together of firms operating at the same stage of production and in the same market.

Morrisons and Safeway

Morrisons, a medium-sized but fast-growing UK supermarket chain, took over its rival Safeway in 2004. The combined firm, with 598 stores and a market share of 16%, aimed to compete with ASDA, Sainsbury's and Tesco — giants of the UK supermarket sector. Morrisons was looking for a way to grow quickly and could afford to fund an acquisition to achieve that goal. The Office of Fair Trading allowed the takeover to go ahead on condition that Morrisons sold off 52 stores following its takeover of the Safeway chain.

Conglomerate integration

The General Electric Company (GE), founded by light bulb inventor Thomas Edison, is a conglomerate. Throughout the 1980s and 1990s, it transformed itself from a simple maker of electrical appliances into a giant conglomerate with interests in sectors from aircraft engines and power generators to financial services, medical imaging, television programmes and plastics.

conglomerate integration: the coming together of firms operating in unrelated markets.

Conglomerate integration results in diversification and thus helps the resulting organisation spread its risks, which is in the long-term interest of both shareholders and employees. It can also lead to a sharing of good practice between different areas of business. However, in some instances, management may have little or no expertise in the newly acquired business area. Studies of corporate growth through conglomeration seem to indicate that unrelated diversification is the fastest route to the growth of sales, but not to the growth of profits. The latter is more likely to come through growth in existing fields.

Conglomerates, by buying up companies, can grow to giant proportions. However, the popularity of the conglomerate form of growth has declined and there have been a number of demergers of conglomerate divisions, often as a result of unsuccessful takeovers and the subsequent need for companies to focus more clearly on their core activities.

DaimlerChrysler

DaimlerChrysler was founded in 1998 when the German Mercedes manufacturer, Daimler-Benz, merged with the US-based Chrysler Corporation. The two businesses complement each other because they operate in different segments of the car market and are prominent in different geographical markets — Chrysler is bigger in the US market than Mercedes, while the German firm has much more presence in Europe and Asia.

In the integration of any businesses, success is about the extent to which they enjoy greater benefits from operating together than they would have done separately. In the case of DaimlerChrysler, Mercedes struggled to blend the contrasting business cultures of the two businesses and the deal failed to produce the transatlantic automotive powerhouse that was anticipated. In 2007, DaimlerChrysler sold Chrysler to a private equity organisation.

FACT FILE

Hewlett-Packard and Compaq

In 2002 the US computer giant Hewlett-Packard completed a merger with Compaq. At the time, there was talk of huge benefits, including greater synergies, economies of scale, improved market share and improved profit margins. The merger resulted in a loss of 15,000 jobs (about 10% of the new company's workforce). The combined group's shares remained stubbornly low and the expected benefits were not realised.

DID YOU KNOW?

Synergy, which means that the whole is greater than the sum of the parts (1 + 1 = 3), is often claimed to be a major advantage of takeovers. The evidence suggests that it is achieved less often than is claimed.

Motives for takeover

- A large company entering a new market may not have the necessary technical expertise and may thus acquire smaller companies with that expertise. In the mid-1990s, Sony did this when it entered the entertainments industry with its PlayStation. While it had the ability needed to produce the hardware, it did not have sufficient software programmers. Its purchase of smaller software producers allowed it to gain a suitably skilled workforce.
- The costs of acquisition or integration may be more favourable than the costs of internal growth, and the speed of growth might be a high priority.
- Brands are expensive to develop, in terms of both time and money, and therefore acquiring companies with prominent brand names is a way to avoid such expense. This was one of the main reasons for Nestlé's takeover of Rowntree.
- The resulting organisation can exploit any patents owned by the company it has acquired. This is particularly important in takeovers in the pharmaceutical and computing industries.
- An organisation may have identified that the market value of a particular company is considerably less than its asset value. Once the company has been acquired, its valuable assets can be sold and the loss-making aspects of the business wound up. This technique is known as **asset stripping**.

Do takeovers work?

Theory suggests that growth via mergers and takeovers will produce synergies, economies of scale, lower unit costs, higher profit levels and increased market share. However, research in the UK and the USA tends to suggest that most takeovers lead to disappointing results.

Many studies show that the majority of takeovers damage the interest of the shareholders of the acquiring company, while rewarding the shareholders of the acquired company, who receive much more for their shares than they were worth before the takeover was announced. Professor Mark Sirower, an adviser to the Boston Consulting Group, in his book *The Synergy Trap: How Companies Lose the Acquisition Game*, says that surveys have repeatedly shown that about 65% of mergers and takeovers fail to benefit the acquiring company, whose shares subsequently underperform in their sector.

The majority of failed mergers and takeovers suffer from poor implementation and the fact that, in a significant proportion of cases, senior management fails to take account of the different cultures of the companies involved. Merging corporate cultures takes time, which senior management does not have, particularly immediately after a merger or takeover. The nature of the problem is not so much that there is direct conflict between the two sides, but that the cultures do not merge quickly enough to take advantage of the available opportunities.

Many consultants refer to how little time companies spend before a merger or takeover thinking about whether their organisations are compatible. The benefits of mergers and takeovers are usually considered in financial or commercial terms rather than human and organisational terms.

If 65% of mergers and takeovers fail to benefit shareholders, what are the conditions that allow the remaining 35% to be successful? Consultants suggest that the combined organisation has to deliver better returns to the shareholders than they would separately — the synergy element. In addition, the merging companies need to decide in advance which partner's way of doing things will prevail — the culture element. Finally, the combined organisation must generate advantages that competitors will find difficult to counter.

FACT FILE

America Online and Time Warner

AOL Time Warner was the result of a merger between America Online (AOL), one of the world's largest internet companies, and Time Warner, the media group that owns Warner Bros film studios, the Warner Music record company, the CNN television news channel and *Time* magazine. The merger in 2001 was, at the time, the largest corporate merger in history and resulted in the world's largest media and entertainment company.

The merger was attractive to AOL as it enabled the company to keep its place as the top internet service provider. To do this, it needed access to a rapid distribution system; and as Time Warner owned one of the USA's largest cable television networks (reaching into 13 million homes), this allowed AOL to offer fast internet services, via cable modems, to millions of households.

The merger was the culmination of AOL's ambition to create a vertically integrated company that would offer consumers everything they needed in the interactive world of the future, from media to films and music. Rupert Murdoch, chairman of

News Corporation, applauded the deal, saying: 'Vertical integration is the way forward. AOL is a distribution company that…took the chance of getting a huge chunk of content.'

However, the internet bubble burst and AOL Time Warner failed to meets its targets. Many of AOL's senior management team failed to cope in the corporate culture of Time Warner and the company failed to exploit many of its advantages. In 2003, shareholders argued that the merger had been a 'grandiose' waste of their money. The company dropped AOL from its orporate name in 2003 and at the same time got rid of most of AOL's management team in an effort to demonstrate that it still valued its core assets. Since then it has sold off non-strategic businesses and assets, and begun to focus more on its core activities.

Analysts suggest that to some extent the merger failed because the claims made for the combined company were foolish, based on wishes rather than any realistic assessment of the market and the world.

FACT FILE

Microsoft's shadow looms over Yahoo's new CEO

In 2008, Microsoft made a $47.5 billion bid for Yahoo that amounted to an offer of $33 a share. The founder of Yahoo, Jerry Yang, rejected the deal, much to the dismay of Yahoo's shareholders. Yang's affinity for the website, which he started as a graduate student in 1994, was viewed as a stumbling block to the talks with Microsoft.

Yahoo's search engine is the second most popular on the Web after Google. Not everyone believes Yahoo will be better off if it hands over its search engine to the software maker because advertising sold alongside search results remain the most lucrative business on the internet. However, since Yang launched Yahoo as a simple internet directory, the company has grown into a mishmash of products that has confused investors, employees, advertisers and consumers.

Yang has now stepped down and analysts are expecting the new chief executive of Yahoo, Carol Bartz, to be the catalyst that brings Microsoft back to the bargaining table. One analyst commented: 'If nothing else, Bartz's fresh perspective should help Yahoo figure out what it does best and then marshal its resources there. Any company that can't define itself to the public in seven to nine words has a problem. Yahoo has had that problem for some time now.'

Source: adapted from an article by Michael Liedtke, Associated Press, www.google.com, 14 January 2009.

Retrenchment

Just as companies encounter problems when becoming larger, so there are problems when they reduce the scale of their operations. Retrenchment can take a range of forms, each of which is likely to have different effects on various stakeholder groups and on the organisation. The overarching problems include possible damage to morale, to relationships and to trust as a result of the inevitable job losses.

KEY TERM

retrenchment: the cutting back of an organisation's scale of operations.

Types of retrenchment

- **Halting recruitment or offering early retirement or voluntary redundancy.** Using this strategy might lessen the feelings of job insecurity among existing employees, as any actions on their part would be voluntary. On the other hand, staff who choose to retire early or take voluntary redundancy may be key people in the organisation and, if they leave, their skills and experience disappear. Cutting back in this way may provide less opportunity for the organisation to introduce change and to restructure.
- **Delayering.** Removing a layer of management from the organisational hierarchy has less impact on operations at shop-floor level and hence on production. It may empower or enrich jobs at the lower level of management, where more responsibility is assumed. However, the workload of the remaining management team will increase, which can add to stress levels and reduce motivation. Motivation might be further affected due to loss of promotion prospects as a layer of opportunities vanishes.

- **Closing a factory, outlet or division of the business.** The effect of this for the business is to reduce overall fixed costs and hence the breakeven point. In addition, depending on the nature of the closure, capacity utilisation may rise in other factories, outlets or divisions. However, this strategy is difficult to reverse if there is an upturn in the economy. Closure will mean a loss of many good staff with valuable skills.
- **Making targeted cutbacks and redundancies throughout the business.** This strategy should allow the company to reorganise to meet objectives — for example, putting more emphasis on e-commerce. It also enables the company to get rid of less productive staff members, which might improve the overall performance of all staff. It will, however, create feelings of job insecurity and lack of trust among the remaining staff.

PRACTICE EXERCISE 1   Total: 50 marks (45 minutes)

1 Distinguish between organic growth and external growth. *(4 marks)*

2 Explain the difference between a merger and a takeover. *(4 marks)*

3 Distinguish between vertical and horizontal integration. *(4 marks)*

4 Explain the term 'conglomerate integration'. *(3 marks)*

5 State two examples of horizontal integration and two examples of conglomerate integration. *(4 marks)*

6 Give two examples of forward vertical integration and two examples of backward vertical integration. *(4 marks)*

7 Explain one possible motive for each of the following types of external growth:
   a horizontal integration   *(3 marks)*   c backward vertical integration   *(3 marks)*
   b forward vertical integration *(3 marks)*   d conglomerate integration   *(3 marks)*

8 Define the term 'retrenchment'. *(3 marks)*

9 Explain two types of retrenchment. *(6 marks)*

10 Explain one positive and one negative effect of retrenchment on an organisation or its stakeholders. *(6 marks)*

CASE STUDY 1 Integration and diversification on the high street

The days when UK clothing retailers manufactured their own garments are long gone. Now only a few retailers, among them Pringle and Jaeger, own factories and control the whole supply process. Even Austin Reed, the epitome of gentlemanly tailoring, has not been in manufacturing since 2000. Laura Ashley still makes curtains and fabrics for soft furnishing, but is no longer a clothing manufacturer.

In the distant past, it made more sense for retailers to make their own clothes. Labour was cheap, the high street was not so competitive and merchandising was less of an art form. How that has changed. The UK textiles industry has crumbled in recent years because of high production costs. Increased competition means that retailers need all of their skills simply to lure shoppers past the window displays. In addition, vertically integrated retailing can be detrimental to flexibility, in terms of the cost of the supply chain and adapting quickly to new styles. Apart from the cost of labour, when a business owns its own factories, it also has to worry about keeping the factories and the staff occupied during quiet periods.

In Europe there is one exception to the rule that vertically integrated retailing does not work — Zara, the cutting-edge Spanish fashion chain. Like many UK retailers, Zara was a clothing producer long before the first store opened in 1975. But, unlike its UK rivals, Zara managed to transform the manufacturing arm into a highly efficient machine, able to cater to the needs of customers, rather than trying to dictate to the market.

Fifty per cent of the retailer's garments and accessories are made up in its own factories in Portugal and Spain. As a result, company executives claim that Zara can translate a catwalk design into high-street fashion within 3 weeks, which means that the company does not have to second-guess what will be fashionable up to 9 months ahead.

There is a much-quoted story that when Madonna played a series of concerts in Spain in 2005, teenagers attending the final performance were able to wear a Zara version of the outfit she had worn at the first show.

Most experts suggest that the Zara model would be difficult to introduce in the UK because of its higher labour costs.

Horizontal integration is more common in the clothing retail sector. Examples include the Arcadia Group and Gap Inc. The Arcadia Group, the largest privately owned clothing retailer, is the result of a series of horizontal integrations, bringing together Burton, Topshop, Topman, Outfit, Miss Selfridge, Evans, Dorothy Perkins, Evans and Wallis. The GAP Inc. retail clothing corporation integrated horizontally to control three distinct companies, Banana Republic, Old Navy and the GAP brand itself.

Questions

Total: 30 marks (40 minutes)

1 According to the case study, 'Vertically integrated retailing can be detrimental to flexibility, in terms of the cost of the supply chain and adapting quickly to new styles.' Discuss this statement in relation to the fashion industry. *(15 marks)*

2 Evaluate the reasons why the Arcadia Group and Gap have chosen to expand through horizontal integration, while other businesses might choose to expand by diversification. *(15 marks)*

ESSAY QUESTIONS

Total: 40 marks (50 minutes)

Answer one of the following questions:

1 Using examples of businesses you are familiar with, assess the implications for a business of organic growth as compared with external growth. *(40 marks)*

2 Research indicates that 65% of mergers and takeovers fail to benefit shareholders. Discuss why the other 35% are successful. *(40 marks)*

New owners and leaders

Managing growth

Growth is a difficult process to manage for a medium-sized business, especially if it is rapid. It often means that owners, who have been in complete control of all aspects of a business, have to plan for, and then adjust to, handing over responsibility to others. In comparison to the leadership of a medium-sized business, the leadership of a large business tends to have a much less hands-on approach and needs to delegate much more. Equally, in a large business, the task of controlling and coordinating activities is much more difficult.

Without strong and effective management, growth can result in a loss of direction and control. The demands placed on a leader or manager in relation to managing and motivating a large team require very different skills from those needed in a medium-sized business. Introducing a solid organisational structure, having an effective management team and carrying out detailed financial and operational planning and forecasting, are vital.

There are a number of issues to consider when a business grows:

- Management structures and hierarchies will need to change so that the business is better positioned to achieve its objectives. A medium-sized business may replace its simple and clear functional structure with a complex matrix structure or, depending on the nature of the business, a product-based or region-based structure. Spans of control are likely to increase and new layers of authority and departments will need to be created. The whole process of management becomes more complex.
- There will be more delegation. The original owners are likely to lose much of the direct contact they had with customers, suppliers and staff, and will take on more of a managing and leading role. Professionals in finance, marketing and personnel will need to be recruited to take on growing specialist responsibilities, and an effective management team will need to be created.
- Staff responsibilities will need to be changed. As the business and workload grows, employees will need to focus on what they do best; jobs will become more clearly defined, with job descriptions, training and development plans, and appraisal systems being introduced.
- Staff motivation may decline, at least in the short term, as the changes that result from growth begin to have an impact, which may in turn affect customer service. For example, in the past employees may have been used to dealing directly with the owner/boss of the business, and the additional layers of management that will be introduced as the business grows may be resented. Managing and motivating a larger team successfully is likely to require a democratic leadership and management style, which may be very different to the previous style. (Leadership style is considered in detail in Chapter 28.)

Ⓔ EXAMINER'S VOICE

When answering questions about the problems associated with business growth, try to take an integrated approach and consider financial, marketing, operations management and human resource issues.

FOTOLIA

Bringing in a management team

As mentioned above, as a business grows it will need restructuring. In most instances, the expertise to build and manage that structure will come from outside the business. A bigger company needs managers to take control of departments and a hierarchy that has the expertise and the time to drive it forward. The Fact File on Alternative Networks below and the case study of Friends Reunited on p. 442 provide examples of how growing businesses can benefit from outside expertise.

Private investors and venture capital firms evaluate management structures and expertise before committing funding, and often insist on recruiting new or interim management. This can be seen as a way of taking control away from the founder, but it is often a means of protecting their investment by ensuring that any skills gaps are plugged and that the necessary structures and experience are in place.

DID YOU KNOW?

Interim managers are employed for a specific task or set period. They can oversee a period of development or the setting up of a new structure, or can come in to run departments until existing members of staff have developed the skills to take over.

FACT FILE

Alternative Networks

James Murray, co-founder of the UK business communications service provider Alternative Networks, wanted to expand the business but had little time to do so. 'As a board we were getting to the size where we needed a senior management team to deal with day-to-day issues. The board had five members which, with eight departments to look after, were spread too thinly and getting bogged down by nitty-gritty activities. We weren't getting the opportunities to look away from the business and work on strategy. We needed to bring people in to look after these areas and then report to the board,' says Murray. In support of its corporate objective to double its sales within 2 years, Alternative Networks appointed an HR director, a head of IT, a finance controller, a head of marketing and a client management director. While still being fully integrated into the company, Murray claims, the board benefited from its new management structure. 'It allowed the board to focus on new ideas, new products, strategy, acquisitions and the overall direction of the business.'

Alternative Networks has achieved a track record of consistently profitable growth over the past 14 years, with a proven and successful strategy that is driven by organic and acquisitive growth. It now employs over 430 people, across four UK regions — London, Reading, Manchester and Leeds.

Source: adapted from www.alternativenetworks.com.

WHAT DO YOU THINK?

Michael Dell, of Dell Computers, once said: 'If you limit a company by its structure or by the people in the company, you will, by definition, limit the full potential of that business.' Do you agree?

Management buyouts and private equity takeovers

Finance for buyouts

Finance for management buyouts can come from managers' personal funds, bank loans and investment funds obtained by selling shares to employees, but more usually it comes from either venture capitalists or private equity firms. Venture capitalists and private equity firms work by lending the MBO the cash it needs and by taking a stake in the company for a return of about 25–30% on their investment over 3–5 years.

Reasons for buyouts

- A large business might sell off a small section to raise cash, refocus the business or get rid of an unprofitable activity. The management team of the parent company's unwanted section might feel it could be successful with a different approach or more finance.
- Owners of a family business who wish to retire might prefer to sell to the management team in the hope of maintaining employment and continuity in the community.
- The firm might be in the hands of the receiver, who must try to keep it going in order to raise money to pay off creditors. One way of doing this is to sell part of it to the management team.

Rewards of buyouts

- Management and employees have more motivation and responsibility.
- Objectives may be clearer because there is no owner–manager conflict.
- There is likely to be less bureaucracy in the form of a head office that might hinder progress.
- Profits will not be diverted to another part of the organisation.
- If successful, the possibility exists of floating the company on the stock market or selling shares in a takeover offer.

Risks of buyouts

- If unsuccessful, personal losses are felt by the new owners or investors.
- The original owners might have been correct in assessing that the business was fundamentally unprofitable.
- There may be little access to capital.
- They often involve considerable rationalisation and job losses, with adverse effects on staff morale.
- Managers have to learn a whole range of new skills immediately, particularly if they have bought out from a large company. Suddenly, they have to do everything that before they took for granted, such as looking after the IT infrastructure, human resources and payroll.

Are buyouts a good thing?

According to figures from the Centre for Management Buy-Out Research at Nottingham University Business School, the value of buyouts rose from just £16 billion in 2003 to a staggering record value of £45.9 billion in 2007. The actual number of buyouts in 2007 was 672.

 KEY TERM

management buyout (MBO): where the managers of a business buy out the existing shareholders in order to gain ownership and control of the business or part of the business.

 YOU KNOW?

Private equity takeovers involve private investors taking over a company and working closely with managers to turn the business around. In many cases they involve **public to private buyouts**: that is, public limited companies being bought out and transformed into private limited companies. This topic was considered in detail in Chapter 7 of the AS textbook.

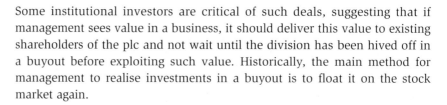
Some institutional investors are critical of such deals, suggesting that if management sees value in a business, it should deliver this value to existing shareholders of the plc and not wait until the division has been hived off in a buyout before exploiting such value. Historically, the main method for management to realise investments in a buyout is to float it on the stock market again.

Some commentators argue that workers may be more at risk with a management buyout than if the company had been purchased by a large organisation. If the company is not successful, workers and managers share the loss, but if the company is successful, it is really only the managers who benefit. Others argue that managers are the real risk takers and that workers' jobs might have disappeared if there had been no management buyout.

From private to public limited company

For many firms, problems arise when growth involves changing from private to public limited company status. Going from a private limited company to a

public limited company usually means floating shares on the stock market. Companies join the stock market all the time, and the more optimistic the economic climate, the more new issues of shares there are. The value of a stock market listing is that a company has a higher profile and access to a large pool of capital. This can provide a more balanced capital structure, especially for highly geared firms.

A drawback of flotation is that public companies are answerable to their shareholders and investment analysts will scrutinise the company prospectus closely. Once the company is floated on the stock market, shareholders may simply be interested in generating quick profits at the cost of longer-term success. The shareholders of a private company tend to be 'in it for the long run', for example, happy to agree to high levels of research spending and accepting relatively low dividend payouts. However, once the shareholder base is widened, the firm comes under severe pressure to generate record levels of profit year by year, even if the 'right' thing to do is to spend heavily on research in the hope of generating future success.

From public to private limited company

A number of companies have changed back from public to private limited companies. Private limited company status has the advantages of more privacy and less pressure on management resulting from share price movements. This allows management to take a longer-term view. Firms go private because, in general, there is a lack of interest in private firms. In such instances, the benefits of being listed are outweighed by the cost of meeting regulatory requirements and by the time that needs to be spent with analysts and fund managers and generally communicating with the market.

ⓔ EXAMINER'S VOICE

The different legal structures of business were covered in Chapter 7 of the AS textbook. Ensure that you are familiar with the characteristics and implications of private and public limited companies.

Poor business performance

Internal change can also come about as a result of the poor performance of a business. Such a situation may lead to a change (usually a decline) in the size of the business and/or it may lead to a change in ownership of the business or changes in leaders and senior managers. Much will depend on the context of the business, but any of the changes and strategies discussed earlier in this chapter may be appropriate. For example, a business that is not performing well and whose share price is falling may be an attractive proposition for another business considering a takeover. As has been seen in a number of the Fact Files, it may be that the business is not performing as well as it could be because the original management did not have the necessary skills or experience. In this case, new leaders may be brought in.

PRACTICE EXERCISE 2   Total: 60 marks (55 minutes)

1 Explain two differences between being the boss of a small business and being the leader or manager of a large business.   *(6 marks)*

2 Explain two types of change that are likely to take place in the organisational structure of a growing business.   *(6 marks)*

3 Distinguish between a functional and a matrix structure.   *(4 marks)*

4 Why might growth lead to a loss of direction and control?   *(5 marks)*

5 Explain one advantage of increasing delegation in a growing firm.   *(4 marks)*

6 Why might the owner of a growing business be reluctant to delegate?   *(4 marks)*

7 Define the term 'management buyout'.   *(3 marks)*

8 Explain one risk and one reward for (a) management and (b) the workforce that might result from a management buyout.   *(8 marks)*

9 Explain the benefit of a stock exchange listing for an organisation.   *(3 marks)*

10 Distinguish between a private limited company and a public limited company.   *(4 marks)*

---

11 Explain two problems that may occur for a growing firm that changes from private limited to public limited company status. *(6 marks)*

12 Explain one reason why a firm might change back from public limited to private limited company status. *(3 marks)*

13 Why might poor performance lead to internal changes for an organisation? *(4 marks)*

CASE STUDY 2 Friends Reunited

Steve Pankhurst, founder of Friends Reunited, realised that he had a business with plenty of potential, but without the expertise to exploit it. 'We quickly became aware of the true value of the company, but we were ideas people and developers who, all of a sudden, had this massive company on our hands. We had a go at growing it ourselves and had taken on 10 people who were mostly friends and family, but we were struggling. We knew we were missing opportunities, such as global expansion, where we simply didn't have the experience.'

Friends Reunited's appointment of a new management team to drive the expansion came from an assessment of their long-term objectives for the business. They received a number of takeover offers. 'The offers we received were tempting and we listened to what they had to say. But it became clear that by selling or giving away some of the company, the site would have become over-commercialised and lost its core values. We didn't want that, so decided to keep control and bring someone in who shared our beliefs.'

Pankhurst and his co-founders appointed former *Financial Times* chief operating officer Michael Murphy as chief executive. 'We liked him because he was down-to-earth and shared our entrepreneurial feelings about not over-commercialising the site, and he had the

experience to grow the site internationally. Michael then brought in someone to take care of the marketing side of the company and made several other management appointments.'

Friends Reunited now operates additional businesses under the umbrella of Happy Group Ltd, with the original founders focused on developing new ideas. 'Bringing in management has allowed us to step away from the running of the business. It's helped stabilise the business and take it to the next level.'

While Pankhurst says the introduction of Friends Reunited's management team went smoothly, it wasn't without its teething problems. 'When Michael came in we were still a bit hands-on, particularly on the technology side, and we were the only people who knew how certain things ran. Initially, Michael wanted to change things, such as the design, and when you've got so close to something, you can become blinkered and defensive about it. It can be difficult to accept criticism about a business you've sweated blood over building. You have to learn to take a step back and accept that's why you've brought these people in.'

ITV bought Friends Reunited in 2005 for £120m.

Source: adapted from **www.friendsreunited.co.uk**.

Question

Total: 15 marks (20 minutes)

Discuss whether Friends Reunited was right to use outside expertise to build and manage the company as it grew.

(15 marks)

CASE STUDY 3   Making it on the market

Almost 2 years on from the flotation of his company, the Wigmore Group, Peter Hewitt, chief executive, feels confident being at the helm of a quoted business. Since he listed the company, which does building maintenance and construction work, Hewitt has raised funds twice more to enable him to make acquisitions. However, he warns other companies not to underestimate the challenges involved in such a move. 'There is no doubt that going public puts the business on a whole different plane,' he says. 'It is like moving from a two-dimensional to a three-dimensional world.'

For Hewitt, the biggest change has been adapting to the world of investor relations. 'You have to remember that the shareholders are your customers and can buy and sell your shares,' he says. 'As a consequence, you are not only having to run the business and make it viable — you also have to go out and sell the business to them and market it in a way that is far beyond the normal trade marketing. That includes everything from meeting investors to lunching the financial journalists.'

Company owners can gain a picture of market sentiment towards their business by reading the literature in which investors look for information. 'Read the magazines and the websites and keep abreast of what people are saying about your business,' he says.

Being in the public eye also means that any mistakes a company owner makes are far more visible. As a result, Hewitt says, company owners need to plan carefully. 'Bear in mind the saying, "Prior planning and preparation prevents poor performance",' he says.

Source: adapted from an article in *The Times*, 18 November 2003.

Question   Total: 15 marks (25 minutes)

Discuss the arguments for and against the flotation of a company such as the Wigmore Group.   *(15 marks)*

ESSAY QUESTION   Total: 40 marks (50 minutes)

Evidence suggests that most entrepreneurs who successfully start and establish a small business do not have the skills to make it into a successful large business. Discuss this statement and evaluate the strategies that might be taken to improve the likelihood of success.   *(40 marks)*

Chapter 27

Planning for change

This chapter considers how businesses plan for change. It identifies the purpose of corporate plans and assesses their value. Internal and external influences on corporate plans are assessed. Contingency planning as part of corporate planning is also considered.

The purpose and value of corporate plans

A firm's mission statement and corporate aims and objectives dictate its future direction. The corporate plan attempts to achieve these aims and objectives and to ensure that the firm's actions match its mission statement.

Aims and objectives start off broad at the corporate level and become more detailed at the level of each functional area, thus encouraging a coordinated approach. The same approach is used in determining the corporate plan or strategy that will be put in place to achieve these aims and objectives. This will have an impact at every level of the firm, from the corporate level to the functional, departmental or operational level. Functional plans will set out what the different functions of the business (including marketing, production, human resource and finance) will do to contribute to the corporate plan and hence the achievement of corporate objectives.

A corporate plan thus clarifies the role of each department in contributing to meeting the aims and objectives of the organisation. As a result, it allows for better coordination of activities within a business. In addition, it helps to identify the resources required by the organisation and so makes it easier to raise finance by providing a clear plan of action, indicating how and why investment is required. Its success depends on a number of issues, including whether it is the right plan for the business in its present circumstances, whether there are adequate financial, human or production resources to implement the plan, the probable actions and reactions of competitors, and how changes in the external environment are likely to affect the plan and the business.

KEY TERM

corporate plan: a strategy detailing how a firm's aims and objectives will be achieved, comprising both medium- and long-term actions.

e EXAMINER'S VOICE

Corporate planning or strategic analysis requires you to bring together many of the concepts and content covered elsewhere in the course — marketing, finance, people, operations.

Don't allow different terms to confuse you. In this area, many terms are used interchangeably and essentially mean the same thing. For example, corporate plan, strategic plan and corporate strategy all refer to the broad corporate-level plans that a business makes in order to achieve its objectives.

e EXAMINER'S VOICE

Try to read a newspaper, listen to the news or log on to the BBC News website regularly so that you are aware of changes taking place in the business environment and are able to identify the dynamic nature of the external environment and how this influences corporate plans.

Strategic decisions

Strategic decisions, which result in the corporate plan, concern the general direction and overall policy of the firm and are likely to influence its performance. These decisions have significant long-term effects on the firm and therefore require detailed consideration and approval at senior management level. They can be high risk because the outcomes are unknown and will remain so for some time.

Strategic decisions often involve moving into new areas and this requires additional resources, new procedures and retraining. Strategic decisions might concern whether the firm should consider expansion by acquisition or organic growth in order to achieve its corporate goal of, say, market dominance. They might also be about how the firm will compete in a way that distinguishes it from its competitors — for example, on the basis of quality and uniqueness or in terms of cost leadership and low prices.

EXAMINER'S VOICE

Just as any decision has an opportunity cost, so choosing one strategy rather than another involves an opportunity cost.

Tactical decisions

In contrast to strategic decisions, tactical decisions tend to be short to medium term and are concerned with specific areas rather than overall policy. Unlike strategic decisions, tactical decisions are calculated and their outcome is more predictable. For example, if a product's sales are below target, a firm may make tactical decisions to remedy this — for example, cutting the price of the product and/or running a sales promotion. Tactical decisions may be used to implement strategic decisions and are usually made by middle management.

Corporate planning process

The corporate planning process involves the following stages:
- **Mission statement.** This stage sets out the purpose of the organisation and its corporate aims (discussed in Chapters 1 and 20).
- **Objectives.** This stage breaks down the corporate aims and indicates how they can be achieved in terms of functional objectives (discussed in Chapters 2, 7, 11 and 16).

To produce a plan of action, the company needs to gather information about the business and its market. Such information comes from internal and external sources.
- **Internal environment.** This stage reviews the organisation's different functional areas, including marketing, finance, operations and human resources, in order to assess its core competencies, what its key resources are and how successful it is in the markets in which it operates. It is through sensible resource utilisation and a focus on its core competencies that a business is best able to take advantage of opportunities in its environment.

■ **External environment.** This stage assesses the key changes that are taking place in the organisation's external environment and makes use of PESTLE analysis (discussed in Chapter 21) and Porter's five forces competitor analysis (discussed in detail in Chapter 34 of the AS textbook and more briefly in Chapter 25 of this book).

■ **SWOT analysis.** This stage identifies the key internal strengths and weaknesses of the organisation and its external opportunities and threats. It analyses what the organisation needs to do to counter threats, seize opportunities, build on its strengths and overcome its weaknesses (covered later in this chapter).

■ **Strategic choice.** This stage identifies a range of options available to the organisation in order to gain a competitive advantage. A range of approaches to decision making can be used (covered in more detail in Chapter 30) and Porter's generic strategies (considered in Chapter 9).

■ **Strategic implementation.** This stage puts a strategy into effect, creating a framework and responsibility for carrying out the strategy at the functional or departmental level. This is where strategies are translated into policies, rules, procedures and operational targets within the different functional areas.

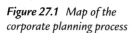

Figure 27.1 Map of the corporate planning process

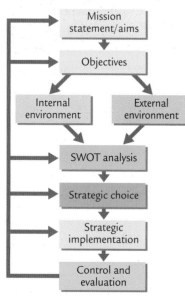

■ **Control and evaluation.** This stage monitors and reviews the success of the strategy and assesses actual performance against what was intended. It enables modifications to be made to the mission, aims and objectives, SWOT analysis, strategic choices and implementation strategies. It is therefore not only a control device but also a means of continuous improvement.

Figure 27.1 illustrates the whole process of corporate or strategic planning and demonstrates how each aspect is linked.

ⓔ EXAMINER'S VOICE

Note how almost all of these stages have been covered in other areas of the A2 specification. Ensure that your knowledge and understanding of all of these areas is sound and that you can apply your understanding of corporate planning effectively, and in an integrated manner, to a given situation.

ⓔ EXAMINER'S VOICE

Ensure that you review your understanding of Porter's five competitive forces and Porter's generic strategies and their relationship to corporate planning.

PRACTICE EXERCISE 1   Total: 25 marks (20 minutes)

1 What is a corporate plan?   *(4 marks)*

2 Explain one advantage of a corporate plan for a business.   *(3 marks)*

3 Identify six stages involved in the corporate planning process.   *(6 marks)*

4 Explain two reasons why a corporate plan might fail.   *(6 marks)*

5 Distinguish between strategic and tactical decisions.   *(6 marks)*

AQA A2 Business Studies

CASE STUDY 1 J Sainsbury plc

Sir Peter Davis became chief executive officer (CEO) of Sainsbury's in March 2000 in what was seen as an attempt by the company to regain market position. During his term, however, Sainsbury's was demoted to third in the UK grocery market and the decline in performance relative to its competitors led the group to make its first ever loss in 2004. Davis also oversaw an almost £3 billion upgrade of stores, distribution and IT equipment.

In March 2004, Davis was replaced as CEO by Justin King, who joined Sainsbury's from Marks and Spencer plc. King had previously been a managing director at ASDA. King ordered a direct-mail campaign to 1 million Sainsbury's customers as part of his 6-month business review, asking them what they wanted from the company and where it could improve. This survey confirmed the commentary of retail analysts that Sainsbury's was not ensuring that shelves were fully stocked. The retailer's supply chain was badly disrupted by problems stemming from the new IT and delivery systems introduced by Peter Davis.

On 18 October 2004, all store managers gathered in Birmingham where King unveiled the results of the business review and his plans to revive the company's fortunes. This was made public on 19 October and was generally well received by both the stock market and the media. Immediate plans included laying off 750 head-quarters staff and recruiting around 3,000 shop-floor staff to improve the quality of service and overcome the firm's main problem of stock availability. At the same meeting, Lawrence Christensen, the newly appointed supply chain director, highlighted the reasons for avail-ability problems and his plan to address them. Immediate supply chain improvements included the reactivation of two distribution centres. Another significant announce-ment was the halving of the dividend to increase funds available to finance price cuts and quality improvements.

Mr King warned that trading in the first quarter of 2005 would be 'challenging', but expressed confidence that customers would notice the improvements made to its stores. Sainsbury's cut prices on 6,000 products during 2005 in an effort to generate more business. It also took action to improve product availability.

J SAINSBURY PLC MEDIA LIBRARY

Sainsbury's market share stabilised in 2005, after declining for much of 2004. Mr King said that the retailer's 3-year recovery plan, which aimed to raise its sales by £2.5 billion by 2007/08, was on track. By the end of 2005, Sainsbury's sales were growing in line with the market, Mr King stressed. 'We said this is a 3-year turnaround. Being successful in this marketplace means you have to be a very good business because we have very good competitors.' Analysts were encouraged by the performance, which indicated that Sainsbury's had turned the corner. Its market share improved but it had yet to convert that to profit.

Despite the improvement, King warned that the group continued to battle in a competitive environ-ment, adding that 'in these circumstances we are particularly pleased that we have seen an improving trend in sales'. 'Our major focus on availability is beginning to show results, with both colleagues and customers noticing improvements in store,' King added. He also said that the group was confident of achieving its sales targets for 2005/06 despite fierce competition.

Sainsbury's did achieve its sales target and is now a much more successful company than it was pre-2005.

Questions

Total: 50 marks (60 minutes)

1 Explain whether the decisions made by Sainsbury's senior management team are strategic or tactical. *(6 marks)*

2 To what extent is Sainsbury's using Porter's generic strategies to achieve its aims? *(14 marks)*

3 Using Sainsbury's as an example, discuss why broad corporate objectives and strategies need to be broken down into functional objectives and strategies if an organisation is to be successful in meeting its aims. *(15 marks)*

4 Discuss the value of a corporate plan such as Sainsbury's '3-year recovery plan' in assisting a company to achieve its objectives. *(15 marks)*

KEY TERMS

SWOT analysis: a technique that allows an organisation to assess its overall position, or the position of one of its divisions, products or activities. It uses an internal audit to assess its strengths and weaknesses, and an external audit to assess its opportunities and threats.

internal audit: assessment of the strengths and weaknesses of a firm in relation to its competitors.

external audit: assessment of the opportunities and threats facing a firm in the general business environment, i.e. the factors that have the potential to benefit the organisation and the factors that have the potential to cause problems for the organisation.

Assessing internal and external influences on corporate plans: SWOT analysis

A SWOT analysis is a structured approach to assessing the internal and external influences on corporate plans. It involves a consideration of the strengths and weaknesses evident in the business (i.e. internal influences) and the opportunities and threats it faces (i.e. external influences).

Internal audit

An internal audit involves looking at current resources, how well they are managed and how well they match up to the demands of the market and to competition. It needs to range across all aspects of each of the functional areas.

External audit

An external audit involves looking at the possibilities for development in different directions in the future. One method of analysing these external factors is to categorise them according to a PESTLE analysis (see Chapter 21).

> **EXAMINER'S VOICE**
>
> Opportunities and threats are about the future. This introduces the issue of uncertainty into any analysis. Remember, therefore, that when considering external factors in a SWOT analysis, the future is uncertain.

> **DID YOU KNOW?**
>
> Remember, PESTLE stands for political, economic, social, technological, legal and environmental factors.

Once the internal and external audits have been carried out, all of the information obtained is presented in such a way as to assist decision making, usually in the form of a SWOT analysis. An example of a SWOT analysis for a hypothetical business is shown in Table 27.1.

INTERNAL FACTORS	
Strengths	**Weaknesses**
• excellent reputation for high-quality products • seen as innovative • highly skilled staff, selected through a well-organised recruitment and selection process • sound investment in fixed assets and modern equipment and methods • an international leader in research and development in its field • an efficient, delayered company structure • very profitable in comparison to similar organisations	• reputation as a poor employer • product portfolio has too many products in decline and growth stages, with a shortage of products in maturity • expertise in a limited range of market segments • limited provision of training for office staff and production-line workers • high levels of staff turnover and absenteeism • poor accessibility to location of main headquarters • communication difficulties between different divisions and subsidiaries • low level of liquidity; cash-flow problems in recent years

EXTERNAL FACTORS	
Opportunities	**Threats**
• change in social attitudes towards environmental protection (e.g. green consumers) • low wages and high unemployment levels among local people with appropriate skills • main competitor experiencing financial difficulties • government economic policy encouraging more spending • recent legislation requires many companies to buy one of the firm's pieces of equipment • increase in skills-based training schemes • a fall in the exchange rate, helping exporters • new markets opening up in other parts of the world • social trends will encourage families to purchase more of certain products	• downturn predicted in the business cycle • high levels of competition within the market • many new products are being released by new entrants into the market • technological changes mean that recent capital purchases will soon become obsolete • an ageing population will mean fewer sales of certain products • pressure group activity against the opening of a new factory • windfall tax on certain companies increase in interest rates

Table 27.1 Example of a SWOT analysis

Advantages of SWOT analysis

The advantages of SWOT analysis are as follows:
- It highlights current and potential changes in the market and encourages an outward-looking approach.
- It encourages firms to develop and build upon existing strengths.
- It relates the present position and future potential of a business to the market in which it operates and the competitive forces within it, and is thus an excellent basis on which to make decisions.
- By determining the organisation's position, it influences the strategy that will be employed in order to achieve the organisation's aims and objectives.

Disadvantages of SWOT analysis

A SWOT analysis can be time consuming and the situation — especially the external factors — may change rapidly. Thus organisations must use the results of a SWOT analysis with caution. What might have been a strength in the past may now be a weakness, or what was previously a threat may now be an opportunity.

DID YOU KNOW?

All firms, whether large or small, will do something similar to a SWOT analysis, even if it is not as formalised as discussed here. A large firm will use a formal approach to establish and maintain competitive advantage. It needs the discipline of this approach to coordinate action and provide a focus for strategic analysis. A small firm, on the other hand, is likely to conduct a SWOT analysis in a much less formal and much more intuitive way.

***e* EXAMINER'S VOICE**

Avoid using bullet points in the examination. You should concentrate on discussing a few points in detail rather than covering a lot of ideas briefly.

PRACTICE EXERCISE 2   Total: 30 marks (25 minutes)

1 What does SWOT stand for? *(4 marks)*

2 Which parts of a SWOT analysis does an internal audit involve? *(2 marks)*

3 Give two examples of possible strengths a business might have in relation to:
  a marketing *(2 marks)*
  b operations management *(2 marks)*

4 Give two examples of possible weaknesses a business might have in relation to:
  a finance and accounting *(2 marks)*
  b people management *(2 marks)*

5 Give two examples of opportunities in the external environment that might be available to a firm. *(2 marks)*

6 Give two examples of threats in the external environment that might confront a firm. *(2 marks)*

7 Which aspects of a SWOT analysis relate to:
  a the present *(2 marks)*
  b the future? *(2 marks)*

8 Why might issues about uncertainty and time be important considerations in relation to a SWOT analysis? *(4 marks)*

9 Explain one advantage to a business of undertaking a SWOT analysis. *(4 marks)*

1 Complete a SWOT analysis of your school/college. In doing so, consider how your school/college can attempt to:
  a minimise the effect of the threats facing it
  b take advantage of the opportunities available to it
  c build on its strengths
  d overcome its weaknesses

2 On the basis of your SWOT analysis, discuss the possible strategies open to your school/college.

Contingency planning

Crisis in business

In a business context, a crisis is any unexpected event that threatens the well-being or survival of a firm. It is possible to distinguish between two types of crisis: those that are fairly predictable and quantifiable, and those that are totally unexpected and have massive implications for business. This is the difference, for example, between sudden fluctuations in exchange rates and natural disasters such as the Asian tsunami. The former can be dealt with by contingency planning and the latter must be dealt with by crisis management.

Examples of crises include:
- physical destruction due to a natural disaster such as the Asian tsunami in December 2004
- environmental disasters, such as an oil spillage that adversely affects coastal areas
- the impact of 'mad cow' disease on the farming industry
- fraudulent activities of employees in financial services organisations
- major customers withdrawing their custom or going into liquidation — for example, the impact on component suppliers of the closure of a car manufacturer
- pressure group activities or unwelcome media attention, such as revelations about child labour used in the production of products for high-profile companies such as Nike
- faulty or dangerous products, such as Coca-Cola's Dasani water, Microsoft's Xbox leads and the illegal dye Sudan 1 in foodstuffs
- strikes by the workforce, such as those by postal workers and London Underground staff
- machine failures causing massive reductions in production capacity
- competitors launching new products
- a severe recession or changes in exchange rates

In the list above, the unexpected crises are towards the top and the more predictable and quantifiable risks are at the bottom.

FILE

Coca-Cola

Dasani purified bottled water is one of the biggest-selling brands in the USA. It was introduced in the UK in February 2004, ahead of a planned pan-European launch. However, the launch proved a major marketing disaster, as it emerged that some bottles in the UK had more than the recommended level of bromate, a potential carcinogen. In addition, the product was exposed in the media as simply being purified tap water, as opposed to mineral water. The media were quick to criticise the brand, especially as it was launched at a premium price. As a result, Coca-Cola recalled all of its stocks and abandoned its plans for the European markets.

Source: adapted from an article in *The Times*, 14 April 2005.

FACT **FILE**

Microsoft

In February 2005, Microsoft had to recall 14 million power leads for its Xbox game console after a defect scorched carpets and burned some users.

FACT **FILE**

Car component manufacturers

In November 2008, as a result of the fall in demand for cars, the components manufacturer Barton Cold Form, based in Worcestershire, experienced a 45% drop in sales. The firm has an annual turnover of about £9.4 million and employs 98 staff. The managing director said that orders had slowed right down because people weren't buying as many cars. His concern was that the situation could get worse because its major customers, BMW and Honda, had reduced production and were taking longer Christmas breaks than usual.

Contingency planning versus crisis management

Contingency planning aims to minimise the impact of foreseeable yet non-critical events. In relation to such events, the organisation usually has weeks in which to prepare and respond. Contingency planning normally involves gathering detailed information on predictable situations and using computer models that provide systematic opportunities to ask and answer 'what if' questions.

KEY **TERM**

contingency planning: preparing for unexpected and usually unwelcome events that are, however, reasonably predictable and quantifiable.

Crisis management normally involves damage limitation strategies and places a heavy emphasis on public relations (PR) and media relationships. It emphasises the need for a flexible response to any situation and the selection of a crisis team to deal with situations as they arise.

KEY TERM

crisis management: responding to a sudden event that poses a significant threat to a firm.

Effects of crises on functional areas

Crises can have effects on marketing, finance, operations and personnel aspects of a business, and each function needs to be able to respond and manage the situation.

- **Marketing.** When a firm's public image is under threat, successful PR often forms a major part of managing a crisis.
- **Finance.** Crisis management usually requires immediate cash expenditure — for example, on advertising campaigns or environmental clean-up campaigns.
- **Operations.** Contingency planning is important in this area, so that customers' needs can be met, especially if the company uses just-in-time production systems.
- **Personnel.** A crisis usually requires direct, authoritarian-type leadership in order to issue instructions and make quick decisions. In addition, effective communication systems are required. Internal communication should be direct, rapid and open; external communication should be informative, truthful and controlled.

Stages in contingency planning

If a firm is prepared for a crisis, it should be in a better position to deal with it. Contingency planning involves the following steps:

- Recognising the need for contingency planning. Without such recognition, a firm is unlikely to be prepared to deal with a crisis.
- Distinguishing between issues that are critical for the future of the business and those that are not critical but will still have an adverse impact. In relation to the former, the business has no choice but to do everything possible before the issues arise. For the latter, it is likely that these problems will be dealt with as and when they occur. For example, if the crisis is a computer crash, banks cannot risk losing records of customer accounts and hospitals cannot close down intensive care facilities; hence, both need back-up facilities at all times. On the other hand, disruption to computerised invoice systems may hit cash flow but is not as critical and could be resolved in the short term by correcting mistakes by hand.
- Listing all possible crisis scenarios and then using sensitivity analysis (see the Fact File overleaf) and 'what if' questions: for example, 'What if the workforce doesn't accept the pay offer and decides to take industrial action?', 'What if a machine failure causes a 35% reduction in capacity and cannot be fixed for the next 12 hours/12 days/12 weeks?', 'What if our largest competitor launches a new product that is more attractive than ours?' and 'What if our firm is the target of a hostile takeover bid?'

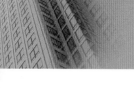

- Searching for ways to prevent each crisis: for example, using extra quality checks and relying less on a single buyer or supplier.
- Formulating plans for dealing with each crisis. This should include planning access to the necessary resources — human, financial and physical — and the establishment of a contingency fund. This is often known as **business continuity planning** or **disaster-recovery planning** (see the Fact Files).
- Simulating each crisis and the operation of each plan. This is usually a computer-based activity, but it can also take the form of role-play exercises.

FACT FILE

Sensitivity analysis

Sensitivity analysis is a technique used to try to reduce uncertainty in decision making. It takes the estimates used in the decision-making process and considers what would happen if the figures were different. It enables managers to evaluate how sensitive the calculations are to changes affecting the inputs to a decision. It asks the question: 'What if?'

Two main methods of applying sensitivity analysis are used. The first asks the question: 'How will the results be affected by a change in each of the variables?' For example, how much will a 10% reduction in sales or a 20% increase in raw material costs affect the expected results?

The second method asks the question: 'What change in the variables will result in the project becoming unacceptable?' This method looks at each of the variables within the calculation and works out how much each of these would have to change to make the project unacceptable. The percentage change in value that makes the project unacceptable is called the **sensitivity margin**. For example, in an investment appraisal, a firm might calculate how much costs and revenues would have to change in order to reduce the net present value (NPV) of a particular project to zero.

Sensitivity analysis is a valuable tool in contingency planning. It gives managers more information to aid decision making and enables them to take a wider view of the risks and to be more prepared for changes. It helps to quantify some of the uncertainties that inevitably accompany business decisions.

FACT FILE

Disaster-recovery planning

When arsonists destroyed the head office of a field marketing agency, its owner ensured the 75 employees were rehoused and the business fully operational within 3 working days.

Having a disaster-recovery plan, which helped to relocate the entire business within days, sent out a strong, positive signal to customers that work would continue as usual. A lot of time was spent making sure that customers' confidence remained strong. Members of the management team held several informal meetings with customers to share ideas and resolve any residual problems. This demonstration of commitment showed that the firm was very much back in business and valued its customers' needs above everything else.

The company's contingency planning routines meant that its data were backed up off site, so it knew this was safe.

AQA A2 Business Studies

Business continuity planning

This is the term that is increasingly used to describe the process of planning for the unexpected. An effective plan will provide a business with procedures to minimise the effects of unexpected disruptive events. The plan should enable a business to recover quickly and efficiently, with the minimum of impact on its day-to-day activities.

Business continuity is particularly important for businesses that are reliant on IT systems, as they provide a process to counteract systems failure. If the IT systems in a business fail or are unavailable, it is likely to have a significant impact on the whole business.

Costs of contingency planning

Contingency planning is a costly activity. In large firms, it can involve huge numbers of highly qualified staff in assessing risk and planning what to do if things go wrong. Like any other form of insurance, it reduces risk but may seem like a waste of money if nothing ultimately goes wrong. The **millennium bug** was a case in point (see the Fact File). For many firms, the potential problems of the millennium bug became very expensive in terms of time and money spent searching for appropriate solutions and strategies.

The 'millennium bug'

The problem of the millennium bug stemmed from computer programmers reducing the space needed for their programs by using shorthand versions of dates. Thus, 31 December 1999 appears in a computer program as 31/12/99. The following day, 1 January 2000, appears as 01/01/00. It was feared that computers would not accept this date as valid because they would be looking for a number in the 'years' space and would not recognise '00' as a year. If a program did not recognise '00', it was feared that the program or even whole computer systems might crash.

It was only in the early 1990s that computer experts identified this problem. Between then and 2000, many programs and operating systems were amended so that they would continue to work as normal on the first day of the year 2000 ('Y2K'). However, some programs, because of their size and complexity, had not been made fully compliant.

At one extreme, as many aircraft are largely controlled by computers, there were fears that the millennium bug could cause widespread disasters as planes fell out of the sky. Other companies were expected to face large bills for the cost of rewriting their computer software or replacing their IT operating systems. Even a company with little or no IT, or whose complete IT package was recent enough to be fully 'Y2K compliant', feared being affected by the bug as their suppliers or customers faced problems that might have knock-on effects.

Thus a potential crisis had been identified, but there was no certainty as to when problems might arise, the exact form they might take or their severity. The millennium problem therefore demonstrated a clear need for detailed contingency planning and preparation so that, when or if problems arose, a firm would know how to respond to minimise the adverse effects.

e EXAMINER'S VOICE

An important aspect of responding promptly to a crisis is to ensure that all functional areas are working together.

Risk management

Business is fraught with risk, and rehearsing the many ways in which things can go wrong is an important management activity. From small start-ups to established global corporations, all companies have to incorporate risk management in every aspect of their business or run the risk of ruin.

Even the smallest slips can have far-reaching consequences. In 1991, jewellery retailer Gerald Ratner gave a speech in which he described some of his company's products as 'total crap'. In doing so, he committed a major PR crime — criticising your own product — and ruined his business. That type of obvious PR disaster can be easily avoided.

Other problems can occur after great planning and consultation, and even government endorsement. For example, Cadbury Schweppes, voted 'Most Admired Company' at the *Management Today* awards in 2004, suffered a severe backlash to its 'Get Active' promotion, in which chocolate wrappers could be redeemed for school sports equipment. Initially, the government's sports minister backed the scheme. But then teachers and health watchdogs criticised the company for linking chocolate consumption with fitness at a time of increasing concern over childhood obesity. As a result, the promotion was dropped.

Once a company's reputation has been damaged, it can take years to restore it because a snowball effect exaggerates the problem. Talented people are less likely to apply for jobs or remain loyal to the company and, as a result, management and morale may suffer. Low staff morale can lead to poor customer service. All of this can have adverse effects on company profits. As a consequence, large companies make risk management a priority.

Some risks are specific to particular industries. For example, mobile phone operators have come under scrutiny over the potential health risks of mobile phone use. At the moment, there is no conclusive evidence that electromagnetic radiation from mobile phones causes ill health, but if such a link were to be established, it would devastate the industry. Mobile operators are managing this risk by spending millions on independent research into the potential health effects of mobile phones and phone masts.

All businesses face risks. But those that assess and manage risk the best are likely to survive the longest.

FACT FILE

Risk management at Diageo

Diageo, the international drinks company, employs thousands of staff simply to assess risk and plan what to do if things go wrong. The company has 'a robust risk-assessment process to capture strategic and operational risk'. It has developed a matrix that allows the company to assess potential events in terms of likelihood and impact.

All aspects of the business are subject to this assessment, from the risk of a fire in a European brewing plant to the potential impact of new European legislation. A lot of time is spent developing practical policies that staff can implement when things go wrong.

WHAT DO YOU THINK?

Given that all businesses face risks, is the alternative for those businesses that fail to assess and manage risk simply to hope for good luck?

FACT FILE

Pepsi and the tsunami

A planned ad for Pepsi, with David Beckham, Ronaldinho and Thierry Henry, among others, was delayed indefinitely following the tsunami in Asia in 2004. Press releases sent out only a few hours before the tsunami happened contained images of the football heroes posing in front of a giant wave. A spokesperson for Pepsi said: 'If we had a crystal ball, we would never have sent out these images.' The image was taken from the commercial, which had a surfing theme, and was meant to be humorous, but it looked frightening immediately after the disaster.

Pepsi had scheduled a glitzy promotional event in Madrid to introduce the ad, which was part of a celebrity-studded campaign employing David Beckham and other athletes and entertainers.

Other firms took similar action. Unilever, the makers of Marmite, ordered the withdrawal of advertisements on London buses. The adverts, which featured people fleeing a huge blob of Marmite, complemented a television campaign as part of Marmite's main winter promotion. The television campaign was virtually finished when the tsunami struck in December, but the campaign on London buses was to have continued into the New Year. American Express, the credit-card provider, decided to withdraw television and cinema advertisements featuring Laird Hamilton, a surfer, talking about the thrill of riding powerful waves.

PRACTICE EXERCISE 3   **Total: 55 marks (50 minutes)**

1 Distinguish between contingency planning and crisis management.   *(6 marks)*

2 Compare the differences in how a firm should deal with a real crisis and with a fairly predictable and quantifiable risk.   *(8 marks)*

3 Explain how the marketing function of a firm needs to be able to respond to a crisis.   *(4 marks)*

4 Explain how the operational function of a firm needs to be able to respond to a crisis.   *(4 marks)*

5 Identify six steps involved in contingency planning.   *(6 marks)*

6 Explain, with an example, the difference between critical and non-critical issues and activities, in the context of contingency planning. *(6 marks)*

7 Briefly explain two approaches to sensitivity analysis. *(6 marks)*

8 What is risk management? *(3 marks)*

9 Explain why a company might wish to introduce 'business continuity planning'. *(4 marks)*

10 Because things rarely go wrong, can the costs of contingency planning be justified? Explain your answer, using examples where possible. *(8 marks)*

CASE STUDY 2 Food alert

In 2005, a large consignment of red chilli, purchased by Premier Foods, was found to contain the illicit dye Sudan 1. The red chilli was used in a vast range of foods, including Crosse and Blackwell Worcester Sauce, in which it was initially found. As a result, millions of food products were recalled from supermarket shelves over concerns that they might be contaminated with the illegal and health-threatening dye. The recall affected all large supermarket chains, including Tesco, Sainsbury's, Marks and Spencer, ASDA and Waitrose, as well as the fast-food chains McDonald's and Pret A Manger.

The UK supplier of the contaminated food products faced very bad PR and a huge bill, although insurers were expected to cover the cost of product recalls, which was estimated at tens of millions of pounds.

The supermarkets acted quickly and the poisoned products were swiftly removed from supermarket shelves. A member of staff from ASDA commented that it was the biggest and quickest recall it had ever had.

The same kind of operation swung into action at all other supermarkets. A member of staff at Tesco said that as soon as the emergency product withdrawal notice arrived from head office, action began to empty the shelves as a matter of urgency. There were checks and cross-checks to make sure these things happened properly.

At Marks and Spencer, a manager said that as the warning was a red alert, the products were off the shelves as soon as they heard about it. All stores were notified at the same time and in the same way.

Source: adapted from an article in *The Times*, 19 February 2005.

Questions
Total: 30 marks (40 minutes)

1 Discuss how effective contingency planning on the part of supermarkets is likely to limit any adverse effects on demand for their products. *(15 marks)*

2 To what extent does the response of supermarkets to the Sudan 1 food scare suggest that rapid operational responses are more important than public relations and strong leadership in a crisis situation? *(15 marks)*

CASE STUDY 3 Heathrow's Terminal 5 (T5)

The £4.3 billion Terminal 5 (T5) at Heathrow airport was opened by the queen on 14 March 2008. Its first day of operations on 27 March was catastrophic.

British Airways chief executive, Mr Willy Walsh, and bosses at airport operator BAA were grilled by MPs from the Commons Transport Committee in May 2008

about the T5 fiasco, which led to hundreds of flights being cancelled and tens of thousands of bags going missing.

Mr Walsh's statement to the committee included the following: 'We let our customers down. We could have done better and should have done better...

AQA A2 Business Studies

We believed that T5 was ready to open and we believed we had prepared sufficiently. With the benefit of hindsight, it was clear we made some mistakes... We compromised on the testing...because of delays in building the terminal...We didn't supply staff with sufficient training and familiarisation. If we did it again, we would do things differently.'

He admitted that the opening of T5 had been 'a disaster' and added: 'I take responsibility for the issues that went wrong...The decisions taken ultimately rest with me. I am prepared to be held responsible.'

Reviewing the press coverage of the situation suggests that there had been a huge failure of planning. For example, no dress rehearsals took place to iron out basic operational problems. As a result, on the day of opening, many staff could not find their car parks, could not get through security and could not find where they were meant to work. Other basic operational problems appear to have been the result of a lack of basic planning. There can be no excuse for

assuming that just because the baggage system worked with one bag, it would work when loaded with 40,000, or that an escalator that glides smoothly when empty will work when full. It was this attention to detail that seems to have been missing. It was in fact a basic failure of management and a failure of the most basic management.

Source: House of Commons Transport Committee: the opening of Heathrow Terminal 5 (2008)(minutes and televised viewing)

Question   Total: 40 marks (50 minutes)

Assess the situation that faced BA on the day Terminal 5 opened. To what extent might effective contingency planning have averted the 'disaster' that took place? Discuss actions that the company might have taken to minimise the impact once the 'disaster' had occurred.   *(40 marks)*

ESSAY QUESTIONS   Total 40 marks (50 minutes)

Select one of the following questions:

1 Assess the value of corporate plans in enabling a business to achieve its aims and objectives. In doing so, evaluate the various stages of the corporate planning process and how each stage contributes to the effectiveness of the overall plan.   *(40 marks)*

2 To what extent is the analysis of internal and external influences on a firm always subject to uncertainty and thus not worth performing?   *(40 marks)*

3 Evaluate the factors that a business might consider before committing itself to a contingency plan that will cost £1 million to implement.   *(40 marks)*

Chapter 28

Key influences on the change process: leadership

This chapter explains the meaning of leadership, its importance in an organisation and how the roles of leaders differ from those of managers. The range of leadership styles are identified and explained. Internal and external factors that influence leadership style are assessed and the role of leadership in managing change is considered.

Leaders or managers?

An old saying states that 'Leadership is doing the right thing and management is doing things right'. Another says that 'Leaders seize opportunities and managers avert threats'. The difference between leaders and managers is not as sharp as these sayings suggest, and both are required for effective corporate growth. For example, the risks taken by leaders create opportunities, which the skills of managers turn into tangible results.

Leadership is about getting people to abandon their old habits and achieve new things, and therefore largely about change — about inspiring, helping, and sometimes enforcing change in people.

Some experts suggest that managers have subordinates but leaders have followers. In this context, managers have a position of authority vested in them by the company, and their subordinates work for them and largely do as they are told. Managers and workers therefore have what is known as a **transactional relationship:** that is, the manager tells the subordinate what to do, and the subordinate does this because they have been promised a reward (their wage or salary) for doing so. Of course, managers are subordinates too and are paid to get things done, often within tight constraints of time and money. They thus naturally pass on this focus on work to their own subordinates.

On the other hand, leaders do not have subordinates, other than those who are also managers. Although leaders have followers, telling people what to do will not inspire them to follow. In order to get people to follow them leaders need to appeal to them and show them how following them will lead to benefits. Charismatic leaders find it easier to attract people to their cause. As a part of their persuasion they typically promise **transformational benefits**. For example, their followers will receive not just extrinsic rewards, such as wages and salaries, but intrinsic benefits, such as somehow becoming better people. Thus, leaders realise the importance of enthusing others to work towards their vision.

An interesting research finding about managers is that they tend to come from stable home backgrounds where they have led relatively normal and comfortable lives. This leads them to be relatively **risk averse**, seeking to avoid conflict where possible and to run a 'happy ship'. Leaders, on the other hand, appear to be **risk seeking**. When pursuing their vision, they consider it natural to encounter problems and hurdles that must be overcome along the way. They are thus comfortable with risk, see routes that others avoid as potential opportunities for advantage, and will happily break rules in order to get things done.

Management skills can be seen as a subset of leadership skills. People who want to lead, but not manage may have wonderful ideas, but without the ability to plan and oversee the necessary work, their ideas are not going to be realised — at least not by them. If their ideas are implemented, it will be done by another leader who embraces the management function.

While management is an important part of leadership, the reverse is not necessarily true. There are many people who are very skilled at implementing someone else's vision but who are not leaders themselves and never could be.

FACT FILE

Jack Welch

Jack Welch was chairman and chief executive officer of General Electric (GE) between 1981 and 2001. Welch gained a reputation for uncanny business acumen and unique leadership strategies at GE. He remains a highly regarded figure in business circles due to his innovative management strategies and leadership style. When he left GE, the company had gone from a market value of $14 billion to one of more than $410 billion, making it the most valuable and largest company in the world.

Jack Welch's goal was to make GE 'the world's most competitive enterprise'. He knew that it would take nothing less than a revolution to transform that dream into a reality. The model of business in the USA in 1980 was that workers worked, managers managed, everyone knew their place and form filling, gaining approval and bureaucracy ruled the day. Welch's 'revolution' meant waging war on GE's old ways of doing things and reinventing the company from top to bottom.

Jack Welch was about leadership, not management. He actually wanted to discard the term 'manager' altogether because it had come to mean someone who 'controls rather than facilitates, complicates rather than simplifies, acts more like a governor than an accelerator'. Welch gave a great deal of thought to how to manage employees effectively so that they were as productive as possible.

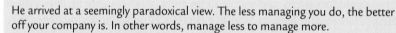

He arrived at a seemingly paradoxical view. The less managing you do, the better off your company is. In other words, manage less to manage more.

Welch decided that GE's leaders, who did too much controlling and monitoring, had to change their management styles. 'Managers slow things down. Leaders spark the business to run smoothly, quickly. Managers talk to one another, write memos to one another. Leaders talk to their employees, talk with their employees, filling them with vision, getting them to perform at levels the employees themselves didn't think possible. Then they simply get out of the way.'

Leadership styles

Leadership styles are concerned with the manner and approach of the head of an organisation or department towards his or her staff. A leader's manner will affect the leader's personal relationships with employees. For example, some leaders will inspire loyalty, some respect and some fear. Leadership style will dictate the extent to which delegation takes place and whether employees are consulted on important decisions.

Four main categories of leadership style are used widely for purposes of analysis: authoritarian (also known as autocratic or dictatorial), paternalistic, democratic and laissez-faire.

 YOU KNOW?

In discussing leadership styles, frequent reference is made to delegation and consultation. Delegation was considered in Chapter 19 of the AS textbook. Consultation means asking employees for their views on various issues that will affect them and the business. Employees' views may be taken into account before decisions are made. The important word here is 'may' and it is this that distinguishes consultation from delegation. Delegation means passing decision-making powers, responsibility and authority down the hierarchy. Consultation means taking into account the views of employees further down the hierarchy, but ultimately the decision-making powers are kept at the top. One of the issues with a detailed consultation process is that decisions can take a long time to be reached.

𝑒 EXAMINER'S VOICE

Because the topic of leadership is closely related to that of motivation, reference is made in this chapter to the work of the motivational theorists F. W. Taylor, Elton Mayo, Maslow and Herzberg. It would be useful to revise your knowledge of these by reading through Chapter 22 of the AS textbook.

Authoritarian leadership

An authoritarian leadership style is an approach which assumes that information and decision making should be kept at the top of the organisation. Authoritarian leaders

KEY TERM

authoritarian leadership: a Taylorite style of leadership in which communication tends to be one-way and top-down.

employ formal systems with strict controls, giving out orders, rather than consulting or delegating. This may happen because leaders have little confidence in the ability of their staff or because they are simply unable to, or prefer not to, relinquish power and control. It may, however, reflect significant pressures on the organisation that force leaders to make rapid and difficult decisions. This is often the case in crisis or emergency situations, where an authoritarian approach is often the most effective.

Authoritarian leadership takes McGregor's Theory X approach (see later in this chapter), using rewards for good behaviour and performance, and penalties for bad performance. The advantages of this approach are that there are clear lines of authority and it can result in quick decisions. However, it can cause frustration and resentment because the system is so dependent on the leader and because of the non-participation of workers in the decision-making process.

Paternalistic leadership

A paternalistic leadership style is essentially an approach where leaders decide what is best for their employees. As its name implies, this style is similar to the approach that parents take with their children. The workforce is treated as a family — there is close supervision, but real attempts are made to gain the respect and acceptance of employees. This is really a type of authoritarian leadership style, but with leaders trying to look after what they perceive to be the needs of their subordinates. Leaders are likely to explain the reasons for their decisions and may consult staff before making them, but delegation is unlikely to be encouraged.

The main advantage of paternalistic leadership is that workers recognise that leaders are trying to support their needs. This style reflects Mayo's work on human relations and the lower- and middle-level needs of Maslow's model.

Democratic leadership

Democratic leadership is related to Maslow's higher-level needs and Herzberg's motivators, and follows McGregor's Theory Y approach (see later in this chapter).

A democratic leadership style means running a business or a department on the basis of decisions agreed by the majority. In some situations, this can mean actually voting on issues, but it is more likely to mean that leaders delegate a great deal, discuss issues, act on advice and explain the reasons for decisions. Democratic leaders not only delegate, but also consult others about their views and take these into account before making a decision.

The major advantage of democratic leadership is that the participation of workers in decision making allows input from people with relevant skills and knowledge, which may lead to improved morale and better-quality decisions. However, the decision-making process might be slower because of the need to consult and discuss, and there might be concern as to where power lies and whether loss of management control is a danger.

KEY TERMS

paternalistic leadership: a leadership style in which employees are consulted but decision making remains firmly at the top.

democratic leadership: a leadership style involving two-way communication and considerable delegation.

DID YOU KNOW?

Participative leadership styles involve consulting with subordinates and evaluating their opinions and suggestions before making a decision. Devolved leadership styles are similar to participative leadership styles.

KEY TERM

laissez-faire leadership:
a leadership style that
abdicates responsibility
and essentially takes a
'hands-off' approach.

Laissez-faire leadership

A laissez-faire leadership style is an approach where the leader has minimal input in the decision-making process and essentially leaves the running of the business to the staff. The term comes from the French for 'leave alone' or 'let be'. Delegation occurs in the sense that decisions are left to people lower down the hierarchy, but such delegation lacks focus and coordination. This style often arises as a result of poor or weak leadership and a failure to provide the framework necessary for a successful democratic approach. However, there may be a conscious decision to give staff the maximum scope to use their initiative and demonstrate their capabilities. How effective it is depends on the staff themselves — some will love the freedom to use their initiative and to be creative, whereas others will hate the unstructured nature of their jobs.

This can be an effective style when employees are highly skilled, experienced and educated, when they take pride in their work and have the drive to do it successfully on their own. The style is less effective when it makes employees feel insecure, when leaders fail to provide regular feedback to employees on how well they are doing, and when leaders themselves do not understand their responsibilities and are hoping that employees can cover for them.

DID YOU KNOW?

Some authors include another style of leadership — bureaucratic leadership — where everything is done according to procedure or policy ('by the book'). Other authors see this as a form of organisational culture (see Chapter 29).

An appropriate leadership style is vitally important if an organisation is to be successful. Probably the worst situation is where an authoritarian approach is used with highly skilled and experienced staff in normal circumstances, as this is likely to alienate staff. Equally, a very democratic or even laissez-faire style of leadership in an emergency situation, or where workers are inexperienced and unskilled, is likely to lead to real problems.

EXAMINER'S VOICE

In most large organisations, there is a clear distinction between senior managers and middle managers. In most cases, senior managers (the marketing director, the finance director etc.) work directly with the chief executive or managing director (the overall leader of the organisation). It is this group who can be defined as the 'leaders'. However, in practice, leadership occurs at all levels. Thus, for example, in a large organisation, branch or departmental managers are actually middle managers in the context of the business as a whole, but in the particular situation they operate in, they are leaders. In the following discussion about McGregor's Theory X and Y, although reference is made to managers, these managers are also likely to be leaders and hence this theory is about both leadership and management style.

McGregor's Theory X and Theory Y

Douglas McGregor (1906–64) was an American psychologist whose book, *The Human Side of Enterprise* (first published in 1960), popularised his view that managers can be grouped into two types: Theory X and Theory Y.

McGregor conducted research into the attitudes of managers towards their employees. He found that the majority of managers assumed that their workers did not enjoy work, did not want to work and were motivated primarily by money; he termed this type of management approach **Theory X** and noted that it was likely to be self-fulfilling. It is an authoritarian approach in which the manager tells workers what to do and supervises them doing it. Such an approach can be useful in a crisis situation or in organisations with many constantly changing or part-time workers, who need clear instructions and clear supervision.

The alternative, minority view that emerged from McGregor's research was that managers assumed that workers enjoyed work, wanted to contribute their ideas and wished to gain satisfaction from employment. He termed this a **Theory Y** approach. It is likely to be a democratic style in which the manager delegates responsibility and authority, and therefore involves staff much more in decision making.

EXAMINER'S VOICE

A common misunderstanding is to think that McGregor's Theory X and Y is a theory about motivation. It is not. It looks at how managers view worker motivation and how this in turn influences their management style.

A Theory X manager assumes that workers:

- are lazy, dislike work and are motivated by money
- need to be supervised and controlled or they will underperform
- have no wish or ability to help make decisions or take on responsibility
- are not interested in the needs of the organisation and lack ambition

In describing Theory X, McGregor commented:

Behind every managerial decision or action are assumptions about human nature and human behaviour. A few of these are remarkably pervasive:
- The average human being has an inherent dislike of work and will avoid it if he can.
- Because of this human characteristic, most people must be coerced to get them to put forth adequate effort towards the achievement of organisational objectives.
- The average human being prefers to be directed, wishes to avoid responsibility, has relatively little ambition, wants security above all.

Source: Douglas McGregor, *The Human Side of Enterprise*, 1987.

A Theory Y manager assumes that:

- workers have many different needs, enjoy work and seek satisfaction from it
- workers will organise themselves and take responsibility if they are trusted to do so
- poor performance is likely to be due to boring or monotonous work or poor management
- workers wish to, and should, contribute to decisions

According to McGregor, in Theory Y:

- The expenditure of physical and mental effort in work is as natural as play or rest...
- The average human being learns, under proper conditions, not only to accept but to seek responsibility...
- The capacity to exercise a relatively high degree of imagination, ingenuity and creativity in the solution of organisational problems is widely, not narrowly, distributed in the population...

Source: Douglas McGregor, *The Human Side of Enterprise*, 1987.

e EXAMINER'S VOICE

Try to integrate topics. In considering leadership styles, relate the use of a particular style to the level of motivation among the workforce, or to the suitability of a particular motivational tool, or to a particular motivational theorist.

McGregor's Theory X approach is clearly linked to the views of Taylor and to Adam Smith's idea of 'economic man'. In practice, many firms use this approach, especially at shop-floor level where money and control may be the main tools of influence. The Theory Y approach is clearly linked to Maslow's higher-level needs and Herzberg's motivators. It was also a forerunner of the later Japanese approach to management.

DID YOU KNOW?

'Economic man' (a term coined by Adam Smith) is an assumption that human behaviour is based on rational economic motives, principally the desire for financial reward.

Tannenbaum and Schmidt's continuum of leadership

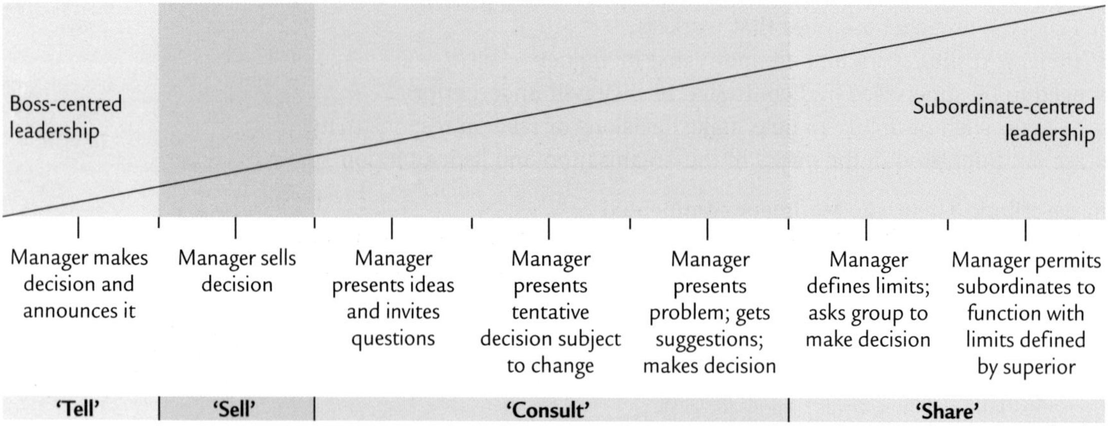

Figure 28.1 *Tannenbaum and Schmidt's continuum of leadership*

Tannenbaum and Schmidt's continuum of leadership (see Figure 28.1) provides a useful model of the impact of different leadership styles on delegation and consultation.

Boss-centred leadership						Subordinate-centred leadership
Manager makes decision and announces it	Manager sells decision	Manager presents ideas and invites questions	Manager presents tentative decision subject to change	Manager presents problem; gets suggestions; makes decision	Manager defines limits; asks group to make decision	Manager permits subordinates to function with limits defined by superior
'Tell'	'Sell'		'Consult'			'Share'

'Team-based' versus 'them and us' styles

Increasingly, firms are employing workers in teams. This is resulting in significant changes to the role of managers. They are seen more as facilitators and supporters than as supervisors, and are there to help teams of employees fulfil their potential and meet company objectives. For this changing role to be effective, managers and employees must have trust and confidence in each other's abilities and be focused on meeting company objectives. To gain this trust, managers need to delegate responsibility to workers to enable them to take full control of their own work. This is a major move away from the more traditional 'them and us' approach. In the latter approach, managers did not communicate regularly with workers — their job was to instruct and closely supervise workers, who obediently carried out tasks without question.

Some organisations try to overcome 'them and us' differences by treating all staff equally. For example, all employees, at whatever level of the organisation, may be known as 'associates' or 'colleagues'. This emphasises the idea of the whole organisation being a team. This is usually linked to a move away from traditional hierarchies and their focus on status.

The Japanese approach to leadership and management

In recent years, the distinctive features of the Japanese approach to leadership and management have had an enormous influence on UK business. The approach is democratic, with an emphasis on trust between leaders, managers and workers, and extensive delegation of responsibility and authority to teams of workers. This is complemented by the development of highly skilled and well-trained workers who are able to take responsibility and control their own work and its quality. The methods used include kaizen/continuous improvement groups and quality circles.

Internal and external factors influencing leadership style

Figure 28.2 identifies a broad range of influences on leadership style. Most of these are internal factors, although 'the particular situation' could include external factors, such as the influence of the competitive market in which the business operates or whether a rival firm is attempting a takeover. If a crisis occurs, for example a natural disaster, or if dangerous faults are found in a product, an authoritarian leadership style is likely to be most appropriate. In a stable situation, with well-trained, skilled and experienced staff, a democratic style of leadership is likely to be best. Thus 'the particular situation' that a business is faced with is likely to be a major influence on leadership style.

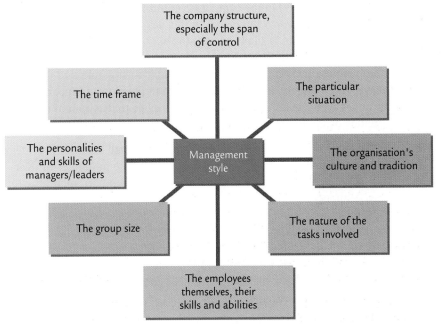

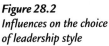

Figure 28.2
Influences on the choice of leadership style

The culture of an organisation affects, and is affected by, the style of leadership, which in turn is a major influence on the degree and effectiveness of delegation and consultation. The culture of an organisation will also affect the amount of resistance to change and therefore the ability of new leaders to impose their style or decisions on subordinates. The importance of culture is discussed in Chapter 29.

Research on leadership style suggests that leaders are likely to be focused either on tasks or on relationships with people. Intuition suggests that authoritarian leaders are more likely to be focused on tasks, while democratic leaders are more likely to be focused on relationships. However, it is more likely that the particular circumstances of the company will dictate the most appropriate approach. For example, if a company is facing massive competition and declining sales, its leadership will probably be very task focused because the company's survival is at stake. This is likely to be the case even if leadership is usually very democratic in its approach.

It might be difficult for leaders to change their style to suit different situations, either because of their personalities or because of internal or external constraints on the organisation. Furthermore, employees might feel insecure if leaders constantly change their style as the situation changes.

The role of leadership in managing change

Change is a constant feature of business activity. The key issues are whether potential change has been foreseen by the company — and therefore planned for — and whether it is within the company's control. For example, significant change will result if there is a huge growth in sales and hence growth in the size of the business. This is likely to require new management structures, more layers of hierarchy and new divisions or departments. In time this may lead to the business becoming very bureaucratic, causing able and creative staff to leave. Alternatively, increased delegation to divisions or departments may have adverse effects on managers as they struggle to live up to their new responsibilities or fail to meet targets.

Unforeseen change is probably more of a problem. If a small business provides a service that suddenly becomes very popular, it may be in danger of over-trading, as it is unable to get the resources needed to support such growth adequately. Management may in turn begin to lose control unless it is well prepared. For example, managers may be unable to delegate because of a lack of appropriate staff, or may be unwilling to delegate effectively because of an inability to 'let go' of power and to trust others. Yet appropriate planning could improve the situation by controlling the rate of growth, by creating an organisational structure that meets the needs of such growth, by developing a leadership style that encourages delegation, and staff who are trained to take on responsibility.

DID YOU KNOW?

Leadership style can greatly influence the attitudes and motivation of employees. McGregor's Theory X and Y clearly indicates this, while Herzberg's motivators suggest that a democratic leadership style is the most appropriate to motivate workers.

External change is usually the hardest to control or even influence, such as when there are changes in tastes or fashions, new laws or taxes, or increased competition. If a firm cannot influence such change, it must ensure that it is prepared to respond quickly and appropriately when it happens. Contingency plans can be drawn up to do just that, but where change develops into a crisis situation, an authoritarian leadership approach might be the most appropriate response, even if the usual style of management and the culture of the organisation suggest a more democratic and participatory approach.

Change management

The key underlying factor in change management is trust. Managers must give staff the skills and training to implement changes. In turn, staff must trust the motives and ability of the managers. Successful management of change therefore requires a number of elements.

> **KEY TERM**
>
> **change management:** the anticipation, organisation, introduction and evaluation of modifications to business strategy and operations.

Organisational structure

Successful change management needs an organisational structure that allows change to be implemented effectively. For example, United Biscuits moved from a geographical to a product category organisational structure and from a decentralised to a more centralised organisation in order to facilitate growth and expansion (see pp. 270–71). An organisation may also change from a functional to a matrix structure (or to cross-functional teams) in order to innovate and relaunch products, as United Biscuits did in the case of Phileas Fogg (see p. 264).

Management

Sensitive handling will be essential if delayering is necessary. As this means removing a layer of management, it is likely to lead to redundancies and to resistance to change among all or some sections of the workforce. In order to reduce resistance to change, leaders should:

- work hard to establish a sense of common purpose or mission and real trust between all levels of the hierarchy
- explain and discuss the reasons for change with all levels of the hierarchy in order to achieve a consensus that such change is essential
- consult widely on the options available for implementing the change, ensuring that employees' views are taken into account and, importantly, are seen to be taken into account in determining the eventual strategy

Leadership

Appropriate leadership should encourage job enrichment by effective delegation and consultation. This should improve staff motivation and trust, which in turn makes staff more willing to accept and possibly even welcome change.

> **DID YOU KNOW?**
>
> Research has shown that, in most organisations, middle managers are the staff who are most resistant to change. This is because middle managers have more to lose in any reorganisation than those below them in the hierarchy.

> **e EXAMINER'S VOICE**
>
> There is no agreement on the best style of leadership. Base your arguments on the circumstances.

PRACTICE EXERCISE   Total: 55 marks (50 minutes)

1 Distinguish between leadership and management.   *(6 marks)*

2 Outline the main characteristics of an authoritarian leadership style.   *(4 marks)*

3 Outline the main characteristics of a paternalistic leadership style.   *(4 marks)*

4 Outline the main characteristics of a democratic leadership style.   *(4 marks)*

5 Outline the main characteristics of a laissez-faire leadership style.   *(4 marks)*

6 Describe the main characteristics of McGregor's Theory X manager.   *(4 marks)*

7 Describe the main characteristics of McGregor's Theory Y manager.   *(4 marks)*

8 Distinguish between team-based styles of leadership and a 'them and us' approach. *(6 marks)*

9 Analyse the link between the Theory X manager and the authoritarian and paternalistic
  leadership styles.   *(9 marks)*

10 Outline the relationship between the different leadership styles and the extent of delegation
   and consultation.   *(10 marks)*

CASE STUDY The Japanese of Europe

Thanks to Sven-Goran Eriksson and his initial success as coach of the England football team, Swedish leadership style is in the news. Similarities with Japanese styles of leadership, such as reaching decisions through a consensual process (agreement among everybody involved), have led to the Swedes being referred to as the Japanese of Europe. Swedish leadership style has a number of distinctive characteristics:

- It is very consensus oriented and fairly pragmatic. Egos do not get in the way of making good decisions.
- It is a funny combination of very plain-speaking discussions as well as very polite ones, whereas in England we tend to talk around issues and can often be quite confrontational.
- It is ultimately an empowerment model: that is to say, dissent is encouraged and senior managers listen to junior people and seek their opinions. These things together mean that good decisions are made.

TOPFOTO

Research suggests that empowerment is a more natural process in Sweden than in the UK or the USA because the Swedes prefer group ideas rather than individual decisions. They are also relatively non-hierarchical, with the power distance between the top of society and the bottom being relatively small.

However, there can be problems with the Swedish leadership style. The risk is that, if you let go and empower people to do as they see fit, you are putting what could be too much trust in the individual. If it backfires, it can lead to devastating effects on a business. Examples include Nick Leeson and Barings Bank in 1995 and Jerome Kerviel and the Société Générale in 2008.

Source: adapted from J. Birkenshaw and S.Crainer, *Leadership the Sven-Goran Eriksson Way: How to Turn your Team into Winners*, 2004.

Questions
Total: 30 marks (40 minutes)

1 Assess the nature of Swedish leadership style in relation to your knowledge of different leadership styles and of McGregor's Theory X and Y.   *(15 marks)*

2 To what extent is the Swedish leadership style appropriate for (a) a football manager such as Sven-Goran Eriksson and (b) the manager of a busy call centre?   *(15 marks)*

ESSAY QUESTIONS
Total: 40 marks (50 minutes)

Answer one of the following questions:

1 To be successful, a business needs a strong leader. To be successful, a strong leader needs good managers. Discuss.   *(40 marks)*

2 To what extent is a particular style of leadership most suited to managing change in an organisation?   *(40 marks)*

Chapter 29

Key influences on the change process: culture

This chapter explains different types of organisational culture, including power, entrepreneurial and task-based cultures. It analyses the reasons for and the problems of changing organisational culture and assesses the importance of organisational culture.

 EXAMINER'S VOICE

Many of the issues raised in this chapter — for example, hierarchical structures, centralised and decentralised structures and delegation — relate to topics about organisational structure you studied at AS and earlier in your A2 studies. Ensure your understanding of all of these areas is secure by referring back to the AS textbook and to earlier chapters in this book.

Leadership style has a huge influence on the philosophy and culture of an organisation. This was considered in detail in Chapter 28.

 TERM

organisational culture: the unwritten code that affects the attitudes and behaviour of staff, approaches to decision making and the leadership style of management.

DID YOU KNOW?

Culture is often described as 'the way that we do things around here', meaning the type of behaviour that is considered acceptable or unacceptable, and is a result of tradition, history and structure.

Types of organisational culture

A key role of organisational culture is to differentiate an organisation from others and to provide a sense of identity for its members: 'who we are', 'what we do' and 'what we stand for'. It is an acquired body of knowledge about how to behave and the shared meanings and symbols that help everyone interpret and understand how to act within an organisation. An organisation's culture shows what it has been good at and what has worked in the past. These values are often accepted without question by long-serving management and employees. Although an organisation can have subgroups with different cultures and with varying agendas, a strong organisational culture is one that is internally consistent, is widely shared, and makes clear what is expected and how people should behave.

Every organisation has its own unique culture. It will have been created unconsciously, based on the values of the founders, senior management and core people who built and now direct the organisation. Over time, the culture may change as new owners and senior management try to impose their own styles and preferences on the organisation or because of changing marketplace conditions. Thus, culture influences the decision-making processes, styles of management and what everyone sees as success. Interpreting and understanding organisational culture is therefore a very important activity for managers because it affects strategic development.

Just as there is no ideal style of leadership or organisational structure, so there is no preferred culture. What is important is that the culture is suited to the environment in which the firm operates, allowing it to react appropriately to market and other changes.

Sources of organisational culture

- **Company routines** — the way everyday decisions and tasks are undertaken. In some organisations, managers regularly walk around and talk to staff; in others, managers are rarely seen. In some organisations, managers communicate and consult with their staff on a routine basis; in others, staff are only informed once decisions have been made.
- **Formal controls** — the rules and procedures governing employee actions. In some organisations, employees have autonomy and independence, and entrepreneurial activity is encouraged; in others, employees are expected to follow procedures closely.
- **Organisational structures** — the way management is organised both vertically, by layers of hierarchy, and horizontally, by functional areas. Some organisational structures are decentralised and place emphasis on delegation; others are more hierarchical and centralised.
- **Power structure** — the interrelationship between individuals or groups who take decisions about how the organisation's resources are allocated. In some organisations, challenging management's views is encouraged; in others, this would be considered disloyal. Some organisations encourage cooperation between different groups, while others encourage a level of competitive rivalry.
- **Symbols** — the emblems representing the organisation's culture. For example, in the professions, the language or jargon that is used can effectively exclude others and thus reinforce professional cultures. Other emblems include the range of pay scales from the highest to the lowest, which indicate status within the organisation, the size and location of managers' offices and whether they have their own secretaries, and whether there are separate canteens, entrances and car parks for management and workers.
- **Rituals and myths** — the patterns of behaviour that have become formalised in the everyday life of the organisation, and the stories that are told of its history. For example, it may be that in a particular organisation, the only training that is considered worthwhile is on-the-job and employees are not seconded to college courses, perhaps because the owner is 'self-made' and values experience over education.

Classifying organisational cultures

Organisational culture has been classified in many different ways. At the simplest level, it is possible to distinguish between a 'them and us' culture in an organisation where strict divisions exist between management and workers, and a more equitable culture in an organisation that tries to reduce barriers, with emphasis being placed on teamwork and more equal treatment of all. Three further approaches to the classification of organisational culture are considered here.

Charles Handy's classification system

Charles Handy, in *Understanding Organisations* (1981), identified four different types of organisational culture: power, role, task and person. Each culture is determined by different assumptions about the basis of power and influence, what motivates people, how people think and learn, and how change should occur.

- **Power culture.** This is where a powerful individual or a small group determines the dominant culture. Power culture is like a web with a ruling spider. Those in the web are dependent on a central power source. Rays of power and influence spread out from the central figure or group. Examples of such an organisation are small, entrepreneurial companies, where power derives from the founder or top person, and a personal relationship with that individual matters more than any formal title or position. However, in some large companies, a charismatic leader like Virgin's Richard Branson can do much to define the culture.
- **Role culture.** An organisation with a role culture is often referred to as a **bureaucracy**. Such organisations are controlled by procedures and role descriptions. Coordination is from the top and job positions are central. Such organisations value predictability and consistency, and may find it hard to adjust to change. Such a culture creates a highly structured, stable company with precise job descriptions, and is often based on a single product.
- **Task culture.** This is where the organisation's values are related to a job or project. Task culture is usually associated with a small team approach. It indicates a network organisation or small organisations cooperating to deliver a project. The emphasis is on results and getting things done. Individuals are empowered with independence and control over their work. Such an organisation is flexible and adaptable, and the culture emphasises talent and ideas, and involves continuous team problem solving and consultation.
- **Person culture.** This culture occurs in universities and in professions, such as accountancy and legal firms, where the organisation exists as a vehicle for people to develop their own careers and expertise. The individual is the central point. If there is a structure, it exists only to serve the individuals within it. Those involved tend to have strong values about how they will work, and they can be very difficult for the organisation to manage.

Bureaucratic and entrepreneurial cultures

Organisational culture can also be classified as either bureaucratic or entrepreneurial. The civil service is an example of an organisation with a **bureaucratic culture**. Characteristics include some or all of the following:

- an emphasis on roles and procedures (rather like Handy's role culture noted above)
- risk averse and anxious to avoid mistakes
- generalised and non-commercial goals
- precisely defined responsibilities and roles
- a hierarchical structure

In general, these characteristics result in organisations that survive for long periods of time, whose staff are unsuited to a dynamic environment and which often have a culture where making the right decision is less important than making decisions in the right way. Bureaucratic cultures tend to be found in large, mature businesses or public sector organisations. Such organisations are likely to discourage risk taking and even penalise managers who introduce unsuccessful projects. As a result, individuals will fear failure and seek to minimise its likely occurrence. Such behaviour may lead to the rejection of interesting or exciting projects because they are judged too risky or uncertain.

Entrepreneurial organisations are found in smaller businesses, profit-centred organisations and conglomerates with local management control. The characteristics of an entrepreneurial culture include:

- an emphasis on results and rewards for individual initiative (rather like Hardy's power culture noted above)
- risk taking
- quantitative and financial goals
- a task culture with flexible roles
- a flatter and more flexible structure, giving more local control

In general, these characteristics result in organisations that have high business mortality (that is, they are less likely to survive in the long term than organisations with bureaucratic cultures) and are focused on commercial results and profit. An entrepreneurial culture often applies to businesses in their early years of development. Such organisations encourage risk taking and the acceptance of occasional failure, on the basis that large gains may be achieved when there is success. Such behaviour may lead to maximum returns on investments if good decisions are made.

Marketing, production and technology orientation

Cultures can be categorised according to whether organisations are marketing, production or technology orientated. **Marketing-orientated** organisations, such as Virgin, place heavy emphasis on meeting the needs of their customers and are continually alert to changes in the market. **Production-orientated** firms place an emphasis on good engineering and high quality in production, as at Dyson. A **technology-orientated** firm tends to define itself in terms of the technology it exploits: for example, Polaroid with its instant picture technology, which it has championed for almost 40 years.

WHAT DO YOU THINK?

Which of the cultures discussed in this chapter best applies to your school or college, or to other organisations with which you are familiar? Try to justify your answer.

Reasons for, and problems of, changing organisational culture

A change in the external environment may require profound changes in the way things are done within an organisation. For example, if the market becomes more competitive, the organisation's values may no longer be appropriate. They may hinder the ability of the organisation to adapt, and thus a change in culture might be needed in order to change the organisation's approach and, ultimately, its performance. However, the existing organisational culture can be a barrier to change and when it is challenged, this can produce strong resistance within the organisation because the fundamental values of staff are under threat.

In bringing about culture change, the role of the leader or senior management is crucial. Leaders and senior management act as role models. If they say one thing and do the opposite, no one will take the culture change seriously and it will quickly lose all credibility. For example, if a firm needs to introduce tighter controls on expenditure, senior management should set an example by practising financial restraint. Similarly, senior management can support the case for change by allocating the necessary resources to bring it about. They can promote and demote staff to signal the desired change. They can communicate the case for change and introduce the necessary training and recruitment policies. Where the organisational structure acts as a barrier to change — for example, where a hierarchical structure may constrain entrepreneurial flair and risk taking — management can restructure the business to help bring about the change in culture.

The importance of organisational culture

Organisational culture is important because it determines how firms respond to changes in their external environment. Though intangible, culture has an important bearing on an organisation's behaviour and performance. A production- or engineering-based culture can lead to a neglect of marketing skills and financial controls. Similarly, an over-concern with financial controls can undermine product development, leaving the firm increasingly exposed to competition from products that are technologically superior.

Culture thus influences the extent to which a business is centralised or decentralised and whether it has a narrow or tall hierarchical structure. However, as well as influencing organisational structure, culture will be influenced by it: for example, whether management is organised vertically by function or geographical or product categories and how many layers there are in the hierarchy. Culture will be influential when it comes to developing mission statements, and, by affecting leadership styles in the business, it will have a major effect on the degree of, and effectiveness of, delegation and consultation. The culture of an organisation will also affect the amount of resistance to change and therefore the ability of new management to impose its style or decisions on subordinates.

There is no 'right' or 'wrong' culture, since the appropriate approach depends on the nature of the business and the environment in which it operates. However, when mergers and takeovers occur, firms with very different cultures, even though they might be operating in similar markets and with similar technologies, are brought together, often leading to managerial confusion and failure (see Chapter 26 for examples of this). Differences in culture can be an important explanation of why so many promising mergers and takeovers fail. Putting it another way, a successful business needs a culture that is appropriate for the environment in which it operates. Failure is often traceable to an inappropriate culture.

e EXAMINER'S VOICE

Corporate culture, change management and the approach of small and large organisations are important concepts to consider when answering questions on management structure and organisation.

PRACTICE EXERCISE   Total: 50 marks (45 minutes)

1 What is meant by the term 'organisational culture'? *(3 marks)*

2 Identify and explain Charles Handy's four different cultures. *(12 marks)*

3 Distinguish between a bureaucratic culture and an entrepreneurial culture. *(6 marks)*

4 How might an organisation's culture influence its attitude to risk taking? *(4 marks)*

5 How might the culture of an organisation influence the degree of resistance to change in that organisation? *(3 marks)*

6 Explain two ways in which management might bring about a change in culture. *(6 marks)*

7 Explain one reason for, and one problem of, changing the culture of an organisation. *(6 marks)*

8 Explain how organisational culture might influence an organisation's ability to cope with external change. *(4 marks)*

9 Consider why an organisation's culture is important. *(6 marks)*

CASE STUDY 1 HSA Healthcare

HSA Healthcare is a financial services company which provides health plans and hospital benefits for individuals and families. Although it has been in business for 80 years and has an excellent reputation with the public, when Des Benjamin, its chief executive, arrived in 2000 he found it 'Dickensian'. The offices had not been redecorated for decades — they were all 'brown, brown, brown' — and equipment was scarce: three members of staff would share a phone. Even worse, the company had an autocratic leadership style. Staff looked downtrodden and, with little or no training, had low confidence, low expectations and low ambitions.

A new board of directors initiated a cultural change exercise. 'We took all 500 people out of the business for a minimum of 2 days and said, "Tell us how this business should be run",' Benjamin says. 'By bringing the culture up from the bowels of the organisation, we got the most powerful backing from workers.'

A staff consultative committee now meets nine times a year and a revised benefits package means that 80% of employees have increased leave, sick pay entitlement and paternity pay, and superior parental leave. All staff are eligible for individual performance-related bonuses, and 80% of them for profit-related pay.

Source: adapted from *The Sunday Times 100 Best Companies to Work For*, 2 March 2003.

Question   Total: 15 marks (25 minutes)

Using the information about HSA Healthcare as an example, discuss the importance of organisational culture in influencing the performance of a business.   *(15 marks)*

CASE STUDY 2 Corporate culture at Starbucks

Read the following information from Starbucks' website and answer the question that follows.

Starbucks' mission statement

Establish Starbucks as the premier purveyor of the finest coffee in the world while maintaining our uncompromising principles while we grow.

The following six guiding principles will help us measure the appropriateness of our decisions:

- Provide a great work environment and treat each other with respect and dignity.
- Embrace diversity as an essential component in the way we do business.
- Apply the highest standards of excellence to the purchasing, roasting and fresh delivery of our coffee.
- Develop enthusiastically satisfied customers all of the time.
- Contribute positively to our communities and our environment.

- Recognise that profitability is essential to our future success.

Starbucks' 'Job Centre'

Our success depends on your success. Our ability to accomplish what we set out to do is based primarily on the people we hire — we call each other 'partners'. We are always focused on our people. We provide opportunities to develop your skills, further your career, and achieve your goals. At Starbucks, you'll find a commitment to excellence among our partners; an emphasis on respect in how we treat our customers and each other; and a dedication to social responsibility. We look for people who are adaptable, self-motivated, passionate, creative team players. We are growing in dynamic new ways and we recognise that the right people, offering their ideas and expertise, will enable us to continue our success.

'The Starbucks experience'

We are devoted to investing in supporting and engaging our partners in the constant reinvention of Starbucks. The first guiding principle in our mission statement (see above) reflects this. Imagine working for a company that constantly aspires to realise this principle. We believe so strongly in embracing diversity that it is the second guiding principle in our mission statement (see above). We strive to create a diverse workplace in which every partner's voice is heard and in which all our partners will succeed while learning from one another. We believe that building understanding, respect and appreciation for different people contributes to our growth and to the growth of our partners.

Source: adapted from information on **www.starbucks.com**.

Question   Total: 15 marks (25 minutes)

On the basis of the information provided, analyse the possible nature of Starbucks' corporate culture and assess how this is likely to influence its leadership style and organisational structure.   *(15 marks)*

ESSAY QUESTION   Total: 40 marks (50 minutes)

(Refer back to the discussion of mergers and takeovers in Chapter 26 on pp. 432–34.)

Surveys show that about 65% of mergers and takeovers fail to benefit the acquiring company. To what extent might conflicting organisational cultures play a part in the failure of more than one third of mergers and takeovers to achieve their expected success?   *(40 marks)*

Chapter 30

Making strategic decisions

This chapter considers the significance of information management. It explains the different approaches to decision making, ranging from intuitive to scientific approaches, and assesses their value. It analyses the influences on corporate decision making, such as whether to adopt an ethical position (real or perceived), the resources available and the relative power of stakeholders.

KEY TERM

information management: the application of management techniques to collect information, communicate it within and outside the organisation, and process it to enable managers to make quicker and better decisions.

The significance of information management

The use of information management improves an organisation's ability to process information and to make decisions. The sophistication of computerised systems means that information management has become a powerful resource for businesses.

Despite this, information management systems do have their limitations. Cost is a major factor, but not just in terms of financial cost. It is not always possible or desirable to access, collect and evaluate every piece of information or evidence that is relevant for taking a certain decision at a reasonable price (i.e. in terms of time and effort). In addition, established organisational rules and procedures, organisational culture and the attitudes of leadership might prevent the optimal, or best, decision from being taken.

The value of different approaches to decision making

Decision making in any business is very important and takes place at every level of the organisation. It varies from short term to long term, and from functional and tactical to strategic and corporate. Decisions are usually constrained by both internal and external factors — for example, by the finance available, the skills of the workforce, competitor activity or government policy. Most decision making includes an element of risk and this is certainly the case with strategic decisions. Just because something is risky does not mean that it should not be pursued. It does mean, however, that careful analysis of the balance of risk and reward should be carried out.

A number of different approaches to decision making are available to assist firms in this process. These range from intuitive to scientific approaches.

A scientific approach to decision making

A scientific approach involves using a systematic process for making decisions in an objective manner. Such a procedure eliminates the practice of decisions being made on the basis of a hunch and removes, as far as possible, bias and subjectivity by ensuring that decisions are made on the basis of well-researched, factual evidence. It therefore reduces risk because decisions are based on hard data, and it allows actions to be reviewed and the most effective course of action to be decided. This does not mean that the decisions made will always be the right ones. Scientific decision making can be criticised as being a rather slow process that lacks creativity and which therefore may fail to lead to innovative and different approaches.

KEY TERM

scientific decision making: a logical and research-based approach to decision making.

A scientific decision-making model similar to that in Figure 30.1 is widely used. The model can be explained by reference to the following hypothetical decision. Assume that a firm is faced with falling demand for its existing product and wishes to cut production of that product and to build up production of an alternative aimed at a different market. It can close down one of its existing factories, making the workforce redundant, and open a new factory abroad. The steps in the decision-making process are as follows:

1 **Set objectives.** The firm must set objectives in relation to what it wants to achieve and where it wants to be within a given time scale, ensuring that this fits well with the corporate mission statement. In relation to the decision, the firm wants production to take place in the most cost-effective location, taking account of long-term training costs, infrastructure costs, building up relationships with customers, suppliers and distributors etc.
2 **Gather data.** Data on costs, demand, location and logistics, available workforce, reputation etc. will be needed and may be gathered through primary and secondary research methods.
3 **Analyse data.** Data that have been gathered need to be analysed in order to provide a recommendation. Various quantitative decision-making techniques or tools are available to do this, such as investment appraisal, cost–benefit analysis, critical path analysis, ratio analysis, elasticity of demand and decision trees (the last are considered later in this chapter).

Figure 30.1 Scientific decision-making model

4 **Select a strategy.** The decision as to which strategy to pursue should be made on the basis of the recommendations that emerge from the data analysis.
5 **Implement and review the decision.** Implementation will itself involve numerous decisions on tactical and operational issues. Reviewing the decision involves looking at how well the outcome has succeeded in achieving the initial objective. For example, if the decision was to retain the existing workforce but it transpires that unit costs are too high and so competitiveness is reduced, the decision not to move abroad may need to be re-examined.

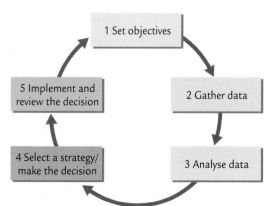

Benefits of using a scientific approach to decision making

The scientific approach offers the following benefits:

- It provides a clear sense of direction. By emphasising the need to set objectives, it ensures that people involved in the decision-making process are aiming for the same goals. SMART (specific, measurable, agreed, reasonable and timed) objectives will help the firm to make decisions that match the aims of the organisation.
- Decisions are based on business logic, involving comparisons between alternative approaches and between pros and cons.
- It is likely that more than one person will be involved in the process, which will reduce the possibility of bias.
- A scientific approach ensures that decisions are monitored continually and reviewed. Although this will not prevent mistakes, it should limit their impact because problems can be identified quickly.
- A major advantage of a scientific approach is its flexibility. At any stage in making a decision, the process can be reviewed and changed if circumstances require.
- If all decisions are based on rational thinking, overall success is more probable.
- It is easier to defend a policy that has been developed on the basis of good planning (and in cooperation with other managers) than one that is based solely on one person's gut feeling.

 FILE

Green Baby

Jill Barker, founder of Green Baby, set up her business on the basis of scientific decision making. With 13 years' experience in City banking and background knowledge of the North American market, Jill recognised the potential for organic, environmentally friendly baby products. Barker chose the first outlet in Islington, north London because 'We were in the kind of area where mothers cared about green issues'.

Source: adapted from an article by Elizabeth Judge in *The Times*, 17 April 2004.

An intuitive approach to decision making

KEY TERM

hunch: a gut feeling held by a manager that is based not on scientific decision making but on the personal views of the manager.

Intuitive approaches involve individuals making decisions on the basis of a 'hunch' (or feeling or instinct). This approach is more likely to be used by small businesses that are owned by a single individual or small group. If the individual or group has a great deal of experience and expertise, this approach may be appropriate. Equally, this approach may lead to more creative and innovative decision making.

However, such decisions are not always informed by evidence and will often involve a level of (mostly unintended) bias and subjectivity, leading to inappropriate or ill-judged outcomes. Examples are deciding to site a factory in a location that is not appropriate but is linked to the owner's childhood, deciding to change the bonus system for all employees because a new system works well for a particular group of employees, and deciding not to upgrade the IT system because everything is working at the moment.

FACT FILE

Red or Dead

Wayne Hemingway and his wife Geraldine founded the Red or Dead fashion house in 1982 by sheer chance: 'We ran out of money one weekend so we emptied our clothes on to Camden Market. We took a load of money and that was it. You should always follow your gut instincts. We had more successes than failures and have never done any kind of market research, although the market is constantly in our minds.'

Source: www.startups.co.uk.

Benefits of using hunches

In general, hunches are used because of problems involved in using a scientific approach to decision making:

- A scientific approach requires a large collection of data and the regular gathering of information to control and review decisions. This can be an expensive process and is hard to justify if there is very little risk involved.
- Following a scientific approach to decision making is time consuming. The constant checking and monitoring means that decisions may be delayed.
- The data collected in a scientific approach to decision making might be flawed. The information may be dated or the original sampling may have a bias. Customers may have just changed their minds.
- Invariably, scientific decisions are based on past information. Decisions may be better if they rely on the instincts of a manager who has a 'qualitative' understanding of the market and can anticipate a change in the trend.

FACT FILE

Knut Eicke

German multi-millionaire Knut Eicke has made a lot of money from hunches. His insurance company, Sir Huckleberry Insurance, offers the usual insurance policies but also provides the world's quirkiest alternatives. Based on a hunch, Knut started offering weird insurance policies against eventualities such as 'choking on pretzels', 'injuries from falling over at a beer festival' and 'being fired from work for playing computer games'. According to Knut, 'insurance against abduction by aliens is the big seller'. For additional premiums, people can also gain compensation for being whisked off to Mars (a payout of £2,500 for a policy that costs less than £20 per annum). Knut does not believe that scientific decision making would have revealed this opportunity. To date Knut has not paid out on the alien abduction policy (a big seller as a novelty gift).

Source: adapted from an article by Allan Hall in the *Evening Standard*, 31 March 2004.

The Body Shop

The Body Shop was set up on a hunch because, according to its founder, Anita Roddick: 'We had no money — I was trying to pay the bills by doing what I was interested in. If I'd had a shed load of money, I'd have done everything wrong — marketing, focus groups, although they are more important now [that the business has grown].'

Source: www.startups.co.uk.

EXAMINER'S VOICE

Review your understanding of opportunity cost, which is an important concept to consider in relation to strategic analysis. It refers to the real cost of a decision in terms of the next best alternative.

Choosing between scientific and hunch-based decision making

The following factors are critical in deciding which approach to use:

- **The speed of the decision.** Where quick decisions are required, there may be insufficient time to analyse the situation and so hunches may be followed. If time is not an issue, a more scientific (but slower) approach can be adopted.
- **Information available.** Where detailed data are not available, hunches and guesswork are more likely to be used. However, if data are held, a more scientific decision is possible.
- **The size of the business.** As a rule, smaller businesses are more likely to follow a hunch. Larger firms have established approaches to decision making that are used by each department. Furthermore, larger firms face more complicated decisions that need a more scientific approach.
- **The predictability of the situation.** In an unpredictable situation, a hunch may be better than following a trend that will not continue. However, if past data are reliable indicators of future changes, a scientific approach is ideal.
- **The character of the person or the culture of the company.** An entrepreneurial risk-taker is more likely to use hunches. A manager (or business) that tries to avoid risk or blame is more likely to use a scientific approach, in order to justify any decisions.

The marketing model, which is considered below, is another example of a scientific approach to decision making. Other decision-making approaches include Ansoff's matrix, Porter's generic strategies, and decision trees. Ansoff's matrix and Porter's generic strategies were considered in Chapter 9. Decision trees are explained later in this chapter.

The marketing model

The marketing model is not dissimilar to the generic scientific approach provided above and can also be applied more generally to assist managers in planning and executing strategy.

The marketing model involves a number of stages:
1 Setting marketing objectives.
2 Gathering the data needed to decide on a strategy.
3 Assessing alternative marketing strategies and implementing the favoured choice.
4 Planning and implementing the marketing mix in accordance with the marketing strategy.
5 Controlling and reviewing the outcome of marketing decisions.

An essential element of the marketing model is the existence of **constraints**. Internal factors (strengths and weaknesses) and external factors (opportunities and threats) are continually monitored at every stage in order to assess their impact. These factors can lead to changes at any stage of the model. For example, feedback gained from stage 2 may help a firm to recognise that its objectives are unrealistic and so stage 1 may be modified. Similarly, control and review (stage 5) might indicate that the wrong strategy had been chosen (stage 3) or that the marketing mix had been implemented incorrectly (stage 4). For these reasons, the marketing model is often represented as a circle surrounded by constraints, to emphasise that marketing decisions do not necessarily follow a set of routine stages every time (see Figure 30.2).

> **KEY TERM**
>
> **marketing model:** a decision-making process that ensures that marketing decisions are taken on a scientific basis. This scientific approach is an alternative to managers taking decisions on the basis of hunches or guesses.

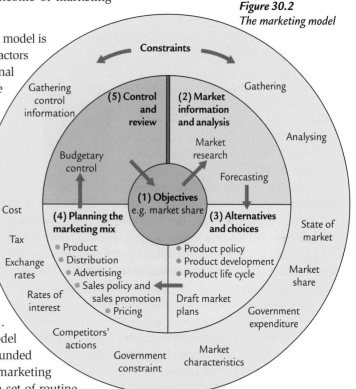

Figure 30.2
The marketing model

Source: P. Tinniswood, *Marketing Decision Making*

PRACTICE EXERCISE 1   Total: 35 marks 30 minutes

1 What is the difference between scientific decision making and decisions based on hunches?   *(6 marks)*

2 Identify the five stages of scientific decision making.   *(5 marks)*

3 Explain two benefits of using scientific decision making.   *(6 marks)*

4 Explain two possible reasons for basing decisions on 'hunches'. *(6 marks)*

5 Consider the factors that an insurance company might consider when deciding whether to use scientific decision making or hunches. *(8 marks)*

6 What is meant by the term 'marketing model'? *(4 marks)*

CASE STUDY 1 Coca-Cola sets out lifestyle stall

In 2004, Coca-Cola UK president, Charlotte Oades, outlined its 'active lifestyle' strategy, aimed to counter the obesity epidemic. The strategy is built on four pillars:

- providing customer choice
- giving customers information to make choices
- responsible sales and marketing
- continuing support for active lifestyles, particularly among young people

Her remarks closely followed McDonald's announcement that it would spend £1 million on an educational campaign aimed at encouraging children to eat a balanced diet and take more exercise, through a series of 2-minute commercials.

'We're suddenly seeing food companies keen to promote a healthier message,' said Food Commission spokesman, Ian Tokelove. However, Labour MP Debra Shipley was sceptical about the motives of brand owners such as Coca-Cola and McDonald's. 'They have been dragged into this position reluctantly because of huge pressure from health experts, politicians and the general public.'

In its defence, Coca-Cola can point out that it has hardly been rushed into a relationship with health and physical fitness. Coke was originally invented for medicinal purposes. The company believed it would benefit from association with the Olympic Games and has been an Olympic sponsor since 1928. It has a policy of not advertising on any television channels aimed at under-12s. Coca-Cola also led the way with diet soft drinks. These decisions have been based on a mixture of market research and individual guesswork by managers.

Coca-Cola has changed its marketing to ensure that promotions give greater prominence to diet brands. In addition, the company announced that it was removing its branding from vending machines in secondary schools. However, this may not harm sales as design experts believe that Coke is so strongly associated with vending machines that the logo on the machine is unimportant.

But how will consumers react? As a company, Coca-Cola has been skilled in anticipating the future, but John Mathers, chief executive of consultancy firm Enterprise IG, believes that the company may have misinterpreted its customers. 'Consumers are seeing initiatives like these in a cynical way. The danger is that they will be seen as attempts to divert attention from the main issues.'

There are other signs that Coca-Cola is beginning to rely on unsupported ideas rather than thorough research. The failure of its bottled water in the UK showed a lack of awareness of the character of UK consumers, who expect bottled water to come from a natural source. The comment, by a senior executive of the company, that it would not have used bottled water in France did not help Coca-Cola's image in the UK.

Source: adapted from an article by Robert Gray in *Marketing*, 14 July 2004.

Questions
Total: 30 marks (40 minutes)

1 To what extent is Coca-Cola's marketing strategy based on hunches rather than scientific decision making? *(15 marks)*

2 Discuss how Coca-Cola might control and review the success of its strategy. *(15 marks)*

CASE STUDY 2 Dyson's magic carpet ride

It took 5 years and 5,127 prototypes for James Dyson to come up with his first bagless cleaner, which started selling in Japan in 1986. Since then, Dyson has expanded the business to 37 countries, shifting his factory from England to Malaysia. The company continues to develop the technology and about a quarter of the 1,300 employees at Dyson's headquarters in England work in research and development.

Within two-and-a-half years of its introduction to the English market, the Dyson vacuum cleaner became England's bestseller. Three years after its US debut, the Dyson became the market-leading upright cleaner. Around two-thirds of its sales now came from overseas.

What lies behind the success of the Dyson cleaners, especially given that they are anything but cheap? A Dyson costs more than twice as much as most rival models. Moreover, the marketing campaign for the cleaners has stayed decidedly low-key.

According to Dyson, superior technology explains his brainstorm's popularity. Because there is no bag or filter to clog, his cleaners stay powerful. 'They maintain constant, maximum suction,' he says. 'All the time it's working to full efficiency, cleaning your home.'

The Dyson has developed an intensely loyal following. The company's research in the UK found that 70% of all users bought the machine after recommendation from friends. Even a brief look at Dyson users' reviews on Amazon.com reveals, in many cases, a level of enthusiasm rarely associated with household appliances. Among the headline comments are: 'I LOVE this vacuum!', 'Believe the hype!' and 'WOW!'

Tim Calkin, a US professor of marketing, says that Dyson has succeeded by bringing something new and innovative to a market that had focused exclusively on price. 'They certainly have set themselves up as a superior vacuum cleaner,' says Calkin. 'They've almost made it an aspirational purchase, but people who buy Dysons really like them. People take pride in their vacuum when they own a Dyson.'

Indeed, Dyson cleaners have benefited from some glamorous associations. They have appeared in episodes of television shows such as *Will and Grace* and *Friends*, and were included in the presenters' gift bag at an Academy Awards ceremony.

In 2005, Dyson unveiled 'the Ball', a vacuum that replaced wheels with a ball to allow easier movement. It took nearly 4 years, 182 patents and £25 million to get the 'Dyson DC15, The Ball' from scribbled sketch into department stores. 'We have no sales target, but personally I believe the Ball will account for 50% of all upright vacuum cleaners we sell,' Mr Dyson said.

Dyson shifted production of its vacuum cleaners from Malmesbury in Wiltshire to Malaysia in 2002, resulting in a loss of 865 manufacturing jobs. At the time, Mr Dyson said he had been forced to shift offshore because of lower costs. He also cited the fact that both component suppliers and some of the cleaners' biggest markets were based in the region. This was followed by an announcement in 2003 that production of Dyson's washing machines would also be transferred to Asia. The move to Malaysia boosted profits and allowed the company to grow and expand in the USA, where it became market leader in just 2 years.

Source: adapted from articles on Business Week and BBC News websites (www.businessweek.com and www.bbc.co.uk), April 2005.

Question

Total: 40 marks (50 minutes)

Assess the extent to which a scientific decision-making model might have benefited the company in deciding on its production move from England to Malaysia.

(40 marks)

Decision trees

A number of models and tools are available to assist businesses in their decision-making processes. For example, investment appraisal can be used to decide between alternative investment projects, while Ansoff's matrix may help to provide strategic direction for a business. The focus of this section, decision tree analysis, is usually applied to problems where numerical data are available and for which the probability of different consequences and the financial outcomes of decisions can be estimated.

Decision tree analysis provides a pictorial approach to decision making — the diagram used resembles the branches of a tree. It maps out the different options available, the possible outcomes of these options and the points where decisions have to be made. Calculations based on the decision tree can be used to determine the best option for the business to select.

Some argue that decision making is most effective when a quantitative approach is taken: that is, when the information on which decisions are based and the outcomes of decisions are expressed as numbers. A decision tree does just this. However, as with all quantitative models, caution must be exercised when considering the nature of the information used and the results themselves.

Constructing and evaluating a decision tree: example

The following business scenario will be used to demonstrate how to construct and evaluate a simple decision tree.

A business wishes to invest in a new plant in order to extend its range of products. It has to decide whether to use the new plant to make product A or product B. Making product A will require a much higher investment (£7 million) than that required for product B (£2 million), but the business estimates that the financial returns look higher for product A than product B. Doing nothing is also an option. Its estimates are as follows:

- If product A is produced and demand is high, the payoff will be £16 million. However, if demand is low, the payoff will only be £6 million. The probability of a high demand for product A is 0.7 and that of a low demand is 0.3.
- If product B is produced and demand is high, the payoff will be £12 million. However, if demand is low, the payoff will only be £4 million. The probability of a high demand for product B is 0.6 and that of a low demand is 0.4.

Constructing the decision tree

1 Start with a small square, to represent the decision, towards the left of your sheet of paper.

2 From the square, draw out lines towards the right for each option or solution that is available and label the option along the line. For example, having to decide between product A and product B will result in a line for product A and a line for product B. Having to decide between a large promotional campaign or a small one or none at all will result in three lines — one for each option. Keep the lines apart so that you can add more lines if necessary. Remember to add a 'Do nothing' option if this is an alternative.

3 At the end of each line, consider the results. If the result of taking that decision is uncertain, draw a small circle. For example, if production of product A may be successful or may result in failure, this is an uncertain outcome. If, on the other hand, the result of a particular option is not uncertain, as is the case with the option 'do nothing', extend the line to the far right. Insert the financial outcome (payoff) of any certain, final outcome.

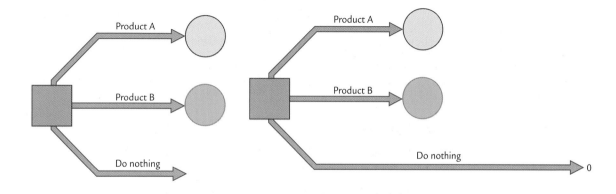

4 From any circle(s), draw lines to the right representing possible outcomes and above each line label the outcome (for example, success or failure, high or low demand). Review your tree diagram and see if there are any options or outcomes that you have missed. If so, draw them in.

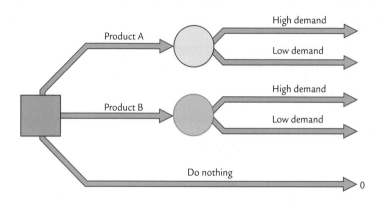

Evaluating the decision tree

This is where you work out which option is financially better.

5 At the end of the line, insert the financial result (payoff) of each outcome.

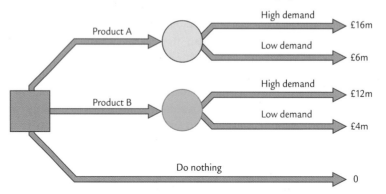

6 Note the probability of each outcome occurring immediately below the line showing that outcome. This will be calculated by considering data on similar events in the past and what experts and forecasts predict. If percentages are being used, the total for each option must add to 100%; if decimals or fractions are used, the total for each option must add to 1.

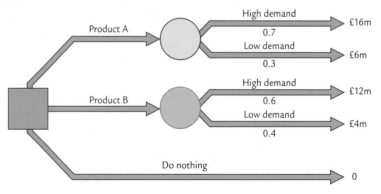

7 If there is a cost involved in selecting a particular option, note this under the line labelled with the option.

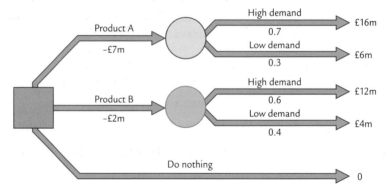

8 Calculate the expected monetary values (EMV) for each outcome and option. Start on the right-hand side of the decision tree. First calculate the expected monetary value of the uncertain outcomes by multiplying the value of the outcome by its probability. Then add the expected monetary values of all the uncertain outcomes of a particular option. Subtract any cost of that option. This gives you a value that represents the benefit of that particular decision or option (the net expected value).

Product A: high demand $0.7 \times £16m = £11.2m$

low demand $0.3 \times £6m = \underline{£1.8m}$

$£13.0m$

$\underline{-£7.0m}$

$£6.0m$

Product B: high demand $0.6 \times £12m = £7.2m$

low demand $0.4 \times £4m = \underline{£1.6m}$

$£8.8m$

$\underline{-£2.0m}$

$£6.8m$

9 When you have calculated the net expected monetary value (EMV) of each option, add them to the diagram and cross through any rejected decisions with two small diagonal lines, leaving untouched the line representing the decision that provides the largest financial benefit.

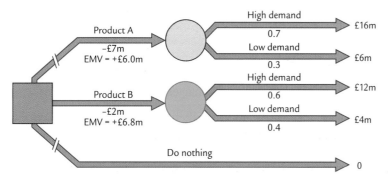

10 Taking into account your decision tree and any non-quantitative (qualitative) factors that might be important, make a final decision on the best approach for the business to take. If quantitative factors only were taken into consideration, product B would be produced, as it has the highest net expected value. However, the relatively narrow difference between £6.0 million and £6.8 million means that qualitative factors will probably be very important in the final decision.

e EXAMINER'S VOICE

Remember that, in a decision tree, squares represent decisions and circles represent uncertain outcomes.

Evaluating decision trees

Once the quantitative analysis using a decision tree has been completed, consider the following questions:

- How reliable are the figures used? For example, how were the estimated costs, probabilities and financial returns arrived at? Who provided them? When? What was their original purpose?
- What market research has been done and how effective is this?
- Are there other non-quantifiable factors that might affect the decision? For example: Are competitors likely to enter the market? Is the economy heading for a recession? What will be the impact on the brand image? Will employees' morale be adversely affected?

Benefits of using decision trees

Decision tree analysis is a useful tool to use when choosing between several options. It provides an effective structure within which to set out the options available and to investigate the possible outcomes of choosing those options. It also helps to form a balanced picture of the risks and rewards associated with each option.

Most decisions cannot be taken with 100% certainty of the outcome. The fact that decisions are rarely based on perfect information means that some risk is usually present. This could be because the business has limited information on which to base the decision, or because the outcome of the decision is uncertain. For example, launching a new product in a new market will be risky, especially if a firm has no experience of selling in that market and if, despite market research, it is unsure about how consumers will react. A given level of risk is not a bad thing if it is balanced by acceptable rewards. Most successful businesses have had to take risks in order to succeed, such as entering a new market in order to gain first-mover advantages.

One of the advantages of decision tree analysis over other decision-making tools, such as investment appraisal, is that it takes into account uncertainty and risk, and tries to quantify these by estimating the probability of a particular outcome occurring. This estimation may be based on past experience, market research or informed guesswork.

By highlighting the issue of uncertainty, decision trees emphasise the fact that every decision can result in a range of possible outcomes, and they ensure that managers make more carefully considered decisions. In addition, using a quantitative approach should ensure a more objective decision-making process than the 'gut reaction' type of decision making based on a hunch.

When faced with a number of different options, a business will usually want to choose the option that gives the highest financial return. When the outcome of each option is uncertain, decision trees can be used to help reach a decision that balances risk and financial return. Table 30.1 summarises the main advantages and disadvantages of using decision trees.

Advantages	Disadvantages
• They set out the problem clearly and encourage a logical approach to decision making.	• They ignore the constantly changing nature of the business environment.
• They encourage careful consideration of all alternatives.	• It is difficult to get accurate and realistic data in order to estimate probabilities.
• They encourage a quantitative approach that may improve the results and also means that the process can be computerised.	• It is quite easy for management bias to influence the estimates of probabilities and financial returns, and for managers to manipulate the data.
• They take risk into account when making decisions and encourage a quantitative assessment of such risk.	• They are less useful in relation to completely new decisions or problems and one-off strategic decisions or problems.
• They are useful when similar scenarios have occurred before, so that realistic estimates of probabilities and financial returns can be made.	• Few decisions can be made on a purely objective basis; most include a subjective element based on managerial experience and intuition.
• They are useful when making tactical or routine decisions rather than strategic decisions.	• They may lead to managers taking less account of important qualitative issues.

Limitations of decision trees

As with all quantitative models, caution must be exercised when considering the nature of the information used. For example, the figures used might be biased or may have been manipulated in order to gain a particular outcome. It is therefore important to consider who produced the figures and to assess their objectivity.

Decision trees are least useful when decisions do not involve clear-cut alternatives, when there are many individuals involved in the decision-making process, when circumstances are very uncertain or changing rapidly, and when completely new or one-off situations exist. In the last two instances, it would be almost impossible to estimate in any realistic or reliable way the probability of a particular outcome occurring.

Because of the disadvantages of using decision tree analysis (see Table 30.1), it should only be part of the decision-making process. Other non-quantitative factors should be taken into account before a final decision is made.

Table 30.1 Advantages and disadvantages of decision trees

FACT FILE

'What if?' or sensitivity analysis

'What if?' or sensitivity analysis can be applied to decision trees by changing either the estimated probabilities of options or the estimated financial returns of outcomes. This type of analysis can be used to answer questions such as: 'How small does the probability of the most optimistic outcome need to be before the other option gives a greater expected monetary value?'

This more detailed analysis helps to reduce the risks involved in the decision-making process by providing a thorough review of each possible outcome, from the most optimistic to the most pessimistic. Sophisticated computer packages are available for this kind of complex procedure — they are able to produce tree diagrams and an array of 'what if?' solutions, once the data have been input.

By using data such as those provided by the Met Office (see the Fact File overleaf), businesses can estimate probabilities (e.g. the chances of bad weather) and their likely financial outcome. When the organisers of Formula One racing changed the date of the British Grand Prix from July to April some years ago, the owners of Silverstone used data of this type to argue successfully for shifting the date back to a time of year in which rainfall was likely to be much lower.

EXAMINER'S VOICE

Given the nature of the Unit 4 examination paper, you are unlikely to be required to set out a decision tree. However, decision trees can be a particularly useful method of decision making in certain situation, so an appreciation of their advantages and disadvantages might be useful.

Influences on corporate decision making

The influences on corporate decision making are the same as the internal and external influences on corporate plans that were discussed in Chapter 27 in the form of a SWOT analysis. Review Chapter 27 to ensure that you are familiar with them. Included in these influences are three factors that the AQA specification identifies specifically: the ethical position ('real or perceived') adopted by the organisation, the resources available to the organisation, and the relative power of the organisation's stakeholders.

Ethical positions

Ethical issues are discussed in Chapter 23. Review the contents of Chapter 23 to ensure you are familiar with issues related to the ethical position adopted by an organisation. Ethics are the set of moral values held by an individual or group, in this case the organisation. A decision made on ethical grounds might reject the most profitable solution for an organisation in favour of one that provides greater benefit to society as a whole, or to particular groups of stakeholders. Such ethical decision making is likely to distinguish a business that is behaving ethically from one focused on profit.

On the other hand, a business may adopt a seemingly ethical position, such as a production or marketing or investment strategy, that is popular with consumers and is likely to lead to increased sales. Whether this is a reflection of the business adopting a 'real' ethical position or a 'perceived' one (i.e. as a PR exercise to gain consumer loyalty and increase sales) is debatable.

Resources

The resources available to a business have a huge influence on corporate plans and thus on corporate decisions. Resources include financial, human and physical resources. Each of these types of resources have been discussed in earlier chapters of this book and in the AS textbook.

If a company is unable to generate sufficient financial resources, this will affect its corporate decision making. For example, decisions about expansion or diversification will depend on the business having sufficient funds to support these developments. Funds may come from retained profit, from the issue of new shares or from loans. Their absence will seriously constrain a company's ability to pursue such developments.

The availability of human resources will also influence an organisation's decision making — whether sufficient trained employees are available within a company, or whether there is a sufficient number of qualified and skilled people interested or available to apply for jobs. Both situations will influence the ability of a business to pursue developments. For example, whether a business decides to introduce a particularly complex piece of computer software might depend on whether it has sufficient trained staff, whether it will be able to recruit such trained and experienced individuals or whether it can provide appropriate training for unskilled, but otherwise suitable staff.

Similarly, if a business is considering expansion or the re-siting of a plant in another area, much will depend on the availability of suitable sites at an affordable price.

The relative power of the stakeholders

Stakeholders are examined in detail in Chapter 20, which discusses the potential conflict and the pressures that stakeholders may bring to decision making. The relative power of individual stakeholder groups and their influence on decision making depends on the nature of the business. For example:
- in some small family businesses, the interests of shareholders may be the major influence on decision making
- for organisations whose location has a major impact on the local environment, local communities or environmental pressure groups may be powerful stakeholders and influence decision making
- for businesses in highly competitive markets, customers will be powerful stakeholders and their needs will be a major influence on decision making

■ in businesses that are dependent on a highly skilled but hard to find workforce, employees may be powerful stakeholders who exert significant influence on the decision making process

Table 20.1 in Chapter 20 identifies the aims of different groups of stakeholders. Their aims and their relative power, in the context of a particular business, will determine the influence they have on corporate decision making.

PRACTICE EXERCISE 2   Total: 50 marks (45 minutes)

1 What is a decision tree? *(4 marks)*

2 Explain two advantages of using decision trees in a business context. *(6 marks)*

3 Explain two disadvantages of using decision trees in a business context. *(6 marks)*

4 Explain two qualitative (non-quantifiable) factors that might be important in making a business decision. *(6 marks)*

5 If the probability of success is 0.6, what is the probability of failure and why? *(2 marks)*

6 A particular outcome has a 40% chance of earning £40,000 and a 60% chance of earning £100,000. What is its expected value? *(4 marks)*

7 Explain one advantage that decision tree analysis has over investment appraisal. *(3 marks)*

8 Outline two situations where decision trees are likely to be a valuable tool. *(6 marks)*

9 Outline one situation where decision trees are unlikely to be useful. *(4 marks)*

10 Explain how the following factors are likely to influence a firm's corporate decision-making.
   a its ethical position *(3 marks)*
   b the resources it has available *(3 marks)*
   c the relative power of its stakeholders *(3 marks)*

PRACTICE EXERCISE 3   Total: 20 marks (30 minutes)

Lynne Lilley has been making crafts in her small studio in Skipton for approximately 10 years. Her products include handmade greeting cards, beeswax candles, pottery and potpourri, most of which she makes herself and much of which she sells to larger shops and stores in Skipton and the surrounding area. The studio is rented and she employs another person on a part-time basis to assist at weekends and during holiday periods. Profit over the years has been reasonable, but during the last few years costs, particularly rents, have started to rise. Skipton, a market town in Yorkshire, attracts many visitors and there have been more businesses setting up in competition with Lynne. As a result of the increased competition, cost increases cannot be passed on to customers through higher prices and thus Lynne has found her profit falling steadily. Lynne believes she has two options available to her — to continue as she is at present or to move to cheaper premises.

If she continues as she is, she envisages three possible outcomes: there is a 30% chance of a downturn in the economy, resulting in a loss of £10,000; there is a 40% chance that the economy will stay the same, resulting in a profit of £30,000; and there is a 30% chance of an upturn in the economy, resulting in a £40,000 profit.

Lynne could move to premises in a less prominent area of the town, where rents are much cheaper. She has built a good reputation and therefore assumes that local customers will still find her, but she realises that she would be less accessible for the tourist trade. Lynne believes it would cost £4,000 to refurbish the premises she is considering and to cover the cost of advertising that would be needed to alert the tourist trade to the presence of the new premises. Again, she faces three possible outcomes: a downturn in the economy, the economy staying the same, or an upturn in the economy. Each of these outcomes has the same probability of occurring as described above, but the expected values are different: if there were a downturn in the economy, she would expect profits of £5,000; if the economic situation stayed the same, she would expect a profit of £35,000; if there were an upturn in the economy, she would expect profits of £50,000.

1 Draw the decision tree and calculate the expected values.   (9 marks)

2 On the basis of your calculations, which option should Lynne choose and why?   (2 marks)

3 Consider how useful a decision tree is in helping Lynne to make her decision?   (9 marks)

ESSAY QUESTIONS   Total: 40 marks (50 minutes)

Answer one of the following questions:

1 Discuss the value of different approaches to decision making that are available to an organisation.   (40 marks)

2 Identify the differing stakeholder perspectives facing a company and discuss the potential for conflict and the pressure that stakeholders may bring to decision making.   (40 marks)

Chapter 31

Implementing and managing change

This chapter considers techniques to implement and manage change successfully, including project champions and project groups. It assesses the factors that promote change and those that resist it, including the clarity of objectives, the availability of resources and the effectiveness of training.

Techniques to implement and manage change

The role of leadership and management of change was discussed in Chapter 28. Techniques to implement and manage change often focus on an area of change as a project; hence the terms 'project champions', 'project management' and 'project groups'. These concepts are discussed below.

Project champions

A saying in project management circles is: 'If you don't have a project champion, you don't have a project.' A successful project requires someone to promote the benefits of pursuing it, while also justifying the organisation's investment. This is the role of the project champion. A project champion is not a formal project team member, but is someone who believes strongly in the project's goals and value.

Project champions have two essential roles in relation to a project:

■ To advocate and promote the benefits of pursuing the project to which they are attached. The project champion actively seeks project support from management and other organisational leaders.
■ To assist the project when it encounters barriers, such as funding constraints or problems with resource allocation.

Desirable characteristics of project champions include:

■ status within the organisation that ensures they carry weight in the organisational decision-making process — the reason why most successful project champions are in mid- to senior-level management
■ a real commitment to pursuing support for the project within the organisation
■ good people skills and the ability to build relationships easily

The role of the project champion must not be confused with that of the project manager. Although the latter is also a project advocate, the project manager's focus is to plan, organise and manage the execution of the project. The project champion, although not a member of the project team, strives to help the project succeed.

Project management and project groups

Good project management means that things get done, on time, within budget, and meet or exceed the expectations of the business. Conversely, a failed project usually means a project that is behind schedule and over budget, and/or that did not meet expectations. It might also mean missed revenue because of delays or cost overruns.

Projects of any size and complexity can be planned by computer. Critical path analysis (explained in Chapter 15) is an integral tool in project management. However, project management is not only about planning, but also about resource management and human attributes like leadership, teamwork and motivation.

Project managers and project groups have grown rapidly, as industry and commerce have realised that much of what business does is project work or the management and implementation of change. One reason for their rapid growth is the need to understand how to look after complex projects, often in high-tech areas, which are critical to business success but also have to use scarce resources efficiently.

The work of project groups provides opportunities for job enlargement, as workers are often allowed to take on a variety of different tasks within the group. They also benefit from the specialist skills of individual group members, which can increase productivity and the possibility of success. Close project group working can also create 'synergy' — a situation in which the combined results of the project group working together as a team of individuals is greater than the individual parts.

External consultants and external specialists

External consultants and specialists are often brought in when an organisation does not have sufficient expertise itself or when its management needs to remain focused on existing business. It is generally agreed that effective change management is best driven by people in the organisation undergoing the change, but they may be supported, where necessary, by external specialists. For example, a change manager or change programme director, with a track record of delivering successful change in similar circumstances, may be brought in as an additional member of the team.

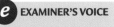

EXAMINER'S VOICE

Refer to Chapter 18, where matrix management is explained. In matrix management, employees report to a team leader on issues linked to the project they are involved in, but are also answerable to their departmental manager for their other roles.

Factors that promote and resist change

A lack of clear objectives or sense of mission or purpose will not help the change process. Appropriate and sufficient resources (including human, financial and physical resources, such as machinery and plant) will be necessary if change is to be implemented and managed successfully. Appropriate trained staff with relevant expertise are necessary during the change process and to ensure that change is successful. For example, for a new IT system to be successfully introduced, there should be SMART objectives to justify its introduction, there should be sufficient resources to ensure its success and there should be provision for ensuring there are sufficient and appropriately trained staff.

> ### e EXAMINER'S VOICE
>
> The AQA specification includes the following three factors that promote and resist change: clarity of objectives, resources and training. These are considered in the above paragraph.

In addition to the above, the following factors also promote or limit change:

- **Resistance to change.** This can impede the ability of a business to serve its customers, to innovate for the future, or to capitalise on a new initiative.
- **Planning.** The firm should consider all possible implications of a proposed initiative, the development of a plan for information and training, and a map for ongoing monitoring of the new environment.
- The **impact on people employed in the business**, and how the business deals with this. For example, different people react differently to change and change often involves a loss — of status, income, friends etc. How a business deals with such issues will determine how successful change is likely to be.
- The **effectiveness of teams** in the organisation and the **skills and commitment** of the people involved.
- The nature of the **organisational structure** — a flat team structure is often most appropriate for implementing and managing change successfully.
- **External factors**, such as the impact of a competitor's actions or changes in the economy. For example, the recession of 2008/09 caused many businesses to cancel their plans for expansion.

> ### e EXAMINER'S VOICE
>
> No exemplar Unit 4 examination paper has been included here because the Unit 4 paper provides pre-issued information and requires a large amount of preparation on the part of students prior to the examination. However, the case study questions and essay questions provided at the end of each chapter in Unit 4 are not dissimilar to those you will meet in the examination.

PRACTICE EXERCISE
Total: 40 marks (35 minutes)

1 Explain the difference between a project manager and a project champion. *(6 marks)*

2 Identify and explain three characteristics of a good project champion. *(9 marks)*

3 Explain two benefits of a project champion to a project that is aimed at initiating change. *(6 marks)*

4 How might a project group contribute to the success of a project? *(4 marks)*

5 What role might external consultants or specialists contribute to a company intent on introducing change? *(3 marks)*

6 Identify and explain four factors that might promote or resist change. *(12 marks)*

CASE STUDY Management of change

Optimal Business Solutions is an IT services business that is considering introducing significant change to its organisation. It wishes to introduce flexible and home-based working for its IT analysts.

IT analysts currently work at four regional offices — based in London, Bristol, Nottingham and Manchester. The plan is to remove these regional offices and focus activity in the central office in London, which accommodates HR, financial, marketing and administrative staff.

The principal reason for the change is to cut costs.

Question
Total: 40 marks (50 minutes)

Discuss the techniques Optimal Business Solutions might use to implement and manage the change it intends, and assess the factors that might promote and hinder the intended change. *(40 marks)*

Index

Note: page numbers in **bold** type refer to key terms (where these occur more than once only the first occurrence is given).

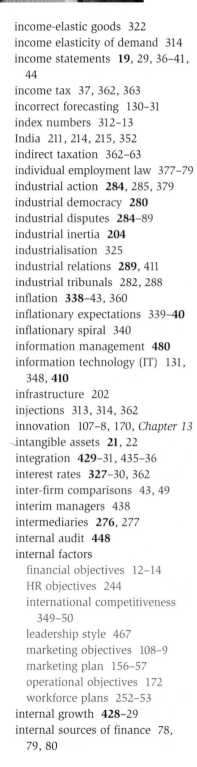